A Dictionary of
CHEMISTRY

A Dictionary of
CHEMISTRY

A.H. Backett

CBS

CBS Publishers & Distributors Pvt. Ltd.

NEW DELHI • BANGALORE • PUNE • COCHIN • CHENNAI (INDIA)

ISBN : 81-239-0897-0

First Indian Edition : 1986
Reprint : 1988
Reprint : 1994
Reprint : 1997
Reprint : 1999
Reprint : 2000
Reprint : 2003

This edition has been published in India by arrangement with Academic Science, Inc., UK

Published by Satish Kumar Jain and produced by V.K. Jain for
CBS Publishers & Distributors Pvt. Ltd.,
CBS Plaza, 4819/XI Prahlad Street, 24 Ansari Road, Daryaganj,
New Delhi - 110002, India.
e-mail: cbspubs@vsnl.com, cbspubs@airtelmail.in, delhi@cbspd.com
Website: www.cbspd.com

Branches:

- ***Bangalore:*** Seema House, 2975, 17th Cross, K.R. Road, Bansankari 2nd Stage, Bangalore - 560070
  Fax: 080-26771680 • e-mail: bangalore@cbspd.com
- ***Pune:*** Shaan Brahmha Complex, 631/632, Basement, Appa Balwant Chowk, Budhwar Peth, Next to Ratan Talkies, Pune - 411002 Fax: 020-24464059 • e-mail: pune@cbspd.com
- ***Cochin:*** 36/14, Kalluvilakam, Lissie Hospital Road, Cochin - 682018, Kerala • e-mail: cochin@cbspd.com
- ***Chennai:*** 20, West Park Road, Shenoy Nagar, Chennai - 600030 • e-mail: chennai@cbspd.com

Printed at:
Somya Printers, Delhi-110053

A

absolute **1.** Not dependent on or relative to anything else, e.g. *absolute zero. **2.** Denoting a temperature measured on an *absolute scale*, a scale of temperature based on absolute zero. The usual absolute scale now is that of thermodynamic *temperature; its unit, the kelvin, was formerly called the degree absolute (°A) and is the same size as the degree Celsius. In British engineering practice an absolute scale with Fahrenheit-size degrees has been used: this is the Rankine scale.

absolute alcohol *See* ethanol.

absolute configuration A way of denoting the absolute structure of an optical isomer (*see* optical activity). Two conventions are in use: The D-L convention relates the structure of the molecule to some reference molecule. In the case of sugars and similar compounds, the dextrorotatory form of glyceraldehyde ($HOCH_2CH(OH)CHO$), 2,3-dihydroxypropanal) was used. The rule is as follow: Write the structure of this molecule down with the asymmetric carbon in the centre, the $-CHO$ group at the top, the $-OH$ on the right, the $-CH_2OH$ at the bottom, and the $-H$ on the left. Now imagine that the central carbon atom is at the centre of a tetrahedron with the four groups at the corners and that the $-H$ and $-OH$ come out of the paper and the $-CHO$ and $-CH_2OH$ groups go into the paper. The resulting three-dimensional structure was taken to be that of *d*-glyceraldehyde and called D-glyceraldehyde. Any compound that contains an asymmetric carbon atom having this configuration belongs to the D-series. One having the opposite configuration belongs to the L-series. It is important to note that the prefixes D- and L- do not stand for dextrorotatory and laevorotatory (i.e. they are not the same as *d*- and *l*-). In fact the arbitrary configuration assigned to D-glyceraldehyde is now known to be the correct one for the dextrorotatory form, although this was not known at the time. However, all D-compounds are not dextrorotatory. For instance, the acid obtained by oxidizing the $-CHO$ group of glyceraldehyde is glyceric acid (1,2-dihydroxypropanoic acid). By convention, this belongs to the D-series, but it is in fact laevorotatory; i.e. its name can be written as D-glyceric acid or *l*-glyceric acid. To avoid confusion it is better to use + (for dextrorotatory) and − (for laevorotatory), as in D-(+)-glyceraldehyde and D-(−)-glyceric acid.

The D-L convention can also be used with alpha amino acids (compounds with the $-NH_2$ group on the same carbon as the $-COOH$ group). In this case the molecule is imagined as being viewed along the H–C bond between the hydrogen and the asymmetric carbon atom. If the clockwise order of the other three groups is $-COOH$, $-R$, $-NH_2$, the amino acid belongs to the D-series; otherwise it belongs to the L-series. This is known as the *CORN rule*.

The R-S convention is a convention based on priority of groups attached to the chiral carbon atom. The order of priority is I, Br, Cl, SO_3H, $OCOCH_3$, OCH_3, OH, NO_2, NH_2, $COOCH_3$, $CONH_2$, $COCH_3$, CHO, CH_2OH, C_6H_5, C_2H_5, CH_3, H, with hydrogen lowest. The molecule is viewed with the group of lowest priority behind the chiral atom. If the clockwise arrangement of the other three groups is in descending priority, the compound belongs to the R-series; if the descending order is anticlockwise it is in the S-series. D-(+)-glyceraldehyde is R-(+)-glyceraldehyde.

absolute temperature *See* absolute; temperature.

absolute zero Zero of thermodynamic *temperature (0 kelvin) and the lowest temperature theoretically attainable. It is the temperature at which the kinetic energy of

ABSORPTION

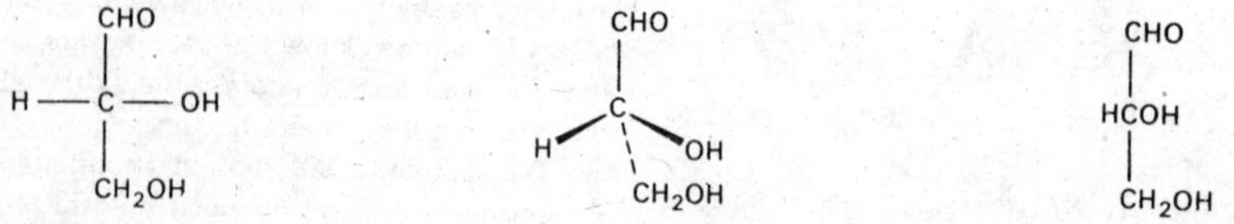

planar formula | structure in 3 dimensions | Fischer projection

D−(+)− glyceraldehyde (2,3-dihydroxypropanal)

D−alanine (R is CH_2 in the CORN rule). The molecule is viewed with H on top

R−configuration S−configuration

R-S system. The lowest priority group is behind the chiral carbon atom

atoms and molecules is minimal. It is equivalent to −273.15°C or −459.67°F. *See also* zero-point energy; cryogenics.

absorption 1. (in chemistry) The take up of a gas by a solid or liquid, or the take up of a liquid by a solid. Absorption differs from *adsorption in that the absorbed substance permeates the bulk of the absorbing substance. **2.** (in physics) The conversion of the energy of electromagnetic radiation, sound, streams of particles, etc., into other forms of energy on passing through a medium. A beam of light, for instance, passing through a medium, may lose intensity because of two effects: scattering of light out of the beam, and absorption of photons by atoms or molecules in the medium. When a photon is absorbed, there is a transition to an excited state.

absorption indicator A type of indicator used in reactions that involve precipitation. The yellow dye fluorescein is a common example, used for the reaction

$$NaCl(aq) + AgNO_3(aq) \rightarrow AgCl(s) + NaNO_3(aq)$$

As silver nitrate solution is added to the sodium chloride, silver chloride precipitates. As long as Cl^- ions are in excess, they adsorb on the precipitate particles. At the end point, no Cl^- ions are left in solution and negative fluorescein ions are then adsorbed, giving a pink colour to the precipitate.

absorption spectrum *See* spectrum.

abundance 1. The ratio of the total mass of a specified element in the earth's crust to the total mass of the earth's crust, often expressed as a percentage. For example, the abundance of aluminium in the earth's crust is about 8%. **2.** The ratio of the number of atoms of a particular isotope of an element to the total number of atoms of all the isotopes present, often expressed as a percentage. For example, the abundance of uranium-235 in natural uranium is 0.71%. This is the *natural abundance*, i.e. the abundance as found in nature before any enrichment has taken place.

accelerator A substance that increases the rate of a chemical reaction, i.e. a catalyst.

acceptor A compound, molecule, ion, etc., to which electrons are donated in the formation of a coordinate bond.

accumulator (secondary cell; storage battery) A type of *voltaic cell or battery that can be recharged by passing a current through it from an external d.c. supply. The charging current, which is passed in the opposite direction to that in which the cell supplies current, reverses the chemical reactions in the cell. The common types are the *lead–acid accumulator and the *nickel–iron accumulator.

acetaldehyde *See* ethanal.

acetals Organic compounds formed by addition of alcohol molecules to aldehyde molecules. If one molecule of aldehyde (RCHO) reacts with one molecule of alcohol (R′OH) a *hemiacetal* is formed (RCH(OH)OR′). The rings of aldose sugars are hemiacetals. Further reaction with a second alcohol molecule produces a full acetal ($RCH(OR')_2$). The formation of acetals is reversible; acetals can be hydrolysed back to aldehydes in acidic solutions. In synthetic organic chemistry aldehyde groups are often converted into acetal groups to protect them before performing other reactions on different groups in the molecule. *See also* ketals.

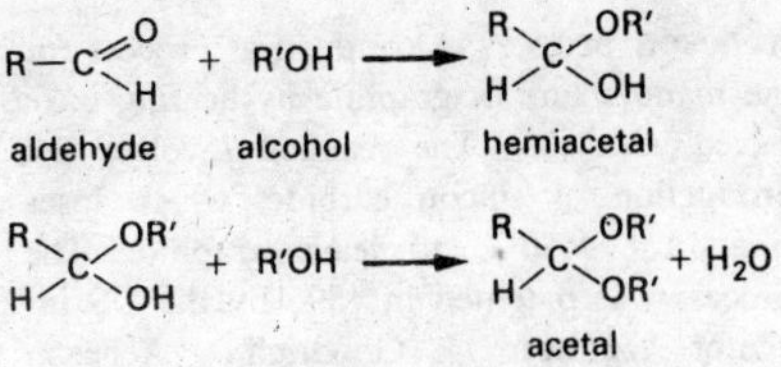

Formation of acetals

acetamide *See* ethanamide.

acetate *See* ethanoate.

acetic acid *See* ethanoic acid.

acetone *See* propanone.

acetylation *See* acylation.

acetyl chloride *See* ethanoyl chloride.

acetylcholine A substance that is released at some (*cholinergic*) nerve endings. Its function is to pass on a nerve impulse to the next nerve (i.e. at a synapse) or to initiate muscular contraction. Once acetylcholine has been released, it has only a transitory effect because it is rapidly broken down by the enzyme *acetylcholinesterase*.

acetylene *See* ethyne.

acetylenes *See* alkynes.

acetyl group *See* ethanoyl group.

acetylide *See* carbide.

Acheson process An industrial process for the manufacture of graphite by heating coke mixed with clay. The reaction involves the production of silicon carbide, which loses silicon at 4150°C to leave graphite. The process was patented in 1896 by the US inventor Edward Goodrich Acheson (1856–1931).

acid 1. A type of compound that contains hydrogen and dissociates in water to produce positive hydrogen ions. The reaction, for an acid HX, is commonly written:

$$HX \rightleftharpoons H^+ + X^-$$

In fact, the hydrogen ion (the proton) is solvated, and the complete reaction is:

$$HX + H_2O \rightleftharpoons H_3O^+ + X^-$$

The ion H_3O^+ is the *oxonium ion* (or *hydroxonium ion* or *hydronium ion*). This definition of acids comes from the *Arrhenius theory*. Such acids tend to be corrosive substances with a sharp taste, which turn litmus red and give colour changes with other *indicators. They are referred to as *protonic acids* and are classified into *strong acids*, which are almost completely dissociated in water (e.g. sulphuric acid and hydrochloric acid), and *weak acids*, which are only partially dissociated (e.g. ethanoic acid and hydrogen sulphide). The strength of an acid depends on the extent to which it dissociates, and is measured by its *dissociation constant. *See also* base.

2. In the *Lowry–Brønsted theory* of acids and bases (1923), the definition was extended to one in which an acid is a proton donor, and a base is a proton acceptor. For example, in

$$HCN + H_2O \rightleftharpoons H_3O^+ + CN^-$$

the HCN is an acid, in that it donates a proton to H_2O. The H_2O is acting as a base in accepting a proton. Similarly, in the reverse reaction H_3O^+ is an acid and CN^- a base. In such reactions, two species related by loss or gain of a proton are said to be *conjugate*. Thus, in the reaction above HCN is the *conjugate acid* of the base CN^-, and CN^- is the *conjugate base* of the acid HCN. Similarly, H_3O^+ is the conjugate acid of the base H_2O. An equilibrium, such as that above, is a competition for protons between an acid and its conjugate base. A strong acid has a weak conjugate base, and vice versa. Under this definition water can act as both acid and base. Thus in

$$NH_3 + H_2O \rightleftharpoons NH_4^+ + OH^-$$

the H_2O is the conjugate acid of OH^-. The definition also extends the idea of acid–base reaction to solvents other than water. For instance, liquid ammonia, like water, has a high dielectric constant and is a good ionizing solvent. Equilibria of the type

$$NH_3 + Na^+Cl^- \rightleftharpoons Na^+NH_2^- + HCl$$

can be studied, in which NH_3 and HCl are acids and NH_2^- and Cl^- are their conjugate bases.

3. A further extension of the idea of acids and bases was made in the *Lewis theory* (G. N. Lewis, 1923). In this, a *Lewis acid* is a compound or atom that can accept a pair of electrons and a *Lewis base* is one that can donate an electron pair. This definition encompasses 'traditional' acid–base reactions. In

$$HCl + NaOH \rightarrow NaCl + H_2O$$

the reaction is essentially

$$H^+ + :OH^- \rightarrow H:OH$$

i.e. donation of an electron pair by OH^-. But it also includes reactions that do not involve ions, e.g.

$$H_3N: + BCl_3 \rightarrow H_3NBCl_3$$

in which NH_3 is the base (donor) and BCl_3 the acid (acceptor). The Lewis theory establishes a relationship between acid–base reactions and *oxidation–reduction reactions.

acid anhydrides (acyl anhydrides) Compounds that react with water to form an acid. For example, carbon dioxide reacts with water to give carbonic acid:

$$CO_2(g) + H_2O(aq) \rightleftharpoons H_2CO_3(aq)$$

A particular group of acid anhydrides are anhydrides of carboxylic acids. They have a general formula of the type R.CO.O.CO.R′, where R and R′ are alkyl or aryl groups.

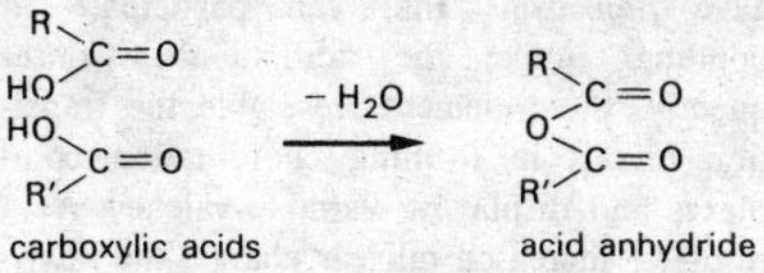

Formation of a carboxylic acid anhydride

For example, the compound ethanoic anhydride ($CH_3.CO.O.CO.CH_3$) is the acid anhydride of ethanoic (acetic) acid. Organic acid anhydrides can be produced by dehydrating acids (or mixtures of acids). They are usually made by reacting an acyl halide with the sodium salt of the acid. They react readily with water, alcohols, phenols, and amines and are used in *acylation reactions.

acid dissociation constant *See* dissociation.

acid dye *See* dye.

acid halides *See* acyl halides.

acidic 1. Describing a compound that is an acid. **2.** Describing a solution that has an excess of hydrogen ions. **3.** Describing a compound that forms an acid when dissolved in water. Carbon dioxide, for example, is an acidic oxide.

acidic hydrogen (acid hydrogen) A hydrogen atom in an *acid that forms a positive ion when the acid dissociates. For instance, in methanoic acid

$$HCOOH \rightleftharpoons H^+ + HCOO^-$$

the hydrogen atom on the carboxylate group is the acidic hydrogen (the one bound directly to the carbon atom does not dissociate).

acidimetry Volumetric analysis using standard solutions of acids to determine the amount of base present.

acidity constant *See* dissociation.

acid rain *See* pollution.

acid salt A salt of a polybasic acid (i.e. an acid having two or more acidic hydrogens) in which not all the hydrogen atoms have been replaced by positive ions. For example, the dibasic acid carbonic acid (H_2CO_3) forms acid salts (hydrogencarbonates) containing the ion HCO_3^-. Some salts of monobasic acids are also known as acid salts. For instance, the compound potassium hydrogendifluoride, KHF_2, contains the ion $[F...H-F]^-$, in which there is hydrogen bonding between the fluoride ion F^- and a hydrogen fluoride molecule.

acid value A measure of the amount of free acid present in a fat, equal to the number of milligrams of potassium hydroxide needed to neutralize this acid. Fresh fats contain glycerides of fatty acids and very little free acid, but the glycerides decompose slowly with time and the acid value increases.

Acrilan A tradename for a synthetic fibre. *See* acrylic resins.

acrylate *See* propenoate.

acrylic acid *See* propenoic acid.

acrylic resins Synthetic resins made by polymerizing esters or other derivatives of acrylic acid (propenoic acid). Examples are poly(propenonitrile) (e.g. *Acrilan*), and poly(methyl 2-methylpropenoate) (polymethyl methacrylate, e.g. *Perspex*).

acrylonitrile *See* propenonitrile.

actinides *See* actinoids.

actinium Symbol Ac. A silvery radioactive metallic element belonging to group IIIB of the periodic table; a.n. 89; mass number of most stable isotope 227 (half-life 21.7 years); m.p. 1050 ± 50°C; b.p. 3300°C (estimated). Actinium-227 occurs in natural uranium to an extent of about 0.715%. Actinium–228 (half-life 6.13 hours) also occurs in nature. There are 22 other artificial isotopes, all radioactive and all with very short half-lives. Its chemistry is similar to that of lanthanum. It has no uses and was discovered by A. Debierne in 1899.

actinium series *See* radioactive series.

actinoid contraction A smooth decrease in atomic or ionic radius with increasing proton number found in the *actinoids.

actinoids (actinides) A series of elements in the *periodic table, generally considered to range in atomic number from thorium (90) to lawrencium (103) inclusive. The actinoids all have two outer *s*-electrons (a $7s^2$ configuration), follow actinium, and are classified together by the fact that increasing proton number corresponds to filling of the $5f$ level. In fact, because the $5f$ and $6d$ levels are close in energy the filling of the $5f$ orbitals is not smooth. The outer electron configurations are as follows:

89 actinium (Ac) $6d^1 7s^2$
90 thorium (Th) $6d^2 7s^2$
91 protactinium (Pa) $5f^2 6d^1 7s^2$
92 uranium (Ur) $5f^3 6d 7s^2$
93 neptunium (Np) $5f^5 7s^2$ (or $5f^4 6d^1 7s^2$)
94 plutonium (Pu) $5f^6 7s^2$
95 americium (Am) $5f^7 7s^2$
96 curium (Cm) $5f^7 6d^1 s^2$
97 berkelium (Bk) $5f^8 6d 7s^2$ (or $5f^9 7s^2$)
98 californium (Cf) $5f^{10} 7s^2$
99 einsteinium (Es) $5f^{11} 7s^2$
100 fermium (Fm) $5f^{12} 7s^2$
101 mendelevium (Md) $5f^{13} 7s^2$
102 nobelium (Nb) $5f^{14} 7s^2$
103 lawrencium (Lw) $5f^{14} 6d^1 s^2$

The first four members (Ac to Ur) occur naturally. All are radioactive and this makes investigation difficult because of self-heating, short lifetimes, safety precautions, etc. Like the *lanthanoids, the actinoids show a smooth decrease in atomic and ionic radius with increasing proton number. The lighter members of the series (up to americium) have *f*-electrons that can participate in bonding, unlike the lanthanoids. Consequently, these elements resemble the transition metals in forming coordination complexes and displaying variable valency. As a result of increased nuclear charge, the heavier members (curium to lawrencium) tend not to use their inner *f*-electrons in forming bonds and resemble the lanthanoids in forming compounds containing the M^{3+} ion. The reason for this is pulling of these inner electrons towards the centre of the atom by the increased nuclear charge. Note that actinium itself does not have a $5f$ electron, but it is usually classified with the actinoids because of its chemical similarities. *See also* transition elements.

actinometer Any of various instruments for measuring the intensity of electromagnetic radiation. Recent actinometers use the *photoelectric effect but earlier instruments depended either on the fluorescence produced by the radiation on a screen or on the amount of chemical change induced in some suitable substance.

action spectrum A graphical plot of the efficiency of electromagnetic radiation in producing a photochemical reaction against the wavelength of the radiation used. For example, the action spectrum for photosynthesis using light shows a peak in the region 670–700 nm. This corresponds to a maximum absorption in the absorption spectrum of chlorophylls in this region.

activated alumina *See* aluminium hydroxide.

activated charcoal *See* charcoal.

activated complex The association of atoms of highest energy formed in the *transition state of a chemical reaction.

activation analysis An analytical technique that can be used to detect most elements when present in a sample in milligram quantities (or less). In *neutron activation analysis* the sample is exposed to a flux of thermal neutrons in a nuclear reactor. Some of these neutrons are captured by nuclides in the sample to form nuclides of the same atomic number but a higher mass number. These newly formed nuclides emit gamma radiation, which can be used to identify the element present by means of a gamma-ray spectrometer. Activation analysis has also been employed using charged particles, such as protons or alpha particles.

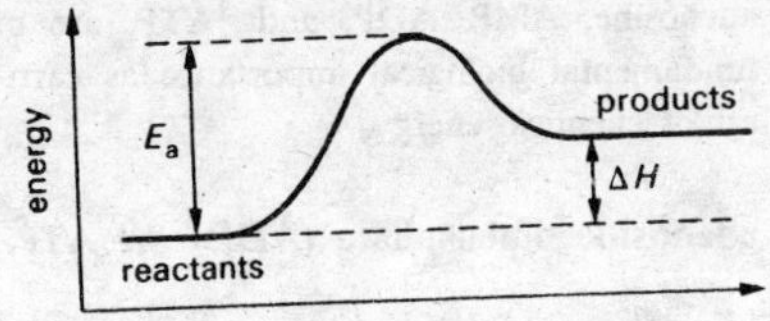

Reaction profile
(for an endothermic reaction)

activation energy The minimum energy required for a chemical reaction to take place. In a reaction, the reactant molecules come together and chemical bonds are stretched, broken, and formed in producing the products. During this process the energy of the system increases to a maximum, then decreases to the energy of the products. The activation energy is the difference between the maximum energy and the energy of the reactants; i.e. it is the energy barrier that has to be overcome for the reaction to proceed. The activation energy determines the way in which the rate of the reaction varies with temperature (*see* Arrhenius equation). It is usual to express activation energies in joules per mole of reactants.

active mass *See* mass action.

active site 1. A site on the surface of a catalyst at which activity occurs. **2.** The site on the surface of an *enzyme molecule that binds the substrate molecule. The properties of an active site are determined by the three-dimensional arrangement of the polypeptide chains of the enzyme and their constituent amino acids. These govern the nature of the interaction that takes place and hence the degree of substrate specificity and susceptibility to *inhibition.

activity 1. Symbol *a*. A thermodynamic function used in place of concentration in equilibrium constants for reactions involving nonideal gases and solutions. For example, in a reaction

$$A \rightleftharpoons B + C$$

the true equilibrium constant is given by

$$K = a_B a_C / a_A$$

where a_A, a_B, and a_C are the activities of the components, which function as concentrations (or pressures) corrected for nonideal behaviour. *Activity coefficients* (symbol γ) are defined for gases by $\gamma = a/p$ (where p is pressure) and for solutions by $\gamma = aX$ (where X is the mole fraction). Thus, the equilibrium constant of a gas reaction has the form

$$K_p = \gamma_B p_B \gamma_C p_C / \gamma_A p_A$$

The equilibrium constant of a reaction in solution is

$$K_c = \gamma_B X_B \gamma_C X_C / \gamma_A X_A$$

The activity coefficients thus act as correction factors for the pressures or concentrations. *See also* fugacity.

2. Symbol *A*. The number of atoms of a radioactive substance that disintegrate per unit time. The *specific activity* (*a*) is the activity per unit mass of a pure radioisotope. *See* radiation units.

acyclic Describing a compound that does not have a ring in its molecules.

acyl anhydrides *See* acid anhydrides.

acylation The process of introducing an acyl group (RCO–) into a compound. The usual method is to react an alcohol with an acyl halide or a carboxylic acid anhydride; e.g.

$$RCOCl + R'OH \rightarrow RCOOR' + HCl$$

The introduction of an acetyl group (CH_3CO-) is *acetylation*, a process used for protecting $-OH$ groups in organic synthesis.

acylglycerol *See* glyceride.

acyl group A group of the type $RCO-$, where R is an organic group. An example is the acetyl group CH_3CO-.

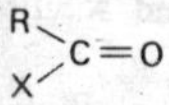

Acyl halide: X is a halogen atom

acyl halides (acid halides) Organic compounds containing the group $-CO.X$, where X is a halogen atom. Acyl chlorides, for instance, have the general formula RCOCl. The group $RCO-$ is the *acyl group*. In systematic chemical nomenclature acyl-halide names end in the suffix *-oyl*; for example, ethanoyl chloride, CH_3COCl. Acyl halides react readily with water, alcohols, phenols, and amines and are used in *acylation reactions. They are made by replacing the $-OH$ group in a carboxylic acid by a halogen using a halogenating agent such as PCl_5.

addition polymerization *See* polymerization.

addition reaction A chemical reaction in which one molecule adds to another. Addition reactions occur with unsaturated compounds containing double or triple bonds, and may be *electrophilic or *nucleophilic. An example of electrophilic addition is the reaction of hydrogen chloride with an alkene, e.g.

$$HCl + CH_2{:}CH_2 \rightarrow CH_3CH_2Cl$$

An example of nucleophilic addition is the addition of hydrogen cyanide across the carbonyl bond in aldehydes to form *cyanohydrins. *Addition–elimination* reactions are ones in which the addition is followed by elimination of another molecule (*see* condensation reaction).

adduct A compound formed by an addition reaction. The term is used particularly for compounds formed by coordination between a Lewis acid (acceptor) and a Lewis base (donor). *See* acid.

adenine A *purine derivative. It is one of the major component bases of *nucleotides and the nucleic acids *DNA and *RNA.

adenosine A nucleoside comprising one adenine molecule linked to a D-ribose sugar molecule. The phosphate-ester derivatives of adenosine, AMP, ADP, and *ATP, are of fundamental biological importance as carriers of chemical energy.

adenosine diphosphate (ADP) *See* ATP.

adenosine monophosphate (AMP) *See* ATP.

adenosine triphosphate *See* ATP.

adhesive A substance used for joining surfaces together. Adhesives are generally colloidal solutions, which set to gels. There are many types including animal glues (based on collagen), vegetable mucilages, and synthetic resins (e.g. *epoxy resins).

adiabatic demagnetization A technique for cooling a paramagnetic salt, such as potassium chrome alum, to a temperature near *absolute zero. The salt is placed between the poles of an electromagnet and the heat produced during magnetization is removed by liquid helium. The salt is then isolated thermally from the surroundings and the field is switched off; the salt is demagnetized adiabatically and its temperature falls. This is because the demagnetized state, being less ordered, involves more energy than the magnetized state. The extra energy can come only from the internal, or thermal, energy of the substance.

adiabatic process Any process that occurs without heat entering or leaving a system. In general, an adiabatic change involves a fall or rise in temperature of the system. For example, if a gas expands under adiabatic conditions, its temperature falls (work is done against the retreating walls of the container). The *adiabatic equation* describes the relationship between the pressure (p) of an ideal gas and its volume (V), i.e. $pV^{\gamma} = K$, where γ is the ratio of the principal specific *heat capacities of the gas and K is a constant.

adipic acid *See* hexanedioic acid.

ADP *See* ATP.

adrenaline (epinephrine) A hormone, produced by the medulla of the adrenal glands, that increases heart activity, improves the power and prolongs the action of muscles, and increases the rate and depth of breathing to prepare the body for 'fright, flight, or fight'. At the same time it inhibits digestion and excretion.

adsorbate A substance that is adsorbed on a surface.

adsorption The formation of a layer of gas on the surface of a solid or, less frequently, of a liquid. There are two types depending on the nature of the forces involved. In *chemisorption* a single layer of molecules, atoms, or ions is attached to the adsorbent surface by chemical bonds. In *physisorption* adsorbed molecules are held by the weaker *van der Waals' forces.

aerosol A colloidal dispersion of a solid or liquid in a gas. The commonly used aerosol sprays contain an inert propellant liquefied under pressure. Halogenated alkanes, such as dichlorodifluoromethane, are commonly used in aerosol cans. This use has been criticized on the grounds that these compounds persist in the atmosphere and may eventually (it is claimed) affect the *ozone layer.

agar An extract of certain species of red seaweeds that is used as a gelling agent in microbiological culture media, foodstuffs, medicines, and cosmetic creams and jellies. *Nutrient agar* consists of a broth made from beef extract or blood that is gelled with agar and used for the cultivation of bacteria, fungi, and some algae.

agate A variety of *chalcedony that forms in rock cavities and has a pattern of concentrically arranged bands or layers that lie parallel to the cavity walls. These layers are frequently alternating tones of brownish-red. *Moss agate* does not show the same banding and is a milky chalcedony containing moss-like or dendritic patterns formed by inclusions of manganese and iron oxides. Agates are used in jewellery and for ornamental purposes.

air *See* earth's atmosphere.

alabaster *See* gypsum.

alanine *See* amino acid.

albumin (albumen) One of a group of globular proteins that are soluble in water but form insoluble coagulates when heated. Albumins occur in egg white, blood, milk, and plants. Serum albumins, which constitute about 55% of blood plasma protein, help regulate the osmotic pressure and hence plasma volume. They also bind and transport fatty acids. α-lactalbumin is one of the proteins in milk.

alcohols Organic compounds that contain the –OH group. In systematic chemical nomenclature alcohol names end in the suffix *-ol*. Examples are methanol, CH_3OH, and ethanol, C_2H_5OH. *Primary alcohols* have two hydrogen atoms on the carbon joined to the –OH group (i.e. they contain the

ALDEHYDES

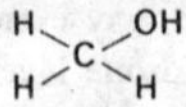

primary alcohol (methanol)

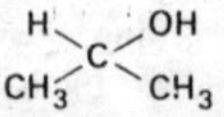

secondary alcohol (methylethanol)

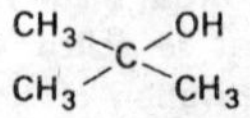

tertiary alcohol (dimethylethylethanol)

Examples of alcohols

group $-CH_2-OH$); *secondary alcohols* have one hydrogen on this carbon (the other two bonds being to carbon atoms, as in $(CH_3)_2CHOH$); *tertiary alcohols* have no hydrogen on this carbon (as in $(CH_3)_3COH$). Primary and secondary alcohols differ in their reactions with potassium dichromate(VI) in sulphuric acid as the following schemes indicate:

primary alcohol → aldehyde → carboxylic acid

secondary alcohol → ketone

tertiary alcohol – no reaction

Other characteristics of alcohols are reaction with acids to give *esters and dehydration to give *alkenes or *ethers. Alcohols that have two –OH groups in their molecules are *diols* (or *dihydric alcohols*), those with three are *triols* (or *trihydric alcohols*), etc.

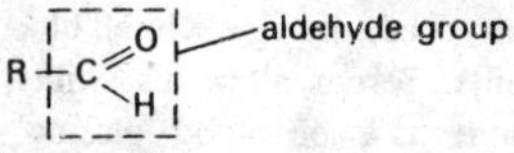

Aldehyde structure

aldehydes Chemical compounds that contain the group –CHO (the *aldehyde group*; i.e. a carbonyl group (C=O) with a hydrogen atom bound to the carbon atom). In systematic chemical nomenclature, aldehyde names end with the suffix *-al*. Examples of aldehydes are methanal (formaldehyde), HCOH, and ethanal (acetaldehyde), CH_3CHO. Aldehydes are formed by oxidation of primary *alcohols; further oxidation yields carboxylic acids. They are reducing agents and tests for aldehydes include *Fehling's test and *Tollen's reagent. Aldehydes have certain characteristic addition and condensation reactions. With sodium hydrogensulphate(IV) they form addition compounds of the type $[RCOH(SO_3)H]^- Na^+$. Formerly these were known as *bisulphite addition compounds.* They also form addition compounds with hydrogen cyanide to give *cyanohydrins and with alcohols to give *acetals and undergo condensation reactions to yield *oximes, *hydrazones, and *semicarbazones. Aldehydes readily polymerize. *See also* ketones.

aldohexose *See* monosaccharide.

aldol *See* aldol reaction.

aldol reaction A reaction of aldehydes of the type

$$2CH_3RCHO \rightarrow CH_3RCH(OH)CH_2RCHO$$

where R represents a hydrocarbon group. The resulting compound is a hydroxyaldehyde (i.e. an aldehyde–alcohol, or *aldol*), containing an alcohol (–OH) group on one carbon atom and an aldehyde group (–CHO) on another carbon atom. The reaction occurs in the presence of hydroxide ions (i.e. it is base-catalysed) and the first step is formation of a negative (carbanion) $^-CH_2RCHO$, which reacts with a molecule of the aldehyde.

aldose *See* monosaccharide.

aldosterone A hormone produced by the adrenal glands that controls excretion of sodium by the kidneys and thereby maintains the balance of salt and water in the body fluids.

alicyclic compound A compound that contains a ring of atoms and is aliphatic. Cyclohexane, C_6H_{12}, is an example.

aliphatic compounds Organic compounds that are *alkanes, *alkenes, or *alkynes or their derivatives. The term is used to denote compounds that do not have the special stability of *aromatic compounds. All noncyclic organic compounds are aliphatic. Cyclic aliphatic compounds are said to be *alicyclic.*

alkali A *base that dissolves in water to give hydroxide ions.

alkali metals (group I elements) The elements of the first group of the *periodic table (group IA): lithium (Li), sodium (Na), potassium (K), rubidium (Rb), caesium (Cs), and francium (Fr). All have a characteristic electron configuration that is a noble gas structure with one outer *s*-electron. They are typical metals (in the chemical sense) and readily lose their outer electron to form stable M^+ ions with noble-gas configurations. All are highly reactive, with the reactivity (i.e. metallic character) increasing down the group. There is a decrease in ionization energy from lithium (520 kJ mol^{-1}) to caesium (380 kJ mol^{-1}). The second ionization energies are much higher and divalent ions are not formed. Other properties also change down the group. Thus, there is an increase in atomic and ionic radius, an increase in density, and a decrease in melting and boiling point. The standard electrode potentials are low and negative, although they do not show a regular trend because they depend both on ionization energy (which decreases down the group) and the hydration energy of the ions (which increases).

All the elements react with water (lithium slowly; the others violently) and tarnish rapidly in air. They can all be made to react with chlorine, bromine, sulphur, and hydrogen. The hydroxides of the alkali metals are strongly alkaline (hence the name) and do not decompose on heating. The salts are generally soluble. The carbonates do not decompose on heating, except at very high temperatures. The nitrates (except for lithium) decompose to give the nitrite and oxygen:

$$2MNO_3(s) \rightarrow 2MNO_2(s) + O_2(g)$$

Lithium nitrate decomposes to the oxide. In fact lithium shows a number of dissimilarities to the other members of group I and in many ways resembles magnesium (*see* diagonal relationship). In general, the stability of salts of oxo acids increases down the group (i.e. with increasing size of the M^+ ion). This trend occurs because the smaller cations (at the top of the group) tend to polarize the oxo anion more effectively than the larger cations at the bottom of the group.

alkalimetry Volumetric analysis using standard solutions of alkali to determine the amount of acid present.

alkaline 1. Describing an alkali. 2. Describing a solution that has an excess of hydroxide ions (i.e. a pH greater than 7).

alkaline-earth metals (group II elements) The elements of the second group of the *periodic table (group IIA): beryllium (Be), magnesium (Mg), calcium (Ca), strontium (Sr), and barium (Ba). The elements are sometimes referred to as the 'alkaline earths', although strictly the 'earths' are the oxides of the elements. All have a characteristic electron configuration that is a noble-gas structure with two outer *s*-electrons. They are typical metals (in the chemical sense) and readily lose both outer electrons to form stable M^{2+} ions; i.e. they are strong reducing agents. All are reactive, with the reactivity increasing down the group. There is a decrease in both first and second ionization energies down the group. Although there is a significant difference between the first and second ionization energies of each element, compounds containing univalent ions are not known. This is because the divalent ions have a smaller size and larger charge, leading to higher hydration energies (in solution) or lattice energies (in solids). Consequently, the overall energy charge favours the formation of divalent compounds. The third ionization energies are much higher than the second ionization energies, and trivalent compounds (containing M^{3+}) are unknown.

Beryllium, the first member of the group, has anomalous properties because of the small size of the ion; its atomic radius (0.112 nm) is much less than that of magnesium (0.16 nm). From magnesium to radium there is a fairly regular increase in atomic and ionic radius. Other regular changes take place in moving down the group from magnesium. Thus, the density and melting and boiling points all increase. Beryllium, on the other hand, has higher boiling and melting points than calcium and its density lies between those of calcium and strontium. The standard electrode potentials are negative and show a regular small decrease from magnesium to barium. In some ways beryllium resembles aluminium (*see* diagonal relationship).

All the metals are rather less reactive than the alkali metals. They react with water and oxygen (beryllium and magnesium form a protective surface film) and can be made to react with chlorine, bromine, sulphur, and hydrogen. The oxides and hydroxides of the metals show the increasing ionic character in moving down the group: beryllium hydroxide is amphoteric, magnesium hydroxide is only very slightly soluble in water and is weakly basic, calcium hydroxide is sparingly soluble and distinctly basic, strontium and barium hydroxides are quite soluble and basic. The hydroxides decompose on heating to give the oxide and water:

$$M(OH)_2(s) \rightarrow MO(s) + H_2O(g)$$

The carbonates also decompose on heating to the oxide and carbon dioxide:

$$MCO_3(s) \rightarrow MO(s) + CO_2(g)$$

The nitrates decompose to give the oxide:

$$2M(NO_3)_2(s) \rightarrow 2MO(s) + 4NO_2(g) + O_2(g)$$

As with the *alkali metals, the stability of salts of oxo acids increases down the group. In general, salts of the alkaline-earth elements are soluble if the anion has a single charge (e.g. nitrates, chlorides). Most salts with a doubly charged anion (e.g. carbonates, sulphates) are insoluble. The solubilities of salts of a particular acid tend to decrease down the group. (Solubilities of hydroxides increase for larger cations.)

alkaloid One of a group of nitrogenous organic compounds derived from plants and having diverse pharmacological properties. Alkaloids include morphine, cocaine, atropine, quinine, and caffeine, most of which are used in medicine as analgesics (pain relievers) or anaesthetics. Some alkaloids are poisonous, e.g. strychnine and coniine, and colchicine inhibits cell division.

alkanes (paraffins) Saturated hydrocarbons with the general formula C_nH_{2n+2}. In systematic chemical nomenclature alkane names end in the suffix *-ane*. They form a *homologous series (the *alkane series*) methane (CH_4), ethane (C_2H_6), propane (C_3H_8), butane (C_4H_{10}), pentane (C_5H_{12}), etc. The lower members of the series are gases; the high-molecular weight alkanes are waxy solids. Alkanes are present in natural gas and petroleum. They can be made by heating the sodium salt of a carboxylic acid with soda lime:

$$RCOO^-Na^+ + Na^+OH^- \rightarrow Na_2CO_3 + RH$$

Other methods include the *Wurtz reaction and *Kolbé's method. Generally the alkanes are fairly unreactive. They form haloalkanes with halogens when irradiated with ultraviolet radiation.

alkenes (olefines; olefins) Unsaturated hydrocarbons that contain one or more double carbon–carbon bonds in their molecules. In systematic chemical nomenclature alkene names end in the suffix *-ene*. Alkenes that have only one double bond form a ho-

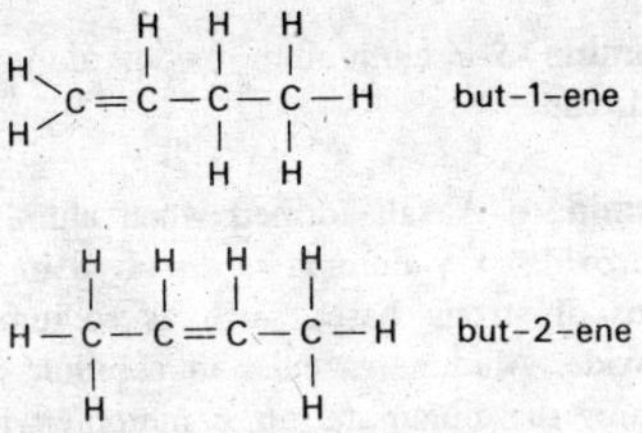

Butene isomers

mologous series (the *alkene series*) starting ethene (ethylene), $CH_2{:}CH_2$, propene, $CH_3CH{:}CH_2$, etc. The general formula is C_nH_{2n}. Higher members of the series show isomerism depending on position of the double bond; for example, butene (C_4H_8) has two isomers, which are (1) but-1-ene ($C_2H_5CH{:}CH_2$) and (2) but-2-ene ($CH_3CH{:}CHCH_3$). Alkenes can be made by dehydration of alcohols (passing the vapour over hot pumice):

$$RCH_2CH_2OH - H_2O \rightarrow RCH{:}CH_2$$

An alternative method is the removal of a hydrogen atom and halogen atom from a haloalkane by potassium hydroxide in hot alcoholic solution:

$$RCH_2CH_2Cl + KOH \rightarrow KCl + H_2O + RCH{:}CH_2$$

Alkenes typically undergo *addition reactions to the double bond. *See also* hydrogenation; oxo reaction; ozonolysis; Ziegler process.

alkoxides Compounds formed by reaction of alcohols with sodium or potassium metal. Alkoxides are saltlike compounds containing the ion $R{-}O^-$

alkylbenzenes Organic compounds that have an alkyl group bound to a benzene ring. The simplest example is methylbenzene (toluene), $CH_3C_6H_5$. Alkyl benzenes can be made by the *Friedel–Crafts reaction.

alkyl group A group obtained by removing a hydrogen atom from an alkane, e.g. methyl group, CH_3-, derived from methane.

alkyl halides *See* haloalkanes.

alkynes (acetylenes) Unsaturated hydrocarbons that contain one or more triple carbon–carbon bonds in their molecules. In systematic chemical nomenclature alkyne names end in the suffix *-yne*. Alkynes that have only one triple bond form a *homologous series: ethyne (acetylene), $CH{\equiv}CH$, propyne, $CH_3CH{\equiv}CH$, etc. They are made by the action of potassium hydroxide in alcohol solution on haloalkanes containing halogen atoms on adjacent carbon atoms; for example:

$$RCHClCH_2Cl + 2KOH \rightarrow 2KCl + 2H_2O + RCH{\equiv}CH$$

Like *alkenes, alkynes undergo addition reactions.

allotropy The existence of elements in two or more different forms (*allotropes*). In the case of oxygen, there are two forms: 'normal' dioxygen (O_2) and ozone, or trioxygen (O_3). These two allotropes have different molecular configurations. More commonly, allotropy occurs because of different crystal structures in the solid, and is particularly prevalent in groups IV, V, and VI of the periodic table. In some cases, the allotropes are stable over a temperature range, with a definite transition point at which one changes into the other. For instance, tin has two allotropes: white (metallic) tin stable above 13.2°C and grey (nonmetallic) tin stable below 13.2°C. This form of allotropy is called *enantiotropy*. Carbon also has two allotropes – diamond and graphite – although graphite is the stable form at all temperatures. This form of allotropy, in which there is no transition temperature at which the two are in equilibrium, is called *monotropy*. *See also* polymorphism.

allowed bands *See* energy bands.

alloy A material consisting of two or more metals (e.g. brass is an alloy of copper and zinc) or a metal and a nonmetal (e.g. steel is an alloy of iron and carbon, sometimes with other metals included). Alloys may be compounds, *solid solutions, or mixtures of the components.

alloy steels *See* steel.

allyl group Formerly, the organic group $CH_2{:}CHCH_2-$. It was used in names such as *allyl alcohol* ($CH_2{:}CHCH_2OH$, prop-2-en-1-ol).

Alnico A tradename for a series of alloys, containing iron, aluminium, nickel, cobalt, and copper, used to make permanent magnets.

alpha-iron *See* iron.

alpha-naphthol test A biochemical test to detect the presence of carbohydrates in solution, also known as *Molisch's test* (after the Austrian chemist H. Molisch (1856–1937), who devised it). A small amount of alcoholic alpha-naphthol is mixed with the test solution and concentrated sulphuric acid is poured slowly down the side of the test tube. A positive reaction is indicated by the formation of a violet ring at the junction of the two liquids.

alpha particle A helium nucleus emitted by a larger nucleus during the course of the type of radioactive decay known as *alpha decay*. As a helium nucleus consists of two protons and two neutrons bound together as a stable entity the loss of an alpha particle involves a decrease in *nucleon number of 4 and decrease of 2 in the *atomic number, e.g. the decay of a uranium–238 nucleus into a thorium–234 nucleus. A stream of alpha particles is known as an *alpha-ray* or *alpha-radiation*.

alum *See* aluminium potassium sulphate; alums.

alumina *See* aluminium oxide; aluminium hydroxide.

aluminate A salt formed when aluminium hydroxide or γ-alumina is dissolved in solutions of strong bases, such as sodium hydroxide. Aluminates exist in solutions containing the aluminate ion, commonly written $[Al(OH)_4]^-$. In fact the ion probably is a complex hydrated ion and can be regarded as formed from a hydrated Al^{3+} ion by removal of four hydrogen ions:

$$[Al(H_2O)_6]^{3+} + 4OH^- \rightarrow 4H_2O + [Al(OH)_4(H_2O)_2]^-$$

Other aluminates and polyaluminates, such as $[Al(OH)_6]^{3-}$ and $[(HO)_3AlOAl(OH)_3]^{2-}$, are also present. *See also* aluminium hydroxide.

aluminium Symbol Al. A silvery-white lustrous metallic element belonging to *group III of the periodic table; a.n. 13; r.a.m. 26.98; r.d. 2.7; m.p. 660°C; b.p. 2467°C. The metal itself is highly reactive but is protected by a thin transparent layer of the oxide, which forms quickly in air. Aluminium and its oxide are amphoteric. The metal is extracted from purified bauxite (Al_2O_3) by electrolysis; the main process uses a *Hall–Heroult cell but other electrolytic methods are under development, including conversion of bauxite with chlorine and electrolysis of the molten chloride. Pure aluminium is soft and ductile but its strength can be increased by work-hardening. A large number of alloys are manufactured; alloying elements include copper, manganese, silicon, zinc, and magnesium. Its lightness, strength (when alloyed), corrosion resistance, and electrical conductivity (62% of that of copper) make it suitable for a variety of uses, including vehicle and aircraft construction, building (window and door frames), and overhead power cables. though it is the third most abundant element in the earth's crust (8.1% by weight) it was not isolated until 1825 by H. C. Oersted (1777–1851).

aluminium acetate *See* aluminium ethanoate.

aluminium chloride A whitish solid, $AlCl_3$, which fumes in moist air and reacts

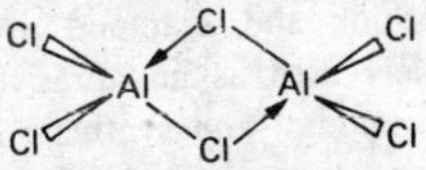

Structure of aluminium trichloride dimer

violently with water (to give hydrogen chloride). It is known as the anhydrous salt (hexagonal; r.d. 2.44 (fused solid); m.p. 190°C (2.5 atm.); sublimes at 178°C) or the hexahydrate $AlCl_3.6H_2O$ (rhombic; r.d. 2.398; loses water at 100°C), both of which are deliquescent. Aluminium chloride may be prepared by passing hydrogen chloride or chlorine over hot aluminium or (industrially) by passing chlorine over heated aluminium oxide and carbon. The chloride ion is polarized by the small positive aluminium ion and the bonding in the solid is intermediate between covalent and ionic. In the liquid and vapour phases dimer molecules exist, Al_2Cl_6, in which there are chlorine bridges making coordinate bonds to aluminium atoms. The $AlCl_3$ molecule can also form compounds with other molecules that donate pairs of electrons (e.g. amines or hydrogen sulphide); i.e. it acts as a Lewis *acid. At high temperatures the Al_2Cl_6 molecules in the vapour dissociate to (planar) $AlCl_3$ molecules. Aluminium chloride is used commercially as a catalyst in the cracking of oils. It is also a catalyst in certain other organic reactions, especially the Friedel–Crafts reaction.

aluminium ethanoate (aluminium acetate) A white solid, $Al(OOCCH_3)_3$, which decomposes on heating, is very slightly soluble in cold water, and decomposes in warm water. The normal salt, $Al(OOCCH_3)_3$, can only be made in the absence of water (e.g. ethanoic anhydride and aluminium chloride at 180°C); in water it forms the basic salts $Al(OH)(OOCCH_3)_2$ and $Al_2(OH)_2(OOCCH_3)_4$. The reaction of aluminium hydroxide with ethanoic acid gives these basic salts directly. The compound is used extensively in dyeing as a mordant, particularly in combination with aluminium sulphate (known as *red liquor*); in the paper and board industry for sizing and hardening; and in tanning. It was previously used as an antiseptic and astringent.

aluminium hydroxide A white crystalline compound, $Al(OH)_3$; r.d. 2.42–2.52. The compound occurs naturally as the mineral *gibbsite* (monoclinic). In the laboratory it can be prepared by precipitation from solutions of aluminium salts. Such solutions contain the hexaquoaluminium(III) ion with six water molecules coordinated, $[Al(H_2O)_6]^{3+}$. In neutral solution this ionizes:

$$[Al(H_2O)_6]^{3+} \rightleftharpoons H^+ + [Al(H_2O)_5OH]^{2+}$$

The presence of a weak base such as S^{2-} or $CO_3^{\ 2-}$ (by bubbling hydrogen sulphide or carbon dioxide through the solution) causes further ionization with precipitation of aluminium hydroxide

$$[Al(H_2O)_6]^{3+}(aq) \rightarrow Al(H_2O)_3(OH)_3(s) + 3H^+(aq)$$

The substance contains coordinated water molecules and is more correctly termed *hydrated aluminium hydroxide*. In addition, the precipitate has water molecules trapped in it and has a characteristic gelatinous form. The substance is amphoteric. In strong bases the *aluminate ion is produced by loss of a further proton:

$$Al(H_2O)_3(OH)_3(s) + OH^-(aq) \rightleftharpoons [Al(H_2O)_2(OH)_4]^-(aq) + H_2O(l)$$

On heating, the hydroxide transforms to a mixed oxide hydroxide, AlO.OH (rhombic; r.d. 3.01). This substance occurs naturally as *diaspore* and *boehmite*. Above 450°C it transforms to γ-alumina.

In practice various substances can be produced that are mixed crystalline forms of $Al(OH)_3$, AlO.OH, and aluminium oxide (Al_2O_3) with water molecules. These are known as *hydrated alumina*. Heating the hydrated hydroxide causes loss of water, and produces various *activated aluminas*, which differ in porosity, number of remaining –OH groups, and particle size. These are used as catalysts (particularly for organic dehydration reactions), as catalyst supports, and in chromatography. Gelatinous freshly precipitated aluminium hydroxide was formerly widely used as a mordant for dyeing and calico printing because of its ability to form insoluble coloured *lakes with vegetable dyes. *See also* aluminium oxide.

aluminium oxide (alumina) A white or colourless oxide of aluminium occurring in two main forms. The stable form α-alumina (r.d. 3.97; m.p. 2020°C; b.p. 2980 ± 60°C) has colourless hexagonal or rhombic crystals; γ-alumina (r.d. 3.5–3.9) transforms to the α-form on heating and is a white microcrystalline solid. The compound occurs naturally as *corundum* or *emery* in the α-form with a hexagonal-close-packed structure of oxide ions with aluminium ions in the octahedral interstices. The gemstones ruby and sapphire are aluminium oxide coloured by minute traces of chromium and cobalt respectively. A number of other forms of aluminium oxide have been described (β-, δ-, and ζ-alumina) but these contain alkali-metal ions. There is also a short-lived spectroscopic suboxide AlO. The highly protective film of oxide formed on the surface of aluminium metal is yet another structural variation, being a defective rock-salt form (every third Al missing).

Pure aluminium oxide is obtained by dissolving the ore bauxite in sodium hydroxide solution; impurities such as iron oxides remain insoluble because they are not amphoteric. The hydrated oxide is precipitated by seeding with material from a previous batch and this is then roasted at 1150–1200°C to give pure α-alumina, or at 500–800°C to give γ-alumina. The bonding in aluminium hydroxide is not purely ionic due to polarization of the oxide ion. Although the compound might be expected to be amphoteric, α-alumina is weakly acidic, dissolving in alkalis to give solutions containing aluminate ions; it is resistant to acid attack. In contrast γ-alumina is typically amphoteric dissolving both in acids to give aluminium salts and in bases to give aluminates. α-alumina is one of the hardest materials known (silicon carbide and diamond are harder) and is widely used as an abrasive in both natural (corundum) and synthetic forms. Its refractory nature makes alumina brick an ideal material for furnace linings and alumina is also used in cements for high-temperature conditions. *See also* aluminium hydroxide.

aluminium potassium sulphate (potash alum; alum) A white or colourless crystalline compound, $Al_2(SO_4)_3.K_2SO_4.24H_2O$; r.d. 1.757; loses $18H_2O$ at 92.5°C; becomes anhydrous at 200°C. It forms cubic or octahedral crystals that are soluble in cold water, very soluble in hot water, and insoluble in ethanol and acetone. The compound occurs naturally as the mineral *kalinite*. It is a double salt and can be prepared by recrystallization from a solution containing equimolar quantities of potassium sulphate and aluminium sulphate. It is used as a mordant for dyeing and in the tanning and finishing of leather goods (for white leather). *See also* alums.

aluminium sulphate A white or colourless crystalline compound, $Al_2(SO_4)_3$, known as the anhydrous compound (r.d. 2.71; decomposes at 770°C) or as the hydrate $Al_2(SO)_3.18H_2O$ (monoclinic; r.d. 1.69; loses water at 86.5°C). The anhydrous salt is soluble in water and slightly soluble in ethanol; the hydrate is very soluble in water and insoluble in ethanol. The compound occurs naturally in the rare mineral *alunogenite* ($Al_2(SO)_3.18H_2O$). It may be prepared by dissolving aluminium hydroxide or china clays (aluminosilicates) in sulphuric acid. It decomposes on heating to sulphur dioxide, sulphur trioxide, and aluminium oxide. Its solutions are acidic because of hydrolysis.

Aluminium sulphate is commercially one of the most important aluminium compounds; it is used in sewage treatment (as a flocculating agent) and in the purification of drinking water, the paper industry, and in the preparation of mordants. It is also a fire-proofing agent. Aluminium sulphate is often wrongly called *alum* in these industries.

aluminium trimethyl *See* trimethylaluminium.

alums A group of double salts with the formula $A_2SO_4.B_2(SO_4)_3.24H_2O$, where A is a monovalent metal and B a trivalent metal. The original example contains potassium and aluminium (called *potash alum* or simply *alum*); its formula is often written $AlK(SO_4)_2.12H_2O$ (aluminium potassium sulphate-12-water). *Ammonium alum* is $AlNH_4(SO_4)_2.12H_2O$, *chrome alum* is $KCr(SO_4)_2.12H_2O$ (*see* potassium chromium sulphate), etc. The alums are isomorphous and can be made by dissolving equivalent amounts of the two salts in water and recrystallizing. *See also* aluminium sulphate.

alunogenite A mineral form of hydrated *aluminium sulphate, $Al_2(SO_4)_3.18H_2O$.

amalgam An alloy of mercury with one or more other metals. Most metals form amalgams (iron and platinum are exceptions), which may be liquid or solid. Some contain definite intermetallic compounds, such as $NaHg_2$.

americium Symbol Am. A radioactive metallic transuranic element belonging to the *actinoids; a.n. 95; mass number of most stable isotope 243 (half-life 7.95×10^3 years); r.d. 13.67 (20°C); m.p. 994 ± 4°C; b.p. 2607°C. Ten isotopes are known. The element was discovered by G. T. Seaborg and associates in 1945, who obtained it by bombarding uranium–238 with alpha particles.

amethyst The purple variety of the mineral *quartz. It is found chiefly in Brazil, the Urals (Soviet Union), Arizona (USA), and Uruguay. The colour is due to impurities, especially iron oxide. It is used as a gemstone.

amides Organic compounds containing the group $-CO.NH_2$ (the *amide group*). Amides are volatile solids; examples are ethanamide, CH_3CONH_2, and propanamide, $C_2H_5CONH_2$. They are made by heating the ammonium salt of the corresponding carboxylic acid.

amination A chemical reaction in which an amino group ($-NH_2$) is introduced into a molecule. Examples of amination reaction include the reaction of halogenated hydrocarbons with ammonia (high pressure and temperature) and the reduction of nitro compounds and nitriles.

amines Organic compounds derived by replacing one or more of the hydrogen atoms in ammonia by organic groups. *Primary amines* have one hydrogen replaced, e.g. methylamine, CH_3NH_2. They contain the functional group $-NH_2$ (the *amino group*). *Secondary amines* have two hydrogens replaced, e.g. methylethylamine, $CH_3(C_2H_5)NH$. The group $=NH$ is the *imino group*. *Tertiary amines* have all three replaced, e.g. trimethylamine, $(CH_3)_3N$. Amines are produced by the decomposition of organic matter. They can be made by reducing nitro compounds or amides.

amine salts Salts similar to ammonium salts in which the hydrogen atoms attached to the nitrogen are replaced by one or more organic groups. Amines readily form salts by reaction with acids, gaining a proton to form a positive ammonium ion, They are named as if they were substituted derivatives of ammonium compounds; for example, dimethylamine ($(CH_3)_2NH$) will react with hydrogen chloride to give dimethylammonium chloride, which is an ionic compound $[(CH_3)_2NH_2]^+Cl^-$. When the amine has a common nonsystematic name the suffix *-ium* can be used; for example, phenylamine (aniline) would give $[C_6H_5NH_3]^+Cl^-$, known as anilinium chloride. Formerly, such compounds were sometimes called *hydrochlorides*, e.g. aniline hydrochloride with the formula $C_6H_5NH_2.HCl$.

Salts formed by amines are crystalline substances that are readily soluble in water. Many insoluble *alkaloids (e.g. quinine and atropine) are used medicinally in the form of soluble salts ('hydrochlorides'). If alkali (sodium hydroxide) is added to solutions of such salts the free amine is liberated.

If all four hydrogen atoms of an ammonium salt are replaced by organic groups a *quaternary ammonium compound* is formed. Such compounds are made by reacting tertiary amines with halogen compounds; for example, trimethylamine ($(CH_3)_3N$) with chloromethane (CH_3Cl) gives tetramethylammonium chloride, $(CH_3)_4N^+Cl^-$. Salts of this type do not liberate the free amine when alkali is added, and quaternary hydroxides (such as $(CH_3)_4N^+OH^-$) can be isolated. Such compounds are strong alkalis, comparable to sodium hydroxide.

amino acid Any of a group of water-soluble organic compounds that possess both a carboxyl ($-COOH$) and an amino ($-NH_2$) group attached to the α-carbon atom. Amino acids can be represented by the general formula $R-CH(NH_2)COOH$. R may be hydrogen or an organic group and determines the properties of any particular amino acid. Through the formation of peptide bonds, amino acids join together to form short chains (*peptides) or much longer chains (*polypeptides). Proteins are composed of various proportions of about 20 commonly occurring amino acids (see table). The sequence of these amino acids in the protein polypeptides determines the shape, properties, and hence biological role of the protein. Some amino acids that never occur in proteins are nevertheless important, e.g. ornithine and citrulline, which are intermediates in the urea cycle.

Plants and many microorganisms can synthesize amino acids from simple inorganic compounds, but animals rely on adequate supplies in their diet. The *essential amino acids must be present in the diet whereas others can be manufactured from them.

aminobenzene *See* phenylamine.

amino group *See* amines.

ammine A coordination *complex in which the ligands are ammonia molecules. An example of an ammine is the tetraamminecopper(II) ion $[Cu(NH_3)_4]^{2+}$.

ammonia A colourless gas, NH_3, with a strong pungent odour; r.d. 0.59 (relative to air); m.p. −74°C; b.p. −30.9°C. It is very soluble in water and soluble in alcohol. The compound may be prepared in the laboratory by the reaction of ammonium salts with bases such as calcium hydroxide, or by the hydrolysis of a nitride. Industrially it is made by the *Haber process and over 80 million tonnes per year are used either directly or in combination. Major uses are the manufacture of nitric acid, ammonium nitrate, ammonium phosphate, and urea (the last three as fertilizers), explosives, dyestuffs and resins.

Liquid ammonia has some similarity to water as it is hydrogen bonded and has a moderate dielectric constant, which permits it to act as an ionizing solvent. It is weakly self-ionized to give ammonium ions, NH_4^+ and amide ions, NH_2^-. It also dissolves electropositive metals to give blue solutions, which are believed to contain solvated electrons. Ammonia is extremely soluble in water giving basic solutions that contain solvated NH_3 molecules and small amounts of the ions NH_4^+ and OH^-. The combustion of ammonia in air yields nitrogen and

amino acid	abbreviation	formula
alanine	ala	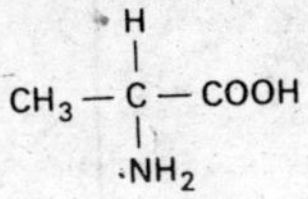
•arginine	arg	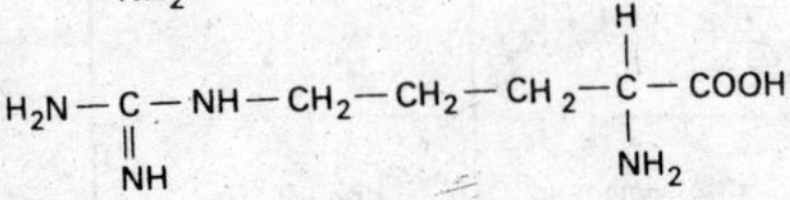
asparagine	asn	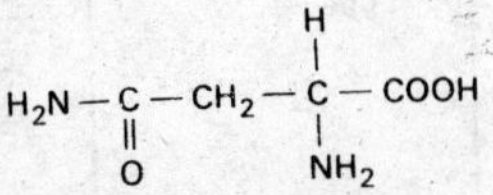
aspartic acid	asp	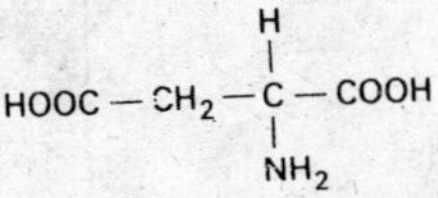
cysteine	cys	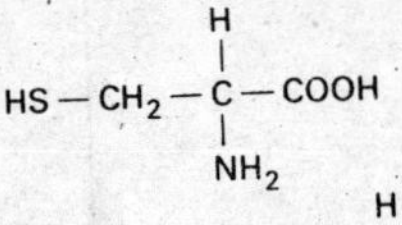
glutamic acid	glu	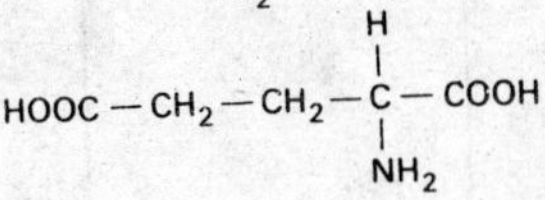
glutamine	gln	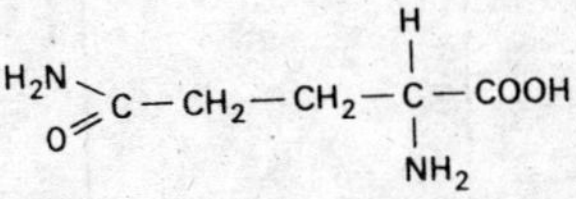
glycine	gly	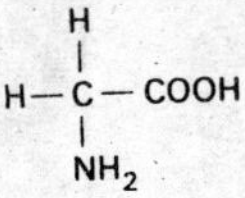
•histidine	his	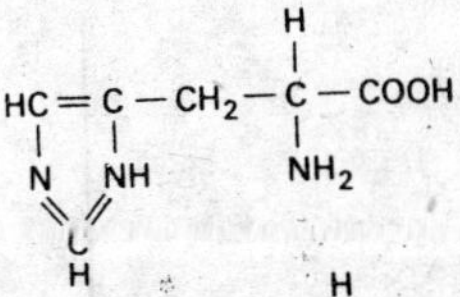
•isoleucine	ile	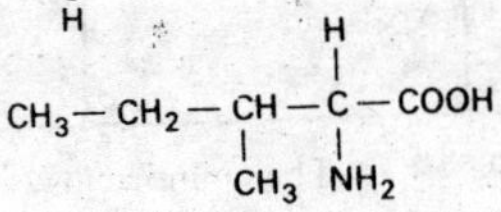
•leucine	leu	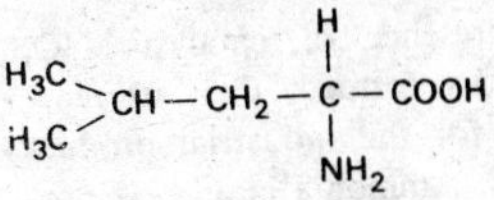

*lysine	lys	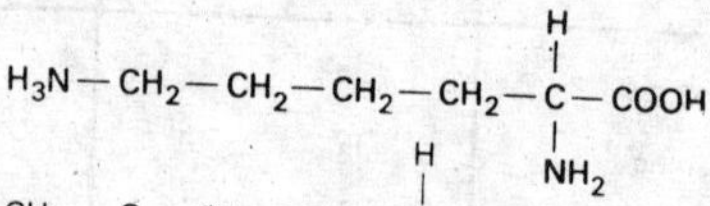
*methionine	met	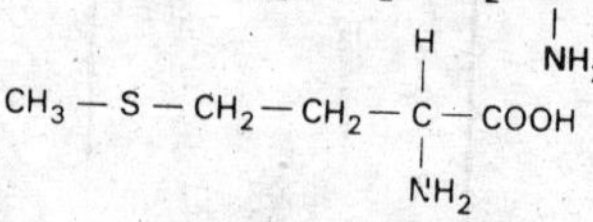
*phenylalanine	phe	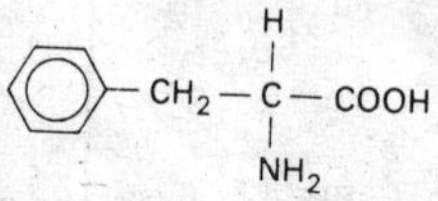
proline	pro	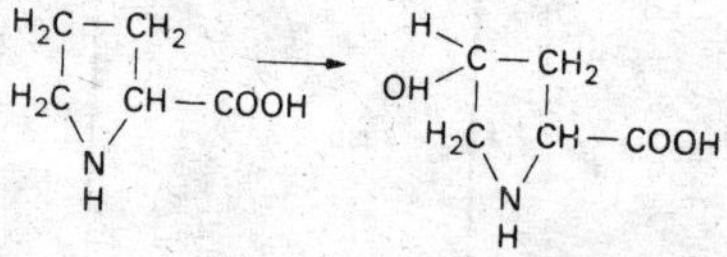 4-hydroxyproline
serine	ser	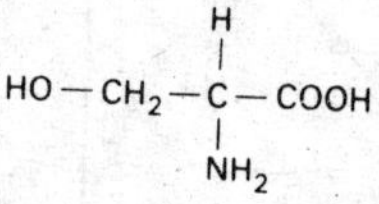
*threonine	thr	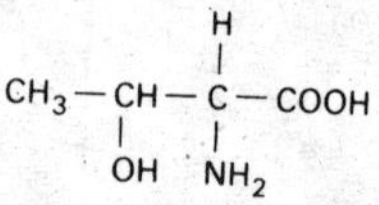
*tryptophan	trp	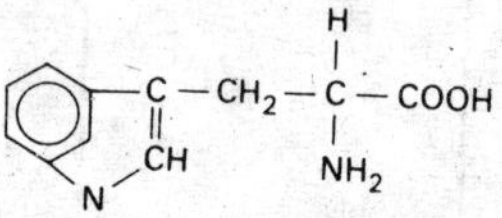
tyrosine	tyr	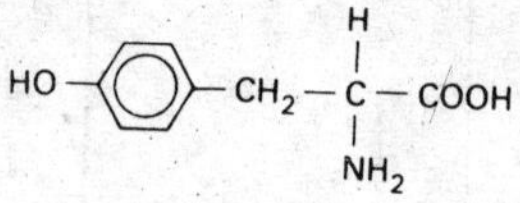
*valine	val	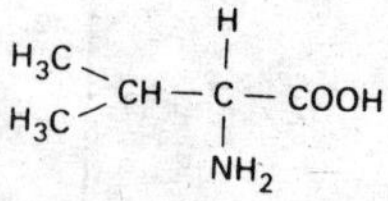

* an essential amino acid

The amino acids occurring in proteins

water. In the presence of catalysts NO, NO_2, and water are formed; this last reaction is the basis for the industrial production of nitric acid. Ammonia is a good proton acceptor (i.e. it is a base) and gives rise to a series of ammonium salts, e.g. NH_3 + HCl → NH_4^+ + Cl^-. It is also a reducing agent. The participation of ammonia in the *nitrogen cycle is a most important natural process. Nitrogen-fixing bacteria are able to achieve similar reactions to those of the Haber process, but under normal conditions of temperature and pressure. These release ammonium ions, which are converted by nitrifying bacteria into nitrite and nitrate ions.

ammoniacal Describing a solution in which the solvent is aqueous ammonia.

ammonia–soda process *See* Solvay process.

ammonium alum *See* alums.

ammonium carbonate A colourless or white crystalline solid, $(NH_4)_2CO_3$, usually encountered as the monohydrate. It is very soluble in cold water. The compound decomposes slowly to give ammonia, water, and carbon dioxide. Commercial 'ammonium carbonate' is a double salt of ammonium hydrogencarbonate and ammonium aminomethanoate (ammonium carbamate), $NH_4HCO_3.NH_2COONH_4$. This material is manufactured by heating a mixture of ammonium chloride and calcium carbonate and recovering the product as a sublimed solid. It readily releases ammonia and is the basis of sal volatile. It is also used in dyeing and wool preparation and in baking powders.

ammonium chloride (sal ammoniac) A white or colourless cubic solid, NH_4Cl; r.d. 1.53; sublimes at 340°C. It is very soluble in water and slightly soluble in ethanol but insoluble in ether. It may be prepared by fractional crystallization from a solution containing ammonium sulphate and sodium chloride or ammonium carbonate and calcium chloride. Pure samples may be made directly by the gas-phase reaction of ammonia and hydrogen chloride. Because of its ease of preparation it can be manufactured industrially alongside any plant that uses or produces ammonia. The compound is used in dry cells, metal finishing, and in the preparation of cotton for dyeing and printing.

ammonium ion The monovalent cation NH_4^+. It may be regarded as the product of the reaction of ammonia (a Lewis base) with a hydrogen ion. The ion has tetrahedral symmetry. The chemical properties of ammonium salts are frequently very similar to those of equivalent alkali-metal salts.

ammonium nitrate A colourless crystalline solid, NH_4NO_3; r.d. 1.72; m.p. 169.6°C; b.p. 210°C. It is very soluble in water and soluble in ethanol. The crystals are rhombic when obtained below 32°C and monoclinic above 32°C. It may be readily prepared in the laboratory by the reaction of nitric acid with aqueous ammonia. Industrially, it is manufactured by the same reaction using ammonia gas. Vast quantities of ammonium nitrate are used as fertilizers (over 20 million tonnes per year) and it is also a component of some explosives.

ammonium sulphate A white rhombic solid, $(NH_4)_2SO_4$; r.d. 1.67; decomposes at 235°C. It is very soluble in water and insoluble in ethanol. It occurs naturally as the mineral *mascagnite*. Ammonium sulphate was formerly manufactured from the 'ammoniacal liquors' produced during coal-gas manufacture but is now produced by the direct reaction between ammonia gas and sulphuric acid. It is decomposed by heating to release ammonia (and ammonium hydrogensulphate) and eventually water, sulphur dioxide, and ammonia. Vast quantities of ammonium sulphate are used as fertilizers.

amorphous Describing a solid that is not crystalline; i.e. one that has no long-range order in its lattice. Many powders that are described as 'amorphous' in fact are composed of microscopic crystals, as can be demonstrated by X-ray diffraction. *Glasses are examples of true amorphous solids.

amount of substance Symbol *n*. A measure of the number of entities present in a substance. The specified entity may be an atom, molecule, ion, electron, photon, etc., or any specified group of such entities. The amount of substance of an element, for example, is proportional to the number of atoms present. For all entities, the constant of proportionality is the *Avogadro constant. The SI unit of amount of substance is the *mole.

AMP *See* ATP; cyclic AMP.

ampere Symbol A. The SI unit of electric current. The constant current that, maintained in two straight parallel infinite conductors of negligible cross section placed one metre apart in a vacuum, would produce a force between the conductors of 2×10^{-7} N m^{-1}. This definition replaced the earlier international ampere defined as the current required to deposit 0.001 118 00 gram of silver from a solution of silver nitrate in one second. The unit is named after A. M. Ampère (1775–1836).

ampere-hour A practical unit of electric charge equal to the charge flowing in one hour through a conductor passing one ampere. It is equal to 3600 coulombs.

ampere-turn The SI unit of magnetomotive force equal to the magnetomotive force produced when a current of one ampere flows through one turn of a magnetizing coil.

amphiboles A large group of rock-forming metasilicate minerals. They have a structure of silicate tetrahedra linked to form double endless chains, in contrast to the single chains of the *pyroxenes, to which they are closely related. They are present in many igneous and metamorphic rocks. The amphiboles show a wide range of compositional variation but conform to the general formula: $X_{2-3}Y_5Z_8O_{22}(OH)_2$, where X = Ca, Na, K, Mg, or Fe^{2+}; Y = Mg, Fe^{2+}, Fe^{3+}, Al, Ti, or Mn; and Z = Si or Al. The hydroxyl ions may be replaced by F, Cl, or O. Most amphiboles are monoclinic, including cummingtonite, $(Mg,Fe^{2+})_7(Si_8O_{22})(OH)_2$; tremolite, $Ca_2Mg_5(Si_8O_{22})(OH,F)_2$; actinolite, $Ca_2(Mg,Fe^{2+})_5(Si_8O_{22})(OH,F)_2$; *hornblende, $NaCa_2(Mg,Fe^{2+},Fe^{3+},Al)_5((Si,Al)_8O_{22})(OH,F)_2$; edenite, $NaCa_2(Mg,Fe^{2+})_5(Si_7AlO_{22})(OH,F)_2$; and riebeckite, $Na_2,Fe_3^{2+}(Si_8O_{22})(OH,F)_2$. Anthophyllite, $(Mg,Fe^{2+})_7(Si_8O_{22})(OH,F)_2$, and gedrite, $(Mg,Fe^{2+})_6Al(Si,Al)_8O_{22}(OH,F)_2$, are orthorhombic amphiboles.

ampholyte A substance that can act as either an acid, in the presence of a strong base, or a base, when in the presence of a strong acid.

ampholyte ion *See* zwitterion.

amphoteric Describing a compound that can act as both an acid and a base (in the traditional sense of the term). For instance, aluminium hydroxide is amphoteric: as a base $Al(OH)_3$ it reacts with acids to form aluminium salts; as an acid H_3AlO_3 it reacts with alkalis to give *aluminates. Oxides of metals are typically basic and oxides of nonmetals tend to be acidic. The existence of amphoteric oxides is sometimes regarded as evidence that an element is a *metalloid.

a.m.u. *See* atomic mass unit.

amylase (diastase) Any of a group of closely related enzymes that degrade starch, glycogen, and other polysaccharides. Plants contain both α- and β-amylases; animals possess only α-amylases, found in pancreatic juice and also (in humans and some other species) in saliva. Amylases cleave the long polysaccharide chains, producing a mixture of glucose and maltose.

amyl group Formerly, any of several isomeric groups with the formula $C_5H_{11}-$.

amylopectin A *polysaccharide comprising highly branched chains of glucose molecules.

It is one of the constituents (the other being amylose) of *starch.

amylose A *polysaccharide consisting of linear chains of between 100 and 1000 linked glucose molecules. Amylose is a constituent of *starch. In water, amylose reacts with iodine to give a characteristic blue colour.

anabolism The metabolic synthesis of proteins, fats, and other constituents of living organisms from molecules or simple precursors. This process requires energy in the form of ATP. *See* metabolism. *Compare* catabolism.

analysis The determination of the components in a chemical sample. *Qualitative analysis* involves determining the nature of a pure unknown compound or the compounds present in a mixture. Various chemical tests exist for different elements or types of compound, and systematic analytical procedures can be used for mixtures. *Quantitative analysis* involves measuring the proportions of known components in a mixture. Chemical techniques for this fall into two main classes: *volumetric analysis and *gravimetric analysis. In addition, there are numerous physical methods of qualitative and quantitative analysis, including spectroscopic techniques, mass spectrometry, polarography, chromatography, activation analysis, etc.

anglesite A mineral form of *lead(II) sulphate, $PbSO_4$.

angstrom Symbol Å. A unit of length equal to 10^{-10} metre. It was formerly used to measure wavelengths and intermolecular distances but has now been replaced by the nanometre. 1 Å = 0.1 nanometre. The unit is named after the Swedish pioneer of spectroscopy A. J. Ångstrom (1814–74).

anhydride A compound that produces a given compound on reaction with water. For instance, sulphur trioxide is the (acid) anhydride of sulphuric acid

$$SO_3 + H_2O \rightarrow H_2SO_4$$

See also acid anhydrides.

anhydrite An important rock-forming anhydrous mineral form of calcium sulphate, $CaSO_4$. It is chemically similar to *gypsum but is harder and heavier and crystallizes in the rhombic form (gypsum is monoclinic). Under natural conditions anhydrite slowly hydrates to form gypsum. It occurs chiefly in white and greyish granular masses and is often found in the caprock of certain salt domes. It is used as a raw material in the chemical industry and in the manufacture of cement and fertilizers.

anhydrous Denoting a chemical compound lacking water: applied particularly to salts lacking their water of crystallization.

aniline *See* phenylamine.

anilinium ion The ion $C_6H_5NH_3^+$, derived from *phenylamine.

animal charcoal *See* charcoal.

animal starch *See* glycogen.

anion A negatively charged *ion, i.e. an ion that is attracted to the *anode in *electrolysis. *Compare* cation.

anionic detergent *See* detergent.

anionic resin *See* ion exchange.

anisotropic Denoting a medium in which certain physical properties are different in different directions. Wood, for instance, is an anisotropic material: its strength along the grain differs from that perpendicular to the grain. Single crystals that are not cubic are anisotropic with respect to some physical properties, such as the transmission of electromagnetic radiation. *Compare* isotropic.

annealing A form of heat treatment applied to a metal to soften it, relieve internal stresses and instabilities, and make it easier to work or machine. It consists of heating the metal to a specified temperature for a specified time, both of which depend on the metal involved, and then allowing it to cool slowly. It is applied to both ferrous and nonferrous metals and a similar process can be applied to other materials, such as glass.

anode A positive electrode. In *electrolysis anions are attracted to the anode. In an electronic vacuum tube it attracts electrons from the *cathode and it is therefore from the anode that electrons flow out of the device. In these instances the anode is made positive by external means; however in a *voltaic cell the anode is the electrode that spontaneously becomes positive and therefore attracts electrons to it from the external circuit.

anode sludge *See* electrolytic refining.

anodizing A method of coating objects made of aluminium with a protective oxide film, by making them the anode in an electrolytic bath containing an oxidizing electrolyte. Anodizing can also be used to produce a decorative finish by formation of an oxide layer that can absorb a coloured dye.

anthocyanin One of a group of *flavonoid pigments. Anthocyanins occur in various plant organs and are responsible for many of the blue, red, and purple colours in plants (particularly in flowers).

anthracene A white crystalline solid, $C_{14}H_{10}$; r.d. 1.25; m.p. 286°C; b.p. 379.8°C. It is an aromatic hydrocarbon with three fused rings, and is obtained by the distillation of crude oils. The main use is in the manufacture of dyes.

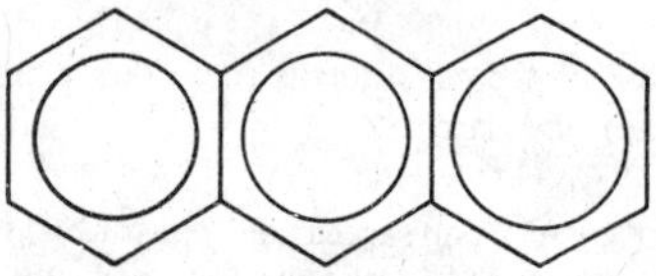

Anthracene

anthracite *See* coal.

antibiotics Substances obtained from microorganisms, especially moulds, that destroy or inhibit the growth of other microorganisms, particularly disease-producing bacteria and fungi. Common antibiotics include penicillin, streptomycin, and tetracyclines. They are used to treat various infections but tend to weaken the body's natural defence mechanisms and can cause allergies. Overuse of antibiotics can lead to the development of resistant strains of microorganisms.

antigorite *See* serpentine.

antimony Symbol Sb. An element belonging to *group VA of the periodic table; a.n. 51; r.a.m. 121.75; r.d. 6.73; m.p. 630.5°C; b.p. 1380°C. Antimony has several allotropes. The stable form is a bluish-white metal. Yellow antimony and black antimony are unstable nonmetallic allotropes made at low temperatures. The main source is stibnite (Sb_2S_3), from which antimony is extracted by reduction with iron metal or by roasting (to give the oxide) followed by reduction with carbon and sodium carbonate. The main use of the metal is as an alloying agent in lead-accumulator plates, type metals, bearing alloys, solders, Britannia metal, and pewter. It is also an agent for producing pearlitic cast iron. Its compounds are used in flame-proofing, paints, ceramics, enamels, glass dyestuffs, and rubber technology. The element will burn in air but is unaffected by water or dilute acids. It is attacked by oxidizing acids and by halogens. It was first reported by Tholden in 1450.

apatite A complex mineral form of *calcium phosphate, $Ca_5(PO_4)_3(OH,F,Cl)$; the commonest of the phosphate minerals. It has a hexagonal structure and occurs widely as an accessory mineral in igneous rocks (e.g. pegmatite) and often in regional and contact metamorphic rocks, especially limestone. Large deposits occur in the Kola Peninsula, USSR. It is used in the production of fertilizers and is a major source of phosphorus. The enamel of teeth is composed chiefly of apatite.

aqua regia A mixture of concentrated nitric acid and concentrated hydrochloric acid in the ratio 1:3 respectively. It is a very powerful oxidizing mixture and will dissolve all metals (except silver, which forms an insoluble chloride) including such noble metals as gold and platinum, hence its name ('royal water'). Nitrosyl chloride (NOCl) is believed to be one of the active constituents.

aqueous Describing a solution in water.

aragonite A rock-forming anhydrous mineral form of calcium carbonate, $CaCO_3$. It is much less stable than *calcite, the commoner form of calcium carbonate, from which it may be distinguished by its greater hardness and specific gravity. Over time aragonite undergoes recrystallization to calcite. Aragonite occurs in cavities in limestone, as a deposit in limestone caverns, as a precipitate around hot springs and geysers, and in high-pressure low-temperature metamorphic rocks; it is also found in the shells of a number of molluscs and corals and is the main constituent of pearls. It is white or colourless when pure but the presence of impurities may tint it grey, blue, green, or pink.

arenes Aromatic hydrocarbons, such as benzene, toluene, and naphthalene.

argentic compounds Compounds of silver in its higher (+2) oxidation state; e.g. argentic oxide is silver(II) oxide (AgO).

argentite A sulphide ore of silver, Ag_2S. It crystallizes in the cubic system but most commonly occurs in massive form. It is dull grey-black in colour but bright when first cut and occurs in veins associated with other silver minerals. Important deposits occur in Mexico, Peru, Chile, Bolivia, Norway, and Czechoslovakia.

argentous compounds Compounds of silver in its lower (+1) oxidation state; e.g. argentous chloride is silver(I) chloride.

arginine *See* amino acid.

argon Symbol Ar. A monatomic noble gas present in air (0.93%); a.n. 18; r.a.m. 39.948; d. 0.00178 g cm^{-3}; m.p. −189°C; b.p. −185°C. Argon is separated from liquid air by fractional distillation. It is slightly soluble in water, colourless, and has no smell. Its uses include inert atmospheres in welding and special-metal manufacture (Ti and Zr), and (when mixed with 20% nitrogen) in gas-filled electric-light bulbs. The element is inert and has no true compounds. Lord Rayleigh and Sir William Ramsey identified argon in 1894.

aromatic compound An organic compound that contains a benzene ring in its molecules or that has chemical properties similar to benzene. Aromatic compounds are unsaturated compounds, yet they do not easily partake in addition reactions. Instead they undergo electrophilic substitution.

Benzene, the archetypal aromatic compound, has an hexagonal ring of carbon atoms and the classical formula (the Kekulé structure) would have alternating double and single bonds. In fact all the bonds in benzene are the same length intermediate between double and single C–C bonds. The properties arise because the electrons in the

π-orbitals are delocalized over the ring, giving an extra stabilization energy of 150 kJ mol^{-1}over the energy of a Kekulé structure. The condition for such delocalization is that a compound should have a planar ring with $(4n + 2)$ pi electrons – this is known as the *Huckel rule*. Aromatic behaviour is also found in heterocyclic compounds such as pyridine. *See also* non-benzenoid aromatic; pseudoaromatic.

aromaticity The property characteristic of *aromatic compounds.

Arrhenius equation An equation of the form

$$k = A\exp(-E_A/RT)$$

where k is the rate constant of a given reaction and E_A the *activation energy. A is a constant for a given reaction, called the *pre-exponential factor*. Often the equation is written in logarithmic form

$$\ln k = \ln A - E_A/RT$$

A graph of $\ln k$ against $1/T$ is a straight line with a gradient $-E_A/R$ and an intercept on the $\ln k$ axis of $\ln A$.

Arrhenius theory *See* acid.

arsenate(III) *See* arsenic(III) oxide.

arsenate(V) *See* arsenic(V) oxide.

arsenic Symbol As. A metalloid element of *group V of the periodic table; a.n. 33; r.a.m. 74.92; r.d. 5.7; sublimes at 613°C. It has three allotropes –yellow, black, and grey. The grey metallic form is the stable and most common one. Over 150 minerals contain arsenic but the main sources are as impurities in sulphide ores and in the minerals orpiment (As_2S_3) and realgar (As_4S_4). Ores are roasted in air to form arsenic oxide and then reduced by hydrogen or carbon to metallic arsenic. Arsenic compounds are used in insecticides and as doping agents in semiconductors. The element is included in some lead-based alloys to promote hardening. Confusion can arise because As_4O_6 is often sold as white arsenic. Arsenic compounds are accumulative poisons. The element will react with halogens, concentrated oxidizing acids, and hot alkalis. Albertus Magnus is believed to have been the first to isolate the element in 1250.

arsenic acid *See* arsenic(V) oxide.

arsenic(III) acid *See* arsenic(III) oxide.

arsenic hydride *See* arsine.

arsenic(III) oxide (arsenic trioxide; arsenious oxide; white arsenic) A white or colourless compound, As_4O_6, existing in three solid forms. The commonest has cubic or octahedral crystals (r.d. 3.85; sublimes at 193°C) and is soluble in water, ethanol, and alkali solutions. It occurs naturally as *arsenolite*. A vitreous form can be prepared by slow condensation of the vapour (r.d. 3.74); its solubility in cold water is more than double that of the cubic form. The third modification, which occurs naturally as *claudetite*, has monoclinic crystals (r.d. 4.15). Arsenic(III) oxide is obtained commercially as a byproduct from the smelting of nonferrous sulphide ores; it may be produced in the laboratory by burning elemental arsenic in air. The structure of the molecule is similar to that of P_4O_6, with a tetrahedral arrangement of As atoms edge linked by oxygen bridges. Arsenic(III) oxide is acidic; its solutions were formerly called *arsenious acid* (technically, *arsenic(III) acid*). It forms *arsenate(III)* salts (formerly called *arsenites*). Arsenic(III) oxide is extremely toxic and is used as a poison for vermin; trace doses are used for a variety of medicinal purposes. It is also used for producing opalescent glasses and enamels.

arsenic(V) oxide (arsenic oxide) A white amorphous deliquescent solid, As_2O_5; r.d. 4.32; decomposes at 315°C. It is soluble in water and ethanol. Arsenic(V) oxide cannot be obtained by direct combination of arsenic and oxygen; it is usually prepared by the reaction of arsenic with nitric acid followed by dehydration of the arsenic acid thus formed. It readily loses oxygen on heating to give arsenic(III) oxide. Arsenic(V) oxide is acidic, dissolving in water to give arsenic(V) acid (formerly called *arsenic acid*), H_3AsO_4; the acid is tribasic and slightly weaker than phosphoric acid and should be visualized as $(HO)_3AsO$. It gives *arsenate (V)* salts (formerly called *arsenates*).

arsenic trioxide *See* arsenic(III) oxide.

arsenious acid *See* arsenic(III) oxide.

arsenious oxide *See* arsenic(III) oxide.

arsenite *See* arsenic(III) oxide.

arsenolite A mineral form of *arsenic(III) oxide, As_4O_6.

arsine (arsenic hydride) A colourless gas, AsH_3; m.p. −116.3°C; b.p. −55°C. It is soluble in water, chloroform, and benzene. Liquid arsine has a relative density of 1.69. Arsine is produced by the reaction of mineral acids with arsenides of electropositive metals or by the reduction of many arsenic compounds using nascent hydrogen. It is extremely poisonous and, like the hydrides of the heavier members of group V, is readily decomposed at elevated temperatures (around 260–300°C). Like ammonia and phosphine, arsine has a pyramidal structure.

Arsine gas has a very important commercial application in the production of modern microelectronic components. It is used in a dilute gas mixture with an inert gas and its ready thermal decomposition is exploited to enable other growing crystals to be doped with minute traces of arsenic to give *n*-type semiconductors.

artinite A mineral form of basic *magnesium carbonate, $MgCO_3.Mg(OH)_2.3H_2O$.

aryl group A group obtained by removing a hydrogen atom from an aromatic compound, e.g. phenyl group, C_6H_5-, derived from benzene.

asbestos Any one of a group of fibrous amphibole minerals (amosite, crocidolite (blue asbestos), tremolite, anthophyllite, and actinolite) or the fibrous serpentine mineral chrysotile. Asbestos has widespread commercial uses because of its resistance to heat, chemical inertness, and high electrical resistance. The fibres may be spun and woven into fireproof cloth for use in protective clothing, curtains, brake linings, etc., or moulded into blocks. Exposure to large amounts of asbestos can cause the respiratory disease asbestosis. Canada and the USSR are the largest producers of asbestos; others include South Africa, Zimbabwe, and China.

ascorbic acid *See* vitamin C.

asparagine *See* amino acid.

aspartic acid *See* amino acid.

astatine Symbol At. A radioactive *halogen element; a.n. 85; r.a.m. 211; m.p. 302°C; b.p. 377°C. It occurs naturally by radioactive decay from uranium and thorium isotopes. Astatine forms at least 20 isotopes, the most stable astatine–210 has a half-life of 8.3 hours. It can also be produced by alpha bombardment of bismuth–200. Astatine is stated to be more metallic than iodine; at least 5 oxidation states are known in aqueous solutions. It will form interhalogen compounds, such as AtI and AtCl. The existence of At_2 has not yet been established. The element was synthesized by nuclear bombardment in 1940 by D. R. Corson, K. R. MacKenzie, and E. Segré at the University of California.

asymmetric atom *See* optical activity.

atactic polymer *See* polymer.

atmolysis The separation of a mixture of gases by means of their different rates of diffusion. Usually, separation is effected by allowing the gases to diffuse through the walls of a porous partition or membrane.

atmosphere 1. (atm.) A unit of pressure equal to 101 325 pascals. This is equal to 760.0 mmHg. The actual *atmospheric pressure fluctuates around this value. The unit is usually used for expressing pressures well in excess of standard atmospheric pressure, e.g. in high-pressure chemical processes. **2.** *See* earth's atmosphere.

atmospheric pressure The pressure exerted by the weight of the air above it at any point on the earth's surface. At sea level the atmosphere will support a column of mercury about 760 mm high. This decreases with increasing altitude. The standard value for the atmospheric pressure at sea level in SI units is 101 325 pascals.

atom The smallest part of an element that can exist chemically. Atoms consist of a small dense nucleus of protons and neutrons surrounded by moving electrons. The number of electrons equals the number of protons so the overall charge is zero. The electrons are considered to move in circular or elliptical orbits (*see* Bohr theory) or, more accurately, in regions of space around the nucleus (*see* orbital).

The *electronic structure* of an atom refers to the way in which the electrons are arranged about the nucleus, and in particular the *energy levels that they occupy. Each electron can be characterized by a set of four quantum numbers, as follows:

(1) The *principal quantum number n* gives the main energy level and has values 1, 2, 3, etc. (the higher the number, the further the electron from the nucleus). Traditionally, these levels, or the orbits corresponding to them, are referred to as *shells* and given letters K, L, M, etc. The K-shell is the one nearest the nucleus.

(2) The *orbital quantum number l*, which governs the angular momentum of the electron. The possible values of l are $(n - 1)$, $(n - 2)$, ... 1, 0. Thus, in the first shell ($n = 1$) the electrons can only have angular momentum zero ($l = 0$). In the second shell ($n = 2$), the values of l can be 1 or 0, giving rise to two *subshells* of slightly different energy. In the third shell ($n = 3$) there are three subshells, with $l = 2$, 1, or 0. The subshells are denoted by letters $s(l = 0)$, $p(l = 1)$, $d(l = 2)$, $f(l = 3)$. The orbital quantum number is sometimes called the *azimuthal quantum number.*

(3) The *magnetic quantum number m*, which governs the energies of electrons in an external magnetic field. This can take values of $+l$, $+(l - 1)$, ... 1, 0, −1, ... $-(l - 1)$, $-l$. In an s-subshell (i.e. $l = 0$) the value of $m = 0$. In a p-subshell ($l = 1$), m can have values +1, 0, and −1; i.e. there are three p-orbitals in the p-subshell, usually designated p_x, p_y, and p_z. Under normal circumstances, these all have the same energy level.

(4) The *spin quantum number* m_s, which gives the spin of the individual electrons and can have the values $+\frac{1}{2}$ or $-\frac{1}{2}$.

According to the *Pauli exclusion principle, no two electrons in the atom can have the same set of quantum numbers. The numbers define the *quantum state* of the electron, and explain how the electronic structures of atoms occur.

atomicity The number of atoms in a given molecule. For example, oxygen (O_2) has an atomicity of 2, ozone (O_3) an atomicity of 3, benzene (C_6H_6) an atomicity of 12, etc.

atomic mass unit (a.m.u.) A unit of mass used to express *relative atomic masses. It is equal to 1/12 of the mass of an atom of the isotope carbon−12 and is equal to $1.660\,33 \times 10^{-27}$ kg. This unit superseded both the physical and chemical mass units based on oxygen–16 and is sometimes called the *unified mass unit* or the *dalton*.

atomic number (proton number) Symbol *Z*. The number of protons in the nucleus of an atom. The atomic number is equal to the number of electrons orbiting the nucleus in a neutral atom.

atomic orbital *See* orbital.

atomic volume The relative atomic mass of an element divided by its density.

atomic weight *See* relative atomic mass.

ATP (adenosine triphosphate) A nucleotide that is of fundamental importance as a carrier of chemical energy in all living organisms. It consists of adenine linked to D-ribose (i.e. adenosine); the D-ribose component bears three phosphate groups, linearly linked together by covalent bonds. These bonds can undergo hydrolysis to yield either a molecule of *ADP* (*adenosine diphosphate*) and inorganic phosphate or a molecule of *AMP* (*adenosine monophosphate*) and pyrophosphate. Both these reactions yield a large amount of energy (about 30.6 kJ mol^{-1}) that is used to bring about such biological processes as muscle contraction, the active transport of ions and molecules across cell membranes, and the synthesis of biomolecules. The reactions bringing about these processes often involve the enzyme-catalysed transfer of the phosphate group to intermediate substrates. Most ATP-mediated reactions require Mg^{2+} ions as *cofactors.

ATP is regenerated by the rephosphorylation of AMP and ADP using the chemical energy obtained from the oxidation of food. This takes place during glycolysis and the Krebs cycle but, most significantly, is also a result of the reduction–oxidation reactions of the electron transport chain, which ultimately reduces molecular oxygen to water (oxidative phosphorylation).

atropine A poisonous crystalline alkaloid, $C_{17}H_{23}NO_3$; m.p. 114–16°C. It can be extracted from deadly nightshade and other solanaceous plants and is used in medicine to treat colic, to reduce secretions, and to dilate the pupil of the eye.

atto- Symbol *a*. A prefix used in the metric system to denote 10^{-18}. For example, 10^{-18} second = 1 attosecond (as).

Aufbau principle A principle that gives the order in which orbitals are filled in successive elements in the periodic table. The order of filling is 1*s*, 2*s*, 2*p*, 3*s*, 3*p*, 4*s*, 3*d*, 4*p*, 5*s*, 4*d*, 5*p*, 6*s*, 4*f*, 5*d*, 6*p*, 7*s*, 5*f*, 6*d*. *See* atom.

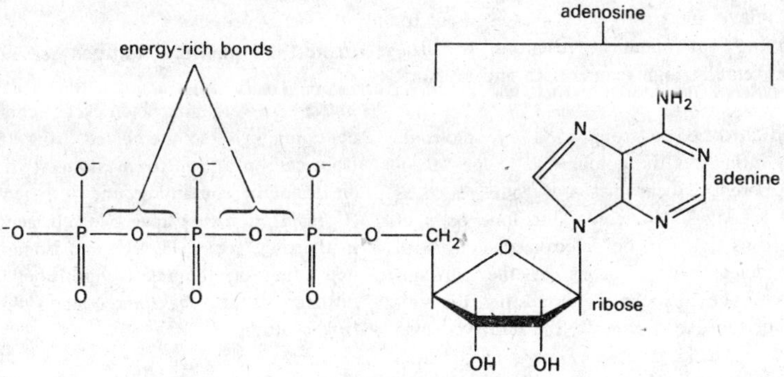

ATP

Auger effect The ejection of an electron from an atom without the emission of an X-or gamma-ray photon, as a result of the de-excitation of an excited electron within the atom. This type of transition occurs in the X-ray region of the emission spectrum. The kinetic energy of the ejected electron, called an *Auger electron*, is equal to the energy of the corresponding X-ray photon minus the binding energy of the Auger electron. The effect was discovered by Pierre Auger (1899–) in 1925.

auric compounds Compounds of gold in its higher (+3) oxidation state; e.g. auric chloride is gold(III) chloride ($AuCl_3$).

aurous compounds Compounds of gold in its lower (+1) oxidation state; e.g. aurous chloride is gold(I) chloride (AuCl).

austenite *See* steel.

autocatalysis *Catalysis in which one of the products of the reaction is a catalyst for the reaction. Reactions in which autocatalysis occurs have a characteristic S-shaped curve for reaction rate against time – the reaction starts slowly and increases as the amount of catalyst builds up, falling off again as the products are used up.

autoclave A strong steel vessel used for carrying out chemical reactions, sterilizations, etc., at high temperature and pressure.

auxochrome A group in a dye molecule that influences the colour due to the *chromophore. Auxochromes are groups, such as $-OH$ and $-NH_2$, containing lone pairs of electrons that can be delocalized along with the delocalized electrons of the chromophore. The auxochrome intensifies the colour of the dye. Formerly, the term was also used of such groups as $-SO_2O^-$, which make the molecule soluble and affect its application.

Avogadro constant Symbol N_A or L. The number of atoms or molecules in one *mole of substance. It has the value $6.022\,52 \times 10^{23}$. Formerly it was called *Avogadro's number*.

Avogadro's law Equal volumes of all gases contain equal numbers of molecules at the same pressure and temperature. The law, often called *Avogadro's hypothesis*, is true only for ideal gases. It was first proposed in 1811 by Count Amadeo Avogadro (1776–1856).

azeotrope (azeotropic mixture; constant-boiling mixture) A mixture of two liquids that boils at constant composition; i.e. the composition of the vapour is the same as that of the liquid. Azeotropes occur because of deviations in Raoult's law leading to a maximum or minimum in the *boiling-point–composition diagram. When the mixture is boiled, the vapour initially has a higher proportion of one component than is present in the liquid, so the proportion of this in the liquid falls with time. Eventually, the maximum and minimum point is reached, at which the two liquids distil together without change in composition. The composition of an azeotrope depends on the pressure.

azides Compounds containing the ion N_3^- or the group $-N_3$.

azimuthal quantum number *See* atom.

azine An organic heterocyclic compound containing a six-membered ring formed from carbon and nitrogen atoms. Pyridine is an example containing one nitrogen atom (C_5H_5N). *Diazines* have two nitrogen atoms in the ring (e.g. $C_4H_4N_2$), and isomers exist depending on the relative positions of the nitrogen atoms. *Triazines* contain three nitrogen atoms.

azo compounds Organic compounds containing the group $-N{=}N-$ linking two other groups. They can be formed by reaction of a diazonium ion with a benzene ring.

azo dye *See* dyes.

azoimide *See* hydrogen azide.

azurite A secondary mineral consisting of hydrated basic copper carbonate, $Cu_3(OH)_2(CO_3)_2$, in monoclinic crystalline form. It is generally formed in the upper zone of copper ore deposits and often occurs with *malachite. Its intense azure-blue colour made it formerly important as a pigment. It is a minor ore of copper and is used as a gemstone.

B

Babbit metal Any of a group of related alloys used for making bearings. They consist of tin containing antimony (about 10%) and copper (1–2%), and often lead. The original alloy was invented in 1839 by the US inventor Isaac Babbit (1799–1862).

Babo's law The vapour pressure of a liquid is decreased when a solute is added, the amount of the decrease being proportional to the amount of solute dissolved. The law was discovered in 1847 by the German chemist Lambert Babo (1818–99). *See also* Raoult's law.

back donation A form of chemical bonding in which a *ligand forms a sigma bond to an atom or ion by donating a pair of electrons, and the central atom donates electrons back by overlap of its *d*-orbitals with empty *p*- or *d*-orbitals on the ligand.

back e.m.f. An electromotive force that opposes the main current flow in a circuit. For example, in an electric cell, *polarization causes a back e.m.f. to be set up by chemical means.

background radiation Low intensity *ionizing radiation present on the surface of the earth and in the atmosphere as a result of *cosmic radiation and the presence of radioisotopes in the earth's rocks, soil, and atmosphere. The radioisotopes are either natural or the result of nuclear fallout or waste gas from power stations. Background counts must be taken into account when measuring the radiation produced by a specified source.

bacteriocidal Capable of killing bacteria. Common bacteriocides are some antibiotics, antiseptics, and disinfectants.

Bakelite A tradename for certain phenol–formaldehyde resins, first introduced in 1909 by the Belgian–American chemist Leo Hendrik Baekeland (1863–1944).

baking soda *See* sodium hydrogencarbonate.

balance An accurate weighing device. The simple *beam balance* consists of two pans suspended from a centrally pivoted beam. Known masses are placed on one pan and the substance or body to be weighed is placed in the other. When the beam is exactly horizontal the two masses are equal. An accurate laboratory balance weighs to the nearest hundredth of a milligram. Specially designed balances can be accurate to a millionth of a milligram. More modern *substitution balances* use the substitution principle. In this calibrated weights are removed from the single lever arm to bring the single pan suspended from it into equilibrium with a fixed counter weight. The substitution balance is more accurate than the two-pan device and enables weighing to be carried out more rapidly. In automatic electronic balances, mass is determined not by mechanical deflection but by electronically controlled compensation of an electric force. A scanner monitors the displacement of the pan support generating a current proportional to the displacement. This current flows through a coil forcing the pan support to return to its original position by means of a magnetic force. The signal generated enables the mass to be read from a digital display. The mass of the empty container can be stored in the balance's computer memory and automatically deducted from the mass of the container plus its contents.

Balmer series *See* hydrogen spectrum.

banana bond Informal name for the type of electron-deficient bond holding the B–H–B bridges in *boranes and similar compounds.

band spectrum *See* spectrum.

band theory *See* energy bands.

bar A c.g.s. unit of pressure equal to 10^6 dynes per square centimetre or 10^5 pascals (approximately 750 mmHg or 0.987 atmosphere). The *millibar* (100 Pa) is commonly used in meteorology.

Barfoed's test A biochemical test to detect monosaccharide (reducing) sugars in solution, devised by the Swedish physician C. T. Barfoed (1815–99). *Barfoed's reagent*, a mixture of ethanoic (acetic) acid and copper(II) acetate, is added to the test solution and boiled. If any reducing sugars are present a red precipitate of copper(II) oxide is formed. The reaction will be negative in the presence of disaccharide sugars as they are weaker reducing agents.

barite *See* barytes.

barium Symbol Ba. A silvery-white reactive element belonging to *group II of the periodic table; a.n. 54; r.a.m. 137.33; r.d. 3.51; m.p. 725°C; b.p. 1640°C. It occurs as the minerals barytes ($BaSO_4$) and witherite. Extraction is by high-temperature reduction of barium oxide with aluminium or silicon in a vacuum, or by electrolysis of fused barium chloride. The metal is used as a getter in vacuum systems. It oxidizes readily in air and reacts with ethanol and water. Soluble barium compounds are extremely poisonous. It was first identified in 1774 by Karl Scheele, and was extracted by Humphry Davy in 1808.

barium bicarbonate *See* barium hydrogencarbonate.

barium carbonate A white insoluble compound, $BaCO_3$; r.d. 4.43. It decomposes on heating to give barium oxide and carbon dioxide:

$$BaCO_3(s) \rightarrow BaO(s) + CO_2(g)$$

The compound occurs naturally as the mineral *witherite* and can be prepared by adding an alkaline solution of a carbonate to a solution of a barium salt. It is used as a raw material for making other barium salts, as a flux for ceramics, and as a raw material in the manufacture of certain types of optical glass.

barium chloride A white compound, $BaCl_2$. The anhydrous compound has two crystalline forms: an α form (monoclinic; r.d. 3.856), which transforms at 962°C to a β form (cubic; r.d. 3.917; m.p. 963°C; b.p. 1560°C). There is also a dihydrate, $BaCl_2.2H_2O$ (cubic; r.d. 3.1), which loses water at 113°C. It is prepared by dissolving barium carbonate (witherite) in hydrochloric acid and crystallizing out the dihydrate. The compound is used in the extraction of barium by electrolysis.

barium hydrogencarbonate (barium bicarbonate) A compound, $Ba(HCO_3)_2$, which is only stable in solution. It can be formed by the action of carbon dioxide on a suspension of barium carbonate in cold water:

$$BaCO_3(s) + CO_2(g) + H_2O(l) \rightarrow Ba(HCO_3)_2(aq)$$

On heating, this reaction is reversed.

barium hydroxide (baryta) A white solid, $Ba(OH)_2$, sparingly soluble in water. The common form is the octahydrate, $Ba(OH)_2.8H_2O$; monoclinic; r.d. 2.18; m.p. 78°C. It can be produced by adding water to barium monoxide or by the action of sodium hydroxide on soluble barium compounds and is used as a weak alkali in volumetric analysis.

barium oxide A white or yellowish solid, BaO, obtained by heating barium in oxygen or by the thermal decomposition of barium carbonate or nitrate; cubic; r.d. 5.72; m.p. 1920°C; b.p. 2000°C. When barium oxide is heated in oxygen the peroxide, BaO_2, is formed in a reversible reaction that was once used as a method for obtaining oxygen (the *Brin process*). Barium oxide is now used in the manufacture of lubricating-oil additives.

barium peroxide A dense off-white solid, BaO_2, prepared by carefully heating *barium oxide in oxygen; r.d. 4.96; m.p. 450°C. It is used as a bleaching agent. With acids, hydrogen peroxide is formed and the reaction is used in the laboratory preparation of hydrogen peroxide.

barium sulphate An insoluble white solid, $BaSO_4$, that occurs naturally as the mineral *barytes (or *heavy spar*) and can be prepared as a precipitate by adding sulphuric acid to barium chloride solution; r.d. 4.50; m.p. 1580°C. The rhombic form changes to a monoclinic form at 1149°C. It is used as a raw material for making other barium salts, as a pigment extender in surface coating materials (called *blanc fixe*), and in the glass and rubber industries. Barium compounds are opaque to X-rays, and a suspension of the sulphate in water is used in medicine to provide a contrast medium for X-rays of the stomach and intestine. Although barium compounds are extremely poisonous, the sulphate is safe to use because it is very insoluble.

baryta *See* barium hydroxide.

barytes (barite) An orthorhombic mineral form of *barium sulphate, $BaSO_4$; the chief ore of barium. It is usually white but may also be yellow, grey, or brown. Large deposits occur in Andalusia, Spain, and in the USA.

basalt A fine-grained basic igneous rock. It is composed chiefly of calcium-rich plagioclase feldspar and pyroxene; other minerals present may be olivine, magnetite, and apatite. Basalt is the commonest type of lava.

base A compound that reacts with a protonic acid to give water (and a salt). The definition comes from the Arrhenius theory of acids and bases. Typically, bases are metal oxides, hydroxides, or compounds (such as ammonia) that give hydroxide ions in aqueous solution. Thus, a base may be either: (1) An insoluble oxide or hydroxide that reacts with an acid, e.g.

$$CuO(s) + 2HCl(aq) \rightarrow CuCl_2(aq) + H_2O(l)$$

Here the reaction involves hydrogen ions from the acid

$$CuO(s) + 2H^+(aq) \rightarrow H_2O(l) + Cu^{2+}(aq)$$

(2) A soluble hydroxide, in which case the solution contains hydroxide ions. The reaction with acids is a reaction between hydrogen ions and hydroxide ions:

$$H^+ + OH^- \rightarrow H_2O$$

(3) A compound that dissolves in water to produce hydroxide ions. For example, ammonia reacts as follows:

$$NH_3(g) + H_2O(l) \rightleftharpoons NH_4^+(aq) + {}^-OH$$

Similar reactions occur with organic *amines (*see also* nitrogenous base; amine salts). A base that dissolves in water to give hydroxide ions is called an *alkali*. Ammonia and sodium hydroxide are common examples.

The original Arrhenius definition of a base has been extended by the Lowry–Brønsted theory and by the Lewis theory. *See* acid.

base dissociation constant *See* dissociation.

base metal A common relatively inexpensive metal, such as iron or lead, that corrodes, oxidizes, or tarnishes on exposure to air, moisture, or heat, as distinguished from precious metals, such as gold and silver.

base unit A unit that is defined arbitrarily rather than being defined by simple combinations of other units. For example, the ampere is a base unit in the SI system defined in terms of the force produced between two current-carrying conductors, whereas the coulomb is a *derived unit*, defined as the quantity of charge transferred by one ampere in one second.

basic 1. Describing a compound that is a base. **2.** Describing a solution containing an excess of hydroxide ions; alkaline.

basic dye *See* dyes.

basicity constant *See* dissociation.

basic-oxygen process (BOP process) A high-speed method of making high-grade steel. It originated in the *Linnz–Donnewitz (L–D) process.* Molten pig iron and scrap are charged into a tilting furnace, similar to the Bessemer furnace except that it has no tuyeres. The charge is converted to steel by blowing high-pressure oxygen onto the surface of the metal through a water-cooled lance. The excess heat produced enables up to 30% of scrap to be incorporated into the charge. The process has largely replaced the Bessemer and open-hearth processes.

basic salt A compound that can be regarded as being formed by replacing some of the oxide or hydroxide ions in a base by other negative ions. Basic salts are thus mixed salt–oxides (e.g. bismuth(III) chloride oxide, BiOCl) or salt–hydroxides (e.g. lead (II) chloride hydroxide, Pb(OH)Cl).

basic slag *Slag formed from a basic flux (e.g. calcium oxide) in a blast furnace. The basic flux is used to remove acid impurities in the ore and contains calcium silicate, phosphate, and sulphide. If the phosphorus content is high the slag can be used as a fertilizer.

basic stains *See* staining.

battery A number of electric cells joined together. The common car battery, or *accumulator, usually consists of six secondary cells connected in series to give a total e.m.f. of 12 volts. A torch battery is usually a dry version of the *Leclanché primary cell, two of which are often connected in series. Batteries may also have cells connected in parallel, in which case they have the same e.m.f. as a single cell, but their capacity is increased, i.e. they will provide more total charge. The capacity of a battery is usually specified in ampere-hours, the ability to supply 1 A for 1 hr, or the equivalent.

bauxite The chief ore of aluminium, consisting of hydrous aluminium oxides and aluminous laterite. It is a claylike amorphous material formed by the weathering of silicate rocks under tropical conditions. The chief producers are Australia, Guinea, Jamaica, USSR, Brazil, and Surinam.

beam balance *See* balance.

Beckmann thermometer A thermometer for measuring small changes of temperature. It consists of a mercury-in-glass thermometer with a scale covering only 5 or 6°C calibrated in hundredths of a degree. It has two

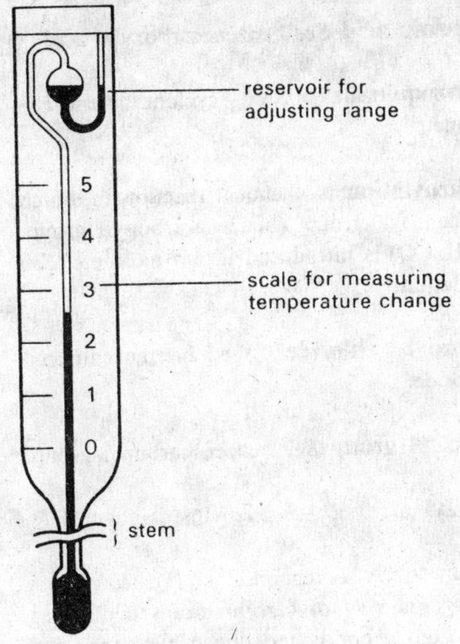

Beckmann thermometer

mercury bulbs, the range of temperature to be measured is varied by running mercury from the upper bulb into the larger lower bulb. It is used particularly for measuring *depression of freezing point or *elevation of boiling point of liquids when solute is added, in order to find relative molecular masses. The instrument was invented by the German chemist E. O. Beckmann (1853–1923).

becquerel Symbol Bq. The SI unit of activity (*see* radiation units). The unit is named after the discoverer of radioactivity A. H. Becquerel (1852–1908).

beet sugar *See* sucrose.

bel Ten *decibels.

bell metal A type of *bronze used in casting bells. It consists of 60–85% copper alloyed with tin, often with some zinc and lead included.

Benedict's test A biochemical test to detect reducing sugars in solution, devised by the US chemist S. R. Benedict (1884–1936). *Benedict's reagent* – a mixture of copper(II) sulphate and a filtered mixture of hydrated sodium citrate and hydrated sodium carbonate – is added to the test solution and boiled. A high concentration of reducing sugars induces the formation of a red precipitate; a lower concentration produces a yellow precipitate. Benedict's test is a more sensitive alternative to *Fehling's test.

beneficiation (ore dressing) The separation of an ore into the valuable components and the waste material (gangue). This may be achieved by a number of processes, including crushing, grinding, magnetic separation, froth flotation, etc. The dressed ore, consisting of a high proportion of valuable components, is then ready for smelting or some other refining process.

benzaldehyde *See* benzenecarbaldehyde.

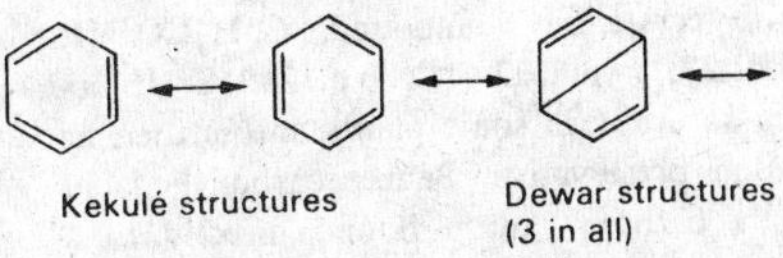

Benzene

benzene A colourless liquid hydrocarbon, C_6H_6; r.d. 0.88; m.p. 5.5°C; b.p. 80.1°C. It is now made from gasoline from petroleum by catalytic reforming (formerly obtained from coal tar). Benzene is the archetypal *aromatic compound. It has an unsaturated molecule, yet will not readily undergo addition reactions. On the other hand, it does undergo substitution reactions in which hydrogen atoms are replaced by other atoms or groups. This behaviour occurs because of delocalization of *p*-electrons over the benzene ring, and all the C–C bonds in benzene are equivalent and intermediate in length between single and double bonds. *See also* Kekulé structure.

benzenecarbaldehyde (benzaldehyde) A yellowish volatile oily liquid, C_6H_5CHO; r.d. 1.04; m.p. −26°C; b.p. 178.1°C. The compound occurs in almond kernels and has an almond-like smell. It is made from methylbenzene (by conversion to dichloromethyl benzene, $C_6H_5CHCl_2$, followed by hydrolysis). Benzenecarbaldehyde is used in flavourings, perfumery, and the dyestuffs industry.

benzenecarbonyl chloride (benzoyl chloride) A colourless liquid, C_6H_5COCl; r.d. 1.21; m.p. 0°C; b.p. 197.2°C. It is an *acyl-halide, used to introduce benzenecarbonyl groups into molecules. *See* acylation.

benzenecarbonyl group (benzoyl group) The organic group C_6H_5CO-.

benzenecarboxylate (benzoate) A salt or ester of benzenecarboxylic acid.

benzenecarboxylic acid (benzoic acid) A white crystalline compound, C_6H_5COOH; r.d. 1.27; m.p. 122.4°C; b.p. 249°C. It occurs naturally in some plants and is used as a food preservative. Benzenecarboxylic acid has a carboxyl group bound directly to a benzene ring. It is a weak carboxylic acid ($K_a = 6.4 \times 10^{-5}$ at 25°C), which is slightly soluble in water. It also undergoes substitution reactions on the benzene ring.

benzene-1,4-diol (hydroquinone; quinol) A white crystalline solid, $C_6H_4(OH)_2$; r.d. 1.33; m.p. 170°C; b.p. 285°C. It is used in making dyes. *See also* quinhydrone electrode.

benzene hexachloride (BHC) A crystalline substance, $C_6H_6Cl_6$, made by adding chlorine to benzene. It is used as a pesticide and, like *DDT, concern has been expressed at its environmental effects.

benzoate *See* benzenecarboxylate.

benzoic acid *See* benzenecarboxylic acid.

benzoquinone *See* cyclohexadiene-1,4-dione.

benzoylation A chemical reaction in which a benzoyl group (benzenecarbonyl group, C_6H_5CO) is introduced into a molecule. *See* acylation.

benzoyl chloride *See* benzenecarbonyl chloride.

benzoyl group *See* benzenecarbonyl group.

benzyl alcohol *See* phenylmethanol.

benzyne A compound, C_6H_4, having a hexagonal ring of carbon atoms containing two double bonds and one triple bond. The compound is highly reactive and cannot be isolated, although benzyne and its derivatives occur as short-lived intermediates in organic reactions.

Bergius process A process for making hydrocarbon mixtures (for fuels) from coal by heating powdered coal mixed with tar and iron(III) oxide catalyst at 450°C under hydrogen at a pressure of about 200 atmospheres. In later developments of the process, the coal was suspended in liquid hydrocarbons and other catalysts were used. The process was developed by the German chemist Friederich Bergius (1884–1949) during World War I as a source of motor fuel.

berkelium Symbol Bk. A radioactive metallic transuranic element belonging to the *actinoids; a.n. 97; mass number of the most stable isotope 247 (half-life 1.4×10^3 years); r.d. (calculated) 14. There are eight known isotopes. It was first produced by G. T. Seborg and associates in 1949 by bombarding americium–241 with alpha particles.

Berthollide compound *See* nonstoichiometric compound.

beryl A hexagonal mineral form of beryllium aluminium silicate, $Be_3Al_2Si_6O_{18}$; the chief ore of beryllium. It may be green, blue, yellow, or white and has long been used as a gemstone. Beryl occurs throughout the world in granite and pegmatites. *Emerald, the green gem variety, occurs more rarely and is of great value. Important sources of beryl are found in Brazil, Madagascar, and the USA.

beryllate A compound formed in solution when beryllium metal, or the oxide or hydroxide, dissolves in strong alkali. The reaction (for the metal) is often written

$$Be + 2OH^-(aq) \rightarrow BeO_2^{2-}(aq) + H_2(g)$$

The ion BeO_2^{2-} is the beryllate ion. In fact, as with the *aluminates, the ions present are probably hydroxy ions of the type $Be(OH)_4^{2-}$ (the *tetrahydroxoberyllate(II)* ion) together with polymeric ions.

beryllia *See* beryllium oxide.

beryllium Symbol Be. A grey metallic element of *group II of the periodic table; a.n. 4; r.a.m. 9.012; r.d. 1.85; m.p. 1285°C; b.p. 2970°C. Beryllium occurs as beryl ($3BeO.Al_2O_3.6SiO_2$) and chrysoberyl ($BeO.Al_2O_3$). The metal is extracted from a fused mixture of BeF_2/NaF by electrolysis or by magnesium reduction of BeF_2. It is used to manufacture Be–Cu alloys, which are used in nuclear reactors as reflectors and moderators because of their low absorption cross section. Beryllium oxide is used in ceramics and in nuclear reactors. Beryllium and its compounds are toxic and can cause serious lung diseases and dermatitis. The metal is resistant to oxidation by air because of the formation of an oxide layer, but will react with dilute hydrochloric and sulphuric acids. Beryllium compounds show high covalent character. The element was isolated independently by F. Wohler and A. A. Bussy in 1828.

beryllium hydroxide A white crystalline compound, $Be(OH)_2$, precipitated from solutions of beryllium salts by adding alkali Like the oxide, it is amphoteric and dissolves in excess alkali to give *beryllates.

beryllium oxide (beryllia) An insoluble solid compound, BeO; hexagonal; r.d. 3.01; m.p. 2550°C; b.p. 4120°C. It occurs naturally as *bromellite*, and can be made by burning beryllium in oxygen or by the decomposition of beryllium carbonate or hydroxide. It is an important amphoteric oxide, reacting with acids to form salts and with alkalis to form compounds known as *beryllates. Beryllium oxide is used in the production of beryllium and beryllium–copper refractories, transistors, and integrated circuits.

Bessemer process A process for converting *pig iron from a *blast furnace into *steel. The molten pig iron is loaded into a refractory-lined tilting furnace (*Bessemer converter*) at about 1250°C. Air is blown into the furnace from the base and *spiegel is added to introduce the correct amount of carbon. Impurities (especially silicon, phosphorus, and manganese) are removed by the converter lining to form a slag. Finally the furnace is tilted so that the molten steel can be poured off. In the modern VLN (very low nitrogen) version of this process, oxygen and steam are blown into the furnace in place of air to minimize the absorption of nitrogen from the air by the steel. The process is named after the British engineer Sir Henry Bessemer (1813–98), who announced it in 1856. *See also* basic-oxygen process.

beta decay A type of radioactive decay in which an unstable atomic nucleus changes into a nucleus of the same mass number but different proton number. The change involves the conversion of a neutron into a proton with the emission of an electron and an antineutrino ($n \rightarrow p + e^- + \bar{\nu}$) or of a proton into a neutron with the emission of a positron and a neutrino ($p \rightarrow n + e^+ + \nu$). An example is the decay of carbon-14:

$$^{14}_{6}C \rightarrow {}^{14}_{7}N + e^- + \bar{\nu}$$

The electrons or positrons emitted are called *beta particles* and streams of beta particles are known as *beta radiation.*

beta-iron A nonmagnetic allotrope of iron that exists between 768°C and 900°C.

beta particle *See* beta decay.

BHC *See* benzene hexachloride.

bicarbonate *See* hydrogencarbonate.

bicarbonate of soda *See* sodium hydrogencarbonate.

bimolecular reaction A step in a chemical reaction that involves two molecules. *See* molecularity.

binary Describing a compound or alloy formed from two elements.

binary acid An *acid in which the acidic hydrogen atom(s) are bound directly to an atom other than oxygen. Examples are hydrogen chloride (HCl) and hydrogen sulphide (H_2S). Such compounds are sometimes called *hydracids. Compare* oxo acid.

biochemical oxygen demand (BOD) The amount of oxygen taken up by microorganisms that decompose organic waste matter in water. It is therefore used as a measure of the amount of certain types of organic pollutant in water. BOD is calculated by keeping a sample of water containing a known amount of oxygen for five days at 20°C. The oxygen content is measured again after this time. A high BOD indicates the presence of a large number of microorganisms, which suggests a high level of pollution.

biochemistry The study of the chemistry of living organisms, especially the structure and function of their chemical components (principally proteins, carbohydrates, lipids, and nucleic acids). Biochemistry has advanced rapidly with the development, from the mid-20th century, of such techniques as chromatography, X-ray diffraction, radioisotopic labelling, and electron microscopy. Using these techniques to separate and analyse biologically important molecules, the steps of the metabolic pathways in which they are involved (e.g. glycolysis) have been determined. This has provided some knowledge of how organisms obtain and store energy, how they manufacture and degrade their biomolecules, and how they sense and respond to their environment.

bioluminescence *See* luminescence.

biosynthesis The production of molecules by a living cell, which is the essential feature of *anabolism.

biotin A vitamin in the *vitamin B complex. It is the *coenzyme for various enzymes that catalyse the incorporation of carbon dioxide into various compounds. Adequate amounts are normally produced by the intestinal bacteria; other sources include cereals, vegetables, milk, and liver.

biotite An important rock-forming silicate mineral, a member of the *mica group of minerals, in common with which it has a sheetlike crystal structure. It is usually black, dark brown, or green in colour.

birefringence *See* double refraction.

Birkeland–Eyde process A process for the fixation of nitrogen by passing air through an electric arc to produce nitrogen oxides. It was introduced in 1903 by the Norwegian chemists Kristian Birkeland (1867–1913) and Samuel Eyde (1866–1940).

The process is economic only if cheap hydroelectricity is available.

bismuth Symbol Bi. A white crystalline metal with a pinkish tinge belonging to *group V of the periodic table; a.n. 83; r.a.m. 208.98; r.d. 9.78; m.p. 271.3°C; b.p. 1560°C. The most important ores are bismuthinite (Bi_2S_3) and bismite (Bi_2O_3). Peru, Japan, Mexico, Bolivia, and Canada are major producers. The metal is extracted by carbon reduction of its oxide. Bismuth is the most diamagnetic of all metals and its thermal conductivity is lower than any metal except mercury. The metal has a high electrical resistance and a high Hall effect when placed in magnetic fields. It is used to make low-melting-point casting alloys with tin and cadmium. These alloys expand on solidification to give clear replication of intricate features. It is also used to make thermally activated safety devices for fire-detection and sprinkler systems. More recent applications include its use as a catalyst for making acrylic fibres, as a constituent of malleable iron, as a carrier of uranium–235 fuel in nuclear reactors, and as a specialized thermocouple material. Bismuth compounds (when lead-free) are used for cosmetics and medical preparations. It is attacked by oxidizing acids, steam (at high temperatures), and by moist halogens. It burns in air with a blue flame to produce yellow oxide fumes. C. G. Junine first demonstrated that it was different from lead in 1753.

bisulphate *See* hydrogensulphate.

bisulphite *See* hydrogensulphite; aldehydes.

bittern The solution of salts remaining when sodium chloride is crystallized from sea water.

bitumen *See* petroleum.

bituminous coal *See* coal.

bituminous sand *See* oil sand.

biuret test A biochemical test to detect proteins in solution, named after the substance *biuret* ($H_2NCONHCONH_2$), which is formed when urea is heated. Sodium hydroxide is mixed with the test solution and drops of 1% copper(II) sulphate solution are then added slowly. A positive result is indicated by a violet ring, caused by the reaction of *peptide bonds in the proteins or peptides. Such a result will not occur in the presence of free amino acids.

bivalent (*or* **divalent**) Having a valency of two.

blackdamp (choke damp) Air left depleted in oxygen following the explosion of firedamp in a mine.

black lead *See* carbon.

blanc fixe *See* barium sulphate.

blast furnace A furnace for smelting iron ores, such as haematite (Fe_2O_3) or magnetite (Fe_3O_4), to make *pig iron. The furnace is a tall refractory-lined cylindrical structure that is charged at the top with the dressed ore (*see* beneficiation), coke, and a flux, usually limestone. The conversion of the iron oxides to metallic iron is a reduction process in which carbon monoxide and hydrogen are the reducing agents. The overall reaction can be summarized thus:

$$Fe_3O_4 + 2CO + 2H_2 \rightarrow 3Fe + 2CO_2 + 2H_2O$$

The CO is obtained within the furnace by blasting the coke with hot air from a ring of tuyeres about two-thirds of the way down the furnace. The reaction producing the CO is:

$$2C + O_2 \rightarrow 2CO$$

In most blast furnaces hydrocarbons (oil, gas, tar, etc.) are added to the blast to provide a source of hydrogen. In the modern *direct-reduction process* the CO and H_2 may be produced separately so that the reduction process can proceed at a lower temperature. The pig iron produced by a blast furnace contains about 4% carbon and further refining is usually required to produce steel or cast iron.

blasting gelatin A high explosive made from nitroglycerine and gun cotton (cellulose nitrate).

bleaching powder A white solid regarded as a mixture of calcium chlorate(I), calcium chloride, and calcium hydroxide. It is prepared on a large scale by passing chlorine gas through a solution of calcium hydroxide. Bleaching powder is sold on the basis of available chlorine, which is liberated when it is treated with a dilute acid. It is used for bleaching paper pulps and fabrics and for sterilizing water.

blende A naturally occurring metal sulphide, e.g. zinc blende ZnS.

block *See* periodic table.

block copolymer *See* polymer.

blue vitriol *See* copper(II) sulphate.

boat conformation *See* conformation.

BOD *See* biochemical oxygen demand.

body-centred cubic (b.c.c.) *See* cubic crystal.

boehmite A mineral form of a mixed aluminium oxide and hydroxide, AlO.OH. It is named after the German scientist J. Böhm. *See* aluminium hydroxide.

Bohr theory The theory published in 1913 by the Danish physicist Niels Bohr (1885–1962) to explain the line spectrum of hydrogen. He assumed that a single electron of mass m travelled in a circular orbit of radius r, at a velocity v, around a positively charged nucleus. The *angular momentum of the electron would then be mvr. Bohr proposed that electrons could only occupy orbits in which this angular momentum had certain fixed values, $h/2\pi$, $2h/2\pi$, $3h/2\pi$, ... $nh/2\pi$, where h is the Planck constant. This means that the angular momentum is quantized, i.e. can only have certain values, each of which is a multiple of n. Each permitted value of n is associated with an orbit of different radius and Bohr assumed that when the atom emitted or absorbed radiation of frequency ν, the electron jumped from one orbit to another; the energy emitted or absorbed by each jump is equal to $h\nu$. This theory gave good results in predicting the series of lines observed in the *hydrogen spectrum but not with any other spectrum. The idea of quantized values of angular momentum was later explained by the wave nature of the electron. Each orbit has to have a whole number of wavelengths around it; i.e. $n\lambda = 2\pi r$, where λ is the wavelength and n a whole number. The wavelength of a particle is given by h/mv, so $nh/mv = 2\pi r$, which leads to $mvr = nh/2\pi$. Modern atomic theory does not allow subatomic particles to be treated in the same way as large objects, and Bohr's reasoning is somewhat discredited. However, the idea of quantized angular momentum has been retained.

boiling point (b.p.) The temperature at which the saturated vapour pressure of a liquid equals the external atmospheric pressure. As a consequence, bubbles form in the liquid and the temperature remains constant until all the liquid has evaporated. As the boiling point of a liquid depends on the external atmospheric pressure, boiling points are usually quoted for standard atmospheric pressure (760 mmHg = 101 325 Pa).

boiling-point–composition diagram A graph showing how the boiling point and vapour composition of a mixture of two liquids depends on the composition of the mixture. The abscissa shows the range of compositions from 100% A at one end to 100% B at the other. The diagram has two curves: the lower one gives the boiling points (at a fixed pressure) for the different compositions. The upper one is plotted by taking the composition of vapour at each temperature on the boiling-point curve. The two curves would coincide for an ideal mixture, but generally they are different because of deviations from *Raoult's law. In some cases, they may show a maximum or minimum and coincide at some intermediate composition, explaining the formation of *azeotropes.

Boltzmann constant Symbol *k*. The ratio of the universal gas constant (*R*) to the Avogadro constant (N_A). It may be thought of therefore as the gas constant per molecule:

$$k = R/N_A = 1.380\,622 \times 10^{-23}\ \mathrm{J\,K^{-1}}$$

It is named after the Austrian physicist Ludwig Boltzmann (1844–1906).

bomb calorimeter An apparatus used for measuring heats of combustion (e.g. calorific values of fuels and foods). It consists of a strong container in which the sample is sealed with excess oxygen and ignited electrically. The heat of combustion at constant volume can be calculated from the resulting rise in temperature.

bond *See* chemical bond.

bond energy An amount of energy associated with a bond in a chemical compound. It is obtained from the heat of atomization. For instance, in methane the bond energy of the C–H bond is one quarter of the enthalpy of the process

$$CH_4(g) \rightarrow C(g) + 4H(g)$$

Bond energies can be calculated from the standard enthalpy of formation of the compound and from the enthalpies of atomization of the elements. Energies calculated in this way are called *average bond energies* or *bond–energy terms*. They depend to some extent on the molecule chosen; the C–H bond energy in methane will differ slightly from that in ethane. The *bond dissociation energy* is a different measurement, being the energy required to break a particular bond: e.g. the energy for the process:

$$CH_4(g) \rightarrow CH_3{\cdot}(g) + H{\cdot}(g)$$

bonding orbital *See* orbital.

bone black *See* charcoal.

Diborane, the simplest of the boranes

borane (boron hydride) Any of a group of compounds of boron and hydrogen, many of which can be prepared by the action of acid on magnesium boride (MgB_2). Others are made by pyrolysis of the products of this reaction in the presence of hydrogen and other reagents. They are all volatile, reactive, and oxidize readily in air, some explosively so. The boranes are a remarkable group of compounds in that their structures cannot be described using the conventional two-electron covalent bond model (*see* electron-deficient compound). The simplest example is *diborane* (B_2H_6). Other boranes include B_4H_{10}, B_5H_9, B_5H_{11}, B_6H_{10}, and $B_{10}H_4$. The larger borane molecules have open or closed polyhedra of boron atoms. In addition, there is a wide range of borane derivatives containing atoms of other elements, such as carbon and phosphorus.

borate Any of a wide range of ionic compounds that have negative ions containing boron and oxygen. Lithium borate, for example, contains the simple anion $B(OH)_4^-$. Most borates, however, are inorganic polymers with rings, chains, or other networks based on the planar BO_3 group or the tetrahedral $BO_3(OH)$ group. 'Hydrated'

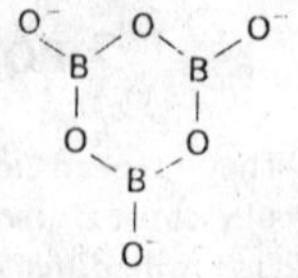

$B_3O_6^{3-}$ as in $Na_3B_3O_6$

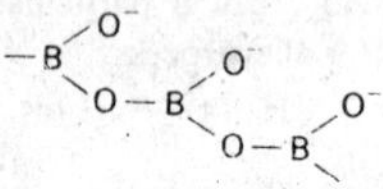

$(BO_2)_n^{n-}$ as in CaB_2O_4

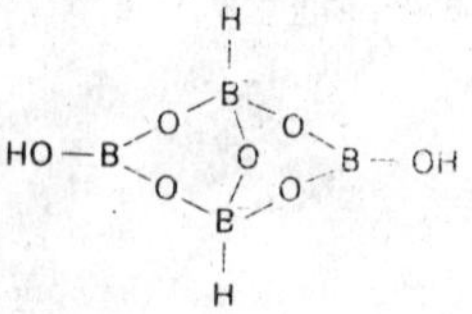

$[B_4O_5(OH)_4]^{2-}$
as in borax $Na_2B_4O_7.10H_2O$

Structure of some typical borate ions

borates are ones containing –OH groups; many examples occur naturally. Anhydrous borates, which contain BO_3 groups, can be made by melting together boric acid and metal oxides.

borax (disodium tetraborate-10-water) A colourless monoclinic solid, $Na_2B_4O_7.10H_2O$, soluble in water and very slightly soluble in ethanol; monoclinic; r.d. 1.73; loses $8H_2O$ at 75°C; loses $10H_2O$ at 320°C. The formula gives a misleading impression of the structure. The compound contains the ion $[B_4O_5(OH)_4]^{2-}$ (*see* borate). Attempts to recrystallize this compound above 60.8°C yield the pentahydrate. The main sources are the borate minerals *kernite* ($Na_2B_4O_7.4H_2O$) and *tincal* ($Na_2B_4O_7.10H_2O$). The ores are purified by carefully controlled dissolution and recrystallization. On treatment with mineral acids borax gives boric acid.

Borax is a very important substance in the glass and ceramics industries as a raw material for making borosilicates. It is also important as a metallurgical flux because of the ability of molten borates to dissolve metal oxides. In solution it partially hydrolyses to boric acid and can thus act as a buffer. For this reason it is used as a laundry pre-soak. It is used medicinally as a mild alkaline antiseptic and astringent for the skin and mucous membranes.

Disodium tetraborate is the source of many industrially important boron compounds, such as barium borate (fungicidal paints), zinc borate (fire-retardant additive in plastics), and boron phosphate (heterogeneous acid catalyst in the petrochemicals industry).

borax–bead test A simple laboratory test for certain metal ions in salts. A small amount of the salt is mixed with borax and a molten bead formed on the end of a piece of platinum wire. Certain metals can be identified by the colour of the bead produced in the oxidizing and reducing parts of a Bunsen flame. For example, iron gives a bead that is red when hot and yellow when cold in the oxidizing flame and a green bead in the reducing flame.

borazon *See* boron nitride.

boric acid Any of a number of acids containing boron and oxygen. Used without qualification the term applies to the compound H_3BO_3 (which is also called *orthoboric acid* or, technically, *trioxoboric (III) acid*). This is a white or colourless solid that is soluble in water and ethanol; triclinic; r.d. 1.435; m.p. 169°C. It occurs naturally in the condensate from volcanic steam vents (suffioni). Commercially, it is made by treating borate minerals (e.g. kernite, $Na_2B_4O_7.4H_2O$) with sulphuric acid followed by recrystallization.

In the solid there is considerable hydrogen bonding between H_3BO_3 molecules resulting in a layer structure, which accounts for the easy cleavage of the crystals. H_3BO_3 molecules also exist in dilute solutions but in more concentrated solutions polymeric acids and ions are formed (e.g. $H_4B_2O_7$; *pyroboric acid* or *tetrahydroxomonoxodiboric (III) acid*). The compound is a very weak acid but also acts as a Lewis *acid in accepting hydroxide ions:

$$B(OH)_3 + H_2O \rightleftharpoons B(OH)_4^- + H^+$$

If solid boric acid is heated it loses water and transforms to another acid at 300°C. This is given the formula HBO_2 but is in fact a polymer $(HBO_2)_n$. It is called *metaboric acid* or, technically, *polydioxoboric (III) acid.*

Boric acid is used in the manufacture of glass (borosilicate glass), glazes and enamels, leather, paper, adhesives, and explosives. It is widely used (particularly in the USA) in detergents, and because of the ability of fused boric acid to dissolve other metal oxides it is used as a flux in brazing and welding. Because of its mild antiseptic properties it is used in the pharmaceutical industry and as a food preservative.

boride A compound of boron with a metal. Most metals form at least one boride of the type MB, MB_2, MB_4, MB_6, or MB_{12}. The compounds have a variety of structures; in particular, the hexaborides contain clusters of B_6 atoms. The borides are all hard high-melting materials with metal-like conductivity. They can be made by direct combination of the elements at high temperatures (over 2000°C) or, more usually, by high-temperature reduction of a mixture of the metal oxide and boron oxide using carbon or aluminium. Chemically, they are stable to nonoxidizing acids but are attacked by strong oxidizing agents and by strong alkalis. Magnesium boride (MgB_2) is unusual in that it can be hydrolysed to boranes. Industrially, metal borides are used as refractory materials. The most important are CrB, CrB_2, TiB_2, and ZnB_2. Generally, they are fabricated using high-temperature powder metallurgy, in which the article is produced in a graphite die at over 2000°C and at very high pressure. Items are pressed as near to final shape as possible as machining requires diamond cutters and is extremely expensive.

Born–Haber cycle A cycle of reactions used for calculating the lattice energies of ionic crystalline solids. For a compound MX, the lattice energy is the enthalpy of the reaction

$$M^+(g) + X^-(g) \rightarrow M^+X^-(s)\ \Delta H_L$$

The standard enthalpy of formation of the ionic solid is the enthalpy of the reaction

$$M(s) + \tfrac{1}{2}X_2(g) \rightarrow M^+X^-(s)\ \Delta H_f$$

The cycle involves equating this enthalpy (which can be measured) to the sum of the enthalpies of a number of steps proceeding from the elements to the ionic solid. The steps are:

(1) Atomization of the metal:

$$M(s) \rightarrow M(g)\ \Delta H_1$$

(2) Atomization of the nonmetal:

$$\tfrac{1}{2}X_2(g) \rightarrow X(g)\ \Delta H_2$$

(3) Ionization of the metal:

$$M(g) \rightarrow M^+(g) + e\ \Delta H_3$$

This is obtained from the ionization potential.

(4) Ionization of the nonmetal:

$$X(g) + e \rightarrow X^-(g)\ \Delta H_4$$

This is the electron affinity.

(5) Formation of the ionic solids:

$$M^+(g) + X^-(g) \rightarrow M^+X^-(s)\ \Delta H_L$$

Equating the enthalpies gives:

from which ΔH_L can be found. It is named after the German physicist Max Born (1882–1970) and the chemist Fritz Haber (1868–1934).

bornite An important ore of copper composed of a mixed copper–iron sulphide, Cu_5FeS_4. Freshly exposed surfaces of the mineral are a metallic reddish-brown but a purplish iridescent tarnish soon develops – hence it is popularly known as *peacock ore.* Bornite is mined in Chile, Peru, Bolivia, Mexico, and the USA.

boron Symbol B. An element of *group III of the periodic table; a.n. 5; r.a.m. 10.81; r.d. 2.35; m.p. 2079°C; b.p. 2550°C. It forms two allotropes: amorphous boron is a brown powder but metallic boron is black. The metallic form is very hard (9.3 on Mohs' scale) and is a poor electrical conductor at room temperature. At least three crystalline forms are possible; two are rhombohedral and the other tetragonal. The element is never found free in nature. It occurs as orthoboric acid in volcanic springs in Tuscany, as borates in kernite ($Na_2B_4O_7.4H_2O$), and as colemanite ($Ca_2B_6O_{11}.5H_2O$) in California. Samples usually contain isotopes in the ratio of 19.78% boron-10 to 80.22% boron-11. Extraction is achieved by vapour-phase reduction of boron trichloride with hydrogen on electrically heated filaments. Amorphous boron can be obtained by reducing the trioxide with magnesium powder. Boron when heated reacts with oxygen, halogens, oxidizing acids, and hot alkalis. It is used in semiconductors and in filaments for specialized aerospace applications. Amorphous boron is used in flares, giving a green coloration. The isotope boron-10 is used in nuclear reactor control rods and shields. The element was discovered in 1808 by Sir Humphry Davy and by J. L. Gay-Lussac and L. J. Thenard.

boron carbide A black solid, B_4C, soluble only in fused alkali; it is extremely hard, over 9½ on Mohs' scale; rhombohedral; r.d. 2.52; m.p. 2350°C; b.p. >3500°C. Boron carbide is manufactured by the reduction of boric oxide with petroleum coke in an electric furnace. It is used largely as an abrasive, but objects can also be fabricated using high-temperature powder metallurgy. Boron nitride is also used as a neutron absorber because of its high proportion of boron-10.

boron hydride *See* borane.

boron nitride A solid, BN, insoluble in cold water and slowly decomposed by hot water; r.d. 2.25 (hexagonal); sublimes above 3000°C. Boron nitride is manufactured by heating boron oxide to 800°C on an acid-soluble carrier, such as calcium phosphate, in the presence of nitrogen or ammonia. It is isoelectronic with carbon and, like carbon, it has a very hard cubic form (*borazon*) and a softer hexagonal form; unlike graphite this is a nonconductor. It is used in the electrical industries where its high thermal conductivity and high resistance are of especial value.

boron trichloride A colourless fuming liquid, BCl_3, which reacts with water to give hydrogen chloride and boric acid; r.d. 1.349; m.p. −107°C; b.p. 12.5°C. Boron trichloride is prepared industrially by the exothermic chlorination of boron carbide at above 700°C, followed by fractional distillation. An alternative, but more expensive, laboratory method is the reaction of dry chlorine with boron at high temperature. Boron trichloride is a Lewis *acid, forming stable addition compounds with such donors as ammonia and the amines and is used in the laboratory to promote reactions that liberate these donors. The compound is important industrially as a source of pure boron (reduction with hydrogen) for the electronics industry. It is also used for the preparation of boranes by reaction with metal hydrides.

borosilicate Any of a large number of substances in which BO_3 and SiO_4 units are linked to form networks with a wide range of structures. Borosilicate glasses are particularly important; the addition of boron to the silicate network enables the glass to be fused at lower temperatures than pure silica and also extends the plastic range of the glass. Thus such glasses as Pyrex have a wider range of applications than soda glasses (narrow plastic range, higher thermal expansion) or silica (much higher melting point). Borosilicates are also used in glazes and enamels and in the production of glass wools.

Bosch process *See* Haber process.

Boyle's law The volume (V) of a given mass of gas at a constant temperature is inversely proportional to its pressure (p), i.e. pV = constant. This is true only for an *ideal gas. This law was discovered in 1662 by the Irish physicist Robert Boyle (1627–91). On the continent of Europe it is known as *Mariotte's law* after E. Mariotte (1620–84), who discovered it independently in 1676. *See also* gas laws.

Brackett series *See* hydrogen spectrum.

branched chain *See* chain.

brass A group of alloys consisting of copper and zinc. A typical yellow brass might contain about 67% copper and 33% zinc.

bridge An atom joining two other atoms in a molecule. *See* aluminium chloride; borane.

Brin process A process formerly used for making oxygen by heating barium oxide in air to form the peroxide and then heating the peroxide at higher temperature (>800°C) to produce oxygen

$$2BaO_2 \rightarrow 2BaO + O_2$$

Britannia metal A silvery alloy consisting of 80–90% tin, 5–15% antimony, and sometimes small percentages of copper, lead, and zinc. It is used in bearings and some domestic articles.

British thermal unit (Btu) The Imperial unit of heat, being originally the heat required to raise the temperature of 1lb of water by 1°F. 1 Btu is now defined as 1055.06 joules.

bromate A salt or ester of a bromic acid.

bromic(I) acid (hypobromous acid) A yellow liquid, HBrO. It is a weak acid but a strong oxidizing agent.

bromic(V) acid A colourless liquid, $HBrO_3$, made by adding sulphuric acid to barium bromate. It is a strong acid.

bromide *See* halide.

bromination A chemical reaction in which a bromine atom is introduced into a molecule. *See also* halogenation.

bromine Symbol Br. A *halogen element; a.n. 35; r.a.m. 79.909; r.d. 3.13; m.p. −7.2°C; b.p. 58.78°C. It is a red volatile liquid at room temperature, having a red-brown vapour. Bromine is obtained from brines in the USA (displacement with chlorine); a small amount is obtained from sea water in Anglesey. Large quantities are used to make 1,2-dibromoethane as a petrol additive. It is also used in the manufacture of many other compounds. Chemically, it is intermediate in reactivity between chlorine and iodine. It forms compounds in which it has oxidation states of 1, 3, 5, or 7. The liquid is harmful to human tissue and the vapour irritates the eyes and throat. The element was discovered in 1826 by Antoine Balard.

bromoethane (ethyl bromide) A colourless flammable liquid, C_2H_5Br; r.d. 1.43; m.p. −119°C; b.p. 38.4°C. It is a typical *haloalkane, which can be prepared from ethene and hydrogen bromide. Bromoethane is used as a refrigerant.

bromoform *See* tribromomethane; haloforms.

bromomethane (methyl bromide) A colourless volatile nonflammable liquid, CH_3Br; r.d. 1.73; m.p. −93°C; b.p. 4.5°C. It is a typical *haloalkane.

bromothymol blue An acid–base *indicator that is yellow in acid solutions and blue in alkaline solutions. It changes colour over the pH range 6–8.

bronze Any of a group of alloys of copper and tin, sometimes with lead and zinc present. The amount of tin varies from 1% to 30%. The alloy is hard and easily cast and extensively used in bearings, valves, and other machine parts. Various improved bronzes are produced by adding other elements; for instance, *phosphor bronzes* contain up to 1% phosphorus. In addition certain alloys of copper and metals other than tin are called bronzes – *aluminium bronze* is a mixture of copper and aluminium. Other special bronzes include *bell metal and *gun metal.

Brownian movement The continuous random movement of microscopic solid particles (of about 1 micrometre in diameter) when suspended in a fluid medium. First observed by the botanist Robert Brown (1773–1858) in 1827 when studying pollen particles, it was originally thought to be the manifestation of some vital force. It was later recognized to be a consequence of bombardment of the particles by the continually moving molecules of the liquid. The smaller the particles the more extensive is the motion. The effect is also visible in particles of smoke suspended in a still gas.

brown-ring test A test for ionic nitrates. The sample is dissolved and iron(II) sulphate solution added in a test tube. Concentrated sulphuric acid is then added slowly so that it forms a separate layer. A brown ring (of $Fe(NO)SO_4$) at the junction of the liquids indicates a positive result.

brucite A mineral form of *magnesium hydroxide, $Mg(OH)_2$.

Buchner funnel A type of funnel with an internal perforated tray on which a flat circular filter paper can be placed, used for filtering by suction. It is named after the German chemist Eduard Buchner (1860–1917).

buffer A solution that resists change in pH when an acid or alkali is added or when the solution is diluted. Acidic buffers consist of a weak acid with a salt of the acid. The salt provides the negative ion A^-, which is the conjugate base of the acid HA. An example is carbonic acid and sodium hydrogencarbonate. Basic buffers have a weak base and a salt of the base (to provide the conjugate acid). An example is ammonia solution with ammonium chloride.

In an acidic buffer, for example, molecules HA and ions A^- are present. When acid is added most of the extra protons are removed by the base:

$$A^- + H^+ \rightarrow HA$$

When base is added, most of the extra hydroxide ions are removed by reaction with undissociated acid:

$$OH^- + HA \rightarrow A^- + H_2O$$

Thus, the addition of acid or base changes the pH very little. The hydrogen-ion concentration in a buffer is given by the expression

$$K_a = [H^+] = [A^-]/[HA]$$

i.e. it depends on the ratio of conjugate base to acid. As this is not altered by dilution, the hydrogen-ion concentration for a buffer does not change much during dilution.

In the laboratory, buffers are used to prepare solutions of known stable pH. Natural buffers occur in living organisms, where the biochemical reactions are very sensitive to change in pH. The main natural buffers are H_2CO_3/HCO_3^- and $H_2PO_4^-/HPO_4^{2-}$. Buffer solutions are also used in medicine (e.g. in intravenous injections), in agriculture, and in many industrial processes (e.g. dyeing, fermentation processes, and the food industry).

bumping Violent boiling of a liquid caused by superheating so that bubbles form at a pressure above atmospheric pressure. It can be prevented by putting pieces of porous pot in the liquid to enable bubbles of vapour to form at the normal boiling point.

Bunsen burner A laboratory gas burner having a vertical metal tube into which the gas is led, with a hole in the side of the base of the tube to admit air. The amount of air can be regulated by a sleeve on the tube. When no air is admitted the flame is luminous and smoky. With air, it has a faintly visible hot outer part (the oxidizing part) and an inner blue cone where combustion is incomplete (the cooler reducing part of the flame). The device is named after the German chemist Robert Bunsen (1811–99), who used a similar device (without a regulating sleeve) in 1855.

Bunsen cell A *primary cell consisting of a zinc cathode immersed in dilute sulphuric acid and a carbon anode immersed in concentrated nitric acid. The electrolytes are separated by a porous pot. The cell gives an e.m.f. of about 1.9 volts.

burette A graduated glass tube with a tap at one end leading to a fine outlet tube, used for delivering known volumes of a liquid (e.g. in titration).

buta-1,3-diene (butadiene) A colourless gaseous hydrocarbon, $CH_2{:}CHCH{:}CH_2$; m.p. 109°C; b.p. –4.5°C. It is made by catalytic dehydrogenation of butane (from petroleum or natural gas) and polymerized in the production of synthetic rubbers. The compound is a conjugated *diene in which the electrons in the pi orbitals are partially delocalized over the whole molecule. It can have trans and cis forms, the latter taking part in *Diels–Alder reactions.

butanal (butyraldehyde) A colourless flammable liquid aldehyde, C_3H_9CHO; r.d. 0.8; m.p. –109°C; b.p. 75.7°C.

butane A gaseous hydrocarbon, C_4H_{10}; d. 0.58 g cm^{-3}; m.p. –135°C; b.p. 0°C. Butane is obtained from petroleum (from refinery gas or by cracking higher hydrocarbons). The fourth member of the *alkane series, it has a straight chain of carbon atoms and is isomeric with 2-methylpropane ($CH_3CH(CH_3)CH_3$, formerly called *isobutane*). It can easily be liquefied under pressure and is supplied in cylinders for use as a fuel gas. It is also a raw material for making buta-1,3-diene (for synthetic rubber).

butanedioic acid (succinic acid) A colourless crystalline fatty acid, $(CH_2)_2(COOH)_2$; r.d. 1.5; m.p. 185°C; b.p. 235°C. A weak carboxylic acid occurring in certain plants, it is produced by fermentation of sugar or ammonium tartrate and used as a sequestrant and in making dyes.

butanoic acid (butyric acid) A colourless liquid water-soluble acid, C_3H_7COOH; r.d. 0.96; b.p. 163°C. It is a weak acid (K_a = 1.5 × 10^{-5} mol dm^{-3} at 25°C) with a rancid odour. Its esters are present in butter and in human perspiration. The acid is used to make esters for flavourings and perfumery.

butanol Either of two aliphatic alcohols with the formula C_4H_9OH. *Butan-1-ol*, $CH_3(CH_2)_3OH$, is a primary alcohol; r.d. 0.81; m.p. –89.5°C; b.p. 117.3°C. *Butan-2-ol*, $CH_3CH(OH)C_2H_5$, is a secondary alcohol; r.d. 0.81; m.p. –114.7°C; b.p. 100°C. Both are colourless volatile liquids obtained from butane and used as solvents.

butanone (methyl ethyl ketone) A colourless flammable water-soluble liquid, $CH_3COC_2H_5$; r.d. 0.8; m.p. –86.4°C; b.p. 77.6°C. It can be made by the catalytic oxidation of butane and is used as a solvent.

butenedioic acid Either of two isomers with the formula HCOOHC:CHCOOH. Both compounds can be regarded as derivatives of ethene in which a hydrogen atom on each carbon has been replaced by a –COOH group. The compounds show cis–trans isomerism. The trans form is *fumaric acid* (r.d. 1.64; sublimes at 200°C) and the cis form is *maleic acid* (r.d. 1.59; m.p. 130°C). Both are colourless crystalline compounds used in making synthetic resins. The cis form is rather less stable than the trans form and converts to the trans form at 120°C. Unlike the trans form it can eliminate water on heating to form a cyclic anhydride containing a –CO.O.CO– group (*maleic anhydride*). Fumaric acid is an intermediate in the Krebs cycle.

butyl group The organic group $CH_3(CH_2)_3$–.

butyl rubber A type of synthetic rubber obtained by copolymerizing 2-methylpropene (CH_2:C(CH_3)CH_3; isobutylene) and methylbuta-1,3-diene (CH_2:C(CH_3)CH:CH_2, isoprene). Only small amounts of isoprene (about 2 mole %) are used. The rubber can be vulcanized. Large amounts were once used for tyre inner tubes.

butyraldehyde *See* butanal.

butyric acid *See* butanoic acid.

by-product A compound formed during a chemical reaction at the same time as the main product. Commercially useful by-products are obtained from a number of industrial processes. For example, calcium chloride is a by-product of the *Solvay process for making sodium carbonate. Propanone is a by-product in the manufacture of *phenol.

C

cadmium Symbol Cd. A soft bluish metal belonging to *group IIB of the periodic table; a.n. 48; r.a.m. 112.41; r.d. 8.65; m.p. 320.9°C; b.p. 765°C. The element's name is derived from the ancient name for calamine, zinc carbonate $ZnCO_3$, and it is usually found associated with zinc ores, such as sphalerite (ZnS), but does occur as the mineral greenockite (CdS). Cadmium is usually produced as an associate product when zinc, copper, and lead ores are reduced. Cadmium is used in low-melting-point alloys to make solders, in Ni–Cd batteries, in bearing alloys, and in electroplating (over 50%). Cadmium compounds are used as phosphorescent coatings in TV tubes. Cadmium and its compounds are extremely toxic at low concentrations; great care is essential where solders are used or where fumes are emitted. It has similar chemical properties to zinc but shows a greater tendency towards complex formation. The element was discovered in 1817 by F. Stromeyer.

cadmium cell *See* Weston cell.

cadmium sulphide A water-insoluble compound, CdS; r.d. 4.82. It occurs naturally as the mineral *greenockite* and is used as a pigment and in semiconductors and fluorescent materials.

caesium Symbol Cs. A soft silvery-white metallic element belonging to *group I of the periodic table; a.n. 55; r.a.m. 132.905; r.d. 1.88; m.p. 28.4°C; b.p. 678°C. It occurs in small amounts in a number of minerals, the main source being carnallite ($KCl.MgCl_2.6H_2O$). It is obtained by electrolysis of molten caesium cyanide. The natural isotope is caesium–133. There are 15 other radioactive isotopes. Caesium–137 (half-life 33 years) is used as a gamma source. As the heaviest alkali metal, caesium has the lowest ionization potential of all elements, hence its use in photoelectric cells, etc.

calcination The formation of a calcium carbonate deposit from hard water. *See* hardness of water.

calcinite A mineral form of *potassium hydrogencarbonate, $KHCO_3$.

calcite One of the most common and widespread minerals, consisting of crystalline calcium carbonate, $CaCO_3$. Calcite crystallizes in the rhombohedral system; it is usually colourless or white and has a hardness of 3 on the Mohs' scale. It has the property of double refraction, which is apparent in Iceland spar – the transparent variety of calcite. It is an important rock-forming mineral and is a major constituent in limestones, marbles, and carbonatites.

calcium Symbol Ca. A soft grey metallic element belonging to *group II of the periodic table; a.n. 20; r.a.m. 40.08; r.d. 1.55; m.p. 840°C; b.p. 1484°C. Calcium compounds are common in the earth's crust; e.g. limestone and marble ($CaCO_3$), gypsum ($CaSO_4.2H_2O$), and fluorite (CaF_2). The element is extracted by electrolysis of fused calcium chloride and is used as a getter in vacuum systems and a deoxidizer in producing nonferrous alloys. It is also used as a reducing agent in the extraction of such metals as thorium, zirconium, and uranium.

Calcium is an essential element for living organisms, being required for normal growth and development.

calcium acetylide *See* calcium dicarbide.

calcium bicarbonate *See* calcium hydrogencarbonate

calcium carbide *See* calcium dicarbide.

calcium carbonate A white solid, $CaCO_3$, which is only sparingly soluble in water. Calcium carbonate decomposes on heating to give *calcium oxide (quicklime) and carbon dioxide. It occurs naturally as the minerals *calcite (rhombohedral; r.d. 2.71) and *aragonite (rhombic; r.d. 2.93). Rocks containing calcium carbonate dissolve slowly in acidified rainwater (containing dissolved CO_2) to cause temporary hardness. In the laboratory, calcium carbonate is precipitated from *limewater by carbon dioxide. Calcium carbonate is used in making lime (calcium oxide) and is the main raw material for the *Solvay process.

calcium chloride A white deliquescent compound, $CaCl_2$, which is soluble in water; r.d. 2.15; m.p. 772°C; b.p. 7600°C. There are a number of hydrated forms, including the monohydrate, $CaCl_2.H_2O$, the dihydrate, $CaCl_2.2H_2O$ (r.d. 0.84), and the hexahydrate, $CaCl_2.6H_2O$ (trigonal; r.d. 1.71; the hexahydrate loses $4H_2O$ at 30°C and the remaining $2H_2O$ at 200°C). Large quantities of it are formed as a byproduct of the *Solvay process and it can be prepared by dissolving calcium carbonate or calcium oxide in hydrochloric acid. Crystals of the anhydrous salt can only be obtained if the hydrated salt is heated in a stream of hydrogen chloride. Solid calcium chloride is used in mines and on roads to reduce dust problems, whilst the molten salt is the electrolyte in the extraction of calcium. An aqueous solution of calcium chloride is used in refrigeration plants.

calcium cyanamide A colourless solid, $CaCN_2$, which sublimes at 1150°C. It is prepared by heating calcium dicarbide at 800°C in a stream of nitrogen:

$$CaC_2(s) + N_2(g) \rightarrow CaCN_2(s) + C(s)$$

The reaction has been used as a method of fixing nitrogen in countries in which cheap electricity is available to make the calcium dicarbide (the *cyanamide process*). Calcium cyanamide can be used as a fertilizer because it reacts with water to give ammonia and calcium carbonate:

$$CaCN_2(s) + 3H_2O(l) \rightarrow CaCO_3(s) + 2NH_3(g)$$

It is also used in the production of melamine, urea, and certain cyanide salts.

calcium dicarbide (calcium acetylide; calcium carbide; carbide) A colourless solid compound, CaC_2; tetragonal; r.d. 2.22; m.p. 450°C; b.p. 2300°C. In countries in which electricity is cheap it is manufactured by heating calcium oxide with either coke or ethyne at temperatures above 2000°C in an electric arc furnace. The crystals consist of Ca^{2+} and C_2^- ions arranged in a similar way to the ions in sodium chloride. When water is added to calcium dicarbide, the important organic raw material ethyne (acetylene) is produced:

$$CaC_2(s) + 2H_2O(l) \rightarrow Ca(OH)_2(s) + C_2H_2(g)$$

calcium fluoride A white crystalline solid, CaF_2; r.d. 3.2; m.p. 1360°C; b.p. 2500°C. It occurs naturally as the mineral *fluorite (or fluorspar) and is the main source of fluorine. The *calcium fluoride structure* (*fluorite structure*) is a crystal structure in which the calcium ions are each surrounded by eight fluoride ions arranged at the corners of a cube. Each fluoride ion is surrounded by four calcium ions at the corners of a tetrahedron.

calcium hydrogencarbonate (calcium bicarbonate) A compound, $Ca(HCO_3)_2$, that is stable only in solution and is formed when water containing carbon dioxide dissolves calcium carbonate:

$$CaCO_3(s) + H_2O(l) + CO_2(g) \rightarrow Ca(HCO_3)_2(aq)$$

It is the cause of temporary *hardness in water, because the calcium ions react with soap to give scum. Calcium hydrogencarbonate is unstable when heated and decomposes to give solid calcium carbonate. This explains why temporary hardness is removed by boiling and the formation of 'scale' in kettles and boilers.

calcium hydroxide (slaked lime) A white solid, $Ca(OH)_2$, which dissolves sparingly in water (*see* limewater); hexagonal; r.d. 2.24. It is manufactured by adding water to calcium oxide, a process that evolves much heat and is known as slaking. It is used as a cheap alkali to neutralize the acidity in certain soils and in the manufacture of mortar, whitewash, bleaching powder, and glass.

calcium nitrate A white deliquescent compound, $Ca(NO_3)_2$, that is very soluble in water; cubic; r.d. 2.50; m.p. 561°C. It can be prepared by neutralizing nitric acid with calcium carbonate and crystallizing it from solution as the tetrahydrate $Ca(NO_3)_2.4H_2O$, which exists in two monoclinic crystalline forms (α, r.d. 1.9; β, r.d. 1.82). There is also a trihydrate, $Ca(NO_3)_2.3H_2O$. The anhydrous salt can be obtained from the hydrate by heating but it decomposes on strong heating to give the oxide, nitrogen dioxide, and oxygen. Calcium nitrate is sometimes used as a nitrogenous fertilizer.

calcium octadecanoate (calcium stearate) An insoluble white salt, $Ca(CH_3(CH_2)_{16}COO)_2$, which is formed when soap is mixed with water containing calcium ions and is the scum produced in hard-water regions.

calcium oxide (quicklime) A white solid compound, CaO, formed by heating calcium in oxygen or by the thermal decomposition of calcium carbonate; cubic; r.d. 3.35; m.p. 2600°C; b.p. 2850°C. On a large scale, calcium carbonate in the form of limestone is heated in a tall tower (lime kiln) to a temperature above 550°C:

$$CaCO_3(s) \rightleftharpoons CaO(s) + CO_2(g)$$

Although the reaction is reversible, the carbon dioxide is carried away by the upward current through the kiln and all the limestone decomposes. Calcium oxide is used to make calcium hydroxide, as a cheap alkali for treating acid soil, and in extractive metallurgy to produce a slag with the impurities (especially sand) present in metal ores.

calcium phosphate(V) A white insoluble powder, $Ca_3(PO_4)_2$; r.d. 3.14. It is found naturally in the mineral *apatite ($Ca_5(PO_4)_3$(OH,F,Cl)) and as rock phosphate. It is also the main constituent of animal bones. Calcium phosphate can be prepared by mixing solutions containing calcium ions and hydrogenphosphate ions in the presence of an alkali:

$$HPO_4^{2-} + OH^- \rightarrow PO_4^{3-} + H_2O$$

$$3Ca^{2+} + 2PO_4^{3-} \rightarrow Ca_3(PO_4)_2$$

It is used extensively as a fertilizer. The compound was formerly called *calcium orthophosphate* (*see* phosphate).

calcium stearate *See* calcium octadecanoate.

calcium sulphate A white solid compound, $CaSO_4$; r.d. 2.96; 1450°C. It occurs naturally as the mineral *anhydrite, which has a rhombic structure, transforming to a monoclinic form at 200°C. More commonly, it is found as the dihydrate, *gypsum, $CaSO_4.2H_2O$ (monoclinic; r.d. 2.32). When heated, gypsum loses water at 128°C to give the hemihydrate, $2CaSO_4.H_2O$, better known as *plaster of Paris. Calcium sulphate is sparingly soluble in water and is a cause of permanent *hardness of water. It is used in the manufacture of certain paints, ceramics, and paper. The naturally occurring forms are used in the manufacture of sulphuric acid.

Calgon Tradename for a water-softening agent. *See* hardness of water.

caliche A mixture of salts found in deposits between gravel beds in the Atacama and Tarapaca regions of Chile. They vary from 4 m to 15 cm thick and were formed by periodic leaching of soluble salts during wet geological epochs, followed by drying out of inland seas in dry periods. They are economically important as a source of nitrates. A typical composition is $NaNO_3$ 17.6%, NaCl 16.1%, Na_2SO_4 6.5%, $CaSO_4$ 5.5%, $MgSO_4$ 3.0%, KNO_3 1.3%, $Na_2B_4O_7$ 0.94%, $KClO_3$ 0.23%, $NaIO_3$ 0.11%, sand and gravel to 100%.

californium Symbol Cf. A radioactive metallic transuranic element belonging to the *actinoids; a.n. 98; mass number of the most stable isotope 251 (half-life about 700 years). Nine isotopes are known; californium-252 is an intense neutron source, which makes it useful in neutron *activation analysis and potentially useful as a radiation source in medicine. The element was first produced by G. T. Seaborg and associates in 1950.

calomel *See* mercury(I) chloride.

calomel half cell (calomel electrode) A type of half cell in which the electrode is mercury coated with calomel (HgCl) and the electrolyte is a solution of potassium chloride and saturated calomel. The standard electrode potential is −0.2415 volt (25°C). In the calomel half cell the reactions are

$$HgCl(s) \rightleftharpoons Hg^+(aq) + Cl^-(aq)$$

$$Hg^+(aq) + e \rightleftharpoons Hg(s)$$

The overall reaction is

$$HgCl(s) + e \rightleftharpoons Hg(s) + Cl^-(aq)$$

This is equivalent to a $Cl_2(g)|Cl^-(aq)$ half cell in which the pressure is the dissociation pressure of HgCl.

calorie The quantity of heat required to raise the temperature of 1 gram of water by 1°C (1 K). The calorie, a c.g.s. unit, is now largely replaced by the *joule, an *SI unit. 1 calorie = 4.186 8 joules.

Calorie (kilogram calorie; kilocalorie) 1000 calories. This unit is still in limited use in estimating the energy value of foods, but is obsolescent.

calorific value The heat per unit mass produced by complete combustion of a given substance. Calorific values are used to express the energy values of fuels; usually these are expressed in megajoules per kilogram ($MJ\,kg^{-1}$). They are also used to measure the energy content of foodstuffs; i.e. the energy produced when the food is oxidized in the body. The units here are kilojoules per gram ($kJ\,g^{-1}$), although Calories (kilocalories) are often still used in nontechnical contexts. Calorific values are measured using a *bomb calorimeter.

calx A metal oxide formed by heating an ore in air.

camphor A white crystalline cyclic ketone, $C_{10}H_{16}O$; r.d. 0.99; m.p. 179°C; b.p. 204°C. It was formerly obtained from the wood of the Formosan camphor tree, but can now be synthesized. The compound has a characteristic odour associated with its use in mothballs. It is a plasticizer in celluloid.

Canada balsam A yellow-tinted resin used for mounting specimens in optical microscopy. It has similar optical properties to glass.

candela Symbol Cd. The *SI unit of luminous intensity equal to the luminous intensity in the perpendicular direction of the *black-body radiation from an area of 1/600 000 square metre at the temperature of freezing platinum under a pressure of 101 325 pascals.

cane sugar *See* sucrose.

Cannizzaro reaction A reaction of aldehydes to give carboxylic acids and alcohols. It occurs in the presence of strong bases with aldehydes that do not have alpha hydrogen atoms. For example, benzenecarbaldehyde gives benzenecarboxylic acid and benzyl alcohol:

$$2C_6H_5CHO \rightarrow C_6H_5COOH + C_6H_5CH_2OH$$

Aldehydes that have alpha hydrogen atoms undergo the *aldol reaction instead. The Cannizzaro reaction is an example of a *disproportionation. It was discovered in 1853 by the Italian chemist Stanislao Cannizzaro (1826–1910).

canonical form One of the possible structures of a molecule that together form a *resonance hybrid.

capric acid *See* decanoic acid.

caproic acid *See* hexanoic acid.

caprolactam A white crystalline substance, $C_6H_{11}NO$; r.d. 1.02; m.p. 170°C; b.p. 150°C. It is a *lactam containing the –NH.CO– group with five CH_2 groups making up the rest of the seven-membered ring. Caprolactam is used in making *nylon.

caprylic acid *See* octanoic acid.

carat 1. A measure of fineness (purity) of gold. Pure gold is described as 24-carat gold. 14-carat gold contains 14 parts in 24 of gold, the remainder usually being copper. **2.** A unit of mass equal to 0.200 gram, used to measure the masses of diamonds and other gemstones.

carbamide *See* urea.

carbanion An organic ion with a negative charge on a carbon atom; i.e. an ion of the type R_3C^-. Carbanions are intermediates in certain types of organic reaction (e.g. the *aldol reaction).

carbene A species of the type R_2C:, in which the carbon atom has two electrons that do not form bonds. *Methylene*, :CH_2, is the simplest example. Carbenes are highly reactive and exist only as transient intermediates in certain organic reactions. They attack double bonds to give cyclopropane derivatives. They also cause insertion reactions, in which the carbene group is inserted between the carbon and hydrogen atoms of a C–H bond:

$$C{-}H + :CR_2 \rightarrow C{-}CR_2{-}H$$

carbide Any of various compounds of carbon with metals or other more electropositive elements. True carbides contain the ion C^{4-} as in Al_4C_3. These are saltlike compounds giving methane on hydrolysis, and were formerly called *methanides*. Compounds containing the ion $C_2^{\ 2-}$ are also saltlike and are known as *dicarbides*. They yield ethyne (acetylene) on hydrolysis and were formerly called *acetylides*. The above types of compound are ionic but have partially covalent bond character, but boron and silicon form true covalent carbides, with giant molecular structures. In addition, the transition metals form a range of interstitial carbides in which the carbon atoms occupy interstitial positions in the metal lattice. These substances are generally hard materials with metallic conductivity. Some transition metals (e.g. Cr, Mn, Fe, Co, and Ni) have atomic radii that are too small to allow individual carbon atoms in the interstitial holes. These form carbides in which the metal lattice is distorted and chains of carbon atoms exist (e.g. Cr_3C_2, Fe_3C). Such compounds are intermediate in character between interstitial carbides and ionic carbides. They give mixtures of hydrocarbons on hydrolysis with water or acids.

carbocyclic *See* cyclic.

carbohydrate One of a group of organic compounds based on the general formula $C_x(H_2O)_y$. The simplest carbohydrates are the *sugars (saccharides), including glucose and sucrose. *Polysaccharides are carbohydrates of much greater molecular weight and complexity; examples are starch, glycogen, and cellulose. Carbohydrates perform many vital roles in living organisms. Sugars, notably glucose, and their derivatives are essential intermediates in the conversion of food to energy. Starch and other polysaccharides serve as energy stores in plants. Cellulose, lignin, and others form the supporting cell walls and woody tissue of plants. Chitin is a structural polysaccharide found in the body shells of many invertebrate animals.

carbolic acid *See* phenol.

carbon Symbol C. A nonmetallic element belonging to *group IV of the periodic table; a.n. 6; r.a.m. 12.011; m.p. ~3550°C; b.p. ~4289°C. Carbon has two main allotropic forms (*see* allotropy).

*Diamond (r.d. 3.52) occurs naturally and small amounts can be produced synthetically. It is extremely hard and has highly refractive crystals. The hardness of diamond results from the covalent crystal structure, in which each carbon atom is linked by covalent bonds to four others situated at the corners of a tetrahedron. The C–C bond length is 0.154 nm and the bond angle is 109.5°.

Graphite (r.d. 2.25), the other allotrope, is a soft black slippery substance (sometimes called *black lead* or *plumbago*). It occurs naturally and can also be made by the *Acheson process. In graphite the carbon atoms are arranged in layers, in which each carbon atom is surrounded by three others to which it is bound by single or double bonds. The layers are held together by much weaker van der Waals' forces. The carbon–carbon bond length in the layers is 0.142 nm and the layers are 0.34 nm apart. Graphite is a good conductor of heat and electricity. It has a variety of uses including electrical contacts, high-temperature equipment, and as a solid lubricant. Graphite mixed with clay is the 'lead' in pencils (hence its alternative name). There are also several amorphous forms of carbon, such as *carbon black and *charcoal.

There are two stable isotopes of carbon (proton numbers 12 and 13) and four radioactive ones (10, 11, 14, 15). Carbon–14 is used in *carbon dating. Chemically, carbon is unique in its ability to form many compounds containing chains and rings of carbon atoms.

carbonate A salt of carbonic acid containing the carbonate ion, CO_3^{2-}. The free ion has a plane triangular structure. Metal carbonates may be ionic or may contain covalent metal–carbonate bonds (complex carbonates) via one or two oxygen atoms. The carbonates of the alkali metals are all soluble but other carbonates are insoluble; they all react with mineral acids to release carbon dioxide.

carbonate minerals A group of common rock-forming minerals containing the anion CO_3^{2-} as the fundamental unit in their structure. The most important carbonate minerals are *calcite, *dolomite, and *magnesite. *See also* aragonite.

carbonation The solution of carbon dioxide in a liquid under pressure.

carbon bisulphide *See* carbon disulphide.

carbon black A fine carbon powder made by burning hydrocarbons in insufficient air. It is used as a pigment and a filler (e.g. for rubber).

carbon cycle One of the major cycles of chemical elements in the environment. Carbon (as carbon dioxide) is taken up from the atmosphere and incorporated into the tissues of plants in photosynthesis. It may then pass into the bodies of animals as the plants are eaten. During the respiration of plants, animals, and organisms that bring about decomposition, carbon dioxide is returned to the atmosphere. The combustion of fossil fuels (e.g. coal and peat) also releases carbon dioxide into the atmosphere.

carbon dating (radiocarbon dating) A method of estimating the ages of archaeological specimens of biological origin. As a result of cosmic radiation a small number of atmospheric nitrogen nuclei are continuously being transformed by neutron bombardment into radioactive nuclei of carbon-14:

$$^{14}_{7}N + n \rightarrow \ ^{14}_{6}C + p$$

Some of these radiocarbon atoms find their way into living trees and other plants in the form of carbon dioxide, as a result of photosynthesis. When the tree is cut down photosynthesis stops and the ratio of radiocarbon atoms to stable carbon atoms begins to fall as the radiocarbon decays. The ratio $^{14}C/^{12}C$ in the specimen can be measured and enables the time that has elapsed since the tree was cut down to be calculated. The method has been shown to give consistent results for specimens up to some 40 000 years old, though its accuracy depends upon assumptions concerning the past intensity of the cosmic radiation. The technique was developed by Willard F. Libby (1908–80) and his coworkers in 1946–47.

carbon dioxide A colourless odourless gas, CO_2, soluble in water, ethanol, and acetone; d. 1.977 g dm^{-3} (0°C); m.p. –56.6°C; b.p. –78.5°C. It occurs in the atmosphere (0.03% by volume) but has a short residence time in this phase as it is both consumed by plants during photosynthesis and produced by respiration and by combustion. It is readily prepared in the laboratory by the action of dilute acids on metal carbonates or of heat on heavy-metal carbonates. Carbon dioxide is a byproduct from the manufacture of lime and from fermentation processes.

Carbon dioxide has a small liquid range and liquid carbon dioxide is produced only at high pressures. The molecule CO_2 is linear with each oxygen making a double bond to the carbon. Chemically, it is unreactive and will not support combustion. It dissolves in water to give *carbonic acid.

Large quantities of solid carbon dioxide (*dry ice*) are used in processes requiring large-scale refrigeration. It is also used in

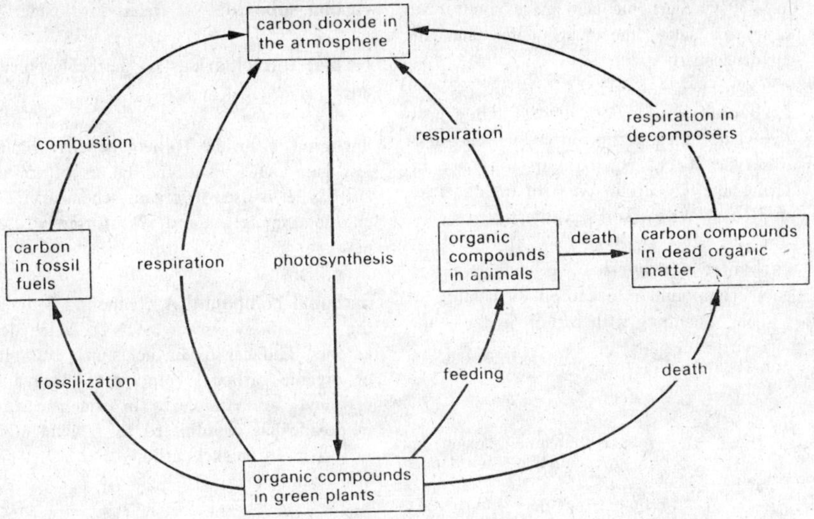

The carbon cycle in nature

fire extinguishers as a desirable alternative to water for most fires, and as a constituent of medical gases as it promotes exhalation. It is also used in carbonated drinks.

The level of carbon dioxide in the atmosphere has been the subject of much environmental controversy as it is argued that extensive burning of fossil fuels will increase the overall CO_2 concentration and then, by the greenhouse effect, increase atmospheric temperatures and cause climatic modification. The full significance of all the factors remains to be established.

carbon disulphide (carbon bisulphide) A colourless highly refractive liquid, CS_2, slightly soluble in water and soluble in ethanol and ether; r.d. 1.261; m.p. −110°C; b.p. 46.3°C. Pure carbon disulphide has an ethereal odour but the commercial product is contaminated with a variety of other sulphur compounds and has a most unpleasant smell. It was previously manufactured by heating a mixture of wood, sulphur, and charcoal; modern processes use natural gas and sulphur. Carbon disulphide is an excellent solvent for oils, waxes, rubber, sulphur, and phosphorus, but its use is decreasing because of its high toxicity and its flammability. It is used for the preparation of xanthates in the manufacture of viscose yarns.

carbon fibres Fibres of carbon in which the carbon has an oriented crystal structure. Carbon fibres are made by heating textile fibres and are used in strong composite materials for use at high temperatures.

carbonic acid A dibasic acid, H_2CO_3, formed in solution when carbon dioxide is dissolved in water:

$$CO_2(aq) + H_2O(l) \rightleftharpoons H_2CO_3(aq)$$

The acid is in equilibrium with dissolved carbon dioxide, and also dissociates as follows:

$$H_2CO_3 \rightleftharpoons H^+ + HCO_3^-$$
$$K_a = 4.5 \times 10^{-7} \text{ mol dm}^{-3}$$
$$HCO_3^- \rightleftharpoons CO_3^{2-} + H^+$$
$$K_a = 4.8 \times 10^{-11} \text{ mol dm}^{-3}$$

The pure acid cannot be isolated, although it can be produced in ether solution at −30°C. Carbonic acid gives rise to two series of salts: the *carbonates and the *hydrogencarbonates.

carbonium ion An organic ion with a positive charge on a carbon atom; i.e. an ion of the type R_3C^+. Carbonium ions are intermediates in certain types of organic reaction (e.g. *Williamson's synthesis).

carbonize (carburize) To change an organic compound into carbon by heating, or to coat something with carbon in this way.

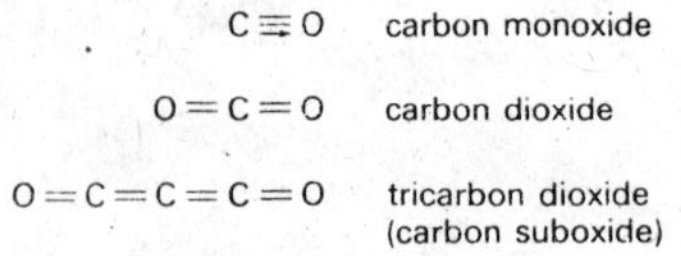

Oxides of carbon

carbon monoxide A colourless odourless gas, CO, sparingly soluble in water and soluble in ethanol and benzene; d. 1.25 g dm^{-3} (0°C); m.p. −199°C; b.p. −191.5°C. It is flammable and highly toxic. In the laboratory it can be made by the dehydration of methanoic acid (formic acid) using concentrated sulphuric acid. Industrially it is produced by the oxidation of natural gas (methane) or (formerly) by the water-gas reaction. It is formed by the incomplete combustion of carbon and is present in car-exhaust gases.

It is a neutral oxide, which burns in air to give carbon dioxide, and is a good reducing agent, used in a number of metallurgical processes. It has the interesting chemical property of forming a range of transition metal carbonyls, e.g. $Ni(CO)_4$. Carbon monoxide is able to use vacant *p*-orbitals in bonding with metals; the stabilization of low oxidation states, including the zero state, is a consequence of this. This also accounts for its toxicity, which is due to the binding of the CO to the iron in haemoglobin, thereby blocking the uptake of oxygen.

carbon suboxide *See* tricarbon dioxide.

carbon tetrachloride *See* tetrachloromethane.

carbonyl chloride (phosgene) A colourless gas, $COCl_2$, with an odour of freshly cut hay. It is used in organic chemistry as a chlorinating agent, and was formerly used as a war gas.

carbonyl compound A compound containing the carbonyl group >C=O. Aldehydes, ketones, and carboxylic acids are examples of organic carbonyl compounds. Inorganic carbonyls are complexes in which carbon monoxide has coordinated to a metal atom or ion, as in *nickel carbonyl, $Ni(CO)_4$. *See also* ligand.

carbonyl group The group >C=O, found in aldehydes, ketones, carboxylic acids, amides, etc., and in inorganic carbonyl complexes (*see* carbonyl compound).

carborundum *See* silicon carbide

carboxyl group The organic group −COOH, present in *carboxylic acids.

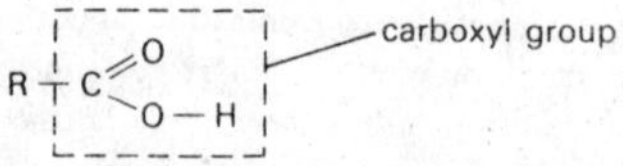

Carboxylic acid structure

carboxylic acids Organic compounds containing the group −CO.OH (the *carboxyl group*; i.e. a carbonyl group attached to a hydroxyl group). In systematic chemical nomenclature carboxylic-acid names end in the suffix *-oic*, e.g. ethanoic acid, CH_3COOH. They are generally weak acids. Many long-chain carboxylic acids occur naturally as esters in fats and oils and are therefore also known as *fatty acids. *See also* glycerides.

carburize *See* carbonize.

carbylamine reaction *See* isocyanide test.

carcinogen Any agent that produces cancer, e.g. tobacco smoke, certain industrial chemicals, and ionizing radiation (such as X-rays and ultraviolet rays).

Carius method A method of determining the amount of sulphur and halogens in an organic compound, by heating the compound in a sealed tube with silver nitrate in concentrated nitric acid. The compound is decomposed and silver sulphide and halides are precipitated, separated, and weighed.

carnallite A mineral consisting of a hydrated mixed chloride of potassium and magnesium, $KCl.MgCl_2.6H_2O$.

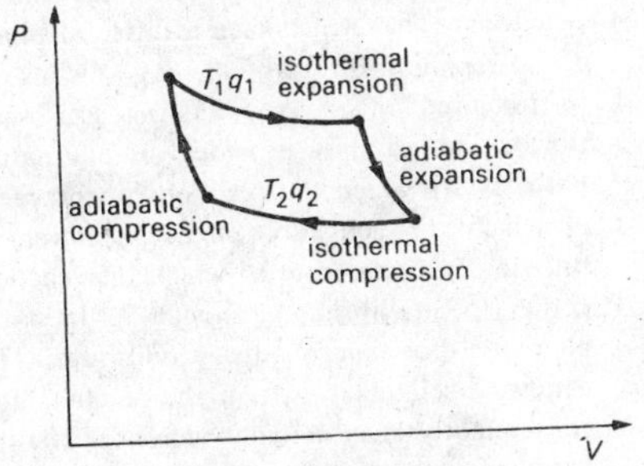

Carnot cycle

Carnot cycle The most efficient cycle of operations for a reversible heat engine. Published in 1824 by the French physicist N. L. S. Carnot (1746–1832), it consists of four operations on the working substance in the engine:

a. Isothermal expansion at thermodynamic temperature T_1 with heat Q_1 taken in.
b. Adiabatic expansion with a fall of temperature to T_2.
c. Isothermal compression at temperature T_2 with heat Q_2 given out.
d. Adiabatic compression with a rise of temperature back to T_1.

According to the *Carnot principle*, the efficiency of any reversible heat engine depends only on the temperature range through which it works, rather than the properties of the working substances. In any reversible engine, the efficiency (η) is the ratio of the work done (W) to the heat input (Q_1), i.e. $\eta = W/Q_1$. As, according to the first law of *thermodynamics, $W = Q_1 - Q_2$, it follows that $\eta = (Q_1 - Q_2)/Q_1$. As the system is reversible, $Q_1/Q_2 = T_1/T_2$, therefore $\eta = (T_1 - T_2)/T_1$. For maximum efficiency T_1 should be as high as possible and T_2 as low as possible.

carnotite A radioactive mineral consisting of hydrated uranium potassium vanadate, $K_2(UO_2)_2(VO_4)_2.nH_2O$. It varies in colour from bright yellow to lemon- or greenish-yellow. It is a source of uranium, radium, and vanadium. The chief occurrences are in the Colorado Plateau, USA; Radium Hill, Australia; and Katanga, Zaîre.

Caro's acid *See* peroxosulphuric(VI) acid.

carotene A member of a class of *carotenoid pigments. Examples are β-carotene and lycopene, which colour carrot roots and ripe tomato fruits respectively. α- and β-carotene yield vitamin A when they are broken down during animal digestion.

carotenoid Any of a group of yellow, orange, red, or brown plant pigments chemically related to terpenes. Carotenoids are responsible for the characteristic colour of many plant organs, such as ripe tomatoes, carrots, and autumn leaves. They also function in the light reactions of photosynthesis.

carrier gas The gas that carries the sample in *gas chromatography.

cascade liquefier An apparatus for liquefying a gas of low *critical temperature. Another gas, already below its critical temperature, is liquified and evaporated at a reduced pressure in order to cool the first gas to below its critical temperature. In practice a series of steps is often used, each step enabling the critical temperature of the next gas to be reached.

cascade process Any process that takes place in a number of steps, usually because the single step is too inefficient to produce the desired result. For example, in various uranium-enrichment processes the separation of the desired isotope is only poorly achieved in a single stage; to achieve better separation the process has to be repeated a number of times, in a series, with the enriched fraction of one stage being fed to the succeeding stage for further enrichment. Another example of cascade process is that operating in a *cascade liquefier.

case hardening The hardening of the surface layer of steel, used for tools and certain mechanical components. The commonest method is to carburize the surface layer by heating the metal in a hydrocarbon or by dipping the red hot metal into molten sodium cyanide. Diffusion of nitrogen into the surface layer to form nitrides is also used.

casein One of a group of phosphate-containing proteins (phosphoproteins) found in milk. Caseins are easily digested by the enzymes of young mammals and represent a major source of phosphorus.

cassiterite A yellow, brown, or black form of tin(IV) oxide, SnO_2, that forms tetragonal, often twinned, crystals; the principal ore of tin. It occurs in hydrothermal veins and metasomatic deposits associated with acid igneous rocks and in alluvial (placer) deposits. The chief producers are Malaysia, Indonesia, Zaîre, and Nigeria.

cast iron A group of iron alloys containing 1.8 to 4.5% of carbon. It is usually cast into specific shapes ready for machining, heat treatment, or assembly. It is sometimes produced direct from the *blast furnace or it may be made from remelted *pig iron.

catabolism The metabolic breakdown of large molecules in living organisms to smaller ones, with the release of energy. Respiration is an example of a catabolic series of reactions. *See* metabolism. *Compare* anabolism.

catalysis The process of changing the rate of a chemical reaction by use of a *catalyst.

catalyst A substance that increases the rate of a chemical reaction without itself undergoing any permanent chemical change (*see also* inhibition). Catalysts that have the same phase as the reactants are *homogeneous catalysts* (e.g. *enzymes in biochemical reactions). Those that have a different phase are *hetereogeneous catalysts* (e.g. metals or oxides used in many industrial gas reactions). The catalyst provides an alternative pathway by which the reaction can proceed, in which the activation energy is lower. It thus increases the rate at which the reaction comes to equilibrium, although it does not alter the position of the equilibrium. The catalyst itself takes part in the reaction and consequently may undergo physical change (e.g. conversion into powder). In certain circumstances, very small quantities of catalyst can speed up very large reactions. Some catalysts are also highly specific in the type of reaction they catalyse, particularly in biochemical reactions.

catalytic cracking *See* cracking.

cataphoresis *See* electrophoresis.

catechol *See* 1,2-dihydroxybenzene.

catecholamine Any of a class of amines (including *dopamine, *adrenaline, and *noradrenaline) that function as neurotransmitters and/or hormones.

catenation The formation of chains of atoms in chemical compounds.

cathetometer A telescope or microscope fitted with crosswires in the eyepiece and mounted so that it can slide along a graduated scale. Cathetometers are used for accurate measurement of lengths without mechanical contact. The microscope type is often called a *travelling microscope.*

cathode A negative electrode. In *electrolysis cations are attracted to the cathode. In vacuum electronic devices electrons are emitted by the cathode and flow to the *anode. It is therefore from the cathode that electrons flow into these devices. However, in a primary or secondary cell the cathode is the electrode that spontaneously becomes negative during discharge, and from which therefore electrons emerge.

cathodic protection *See* sacrificial protection.

cation A positively charged ion, i.e. an ion that is attracted to the cathode in *electrolysis. *Compare* anion.

cationic detergent *See* detergent.

cationic dye *See* dyes.

cationic resin *See* ion exchange.

caustic Describing a substance that is strongly alkaline (e.g. caustic soda).

caustic potash *See* potassium hydroxide.

caustic soda *See* sodium hydroxide.

celestine A mineral form of strontium sulphate, $SrSO_4$.

cell 1. A system in which two electrodes are in contact with an electrolyte. The electrodes are metal or carbon plates or rods or, in some cases, liquid metals (e.g. mercury). In an *electrolytic cell a current from an outside source is passed through the electrolyte to produce chemical change (*see* electrolysis). In a *voltaic cell, spontaneous reactions between the electrodes and electrolyte(s) produce a potential difference between the two electrodes.

Voltaic cells can be regarded as made up of two *half cells, each composed of an electrode in contact with an electrolyte. For instance, a zinc rod dipped in zinc sulphate solution is a $Zn|Zn^{2+}$ half cell. In such a system zinc atoms dissolve as zinc ions, leaving a negative charge on the electrode

$$Zn(s) \rightarrow Zn^{2+}(aq) + 2e$$

The solution of zinc continues until the charge build-up is sufficient to prevent further ionization. There is then a potential difference between the zinc rod and its solution. This cannot be measured directly, since measurement would involve making contact with the electrolyte, thereby introducing another half cell (*see* electrode potential). A rod of copper in copper sulphate solution comprises another half cell. In this case the spontaneous reaction is one in which copper ions in solution take electrons from the electrode and are deposited on the electrode as copper atoms. In this case, the copper acquires a positive charge.

The two half cells can be connected by using a porous pot for the liquid junction (as in the *Daniell cell) or by using a *salt bridge. The resulting cell can then supply current if the electrodes are connected through an external circuit. The cell is written

$$Zn(s)|Zn^{2+}(aq)|Cu^{2+}(aq)|Cu \quad E = 1.10\ V$$

Here, E is the e.m.f. of the cell equal to the potential of the right-hand electrode minus that of the left-hand electrode for zero current. Note that 'right' and 'left' refer to the cell as written. Thus, the cell could be written

$$Cu(s)|Cu^{2+}(aq)|Zn^{2+}(aq)|Zn(s) \quad E = -1.10\ V$$

The overall reaction for the cell is

$Zn(s) + Cu^{2+}(aq) \rightarrow Cu(s) + Zn^{2+}(aq)$
This is the direction in which the cell reaction occurs for a positive e.m.f.

The cell above is a simple example of a *chemical cell*; i.e. one in which the e.m.f. is produced by a chemical difference. *Concentration cells* are cells in which the e.m.f. is caused by a difference of concentration. This may be a difference in concentration of the electrolyte in the two half cells. Alternatively, it may be an electrode concentration difference (e.g. different concentrations of metal in an amalgam, or different pressures of gas in two gas electrodes). Cells are also classified into cells *without transport* (having a single electrolyte) and *with transport* (having a liquid junction across which ions are transferred). Various types of voltaic cell exist, used as sources of current, standards of potential, and experimental set-ups for studying electrochemical reactions.
2. *See* photoelectric cell.

celluloid A transparent highly flammable substance made from cellulose nitrate with a camphor plasticizer. It was formerly widely used as a thermoplastic material, especially for film, (a use now discontinued owing to the inflammability of celluloid).

cellulose A polysaccharide that consists of a long unbranched chain of glucose units. It is the main constituent of the cell walls of all higher plants, many algae, and some fungi and is responsible for providing the rigidity of the cell wall. The fibrous nature of extracted cellulose has led to its use in the textile industry for the production of cotton, artificial silk, etc.

cellulose acetate *See* cellulose ethanoate.

cellulose ethanoate (cellulose acetate) A compound prepared by treating cellulose (cotton linters or wood pulp) with a mixture of ethanoic anhydride, ethanoic acid, and concentrated sulphuric acid. Cellulose in the cotton is ethanoylated and when the resulting solution is treated with water, cellulose ethanoate forms as a flocculent white mass. It is used in lacquers, nonshatterable glas. varnishes, and as a fibre (*see also* rayon).

cellulose nitrate A highly flammable material made by treating cellulose (wood pulp) with concentrated nitric acid. Despite the alternative name *nitrocellulose*, the compound is in fact an ester (containing $CONO_2$ groups), not a nitro compound (which would contain $C\text{-}NO_2$). It is used in explosives (as *guncotton*) and celluloid.

Celsius scale A *temperature scale in which the fixed points are the temperatures at standard pressure of ice in equilibrium with water (0°C) and water in equilibrium with steam (100°C). The scale, between these two temperatures, is divided in 100 degrees. The degree Celsius (°C) is equal in magnitude to the *kelvin. This scale was formerly known as the *centigrade scale*; the name was officially changed in 1948 to avoid confusion with a hundredth part of a grade. It is named after the Swedish astronomer Anders Celsius (1701–44), who devised the inverted form of this scale (ice point 100°, steam point 0°) in 1742.

cement Any of various substances used for bonding or setting to a hard material. Portland cement is a mixture of calcium silicates and aluminates made by heating limestone ($CaCO_3$) with clay (containing aluminosilicates) in a kiln. The product is ground to a fine powder. When mixed with water it sets in a few hours and then hardens over a longer period of time due to the formation of hydrated aluminates and silicates.

cementation Any metallurgical process in which the surface of a metal is impregnated by some other substance, especially an obsolete process for making steel by heating bars of wrought iron to red heat for several days in a bed of charcoal. *See also* case hardening.

cementite *See* steel.

centi- Symbol c. A prefix used in the metric system to denote one hundredth. For example, 0.01 metre = 1 centimetre (cm).

centigrade scale *See* Celsius scale.

centrifugal pump *See* pump.

centrifuge A device in which solid or liquid particles of different densities are separated by rotating them in a tube in a horizontal circle. The denser particles tend to move along the length of the tube to a greater radius of rotation, displacing the lighter particles to the other end.

ceramics Inorganic materials, such as pottery, enamels, and refractories. Ceramics are metal silicates, oxides, nitrides, etc.

cerium Symbol Ce. A silvery metallic element belonging to the *lanthanoids; a.n. 58; r.a.m. 140.12; r.d. 6.77 (20°C); m.p. 798°C; b.p. 3433°C. It occurs in allanite, bastnasite, cerite, and monazite. Four isotopes occur naturally: cerium-136, -138, -140, and -142; fifteen radioisotopes have been identified. Cerium is used in mischmetal, a rare-earth metal containing 25% cerium, for use in lighter flints. The oxide is used in the glass industry. It was discovered by M. H. Klaproth in 1803.

cermet A composite material consisting of a ceramic in combination with a sintered metal, used when a high resistance to temperature, corrosion, and abrasion is needed.

cerussite An ore of lead consisting of lead carbonate, $PbCO_3$. It is usually of secondary origin, formed by the weathering of *galena. Pure cerussite is white but the mineral may be grey due to the presence of impurities. It forms well-shaped orthorhombic crystals. It occurs in the USA, Spain, and SW Africa.

cetane *See* hexadecane.

cetane number A number that provides a measure of the ignition characteristics of a Diesel fuel when it is burnt in a standard Diesel engine. It is the percentage of cetane (hexadecane) in a mixture of cetane and 1-methylnaphthalene that has the same ignition characteristics as the fuel being tested *Compare* octane number.

c.g.s. units A system of *units based on the centimetre, gram, and second. Derived from the metric system, it was badly adapted to use with thermal quantities (based on the inconsistently defined *calorie) and with electrical quantities (in which two systems, based respectively on unit permittivity and unit permeability of free space, were used). For scientific purposes c.g.s. units have now been replaced by *SI units.

chain A line of atoms of the same type in a molecule. In a *straight chain* the atoms are attached only to single atoms, not to groups. Propane, for instance, is a straight-chain alkane, $CH_3CH_2CH_3$, with a chain of three carbon atoms. A *branched chain* is one in which there are side groups attached to the chain. Thus, 3-ethyloctane, $CH_3CH_2CH(C_2H_5)C_5H_{11}$, is a branched-chain alkane in which there is a *side chain* (C_2H_5) attached to the third carbon atom. A *closed chain* is a *ring of atoms in a molecule; otherwise the molecule has an *open chain*.

chain reaction A reaction that is self-sustaining as a result of the products of one step initiating a subsequent step. Chemical chain reactions usually involve free radicals as intermediates. An example is the reaction of chlorine with hydrogen initiated by ultraviolet radiation. A chlorine molecule is first split into atoms:

$$Cl_2 \rightarrow Cl\cdot + Cl\cdot$$

These react with hydrogen as follows

$$Cl\cdot + H_2 \rightarrow HCl + H\cdot$$
$$H\cdot + Cl_2 \rightarrow HCl + Cl\cdot \text{ etc.}$$

Combustion and explosion reactions involve similar free-radical chain reactions.

chair conformation *See* conformation.

chalcedony A mineral consisting of a microcrystalline variety of *quartz. It occurs in several forms, including a large number of semiprecious gemstones; for example, sard, carnelian, jasper, onyx, chrysoprase, agate, and tiger's-eye.

chalcogens *See* group VI elements.

chalconides Binary compounds formed between metals and group VI elements; i.e. oxides, sulphides, selenides, and tellurides.

chalcopyrite (copper pyrites) A brassy yellow mineral consisting of a mixed copper–iron sulphide, $CuFeS_2$, crystallizing in the tetragonal system; the principal ore of copper. It is similar in appearance to pyrite and gold. It crystallizes in igneous rocks and hydrothermal veins associated with the upper parts of acid igneous intrusions. Chalcopyrite is the most widespread of the copper ores, occurring, for example, in Cornwall (UK), Sudbury (Canada), Chile, Tasmania (Australia), and Rio Tinto (Spain).

chalk A very fine-grained white rock composed of the skeletal remains of microscopic sea creatures, such as plankton, and consisting largely of *calcium carbonate ($CaCO_3$). It is used in toothpaste and cosmetics. It should not be confused with blackboard 'chalk', which is made from calcium sulphate.

change of phase (change of state) A change of matter in one physical *phase (solid, liquid, or gas) into another. The change is invariably accompanied by the evolution or absorption of energy, even if it takes place at constant temperature (*see* latent heat).

charcoal A porous form of carbon produced by the destructive distillation of organic material. Charcoal from wood is used as a fuel. All forms of charcoal are porous and are used for adsorbing gases and purifying and clarifying liquids. There are several types depending on the source. Charcoal from coconut shells is a particularly good gas adsorbent. *Animal charcoal* (or *bone black*) is made by heating bones and dissolving out the calcium phosphates and other mineral salts with acid. It is used in sugar refining. *Activated charcoal* is charcoal that has been activated for adsorption by steaming or by heating in a vacuum.

charge A property of some *elementary particles that gives rise to an interaction between them and consequently to the host of material phenomena described as electrical. Charge occurs in nature in two forms, conventionally described as *positive* and *negative* in order to distinguish between the two kinds of interaction between particles. Two particles that have similar charges (both negative or both positive) interact by repelling each other; two particles that have dissimilar charges (one positive, one negative) interact by attracting each other.

The natural unit of negative charge is the charge on an *electron, which is equal but opposite in effect to the positive charge on the proton. Large-scale matter that consists of equal numbers of electrons and protons is electrically neutral. If there is an excess of electrons the body is negatively charged; an excess of protons results in a positive charge. A flow of charged particles, especially a flow of electrons, constitutes an electric current. Charge is measured in coulombs, the charge on an electron being 1.602×10^{-19} coulombs.

Charles' law The volume of a fixed mass of gas at constant pressure expands by a constant fraction of its volume at 0°C for each Celsius degree or kelvin its temperature is raised. For any *ideal gas the fraction is approximately 1/273. This can be expressed by the equation $V = V_0(1 + t/273)$, where V_0 is the volume at 0°C and V is its volume at t°C. This is equivalent to the statement that the volume of a fixed mass of gas at constant pressure is proportional to its thermodynamic temperature, $V = kT$, where k is a constant. The law resulted from experiments begun around 1787 by the French scientist J. A. C. Charles (1746–1823) but was properly established only by the more accurate results published in 1802 by the French scientist Joseph Gay-Lussac (1778–1850). Thus the law is also known as *Gay-Lussac's law*. An equation similar to that given above applies to pressures for ideal gases: $p = p_0(1 + t/273)$, a relationship known as *Charles' law of pressures*. *See also* gas laws.

cheddite Any of a group of high explosives made from nitro compounds mixed with sodium or potassium chlorate.

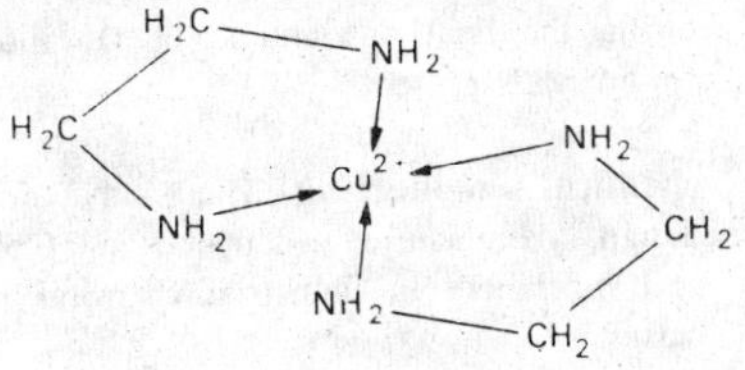

Chelate formed by coordination of two molecules of $H_2N(CH_2)_2NH_2$

chelate An inorganic complex in which a *ligand is coordinated to a metal ion at two (or more) points, so that there is a ring of atoms including the metal. The process is known as *chelation*. The bidentate ligand diaminoethane forms chelates with many ions. *See also* sequestration.

chemical bond A strong force of attraction holding atoms together in a molecule or crystal. Typically chemical bonds have energies of about 1000 kJ mol^{-1} and are distinguished from the much weaker forces between molecules (*see* van der Waals' forces). There are various types.

Ionic (or *electrovalent*) bonds can be formed by transfer of electrons. For instance, the calcium atom has an electron configuration of [Ar]$4s^2$, i.e. it has two electrons in its outer shell. The chlorine atom is [Ne]$3s^2 3p^5$, with seven outer electrons. If the calcium atom transfers two electrons, one to each chlorine atom, it becomes a Ca^{2+} ion with the stable configuration of an inert gas [Ar]. At the same time each chlorine, having gained one electron, becomes a Cl^- ion, also with an inert-gas configuration [Ar]. The bonding in calcium chloride is the electrostatic attraction between the ions.

Covalent bonds are formed by sharing of valence electrons rather than by transfer. For instance, hydrogen atoms have one outer electron ($1s^1$). In the hydrogen molecule, H_2, each atom contributes 1 electron to the bond. Consequently, each hydrogen atom has control of 2 electrons – one of its own and the second from the other atom – giving it the electron configuration of an inert gas [He]. In the water molecule, H_2O, the oxygen atom, with six outer electrons, gains control of an extra two electrons supplied by the two hydrogen atoms. This gives it the configuration [Ne]. Similarly, each hydrogen atom gains control of an extra electron from the oxygen, and has the [He] electron configuration.

A particular type of covalent bond is one in which one of the atoms supplies both the electrons. These are known as *coordinate* (*semipolar* or *dative*) bonds, and written A→B, where the direction of the arrow denotes the direction in which electrons are donated.

Covalent or coordinate bonds in which one pair of electrons is shared are *electron-pair bonds* and are known as *single bonds*. Atoms can also share two pairs of electrons to form *double bonds* or three pairs in *triple bonds*. *See* orbital.

In a compound such as sodium chloride, Na^+Cl^-, there is probably complete transfer of electrons in forming the ionic bond (the bond is said to be *heteropolar*). Alternatively, in the hydrogen molecule H–H, the pair of electrons is equally shared between the two atoms (the bond is *homopolar*). Between these two extremes, there is a whole range of *intermediate bonds*, which have both ionic and covalent contributions. Thus, in hydrogen chloride, H–Cl, the bonding is predominantly covalent with one pair of electrons shared between the two atoms. However, the chlorine atom is more electronegative than the hydrogen and has more control over the electron pair; i.e. the molecule is polarized with a positive charge on the hydrogen and a negative charge on the chlorine. *See also* hydrogen bond; metallic bond.

chemical cell *See* cell.

chemical combination The combination of elements to give compounds. There are three laws of chemical combination.

(1) The *law of constant composition* states that the proportions of the elements in a compound are always the same, no matter how the compound is made. It is also called the *law of constant proportions* or *definite proportions*.

(2) The *law of multiple proportions* states that when two elements A and B combine to form more than one compound, then the masses of B that combine with a fixed mass of A are in simple ratio to one another. For example, carbon forms two oxides. In one, 12 grams of carbon is combined with 16 grams of oxygen (CO); in the other 12 g of carbon is combined with 32 grams of oxygen (CO_2). The oxygen masses combining with a fixed mass of carbon are in the ratio 16:32, i.e. 1:2.

(3) The *law of equivalent proportions* states that if two elements A and B each form a compound with a third element C, then a compound of A and B will contain A and B in the relative proportions in which they react with C. For example, sulphur and carbon both form compounds with hydrogen. In methane 12 g of carbon react with 4 g of hydrogen. In hydrogen sulphide, 32 g of sulphur react with 2 g of hydrogen (i.e. 64 g of S for 4 g of hydrogen). Sulphur and carbon form a compound in which the C:S ratio is 12:64 (i.e. CS_2). The law is sometimes called the law of *reciprocal proportions*.

chemical dating An absolute *dating technique that depends on measuring the chemical composition of a specimen. Chemical dating can be used when the specimen is known to undergo slow chemical change at a known rate. For instance, phosphate in buried bones is slowly replaced by fluoride ions from the ground water. Measurement of the proportion of fluorine present gives a rough estimate of the time that the bones have been in the ground. Another, more accurate, method depends on the fact that amino acids in living organisms are L- optical isomers. After death, these racemize and the age of bones can be estimated by measuring the relative amounts of D- and L amino acids present.

chemical engineering The study of the design, manufacture, and operation of plant and machinery in industrial chemical processes.

chemical equation A way of denoting a chemical reaction using the symbols for the participating particles (atoms, molecules, ions, etc.); for example,

$$xA + yB \rightarrow zC + wD$$

The single arrow is used for an irreversible reaction; double arrows ($\rightleftharpoons$) are used for reversible reactions. When reactions involve different phases it is usual to put the phase in brackets after the symbol (s = solid; l = liquid; g = gas; aq = aqueous). The numbers x, y, z, and w, showing the relative numbers of molecules reacting, are called the *stoichiometric coefficients*. The sum of the coefficients of the reactants minus the sum of the coefficients of the products (x +

$y - z - w$ in the example) is the *stoichiometric sum*. If this is zero the equation is balanced. Sometimes a generalized chemical equation is considered

$$\nu_1 A$$

In this case the reaction can be written $\Sigma\nu_i A_i = 0$, where the convention is that stoichiometric coefficients are positive for reactants and negative for products. The stoichiometric sum is $\Sigma\nu_i$.

chemical equilibrium A reversible chemical reaction in which the concentrations of reactants and products are not changing with time because the system is in thermodynamic equilibrium. For example, the reversible reaction

$$3H_2 + N_2 \rightleftharpoons 2NH_3$$

is in chemical equilibrium when the rate of the *forward reaction*

$$3H_2 + N_2 \rightarrow 2NH_3$$

is equal to the rate of the *back reaction*

$$2NH_3 \rightarrow 3H_2 + N_2$$

See also equilibrium constant.

chemical equivalent *See* equivalent weight.

chemical fossil Any of various organic compounds found in ancient geological strata that appear to be biological in origin and are assumed to indicate that life existed when the rocks were formed. The presence of chemical fossils in Precambrian strata indicates that life existed over 3000 million years ago.

chemical potential Symbol: μ. For a given component in a mixture, the coefficient $\partial G/\partial n$, where G is the Gibbs free energy and n the amount of substance of the component. The chemical potential is the change in Gibbs free energy with respect to change in amount of the component, with pressure, temperature, and amounts of other components being constant. Components are in equilibrium if their chemical potentials are equal.

chemical reaction A change in which one or more chemical elements or compounds (the *reactants*) form new compounds (the *products*). All reactions are to some extent *reversible*; i.e. the products can also react to give the original reactants. However, in many cases the extent of this back reaction is negligibly small, and the reaction is regarded as *irreversible*.

chemiluminescence *See* luminescence.

chemisorption *See* adsorption.

chemistry The study of the elements and the compounds they form. Chemistry is mainly concerned with effects that depend on the outer electrons in atoms. *See* biochemistry; geochemistry; inorganic chemistry; organic chemistry; physical chemistry.

chert *See* flint.

Chile saltpetre A commercial mineral largely composed of *sodium nitrate from the caliche deposits in Chile. Before the ammonia-oxidation process for nitrates most imported Chilean saltpetre was used by the chemical industry; its principal use today is as an agricultural source of nitrogen.

china clay *See* kaolin.

Chinese white *See* zinc oxide.

chirality The property of existing in left- and right-handed structural forms. *See* optical activity.

chitin A *polysaccharide comprising chains of N-acetyl-D-glucosamine, a derivative of glucose. Chitin is structurally very similar to cellulose and serves to strengthen the supporting structures of various invertebrates. It also occurs in fungi.

chloral *See* trichloroethanal.

chloral hydrate *See* 2,2,2-trichloroethanediol.

chlorates Salts of the chloric acids; i.e. salts containing the ions ClO^- (chlorate(I) or *hypochlorite*), ClO_2^- (chlorate(III) or *chlorite*), ClO_3^- (chlorate(V)), or ClO_4^- (chlorate(VII) or *perchlorate*). When used without specification of an oxidation state the term 'chlorate' refers to a chlorate(V) salt.

chloric acid Any of the oxoacids of chlorine: *chloric(I) acid, *chloric(III) acid, *chloric(V) acid, and *chloric(VII) acid. The term is commonly used without specification of the oxidation state of chlorine to mean chloric(V) acid, $HClO_3$.

chloric(I) acid (hypochlorous acid) A liquid acid that is stable only in solution, HOCl. It may be prepared by the reaction of chlorine with an agitated suspension of mercury(II) oxide. Because the disproportionation of the ion ClO^- is slow at low temperatures chloric(I) acid may be produced, along with chloride ions by the reaction of chlorine with water at 0°C. At higher temperatures disproportionation to the chlorate(˘) ion, ClO_3^-, takes place. Chloric(I) acid is a very weak acid but is a mild oxidizing agent and is widely used as a bleaching agent.

chloric(III) acid (chlorous acid) A pale-yellow acid known only in solution, $HClO_2$. It is formed by the reaction of chlorine dioxide and water and is a weak acid and an oxidizing agent.

chloric(V) acid (chloric acid) A colourless unstable liquid, $HClO_3$; r.d. 1.2; m.p. <−20°C; decomposes at 40°C. It is best prepared by the reaction of barium chlorate with sulphuric acid although chloric(V) acid is also formed by the disproportionation of chloric(I) acid in hot solutions. It is both a strong acid and a powerful oxidizing agent; hot solutions of the acid or its salts have been known to detonate in contact with readily oxidized organic material.

chloric(VII) acid (perchloric acid) An unstable liquid acid, $HClO_4$; r.d. 1.76; m.p. −112°C; b.p. 39°C (50 mmHg); explodes at about 90°C at atmospheric pressure. There is also a monohydrate (r.d. 1.88 (solid), 1.77 (liquid); m.p. 48°C; explodes at about 110°C) and a dihydrate (r.d. 1.65; m.p. −17.8°C; b.p. 200°C). Commercial chloric(VII) acid is a water azeotrope, which is 72.5% $HClO_4$, boiling at 203°C. The anhydrous acid may be prepared by vacuum distillation of the concentrated acid in the presence of magnesium perchlorate as a dehydrating agent. Chloric(VII) acid is both a strong acid and a strong oxidizing agent. It is widely used to decompose organic materials prior to analysis, e.g. samples of animal or vegetable matter requiring heavy-metal analysis.

chloride *See* halide.

chlorination **1.** A chemical reaction in which a chlorine atom is introduced into a compound. *See* halogenation. **2.** The treatment of water with chlorine to disinfect it.

chlorine Symbol Cl. A *halogen element; a.n. 17; r.a.m. 35.453; d. 3.214 g dm^{-3}; m.p. −100.98°C; b.p. −34.6°C. It is a poisonous greenish-yellow gas and occurs widely in nature as sodium chloride in seawater and as halite (NaCl), carnallite ($KCl.MgCl_2.6H_2O$), and sylvite (KCl). It is manufactured by the electrolysis of brine and also obtained in the *Downs process for making sodium. It has many applications, including the chlorination of drinking water, bleaching, and the manufacture of a large number of organic chemicals.

It reacts directly with many elements and compounds and is a strong oxidizing agent. Chlorine compounds contain the element in the 1, 3, 5, and 7 oxidation states. It was discovered by Karl Scheele in 1774 and Humphry Davy confirmed it as an element in 1810.

chlorine dioxide A yellowish-red explosive gas, ClO_2; d. 3.09 g dm^{-3}; m.p. −59.5°C; b.p. 9.9°C. It is soluble in cold water but decomposed by hot water to give chloric (VII) acid, chlorine, and oxygen. Because of its high reactivity, chlorine dioxide is best prepared by the reaction of sodium chlorate and moist oxalic acid at 90°–100°C, as the product is then diluted by liberated carbon dioxide. Commercially the gas is produced by the reaction of sulphuric acid containing chloride ions with sulphur dioxide. Chlorine dioxide is widely used as a bleach in flour milling and in wood pulping and also finds application in water purification.

chlorine monoxide *See* dichlorine oxide.

chlorite 1. *See* chlorates. **2.** A group of layered silicate minerals, usually green or white in colour, that are similar to the micas in structure and crystallize in the monoclinic system. Chlorites are composed of complex silicates of aluminium, magnesium, and iron in combination with water, with the formula $(Mg,Al,Fe)_{12}(Si,Al)_8O_{20}(OH)_{16}$. They are most common in low-grade metamorphic rocks and also occur as secondary minerals in igneous rocks as alteration products of pyroxenes, amphiboles, and micas. The term is derived from *chloros*, the Greek word for green.

chloroacetic acids *See* chloroethanoic acids.

chlorobenzene A colourless highly inflammable liquid, C_6H_5Cl; r.d. 1.106; m.p. −45.43°C; b.p. 131.85°C. It is prepared by the direct chlorination of benzene using a halogen carrier (*see* Friedel–Crafts reaction), or manufactured by the *Raschig process. It is used mainly as an industrial solvent.

2-chlorobuta-1,3-diene (chloroprene) A colourless liquid chlorinated diene, $CH_2{:}CClCH{:}CH_2$; r.d. 0.96; b.p. 59°C. It is polymerized to make synthetic rubbers (e.g. neoprene).

chloroethane (ethyl chloride) A colourless flammable gas, C_2H_5Cl; m.p. −45°C; b.p. 132°C. It is made by reaction of ethene and hydrogen chloride and used in making lead tetraethyl for petrol.

chloroethanoic acids (chloroacetic acids) Three acids in which hydrogen atoms in the methyl group of ethanoic acid have been replaced by chlorine atoms. They are: *monochloroethanoic acid* ($CH_2ClCOOH$); *dichloroethanoic acid* ($CHCl_2COOH$); *trichloroethanoic acid* (CCl_3COOH). The presence of chlorine atoms in the methyl group causes electron withdrawal from the COOH group and makes the chloroethanoic acids stronger acids than ethanoic acid itself. The K_a values (in moles dm^{-3} at 25°C) are

CH_3COOH 1.7×10^{-5}

$CH_2ClCOOH$ 1.3×10^{-3}

$CHCl_2COOH$ 5.0×10^{-2}

CCl_3COOH 2.3×10^{-1}

chloroethene (vinyl chloride) A gaseous compound, $CH_2{:}CHCl$; r.d. 0.911; m.p. −153.8°C; b.p. −13.37°C. It is made by chlorinating ethene to give dichloroethane, then removing HCl:

$$C_2H_4 + Cl_2 \rightarrow CH_2ClCH_2Cl \rightarrow CH_2CHCl$$

The compound is used in making PVC.

chloroform *See* trichloromethane.

chloromethane (methyl chloride) A colourless flammable gas, CH_3Cl; r.d. 0.916; m.p. −97°C; b.p. −24°C. It is a *haloalkane, made by direct chlorination of methane and used as a local anaesthetic and refrigerant.

chlorophyll The pigment responsible for the green colour of most plants. The chlorophyll molecule is the principal site of light absorption in the light reactions of photosynthesis. It is a magnesium-containing *porphyrin, chemically related to cytochrome and haemoglobin.

chloroplatinic acid A reddish crystalline compound, H_2PtCl_6, made by dissolving platinum in aqua regia.

chloroprene *See* 2-chlorobuta-1,3-diene.

chlorosulphanes *See* disulphur dichloride.

chlorous acid *See* chloric(III) acid.

choke damp *See* blackdamp.

cholecalciferol *See* vitamin D.

cholesteric crystal *See* liquid crystal.

cholesterol A *sterol occurring widely in animal tissues and also in some higher plants and algae. It can exist as a free sterol or esterified with a long-chain fatty acid. Cholesterol is absorbed through the intestine or manufactured in the liver. It serves principally as a constituent of blood plasma lipoproteins and of the lipid–protein complexes that form cell membranes. It is also important as a precursor of various steroids, especially the bile acids, sex hormones, and adrenocorticoid hormones. The derivative 7-dehydrocholesterol is converted to vitamin D_3 by the action of sunlight on skin. Increased levels of dietary and blood cholesterol have been associated with *atherosclerosis*, a condition in which lipids accumulate on the inner walls of arteries and eventually obstruct blood flow.

choline An amino alcohol, $CH_2OHCH_2N(CH_3)_3OH$. It occurs widely in living organisms as a constituent of certain types of phospholipids – the lecithins and sphingomyelins. It is sometimes classified as a member of the vitamin B complex.

chromate A salt containing the ion CrO_4^{2-}.

chromatogram A record obtained by chromatography. The term is applied to the developed records of *paper chromatography and *thin-layer chromatography and also to the graphical record produced in *gas chromatography.

chromatography A technique for analysing or separating mixtures of gases, liquids, or dissolved substances. The original technique (invented by the Russian botanist Mikhail Tsvet in 1906) is a good example of *column chromatography*. A vertical glass tube is packed with an adsorbing material, such as alumina. The sample is poured into the column and continuously washed through with a solvent (a process known as *elution*). Different components of the sample are adsorbed to different extents and move down the column at different rates. In Tsvet's original application, plant pigments were used and these separated into coloured bands in passing down the column (hence the name chromatography). The usual method is to collect the liquid (the *eluate*) as it passes out from the column in fractions.

In general, all types of chromatography involve two distinct phases – the *stationary phase* (the adsorbent material in the column in the example above) and the *moving phase* (the solution in the example). The separation depends on competition for molecules of sample between the moving phase and the stationary phase. The form of column chromatography above is an example of *adsorption chromatography*, in which the sample molecules are adsorbed on the alumina. In *partition chromatography*, a liquid (e.g. water) is first absorbed by the stationary phase and the moving phase is an immiscible liquid. The separation is then by *partition between the two liquids. In ion-exchange chromatography (*see* ion exchange), the process involves competition between different ions for ionic sites on the stationary phase. *Gel filtration is another chromatographic technique in which the size of the sample molecules is important.

See also gas chromatography; paper chromatography; thin-layer chromatography.

chrome alum *See* potassium chromium sulphate.

chrome iron ore A mixed iron–chromium oxide, $FeO.Cr_2O_3$, used to make ferrochromium for chromium steels.

chrome red A basic lead chromate, $PbO.PbCrO_4$, used as a red pigment.

chrome yellow Lead chromate, $PbCrO_4$, used as a pigment.

chromic acid A hypothetical acid, H_2CrO_4, known only in chromate salts.

chromic anhydride *See* chromium(VI) oxide.

chromic compounds Compounds containing chromium in a higher (+3 or +6) oxidation state; e.g. chromic oxide is chromium (VI) oxide (CrO_3).

chromite A spinel mineral, $FeCr_2O_4$; the principal ore of chromium. It is black with a metallic lustre and usually occurs in massive form. It is a common constituent of peridotites and serpentines. The chief producing countries are Turkey, South Africa, the USSR, the Philippines, and Zimbabwe.

chromium Symbol Cr. A hard silvery *transition element; a.n. 24; r.a.m. 52.00; r.d. 7.19; m.p. 1900°C; b.p. 2640°C. The main ore is chromite ($FeCr_2O_4$). The metal is extracted by heating chromite with sodium chromate, from which chromium can be obtained by electrolysis. Alternatively, chromite can be heated with carbon in an electric furnace to give ferrochrome, which is used in making alloy steels. The metal is also used as a shiny decorative electroplated coating and in the manufacture of certain chromium compounds.

At normal temperatures the metal is corrosion-resistant. It reacts with dilute hydrochloric and sulphuric acids to give chromium(II) salts. These readily oxidize to the more stable chromium(III) salts. Chromium also forms compounds with the +6 oxidation state, as in chromates, which contain the CrO_4^{2-} ion. The element was discovered in 1797 by Vauquelin.

chromium(II) oxide A black insoluble powder, CrO. Chromium(II) oxide is prepared by oxidizing chromium amalgam with air. At high temperatures hydrogen reduces it to the metal.

chromium(III) oxide A green crystalline water-insoluble salt, Cr_2O_3; r.d. 5.21; m.p. 2266°C; b.p. 4000°C. It is obtained by heating chromium in a stream of oxygen or by heating ammonium dichromate. The industrial preparation is by reduction of sodium dichromate with carbon. Chromium(III) oxide is amphoteric, dissolving in acids to give chromium(III) ions and in concentrated solutions of alkalis to give *chromites*. It is used as a green pigment in glass, porcelain, and oil paint.

chromium(IV) oxide (chromium dioxide) A black insoluble powder, CrO_2; m.p. 300°C. It is prepared by the action of oxygen on chromium(VI) oxide or chromium (III) oxide at 420–450°C and 200–300 atmospheres. The compound is unstable.

chromium(VI) oxide (chromium trioxide; chromic anhydride) A red compound, CrO_3; rhombic; r.d. 2.70; m.p. 196°C. It can be made by careful addition of concentrated sulphuric acid to an ice-cooled strong aqueous solution of sodium dichromate with stirring. The mixture is then filtered through sintered glass, washed with nitric acid, then dried out 120°C in a desiccator.

Chromium(VI) oxide is an extremely powerful oxidizing agent, especially to organic matter; it immediately inflames ethanol. It is an acidic oxide and dissolves in water to form 'chromic acid', a powerful oxidizing agent and cleansing fluid for glassware. At 400°C, chromium(VI) oxide loses oxygen to give chromium(III) oxide.

chromium potassium sulphate A red crystalline solid, $K_2SO_4.Cr_2(SO_4)_3.24H_2O$; r.d. 1.91. It is used as a mordant *See also* alums.

chromium steel Any of a group of *stainless steels containing 8–25% of chromium. A typical chromium steel might contain 18% of chromium, 8% of nickel, and 0.15% of carbon. Chromium steels are highly resistant to corrosion and are used for cutlery, chemical plant, ball bearings, etc.

chromophore A group causing coloration in a *dye. Chromophores are generally groups of atoms having delocalized electrons.

chromous compounds Compounds containing chromium in its lower (+2) oxidation state; e.g. chromous chloride is chromium(II) chloride ($CrCl_2$).

chromyl chloride (chromium oxychloride) A dark red liquid, CrO_2Cl_2; r.d. 1.911; m.p. −96.5°C; b.p. 117°C. It is evolved as a dark-red vapour on addition of concentrated sulphuric acid to a mixture of solid potassium dichromate and sodium chloride; it condenses to a dark-red covalent liquid, which is immediately hydrolysed by solutions of alkalis to give the yellow chromate. Since bromides and iodides do not give analogous compounds this is a specific test for chloride ions. The compound is a powerful oxidizing agent, exploding on contact with phosphorus and inflaming sulphur and many organic compounds.

chrysotile *See* serpentine.

cinnabar A bright red mineral form of mercury(II) sulphide, HgS, crystallizing in the hexagonal system; the principal ore of mercury. It is deposited in veins and impregnations near recent volcanic rocks and hot springs. The chief sources include Spain, Italy, and Yugoslavia.

cinnamic acid (3-phenylpropenoic acid) A white crystalline aromatic *carboxylic acid, $C_6H_5CH{:}CHCOOH$; r.d. 1.28 (trans isomer); m.p. 133°C; b.p. 300°C. Esters of cinnamic acid occur in some essential oils.

circular polarization *See* polarization of light.

cis–trans isomerism *See* isomerism.

citrate A salt or ester of citric acid.

citric acid A white crystalline hydroxycarboxylic acid, $HOOCCH_2C(OH)(COOH)CH_2COOH$; r.d. 1.67; m.p. 153°C. It is present in citrus fruits and is an intermediate in the *Krebs cycle in plant and animal cells.

citric-acid cycle *See* Krebs cycle.

Claisen condensation A reaction of esters in which two molecules of the ester react to give a keto ester, e.g.

$$2CH_3COOR \rightarrow CH_3COCH_2COOR + ROH$$

The reaction is catalysed by sodium ethoxide, the mechanism being similar to that of the *aldol reaction.

Clark cell A type of *voltaic cell consisting of an anode made of zinc amalgam and a cathode of mercury both immersed in a saturated solution of zinc sulphate. The Clark cell was formerly used as a standard of e.m.f.; the e.m.f. at 15°C is 1.4345 volts. It is named after the British scientist Hosiah Clark (*d.* 1898).

Clark process *See* hardness of water.

clathrate A solid mixture in which small molecules of one compound or element are trapped in holes in the crystal lattice of another substance. Clathrates are sometimes called *enclosure compounds*, but they are not true compounds (the molecules are not held by chemical bonds). Quinol and ice both form clathrates with such substances as sulphur dioxide and xenon.

Claude process A process for liquefying air on a commercial basis. Air under pressure is used as the working substance in a piston engine, where it does external work and cools adiabatically. This cool air is fed to a counter-current heat exchanger, where it reduces the temperature of the next intake of high-pressure air. The same air is re-compressed and used again, and after several cycles eventually liquefies. The process was perfected in 1902 by the French scientist Georges Claude (1870–1960).

claudetite A mineral form of *arsenic(III) oxide, As_4O_6.

clay A fine-grained deposit consisting chiefly of *clay minerals. It is characteristically plastic and virtually impermeable when wet and cracks when it dries out. In geology the size of the constituent particles is usually taken to be less than 1/256 mm. In soil science clay is regarded as a soil with particles less than 0.002 mm in size.

clay minerals Very small particles, chiefly hydrous silicates of aluminium, sometimes with magnesium and/or iron substituting for all or part of the aluminium, that are the major constituents of clay materials. The particles are essentially crystalline (either platy or fibrous) with a layered structure, but may be amorphous or metalloidal. The clay minerals are responsible for the plastic properties of clay; the particles have the property of being able to hold water. The chief groups of clay minerals are: *kaolinite*, $Al_4Si_4O_{10}(OH)_8$, the chief constituent of *kaolin; *halloysite*, $Al_4Si_4(OH)_8O_{10}.4H_2O$; *illite*, $KAl_4(Si,Al)_8O_{18}.2H_2O$; *montmorillonite*, $(Na,Ca)_{0.33}(Al,Mg)_2Si_4O_{10}(OH)_2.nH_2O$, formed chiefly through alteration of volcanic ash; *vermiculite*, $(Mg,Fe,Al)_3(Al,Si)_4O_{10}(OH)_2.4H_2O$, used as an insulating material and potting soil.

cleavage The splitting of a crystal along planes of atoms in the lattice.

closed chain *See* chain; ring.

close packing The packing of spheres so as to occupy the minimum amount of space. In a single plane, each sphere is surrounded by six close neighbours in a hexagonal arrangement. The spheres in the second plane fit into depressions in the first layer, and so on. Each sphere has 12 other touching spheres. There are two types of close packing. In *hexagonal close packing* the spheres in the third layer are directly over those in the first, etc., and the arrangement of planes is ABAB.... In *cubic close packing* the spheres in the third layer occupy a different set of depressions than those in the first. The arrangement is ABCABC.... *See also* cubic crystal.

Clusius column A device for separating isotopes by thermal diffusion. One form consists of a vertical column some 30 metres high with a heated electric wire running along its axis. The lighter isotopes in a gaseous mixture of isotopes diffuse faster than the heavier isotopes. Heated by the axial wire, and assisted by natural convection, the lighter atoms are carried to the top of the column, where a fraction rich in lighter isotopes can be removed for further enrichment.

coagulation The process in which colloidal particles come together to form larger masses. Coagulation can be brought about by adding ions to neutralize the charges stabilizing the colloid. Ions with a high charge are particularly effective (e.g. alum, containing Al^{3+}, is used in styptics to coagulate blood). Another example of ionic coagulation is in the formation of river deltas, which occurs when colloidal silt particles in rivers are coagulated by ions in sea water. Heating is another way of coagulating certain colloids (e.g. boiling an egg coagulates the albumin).

coal A brown or black carbonaceous deposit derived from the accumulation and alteration of ancient vegetation, which originated largely in swamps or other moist environments. As the vegetation decomposed it formed layers of peat, which were subsequently buried (for example, by marine sediments following a rise in sea level or subsidence of the land). Under the increased pressure and resulting higher temperatures the peat was transformed into coal. Two types of coal are recognized: *humic* (or *woody*) *coals*, derived from plant remains; and *sapropelic coals*, which are derived from algae, spores, and finely divided plant material.

As the processes of coalification (i.e. the transformation resulting from the high temperatures and pressures) continue, there is a progressive transformation of the deposit: the proportion of carbon relative to oxygen rise and volatile substances and water are driven out. The various stages in this process are referred to as the *ranks* of the coal. In ascending order, the main ranks of coal are: *lignite* (or *brown coal*), which is soft, brown, and has a high moisture content; *subbituminous coal*, which is used chiefly by generating stations; *bituminous coal*, which is the most abundant rank of coal; *semibituminous coal*; *semianthracite coal*, which has a fixed carbon content of between 86% and 92%; and *anthracite coal*, which is hard and black with a fixed carbon content of between 92% and 98%.

Most deposits of coal were formed during the Carboniferous and Permian periods. More recent periods of coal formation occurred during the early Jurassic and Tertiary periods. Coal deposits occur in all the major continents; the leading producers include the USA, China, USSR, Poland, UK, South Africa, India, Australia, and West Germany. Coal is used as a fuel and in the chemical industry; by-products include coke and coal tar.

coal gas A fuel gas produced by the destructive distillation of coal. In the late-19th and early-20th centuries coal gas was a major source of energy and was made by heating coal in the absence of air in local gas works. Typically, it contained hydrogen (50%), methane (35%), and carbon monoxide (8%). By-products of the process were *coal tar and coke. The use of this type of gas declined with the increasing availability of natural gas, although since the early 1970s interest has developed in using coal in making *SNG.

coal tar A tar obtained from the destructive distillation of coal. Formerly, coal tar was obtained as a by-product in manufacturing *coal gas. Now it is produced in making coke for steel making. The crude tar contains a large number of organic compounds, such as benzene, naphthalene, methylbenzene, phenols, etc., which can be obtained by distillation. The residue is *pitch*. At one time coal tar was the major source of organic chemicals, most of which are now derived from petroleum and natural gas.

cobalt Symbol Co. A light-grey *transition element; a.n. 27; r.a.m. 58.933; r.d. 8.9; m.p. 1495°C; b.p. 2870°C. Cobalt is ferromagnetic below its Curie point of 1150°C. Small amounts of metallic cobalt are present in meteorites but it is usually extracted from ore deposits worked in Canada, Morocco, and Zaîre. It is present in the minerals cobaltite, smaltite, and erythrite but also associated with copper and nickel as sulphides and arsenides. Cobalt ores are usually roasted to the oxide and then reduced with carbon or water gas. Cobalt is usually alloyed for use. Alnico is a well-known magnetic alloy and cobalt is also used to make stainless steels and in high-strength alloys that are resistant to oxidation at high temperatures (for turbine blades and cutting tools).

The metal is oxidized by hot air and also reacts with carbon, phosphorus, sulphur, and dilute mineral acids. Cobalt salts, usual oxidation states II and III, are used to give a brilliant blue colour in glass, tiles, and pottery. Anhydrous cobalt(II) chloride paper is used as a qualitative test for water and as a heat-sensitive ink. Small amounts of cobalt salts are essential in a balanced diet for mammals (*see* essential element). Artificially produced cobalt-60 is an important radioactive tracer and cancer-treatment agent. The element was discovered by G. Brandt in 1737.

cobalt(II) oxide A pink solid, CoO; cubic; r.d. 6.45; m.p. 1795°C. The addition of potassium hydroxide to a solution of cobalt(II) nitrate gives a bluish-violet precipitate, which on boiling is converted to pink impure cobalt(II) hydroxide. On heating this in the absence of air, cobalt(II) oxide is formed. The compound is readily oxidized in air to form tricobalt tetroxide, Co_3O_4, and is readily reduced by hydrogen to the metal.

cobalt(III) oxide (cobalt sesquioxide) A black grey insoluble solid, Co_2O_3; hexagonal or rhombic; r.d. 5.18; decomposes at 895°C. It is produced by the ignition of cobalt nitrate; the product however never has the composition corresponding exactly to cobalt(III) oxide. On heating it readily forms Co_3O_4, which contains both Co(II) and Co(III), and is easily reduced to the metal by hydrogen. Cobalt(III) oxide dissolves in strong acid to give unstable brown solutions of trivalent cobalt salts. With dilute acids cobalt(II) salts are formed.

cobalt steel Any of a group of *alloy steels containing 5–12% of cobalt, 14–20% of tungsten, usually with 4% of chromium and 1–2% of vanadium. They are very hard but somewhat brittle. Their main use is in high-speed tools.

coenzyme An organic nonprotein molecule that associates with an enzyme molecule in catalysing biochemical reactions. Coenzymes usually participate in the substrate–enzyme interaction by donating or accepting certain chemical groups. Many vitamins are precursors of coenzymes. *See also* cofactor.

coenzyme A (CoA) A complex organic compound that acts in conjunction with enzymes involved in various biochemical reactions, notably the oxidation of pyruvate via the *Krebs cycle and fatty-acid oxidation and synthesis. It comprises principally the B vitamin pantothenic acid, the nucleotide adenine, and a ribose-phosphate group.

coenzyme Q (ubiquinone) Any of a group of related quinone-derived compounds that serve as electron carriers in the *electron transport chain reactions of cellular respiration. Coenzyme Q molecules have side chains of different lengths in different types of organisms but function in similar ways.

cofactor A nonprotein component essential for the normal catalytic activity of an enzyme. Cofactors may be organic molecules (*coenzymes) or inorganic ions. They may activate the enzyme by altering its shape or they may actually participate in the chemical reaction.

coherent units A system of *units of measurement in which derived units are obtained by multiplying or dividing base units without the use of numerical factors. *SI units form a coherent system; for example the unit of force is the newton, which is equal to 1 kilogram metre per second squared ($kg\,m\,s^{-2}$), the kilogram, metre, and second all being base units of the system.

coinage metals A group of three malleable ductile metals forming subgroup IB of the *periodic table: copper (Cu), silver (Ag), and gold (Au). Their outer electronic configurations have the form $nd^{10}(n+1)s^1$. Although this is similar to that of alkali metals, the coinage metals all have much higher ionization energies and higher (and positive) standard electrode potentials. Thus, they are much more difficult to oxidize and are more resistant to corrosion. In addition, the fact that they have *d*-electrons makes them show variable valency (Cu^{I}, Cu^{II}, and Cu^{III}; Ag^{I} and Ag^{II}; $Au^{I}$and Au^{III}) and form a wide range of coordination compounds. They are generally classified with the *transition elements.

coke A form of carbon made by the destructive distillation of coal. Coke is used for blast-furnaces and other metallurgical and chemical processes requiring a source of carbon. Lower-grade cokes, made by heating the coal to a lower temperature, are used as smokeless fuels for domestic heating.

colchicine An *alkaloid derived from the autumn crocus, *Colchicum autumnale*. It inhibits cell division. Colchicine is used in genetics, cytology, and plant-breeding research, and also in cancer therapy to inhibit cell division.

collagen An insoluble fibrous protein found extensively in the connective tissue of skin, tendons, and bone. The polypeptide chains of collagen (containing the amino acids glycine and proline predominantly) form triple-stranded helical coils that are bound together to form fibrils, which have great strength and limited elasticity. Collagen accounts for over 30% of the total body protein of mammals.

colligative properties Properties that depend on the concentration of particles (molecules, ions, etc.) present in a solution, and not on the nature of the particles. Examples of colligative properties are osmotic pressure (*see* osmosis), *lowering of vapour pressure, *depression of freezing point, and *elevation of boiling point.

collodion A thin film of cellulose nitrate made by dissolving the cellulose nitrate in ethanol or ethoxyethane, coating the surface, and evaporating the solvent.

colloids Colloids were originally defined by Thomas Graham in 1861 as substances, such as starch or gelatin, which will not diffuse through a membrane. He distinguished them from *crystalloids* (e.g. inorganic salts), which would pass through membranes. Later it was recognized that colloids were distinguished from true solutions by the presence of particles that were too small to be observed with a normal microscope yet were much larger than normal molecules. Colloids are now regarded as systems in which there are two or more phases, with one (the *dispersed phase*) distributed in the other (the *continuous phase*). Moreover, at least one of the phases has small dimensions (in the range 10^{-9}–10^{-6} m). Colloids are classified in various ways.

Sols are dispersions of small solid particles in a liquid. The particles may be macromolecules or may be clusters of small molecules. *Lyophobic sols* are those in which there is no affinity between the dispersed phase and the liquid. An example is silver chloride dispersed in water. In such colloids the solid particles have a surface charge, which tends to stop them coming together. Lyophobic sols are inherently unstable and in time the particles aggregate and form a precipitate. *Lyophilic sols*, on the other hand, are more like true solutions in which the solute molecules are large and have an affinity for the solvent. Starch in water is an example of such a system. *Association colloids* are systems in which the dispersed phase consists of clusters of molecules that have lyophobic and lyophilic parts. Soap in water is an association colloid (*see* micelle).

Emulsions are colloidal systems in which the dispersed and continuous phases are both liquids, e.g. oil-in-water or water-in-oil. Such systems require an emulsifying agent to stabilize the dispersed particles.

Gels are colloids in which both dispersed and continuous phases have a three-dimensional network throughout the material, so that it forms a jelly-like mass. Gelatin is a common example. One component may sometimes be removed (e.g. by heating) to leave a rigid gel (e.g. silica gel).

Other types of colloid include *aerosols* (dispersions of liquid or solid particles in a gas, as in a mist or smoke) and foams (dispersions of gases in liquids or solids).

colorimetric analysis Quantitative analysis of solutions by estimating their colour, e.g. by comparing it with the colours of standard solutions.

columbium A former name for the element *niobium.

column chromatography *See* chromatography.

combustion A chemical reaction in which a substance reacts rapidly with oxygen with the production of heat and light. Such reactions are often free-radical chain reactions, which can usually be summarized as the oxidation of carbon to form its oxides and the oxidation of hydrogen to form water. *See also* flame.

common salt *See* sodium chloride.

complex A compound in which molecules or ions form coordinate bonds to a metal atom or ion. The complex may be a positive ion (e.g. $[Cu(H_2O)_6]^{2+}$), a negative ion (e.g. $Fe[(CN)_6]^{3-}$), or a neutral molecule (e.g. $PtCl_2(NH_3)_2$). The formation of such coordination complexes is typical behaviour of transition metals. The complexes formed are often coloured and have unpaired electrons (i.e. are paramagnetic). *See also* ligand; chelate.

complexometric analysis A type of volumetric analysis in which the reaction involves the formation of an inorganic *complex.

component A distinct chemical species in a mixture. If there are no reactions taking place, the number of components is the number of separate chemical species. A mixture of water and ethanol, for instance, has two components (but is a single phase). A mixture of ice and water has two phases but one component (H_2O). If an equilibrium reaction occurs, the number of components is taken to be the number of chemical species minus the number of reactions. Thus, in

$$H_2 + I_2 \rightleftharpoons 2HI$$

there are two components. *See also* phase rule.

compound A substance formed by the combination of elements in fixed proportions. The formation of a compound involves a chemical reaction; i.e. there is a change in the configuration of the valence electrons of the atoms. Compounds, unlike mixtures, cannot be separated by physical means. *See also* molecule.

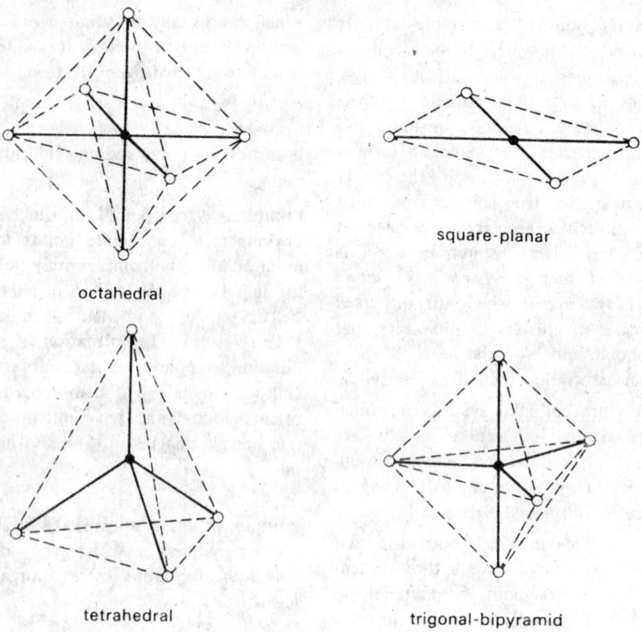

Some common shapes of coordination complexes

concentrated Describing a solution that has a relatively high concentration of solute.

concentration The quantity of dissolved substance per unit quantity of solvent in a solution. Concentration is measured in various ways. The amount of substance dissolved per unit volume (symbol c) has units of mol dm^{-3} or mol l^{-1}. It is now called 'concentration' (formerly *molarity*). The *mass concentration* (symbol ρ) is the mass of solute per unit volume of solvent. It has units of kg dm^{-3}, g cm^{-3}, etc. The *molal concentration* (or *molality*; symbol m) is the amount of substance per unit mass of solvent, commonly given in units of mol kg^{-1} *See also* mole fraction.

concentration cell *See* cell.

condensation The change of a vapour or gas into a liquid. The change of phase is accompanied by the evolution of heat (*see* latent heat).

condensation polymerization *See* polymer.

condensation pump *See* diffusion pump.

condensation reaction A chemical reaction in which two molecules combine to form a larger molecule with elimination of a small molecule (e.g. H_2O). *See* aldehydes; ketones.

condenser A device used to cool a vapour to cause it to condense to a liquid. *See* Liebig condenser.

conductiometric titration A type of titration in which the electrical conductivity of the reaction mixture is continuously monitored as one reactant is added. The equivalence point is the point at which this undergoes a sudden change. The method is used for titrating coloured solutions, which cannot be used with normal indicators.

conduction band *See* energy bands.

conductivity water *See* distilled water.

Condy's fluid A mixture of calcium and potassium permanganates (manganate(VII)) used as an antiseptic.

configuration 1. The arrangement of atoms or groups in a molecule. **2.** The arrangement of electrons about the nucleus of an *atom.

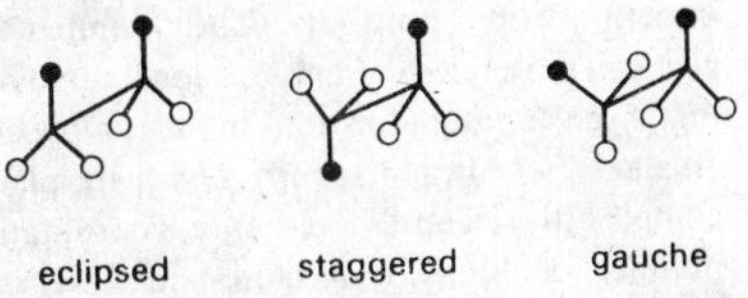

Conformation for rotation about a single bond

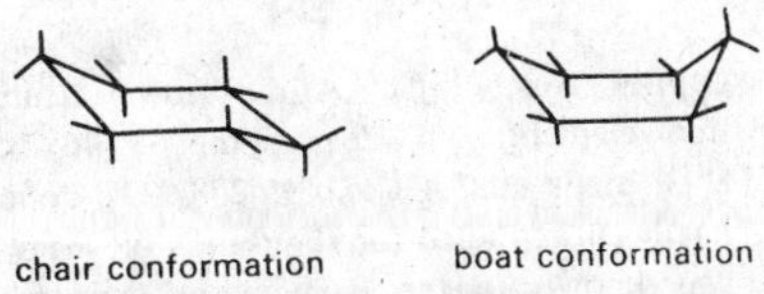

Conformations of cyclohexane ring

conformation Any of the large number of possible shapes of a molecule resulting from rotation of one part of the molecule about a single bond. See illustration.

congeners Elements that belong to the same group in the periodic table.

conjugate acid *or* **base** *See* acids.

conjugated Describing double or triple bonds in a molecule that are separated by one single bond. For example, the organic compound buta-1,3-diene, $H_2C{=}CH{-}CH{=}CH_2$, has conjugated double bonds. In such molecules, there is some delocalization of electrons in the pi orbitals between the carbon atoms linked by the single bond.

conservation law A law stating that the total magnitude of a certain physical property of a system, such as its mass, energy, or charge, remain unchanged even though there may be exchanges of that property between components of the system. For example, imagine a table with a bottle of salt solution (NaCl), a bottle of silver nitrate solution ($AgNO_3$), and a beaker standing on it. The mass of this table and its contents will not change even when some of the contents of the bottles are poured into the beaker. As a result of the reaction between the chemicals two new substances (silver chloride and sodium nitrate) will appear in the beaker:

$$NaCl + AgNO_3 \rightarrow AgCl + NaNO_3,$$

but the total mass of the table and its contents will not change. This *conservation of mass* is a law of wide and general applicability, which is true for the universe as a whole, provided that the universe can be considered a closed system (nothing escaping from it, nothing being added to it). According to Einstein's mass–energy relationship, every quantity of energy (E) has a mass (m), which is given by E/c^2, where c is the speed of light. Therefore if mass is conserved, the law of *conservation of energy* must be of equally wide application.

consolute temperature The temperature at which two partially miscible liquids become fully miscible as the temperature is increased.

constantan An alloy having an electrical resistance that varies only very slightly with temperature (over a limited range around normal room temperatures). It consists of copper (50–60%) and nickel (40–50%) and is used in resistance wire, thermocouples, etc.

constant-boiling mixture *See* azeotrope.

constant proportions *See* chemical combination.

contact process A process for making sulphuric acid from sulphur dioxide (SO_2), which is made by burning sulphur or by roasting sulphide ores. A mixture of sulphur dioxide and air is passed over a hot catalyst

$$2SO_2 + O_2 \rightarrow 2SO_3$$

The reaction is exothermic and the conditions are controlled to keep the temperature at an optimum 450°C. Formerly, platinum catalysts were used but vanadium–vanadium oxide catalysts are now mainly employed (although less efficient, they are less susceptible to poisoning). The sulphur trioxide is dissolved in sulphuric acid

$$H_2SO_4 + SO_3 \rightarrow H_2S_2O_7$$

and the oleum is then diluted.

continuous phase *See* colloid.

continuous spectrum *See* spectrum.

convection A process by which heat is transferred from one part of a fluid to another by movement of the fluid itself. In *natural convection* the movement occurs as a result of gravity: the hot part of the fluid expands, becomes less dense, and is displaced by the colder denser part of the fluid as this drops below it. This is the process that occurs in most domestic hot-water systems between the boiler and the hot-water cylinder. A natural convection current is set up transferring the hot water from the boiler up to the cylinder (always placed above the boiler) so that the cold water from the cylinder can move down into the boiler to be heated. In some modern systems, where small-bore pipes are used or it is inconvenient to place the cylinder above the boiler, the circulation between boiler and hot-water cylinder relies upon a pump. This is an example of *forced convection*, where hot fluid is transferred from one region to another by a pump or fan.

converter The reaction vessel in the *Bessemer process or some similar steel-making process.

coordinate bond *See* chemical bond.

coordination compound A compound in which coordinate bonds are formed (*see* chemical bond). The term is used especially for inorganic *complexes.

coordination number The number of groups, molecules, atoms, or ions surrounding a given atom or ion in a complex or crystal. For instance, in a square-planar complex the central ion has a coordination number of four. In a close-packed crystal (*see* close packing) the coordination number is twelve.

copolymer *See* polymer.

copper Symbol Cu. A red-brown *transition element; a.n. 29; r.a.m. 63.546; r.d. 8.93; m.p. 1083.4°C; b.p. 2582°C. Copper has been extracted for thousands of years; it was known to the Romans as cuprum, a name linked with the island of Cyprus. The metal is malleable and ductile and an excellent conductor of heat and electricity. Copper-containing minerals include cuprite (Cu_2O), azurite ($2CuCO_3.Cu(OH)_2$), chalcopyrite ($CuFeS_2$), and malachite ($CuCO_3.Cu(OH)_2$). Native copper appears in isolated pockets in some parts of the world. The large mines in the USA, Chile, Canada, Zambia, Zaîre, and Peru extract ores containing sulphides, oxides, and carbonates. They are usually worked by smelting, leaching, and electrolysis. Copper metal is used to make electric cables and wires. Its alloys, brass (copper–zinc) and bronze (copper–tin), are used extensively.

Water does not attack copper but in moist atmospheres it slowly forms a characteristic green surface layer (patina). The metal will not react with dilute sulphuric or hydrochloric acids, but with nitric acid oxides of nitrogen are formed. Copper compounds contain the element in the +1 and +2 oxidation states. Copper(I) compounds are mostly white (the oxide is red). Copper (II) salts are blue in solution. The metal also forms a large number of coordination complexes.

copperas *See* iron(II) sulphate.

copper(I) chloride A white solid compound, CuCl; cubic; r.d. 4.14; m.p. 430°C; b.p. 1490°C. It is obtained by boiling a solution containing copper(II) chloride, excess copper turnings, and hydrochloric acid. Copper(I) is present as the $[CuCl_2]^-$ complex ion. On pouring the solution into air-free distilled water copper(I) chloride precipitates. It must be kept free of air and moisture since it oxidizes to copper(II) chloride under those conditions.

Copper(I) chloride is essentially covalent and its structure is similar to that of diamond; i.e. each copper atom is surrounded tetrahedrally by four chlorine atoms and vice versa. In the vapour phase, dimeric and trimeric species are present. Copper(I) chloride is used in conjunction with ammonium chloride as a catalyst in the dimerization of ethyne to but-1-ene-3-yne (vinyl acetylene), which is used in the production of synthetic rubber. In the laboratory a mixture of copper(I) chloride and hydrochloric acid is used for converting benzene diazonium chloride to chlorobenzene – the Sandmeyer reaction.

copper(II) chloride A brown-yellow powder, $CuCl_2$; r.d. 3.386; m.p. 620°C. It exists as a blue-green dihydrate (rhombic; r.d. 2.54; loses H_2O at 100°C). The anhydrous solid is obtained by passing chlorine over heated copper. It is predominantly covalent and adopts a layer structure in which each copper atom is surrounded by four chlorine atoms at a distance of 0.23 and two more at a distance of 0.295. A concentrated aqueous solution is dark brown in colour due to the presence of complex ions such as $[CuCl_4]^{2-}$. On dilution the colour changes to green and then blue because of successive replacement of chloride ions by water molecules, the final colour being that of the $[Cu(H_2O)_6]^{2+}$ ion. The dihydrate can be obtained by crystallizing the solution.

copper glance A mineral form of copper(I) sulphide, Cu_2S.

copper(II) nitrate A blue deliquescent solid, $Cu(NO_3)_2.3H_2O$; r.d. 2.32; m.p. 114.5°C. It may be obtained by reacting either copper(II) oxide or copper(II) carbonate with dilute nitric acid and crystallizing the resulting solution. Other hydrates containing 6 or 9 molecules of water are known. On heating it readily decomposes to give copper(II) oxide, nitrogen dioxide, and oxygen. The anhydrous form can be obtained by reacting copper with a solution of nitrogen dioxide in ethyl ethanoate. It sublimes on heating suggesting that it is appreciably covalent.

copper(I) oxide A red insoluble solid, Cu_2O; r.d. 6.0; m.p. 1235°C. It is obtained by reduction of an alkaline solution of copper(II) sulphate. Since the addition of alkalis to a solution of copper(II) salt results in the precipitation of copper(II) hydroxide the copper(II) ions are complexed with tartrate ions; under such conditions the concentration of copper(II) ions is so low that the solubility product of copper(II) hydroxide is not exceeded.

When copper(I) oxide reacts with dilute sulphuric acid a solution of copper(II) sulphate and a deposit of copper results, i.e. disproportionation occurs.

$$Cu_2O + 2H^+ \rightarrow Cu^{2+} + Cu + H_2O$$

When dissolved in concentrated hydrochloric acid the $[CuCl_2]^-$ complex ion is formed. Copper(I) oxide is used in the manufacture of rectifiers and the production of red glass.

copper(II) oxide A black insoluble solid, CuO; monoclinic; r.d. 6.3; m.p. 1326°C. It is obtained by heating either copper(II) carbonate or copper(II) nitrate. It decomposes on heating above 800°C to copper(I) oxide and oxygen. Copper(II) oxide reacts readily with mineral acids on warming, with the formation of copper(II) salts; it is also readily reduced to copper on heating in a stream of hydrogen. Copper(II) oxide is soluble in dilute acids forming blue solutions of cupric salts.

copper pyrites *See* chalcopyrite.

copper(II) sulphate A blue crystalline solid, $CuSO_4.5H_2O$; triclinic; r.d. 2.284. The pentahydrate loses $4H_2O$ at 110°C and the fifth H_2O at 150°C to form the white anhydrous compound (rhombic; r.d. 3.6; decomposes above 200°C). The pentahydrate is prepared either by reacting copper(II) oxide or copper(II) carbonate with dilute sulphuric acid; the solution is heated to saturation and the blue pentahydrate crystallizes out on cooling (a few drops of dilute sulphuric acid are generally added to prevent hydrolysis). It is obtained on an industrial scale by forcing air through a hot mixture of copper and dilute sulphuric acid. In the pentahydrate each copper(II) ion is surrounded by four water molecules at the corner of a square, the fifth and sixth octahedral positions are occupied by oxygen atoms from the sulphate anions, and the fifth water molecule is held in place by hydrogen bonding. Copper(II) sulphate has many industrial uses, including the preparation of the Bordeaux mixture (a fungicide) and the preparation of other copper compounds. It is also used in electroplating and textile dying and as a timber preservative. The anhydrous form is used in the detection of traces of moisture.

Copper(II) sulphate pentahydrate is also known as *blue vitriol.*

cordite An explosive mixture of cellulose nitrate and nitroglycerin, with added plasticizers and stabilizers, used as a propellant for guns.

CORN rule *See* absolute configuration.

corrosion Chemical or electrochemical attack on the surface of a metal. *See also* electrolytic corrosion; rusting.

corundum A mineral form of aluminium oxide, Al_2O_3. It crystallizes in the trigonal system and occurs as well-developed hexagonal crystals. It is colourless and transparent when pure but the presence of other elements gives rise to a variety of colours. *Ruby is a red variety containing chromium; *sapphire is a blue variety containing iron and titanium. Corundum occurs as a rock-forming mineral in both metamorphic and igneous rocks. It is chemically resistant to weathering processes and so also occurs in alluvial (placer) deposits. The second hardest mineral after diamond (it has a hardness of 9 on the Mohs' scale), it is used as an abrasive.

coulomb Symbol C. The *SI unit of electric charge. It is equal to the charge transferred by a current of one ampere in one second. The unit is named after Charles de Coulomb (1736–1806), a French physicist.

coupling A type of chemical reaction in which two molecules join together; for example, the formation of an *azo compound by coupling of a diazonium ion with a benzene ring.

covalent bond *See* chemical bond.

covalent crystal A crystal in which the atoms are held together by covalent bonds. Covalent crystals are sometimes called *macromolecular* or *giant-molecular crystals.* They are hard high-melting substances. Examples are diamond and boron nitride.

covalent radius An effective radius assigned to an atom in a covalent compound. In the case of a simple diatomic molecule, the covalent radius is half the distance between the nuclei. Thus, in Cl_2 the internuclear distance is 0.198 nm so the covalent radius is taken to be 0.099 nm. Covalent radii can also be calculated for multiple bonds; for instance, in the case of carbon the values are 0.077 nm for single bonds, 0.0665 nm for double bonds, and 0.0605 nm for triple bonds. The values of different covalent radii can sometimes be added to give internuclear distances. For example, the length of the bond in interhalogens (e.g. ClBr) is nearly equal to the sum of the covalent radii of the halogens involved. This, however, is not always true because of other effects (e.g. ionic contributions to the bonding).

cracking The process of breaking down chemical compounds by heat. The term is applied particularly to the cracking of hydrocarbons in the kerosine fraction obtained from *petroleum refining to give smaller hydrocarbons and alkenes. It is an important process, both as a source of branched-chain hydrocarbons suitable for gasoline (for motor fuel) and as a source of ethene and other alkenes. *Catalytic cracking* is a similar process in which a catalyst is used to lower the temperature required and to modify the products obtained.

cream of tartar *See* potassium hydrogentartrate.

creosote 1. (wood creosote) An almost colourless liquid mixture of phenols obtained by distilling tar obtained by the destructive distillation of wood. It is used medically as an antiseptic and expectorant. **2. (coal-tar creosote)** A dark liquid mixture of phenols and cresols obtained by distilling coal tar. It is used for preserving timber.

cresols *See* methylphenols.

cristobalite A mineral form of *silicon(IV) oxide, SiO_2.

critical pressure The pressure of a fluid in its *critical state; i.e. when it is at its critical temperature and critical volume.

critical state The state of a fluid in which the liquid and gas phases both have the same density. The fluid is then at its critical temperature, critical pressure, and critical volume.

critical temperature 1. The temperature above which a gas cannot be liquefied by an increase of pressure. *See also* critical state. **2.** *See* transition point.

critical volume The volume of a fixed mass of a fluid in its *critical state; i.e. when it is at its critical temperature and critical pressure. The *critical specific volume* is its volume per unit mass in this state: in the past this has often been called the critical volume.

cross linkage A short side chain of atoms linking two longer chains in a polymeric material.

crucible A dish or other vessel in which substances can be heated to a high temperature.

crude oil *See* petroleum.

cryogenic pump A *vacuum pump in which pressure is reduced by condensing gases on surfaces maintained at about 20 K by means of liquid hydrogen or at 4 K by means of liquid helium. Pressures down to 10^{-8} mmHg (10^{-6} Pa) can be maintained; if they are used in conjunction with a *diffusion pump, pressures as low as 10^{-15} mmHg (10^{-13} Pa) can be reached.

cryohydrate A eutectic mixture of ice and some other substance (e.g. an ionic salt) obtained by freezing a solution.

cryolite A rare mineral form of sodium aluminofluoride, Na_3AlF_6, which crystallizes in the monoclinic system. It is usually white but may also be colourless. The only important occurrence of the mineral is in Greenland. It is used chiefly as a flux in the production of aluminium from bauxite.

cryoscopic constant *See* depression of freezing point.

cryostat A vessel enabling a sample to be maintained at a very low temperature. The *Dewar flask is the most satisfactory vessel for controlling heat leaking in by radiation, conduction, or convection. Cryostats usually consist of two or more Dewar flasks nesting in each other. For example, a liquid nitrogen bath is often used to cool a Dewar flask containing a liquid helium bath.

crystal A solid with a regular polyhedral shape. All crystals of the same substance grow so that they have the same angles between their faces. However, they may not have the same external appearance because different faces can grow at different rates, depending on the conditions. The external form of the crystal is referred to as the *crystal habit*. The atoms, ions, or molecules forming the crystal have a regular arrangement and this is the *crystal structure*.

crystal-field theory A theory of the electronic structures of inorganic *complexes, in which the complex is assumed to consist of a central metal atom or ion surrounded by ligands that are negative ions. For example, the complex $[PtCl_4]^{2-}$ is thought of as a Pt^{2+} ion surrounded by four Cl^- ions at the corners of a square. The presence of these ions affects the energies of the *d*-orbitals, causing a splitting of energy levels. The theory can be used to explain the spectra of complexes and their magnetic properties. *Ligand-field theory* is a development of crystal-field theory in which the overlap of orbitals is taken into account.

crystal habit *See* crystal.

crystal lattice The regular pattern of atoms, ions, or molecules in a crystalline substance. A crystal lattice can be regarded as produced by repeated translations of a *unit cell* of the lattice. *See also* crystal system.

crystalline Having the regular internal arrangement of atoms, ions, or molecules characteristic of crystals. Crystalline materials need not necessarily exist as crystals; all metals, for example, are crystalline although they are not usually seen as regular geometric crystals.

crystallite A small crystal, e.g. one of the small crystals forming part of a microcrystalline substance.

crystallization The process of forming crystals from a liquid or gas.

crystallography The study of crystal form and structure. *See also* X-ray crystallography.

crystalloids *See* colloids.

crystal structure *See* crystal.

crystal system A method of classifying crystalline substances on the basis of their unit cell. There are seven crystal systems. If the cell is a parallelopiped with sides *a*, *b*, and *c* and if α is the angle between *b* and *c*, β the angle between *a* and *c*, and γ the angle between *a* and *b*, the systems are:
(1) *cubic* $a=b=c$ and $\alpha=\beta=\gamma=90°$
(2) *tetragonal* $a=b=c$ and $\alpha=\beta=\gamma=90°$
(3) *rhombic* (or *orthorhombic*) $a=b=c$ and $\alpha=\beta=\gamma=90°$
(4) *hexagonal* $a=b=c$ and $\alpha=\beta=\gamma=90°$
(5) *trigonal* $a=b=c$ and $\alpha=\beta=\gamma=90°$
(6) *monoclinic* $a=b=c$ and $\alpha=\gamma=90°=\beta$
(7) *triclinic* $a=b=c$ and $\alpha=\beta=\gamma$

CS gas The vapour from a white solid, $C_6H_4(Cl)CH{:}C(CN)_2$, causing tears and choking, used in 'crowd control'.

cubic close packing *See* close packing.

cubic crystal A crystal in which the unit cell is a cube (*see* crystal system). There are three possible packings for cubic crystals: *simple cubic*, *face-centred cubic*, and *body-centred cubic*. See illustration.

cumene process An industrial process for making phenol from benzene. A mixture of benzene vapour and propene is passed over a phosphoric acid catalyst at 250°C and high pressure

$$C_6H_6 + CH_3CH{:}CH_2 \rightarrow C_6H_5CH(CH_3)_2$$

The product is called *cumene*, and it can be oxidized in air to a peroxide, $C_6H_5C(CH_3)_2O_2H$. This reacts with dilute acid to give phenol (C_6H_5OH) and propanone (acetone, CH_3OCH_3), which is a valuable by-product.

cupellation A method of separating noble metals (e.g. gold or silver) from base metals (e.g. lead) by melting the mixture with a blast of hot air in a shallow porous dish (the *cupel*). The base metals are oxidized, the oxide being carried away by the blast of air or absorbed by the porous container.

cuprammonium ion The tetraamminecopper(II) ion $[Cu(NH_3)_4]^{2+}$. *See* ammine.

cupric compounds Compounds containing copper in its higher (+2) oxidation state; e.g. cupric chloride is copper(II) chloride ($CuCl_2$).

cuprite A red mineral cubic form of copper (I) oxide, Cu_2O; an important ore of copper. It occurs where deposits of copper have been subjected to oxidation. The mineral has been mined as a copper ore in Chile, Zaïre, Bolivia, Australia, the USSR, and the USA.

cuprous compounds Compounds containing copper in its lower (+1) oxidation state; e.g. cuprous chloride is copper(I) chloride (CuCl).

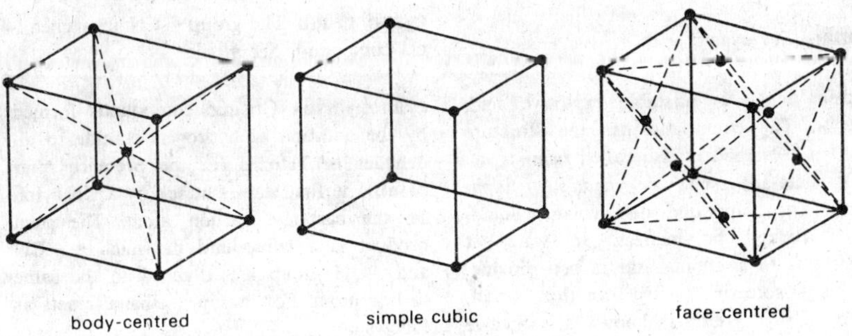

Cubic crystal structures

curie The former unit of *activity (*see* radiation units). It is named after the Polish-born French physicist Marie Curie (1867–1934).

Curie point (Curie temperature) The temperature at which a ferromagnetic substance loses its ferromagnetism and becomes only paramagnetic. For iron the Curie point is 760°C and for nickel 356°C.

curium Symbol Cm. A radioactive metallic transuranic element belonging to the *actinoids; a.n. 96; mass number of the most stable isotope 247 (half-life 1.64×10^7 years); r.d. (calculated) 13.51; m.p. 1340±40°C. There are nine known isotopes. The element was first identified by G. T. Seaborg and associates in 1944 and first produced by L. B. Werner and I. Perlman in 1947 by bombarding americium-241 with neutrons.

cyanamide 1. An inorganic salt containing the ion CN_2^{2-}. *See* calcium cyanamide. **2.** A colourless crystalline solid, H_2NCN, made by the action of carbon dioxide on hot sodamide. It is a weakly acidic compound (the parent acid of cyanamide salts) that is soluble in water and ethanol. It is hydrolysed to urea in acidic solutions.

cyanamide process *See* calcium cyanamide.

cyanate *See* cyanic acid.

cyanic acid An unstable explosive acid, HOCN. The compound has the structure H–O–C≡N, and is also called *fulminic acid.* Its salts and esters are *cyanates* (or *fulminates*). The compound is a volatile liquid, which readily polymerizes. In water it hydrolyses to ammonia and carbon dioxide. It is isomeric with another acid, H–N=C=O, which is known as *isocyanic acid.* Its salts and esters are *isocyanates.*

cyanide 1. An inorganic salt containing the cyanide ion CN^-. Cyanides are extremely poisonous because of the ability of the CN^- ion to coordinate with the iron in haemoglobin, thereby blocking the uptake of oxygen by the blood. **2.** A metal coordination complex formed with cyanide ions.

cyanide process A method of extracting gold by dissolving it in potassium cyanide (to form the complex ion $[Au(CN)_2]^-$). The ion can be reduced back to gold with zinc.

cyanine dyes A class of dyes that contain a –CH= group linking two nitrogen-containing heterocyclic rings. They are used as sensitizers in photography.

cyanocobalamin *See* vitamin B complex.

cyanogen A colourless gas, $(CN)_2$, with a pungent odour; soluble in water, ethanol, and ether; d. 2.335 g dm^{-3}; m.p. –27.9°C; b.p. –20.7°C. The compound is very toxic. It may be prepared in the laboratory by heating mercury(II) cyanide; industrially it is made by gas-phase oxidation of hydrogen cyanide using air over a silver catalyst, chlorine over activated silicon(IV) oxide, or nitrogen dioxide over a copper(II) salt. Cyanogen is an important intermediate in the preparation of various fertilizers and is also used as a stabilizer in making nitrocellulose. It is an example of a *pseudohalogen.

cyano group The group –CN in a chemical compound. *See* nitrile.

cyanohydrins Organic compounds formed by the addition of hydrogen cyanide to aldehydes or ketones (in the presence of a base). The first step is attack by a CN^- ion on the carbonyl carbon atom. The final product is a compound in which a –CN and –OH group are attached to the same carbon atom. For example, ethanal reacts as follows

$$CH_3CHO + HCN \rightarrow$$

$CH_3CH(OH)(CN)$

The product is 2-hydroxypropanonitrile. Cyanohydrins of this type can be oxidized to α-hydroxy carboxylic acids.

cyanuric acid A white crystalline water-soluble trimer of cyanic acid, $(HNCO)_3$. It is a cyclic compound having a six-membered ring made of alternating imide (NH) and carbonyl (CO) groups.

cyclamates Salts of the acid, $C_6H_{11}.NH.SO_3H$, where C_6H_{11}–is a cyclohexyl group. Sodium and calcium cyclamates were formerly used as sweetening agents in soft drinks, etc, until their use was banned when they were suspected of causing cancer.

cyclic Describing a compound that has a ring of atoms in its molecules. In *homocyclic* compounds all the atoms in the ring are the same type, e.g. benzene (C_6H_6) and cyclohexane (C_6H_{12}). These two examples are also examples of *carbocyclic* compounds; i.e. the rings are of carbon atoms. If different atoms occur in the ring, as in pyridine (C_5H_5N), the compound is said to be *heterocyclic*.

cyclic AMP A derivative of *ATP that is widespread in animal cells as an intermediate messenger in many biochemical reactions induced by hormones. Upon reaching their target cells, the hormones activate the enzyme that catalyses cyclic AMP production. Cyclic AMP ultimately activates the enzymes of the reaction induced by the hormone concerned. Cyclic AMP is also involved in controlling gene expression and cell division, in immune responses, and in nervous transmission.

cyclization The formation of a cyclic compound from an open-chain compound. *See* ring.

cyclo- Prefix designating a cyclic compound, e.g. a cycloalkane or a cyclosilicate.

cycloalkanes Cyclic saturated hydrocarbons containing a ring of carbon atoms joined by single bonds. They have the general formula C_nH_{2n}, for example cyclohexane, C_6H_{12}, etc. In general they behave like the *alkanes but are rather less reactive.

cyclohexadiene-1,4-dione (benzoquinone; quinone) A yellow solid, $C_6H_4O_2$; r.d. 1.3; m.p. 116°C. It has a six-membered ring of carbon atoms with two opposite carbon atoms linked to oxygen atoms (C=O) and the other two pairs of carbon atoms linked by double bonds (HC=CH). The compound is used in making dyes. *See also* quinhydrone electrode.

cyclohexane A colourless liquid *cycloalkane, C_6H_{12}; r.d. 0.78; m.p. 6.5°C; b.p. 81°C. It occurs in petroleum and is made by passing benzene and hydrogen under pressure over a heated Raney nickel catalyst at 150°C, or by the reduction of cyclohexanone. It is used as a solvent and paint remover and can be oxidized using hot concentrated nitric acid to hexanedioic acid (adipic acid). The cyclohexane ring is not planar and can adopt boat and chain *conformations; in formulae it is represented by a single hexagon.

cyclonite (RDX) A highly explosive nitro compound, $(CH_2N.NO_2)_3$. It has a cyclic structure with a six-membered ring of alternating CH_2 groups and nitrogen atoms, with each nitrogen being attached to a NO_2 group. It is made by nitrating hexamine, $C_6H_{12}N_4$, which is obtained from ammonia and methanal. Cyclonite is a very powerful explosive used mainly for military purposes.

cyclopentadiene A colourless liquid cyclic *alkene, C_5H_6; r.d. 0.8047; b.p. 42.5°C. It is prepared as a by-product during the fractional distillation of crude benzene from coal tar. It undergoes condensation reactions with ketones to give highly coloured compounds (fulvenes) and readily undergoes polymerization at room temperature to give the dimer, dicyclopentadiene. The compound itself is not *aromatic because it does not have the required number of pi electrons. However, removal of a hydrogen atom produces the stable *cyclopentadienyl ion*, $C_5H_5^-$, which does have aromatic properties. In particular, the ring can coordinate to positive ions in such compounds as *ferrocene.

cyclopentadienyl ion *See* cyclopentadiene.

cysteine *See* amino acid.

cystine A molecule resulting from the oxidation reaction between the sulphydryl (–SH) groups of two cysteine molecules (*see* amino acid). This often occurs between adjacent cysteine residues in polypeptides. The resultant *disulphide bonds* (–S–S–) are important in stabilizing the structure of protein molecules.

cytidine A nucleoside comprising one cytosine molecule linked to a D-ribose sugar molecule. The derived nucleotides, cytidine mono-, di-, and triphosphate (CMP, CDP, and CTP respectively) participate in various biochemical reactions, notably in phospholipid synthesis.

cytochrome Any of a group of proteins, each with an iron-containing *haem group, that form part of the electron transport chain in mitochondria and chloroplasts. Electrons are transferred by reversible changes in the iron atom between the reduced Fe(II) and oxidized Fe(III) states.

cytosine A *pyrimidine derivative. It is one of the principal component bases of *nucleotides and the nucleic acids *DNA and *RNA.

D

dalton *See* atomic mass unit.

Dalton's atomic theory A theory of *chemical combination, first stated by the British chemist John Dalton (1766–1844) in 1803. It involves the following postulates:
(1) Elements consist of indivisible small particles (atoms).
(2) All atoms of the same element are identical; different elements have different types of atom.
(3) Atoms can neither be created nor destroyed.
(4) 'Compound elements' (i.e. compounds) are formed when atoms of different elements join in simple ratios to form 'compound atoms' (i.e. molecules).

Dalton also proposed symbols for atoms of different elements (later replaced by the present notation using letters).

Dalton's law The total pressure of a mixture of gases or vapours is equal to the sum of the partial pressures of its components, i.e. the sum of the pressures that each component would exert if it were present alone and occupied the same volume as the mixture of gases. Strictly speaking, the principle is true only for ideal gases.

Daniell cell A type of primary *voltaic cell with a copper positive electrode and a negative electrode of a zinc amalgam. The zinc-amalgam electrode is placed in an electrolyte of dilute sulphuric acid or zinc sulphate solution in a porous pot, which stands in a solution of copper sulphate in which the copper electrode is immersed. While the reaction takes place ions move through the porous pot, but when it is not in use the cell should be dismantled to prevent the diffusion of one electrolyte into the other. The e.m.f. of the cell is 1.08 volts with sulphuric acid and 1.10 volts with zinc sulphate. It was invented in 1836 by the British chemist John Daniell (1790–1845).

dating techniques Methods of estimating the age of rocks, palaeontological specimens, archaeological sites, etc. *Relative dating techniques* date specimens in relation to one another; for example, *stratigraphy is used to establish the succession of fossils. *Absolute* (or *chronometric*) *techniques* give an absolute estimate of the age and fall into two main groups. The first depends on the existence of something that develops at a seasonally varying rate, as in *dendrochronology and *varve dating. The other uses some measurable change that occurs at a known rate, as in *chemical dating, *radioactive* (or *radiometric*) *dating* (*see* carbon dating; fission-track dating; potassium–argon dating; rubidium–strontium dating; uranium–lead dating), and thermoluminescence.

dative bond *See* chemical bond.

daughter 1. A nuclide produced by radioactive *decay of some other nuclide (the *parent*). **2.** An ion or free radical produced by dissociation or reaction of some other (*parent*) ion or radical.

Davy lamp An oil-burning miner's safety lamp invented by Sir Humphry Davy (1778–1829) in 1816 when investigating firedamp (methane) explosions in coal mines. The lamp has a metal gauze surrounding the flame, which cools the hot gases by conduction and prevents ignition of gas outside the gauze. If firedamp is present it burns within the gauze cage, and lamps of this type are still used for testing for gas.

***d*-block elements** The block of elements in the *periodic table consisting of scandium, yttrium, and lanthanum together with the three periods of transition elements: titanium to zinc, zirconium to cadmium, and hafnium to mercury. These elements all have two outer *s*-electrons and have *d*-electrons in their penultimate shell; i.e. an outer electron configuration of the form $(n-1)d^xns^2$, where x is 1 to 10. *See also* transition elements.

DDT Dichlorodiphenyltrichloroethane; a colourless organic crystalline compound, $(ClC_6H_4)_2CH(CCl_3)$, made by the reaction of trichloromethanal with chlorobenzene. DDT is the best known of a number of chlorine-containing pesticides used extensively in agriculture in the 1940s and 50s. The compound is stable, accumulates in the soil, and concentrates in fatty tissue, reaching dangerous levels in carnivores high in the food chain. Restrictions are now placed on the use of DDT and similar pesticides.

Deacon process A former process for making chlorine by oxidizing hydrogen chloride in air at 450°C using a copper chloride catalyst. It was patented in 1870 by Henry Deacon (1822–76).

deamination The removal of an amino group ($-NH_2$) from a compound. Enzymatic deamination occurs in the liver and is important in amino-acid metabolism, especially in their degradation and subsequent oxidation. The amino group is removed as ammonia and excreted, either unchanged or as urea or uric acid.

de Broglie wavelength The wavelength of the wave associated with a moving particle. The wavelength (λ) is given by $\lambda = h/mv$, where h is the Planck constant, m is the mass of the particle, and v its velocity. The *de Broglie wave* was first suggested by the French physicist Louis de Broglie (1892–) in 1924 on the grounds that electromagnetic waves can be treated as particles (photons) and one could therefore expect particles to behave in some circumstances like waves. The subsequent observation of electron diffraction substantiated this argument and the de Broglie wave became the basis of *wave mechanics.

debye A unit of electric dipole moment in the electrostatic system, used to express dipole moments of molecules. It is the dipole moment produced by two charges of opposite sign, each of 1 statcoulomb and placed 10^{-18} cm apart, and has the value 3.335 64 $\times 10^{-30}$ coulomb metre.

deca- Symbol da. A prefix used in the metric system to denote ten times. For example, 10 coulombs = 1 decacoulomb (daC).

decahydrate A crystalline hydrate containing ten molecules of water per molecule of compound.

decanoic acid (capric acid) A white crystalline straight-chain saturated *carboxylic acid, $CH_3(CH_2)_8COOH$; m.p. 315°C. Its esters are used in perfumes and flavourings.

decay The spontaneous transformation of one radioactive nuclide into a daughter nuclide, which may be radioactive or may not, with the emission of one or more particles or photons. The decay of N_0 nuclides to give N nuclides after time t is given by $N = N_0 \exp(-\gamma t)$, where γ is called the *decay constant* or the *disintegration constant*. The reciprocal of the decay constant is the *mean life*. The time required for half the original nuclides to decay (i.e. $N = \frac{1}{2}N_0$) is called the *half-life* of the nuclide. The same terms are applied to elementary particles that spontaneously transform into other particles. For example, a free neutron decays into a proton and an electron.

deci- Symbol d. A prefix used in the metric system to denote one tenth. For example, 0.1 coulomb = 1 decicoulomb (dC).

decomposition Chemical reaction in which a compound breaks down into simpler compounds or into elements.

decrepitation A crackling noise produced when certain crystals are heated, caused by changes in structure resulting from loss of water of crystallization.

defect A discontinuity in a crystal lattice. A *point defect* consists either of a missing atom or ion creating a *vacancy* in the lattice (a vacancy is sometimes called a *Schottky defect*) or an extra atom or ion between two normal lattice points creating an *interstitial*. A *Frenkel defect* consists of a vacancy in which the missing atom or ion has moved to an interstitial position. If more than one adjacent point defect occurs in a crystal there may be a slip along a surface causing a *line defect* (or *dislocation*). Defects are caused by strain or, in some cases, by irradiation. All crystalline solids contain an equilibrium number of point defects above absolute zero; this number increases with temperature. The existence of defects in crystals is important in the conducting properties of semiconductors.

definite proportions *See* chemical combination.

degradation A type of organic chemical reaction in which a compound is converted into a simpler compound in stages.

degree A division on a *temperature scale.

degrees of freedom 1. The number of independent parameters required to specify the configuration of a system. This concept is applied in the *kinetic theory to specify the number of independent ways in which an atom or molecule can take up energy. There are however various sets of parameters that may be chosen, and the details of the consequent theory vary with the choice. For example, in a monatomic gas each atom may be allotted three degrees of freedom, corresponding to the three coordinates in space required to specify its position. The mean energy per atom for each degree of freedom is the same, according to the principle of the *equipartition of energy, and is equal to $kT/2$ for each degree of freedom (where k is the *Boltzmann constant and T is the thermodynamic temperature). Thus for a monatomic gas the total molar energy is $3LkT/2$, where L is the Avogadro constant (the number of atoms per mole). As $k = R/L$, where R is the molar gas constant, the total molar energy is $3RT/2$.

In a diatomic gas the two atoms require six coordinates between them, giving six degrees of freedom. Commonly these are interpreted as six independent ways of storing energy: on this basis the molecule has three degrees of freedom for different directions of translational motion, and in addition there are two degrees of freedom for rotation of the molecular axis and one vibrational degree of freedom along the bond between the atoms. The rotational degrees of freedom each contribute their share, $kT/2$, to the total energy; similarly the vibrational degree of freedom has an equal share of kinetic energy and must on average have as much potential energy. The total energy per molecule for a diatomic gas is therefore $3kT/2$ (for translational energy of the whole molecule) plus $2kT/2$ (for rotational energy of each atom) plus $2kT/2$ (for vibrational energy), i.e. a total of $7kT/2$.

2. The least number of independent variables required to define the state of a system in the *phase rule. In this sense a gas has two degrees of freedom (e.g. temperature and pressure).

dehydration **1.** Removal of water from a substance. **2.** A chemical reaction in which a compound loses hydrogen and oxygen in the ratio 2:1. For instance, ethanol passed over hot pumice undergoes dehydration to ethene:

$$C_2H_5OH - H_2O \rightarrow CH_2{:}CH_2$$

Substances such as concentrated sulphuric acid, which can remove H_2O in this way, are known as *dehydrating agents*. For example, with sulphuric acid, methanoic acid gives carbon monoxide:

$$HCOOH - H_2O \rightarrow CO$$

dehydrogenase Any enzyme that catalyses the removal of hydrogen atoms in biological reactions. Dehydrogenases occur in many biochemical pathways but are particularly important in driving the electron-transport-chain reactions of cell respiration. They work in conjunction with the hydrogen-accepting coenzymes NAD and FAD.

deliquescence The absorption of water from the atmosphere by a hygroscopic solid to such an extent that a concentrated solution of the solid eventually forms.

delocalization In certain chemical compounds the valence electrons cannot be regarded as restricted to definite bonds between the atoms but are 'spread' over several atoms in the molecule. Such electrons are said to be *delocalized*. Delocalization occurs particularly when the compound contains alternating (conjugated) double or triple bonds, the delocalized electrons being those in the pi *orbitals. The molecule is then more stable than it would be if the electrons were localized, an effect accounting for the properties of benzene and other aromatic compounds. Another example is in the ions of carboxylic acids, containing the carboxylate group $-COO^-$. In terms of a simple model of chemical bonding, this group would have the carbon joined to one oxygen by a double bond (i.e. $C=O$) and the other joined to O^- by a single bond ($C-O^-$). In fact, the two $C-O$ bonds are identical because the extra electron on the O^- and the electrons in the pi bond of $C=O$ are delocalized over the three atoms.

delta-iron *See* iron.

denature **1.** To add a poisonous or unpleasant substance to ethanol to make it unsuitable for human consumption (*see* methylated spirits). **2.** To produce a structural change in a protein or nucleic acid that results in the reduction or loss of its biological properties. Denaturation is caused by heat, chemicals, and extremes of pH. The differences between raw and boiled eggs are largely a result of denaturation. 3. To add another isotope to a fissile material to make it unsuitable for use in a nuclear weapon.

dendrite A crystal that has branched in growth into two parts. Crystals that grow in this way (*dendritic growth*) have a branching treelike appearance.

dendrochronology An absolute *dating technique using the growth rings of trees. It depends on the fact that trees in the same locality show a characteristic pattern of growth rings resulting from climatic conditions. Thus it is possible to assign a definite date for each growth ring in living trees, and to use the ring patterns to date fossil trees or specimens of wood (e.g. used for buildings or objects on archaeological sites) with lifespans that overlap those of living trees. The bristlecone pine (*Pinus aristata*), which lives for up to 5000 years, has been used to date specimens over 8000 years old. Fossil specimens accurately dated by dendrochronology have been used to make corrections to the *carbon-dating technique. Dendrochronology is also helpful in studying past climatic conditions. Analysis of trace elements in sections of rings can also provide information on past atmospheric pollution.

denitrification A chemical process in which nitrates in the soil are reduced to molecular nitrogen, which is released into the atmosphere. This process is effected by the bacterium *Pseudomonas denitrificans*, which uses nitrates as a source of energy for other chemical reactions in a manner similar to respiration in other organisms. *Compare* nitrification. *See* nitrogen cycle.

density The mass of a substance per unit of volume. In *SI units it is measured in kg m^{-3}. *See also* relative density; vapour density.

deoxyribonucleic acid *See* DNA.

depolarization The prevention of *polarization in a *primary cell. For example, maganese(IV) oxide (the *depolarizer*) is placed around the positive electrode of a *Leclanché cell to oxidize the hydrogen released at this electrode.

depression of freezing point The reduction in the freezing point of a pure liquid when another substance is dissolved in it. It is a *colligative property – i.e. the lowering of the freezing point is proportional to the number of dissolved particles (molecules or ions), and does not depend on their nature. It is given by $\Delta t = K_f C_m$, where C_m is the molar concentration of dissolved solute and K_f is a constant (the *cryoscopic constant*) for the solvent used. Measurements of freezing-point depression (using a Beckmann thermometer) can be used for finding relative molecular masses of unknown substances.

derivative A compound that is derived from some other compound and usually maintains its general structure, e.g. trichloromethane (chloroform) is a derivative of methane.

derived unit *See* base unit.

desalination The removal of salt from sea water for irrigation of the land or to provide drinking water. The process is normally only economic if a cheap source of energy, such as the waste heat from a nuclear power station, can be used. Desalination using solar energy has the greatest economic potential since shortage of fresh water is most acute in hot regions. The methods employed include evaporation, often under reduced pressure (flash evaporation); freezing (pure ice forms from freezing brine); *reverse osmosis; *electrodialysis; and *ion exchange.

desiccator A container for drying substances or for keeping them free from moisture. Simple laboratory desiccators are glass vessels containing a drying agent, such as silica gel. They can be evacuated through a tap in the lid.

desorption The removal of adsorbed atoms, molecules, or ions from a surface.

destructive distillation The process of heating complex organic substances in the absence of air so that they break down into a mixture of volatile products, which are condensed and collected. At one time the destructive distillation of coal (to give coke, coal tar, and coal gas) was the principal source of industrial organic chemicals.

detergent A substance added to water to improve its cleaning properties. Although water is a powerful solvent for many compounds, it will not dissolve grease and natural oils. Detergents are compounds that cause such nonpolar substances to go into solution in water. *Soap is the original example, owing its action to the presence of ions formed from long-chain fatty acids (e.g. the octadecanoate (stearate) ion, $CH_3(CH_2)_{16}COO^-$). These have two parts: a nonpolar part (the hydrocarbon chain), which attaches to the grease; and a polar part (the $-COO^-$ group), which is attracted to the water. A disadvantage of soap is that it forms a scum with hard water (*see* hardness of water) and is relatively expensive to make. Various synthetic ('soapless') detergents have been developed from petrochemicals. The commonest, used in washing powders, is sodium dodecylbenzenesulphonate, which contains $CH_3(CH_2)_{11}C_6H_4SO_2O^-$ ions. This, like soap, is an example of an *anionic detergent*, i.e. one in which the active part is a negative ion. *Cationic detergents* have a long hydrocarbon chain connected to a positive ion. Usually they are amine salts, as in $CH_3(CH_2)_{15}N(CH_3)_3{}^+Br^-$, in which the polar part is the $-N(CH_3)_3{}^+$ group. *Nonionic detergents* have nonionic polar groups of the type $-C_2H_4-O-C_2H_4-OH$, which form hydrogen bonds with the water. Synthetic detergents are also used as wetting agents emulsifiers, and stabilizers for foam.

deuterated compound A compound in which some or all of the hydrogen-1 atoms have been replaced by deuterium atoms.

deuterium (heavy hydrogen) Symbol D. The isotope of hydrogen that has a mass number 2 (r.a.m. 2.0144). Its nucleus contains one proton and one neutron. The abundance of deuterium in natural hydrogen is about 0.015%. It is present in water as the oxide, deuterium oxide (*see* heavy water), from which it is usually obtained by electrolysis or fractional distillation. Its chemical behaviour is almost identical to hydrogen although deuterium compounds tend to react rather more slowly than the corresponding hydrogen compounds. Its physical properties are slightly different from those of hydrogen, e.g. b.p. 23.6 K (hydrogen 20.4 K).

deuterium oxide *See* heavy water.

devitrification Loss of the amorphous nature of glass as a result of crystallization.

Dewar flask A vessel for storing hot or cold liquids so that they maintain their temperature independently of the surroundings. Heat transfer to the surroundings is reduced to a minimum: the walls of the vessel consist of two thin layers of glass (or, in large vessels, steel) separated by a vacuum to reduce conduction and convection; the inner surface of a glass vessel is silvered to reduce radiation; and the vessel is stoppered to prevent evaporation. It was devised around 1872 by the British physicist Sir James Dewar (1842–1923) and is also known by its first trade name *Thermos flask*. *See also* cryostat.

Dewar structure A proposed structure of *benzene, having a hexagonal ring of six carbon atoms with two opposite atoms joined by a long single bond across the ring and with two double C–C bonds, one on each side of the hexagon. Dewar structures contribute to the resonance hybrid of benzene.

dextrorotatory Denoting a chemical compound that rotates the plane of polarization of plane-polarized light to the right (clockwise as observed by someone facing the oncoming radiation). *See* optical activity.

dextrose *See* glucose.

***d*-form** *See* optical activity.

diagonal relationship A relationship within the periodic table by which certain elements in the second period have a close chemical similarity to their diagonal neighbours in the next group of the third period. This is particularly noticeable with the following pairs.

Lithium and magnesium:

(1) both form chlorides and bromides that hydrolyse slowly and are soluble in ethanol;

(2) both form colourless or slightly coloured crystalline nitrides by direct reaction with nitrogen at high temperatures;

(3) both burn in air to give the normal oxide only;

(4) both form carbonates that decompose on heating.

Beryllium and aluminium:

(1) both form highly refractory oxides with polymorphs;

(2) both form crystalline nitrides that are hydrolysed in water;

(3) addition of hydroxide ion to solutions of the salts gives an amphoteric hydroxide, which is soluble in excess hydroxide giving beryllate or aluminate ions $[Be(OH)_4]^{2-}$ and $[Al(OH)_4]^-$;

(4) both form covalent halides and covalent alkyl compounds that display bridging structures;

(5) both metals dissolve in alkalis.

Boron and silicon:

(1) both display semiconductor properties;

(2) both form hydrides that are unstable in air and chlorides that hydrolyse in moist air;

(3) both form acidic oxides with covalent crystal structures, which are readily incorporated along with other oxides into a wide range of glassy materials.

The reason for this relationship is a combination of the trends to increase size down a group and to decrease size along a period, and a similar, but reversed, effect in electronegativity, i.e. decrease down a group and increase along a period.

dialysis A method by which large molecules (such as starch or protein) and small molecules (such as glucose or amino acids) in solution may be separated by selective diffusion through a semipermeable membrane. For example, if a mixed solution of starch and glucose is placed in a closed container made of a semipermeable substance (such as Cellophane), which is then immersed in a beaker of water, the smaller glucose molecules will pass through the membrane into the water while the starch molecules remain behind. The cell membranes of living organisms are semipermeable, and dialysis takes place naturally in the kidneys for the excretion of nitrogenous waste. An artificial kidney (*dialyser*) utilizes the principle of dialysis by taking over the functions of diseased kidneys.

1,6-diaminohexane (hexamethylenediamine) A solid colourless amine, $H_2N(CH_2)_6NH_2$; m.p. 41°C; b.p. 204°C. It is made by oxidizing cyclohexane to hexanedioic acid, reacting this with ammonia to give the ammonium salt, and dehydrating the salt to give hexanedionitrile ($NC(CH_2)_6CN$). This is reduced with hydrogen to the diamine. The compound is used, with hexanedioic acid, in the production of *nylon 6,6.

diamond The hardest known mineral (with a hardness of 10 on Mohs' scale). It is an allotropic form of pure *carbon that has crystallized in the cubic system, usually as octahedra or cubes, under great pressure. Diamond crystals may be colourless and transparent or yellow, brown, or black. They are highly prized as gemstones but also have extensive uses in industry, mainly for cutting and grinding tools. Diamonds occur in ancient volcanic pipes of kimberlite; the most important deposits are in South Africa but others are found in Tanzania, the USA, USSR, and Australia. Diamonds also occur in river deposits that have been derived from weathered kimberlite, notably in Brazil, Zaîre, Sierra Leone, and India. Industrial diamonds are increasingly being produced synthetically.

diaspore A mineral form of a mixed aluminium oxide and hydroxide, AlO.OH. *See* aluminium hydroxide.

diastase *See* amylase.

diastereoisomers Stereoisomers that are not identical and yet not mirror images. For instance, the *d*-form of tartaric acid and the meso form constitute a pair of diastereoisomers. *See* optical activity.

diatomic molecule A molecule formed from two atoms (e.g. H_2 or HCl).

diazine *See* azine.

diazo compounds Organic compounds containing two linked nitrogen compounds. The term includes *azo compounds, diazonium compounds, and also such compounds as diazomethane, CH_2N_2.

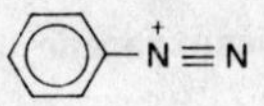

Structure of diazonium ion $C_6H_5N_2^+$

diazonium salts Unstable salts containing the ion $C_6H_5N_2^+$ (the *diazonium ion*). They are formed by *diazotization reactions.

diazotization The formation of a *diazonium salt by reaction of an aromatic amine with nitrous acid at low temperature (below 5°C). The nitrous acid is produced in the reaction mixture from sodium nitrite and hydrochloric acid:

$$ArNH_2 + NaNO_2 + HCl \rightarrow$$
$$ArN^+N + Cl^- + Na^+ + OH^- + H_2O$$

dibasic acid An *acid that has two acidic hydrogen atoms in its molecules. Sulphuric (H_2SO_4) and carbonic (H_2CO_3) acids are common examples.

1,2-dibromoethane A colourless liquid *haloalkane, $BrCH_2CH_2Br$; r.d. 2.2; m.p. 9°C; b.p. 121°C. It is made by addition of bromine to ethene and used as an additive in petrol to remove lead as the volatile lead bromide.

dicarbide *See* carbide.

dicarboxylic acid A *carboxylic acid having two carboxyl groups in its molecules. In systematic chemical nomenclature, dicarboxylic acids are denoted by the suffix *-dioic*; e.g. hexanedioic acid, $HOOC(CH_2)_4COOH$.

dichlorine oxide (chlorine monoxide) A strongly oxidizing orange gas, Cl_2O, made by oxidation of chlorine using mercury(II) oxide. It is the acid anhydride of chloric(I) acid.

dichloroethanoic acid *See* chloroethanoic acids.

2,4-dichlorophenoxyacetic acid *See* 2,4-D.

dichroism The property of some crystals, such as tourmaline, of selectively absorbing light vibrations in one plane while allowing light vibrations at right angles to this plane to pass through. Polaroid is a synthetic dichroic material. *See* polarization.

dichromate(VI) A salt containing the ion $Cr_2O_7^{-}$. Solutions containing dichromate (VI) ions are strongly oxidizing.

Diels–Alder reaction A type of chemical reaction in which a compound containing two double bonds separated by a single bond (i.e. a conjugated *diene) adds to a suitable compound containing one double bond (known as the *dienophile*) to give a ring compound. In the dienophile, the double bond must have a carbonyl group on each side. It is named after the German chemists Otto Diels (1876–1954) and Kurt Alder (1902–58), who discovered it in 1928.

diene An *alkene that has two double bonds in its molecule. If the two bonds are separated by one single bond, as in buta-1,3-diene CH_2:CHCH:CH_2, the compound is a *conjugated diene*.

dienophile *See* Diels–Alder reaction.

diethyl ether *See* ethoxyethane.

diffusion 1. The process by which different substances mix as a result of the random motions of their component atoms, molecules, and ions. In gases, all the components are perfectly miscible with each other and mixing ultimately becomes nearly uniform, though slightly affected by gravity (*see also* Graham's law). The diffusion of a solute through a solvent to produce a solution of uniform concentration is slower, but otherwise very similar to the process of gaseous diffusion. In solids, however, diffusion occurs very slowly at normal temperatures. **2.** The passage of elementary particles through matter when there is a high probability of scattering and a low probability of capture.

diffusion pump (condensation pump) A *vacuum pump in which oil or mercury vapour is diffused through a jet, which entrains the gas molecules from the container in which the pressure is to be reduced. The diffused vapour and entrained gas molecules are condensed on the cooled walls of the pump. Pressures down to 10^{-7} Pa can be reached by sophisticated forms of the diffusion pump.

dihedral (dihedron) An angle formed by the intersection of two planes (e.g. two faces of a polyhedron). The *dihedral angle* is the angle formed by taking a point on the line of intersection and drawing two lines from this point, one in each plane, perpendicular to the line of intersection.

dihydrate A crystalline hydrate containing two molecules of water per molecule of compound.

dihydric alcohol *See* diol.

1,2-dihydroxybenzene (catechol) A colourless crystalline phenol, $C_6H_4(OH)_2$; r.d. 1.4; m.p. 105°C; b.p. 240°C. It is used as a photographic developer.

2,3-dihydroxybutanedioic acid *See* tartaric acid.

dilead(II) lead(IV) oxide A red amorphous powder, Pb_3O_4; r.d. 9.1; decomposes at 500°C to lead(II) oxide. It is prepared by heating lead(II) oxide to 400°C and has the unusual property of being black when hot and red-orange when cold. The compound is nonstoichiometric, generally containing less oxygen than implied by the formula. It is largely covalent and has Pb(IV)O_6 octahedral groups linked together by Pb(II) atoms, each joined to three oxygen atoms. It is used in glass making but its use in the paint industry has largely been discontinued because of the toxicity of lead. Dilead(II) lead(IV) oxide is commonly called *red lead* or, more accurately, *red lead oxide*.

dilute Describing a solution that has a relatively low concentration of solute.

dilution The volume of solvent in which a given amount of solute is dissolved.

dilution law *See* Ostwald's dilution law.

dimer An association of two identical molecules linked together. The molecules may react to form a larger molecule, as in the formation of dinitrogen tetroxide (N_2O_4) from nitrogen dioxide (NO_2), or the formation of an *aluminium chloride dimer (Al_2Cl_6) in the vapour. Alternatively, they may be held by hydrogen bonds. For example, carboxylic acids form dimers in organic solvents, in which hydrogen bonds exist between the O of the C=O group and the H of the –O–H group.

dimethylbenzenes (xylenes) Three compounds with the formula $(CH_3)_2C_6H_4$, each having two methyl groups substituted on the benzene ring. 1,2-dimethylbenzene is *o*-xylene, etc. A mixture of the isomers (b.p. 135–145°C) is obtained from petroleum.

dimorphism *See* polymorphism.

dinitrogen oxide (nitrous oxide) A colourless gas, N_2O, d. 1.97 g dm^{-3}; m.p. –90.8°C; b.p. –88.5°C. It is soluble in water, ethanol, and sulphuric acid. It may be prepared by the controlled heating of ammonium nitrate (chloride free) to 250°C and passing the gas produced through solutions of iron(II) sulphate to remove impurities of nitrogen monoxide. It is relatively unreactive, being inert to halogens, alkali metals, and ozone at normal temperatures. It is decomposed on heating above 520°C to nitrogen and oxygen and will support the combustion of many compounds. Dinitrogen oxide is used as an anaesthetic gas ('laughing gas') and as an aerosol propellant.

dinitrogen tetroxide A colourless to pale yellow liquid or a brown gas, N_2O_4; r.d. 1.45 (liquid); m.p. –11.2°C; b.p. 21.2°C. It dissolves in water with reaction to give a mixture of nitric acid and nitrous acid. It may be readily prepared in the laboratory by the reaction of copper with concentrated nitric acid; mixed nitrogen oxides containing dinitrogen oxide may also be produced by heating metal nitrates. The solid compound is wholly N_2O_4 and the liquid is about 99% N_2O_4 at the boiling point; N_2O_4 is diamagnetic. In the gas phase it dissociates to give *nitrogen dioxide*

$$N_2O_4 \rightleftharpoons 2NO_2$$

Because of the unpaired electron this is paramagnetic and brown. Liquid N_2O_4 has been widely studied as a nonaqueous solvent system (self-ionizes to NO^+ and NO_3^-). Dinitrogen tetroxide, along with other nitrogen oxides, is a product of combustion engines and is thought to be involved in the depletion of stratospheric ozone.

diol (dihydric alcohol) An *alcohol containing two hydroxyl groups per molecule.

dioxan A colourless toxic liquid, $C_4H_8O_2$; r.d. 1.03; m.p. 11°C; b.p. 101.5°C. The molecule has a six-membered ring containing four CH_2 groups and two oxygen atoms at opposite corners. It can be made from ethane-1,2-diol and is used as a solvent.

dioxonitric(III) acid *See* nitrous acid.

dioxygenyl compounds Compounds containing the positive ion O_2^+, as in dioxygenyl hexafluoroplatinate O_2PtF_6 – an orange solid that sublimes in vacuum at 100°C. Other ionic compounds of the type

$O_2^+[MF_6]^-$ can be prepared, where M is P, As, or Sb.

diphosphane (diphosphine) A yellow liquid, P_2H_4, which is spontaneously flammable in air. It is obtained by hydrolysis of calcium phosphide. Many of the references to the spontaneous flammability of phosphine (PH_3) are in fact due to traces of P_2H_4 as impurities.

diphosphine *See* diphosphane.

direct dye *See* dye.

disaccharide A sugar consisting of two linked *monosaccharide molecules. For example, sucrose comprises one glucose molecule and one fructose molecule bonded together.

disilane *See* silane.

dislocation *See* defect.

disodium hydrogenphosphate(V) (disodium orthophosphate) A colourless crystalline solid, Na_2HPO_4, soluble in water and insoluble in ethanol. It is known as the dihydrate (r.d. 2.066), heptahydrate (r.d. 1.68), and dodecahydrate (r.d. 1.52). It may be prepared by titrating phosphoric acid with sodium hydroxide to an alkaline end point (phenolphthalein) and is used in treating boiler feed water and in the textile industry.

disodium orthophosphate *See* disodium hydrogenphosphate(V).

disodium tetraborate-10-water *See* borax.

disperse dye *See* dye.

disperse phase *See* colloids.

displacement reaction *See* substitution reaction.

disproportionation A type of chemical reaction in which the same compound is simultaneously reduced and oxidized. For example, copper(I) chloride disproportionates thus:

$$2CuCl \rightarrow Cu + CuCl_2$$

The reaction involves oxidation of one molecule

$$Cu^{I} \rightarrow Cu^{II} + e$$

and reduction of the other

$$Cu^{I} + e \rightarrow Cu$$

The reaction of halogens with hydroxide ions is another example of a disproportionation reaction, for example

$$Cl_2(g) + 2OH^-(aq) \rightleftharpoons Cl^-(aq) + ClO^-(aq) + H_2O(l)$$

dissociation The breakdown of a molecule, ion, etc., into smaller molecules, ions, etc. An example of dissociation is the reversible reaction of hydrogen iodide at high temperatures

$$2HI(g) \rightleftharpoons H_2(g) + I_2(g)$$

The *equilibrium constant of a reversible dissociation is called the *dissociation constant*. The term 'dissociation' is also applied to ionization reactions of *acids and *bases in water; for example

$$HCN + H_2O \rightleftharpoons H_3O^+ + CN^-$$

which is often regarded as a straightforward dissociation into ions

$$HCN \rightleftharpoons H^+ + CN^-$$

The equilibrium constant of such a dissociation is called the *acid dissociation constant* or *acidity constant*, given by

$$K_a = [H^+][A^-]/[HA]$$

for an acid HA (the concentration of water $[H_2O]$ can be taken as constant). K_a is a measure of the strength of the acid. Similarly, for a nitrogenous base B, the equilibrium

$$B + H_2O \rightleftharpoons BH^+ + OH^-$$

is also a dissociation; with the *base dissociation constant*, or *basicity constant*, given by

$$K_b = [BH^+][OH^-]/[B]$$

For a hydroxide MOH,

$$K_b = [M^+][OH^-]/[MOH]$$

dissociation pressure When a solid compound dissociates to give one or more gaseous products, the dissociation pressure is the pressure of gas in equilibrium with the solid at a given temperature. For example, when calcium carbonate is maintained at a constant high temperature in a closed container, the dissociation pressure at that temperature is the pressure of carbon dioxide from the equilibrium

$$CaCO_3(s) \rightleftharpoons CaO(s) + CO_2(g)$$

distillation The process of boiling a liquid and condensing and collecting the vapour. The liquid collected is the *distillate*. It is used to purify liquids and to separate liquid mixtures (*see* fractional distillation; steam distillation). *See also* destructive distillation.

distilled water Water purified by distillation so as to free it from dissolved salts and other compounds. Distilled water in equilibrium with the carbon dioxide in the air has a conductivity of about 0.8×10^{-6} siemens cm^{-1}. Repeated distillation in a vacuum can bring the conductivity down to 0.043×10^{-6} siemens cm^{-1} at 18°C (sometimes called *conductivity water*). The remaining conductivity is due to self ionization: $H_2O \rightleftharpoons H^+ + OH^-$.

disulphur dichloride (sulphur monochloride) An orange–red liquid, S_2Cl_2, which is readily hydrolysed by water and is soluble in benzene and ether; r.d. 1.678; m.p. −80°C; b.p. 136°C. It may be prepared by passing chlorine over molten sulphur; in the presence of iodine or metal chlorides *sulphur dichloride*, SCl_2, is also formed. In the vapour phase S_2Cl_2 molecules have Cl–S–S–Cl chains. The compound is used as a solvent for sulphur and can form higher *chlorosulphanes* of the type Cl–$(S)_n$–Cl ($n < 100$), which are of great value in *vulcanization processes.

disulphuric(VI) acid (pyrosulphuric acid) A colourless hygroscopic crystalline solid, $H_2S_2O_7$; r.d. 1.9; m.p. 35°C. It is commonly encountered mixed with sulphuric acid as it is formed by dissolving sulphur trioxide in concentrated sulphuric acid. The resulting fuming liquid, called *oleum* or *Nordhausen sulphuric acid*, is produced during the *contact process and is also widely used in the *sulphonation of organic compounds. *See also* sulphuric acid.

dithionate A salt of dithionic acid, containing the ion $S_2O_6^{2-}$, usually formed by the oxidation of a sulphite using manganese(IV) oxide. The ion has neither pronounced oxidizing nor reducing properties.

dithionic acid An acid, $H_2S_2O_6$, known in the form of its salts (dithionates).

dithionite *See* sulphinate.

dithionous acid *See* sulphinic acid.

divalent (bivalent) Having a valency of two.

***dl*-form** *See* optical activity; racemic mixture.

D-lines Two close lines in the yellow region of the visible spectrum of sodium, having wavelengths 589.0 and 589.6 nm. As they are prominent and easily recognized they are used as a standard in spectroscopy.

DNA (deoxyribonucleic acid) The genetic material of most living organisms, which is a major constituent of the chromosomes within the cell nucleus and plays a central role in the determination of hereditary characteristics by controlling protein synthesis in cells. DNA is a nucleic acid composed of two chains of *nucleotides in which the sugar is *deoxyribose* and the bases are *adenine, *cytosine, *guanine, and *thymine (*compare* RNA). The two chains are wound round each other and linked together by hydrogen bonds between specific complementary bases

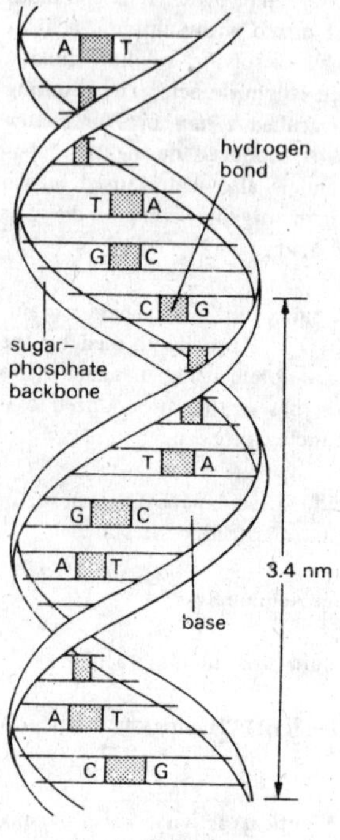

Double helical structure of DNA

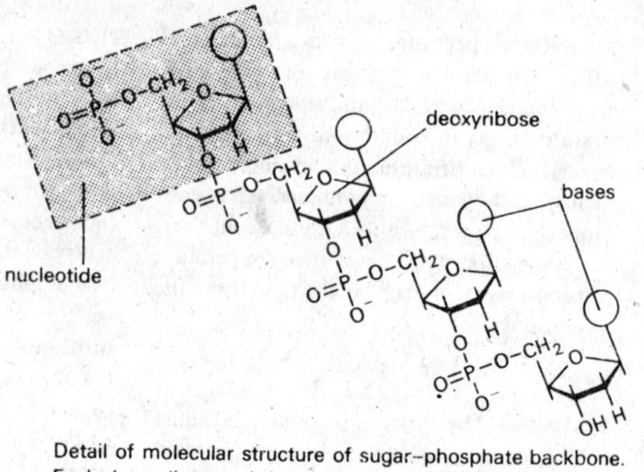

Detail of molecular structure of sugar-phosphate backbone. Each deoxyribose unit is attached to a phosphate group and a base, forming a nucleotide

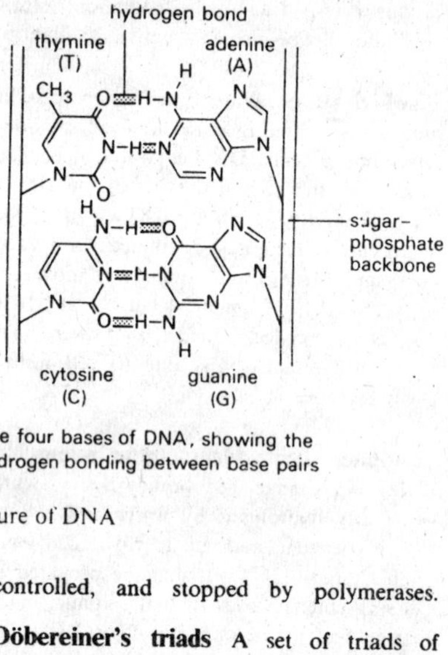

The four bases of DNA, showing the hydrogen bonding between base pairs

Molecular structure of DNA

to form a spiral ladder-shaped molecule (*double helix*).

When the cell divides, its DNA also replicates in such a way that each of the two daughter molecules is identical to the parent molecule. The hydrogen bonds between the complementary bases on the two strands of the parent molecule break and the strands unwind. Using as building bricks nucleotides present in the nucleus, each strand directs the synthesis of a new one complementary to itself. Replication is initiated, controlled, and stopped by polymerases.

Döbereiner's triads A set of triads of chemically similar elements noted by J. W. Döbereiner in 1817. Even with the inaccurate atomic mass data of the day it was observed that when each triad was arranged in order of increasing atomic mass, then the mass of the central member was approximately the average of the values for the other two. The chemical and physical properties were similarly related. The triads are now recognized as consecutive members of the groups of the periodic table. Examples are: lithium, sodium, and potassium; calcium, strontium, and barium; and chlorine, bromine, and iodine.

dodecanoic acid (lauric acid) A white crystalline *fatty acid, $CH_3(CH_2)_{10}COOH$; r.d. 0.8; m.p. 44°C; b.p. 225°C. Glycerides of the acid are present in natural fats and oils (e.g. coconut and palm-kernel oil).

dodecene A straight-chain alkene, $CH_3(CH_2)_9CH{:}CH_2$, obtained from petroleum and used in making *dodecylbenzene.

dodecylbenzene A hydrocarbon, $CH_3(CH_2)_{11}C_6H_5$, manufactured by a Friedel–Crafts reaction between dodecene ($CH_3(CH_2)_9CH{:}CH_2$) and benzene. It can be sulphonated, and the sodium salt of the sulphonic acid is the basis of common *detergents.

dolomite A carbonate mineral consisting of a mixed calcium–magnesium carbonate, $CaCO_3.MgCO_3$, crystallizing in the rhombohedral system. It is usually white or colourless. The term is also used to denote a rock with a high ratio of magnesium to calcium carbonate. *See* limestone.

donor An ion or molecule that provides a pair of electrons in forming a coordinate bond.

dopa (dihydroxyphenylalanine) A derivative of the amino acid tyrosine. It is found in particularly high levels in the adrenal glands and is a precursor in the synthesis of *dopamine, *noradrenaline, and *adrenaline. The laevorotatory form, *L-dopa*, is administered in the treatment of Parkinson's disease, in which brain levels of dopamine are reduced.

dopamine A *catecholamine that is a precursor in the synthesis of *noradrenaline and *adrenaline. It is also believed to function as a neurotransmitter in the brain.

***d*-orbital** *See* orbital.

double bond *See* chemical bond.

double decomposition (metathesis) A chemical reaction involving exchange of radicals, e.g.

$$AgNO_3(aq) + KCl(aq) \rightarrow KNO_3(aq) + AgCl(s)$$

double refraction The property, possessed by certain crystals (notably calcite), of forming two refracted rays from a single incident ray. The *ordinary ray* obeys the normal laws of refraction. The other refracted ray, called the *extraordinary ray*, follows different laws. The light in the ordinary ray is polarized at right angles to the light in the extraordinary ray. Along an optic axis the ordinary and extraordinary rays travel with the same speed. Some crystals, such as calcite, quartz, and tourmaline, have only one optic axis; they are *uniaxial crystals*. Others, such as mica and selenite, have two optic axes; they are *biaxial crystals*. The phenomenon is also known as *birefringence* and the double-refracting crystal as a *birefringent crystal*. *See also* polarization.

double salt A crystalline salt in which there are two different anions and/or cations. An example is the mineral dolomite, $CaCO_3.MgCO_3$, which contains a regular arrangement of Ca^{2+} and Mg^{2+} ions in its crystal lattice. *Alums are double sulphates. Double salts only exist in the solid; when dissolved they act as a mixture of the two separate salts. *Double oxides* are similar.

doublet A pair of associated lines in certain spectra, e.g. the two lines that make up the sodium D-lines.

Downs process A process for extracting sodium by the electrolysis of molten sodium chloride. The *Downs cell* has a central graphite anode surrounded by a cylindrical steel cathode. Chlorine released is led away through a hood over the anode. Molten sodium is formed at the cathode and collected through another hood around the top of the cathode cylinder (it is less dense than the sodium chloride). The two hoods and electrodes are separated by a coaxial cylindrical steel gauze. A small amount of calcium chloride is added to the sodium chloride to lower its melting point. The sodium chloride is melted electrically and kept molten by the current through the cell. More sodium chloride is added as the electrolysis proceeds.

dry cell A primary or secondary cell in which the electrolytes are in the form of a paste. Many torch, radio, and calculator batteries are *Leclanché cells in which the electrolyte is an ammonium chloride paste and the container is the negative zinc electrode (with an outer plastic wrapping).

dry ice Solid carbon dioxide used as a refrigerant. It is convenient because it sublimes at −78°C (195 K) at standard pressure rather than melting.

drying oil A natural oil, such as linseed oil, that hardens on exposure to the air. Drying oils contain unsaturated fatty acids, such as linoleic and linolenic acids, which polymerize on oxidation. They are used in paints, varnishes, etc.

D-series *See* absolute configuration.

Dulong and Petit's law For a solid element the product of the relative atomic mass and the specific heat capacity is a constant equal to about 25 J mol^{-1} K^{-1}. Formulated in these terms in 1819 by the French scientists Pierre Dulong (1785–1838) and A. T. Petit (1791–1820), the law in modern terms states: the molar heat capacity of a solid element is approximately equal to $3R$, where R is the *gas constant. The law is only approximate but applies with fair accuracy at normal temperatures to elements with a simple crystal structure.

Dumas' method 1. A method of finding the amount of nitrogen in an organic compound. The sample is weighed, mixed with copper(II) oxide, and heated in a tube. Any nitrogen present in the compound is converted into oxides of nitrogen, which are led over hot copper to reduce them to nitrogen gas. This is collected and the volume measured, from which the mass of nitrogen in a known mass of sample can be found. **2.** A method of finding the relative molecular masses of volatile liquids by weighing. A thin-glass bulb with a long narrow neck is used. This is weighed full of air at known temperature, then a small amount of sample is introduced and the bulb heated (in a bath) so that the liquid is vaporized and the air is driven out. The tip of the neck is sealed and the bulb cooled and weighed at known (room) temperature. The volume of the bulb is found by filling it with water and weighing again. If the density of air is known, the mass of vapour in a known volume can be calculated.

The techniques are named after the French chemist Jean Baptiste André Dumas (1800–84).

duplet A pair of electrons in a covalent chemical bond.

dyes Substances used to impart colour to textiles, leather, paper, etc. Compounds used for dyeing (*dyestuffs*) are generally organic compounds containing conjugated double bonds. The group producing the colour is the *chromophore; other noncoloured groups that influence or intensify the colour are called *auxochromes. Dyes can be classified according to the chemical structure of the dye molecule. For example, *azo dyes* contain the $-N{=}N-$ group (*see* azo compounds). In practice, they are classified according to the way in which the dye is applied or is held on the substrate.

Acid dyes are compounds in which the chromophore is part of a negative ion (usually an organic sulphonate RSO_2O^-). They can be used for protein fibres (e.g. wool and silk) and for polyamide and acrylic fibres. Originally, they were applied from an acidic bath. *Metallized dyes* are forms of acid dyes in which the negative ion contains a chelated metal atom. *Basic dyes* have chromophores that are part of a positive ion (usually an amine salt or ionized imino group). They are used for acrylic fibres and also for wool and silk, although they have only moderate fastness with these materials.

Direct dyes are dyes that have a high affinity for cotton, rayon, and other cellulose fibres. They are applied directly from a neutral bath containing sodium chloride or sodium sulphate. Like acid dyes, they are usually sulphonic acid salts but are distinguished by their greater substantivity (affinity for the substrate), hence the alternative name *substantive dyes*.

Vat dyes are insoluble substances used for cotton dyeing. They usually contain keto groups, C=O, which are reduced to C–OH groups, rendering the dye soluble (the *leuco form* of the dye). The dye is applied in this form, then oxidized by air or oxidizing agents to precipitate the pigment in the fibres. Indigo and anthroquinone dyes are examples of vat dyes. *Sulphur dyes* are dyes applied by this technique using sodium sulphide solution to reduce and dissolve the dye. Sulphur dyes are used for cellulose fibres.

Disperse dyes are insoluble dyes applied in the form of a fine dispersion in water. They are used for cellulose acetate and other synthetic fibres.

Reactive dyes are compounds that contain groups capable of reacting with the substrate to form covalent bonds. They have high substantivity and are used particularly for cellulose fibres.

dynamic equilibrium *See* equilibrium.

dynamite Any of a class of high explosives based on nitroglycerin. The original form, invented in 1867 by Alfred Nobel, consisted of nitroglycerin absorbed in kieselguhr. Modern dynamites, which are used for blasting, contain sodium or ammonium nitrate sensitized with nitroglycerin and use other absorbers (e.g. wood pulp).

dysprosium Symbol Dy. A soft silvery metallic element belonging to the *lanthanoids; a.n. 66; r.a.m. 162.50; r.d. 8.551 (20°C); m.p. 1412°C; b.p. 2567°C. It occurs in apatite, gadolinite, and xenotime, from which it is extracted by an ion-exchange process. There are seven natural isotopes and twelve artificial isotopes have been identified. It finds limited use in some alloys as a neutron absorber, particularly in nuclear technology. It was discovered by François Lecoq de Boisbaudran in 1886.

dystectic mixture A mixture of substances that has a constant maximum melting point.

E

earth The planet that orbits the sun between the planets Venus and Mars. The earth consists of three layers: the gaseous atmosphere (*see* earth's atmosphere), the liquid *hydrosphere*, and the solid *lithosphere*. The solid part of the earth also consists of three layers: the *crust* with a mean thickness of about 32 km under the land and 10 km under the seas; the *mantle*, which extends some 2900 km below the crust; and the *core*, part of which is believed to be liquid. The composition of the crust is: oxygen 47%, silicon 28%, aluminium 8%, iron 4.5%, calcium 3.5%, sodium and potassium 2.5% each, and magnesium 2.2%. Hydrogen, carbon, phosphorus, and sulphur are all present to an extent of less than 1%.

earth's atmosphere The gas that surrounds the earth. The composition of dry air at sea level is: nitrogen 78.08%, oxygen 20.95%, argon 0.93%, carbon dioxide 0.03%, neon 0.0018%, helium 0.0005%, krypton 0.0001%, and xenon 0.00001%. In addition to water vapour, air in some localities contains sulphur compounds, hydrogen peroxide, hydrocarbons, and dust particles.

ebonite *See* vulcanite.

ebullioscopic constant *See* elevation of boiling point.

echelon A form of interferometer consisting of a stack of glass plates arranged stepwise with a constant offset. It gives a high resolution and is used in spectroscopy to study hyperfine line structure.

eclipsed conformation *See* conformation.

Edison cell *See* nickel–iron accumulator.

EDTA Ethylenediaminetetracetic acid,

$$(HOOCCH_2)_2N(CH_2)_2N(CH_2COOH)_2$$

A compound used as a chelating agent in inorganic chemistry.

effective temperature *See* luminosity.

effervescence The formation of gas bubbles in a liquid by chemical reaction.

efflorescence The process in which a crystalline hydrate loses water, forming a powdery deposit on the crystals.

effusion The flow of a gas through a small aperture. The relative rates at which gases effuse, under the same conditions, is approximately inversely proportional to the square roots of their densities.

eigenfunction An allowed *wave function of a system in quantum mechanics. The associated energies are *eigenvalues.*

Einstein equation 1. The mass–energy relationship announced by Einstein in 1905 in the form $E = mc^2$, where E is a quantity of energy, m its mass, and c is the speed of light. It presents the concept that energy possesses mass. **2.** The relationship $E_{max} = hf - W$, where E_{max} is the maximum kinetic energy of electrons emitted in the photoemissive effect, h is the Planck constant, f the frequency of the incident radiation, and W the *work function of the emitter. This is also written $E_{max} = hf - \phi e$, where e is the electronic charge and ϕ a potential difference, also called the work function. (Sometimes W and ϕ are distinguished as *work function energy* and *work function potential.*) The equation can also be applied to photoemission from gases, when it has the form: $E = hf - I$, where I is the ionization potential of the gas.

einsteinium Symbol Es. A radioactive metallic transuranic element belonging to the *actinoids; a.n. 99; mass number of the most stable isotope 254 (half-life 270 days). Eleven isotopes are known. The element was first identified by A. Ghiorso and associates in debris from the first hydrogen bomb explosion in 1952. Microgram quantities of the element did not become available until 1961.

elastomer A natural or synthetic rubber or rubberoid material, which has the ability to undergo deformation under the influence of a force and regain its original shape once the force has been removed.

electret A permanently electrified substance or body that has opposite charges at its extremities. Electrets resemble permanent magnets in many ways. An electret can be made by cooling certain waxes in a strong electric field.

electric-arc furnace A furnace used in melting metals to make alloys, especially in steel manufacture, in which the heat source is an electric arc. In the direct-arc furnace, such as the Héroult furnace, an arc is formed between the metal and an electrode. In the indirect-arc furnace, such as the Stassano furnace, the arc is formed between two electrodes and the heat is radiated onto the metal.

electrochemical cell *See* cell.

electrochemical equivalent Symbol *z*. The mass of a given element liberated from a solution of its ions in electrolysis by one coulomb of charge. *See* Faraday's laws (of electrolysis).

electrochemical series *See* electromotive series.

electrochemistry The study of chemical properties and reactions involving ions in solution, including electrolysis and electric cells.

electrochromatography *See* electrophoresis.

electrode 1. A conductor that emits or collects electrons in a cell, thermionic valve, semiconductor device, etc. The *anode* is the positive electrode and the *cathode* is the negative electrode. **2.** *See* half cell.

electrodeposition The process of depositing one metal on another by electrolysis, as in *electroforming and *electroplating.

electrode potential The potential difference produced between the electrode and the solution in a *half cell. It is not possible to measure this directly since any measurement involves completing the circuit with the electrolyte, thereby introducing another half cell. *Standard electrode potentials* E are defined by measuring the potential relative to a standard *hydrogen half cell using 1.0 molar solution at 25°C. The convention is to designate the cell so that the oxidized form is written first. For example,

$$Pt(s)|H_2(g)H^+(aq)|Zn^{2+}(aq)|Zn(s)$$

The e.m.f. of this cell is −0.76 volt (i.e. the zinc electrode is negative). Thus the standard electrode potential of the $Zn^{2+}|Zn$ half cell is −0.76 V. Electrode potentials are also called *reduction potentials*. *See also* electromotive series.

electrodialysis A method of obtaining pure water from water containing a salt, as in *desalination. The water to be purified is fed into a cell containing two electrodes. Between the electrodes is placed an array of *semipermeable membranes alternately semipermeable to positive ions and negative ions. The ions tend to segregate between alternate pairs of membranes, leaving pure water in the other gaps between membranes. In this way, the feed water is separated into two streams: one of pure water and the other of more concentrated solution.

electroforming A method of forming intricate metal articles or parts by *electrodeposition of the metal on a removable conductive mould.

electroluminescence *See* luminescence.

electrolysis The production of a chemical reaction by passing an electric current through an electrolyte. In electrolysis, positive ions migrate to the cathode and negative ions to the anode. The reactions occurring depend on electron transfer at the electrodes and are therefore redox reactions. At the anode, negative ions in solution may lose electrons to form neutral species. Alternatively, atoms of the electrode can lose electrons and go into solution as positive ions. In either case the reaction is an oxidation. At the cathode, positive ions in solution can gain electrons to form neutral species. Thus cathode reactions are reductions.

electrolyte A liquid that conducts electricity as a result of the presence of positive or negative ions. Electrolytes are molten ionic compounds or solutions containing ions, i.e. solutions of ionic salts or of compounds that ionize in solution. Liquid metals, in which the conduction is by free electrons, are not usually regarded as electrolytes.

electrolytic cell A cell in which electrolysis occurs; i.e. one in which current is passed through the electrolyte from an external source.

electrolytic corrosion Corrosion that occurs through an electrochemical reaction. *See* rusting.

electrolytic gas The highly explosive gas formed by the electrolysis of water. It consists of two parts hydrogen and one part oxygen by volume.

electrolytic refining The purification of metals by electrolysis. It is commonly applied to copper. A large piece of impure copper is used as the anode with a thin strip of pure copper as the cathode. Copper (II) sulphate solution is the electrolyte. Copper dissolves at the anode: $Cu \rightarrow Cu^{2+} + 2e$, and is deposited at the cathode. The net result is transfer of pure copper from anode to cathode. Gold and silver in the impure copper form a so-called *anode sludge* at the bottom of the cell, which is recovered.

electromagnetic spectrum The range of wavelengths over which electromagnetic radiation extends. The longest waves (10^5-10^{-3} metres) are radio waves, the next longest ($10^{-3}-10^{-6}$ m) are infrared waves, then comes the narrow band ($4-7 \times 10^{-7}$ m) of visible radiation, followed by ultraviolet waves ($10^{-7}-10^{-9}$ m), X-rays ($10^{-9}-10^{-11}$ m), and gamma rays ($10^{-11}-10^{-14}$ m).

electrometallurgy The uses of electrical processes in the separation of metals from their ores, the refining of metals, or the forming or plating of metals.

electromotive force (e.m.f.) The greatest potential difference that can be generated by a particular source of electric current. In practice this may be observable only when the source is not supplying current, because of its internal resistance.

electromotive series (electrochemical series) A series of chemical elements arranged in order of their *electrode potentials. The hydrogen electrode ($H^+ + e \rightarrow \frac{1}{2}H_2$) is taken as having zero electrode potential. Elements that have a greater tendency than hydrogen to lose electrons to their solution are taken as *electropositive*; those that gain electrons from their solution are below hydrogen in the series and are called *electronegative*. The series shows the order in which metals replace one another from their salts; electropositive metals will replace hydrogen from acids. The chief metals and hydrogen, placed in order in the series, are: potassium, calcium, sodium, magnesium, aluminium, zinc, cadmium, iron, nickel, tin, lead, hydrogen, copper, mercury, silver, platinum, gold.

electron An *elementary particle with a rest mass of $9.109\,558 \times 10^{-31}$ kg and a negative charge of $1.602\,192 \times 10^{-19}$ coulomb. Electrons are present in all atoms in groupings called shells around the nucleus; when they are detached from the atom they are called *free electrons*. The antiparticle of the electron is the *positron*.

electron affinity Symbol *A*. The energy change occurring when an atom or molecule gains an electron to form a negative ion. For an atom or molecule X, it is the energy released for the electron-attachment reaction

$$X(g) + e \rightarrow X^-(g)$$

Often this is measured in electronvolts. Alternatively, the molar enthalpy change, ΔH, can be used.

electron capture **1.** The formation of a negative ion by an atom or molecule when it acquires an extra free electron. **2.** A radioactive transformation in which a nucleus acquires an electron from an inner orbit of the atom, thereby transforming, initially, into a nucleus with the same mass number but an atomic number one less than that of the original nucleus (capture of the electron transforms a proton into a neutron). This type of capture is accompanied by emission of an X-ray photon or Auger electron as the vacancy in the inner orbit is filled by an outer electron.

electron-deficient compound A compound in which there are fewer electrons forming the chemical bonds than required in normal electron-pair bonds. *See* borane.

electron diffraction Diffraction of a beam of electrons by atoms or molecules. The fact that electrons can be diffracted in a similar way to light and X-rays shows that particles can act as waves (*see* de Broglie wavelength). An electron (mass m, charge e) accelerated through a potential difference V acquires a kinetic energy $mv^2/2 = eV$, where v is the velocity of the electron. Thus, the momentum (p) of the electron is $\surd(2eVm)$. As the de Broglie wavelength (λ) of an electron is given by h/p, where h is the Planck constant, then $\lambda = h/\surd(2eVm)$. For an accelerating voltage of 3600 V, the wavelength of the electron beam is 0.02 nanometre, some 3×10^4 times shorter than visible radiation.

Electrons then, like X-rays, show diffraction effects with molecules and crystals in which the interatomic spacing is comparable to the wavelength of the beam. They have the advantage that their wavelength can be set by adjusting the voltage. Unlike X-rays they have very low penetrating power. The first observation of electron diffraction was by George Thomson (1892–1975) in 1927, in an experiment in which he passed a beam of electrons in a vacuum through a very thin gold foil onto a photographic plate. Concentric circles were produced by diffraction of electrons by the lattice. The same year Clinton J. Davisson (1881–1958) and Lester Germer (1896–1971) performed a classic experiment in which they obtained diffraction patterns by glancing an electron beam off the surface of a nickel crystal. Both experiments were important verifications of de Broglie's theory and the new quantum theory.

Electron diffraction, because of the low penetration, cannot easily be used to investigate crystal structure. It is, however, employed to measure bond lengths and angles of molecules in gases. Moreover, it is extensively used in the study of solid surfaces and absorption. The main techniques are low-energy electron diffraction (*LEED*) in which the electron beam is reflected onto a fluorescent screen, and high-energy electron diffraction (*HEED*) used either with reflection or transmission in investigating thin films.

electronegative Describing elements that tend to gain electrons and form negative ions. The halogens are typical electronegative elements. For example, in hydrogen chloride, the chlorine atom is more electronegative than the hydrogen and the molecule is polar, with negative charge on the chlorine atom. There are various ways of assigning values for the *electronegativity* of an element. *Mulliken electronegativities* are calculated from $E = (I + A)/2$, where I is ionization potential and A is electron affinity. More commonly, *Pauling electronegativities* are used. These are based on bond dissociation energies using a scale in which fluorine, the most electronegative element, has a value 4. Some other values on this scale are B 2, C 2.5, N 3.0, O 3.5, Si 1.8, P 2.1, S 2.5, Cl 3.0, Br 2.8.

electron microscope A form of microscope that uses a beam of electrons instead of a beam of light (as in the optical microscope) to form a large image of a very small object. In optical microscopes the resolution is limited by the wavelength of the light. High-energy electrons, however, can be associated with a considerably shorter wavelength than light; for example, electrons accelerated to an energy of 10^5 electronvolts have a wavelength of 0.04 nanometre (*see* de Broglie wavelength) enabling a resolution of 0.2–0.5 nm to be achieved. The *transmission electron microscope* has an electron beam, sharply focused by electron lenses, passing through a very thin metallized specimen (less than 50 nanometres thick) onto a fluorescent screen, where a visual image is formed. This image can be photographed. The *scanning electron microscope* can be used with thicker specimens and forms a perspective image, although the resolution and magnification are lower. In this type of instrument a beam of primary electrons scans the specimen and those that are reflected, together with any secondary electrons emitted, are collected. This current is used to modulate a separate electron beam in a TV monitor, which scans the screen at the same frequency, consequently building up a picture of the specimen. The resolution is limited to about 10–20 nm.

electron probe microanalysis (EPM) A method of analysing a very small quantity of a substance (as little as 10^{-13} gram). The method consists of directing a very finely focused beam of electrons on to the sample to produce the characteristic X-ray spectrum of the elements present. It can be used quantitatively for elements with atomic numbers in excess of 11.

electron-spin resonance (ESR) A spectroscopic method of locating electrons within the molecules of a paramagnetic substance (*see* magnetism) in order to provide information regarding its bonds and structure. The spin of an unpaired electron is associated with a magnetic moment that is able to align itself in one of two ways with an applied external magnetic field. These two alignments correspond to different energy levels, with a statistical probability, at normal temperatures, that there will be slightly more in the lower state than in the higher. By applying microwave radiation to the sample a transition to the higher state can be achieved. The precise energy difference between the two states of an electron depends on the surrounding electrons in the atom or molecule. In this way the position of unpaired electrons can be investigated. The technique is used particularly in studying free radicals and paramagnetic substances such as inorganic complexes. *See also* nuclear magnetic resonance.

electron transport chain (respiratory chain) A sequence of biochemical oxidation-reduction reactions that forms the final stage of aerobic respiration. It results in the transfer of electrons or hydrogen atoms derived from the *Krebs cycle to molecular oxygen, with the formation of water. At the same time it conserves energy from good or light in the form of ATP. The chain comprises a series oı electron carriers that undergo reversible oxidation-reduction reactions, accepting electrons and then donating them to the next carrier in the chain. In the mitochondria, NADH and $FADH_2$, generated by the Krebs cycle, transfer their electrons to a chain comprising flavin mononucleotide (FMN), *coenzyme Q, and a series of *cytochromes. This process is coupled to the formation of ATP at three sites along the chain. The ATP is then carried across the mitochondrial membrane in exchange for ADP. An electron transport chain also occurs in the light reaction of photosynthesis.

electronvolt Symbol eV. A unit of energy equal to the work done on an electron in moving it through a potential difference of one volt. It is used as a measure of particle energies although it is not an *SI unit. 1 eV = 1.602×10^{-19} joule.

electrophile An ion or molecule that is electron deficient and can accept electrons. Electrophiles are often reducing agents and Lewis *acids. They are either positive ions (e.g. NO_2^+) or molecules that have a positive charge on a particular atom (e.g. SO_3, which has an electron-deficient sulphur atom). In organic reactions they tend to attack negatively charged parts of a molecule. *Compare* nucleophile.

electrophilic addition An *addition reaction in which the first step is attack by an electrophile (e.g. a positive ion) on an electron-rich part of the molecule. An example is addition to the double bonds in alkenes.

electrophilic substitution A *substitution reaction in which the first step is attack by an electrophile. Electrophilic substitution is a feature of reactions of benzene (and its compounds) in which a positive ion approaches the delocalized pi electrons on the benzene ring.

electrophoresis (cataphoresis) A technique for the analysis and separation of colloids, based on the movement of charged colloidal particles in an electric field. There are various experimental methods. In one the sample is placed in a U-tube and a buffer solution added to each arm, so that there are sharp boundaries between buffer and sample. An electrode is placed in each arm, a voltage applied, and the motion of the boundaries under the influence of the field is observed. The rate of migration of the particles depends on the field, the charge on the particles, and on other factors, such as the size and shape of the particles. More simply, electrophoresis can be carried out using an adsorbent, such as a strip of filter paper, soaked in a buffer with two electrodes making contact. The sample is placed between the electrodes and a voltage applied. Different components of the mixture migrate at different rates, so the sample separates into zones. The components can be identified by the rate at which they move. This technique has also been called *electrochromatography*.

Electrophoresis is used extensively in studying mixtures of proteins, nucleic acids, carbohydrates, enzymes, etc. In clinical medicine it is used for determining the protein content of body fluids.

electroplating A method of plating one metal with another by *electrodeposition. The articles to be plated are made the cathode of an electrolytic cell and a rod or bar of the plating metal is made the anode. Electroplating is used for covering metal with a decorative, more expensive, or corrosion-resistant layer of another metal.

electropositive Describing elements that tend to lose electrons and form positive ions. The alkali metals are typical electropositive elements.

electrovalent bond *See* chemical bond.

electrum **1.** An alloy of gold and silver containing 55–88% of gold. **2.** A *German silver alloy containing 52% copper, 26% nickel, and 22% zinc.

element A substance that cannot be decomposed into simpler substances. In an element, all the atoms have the same number of protons or electrons, although the number of neutrons may vary. There are 92 naturally occurring elements. *See also* periodic table; transuranic element.

elevation of boiling point An increase in the boiling point of a liquid when a solid is dissolved in it. The elevation is proportional to the number of particles dissolved (molecules or ions) and is given by $\Delta t = k_B C$, where C is the molal concentration of solute. The constant k_B is the *ebullioscopic constant* of the solvent and if this is known, the molecular weight of the solute can be calculated from the measured value of Δt. The elevation is measured by a Beckmann thermometer. *See also* colligative property.

elimination reaction A reaction in which a molecule decomposes to two molecules, one smaller than the other.

Elinvar Trade name for a nickel–chromium steel containing about 36% nickel, 12% chromium, and smaller proportions of tungsten and manganese. Its elasticity does not vary with temperature and it is therefore used to make hairsprings for watches.

elliptical polarization *See* polarization of light.

eluate *See* chromatography; elution.

eluent *See* chromatography; elution.

elution The process of removing an adsorbed material (*adsorbate*) from an adsorbent by washing it in a liquid (*eluent*). The solution consisting of the adsorbate dissolved in the eluent is the *eluate*. Elution is the process used to wash components of a mixture through a *chromatography column.

elutriation. The process of suspending finely divided particles in an upward flowing stream of air or water to wash and separate them into sized fractions.

emanation The former name for the gas radon, of which there are three isotopes: Rn–222 (radium emanation), Rn–220 (thoron emanation), and Rn–219 (actinium emanation).

emerald The green gem variety of *beryl: one of the most highly prized gemstones. The finest specimens occur in the Muzo mines, Colombia. Other occurrences include the Ural Mountains, the Transvaal in South Africa, and Kaligunan in India. Emeralds can also be successfully synthesized.

emery A rock composed of corundum (natural aluminium oxide, Al_2O_3) with magnetite, haematite, or spinel. It occurs on the island of Naxos (Greece) and in Turkey. Emery is used as an abrasive and polishing material and in the manufacture of certain concrete floors.

e.m.f. *See* electromotive force.

emission spectrum *See* spectrum.

empirical Denoting a result that is obtained by experiment or observation rather than from theory.

empirical formula *See* formula.

emulsion A *colloid in which small particles of one liquid are dispersed in another liquid. Usually emulsions involve a dispersion of water in an oil or a dispersion of oil in water, and are stabilized by an *emulsifier*. Commonly emulsifiers are substances, such as *detergents, that have lyophobic and lyophilic parts in their molecules.

enantiomers *See* optical activity.

enantiomorphism *See* optical activity.

endothermic Denoting a chemical reaction that takes heat from its surroundings. *Compare* exothermic.

end point The point in a titration at which reaction is complete as shown by the *indicator.

energy A measure of a system's ability to do work. Like work itself, it is measured in joules. Energy is conveniently classified into two forms: *potential energy* is the energy stored in a body or system as a consequence of its position, shape, or state (this includes gravitational energy, electrical energy, nuclear energy, and chemical energy); *kinetic energy* is energy of motion and is usually defined as the work that will be done by the body possessing the energy when it is brought to rest. For a body of mass m having a speed v, the kinetic energy is $mv^2/2$. The rotational kinetic energy of a body having an angular velocity ω is $I\omega^2/2$, where I is its moment of inertia.

The *internal energy of a body is the sum of the potential energy and the kinetic energy of its component atoms and molecules.

energy band A range of energies that electrons can have in a solid. In a single atom, electrons exist in discrete *energy levels. In a crystal, in which large numbers of atoms are held closely together in a lattice, electrons are influenced by a number of adjacent nuclei and the sharply defined levels of the atoms become bands of allowed energy; this approach to energy levels in solids is often known as the *band theory*. Each band represents a large number of allowed quantum states. Between the bands are *forbidden bands*. The outermost electrons of the atoms (i.e. the ones responsible for chemical bonding) form the *valence band* of the solid. This is the band, of those occupied, that has the highest energy.

The band structure of solids accounts for their electrical properties. In order to move through the solid, the electrons have to change from one quantum state to another. This can only occur if there are empty quantum states close to the electrons. In general, if the valence band is full, electrons cannot change to new quantum states in the same band. For conduction to occur, the electrons have to be in an unfilled band – the *conduction band*. Metals are good conductors either because the valence band and the conduction band are only half-filled or because the conduction band overlaps with the valence band; in either case vacant states are available. In insulators the conduction band and valence band are separated by a wide forbidden band and electrons do not have enough energy to 'jump' from one to the other.

In intrinsic semiconductors the forbidden gap is narrow and, at normal temperatures, electrons at the top of the valence band can move by thermal agitation into the conduction band (at absolute zero, a semiconductor would act as an insulator). Doped semiconductors have extra bands in the forbidden gap.

energy level A definite fixed energy that a molecule, atom, electron, or nucleus can have. In an atom, for example, the atom

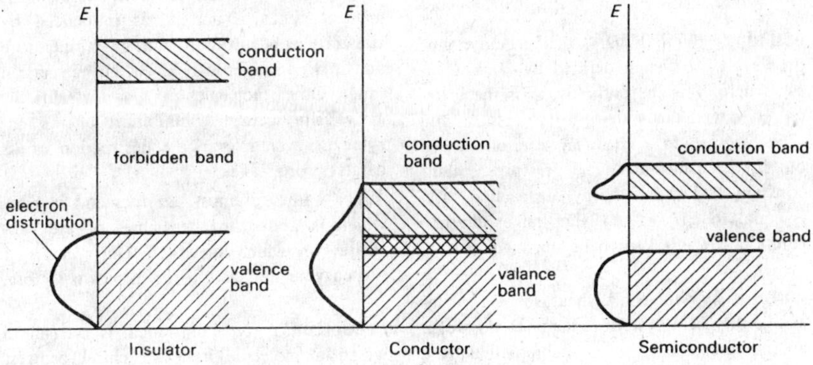

Energy bands

has a fixed energy corresponding to the *orbitals in which its electrons move around the nucleus. The atom can accept a quantum of energy to become an excited atom (*see* excitation) if that extra energy will raise an electron to a permitted orbital. Between the *ground state*, which is the lowest possible energy level for a particular system, and the first excited state there are no permissible energy levels. According to the *quantum theory, only certain energy levels are possible. An atom passes from one energy level to the next without passing through fractions of that energy transition. These levels are usually described by the energies associated with the individual electrons in the atoms, which are always lower than an arbitrary level for a free electron. The energy levels of molecules also involve quantized vibrational and rotational motion.

Engel's salt *See* potassium carbonate.

enols Compounds containing the group $-CH{=}C(OH)-$ in their molecules. *See also* keto–enol tautomerism.

enrichment The process of increasing the abundance of a specified isotope in a mixture of isotopes. It is usually applied to an increase in the proportion of U–235, or the addition of Pu–239 to natural uranium for use in a nuclear reactor or weapon.

enthalpy Symbol H. A thermodynamic property of a system defined by $H = U + pV$, where H is the enthalpy, U is the internal energy of the system, p its pressure, and V its volume. In a chemical reaction carried out in the atmosphere the pressure remains constant and the enthalpy of reaction, ΔH, is equal to $\Delta U + p\Delta V$. For an exothermic reaction ΔH is taken to be negative.

entropy Symbol S. A measure of the unavailability of a system's energy to do work; an increase in entropy is accompanied by a decrease in energy availability. When a system undergoes a reversible change the entropy (S) changes by an amount equal to the energy (Q) absorbed by the system divided by the thermodynamic temperature (T) at which the energy is absorbed, i.e. $\Delta S = \Delta Q/T$. However, all real processes are to a certain extent irreversible changes and in any closed system an irreversible change is always accompanied by an increase in entropy.

In a wider sense entropy can be interpreted as a measure of a system's disorder; the higher the entropy the greater the disorder. As any real change to a closed system tends towards higher entropy, and therefore higher disorder, it follows that the entropy of the universe (if it can be considered a closed system) is increasing and its available energy is decreasing. This increase in the entropy of the universe is one way of stating the second law of *thermodynamics.

enzyme A protein that acts as a *catalyst in biochemical reactions. Each enzyme is specific to a particular reaction or group of similar reactions. Many require the association of certain nonprotein *cofactors in order to function. The molecule undergoing reaction (the *substrate*) binds to a specific *active site on the enzyme molecule to form a short-lived intermediate: this greatly increases (by a factor of up to 10^{20}) the rate at which the reaction proceeds to form the product. Enzyme activity is influenced by substrate concentration and by temperature and pH, which must lie within a certain range. Other molecules may compete for the active site, causing *inhibition of the enzyme or even irreversible destruction of its catalytic properties.

The names of most enzymes end in *-ase*, which is added to the names of the substrates on which they act. Thus *lactase* is the enzyme that acts to break down lactose.

epimerism A type of optical isomerism in which a molecule has two chiral centres; two optical isomers (*epimers*) differ in the arrangement about one of these centres. *See also* optical activity.

epinephrine *See* adrenaline.

epitaxy (epitaxial growth) Growth of a layer of one substance on a single crystal of another, such that the crystal structure in the layer is the same as that in the substrate. It is used in making semiconductor devices.

EPM *See* electron probe microanalysis.

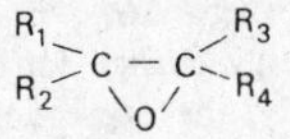

The functional group in epoxides

epoxides Compounds that contain oxygen atoms in their molecules as part of a three-membered ring. Epoxides are thus *cyclic ethers.*

epoxyethane (ethylene oxide) A colourless flammable gas, C_2H_4O; m.p. $-111°C$; b.p. 11°C. It is a cyclic ether (*see* epoxides), made by the catalytic oxidation of ethene. It can be hydrolysed to ethane-1,2-diol and also polymerizes to:
$\ldots -O-C_2H_4-O-C_2H_4- \ldots$, which is used for lowering the viscosity of water (e.g. in fire fighting).

epoxy resins Synthetic resins produced by copolymerizing epoxide compounds with phenols. They contain –O– linkages and epoxide groups and are usually viscous liquids. They can be hardened by addition of agents, such as polyamines, that form cross-linkages. Alternatively, catalysts may be used to induce further polymerization of the resin. Epoxy resins are used in electrical equipment and in the chemical industry (because of resistance to chemical attack). They are also used as adhesives.

epsomite A mineral form of *magnesium sulphate heptahydrate, $MgSO_4.7H_2O$.

Epsom salt *See* magnesium sulphate.

equation of state An equation that relates the pressure p, volume V, and thermodynamic temperature T of an amount of substance n. The simplest is the ideal *gas law:

$$pV = nRT,$$

where R is the universal gas constant. Applying only to ideal gases, this equation takes no account of the volume occupied by the gas molecules (according to this law if the pressure is infinitely great the volume becomes zero), nor does it take into account any forces between molecules. A more accurate equation of state would therefore be

$$(p + k)(V - nb) = nRT,$$

where k is a factor that reflects the decreased pressure on the walls of the container as a result of the attractive forces between particles, and nb is the volume occupied by the particles themselves when the pressure is infinitely high. In the *van der Waals equation of state*, proposed by the Dutch physicist J. D. van der Waals (1837–1923),

$$k = n^2a/V^2,$$

where a is a constant. This equation more accurately reflects the behaviour of real gases; several others have done better but are more complicated.

equilibrium A state in which a system has its energy distributed in the statistically most probable manner; a state of a system in which forces, influences, reactions, etc., balance each other out so that there is no net change. A body is said to be in *thermal equilibrium* if no net heat exchange is taking place within it or between it and its surroundings. A system is in *chemical equilibrium when a reaction and its reverse are proceeding at equal rates (*see also* equilibrium constant). These are examples of *dynamic equilibrium*, in which activity in one sense or direction is in aggregate balanced by comparable reverse activity.

equilibrium constant For a reversible reaction of the type

$$xA + yB \rightleftharpoons zC + wD$$

chemical equilibrium occurs when the rate of the forward reaction equals the rate of the back reaction, so that the concentrations of products and reactants reach steady-state values. It can be shown that at equilibrium the ratio of concentrations

$$[C]^z[D]^w/[A]^x[B]^y$$

is a constant for a given reaction and fixed temperature, called the equilibrium constant K_c (where the *c* indicates concentrations have been used). Note that, by convention, the products on the right-hand side of the reaction are used on the top line of the expression for equilibrium constant. This form of the equilibrium constant was originally introduced in 1863 by C. M. Guldberg and P. Waage using the law of *mass action. They derived the expression by taking the rate of the forward reaction

$$k_f[A]^x[B]^y$$

and that of the back reaction

$$k_b[C]^z[D]^w$$

Since the two rates are equal at equilibrium, the equilibrium constant K_c is the ratio of the rate constants k_f/k_b. The principle that the expression is a constant is known as the *equilibrium law* or *law of chemical equilibrium.*

The equilibrium constant shows the *position* of equilibrium. A low value of K_c indicates that [C] and [D] are small compared to [A]and [B]; i.e. that the back reaction predominates. It also indicates how the equilibrium shifts if concentration changes. For example, if [A] is increased (by adding A) the equilibrium shifts towards the right so that [C] and [D] increase, and K_c remains constant.

For gas reactions, partial pressures are used rather than concentrations. The symbol K_p is then used. Thus, in the example above

$$K_p = p_C{}^z p_D{}^w / p_A{}^x p_B{}^y$$

It can be shown that, for a given reaction $K_p = K_c(RT)^{\Delta\nu}$, where $\Delta\nu$ is the difference in stoichiometric coefficients for the reaction (i.e. $z + w - x - y$). Note that the units of K_p and K_c depend on the numbers of molecules appearing in the stoichiometric equation. The value of the equilibrium constant depends on the temperature. If the forward reaction is exothermic, the equilibrium constant decreases as the temperature rises; if endothermic it increases (*see also* van't Hoff's isochore).

The expression for the equilibrium constant can also be obtained by thermodynamics; it can be shown that the standard equilibrium constant K is given by exp ($-\Delta G$ $/RT$), where ΔG is the standard Gibbs free energy change for the complete reaction. Strictly, the expressions above for equilibrium constants are true only for ideal gases (pressure) or infinite dilution (concentration). For accurate work *activities are used.

equilibrium law *See* equilibrium constant.

equipartition of energy The theory, proposed by Ludwig Boltzmann (1844–1906) and given some theoretical support by James Clerk Maxwell (1831–79), that the energy of gas molecules in a large sample under thermal *equilibrium is equally divided among their available *degrees of freedom, the average energy for each degree of freedom being $kT/2$, where k is the *Boltzmann constant and T is the thermodynamic temperature. The proposition is not generally true if quantum considerations are important, but is frequently a good approximation.

equivalence point The point in a titration at which reaction is complete. *See* indicator.

equivalent proportions *See* chemical combination.

equivalent weight The mass of an element or compound that could combine with or displace one gram of hydrogen (or eight grams of oxygen or 35.5 grams of chlorine) in a chemical reaction. The equivalent weight represents the 'combining power' of the substance. For an element it is the relative atomic mass divided by the valency. For a compound it depends on the reaction considered.

erbium Symbol Er. A soft silvery metallic element belonging to the *lanthanoids; a.n. 68; r.a.m. 167.26; r.d. 9.066 (20°C); m.p. 1529°C; b.p. 2868°C. It occurs in apatite, gadolinite, and xenotine from certain sources. There are six natural isotopes, which are stable, and twelve artificial isotopes are known. It has been used in alloys for nuclear technology as it is a neutron absorber; it is being investigated for other potential uses. It was discovered by C. G. Mosander in 1843.

ergocalciferol *See* vitamin D.

ergosterol A *sterol occurring in fungi, bacteria, algae, and higher plants. It is converted into vitamin D_2 by the action of ultraviolet light.

ESCA *See* photoelectron spectroscopy.

ESR *See* electron-spin resonance.

essential amino acid An *amino acid that an organism is unable to synthesize in sufficient quantities. It must therefore be present in the diet. In man the essential amino acids are arginine, histidine, lysine, threonine, methionine, isoleucine, leucine, valine, phenylalanine, and tryptophan. These are required for protein synthesis and deficiency leads to retarded growth and other symptoms. Most of the amino acids required by man are also essential for all other multicellular animals and for most protozoans.

essential element Any of a number of elements required by living organisms to ensure normal growth, development, and maintenance. Apart from the elements found in organic compounds (i.e. carbon, hydrogen, oxygen, and nitrogen), plants, animals, and microorganisms all require a range of elements in inorganic forms in varying amounts, depending on the type of organism. The *major elements*, present in tissues in relatively large amounts (greater than 0.005%), are calcium, phosphorus, potassium, sodium, chlorine, sulphur, and magnesium. The *trace elements* occur at much lower concentrations and thus requirements are much less. The most important are iron, manganese, zinc, copper, iodine, cobalt, selenium, molybdenum, chromium, and silicon. Each element may fulfil one or more of a variety of metabolic roles.

essential fatty acids *Fatty acids that must normally be present in the diet of certain animals, including man. Essential fatty acids, which include *linoleic and *linolenic acids, all possess double bonds at the same two positions along their hydrocarbon chain and so can act as precursors of *prostaglandins. Deficiency of essential fatty acids can cause dermatosis, weight loss, irregular oestrus, etc. An adult human requires 2–10 g linoleic acid or its equivalent per day.

essential oil A natural oil with a distinctive scent secreted by the glands of certain aromatic plants. *Terpenes are the main constituents. Essential oils are extracted from plants by steam distillation, extraction with cold neutral fats or solvents (e.g. alcohol), or pressing and used in perfumes, flavourings, and medicine. Examples are citrus oils, flower oils (e.g. rose, jasmine), and oil of cloves.

esterification A reaction of an alcohol with an acid to produce an ester and water; e.g.

$$CH_3OH + C_6H_5COOH \rightleftharpoons CH_3OOCC_6H_5 + H_2O$$

The reaction is an equilibrium and is slow under normal conditions, but can be speeded up by addition of a strong acid catalyst. The ester can often be distilled off so that the reaction can proceed to completion. The reverse reaction is ester hydrolysis or *saponification. *See also* labelling.

esters Organic compounds formed by reaction between alcohols and acids. Esters formed from carboxylic acids have the general formula RCOOR′. Examples are ethyl ethanoate, $CH_3COOC_2H_5$, and methyl propanoate, $C_2H_5COOCH_3$. Esters containing simple hydrocarbon groups are volatile fragrant substances used as flavourings in the food industry. Triesters, molecules containing three ester groups, occur in nature as oils and fats. *See also* glycerides.

ethanal (acetaldehyde) A colourless highly flammable liquid aldehyde, CH_3CHO; r.d. 0.78; m.p. −124.6°C; b.p. 20.8°C. It is made from ethene by the *Wacker process and used as a starting material for making many organic compounds. The compound polymerizes if dilute acid is added to give *ethanal trimer* (or *paraldehyde*), which contains a six-membered ring of alternating carbon and oxygen atoms with a hydrogen atom and a methyl group attached to each carbon atom. It is used as a drug for inducing sleep. Addition of dilute acid below 0°C gives *ethanal tetramer* (or *metaldehyde*), which has a similar structure to the trimer but with an eight-membered ring. It is used as a solid fuel in portable stoves and in slug pellets.

ethanamide (acetamide) A colourless solid crystallizing in the form of long white crystals with a characteristic smell of mice, CH_3CONH_2; r.d. 1.159; m.p. 82.3°C; b.p. 221.25°C. It is made by the dehydration of ammonium ethanoate or by the action of ammonia on ethanoyl chloride, ethanoic anhydride, or ethyl ethanoate.

ethane A colourless flammable gaseous hydrocarbon, C_2H_6; m.p. −183°C; b.p. −89°C. It is the second member of the *alkane series of hydrocarbons and occurs in natural gas.

ethanedioic acid *See* oxalic acid.

ethane-1,2-diol (ethylene glycol; glycol) A colourless viscous hygroscopic liquid, CH_2OHCH_2OH; m.p. −13°C; b.p. 197°C. It is made by hydrolysis of epoxyethane (from ethene) and used as an antifreeze and a raw material for making *polyesters (e.g. Terylene).

ethanoate (acetate) A salt or ester of ethanoic acid (acetic acid).

ethanoic acid (acetic acid) A clear viscous liquid or glassy solid *carboxylic acid, CH_3COOH, with a characteristically sharp odour of vinegar; r.d. 1.049; m.p. 16.7°C; b.p. 118.5°C. The pure compound is called *glacial ethanoic acid.* It is manufactured by the oxidation of ethanol or by the oxidation of butane in the presence of dissolved manganese(II) or cobalt(II) ethanoates at 200°C, and is used in making ethanoic anhydride for producing cellulose ethanoates. It is also used in making ethenyl ethanoate (for polyvinylacetate). The compound is formed by the fermentation of alcohol and is present in vinegar, which is made by fermenting beer or wine. 'Vinegar' made from ethanoic acid with added colouring matter is called 'nonbrewed condiment'.

ethanol (ethyl alcohol) A colourless water-soluble *alcohol, C_2H_5OH; r.d. 0.61

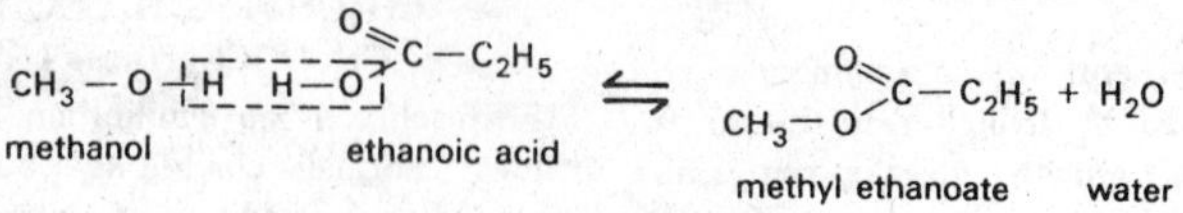

Ester formation

(0°C); m.p. −169°C; b.p. −102°C. It is the active principle in intoxicating drinks, in which it is produced by fermentation of sugar using yeast

$$C_6H_{12}O_6 \rightarrow 2C_2H_5OH + 2CO_2$$

The ethanol produced kills the yeast and fermentation alone cannot produce ethanol solutions containing more than 15% ethanol by volume. Distillation can produce a constant-boiling mixture containing 95.6% ethanol and 4.4% water. Pure ethanol (*absolute alcohol*) is made by removing this water by means of drying agents.

The main industrial use of ethanol is as a solvent although at one time it was a major starting point for making other chemicals. For this it was produced by fermentation of molasses. Now ethene has replaced ethanol as a raw material and industrial ethanol is made by hydrolysis of ethene.

ethanoyl chloride (acetyl chloride) A colourless liquid acyl chloride (*see* acyl halides), CH_3COCl, with a pungent smell; r.d. 1.104; m.p. −112.15°C; b.p. 55°C. It is made by reacting ethanoic acid with a halogenating agent such as phosphorus(III) chloride, phosphorus(V) chloride, or sulphur dichloride oxide and is used to introduce ethanoyl groups into organic compounds containing −OH, $-NH_2$, and −SH groups. *See* acylation.

ethanoyl group (acetyl group) The organic group CH_3CO-.

ethene (ethylene) A colourless flammable gaseous hydrocarbon, C_2H_4; m.p. −169°C; b.p. −102°C. It is the first member of the *alkene series of hydrocarbons. It is made by cracking hydrocarbons from petroleum and is now a major raw material for making other organic chemicals (e.g. ethanal, ethanol, ethane-1,2-diol). It can be polymerized to *polyethene. It occurs naturally in plants, in which it acts as a *growth substance promoting the ripening of fruits.

ethenyl ethanoate (vinyl acetate) An unsaturated organic ester, $CH_2{:}CHOOCCH_3$; r.d. 0.9; m.p. −100°C; b.p. 73°C. It is made by catalytic reaction of ethanoic acid and ethene and used to make polyvinylacetate.

ether *See* ethoxyethane; ethers.

ethers Organic compounds containing the group −O− in their molecules. Examples are dimethyl ether, CH_3OCH_3, and diethyl ether, $C_2H_5OC_2H_5$ (*see* ethoxyethane). They are volatile highly flammable compounds made by dehydrating alcohols using sulphuric acid.

ethoxyethane (diethyl ether; ether) A colourless flammable volatile *ether, $C_2H_5OC_2H_5$; r.d. 0.71; m.p. −116°C; b.p. 34.5°C. It can be made by *Williamson's synthesis. It is an anaesthetic and useful organic solvent.

ethyl acetate *See* ethyl ethanoate.

ethyl alcohol *See* ethanol.

ethylamine A colourless flammable volatile liquid, $C_2H_5NH_2$; r.d. 0.69; m.p. −81°C; b.p. 16.6°C. It is a primary amine made by reacting chloroethane with ammonia and used in making dyes.

ethylbenzene A colourless flammable liquid, $C_6H_5C_2H_5$; r.d. 0.8; m.p. −95°C; b.p. 136°C. It is made from ethene and benzene by a *Friedel–Crafts reaction and is used in making phenylethene (for polystyrene).

ethyl bromide *See* bromoethane.

ethylene *See* ethene.

ethylene glycol *See* ethane-1,2-diol.

ethylene oxide *See* epoxyethane.

ethyl ethanoate (ethyl acetate) A colourless flammable liquid ester, $C_2H_5OOCCH_3$; r.d. 0.69; m.p. −81°C; b.p. 16.6°C. It is used as a solvent and in flavourings and perfumery.

ethyl group The organic group C_2H_5-.

ethyl iodide *See* iodoethane.

ethyne (acetylene) A colourless unstable gas, C_2H_2, with a characteristic sweet odour; r.d. 0.618; m.p. −83.25°C; b.p. −79.85°C. It is the simplest member of the *alkyne series of unsaturated hydrocarbons, and is prepared by the action of water on calcium dicarbide or by adding alcoholic potassium hydroxide to 1,2-dibromoethane. It can be manufactured by heating methane to 1500°C in the presence of a catalyst. It is used in oxyacetylene welding and in the manufacture of ethanal and ethanoic acid. Ethyne can be polymerized easily at high temperatures to give a range of products. The inorganic saltlike dicarbides contain the ion $C_2{}^{2-}$, although ethyne itself is a neutral compound (i.e. not a protonic acid).

eudiometer An apparatus for measuring changes in volume of gases during chemical reactions. A simple example is a graduated glass tube sealed at one end and inverted in mercury. Wires passing into the tube allow the gas mixture to be sparked to initiate the reaction between gases in the tube.

europium Symbol Eu. A soft silvery metallic element belonging to the *lanthanoids; a.n. 63; r.a.m. 151.96; r.d. 5.245 (20°C); m.p. 822°C; b.p. 1529°C. It occurs in small quantities in bastanite and monazite. Two stable isotopes occur naturally: europium−151 and europium−153, both of which are neutron absorbers. Experimental europium alloys have been tried for nuclear-reactor parts but until recently the metal has not been available in sufficient quantities. Additional uses are being researched since the metal became available in larger quantities. It was discovered by Sir William Crookes in 1889.

eutectic mixture A solid solution consisting of two or more substances and having the lowest freezing point of any possible mixture of these components. The minimum freezing point for a set of components is called the *eutectic point*. Low-melting-point alloys are usually eutectic mixtures.

evaporation The change of state of a liquid into a vapour at a temperature below the boiling point of the liquid. Evaporation occurs at the surface of a liquid, some of those molecules with the highest kinetic energies escaping into the gas phase. The result is a fall in the average kinetic energy of the molecules of the liquid and consequently a fall in its temperature.

exa- Symbol E. A prefix used in the metric system to denote 10^{18} times. For example, 10^{18} metres = 1 exametre (Em).

excitation A process in which a nucleus, electron, atom, ion, or molecule acquires energy that raises it to a quantum state (*excited state*) higher than that of its *ground state. The difference between the energy in the ground state and that in the excited state is called the *excitation energy*. *See* energy level.

exclusion principle *See* Pauli exclusion principle.

exothermic Denoting a chemical reaction that releases heat into its surroundings. *Compare* endothermic.

explosives Substances that undergo rapid chemical reaction evolving heat and causing a sudden increase in pressure. The volume of gas produced by an explosive is great compared with the volume of the original substance. Examples of explosive substances are gunpowder, cellulose nitrate, TNT, nitroglycerin, and cyclonite.

extender An inert substance added to a product (paint, rubber, washing powder, etc.) to dilute it (for economy) or to modify its physical properties.

extraordinary ray *See* double refraction.

F

face-centred cubic (f.c.c.) *See* cubic crystal.

FAD (flavin adenine dinucleotide) A *coenzyme important in various biochemical reactions. It comprises a phosphorylated vitamin B_2(riboflavin) molecule linked to the nucleotide adenine monophosphate (AMP). FAD is usually tightly bound to the enzyme forming a *flavoprotein*. It functions as a hydrogen acceptor in dehydrogenation reactions, being reduced to $FADH_2$. This in turn is oxidized to FAD by the *electron transport chain, thereby generating ATP (two molecules of ATP per molecule of $FADH_2$).

Fahrenheit scale A temperature scale in which (by modern definition) the temperature of boiling water is taken as 212 degrees and the temperature of melting ice as 32 degrees. It was invented in 1714 by the German scientist G. D. Fahrenheit (1686–1736), who set the zero at the lowest temperature he knew how to obtain in the laboratory (by mixing ice and common salt) and took his own body temperature as 96°F. The scale is no longer in scientific use. To convert to the *Celsius scale the formula is $C = 5(F - 32)/9$.

Fajans' rules Rules indicating the extent to which an ionic bond has covalent character caused by polarization of the ions. Covalent character is more likely if:

(1) the charge of the ions is high;

(2) the positive ion is small or the negative ion is large;

(3) the positive ion has an outer electron configuration that is not a noble-gas configuration.

The rules were introduced by the Polish–American chemist Kasimir Fajans (1887–).

fall-out 1. (*or* **radioactive fall-out**) Radioactive particles deposited from the atmosphere either from a nuclear explosion or from a nuclear accident. *Local fall-out*, within 250 km of an explosion, falls within a few hours of the explosion. *Tropospheric fall-out* consists of fine particles deposited all round the earth in the approximate latitude of the explosion within about one week. *Stratospheric fall-out* may fall anywhere on earth over a period of years. The most dangerous radioactive isotopes in fall-out are the fission fragments iodine–131 and strontium–90. Both can be taken up by grazing animals and passed on to human populations in milk, milk products, and meat. Iodine–131 accumulates in the thyroid gland and strontium–90 accumulates in bones. **2.** (*or* **chemical fall-out**) Hazardous chemicals discharged into and subsequently released from the atmosphere, especially by factory chimneys.

farad Symbol F. The SI unit of capacitance, being the capacitance of a capacitor that, if charged with one coulomb, has a potential difference of one volt between its plates. $1\ F = 1\ C\ V^{-1}$. The farad itself is too large for most applications; the practical unit is the microfarad (10^{-6} F). The unit is named after Michael Faraday (1791–1867).

Faraday constant Symbol *F*. The electric charge carried by one mole of electrons or singly ionized ions, i.e. the product of the *Avogadro constant and the charge on an electron (disregarding sign). It has the value $9.648\,670 \times 10^4$ coulombs per mole. This number of coulombs is sometimes treated as a unit of electric charge called the *faraday*.

Faraday's laws Two laws describing electrolysis:
(1) The amount of chemical change during electrolysis is proportional to the charge passed.
(2) The charge required to deposit or liberate a mass m is given by $Q = Fmz/M$, where F is the Faraday constant, z the charge of the ion, and M the relative ionic mass.

These are the modern forms of the laws. Originally, they were stated by Faraday in a different form:
(1) The amount of chemical change produced is proportional to the quantity of electricity passed.
(2) The amount of chemical change produced in different substances by a fixed quantity of electricity is proportional to the electrochemical equivalent of the substance.

fat A mixture of lipids, chiefly *triglycerides, that is solid at normal body temperatures. Fats occur widely in plants and animals as a means of storing food energy, having twice the calorific value of carbohydrates. In mammals, fat is deposited in a layer beneath the skin (subcutaneous fat) and deep within the body as a specialized adipose tissue.

Fats derived from plants and fish generally have a greater proportion of unsaturated *fatty acids than those from mammals. Their melting points thus tend to be lower, causing a softer consistency at room temperatures. Highly unsaturated fats are liquid at room temperatures and are therefore more properly called *oils.

fatty acid An organic compound consisting of a hydrocarbon chain and a terminal carboxyl group (*see* carboxylic acids). Chain length ranges from one hydrogen atom (methanoic, or formic, acid, HCOOH) to nearly 30 carbon atoms. Ethanoic (acetic), propanoic (propionic), and butanoic (butyric) acids are important in metabolism. Long-chain fatty acids (more than 8–10 carbon atoms) most commonly occur as constituents of certain lipids, notably glycerides, phospholipids, sterols, and waxes, in which they are esterified with alcohols. These long-chain fatty acids generally have an even number of carbon atoms; unbranched chains predominate over branched chains. They may be saturated (e.g. *palmitic (hexadecanoic) acid and *stearic (octadecanoic) acid) or unsaturated, with one double bond (e.g. *oleic (cis-octodec-9-enoic) acid) or two or more double bonds, in which case they are called *polyunsaturated fatty acids* (e.g. *linoleic acid and *linolenic acid). *See also* essential fatty acids.

The physical properties of fatty acids are determined by chain length, degree of unsaturation, and chain branching. Short-chain acids are pungent liquids, soluble in water. As chain length increases, melting points are raised and water-solubility decreases. Unsaturation and chain branching tend to lower melting points.

***f*-block elements** The block of elements in the *periodic table consisting of the lanthanoid series (from cerium to lutetium) and the actinoid series (from thorium to lawrencium). They are characterized by having two *s*-electrons in their outer shell (n) and *f*-electrons in their inner ($n-1$) shell.

f.c.c. Face-centred cubic. *See* cubic crystal.

Fehling's test A chemical test to detect reducing sugars and aldehydes in solution, devised by the German chemist H. C. von Fehling (1812–85). *Fehling's solution* consists of Fehling's A (copper(II) sulphate solution) and Fehling's B (alkaline sodium tartrate 2,3-dihydroxybutanedioate solution), equal amounts of which are added to the test solution. After boiling, a positive result is indicated by the formation of a brick-red precipitate of copper(I) oxide. Methanal, being a strong reducing agent, also produces copper metal; ketones do not react.

feldspars A group of silicate minerals, the most abundant minerals in the earth's crust. They have a structure in which $(Si,Al)O_4$ tetrahedra are linked together with potassium, sodium, and calcium and very occasionally barium ions occupying the large spaces in the framework. The chemical composition of feldspars may be expressed as combinations of the four components:
anorthite (An), $CaAl_2Si_2O_8$;
albite (Ab), $NaAlSi_3O_8$;
orthoclase (Or), $KAlSi_3O_8$; and
celsian (Ce), $BaAl_2Si_2O_8$.
The feldspars are subdivided into two groups: the *alkali feldspars* (including microcline, orthoclase, and sanidine), in which potassium is dominant with a smaller proportion of sodium and negligible calcium; and the *plagioclase feldspars*, which vary in composition in a series that ranges from pure sodium feldspar (albite) through to pure calcium feldspar (anorthite) with negligible potassium. Feldspars form colourless, white, or pink crystals with a hardness of 6 on the Mohs' scale.

feldspathoids A group of alkali aluminosilicate minerals that are similar in chemical composition to the *feldspars but are relatively deficient in silica and richer in alkalis. The structure consists of a framework of $(Si,Al)O_4$ tetrahedra with aluminium and silicon atoms at their centres. The feldspathoids occur chiefly with feldspars but do not coexist with free quartz (SiO_2) as they react with silica to yield feldspars. The chief varieties of feldspathoids are:
nepheline, $KNa_3(AlSiO_4)_4$;
leucite, $KAlSi_2O_6$;
analcime, $NaAlSi_2O_6.H_2O$;
cancrinite, $Na_8(AlSiO_4)_6(HCO_3)_2$;
and the sodalite subgroup comprising
sodalite, $3(NaAlSiO_4).NaCl$;
nosean, $3(NaAlSiO_4).Na_2SO_4$;
haüyne, $3(NaAlSiO_4).CaSO_4$;
and lazurite, $(Na,Ca)_8(Al,Si)_{12}O_{24}(S,SO_4)$ (*see* *lapis lazuli*).

femto- Symbol f. A prefix used in the metric system to denote 10^{-15}. For example, 10^{-15} second = 1 femtosecond (fs).

fermentation A form of anaerobic respiration occurring in certain microorganisms, e.g. yeasts. It comprises a series of biochemical reactions by which sugar is converted to ethanol and carbon dioxide. Fermentation is the basis of the baking, wine, and beer industries.

fermi A unit of length formerly used in nuclear physics. It is equal to 10^{-15} metre. In SI units this is equal to 1 femtometre (fm). It was named after the Italian-born US physicist Enrico Fermi (1901–54).

Fermi–Dirac statistics *See* quantum statistics.

Fermi level The energy level in a solid at which the probability of finding an electron is 1/2. The Fermi level in conductors lies in the conduction band (*see* energy bands), in insulators it lies in the valence band, and in semiconductors it falls in the gap between the conduction band and the valence band. At absolute zero all the electrons would occupy energy levels up to the Fermi level and no higher levels would be occupied.

fermium Symbol Fm. A radioactive metallic transuranic element belonging to the *actinoids; a.n. 100; mass number of the most stable isotope 257 (half-life 10 days). Ten isotopes are known. The element was first identified by A. Ghiorso and associates in debris from the first hydrogen-bomb explosion in 1952.

ferric compounds Compounds of iron in its +3 oxidation state; e.g. ferric chloride is iron(III) chloride, $FeCl_3$.

ferricyanide A compound containing the complex ion $[Fe(CN)_6]^{3-}$, i.e. the hexacyanoferrate(III) ion.

ferrite 1. A member of a class of mixed oxides $MO.Fe_2O_3$, where M is a metal such as cobalt, manganese, nickel, or zinc. The ferrites are ceramic materials that show either ferrimagnetism or ferromagnetism, but are not electrical conductors. For this reason they are used in high-frequency circuits as magnetic cores. **2.** *See* steel.

ferroalloys Alloys of iron with other elements made by smelting mixtures of iron ore and the metal ore; e.g. ferrochromium, ferrovanadium, ferromanganese, ferrosilicon, etc. They are used in making alloy *steels.

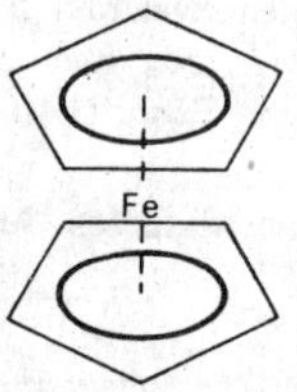

Ferrocene

ferrocene An orange-red crystalline solid, $Fe(C_5H_5)_2$; m.p. 173°C. It can be made by adding the ionic compound $Na^+C_5H_5^-$ (cyclopentadienyl sodium, made from sodium and cyclopentadiene) to iron(III) chloride. In ferrocene, the two rings are parallel, with the iron ion sandwiched between them (hence the name *sandwich compound*). The bonding is between pi orbitals on the rings and *d*-orbitals on the Fe^{2+} ion. The compound can undergo electrophilic substitution on the C_5H_5 rings (they have some aromatic character). It can also be oxidized to the blue ion $(C_5H_5)_2Fe^+$. Ferrocene is the first of a class of similar complexes called *metallocenes*. Its systematic name is *di-π-cyclopentadienyl iron(II)*.

ferrocyanide A compound containing the complex ion $[Fe(CN)_6]^{4-}$, i.e. the hexacyanoferrate(II) ion.

ferroelectric materials Ceramic dielectrics, such as Rochelle salt and barium titanate, that have a domain structure making them analogous to ferromagnetic materials. They exhibit hysteresis and usually the piezoelectric effect.

ferrosoferric oxide *See* tri-iron tetroxide.

ferrous compounds Compounds of iron in its +2 oxidation state; e.g. ferrous chloride is iron(II) chloride, $FeCl_2$.

filler A solid inert material added to a synthetic resin or rubber, either to change its physical properties or simply to dilute it for economy.

film badge A lapel badge containing masked photographic film worn by personnel who could be exposed to ionizing radiation. The film is developed to indicate the extent that the wearer has been exposed to harmful radiation.

filter A device for separating solid particles from a liquid or gas. The simplest laboratory filter for liquids is a funnel in which a cone of paper (*filter paper*) is placed. Special containers with a porous base of sintered glass are also used. *See also* Gooch crucible.

filter pump A simple laboratory vacuum pump in which air is removed from a system by a jet of water forced through a narrow nozzle. The lowest pressure possible is the vapour pressure of water.

filtrate The clear liquid obtained by filtration.

filtration The process of separating solid particles using a filter. In vacuum filtration, the liquid is drawn through the filter by a vacuum pump.

fine chemicals Chemicals produced industrially in relatively small quantities and with a high purity; e.g. dyes and drugs.

fineness of gold A measure of the purity of a gold alloy, defined as the parts of gold in 1000 parts of the alloy by mass. Gold with a fineness of 750 contains 75% gold, i.e. 18 *carat gold.

fine structure Closely spaced spectral lines arising from transitions between energy levels that are split by the vibrational or rotational motion of a molecule or by electron spin. They are visible only at high resolution. *Hyperfine structure*, visible only at very high resolution, results from the influence of the atomic nucleus on the allowed energy levels of the atom.

firedamp Methane formed in coal mines.

first-order reaction *See* order.

Fischer–Tropsch process An industrial method of making hydrocarbon fuels from carbon monoxide and hydrogen. The process was invented in 1933 and used by Germany in World War II to produce motor fuel. Hydrogen and carbon monoxide are mixed in the ratio 2:1 (water gas was used with added hydrogen) and passed at 200°C over a nickel or cobalt catalyst. The resulting hydrocarbon mixture can be separated into a higher-boiling fraction for Diesel engines and a lower-boiling gasoline fraction. The gasoline fraction contains a high proportion of straight-chain hydrocarbons and has to be reformed for use in motor fuel. Alcohols, aldehydes, and ketones are also present. The process is also used in the manufacture of SNG from coal. It is named after the German chemist Franz Fischer (1852–1932) and the Czech Hans Tropsch (1839–1935).

fission-track dating A method of estimating the age of glass and other mineral objects by observing the tracks made in them by the fission fragments of the uranium nuclei that they contain. By irradiating the objects with neutrons to induce fission and comparing the density and number of the tracks before and after irradiation it is possible to estimate the time that has elapsed since the object solidified.

Fittig reaction *See* Wurtz reaction

fixation *See* nitrogen fixation.

fixed point A temperature that can be accurately reproduced to enable it to be used as the basis of a *temperature scale.

flame A hot luminous mixture of gases undergoing combustion. The chemical reactions in a flame are mainly free-radical chain reactions and the light comes from fluorescence of excited molecules or ions or from incandescence of small solid particles (e.g. carbon).

flame test A simple test for metals, in which a small amount of the sample (usually moistened with hydrochloric acid) is placed on the end of a platinum wire and held in a Bunsen flame. Certain metals can be detected by the colour produced: barium (green), calcium (brick red), lithium (crimson), potassium (lilac), sodium (yellow), strontium (red).

flash photolysis A technique for studying free-radical reactions in gases. The apparatus used typically consists of a long glass or quartz tube holding the gas, with a lamp outside the tube suitable for producing an intense flash of light. This dissociates molecules in the sample creating free radicals, which can be detected spectroscopically by a beam of light passed down the axis of the tube. It is possible to focus the spectrometer on an absorption line for a particular product and measure its change in intensity with time using an oscilloscope. In this way the kinetics of very fast free-radical gas reactions can be studied.

flash point The temperature at which the vapour above a volatile liquid forms a combustible mixture with air. At the flash point the application of a naked flame gives a momentary flash rather than sustained combustion, for which the temperature is too low.

flavin adenine dinucleotide *See* FAD.

flavonoid One of a group of naturally occurring phenolic compounds many of which are plant pigments. They include the anthocyanins, flavonols, and flavones. Patterns of flavonoid distribution have been used in taxonomic studies of plant species.

flavoprotein *See* FAD.

flint (chert) Very hard dense nodules of microcrystalline quartz and chalcedony found in chalk and limestone.

flocculation The process of aggregating into larger clumps.

flocculent Aggregated in woolly masses; used to describe precipitates.

fluidization A technique used in some industrial processes in which solid particles suspended in a stream of gas are treated as if they were in the liquid state. Fluidization is useful for transporting powders, such as coal dust. *Fluidized beds*, in which solid particles are suspended in an upward stream, are extensively used in the chemical industry, particularly in catalytic reactions where the powdered catalyst has a high surface area.

fluorescein A yellowish-red dye that produces yellow solutions with a green fluorescence. It is used in tracing water flow and as an *absorption indicator.

fluorescence *See* luminescence.

fluoridation The process of adding very small amounts of fluorine salts (e.g. sodium fluoride, NaF) to drinking water to prevent tooth decay.

fluoride *See* halide.

fluorination A chemical reaction in which a fluorine atom is introduced into a molecule. *See* halogenation.

fluorine Symbol F. A poisonous pale yellow gaseous element belonging to group VII of the periodic table (the *halogens); a.n. 9; r.a.m. 18.9984; d. 1.7 $g\,dm^{-3}$; m.p. −219.62°C; b.p. −188.1°C. The main mineral sources are *fluorite (CaF_2) and *cryolite (Na_3AlF). The element is obtained by electrolysis of a molten mixture of potassium fluoride and hydrogen fluoride. It is used in the synthesis of organic fluorine compounds. Chemically, it is the most reactive and electronegative of all elements. It is a highly dangerous compound, causing severe chemical burns on contact with the skin. The element was identified by Scheele in 1771 and first isolated by Moissan in 1886.

fluorite (fluorspar) A mineral form of calcium fluoride, CaF_2, crystallizing in the cubic system. It is variable in colour; the most common fluorites are green and purple (blue john), but other forms are white, yellow, or brown. Fluorite is used chiefly as a flux material in the smelting of iron and steel; it is also used as a source of fluorine and hydrofluoric acid and in the ceramic and optical-glass industries.

fluorite structure *See* calcium fluoride structure.

fluorocarbons Compounds obtained by replacing the hydrogen atoms of hydrocarbons by fluorine atoms. Their high stability to temperature makes them suitable for a variety of uses, including aerosol propellants, oils, polymers, etc. They are often known as *freons*. There has been some concern that their use in aerosols may cause depletion of the ozone layer.

foam A dispersion of bubbles in a liquid. Foams can be stabilized by *surfactants. Solid foams (e.g. expanded polystyrene or foam rubber) are made by foaming the liquid and allowing it to set. *See also* colloid.

folacin *See* folic acid.

folic acid (folacin) A vitamin of the *vitamin B complex. In its active form, tetrahydrofolic acid, it is a *coenzyme in various reactions involved in the metabolism of amino acids, purines, and pyrimidines. It is synthesized by intestinal bacteria and is widespread in food, especially green leafy vegetables. Deficiency causes poor growth and nutritional anaemia.

fool's gold *See* pyrite.

forbidden band *See* energy bands.

forced convection *See* convection.

formaldehyde *See* methanal.

formalin A colourless solution of methanal (formaldehyde) in water with methanol as a stabilizer; r.d. 1.075–1.085. When kept at temperatures below 25°C a white polymer of methanal separates out. It is used as a disinfectant and preservative for biological specimens.

formate *See* methanoate.

formic acid *See* methanoic acid.

formula A way of representing a chemical compound using symbols for the atoms present. Subscripts are used for the numbers of atoms. The *molecular formula* simply gives the types and numbers of atoms present. For example, the molecular formula of ethanoic acid is $C_2H_4O_2$. The *empirical formula* gives the atoms in their simplest ratio; for ethanoic acid it is CH_2O. The *structural formula* gives an indication of the way the atoms are arranged. Commonly, this is done by dividing the formula into groups; ethanoic acid can be written $CH_3.CO.OH$ (or more usually simply CH_3COOH). Structural formulae can also show the arrangement of atoms or groups in space.

formula weight The relative molecular mass of a compound as calculated from its molecular formula.

formyl group The group HCO–.

Fortin barometer *See* barometer.

fossil fuel Coal, oil, and natural gas, the fuels used by man as a source of energy. They are formed from the remains of living organisms and all have a high carbon or hydrogen content. Their value as fuels relies on the exothermic oxidation of carbon to form carbon dioxide ($C + O_2 \rightarrow CO_2$) and the oxidation of hydrogen to form water ($H_2 + \frac{1}{2}O_2 \rightarrow H_2O$).

fraction *See* fractional distillation.

fractional crystallization A method of separating a mixture of soluble solids by dissolving them in a suitable hot solvent and then lowering the temperature slowly. The least soluble component will crystallize out first, leaving the other components in solution. By controlling the temperature, it is sometimes possible to remove each component in turn.

fractional distillation (fractionation) The separation of a mixture of liquids by distillation. Effective separation can be achieved by using a long vertical column (*fractionating column*) attached to the distillation vessel and filled with glass beads. Vapour from the liquid rises up the column until it condenses and runs back into the vessel. The rising vapour in the column flows over the descending liquid, and eventually a steady state is reached in which there is a decreasing temperature gradient up the column. The vapour in the column has more volatile components towards the top and less volatile components at the bottom. Various *fractions* of the mixture can be drawn off at points on the column. Industrially, fractional distillation is performed in large towers containing many perforated trays. It is used extensively in petroleum refining.

fractionating column *See* fractional distillation.

fractionation *See* fractional distillation.

francium Symbol Fr. A radioactive element belonging to *group I of the periodic table; a.n. 87; r.d. 2.4; m.p. 27±1°C; b.p. 677±1°C. The element is found in uranium and thorium ores. All 22 known isotopes are radioactive, the most stable being francium-223. The existence of francium was confirmed by Marguerite Perey in 1939.

Frasch process A method of obtaining sulphur from underground deposits using a tube consisting of three concentric pipes. Superheated steam is passed down the outer pipe to melt the sulphur, which is forced up through the middle pipe by compressed air fed through the inner tube. The steam in the outer casing keeps the sulphur molten in the pipe.

Fraunhofer lines Dark lines in the solar spectrum that result from the absorption by elements in the solar chromosphere of some of the wavelengths of the visible radiation emitted by the hot interior of the sun.

free electron *See* electron.

free energy A measure of a system's ability to do work. The *Gibbs free energy* (or *Gibbs function*), G, is defined by $G = H - TS$, where G is the energy liberated or absorbed in a reversible process at constant pressure and constant temperature (T), H is the *enthalpy and S the *entropy of the system. Changes in Gibbs free energy, ΔG, are useful in indicating the conditions under which a chemical reaction will occur. If ΔG is positive the reaction will only occur if energy is supplied to force it away from the equilibrium position (i.e. when $\Delta G = 0$). If ΔG is negative the reaction will proceed spontaneously to equilibrium.

The *Helmholtz free energy* (or *Helmholtz function*), F, is defined by $F = U - TS$, where U is the *internal energy. For a reversible isothermal process, ΔF represents the useful work available.

free radical An atom or group of atoms with an unpaired valence electron. Free radicals can be produced by photolysis or pyrolysis in which a bond is broken without forming ions (*see* homolytic fission). Because of their free valency, most free radicals are extremely reactive. *See also* chain reaction.

freeze drying A process used in dehydrating food, blood plasma, and other heat-sensitive substances. The product is deep-frozen and the ice trapped in it is removed by reducing the pressure and causing it to sublime. The water vapour is then removed, leaving an undamaged dry product.

freezing mixture A mixture of components that produces a low temperature. For example, a mixture of ice and sodium chloride gives a temperature of −20°C.

freons *See* fluorocarbons.

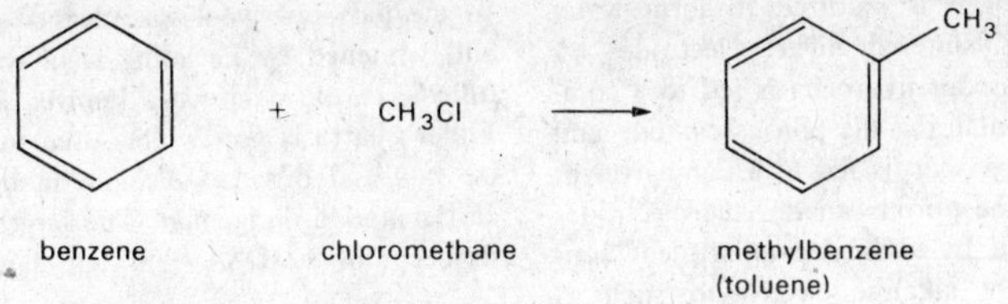

Friedel–Crafts methylation

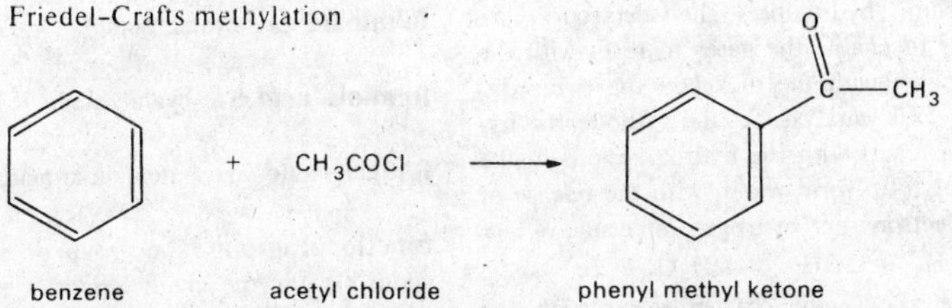

Friedel–Crafts acetylation

Friedel–Crafts reaction A type of reaction in which an alkyl group (from a haloalkane) or an acyl group (from an acyl halide) is substituted on a benzene ring. The product is an alkylbenzene (for alkyl substitution) or an alkyl aryl ketone (for acyl substitution). The reactions occur at high temperature (about 100°C) with an aluminium chloride catalyst. The catalyst acts as an electron acceptor for a lone pair on the halide atom. This polarizes the haloalkane or acyl halide, producing a positive charge on the alkyl or acyl group. The mechanism is then electrophilic substitution. Alcohols and alkenes can also undergo Friedel–Crafts reactions. The reaction is named after the French chemist Charles Friedel (1832–99) and the US chemist James M. Craft (1839–1917).

froth flotation A method of separating mixtures of solids, used industrially for separating ores from the unwanted gangue. The mixture is ground to a powder and water and a frothing agent added. Air is blown through the water. With a suitable frothing agent, the bubbles adhere only to particles of ore and carry them to the surface, leaving the gangue particles at the bottom.

fructose (fruit sugar; laevulose) A simple sugar, $C_6H_{12}O_6$, stereoisomeric with glucose. (Although natural fructose is the D-form, it is in fact laevorotatory.) Fructose occurs in green plants, fruits, and honey and tastes sweeter than sucrose (cane sugar), of which it is a constituent. Derivatives of fructose are important in the energy metabolism of living organisms. Some polysaccharide derivatives (fructans) are carbohydrate energy stores in certain plants.

fruit sugar *See* fructose.

fuel A substance that is oxidized or otherwise changed in a furnace or heat engine to release useful heat or energy. For this purpose wood, vegetable oil, and animal products have largely been replaced by *fossil fuels since the 18th century.

The limited supply of fossil fuels and the expense of extracting them from the earth has encouraged the development of nuclear fuels to produce electricity (*see* nuclear energy).

fuel cell A cell in which the chemical energy of a fuel is converted directly into electrical energy. The simplest fuel cell is one in which hydrogen is oxidized to form water over porous sintered nickel electrodes. A supply of gaseous hydrogen is fed to a compartment containing the porous cathode and a supply of oxygen is fed to a compartment containing the porous anode; the electrodes are separated by a third compartment containing a hot alkaline electrolyte, such as potassium hydroxide. The electrodes are porous to enable the gases to react with the electrolyte, with the nickel in the electrodes acting as a catalyst. At the cathode the hydrogen reacts with the hydroxide ions in the electrolyte to form water, with the release of two electrons per hydrogen molecule:

$$H_2 + 2OH^- \rightarrow 2H_2O + 2e^-$$

At the anode, the oxygen reacts with the water, taking up electrons, to form hydroxide ions:

$$\tfrac{1}{2}O_2 + H_2O + 2e^- \rightarrow 2OH^-$$

The electrons flow from the cathode to the anode through an external circuit as an electric current. The device is a more efficient converter of electric energy than a heat engine, but it is bulky and requires a continuous supply of gaseous fuels. Their use to power electric vehicles is being actively explored.

fugacity Symbol *f*. A thermodynamic function used in place of partial pressure in reactions involving real gases and mixtures. For a component of a mixture, it is defined by $d\mu = RTd(\ln f)$, where μ is the chemical potential. It has the same units as pressure and the fugacity of a gas is equal to the pressure if the gas is ideal. The fugacity of a liquid or solid is the fugacity of the vapour with which it is in equilibrium. The ratio of the fugacity to the fugacity in some standard state is the *activity. For a gas, the standard state is chosen to be the state at which the fugacity is 1. The activity then equals the fugacity.

fuller's earth A naturally occurring clay material (chiefly montmorillonite) that has the property of decolorizing oil and grease. In the past raw wool was cleaned of grease and whitened by kneading it in water with fuller's earth; a process known as *fulling*. Fuller's earth is now widely used to decolorize fats and oils and also as an insecticide carrier and drilling mud. The largest deposits occur in the USA, UK, and Japan.

fulminate *See* cyanic acid.

fulminic acid *See* cyanic acid.

fumaric acid *See* butenedioic acid.

functional group The group of atoms responsible for the characteristic reactions of a compound. The functional group is –OH for alcohols, –CHO for aldehydes, –COOH for carboxylic acids, etc.

fundamental constants (universal constants) Those parameters that do not change throughout the universe. The charge on an electron, the speed of light in free space, the Planck constant, the gravitational constant, the electric constant, and the magnetic constant are all thought to be examples.

fundamental units A set of independently defined *units of measurement that forms the basis of a system of units. Such a set requires three mechanical units (usually of length, mass, and time) and one electrical unit; it has also been found convenient to treat certain other quantities as fundamental, even though they are not strictly independent. In the metric system the centimetre–gram–second (c.g.s.) system was replaced by the metre–kilogram–second (m.k.s.) system; the latter has now been adapted to provide the basis for *SI units. In British Imperial units the foot–pound–second (f.p.s.) system was formerly used.

furan A colourless liquid compound, C_4H_4O; r.d. 0.94; m.p. –86°C; b.p. 31.4°C.

It has a five-membered ring consisting of four CH_2 groups and one oxygen atom.

furanose A *sugar having a five-membered ring containing four carbon atoms and one oxygen atom.

fused ring *See* ring.

fusible alloys Alloys that melt at low temperature (around 100°C). They have a number of uses, including constant-temperature baths, pipe bending, and automatic sprinklers to provide a spray of water to prevent fires from spreading. Fusible alloys are usually *eutectic mixtures of bismuth, lead, tin, and cadmium. Wood's metal and Lipowitz's alloy are examples of alloys that melt at about 70°C.

fusion 1. Melting. **2.** *See* nuclear fusion.

G

gadolinium Symbol Gd. A soft silvery metallic element belonging to the *lanthanoids; a.n. 64; r.a.m. 157.25; r.d. 7.901 (20°C); m.p. 1312°C; b.p. 3273°C. It occurs in gadolinite, xenotime, monazite, and residues from uranium ores. There are seven stable natural isotopes and eleven artificial isotopes are known. Two of the natural isotopes, gadolinium–155 and gadolinium–157, are the best neutron absorbers of all the elements. The metal has found limited applications in nuclear technology and in ferromagnetic alloys (with cobalt, copper, iron, and cerium). It was discovered by J. C. G. Marignac in 1880.

galactose A simple sugar, $C_6H_{12}O_6$, stereoisomeric with glucose, that occurs naturally as one of the products of the enzymic digestion of milk sugar (lactose) and as a constituent of gum arabic.

galena A mineral form of lead(II) sulphide, PbS, crystallizing in the cubic system; the chief ore of lead. It usually occurs as grey metallic cubes, frequently in association with silver, arsenic, copper, zinc, and antimony. Important deposits occur in Australia (at Broken Hill), Germany, the USA (especially in Missouri, Kansas, and Oklahoma), and the UK.

gallium Symbol Ga. A soft silvery metallic element belonging to group IIIA of the periodic table; a.n. 31; r.a.m. 69.72; r.d. 5.90 (20°C); m.p. 29.78°C; b.p. 2403°C. It occurs in zinc blende, bauxite, and kaolin, from which it can be extracted by fractional electrolysis. It also occurs in gallite, $CuGaS_2$, to an extent of 1%; although bauxite only contains 0.01% this is the only commercial source. The two stable isotopes are gallium–69 and gallium–71; there are eight radioactive isotopes, all with short half-lives. The metal has only a few minor uses (e.g. as an activator in luminous paints), but gallium arsenide is extensively used as a semiconductor in many applications. Gallium corrodes most other metals because it rapidly diffuses into their lattices. Most gallium(I) and some gallium(II) compounds are unstable. The element was first identified by François Lecoq de Boisbaudran in 1875.

galvanized iron Iron or steel that has been coated with a layer of zinc to protect it from corrosion. Corrugated mild-steel sheets for roofing and mild-steel sheets for dustbins, etc., are usually galvanized by dipping them in molten zinc. The formation of a brittle zinc–iron alloy is prevented by the addition of small quantities of aluminium or magnesium. Wire is often galvanized by a cold electrolytic process as no alloy forms in this process. Galvanizing is an effective method of protecting steel because even if the surface is scratched, the zinc still protects the underlying metal. *See* sacrificial protection.

gamma-iron *See* iron.

gamma radiation Electromagnetic radiation emitted by excited atomic nuclei during the process of passing to a lower excitation state. Gamma radiation ranges in energy from about 10^{-15} to 10^{-11} joule (10 keV to 100 MeV) corresponding to a wavelength range of about 10^{-10} to 10^{-14} metre. A common source of gamma radiation is cobalt-60, the decay process of which is:

$$^{60}_{27}Co \rightarrow {}^{60}_{28}Ni \rightarrow Ni$$

The de-excitation of nickel-60 is accompanied by the emission of a gamma-ray photon having an energy of 1.87×10^{-13} J (1.17 MeV).

gangue Rock and other waste material present in an ore.

garnet Any of a group of silicate minerals that conform to the general formula $A_3B_2(SiO_4)_3$. The elements representing A may include magnesium, calcium, manganese, and iron(II); those representing B may include aluminium, iron(III), chromium, or titanium. Six varieties of garnet are generally recognized:
pyrope, $Mg_3Al_2Si_3O_{12}$;
almandine, $Fe^{2+}_3Al_2Si_3O_{12}$;
spessartite, $Mn_3Al_2Si_3O_{12}$;
grossularite, $Ca_3Al_2Si_3O_{12}$;
andradite, $Ca_3(Fe^{3+},Ti)_2Si_3O_{12}$;
and uvarovite, $Ca_3Cr_2Si_3O_{12}$.
Varieties of garnet are used as gemstones and abrasives.

gas A state of matter in which the matter concerned occupies the whole of its container irrespective of its quantity. In an *ideal gas, which obeys the *gas laws exactly, the molecules themselves would have a negligible volume and negligible forces between them, and collisions between molecules would be perfectly elastic. In practice, however, the behaviour of real gases deviates from the gas laws because their molecules occupy a finite volume, there are small forces between molecules, and in polyatomic gases collisions are to a certain extent inelastic (*see* equation of state).

gas chromatography A technique for separating or analysing mixtures of gases by *chromatography. The apparatus consists of a very long tube containing the stationary phase. This may be a solid, such as kieselguhr (*gas–solid chromatography*, or *GSC*), or a nonvolatile liquid, such as a hydrocarbon oil coated on a solid support (*gas–liquid chromatography*, or *GLC*). The sample is often a volatile liquid mixture, which is vaporized and swept through the column by a carrier gas (e.g. hydrogen). The components of the mixture pass through the column at different rates and are detected as they leave, either by measuring the thermal conductivity of the gas or by a flame detector.

Gas chromatography is usually used for analysis; components can be identified by the time they take to pass through the column. It is sometimes also used for separating mixtures.

gas constant (universal molar gas constant) Symbol *R*. The constant that appears in the *universal gas equation* (*see* gas laws). It has the value 8.314 34 J K^{-1} mol^{-1}.

gas equation *See* gas laws.

gas laws Laws relating the temperature, pressure, and volume of an *ideal gas. *Boyle's law states that the pressure (p) of a specimen is inversely proportional to the volume (V) at constant temperature (pV = constant). The modern equivalent of *Charles' law states that the volume is directly proportional to the thermodynamic temperature (T) at constant pressure (V/T = constant); originally this law stated the constant expansivity of a gas kept at constant pressure. The pressure law states that the pressure is directly proportional to the thermodynamic temperature for a specimen kept at constant volume. The three laws can be combined in the *universal gas equation*, $pV = nRT$, where n is the amount of gas in the specimen and R is the *gas constant. The gas laws were first established experimentally for real gases, although they are obeyed by real gases to only a limited extent; they are obeyed best at high temperatures and low pressures. *See also* equation of state.

gasoline *See* petroleum.

gas thermometer A device for measuring temperature in which the working fluid is a gas. It provides the most accurate method of measuring temperatures in the range 2.5 to 1337 K. Using a fixed mass of gas a *constant-volume thermometer* measures the pressure of a fixed volume of gas at relevant temperatures, usually by means of a mercury manometer and a barometer.

Gattermann reaction A variation of the *Sandmeyer reaction for preparing chloro- or bromoarenes by reaction of the diazonium compound. In the Gattermann reaction the aromatic amine is added to sodium nitrite and the halogen acid (10°C), then fresh copper powder (e.g. from Zn + $CuSO_4$) is added and the solution warmed. The diazonium salt then forms the haloarene, e.g.

$$C_6H_5N_2^+Cl^- \rightarrow C_6H_5Cl + N_2$$

The copper acts as a catalyst. The reaction is easier to perform than the Sandmeyer reaction and takes place at lower temperature, but generally gives lower yields. It was discovered in 1890 by the German chemist Ludwig Gattermann (1860–1920).

gauche conformation *See* conformation.

Gay Lussac's law 1. When gases combine chemically the volumes of the reactants and the volume of the product, if it is gaseous, bear simple relationships to each other when measured under the same conditions of temperature and pressure. The law was first stated in 1808 by J. L. Gay Lussac (1778–1850) and led to *Avogadro's law. **2.** *See* Charles' law.

gaylussite A mineral consisting of a hydrated mixed carbonate of sodium and calcium, $Na_2CO_3.CaCO_3.5H_2O$.

Geiger counter (Geiger–Müller counter) A device used to detect and measure ionizing radiation. It consists of a tube containing a low-pressure gas (usually argon or neon and methane) and a cylindrical hollow cathode through the centre of which runs a fine-wire anode. A potential difference of about 1000 volts is maintained between the electrodes. An ionizing particle or photon passing through a window into the tube will cause an ion to be produced and the high p.d. will accelerate it towards its appropriate electrode, causing an avalanche of further ionizations by collision. The consequent current pulses can be counted in electronic circuits or simply amplified to work a small loudspeaker in the instrument. It was first devised in 1908 by Hans Geiger (1882–1947). Geiger and W. Müller produced an improved design in 1928.

gel A lyophilic *colloid that has coagulated to a rigid or jelly-like solid. In a gel, the disperse medium has formed a loosely-held network of linked molecules through the dispersion medium. Examples of gels are silica gel and gelatin.

gelatin(e) A colourless or pale yellow water-soluble protein obtained by boiling collagen with water and evaporating the solution. It swells when water is added and dissolves in hot water to form a solution that sets to a gel on cooling. It is used in photographic emulsions and adhesives, and in jellies and other foodstuffs.

gel filtration A type of column *chromatography in which a mixture of liquids is passed down a column containing a gel.

Small molecules in the mixture can enter pores in the gel and move slowly down the column; large molecules, which cannot enter the pores, move more quickly. Thus, mixtures of molecules can be separated on the basis of their size. The technique is used particularly for separating proteins but it can also be applied to other polymers and to cell nuclei, viruses, etc.

gelignite A high explosive made from nitroglycerin, cellulose nitrate, sodium nitrate, and wood pulp.

gem Designating molecules in which two functional groups are attached to the same atom in a molecule. For example, chloral hydrate, $CCl_3CH(OH)_2$, is a gem diol in which both hydroxyl groups are on the same carbon atom.

geochemistry The scientific study of the chemical composition of the earth. It includes the study of the abundance of the earth's elements and their isotopes and the distribution of the elements in environments of the earth (lithosphere, atmosphere, biosphere, and hydrosphere).

geometrical isomerism *See* isomerism.

geraniol An alcohol, $C_9H_{15}CH_2OH$, present in a number of essential oils.

germanium Symbol Ge. A lustrous hard metalloid element belonging to group IV of the periodic table; a.n. 32; r.a.m. 72.59; r.d. 5.36; m.p. 937°C; b.p. 2830°C. It is found in zinc sulphide and in certain other sulphide ores, and is mainly obtained as a by-product of zinc smelting. It is also present in some coal (up to 1.6%). Small amounts are used in specialized alloys but the main use depends on its semiconductor properties. Chemically, it forms compounds in the +2 and +4 oxidation states, the germanium(IV) compounds being the more stable. The element also forms a large number of organometallic compounds. Predicted in 1871 by Mendeleev (eka-silicon), it was discovered by Winkler in 1886.

German silver (nickel silver) An alloy of copper, zinc, and nickel, often in the proportions 5:2:2. It resembles silver in appearance and is used in cheap jewellery and cutlery and as a base for silver-plated wire. *See also* electrum.

Gibbs free energy (Gibbs function) *See* free energy. It is named after the US chemist J. W. Gibbs (1839–1903).

gibbsite A mineral form of hydrated *aluminium hydroxide ($Al(OH)_3$). It is named after the US mineralogist George Gibbs (d. 1833).

giga- Symbol G. A prefix used in the metric system to denote one thousand million times. For example, 10^9 joules = 1 gigajoule (GJ).

glacial ethanoic (*or* acetic) acid *See* ethanoic acid.

glass Any noncrystalline solid; i.e. a solid in which the atoms are random and have no long-range ordered pattern. Glasses are often regarded as supercooled liquids. Characteristically they have no definite melting point, but soften over a range of temperatures.

The common glass used in windows, bottles, etc., is *soda glass*, which is made by heating a mixture of lime (calcium oxide), soda (sodium carbonate), and sand (silicon (IV) oxide). It is a form of calcium silicate. Borosilicate glasses (e.g. *Pyrex*) are made by incorporating some boron oxide, so that silicon atoms are replaced by boron atoms. They are tougher than soda glass and more resistant to temperature changes, hence their use in cooking utensils and laboratory apparatus. Glasses for special purposes (e.g. optical glass) have other elements added (e.g. barium, lead).

glass electrode A type of *half cell having a glass bulb containing an acidic solution of fixed pH, into which dips a platinum wire. The glass bulb is thin enough for hydrogen ions to diffuse through. If the bulb is placed in a solution containing hydrogen ions, the electrode potential depends on the hydrogen-ion concentration. Glass electrodes are used in pH measurement.

glass fibres Melted glass drawn into thin fibres some 0.005 mm–0.01 mm in diameter. The fibres may be spun into threads and woven into fabrics, which are then impregnated with resins to give a material that is both strong and corrosion resistant for use in car bodies and boat building.

glauberite A mineral consisting of a mixed sulphate of sodium and calcium, $Na_2SO_4.CaSO_4$.

Glauber's salt *Sodium sulphate decahydrate, $Na_2SO_4.10H_2O$, used as a laxative. It is named after J. R. Glauber (1604–68).

GLC (gas–liquid chromatography) *See* gas chromatography.

globulin Any of a group of globular proteins that are generally insoluble in water and present in blood, eggs, milk, and as a reserve protein in seeds. Blood serum globulins comprise four types: α_1-, α_2-, and β-globulins, which serve as carrier proteins; and γ-globulins, which include the immunoglobulins responsible for immune responses.

gluconic acid An optically active hydroxycarboxylic acid, $CH_2(OH)(CHOH)_4COOH$. It is the carboxylic acid corresponding to the aldose sugar glucose, and can be made by the action of certain moulds.

glucose (dextrose; grape sugar) A white crystalline sugar, $C_6H_{12}O_6$, occurring widely in nature. Like other *monosaccharides, glucose is optically active: most naturally occurring glucose is dextrorotatory. Glucose and its derivatives are crucially important in the energy metabolism of living organisms. Glucose is also a constituent of many polysaccharides, most notably starch and cellulose. These yield glucose when broken down, for example by enzymes during digestion.

glutamic acid *See* amino acid.

glutamine *See* amino acid.

glyceride (acylglycerol) A fatty-acid ester of glycerol. Esterification can occur at one, two, or all three hydroxyl groups of the glycerol molecule producing mono-, di-, and triglycerides respectively. *Triglycerides are the major constituent of fats and oils found in living organisms. Alternatively, one of the hydroxyl groups may be esterified with a phosphate group forming a phosphoglyceride (*see* phospholipid) or to a sugar forming a *glycolipid*.

glycerine *See* glycerol.

glycerol (glycerine; propane-1,2,3,-triol) A trihydric alcohol, $HOCH_2CH(OH)CH_2OH$. Glycerol is a colourless sweet-tasting viscous liquid, miscible with water but insoluble in ether. It is widely distributed in all living organisms as a constituent of the *glycerides, which yield glycerol when hydrolysed.

glycine *See* amino acid.

glycogen (animal starch) A *polysaccharide consisting of a highly branched polymer of glucose occurring in animal tissues, especially in liver and muscle cells. It is the major store of carbohydrate energy in animal cells and is present as granular clusters of minute particles.

glycol *See* ethane-1,2-diol.

glycolipid *See* glyceride.

goethite A yellow-brown mineral, FeO.OH, crystallizing in the orthorhombic system. It is formed as a result of the oxidation and hydration of iron minerals or as a direct precipitate from marine or fresh water (e.g. in swamps and bogs). Most *limonite is composed largely of cryptocrystalline goethite. Goethite is mined as an ore of iron.

gold Symbol Au. A soft yellow malleable metallic *transition element; a.n. 79; r.a.m. 196.967; r.d. 19.32; m.p. 1064.43°C; b.p. 2807±2°C. It is found as the free metal in gravel or in quartz veins, and is also present in some lead and copper sulphide ores. It also occurs combined with silver in the telluride sylvanite, $(Ag,Au)Te_2$. It is used in jewellery, dentistry, and electronic devices. Chemically, it is unreactive, being unaffected by oxygen. It reacts with chlorine at 200°C to form gold(III) chloride. It forms a number of complexes with gold in the +1 and +3 oxidation states.

Goldschmidt process A method of extracting metals by reducing the oxide with aluminium powder, e.g.

$$Cr_2O_3 + 2Al \rightarrow 2Cr + Al_2O_3$$

The reaction can also be used to produce molten iron (*see* thermite). It was discovered by the German chemist Hans Goldschmidt (1861–1923).

Gooch crucible A porcelain dish with a perforated base over which a layer of asbestos is placed, used for filtration in gravimetric analysis.

graft copolymer *See* polymer.

Graham's law The rates at which gases diffuse is inversely proportional to the square roots of their densities. This principle is made use of in the diffusion method of separating isotopes. The law was formulated in 1829 by Thomas Graham (1805–69).

gram Symbol g. One thousandth of a kilogram. The gram is the fundamental unit of mass in *c.g.s. units and was formerly used in such units as the *gram-atom*, *gram-molecule*, and *gram-equivalent*, which have now been replaced by the *mole.

graphite *See* carbon.

gravimetric analysis A type of quantitative analysis that depends on weighing. For instance, the amount of silver in a solution of silver salts could be measured by adding excess hydrochloric acid to precipitate silver chloride, filtering the precipitate, washing, drying, and weighing.

gray Symbol Gy. The derived SI unit of absorbed *dose of ionizing radiation (*see* radiation units). It is named after the British radiobiologist L. H. Gray (1905–65).

greenockite A mineral form of cadmium sulphide, CdS.

green vitriol *See* iron(II) sulphate.

Grignard reagents A class of organometallic compounds of magnesium, with the general formula RMgX, where R is an organic group and X a halogen atom (e.g. CH_3MgCl, C_2H_5MgBr, etc.). They actually have the structure $R_2Mg.MgCl_2$, and can be made by reacting a haloalkane with magnesium in ether; they are rarely isolated but are extensively used in organic synthesis, when they are made in one reaction mixture. Grignard reagents have a number of reactions that make them useful in organic synthesis. With methanal they give a primary alcohol

$CH_3MgCl + HCHO \rightarrow CH_3CH_2OH$

Other aldehydes give a secondary alcohol

$CH_3CHO + CH_3MgCl \rightarrow (CH_3)_2CHOH$

With alcohols, hydrocarbons are formed

$CH_3MgCl + C_2H_5OH \rightarrow C_2H_5CH_3$

Water also gives a hydrocarbon

$CH_3MgCl + H_2O \rightarrow CH_4$

The compounds are named after their discoverer, the French chemist F. A. V. Grignard (1871–1935).

ground state The lowest stable energy state of a system, such as a molecule, atom, or nucleus. *See* energy level.

group (in chemistry) *See* periodic table.

group 0 elements *See* noble gases.

group I elements A group of elements in the *periodic table, divided into two subgroups: group IA (the main group, *see* alkali metals) and group IB. Group IB consists of the *coinage metals, copper, silver, and gold, which are usually classified with the *transition elements.

group II elements A group of elements in the *periodic table, divided into two subgroups: group IIA (the main group, *see* alkaline-earth metals) and group IIB. Group IIB consists of the three metals zinc (Zn), cadmium (Cd), and mercury (Hg), which have two *s*-electrons outside filled *d*-subshells. Moreover, none of their compounds have unfilled *d*-levels, and the metals are regarded as nontransition elements. They are sometimes called the *zinc group*. Zinc and cadmium are relatively electropositive metals, forming compounds containing divalent ions Zn^{2+} or Cd^{2+}. Mercury is more unreactive and also unusual in forming mercury(I) compounds, which contain the ion Hg_2^{2+}.

group III elements A group of elements in the *periodic table, divided into subgroup IIIB (the main group) and subgroup IIIA. The IIIA subgroup consists of scandium (Sc), yttrium (Y), and lanthanum (La), which are generally classified with the *lanthanoids, and actinium (Ac), generally classified with the *actinoids. The term *group III elements* usually refers to the main-group elements: boron (B), aluminium (Al), gallium (Ga), indium (In), and thallium (Tl), which all have outer electronic configurations ns^2np^1 with no partly filled inner levels. They are the first members of the *p*-block. The group differs from the alkali metals and alkaline-earth metals in displaying a considerable variation in properties as the group is descended.

Boron has a small atomic radius and a relatively high ionization energy. In consequence its chemistry is largely covalent and it is generally classed as a metalloid. It forms a large number of volatile hydrides, some of which have the uncommon bonding characteristic of *electron-deficient compounds. It also forms a weakly acidic oxide. In some ways, boron resembles silicon (*see* diagonal relationship).

As the group is descended, atomic radii increase and ionization energies are all lower than for boron. There is an increase in polar interactions and the formation of distinct M^{3+} ions. This increase in metallic character is clearly illustrated by the increasing basic character of the hydroxides: boron hydroxide is acidic, aluminium and gallium hydroxides are amphoteric, indium hydroxide is basic, and thallium forms only the oxide. As the elements of group III have a vacant *p*-orbital they display many electron-acceptor properties. For example, many boron compounds form adducts with donors such as ammonia and organic amines (acting as Lewis acids). A large number of complexes of the type $[BF_4]^-$, $[AlCl_4]^-$, $[InCl_4]^-$, $[TlI_4]^-$ are known and the heavier members can expand their coordination numbers to six as in $[AlF_6]^{3-}$ and $[TlCl_6]^{3-}$. This acceptor property is also seen in bridged dimers of the type Al_2Cl_6. Another feature of group III is the increasing stability of the monovalent state down the group. The electron configuration ns^2np^1 suggests that only one electron could be lost or shared in forming compounds. In fact, for the lighter members of the group the energy required to promote an electron from the *s*-subshell to a vacant *p*-subshell is small. It is more than compensated for by the resulting energy gain in forming three bonds rather than one. This energy gain is less important for the heavier members of the group. Thus, aluminium forms compounds of the type AlCl in the gas phase at high temperatures. Gallium similarly forms such compounds and gallium(I) oxide (Ga_2O) can be isolated. Indium has a number of known indium(I) compounds (e.g. InCl, In_2O, $In^I[In^{III}Cl_6]$). Thallium has stable monovalent compounds. In aqueous solution, thallium(I) compounds are more stable than the corresponding thallium (III) compounds. *See* inert-pair effect.

group IV elements A group of elements in the *periodic table, divided into subgroup IVB (the main group) and subgroup IVA. The IVA subgroup consists of titanium (Ti), zirconium (Zr), and hafnium (Hf), which are generally classified with the *transition elements. The term *group IV elements* usually refers to the main-group elements: carbon (C), silicon (Si), germanium (Ge), tin (Sn), and lead (Pb), which all have outer electronic configurations ns^2np^2 with no partly filled inner levels.

The main valency of the elements is 4, and the members of the group show a variation from nonmetallic to metallic behaviour in moving down the group. Thus, carbon is a nonmetal and forms an acidic oxide (CO_2) and a neutral oxide. Carbon compounds are mostly covalent. One allotrope (diamond) is an insulator, although graphite is a fairly good conductor. Silicon and germanium are metalloids, having semiconductor properties. Tin is a metal, but does have a nonmetallic allotrope (grey tin). Lead is definitely a metal. Another feature of the group is the tendency to form divalent compounds as the size of the atom increases. Thus carbon has only the highly reactive carbenes. Silicon forms analogous silylenes. Germanium has an unstable hydroxide (Ge$(OH)_2$), a sulphide (GeS), and halides. The sulphide and halides disproportionate to germanium and the germanium(IV) compound. Tin has a number of tin(II) compounds, which are moderately reducing, being oxidized to the tin(IV) compound. Lead has a stable lead(II) state. *See* inert-pair effect.

In general, the reactivity of the elements increases down the group from carbon to lead. All react with oxygen on heating. The first four form the dioxide; lead forms the monoxide (i.e. lead(II) oxide, PbO). Similarly, all will react with chlorine to form the tetrachloride (in the case of the first four) or the dichloride (for lead). Carbon is the only one capable of reacting directly with hydrogen. The hydrides all exist from the stable methane (CH_4) to the unstable plumbane (PbH_4).

group V elements A group of elements in the *periodic table, divided into subgroup VB (the main group) and subgroup VA. The VA subgroup consists of vanadium (V), niobium (Nb), and tantalum (Ta), which are generally classified with the *transition elements. The term *group V elements* usually refers to the main-group elements: nitrogen (N), phosphorus (P), arsenic (As), antimony (Sb), and bismuth (Bi), which all have outer electronic configurations ns^2np^3 with no partly filled inner levels.

The lighter elements (N and P) are nonmetals; the heavier elements are metalloids. The lighter elements are electronegative in character and have fairly large ionization energies. Nitrogen has a valency of 3 and tends to form covalent compounds. The other elements have available *d*-sublevels and can promote an *s*-electron into one of these to form compounds with the V oxidation state. Thus, they have two oxides

P_2O_3, P_2O_5, Sb_2O_3, Sb_2O_5, etc. In the case of bismuth, the pentoxide Bi_2O_5 is difficult to prepare and unstable – an example of the increasing stability of the III oxidation state in going from phosphorus to bismuth. The oxides also show how there is increasing metallic (electropositive) character down the group. Nitrogen and phosphorus have oxides that are either neutral (N_2O, NO) or acidic. Bismuth trioxide (Bi_2O_3) is basic. Bismuth is the only member of the group that forms a well-characterized positive ion Bi^{3+}.

group VI elements A group of elements in the *periodic table, divided into group VIB (the main group) and group VIA. The VIA subgroup consists of chromium (Cr), molybdenum (Mo), and tungsten (W), which are generally classified with the *transition elements. The term *group VI elements* usually refers to the main-group elements: oxygen (O), sulphur (S), selenium (Se), tellurium (Te), and polonium (Po), which all have outer electronic configurations ns^2np^4 with no partly filled inner levels. They are also called the *chalcogens*.

The configurations are just two electrons short of the configuration of a noble gas and the elements are characteristically electronegative and almost entirely nonmetallic. Ionization energies are high, (O 1314 to Po 813 kJ mol^{-1}) and monatomic cations are not known. Polyatomic cations do exist, e.g. O_2^+, S_8^{2+}, Se_8^{2+}, Te_4^{2+}. Electronegativity decreases down the group but the nearest approach to metallic character is the occurrence of 'metallic' allotropes of selenium, tellurium, and polonium along with some metalloid properties, in particular, marked photoconductivity. The elements of group VI combine with a wide range of other elements and the bonding is largely covalent. The elements all form hydrides of the type XH_2. Apart from water, these materials are all toxic foul-smelling gases; they show decreasing thermal stability with increasing relative atomic mass of X. The hydrides dissolve in water to give very weak acids (acidity increases down the group). Oxygen forms the additional hydride H_2O_2 (hydrogen peroxide), but sulphur forms a range of sulphanes, such as H_2S_2, H_2S_4, H_2S_6.

Oxygen forms the fluorides O_2F_2 and OF_2, both powerful fluorinating agents; sulphur forms analogous fluorides along with some higher fluorides, S_2S_2, SF_2, SF_4, SF_6, S_2F_{10}. Selenium and tellurium form only the higher fluorides MF_4 and MF_6; this is in contrast to the formation of lower valence states by heavier elements observed in groups III, IV, and V. The chlorides are limited to M_2Cl_2 and MCl_4; the bromides are similar except that sulphur only forms S_2Br_2. All metallic elements form oxides and sulphides and many form selenides.

group VII elements A group of elements in the *periodic table divided into two subgroups: group VIIA and group VIIB. Group VIIB is the main group (*see* halogens) and group VIIA consists of the elements manganese (Mn), technetium (Tc), and rhenium (Re), which are usually classified with the *transition elements.

group VIII elements A group of nine elements in the *periodic table consisting of the *platinum metals – cobalt (Co), rhodium (Rh), iridium (Ir), nickel (Ni), palladium (Pd), and platinum (Pt) – together with iron (Fe), ruthenium (Ru), and osmium (Os). These metals are now classified with the *transition elements.

GSC (gas–solid chromatography) *See* gas chromatography.

guanidine A crystalline basic compound $HN{:}C(NH_2)_2$, related to urea.

guanine A *purine derivative. It is one of the major component bases of *nucleotides and the nucleic acids *DNA and *RNA.

gum Any of a variety of substances obtained from plants. Typically they are insoluble in organic solvents but form gelatinous or sticky solutions with water. Gum resins are mixtures of gums and natural resins. Gums are produced by the young xylem vessels of some plants (mainly trees) in response to wounding or pruning. The exudate hardens when it reaches the plant surface and thus provides a temporary protective seal while the cells below divide to form a permanent repair. Excessive gum formation is a symptom of some plant diseases. *See also* mucilage.

guncotton *See* cellulose nitrate.

gun metal A type of bronze usually containing 88–90% copper, 8–10% tin, and 2–4% zinc. Formerly used for cannons, it is still used for bearings and other parts that require high resistance to wear and corrosion.

gunpowder An explosive consisting of a mixture of potassium nitrate, sulphur, and charcoal.

gypsum A monoclinic mineral form of hydrated *calcium sulphate, $CaSO_4.2H_2O$. It occurs in five varieties: *rock gypsum*, which is often red stained and granular; *gypsite*, an impure earthy form occurring as a surface deposit; *alabaster*, a pure fine-grained translucent form; *satin spar*, which is fibrous and silky; and *selenite*, which occurs as transparent crystals in muds and clays. It is used in the building industry and in the manufacture of cement, rubber, paper, and plaster of Paris.

H

Haber process An industrial process for producing ammonia by reaction of nitrogen with hydrogen:

$$N_2 + 3H_2 \rightleftharpoons 2NH_3$$

The reaction is reversible and exothermic, so that a high yield of ammonia is favoured by low temperature (*see* Le Chatelier's principle). However, the rate of reaction would be too slow for equilibrium to be reached at normal temperatures, so an optimum temperature of about 450°C is used, with a catalyst of iron containing potassium and aluminium oxide promoters. The higher the pressure the greater the yield, although there are technical difficulties in using very high pressures. A pressure of about 250 atmospheres is commonly employed.

The process is of immense importance for the fixation of nitrogen for fertilizers. It was developed in 1908 by the German chemist Fritz Haber (1886–1934) and was developed for industrial use by Carl Bosch (1874–1940), hence the alternative name *Haber–Bosch process*. The nitrogen is obtained from liquid air. Formerly, the hydrogen was from *water gas and the water–gas shift reaction (the *Bosch process*) but now the raw material (called *synthesis gas*) is obtained by steam *reforming natural gas.

habit *See* crystal habit.

haem (heme) An iron-containing molecule that binds with proteins as a *cofactor or *prosthetic group to form the *haemoproteins*. These are *haemoglobin, *myoglobin, and the *cytochromes. Essentially, haem comprises a *porphyrin with its four nitrogen atoms holding the iron(II) atom as a chelate. This iron can reversibly bind oxygen (as in haemoglobin and myoglobin) or (as in the cytochromes) conduct electrons by conversion between the iron(II) and iron (III) series.

haematite A mineral form of iron(III) oxide, Fe_2O_3. It is the most important ore of iron and usually occurs in two main forms: as a massive red kidney-shaped ore (*kidney ore*) and as grey to black metallic crystals known as *specular iron ore*. Haematite is the major red colouring agent in rocks; the largest deposits are of sedimentary origin. In industry haematite is also used as a polishing agent (jeweller's rouge) and in paints.

haemoglobin One of a group of globular proteins occurring widely in animals as oxygen carriers in blood. Vertebrate haemoglobin comprises two pairs of polypeptide chains (forming the *globin* protein) with each chain folded to provide a binding site for a *haem group. Each of the four haem groups binds one oxygen molecule to form *oxyhaemoglobin*. Dissociation occurs in oxygen-depleted tissues: oxygen is released and haemoglobin is reformed. The haem groups also bind other inorganic molecules, including carbon monoxide. This binds more strongly than oxygen and competes with it (hence its toxicity). In vertebrates, haemoglobin is contained in the red blood cells (erythrocytes).

hafnium Symbol Hf. A silvery lustrous metallic *transition element; a.n. 72; r.a.m. 178.49; r.d. 13.3; m.p. 2230±20°C; b.p. 4602°C. The element is found with zirconium and is extracted by formation of the chloride and reduction by the Kroll process. It is used in tungsten alloys in filaments and electrodes and as a neutron absorber. The metal forms a passive oxide layer in air. Most of its compounds are hafnium(IV) complexes; less stable hafnium(III) complexes also exist. The element was first reported by Urbain in 1911, and its existence was finally established by D. Coster and G. C. de Hevesey in 1923.

half cell An electrode in contact with a solution of ions, forming part of a *cell. Various types of half cell exist, the simplest consisting of a metal electrode immersed in a solution of metal ions. Gas half cells have a gold or platinum plate in a solution with gas bubbled over the metal plate. The commonest is the *hydrogen half cell. Half cells can also be formed by a metal in contact with an insoluble salt or oxide and a solution. The *calomel half cell is an example of this. Half cells are commonly referred to as *electrodes*.

half-thickness The thickness of a specified material that reduces the intensity of a beam of radiation to half its original value.

half-width Half the width of a spectrum line (or in some cases the full width) measured at half its height.

halide A compound of a halogen with another element or group. The halides of typical metals are ionic (e.g. sodium fluoride, Na^+F^-). Metals can also form halides in which the bonding is largely covalent (e.g. aluminium chloride, $AlCl_3$). Organic compounds are also sometimes referred to as halides; e.g. the alkyl halides (*see* haloalkanes) and the *acyl halides. Halides are named *fluorides*, *chlorides*, *bromides*, or *iodides*.

halite (rock salt) Naturally occurring *sodium chloride (common salt, NaCl), crystallizing in the cubic system. It is chiefly colourless or white (sometimes blue) when pure but the presence of impurities may colour it grey, pink, red, or brown. Halite often occurs in association with anhydrite and gypsum.

Hall–Heroult cell An electrolytic cell used industrially for the extraction of aluminium from bauxite. The bauxite is first purified by dissolving it in sodium hydroxide and filtering off insoluble constituents. Aluminium hydroxide is then precipitated (by adding CO_2) and this is decomposed by heating to obtain pure Al_2O_3. In the

Hall–Heroult cell, the oxide is mixed with cryolite (to lower its melting point) and the molten mixture electrolysed using graphite anodes. The cathode is the lining of the cell, also of graphite. The electrolyte is kept in a molten state (about 850°C) by the current. Molten aluminium collects at the bottom of the cell and can be tapped off. Oxygen forms at the anode, and gradually oxidizes it away. The cell is named after the US chemist Charles Martin Hall (1863–1914), who discovered the process in 1886, and the French chemist Paul Heroult (1863–1914), who discovered it independently in the same year.

haloalkanes (alkyl halides) Organic compounds in which one or more hydrogen atoms of an alkane have been substituted by halogen atoms. Examples are chloromethane, CH_3Cl, dibromoethane, CH_2BrCH_2Br, etc. Haloalkanes can be formed by direct reaction between alkanes and halogens using ultraviolet radiation. They are usually made by reaction of an alcohol with a halogen carrier.

haloform reaction A reaction for producing haloforms from methyl ketones. An example is the production of chloroform from propanone using sodium chlorate(I) (or bleaching powder):

$$CH_3COCH_3 + 3NaOCl \rightarrow CH_3COCl_3 + 3NaOH$$

The substituted ketone then reacts to give chloroform (trichloromethane):

$$CH_3COCCl_3 + NaOH \rightarrow NaOCOCH_3 + CHCl_3$$

The reaction can also be used for making carboxylic acids, since $RCOCH_3$ gives the product NaOCOR. It is particularly useful for aromatic acids as the starting ketone can be made by a Friedel–Crafts acylation.

The reaction of methyl ketones with sodium iodate(I) gives iodoform (triiodomethane), which is a yellow solid with a characteristic smell. This reaction is used in the *iodoform test* to identify methyl ketones. It also gives a positive result with a secondary alcohol of the formula $RCH(OH)CH_3$ (which is first oxidized to a methylketone) or with ethanol (oxidized to ethanal, which also undergoes the reaction).

haloforms The four compounds with formula CHX_3, where X is a halogen atom. They are *chloroform* ($CHCl_3$), and, by analogy, *fluoroform* (CHF_3), *bromoform* ($CHBr_3$), and *iodoform* (CHI_3). The systematic names are trichloromethane, trifluoromethane, etc.

halogenating agent *See* halogenation.

halogenation A chemical reaction in which a halogen atom is introduced into a compound. Halogenations are described as *chlorination*, *fluorination*, *bromination*, etc., according to the halogen involved. Halogenation reactions may take place by direct reaction with the halogen. This occurs with alkanes, where the reaction involves free radicals and requires high temperature, ultraviolet radiation, or a chemical initiator; e.g.

$$C_2H_6 + Br_2 \rightarrow C_2H_5Br + HBr$$

The halogenation of aromatic compounds can be effected by electrophilic substitution using an aluminium chloride catalyst:

$$C_6H_6 + Cl_2 \rightarrow C_6H_5Cl + HCl$$

Halogenation can also be carried out using compounds, such as phosphorus halides (e.g. PCl_3) or sulphur dihalide oxides (e.g. $SOCl_2$), which react with –OH groups. Such compounds are called *halogenating agents*. Addition reactions are also referred to as halogenations; e.g.

$$C_2H_4 + Br_2 \rightarrow CH_2BrCH_2Br$$

halogens (group VII elements) A group of elements in the *periodic table (group VIIB): fluorine (F), chlorine (Cl), bromine (Br), iodine (I), and astatine (At). All have a characteristic electron configuration of noble gases but with outer ns^2np^5 electrons. The outer shell is thus one electron short of a noble-gas configuration. Consequently, the halogens are typical nonmetals; they have high electronegativities – high electron affinities and high ionization energies. They form compounds by gaining an electron to complete the stable configuration; i.e. they are good oxidizing agents. Alternatively, they share their outer electrons to form covalent compounds, with single bonds.

All are reactive elements with the reactivity decreasing down the group. The electron affinity decreases down the group and other properties also show a change from fluorine to astatine. Thus, the melting and boiling points increase; at 20°C, fluorine and chlorine are gases, bromine a liquid, and iodine and astatine are solids. All exist as diatomic molecules.

The name 'halogen' comes from the Greek 'salt-producer', and the elements react with metals to form ionic halide salts. They also combine with nonmetals, the activity decreasing down the group: fluorine reacts with all nonmetals except nitrogen and the noble gases helium, neon, and argon; iodine does not react with any noble gas, nor with carbon, nitrogen, oxygen, or sulphur. The elements fluorine to iodine all react with hydrogen to give the acid, with the activity being greatest for fluorine, which reacts explosively. Chlorine and hydrogen react slowly at room temperature in the dark (sunlight causes a free-radical chain reaction). Bromine and hydrogen react if heated in the presence of a catalyst. Iodine and hydrogen react only slowly and the reaction is not complete. There is a decrease in oxidizing ability down the group from fluorine to iodine. As a consequence, each halogen will displace any halogen below it from a solution of its salt, for example:

$$Cl_2 + 2Br^- \rightarrow Br_2 + 2Cl^-$$

The halogens also form a wide variety of organic compounds in which the halogen atom is linked to carbon. In general, the aryl compounds are more stable than the alkyl compounds and there is decreasing resistance to chemical attack down the group from the fluoride to the iodide.

Fluorine has only a valency of 1, although the other halogens can have higher oxidation states using their vacant *d*-electron levels. There is also evidence for increasing metallic behaviour down the group. Chlorine and bromine form compounds with oxygen in which the halogen atom is assigned a positive oxidation state. Only iodine, however, forms positive ions, as in $I^+NO_3^-$.

hardening of oils The process of converting unsaturated esters of *fatty acids into (more solid) saturated esters by hydrogenation using a nickel catalyst. It is used in the manufacture of margarine from vegetable oils.

hardness of water The presence in water of dissolved calcium or magnesium ions, which form a scum with soap and prevent the formation of a lather. The main cause of hard water is dissolved calcium hydrogencarbonate ($Ca(HCO_3)_2$), which is formed in limestone or chalk regions by the action of dissolved carbon dioxide on calcium carbonate. This type is known as *temporary hardness* because it is removed by boiling:

$$Ca(HCO_3)_2(aq) \rightarrow CaCO_3(s) + H_2O(l) + CO_2(g)$$

The precipitated calcium carbonate is the 'fur' (or 'scale') formed in kettles, boilers, pipes, etc. In some areas, hardness also results from dissolved calcium sulphate ($CaSO_4$), which cannot be removed by boiling (*permanent hardness*).

Hard water is a considerable problem in washing, reducing the efficiency of boilers, heating systems, etc., and in certain industrial processes. Various methods of *water softening* are used. In public supplies, the temporary hardness can be removed by adding lime (calcium hydroxide), which precipitates calcium carbonate

$$Ca(OH)_2(aq) + Ca(HCO_3)_2(aq) \rightarrow 2CaCO_3(s) + 2H_2O(l)$$

This is known as the *Clark process* (or as '*clarking*'). It does not remove permanent hardness. Both temporary and permanent hardness can be treated by precipitating calcium carbonate by added sodium carbonate – hence its use as a washing soda and in bath salts. Calcium (and other) ions can also be removed from water by ion-exchange using zeolites (e.g. *Permutit*). This method is used in small domestic water-softeners. Another technique is not to remove the Ca^{2+} ions but to complex them and prevent them reacting further. For domestic use polyphosphates (containing the ion $P_6O_{18}^{6-}$, e.g. *Calgon*) are added. Other sequestering agents are also used for industrial water. *See also* sequestration.

heat capacity (thermal capacity) The ratio of the heat supplied to an object or specimen to its consequent rise in temperature. The *specific heat capacity* is the ratio of the heat supplied to unit mass of a substance to its consequent rise in temperature. The *molar heat capacity* is the ratio of the heat supplied to unit amount of a substance to its consequent rise in temperature. In practice, heat capacity (C) is measured in joules per kelvin, specific heat capacity (c) in $J K^{-1} kg^{-1}$, and molar heat capacity (C_m) in $J K^{-1} mol^{-1}$. For a gas, the values of c and C_m are commonly given either at *constant volume*, when only its *internal energy is increased, or at *constant pressure*, which requires a greater input of heat as the gas is allowed to expand and do work against the surroundings. The symbols for the specific and molar heat capacities at constant volume are c_v and C_v, respectively; those for the specific and molar heat capacities at constant pressure are c_p and C_p.

heat of atomization The energy required to dissociate one mole of a given substance into atoms.

heat of combustion The energy liberated when one mole of a given substance is completely oxidized.

heat of formation The energy liberated or absorbed when one mole of a compound is formed from its constituent elements.

heat of neutralization The energy liberated in neutralizing one mole of an acid or base.

heat of reaction The energy liberated or absorbed as a result of the complete chemical reaction of molar amounts of the reactants.

heat of solution The energy liberated or absorbed when one mole of a given substance is completely dissolved in a large volume of solvent (strictly, to infinite dilution).

heavy hydrogen *See* deuterium.

heavy spar A mineral form of *barium sulphate, $BaSO_4$.

heavy water (deuterium oxide) Water in which hydrogen atoms, ^1H, are replaced by the heavier isotope deuterium, ^2H. It is a colourless liquid, which forms hexagonal crystals on freezing. Its physical properties differ from those of 'normal' water; r.d. 1.105; m.p. 3.8°C; b.p. 101.4°C. Deuterium oxide occurs to a small extent (about 0.003% by weight) in natural water, from which it can be separated by fractional distillation or by electrolysis. It is particularly useful in the nuclear industry because of its ability to reduce the energies of fast neutrons to thermal energies and because its quenching cross-section is lower than that of hydrogen and consequently it does not appreciably reduce the neutron flux. In the laboratory it is used for *labelling other molecules for studies of reaction mechanisms.

hecto- Symbol h. A prefix used in the metric system to denote 100 times. For example, 100 coulombs = 1 hectocoulomb (hC).

Heisenberg uncertainty principle *See* uncertainty principle.

helium Symbol He. A colourless odourless gaseous nonmetallic element belonging to group 0 of the periodic table (*see* noble gases); a.n. 2; r.a.m. 4.0026; d. 0.178 g dm^{-3}; m.p. −272.2°C (at 20 atm.); b.p. −268.93°C. The element has the lowest boiling point of all substances and can be solidified only under pressure. Natural helium is mostly helium−4, with a small amount of helium−3. There are also two short-lived radioactive isotopes: helium−5 and −6. It occurs in ores of uranium and thorium and in some natural-gas deposits. It has a variety of uses, including the provision of inert atmospheres for welding and semiconductor manufacture, as a refrigerant for superconductors, and as a diluent in breathing apparatus. It is also used in filling balloons. Chemically it is totally inert and has no known compounds. It was discovered in the solar spectrum in 1868 by Lockyer.

Helmholtz free energy *See* free energy.

hemiacetals *See* acetals.

hemihydrate A crystalline hydrate containing two molecules of compound per molecule of water (e.g. $2CaSO_4.H_2O$).

hemiketals *See* ketals.

henry Symbol H. The *SI unit of inductance equal to the inductance of a closed circuit in which an e.m.f. of one volt is produced when the electric current in the circuit varies uniformly at a rate of one ampere per second. It is named after Joseph Henry (1797−1878), a US physicist.

heptahydrate A crystalline hydrate that has seven molecules of water per molecule of compound.

heptane A liquid straight-chain alkane obtained from petroleum, C_7H_{16}; r.d. 0.684; m.p. 182°C; b.p. 371°C. In standardizing *octane numbers, heptane is given a value zero.

heptaoxodiphosphoric(V) acid *See* phosphoric(V) acid.

heptavalent (septivalent) Having a valency of seven.

hertz Symbol Hz. The *SI unit of frequency equal to one cycle per second. It is named after Heinrich Hertz (1857−94), a German physicist.

Hess's law If reactants can be converted into products by a series of reactions, the sum of the heats of these reactions (with due regard to their sign) is equal to the heat of reaction for direct conversion from reactants to products. More generally, the overall energy change in going from reactants to products does not depend on the route taken. The law can be used to obtain thermodynamic data that cannot be measured directly. For example, the heat of formation of ethane can be found by considering the reactions:

$$2C(s) + 3H_2(g) + 3\tfrac{1}{2}O_2(g) \rightarrow 2CO_2(g) + 3H_2O(l)$$

The heat of this reaction is $2\Delta H_C + 3\Delta H_H$, where ΔH_C and ΔH_H are the heats of combustion of carbon and hydrogen respectively, which can be measured. By Hess' law, this is equal to the sum of the energies for two stages:

$$2C(s) + 3H_2(g) \rightarrow C_2H_6(g)$$

(the heat of formation of ethane, ΔH_f) and

$$C_2H_6(g) + 3\tfrac{1}{2}O_2 \rightarrow 2CO_2(g) + 3H_2O(l)$$

(the heat of combustion of ethane, ΔH_E). As ΔH_E can be measured and as

$$\Delta H_f + \Delta H_E = 2\Delta H_c + 3\Delta H_H$$

ΔH_f can be found. Another example is the use of the *Born–Haber cycle to obtain lattice energies. The law was first put forward in 1840 by the Russian chemist Germain Henri Hess (1802–50). It is sometimes called the *law of constant heat summation* and is a consequence of the law of conservation of energy.

hetero atom An odd atom in the ring of a heterocyclic compound. For instance, nitrogen is the hetero atom in pyridine.

heterocyclic *See* cyclic.

heterogeneous catalysis *See* catalysis.

heterolytic fission The breaking of a bond in a compound in which the two fragments are oppositely charged ions. For example, $HCl \rightarrow H^+ + Cl^-$. *Compare* homolytic fission.

heteropolar bond *See* chemical bond.

heteropolymer *See* polymer.

Heusler alloys Ferromagnetic alloys containing no ferromagnetic elements. The original alloys contained copper, manganese, and tin and were first made by Conrad Heusler (19th-century mining engineer).

hexadecane (cetane) A colourless liquid straight-chain alkane hydrocarbon, $C_{16}H_{34}$, used in standardizing *cetane ratings of Diesel fuel.

hexadecanoate *See* palmitate.

hexadecanoic acid *See* palmitic acid.

hexagonal close packing *See* close packing.

hexagonal crystal *See* crystal system.

hexanedioate (adipate) A salt or ester of hexanedioic acid.

hexanedioic acid (adipic acid) A carboxylic acid, $(CH_2)_4(COOH)_2$; r.d. 1.366; m.p. 149°C; b.p. 265°C (100 mmHg). It is used in the manufacture of *nylon 6,6. *See also* polymerization.

hexanoate (caproate) A salt or ester of hexanoic acid.

hexanoic acid (caproic acid) A liquid fatty acid, $CH_3(CH_2)_4COOH$; r.d. 0.93; m.p. −3.4°C; b.p. 205°C. Glycerides of the acid occur naturally in cow and goat milk and in some vegetable oils.

hexose A *monosaccharide that has six carbon atoms in its molecules.

high-speed steel A steel that will remain hard at dull red heat and can therefore be used in cutting tools for high-speed lathes. It usually contains 12–22% tungsten, up to 5% chromium, and 0.4–0.7% carbon. It may also contain small amounts of vanadium, molybdenum, and other metals.

histidine *See* amino acid.

histochemistry The study of the distribution of the chemical constituents of tissues by means of their chemical reactions. It utilizes such techniques as staining, light and electron microscopy, autoradiography, and *chromatography.

holmium Symbol Ho. A soft silvery metallic element belonging to the *lanthanoids; a.n. 67; r.a.m. 164.93; r.d. 8.795 (20°C); m.p. 1472°C; b.p. 2700°C. It occurs in apatite, xenotime, and some other rare-earth minerals. There is one natural isotope, holmium–165; eighteen artificial isotopes have been produced. There are no uses for the element, which was discovered by P. T. Cleve and J. L. Soret in 1879.

homocyclic *See* cyclic.

homologous series A series of related chemical compounds that have the same functional group(s) but differ in formula by a fixed group of atoms. For instance, the simple carboxylic acids: methanoic (HCOOH), ethanoic (CH_3COOH), propanoic (C_2H_5COOH), etc., form a homologous series in which each member differs from the next by CH_2. Successive members of such a series are called *homologues*.

homolytic fission The breaking of a bond in a compound in which the fragments are uncharged free radicals. For example, $Cl_2 \rightarrow Cl\cdot + Cl\cdot$. *Compare* heterolytic fission.

homopolar bond *See* chemical bond.

homopolymer *See* polymer.

hormone A substance that is manufactured and secreted in very small quantities into the bloodstream by an endocrine gland or a specialized nerve cell and regulates the growth or functioning of a specific tissue or organ in a distant part of the body. For example, the hormone insulin controls the rate and manner in which glucose is used by the body.

hornblende Any of a group of common rock-forming minerals of the amphibole group with the generalized formula:

$$(Ca,Na)_2(Mg,Fe,Al)_5(Al,Si)_8O_{22}(OH,F)_2$$

Hornblendes consist mainly of calcium, iron, and magnesium silicate.

hybrid orbital *See* orbital.

hydracid *See* binary acid.

hydrate A substance formed by combination of a compound with water. *See* water of crystallization.

hydrated alumina *See* aluminium hydroxide.

hydrated aluminium hydroxide. *See* aluminium hydroxide.

hydration *See* solvation.

hydrazine A colourless liquid or white crystalline solid, N_2H_4; r.d. 1.01 (liquid); m.p. 1.4°C; b.p. 113.5°C. It is very soluble in water and soluble in ethanol. Hydrazine is prepared by the *Raschig synthesis* in which ammonia reacts with sodium(I) chlorate (sodium hypochlorite) to give NH_2Cl, which then undergoes further reaction with ammonia to give N_2H_4. Industrial production must be carefully controlled to avoid a side reaction leading to NH_4Cl. The compound is a weak base giving rise to two series of salts, those based on $N_2H_5^+$, which are stable in water (sometimes written in the form $N_2H_4.HCl$ rather than $N_2H_5^+Cl^-$), and a less stable and extensively hydrolysed series based on $N_2H_6^{2+}$. Hydrazine is a powerful reducing agent and reacts violently with many oxidizing agents, hence its use as a rocket propellant.

hydrazoic acid *See* hydrogen azide.

hydrazones Organic compounds containing the group $=C{:}NNH_2$, formed by condensation of substituted hydrazines with with aldehydes and ketones. *Phenylhydrazones* contain the group $=C{:}NNHC_6H_5$.

hydrobromic acid *See* hydrogen bromide.

hydrocarbons Chemical compounds that contain only carbon and hydrogen. A vast number of different hydrocarbon compounds exist, the main types being the *alkanes, *alkenes, *alkynes, and *arenes.

hydrochloric acid *See* hydrogen chloride.

hydrochloride *See* amine salts.

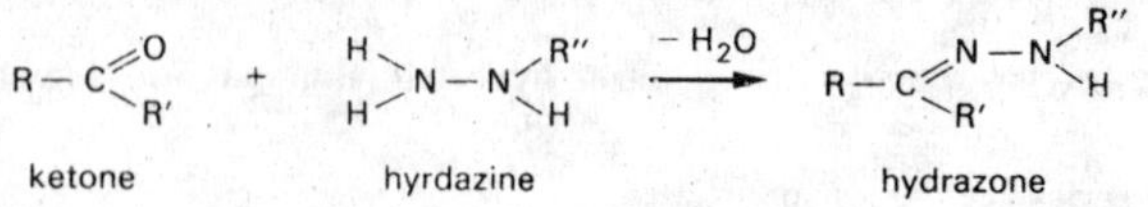

Formation of a hydrazone from a ketone. The same reaction occurs with an aldehyde ($R'=H$). If $R''=C_6H_5$, the product is phenylhydrazone

hydrocyanic acid *See* hydrogen cyanide.

hydrofluoric acid *See* hydrogen fluoride.

hydrogen Symbol H. A colourless odourless gaseous chemical element; a.n. 1; r.a.m. 1.008; d. 0.0899 g dm^{-3}; m.p. −259.14°C; b.p. −252.87°C. It is the lightest element and the most abundant in the universe. It is present in water and in all organic compounds. There are three isotopes: naturally occurring hydrogen consists of the two stable isotopes hydrogen-1 (99.985%) and *deuterium. The radioactive *tritium is made artificially. The gas is diatomic and has two forms: *orthohydrogen*, in which the nuclear spins are parallel, and *parahydrogen*, in which they are antiparallel. At normal temperatures the gas is 25% parahydrogen. In the liquid it is 99.8% parahydrogen. The main source of hydrogen is steam *reforming of natural gas. It can also be made by the Bosch process (*see* Haber process) and by electrolysis of water. The main use is in the Haber process for making ammonia. Hydrogen is also used in various other industrial processes, such as the reduction of oxide ores, the refining of petroleum, the production of hydrocarbons from coal, and the hydrogenation of vegetable oils. Considerable interest has also been shown in its potential use in a 'hydrogen fuel economy' in which primary energy sources not based on fossil fuels (e.g. nuclear, solar, or geothermal energy) are used to produce electricity, which is employed in electrolysing water. The hydrogen formed is stored as liquid hydrogen or as metal *hydrides. Chemically, hydrogen reacts with most elements. It was discovered by Henry Cavendish in 1776.

hydrogenation 1. A chemical reaction with hydrogen; in particular, an addition reaction in which hydrogen adds to an unsaturated compound. Nickel is a good catalyst for such reactions. **2.** The process of converting coal to oil by making the carbon in the coal combine with hydrogen to form hydrocarbons. *See* Fischer–Tropsch process; Bergius process.

hydrogen azide (hydrazoic acid; azoimide) A colourless liquid, HN_3; r.d. 1.09; m.p. −80°C; b.p. 37°C. It is highly toxic and a powerful reductant, which explodes in the presence of oxygen and other oxidizing agents. It may be prepared by the reaction of sodium amide and sodium nitrate at 175°C followed by distillation of a mixture of the resulting sodium azide and a dilute acid. *See also* azides.

hydrogen bond A type of electrostatic interaction between molecules occurring in molecules that have hydrogen atoms bound to electronegative atoms (F, N, O). It is a strong dipole–dipole attraction caused by the electron-withdrawing properties of the electronegative atom. Thus, in the water molecule the oxygen atom attracts the electrons in the O–H bonds. The hydrogen atom has no inner shells of electrons to shield the nucleus, and there is an electrostatic interaction between the hydrogen proton and a lone pair of electrons on an oxygen atom in a neighbouring molecule. Each oxygen atom has two lone pairs and can make hydrogen bonds to two different hydrogen atoms. The strengths of hydrogen bonds are about one tenth of the strengths of normal covalent bonds. Hydrogen bonding does, however, have significant effects on physical properties. Thus it accounts for the unusual properties of *water and for the relatively high boiling points of H_2O, HF, and NH_3 (compared with H_2S, HCl, and PH_3). It is also of great importance in living organisms. Hydrogen bonding occurs between bases in the chains of DNA. It also occurs between the C=O and N–H groups in proteins, and is responsible for maintaining the secondary structure.

hydrogen bromide A colourless gas, HBr; m.p. −86°C; b.p. −66.4°C. It can be made by direct combination of the elements using a platinum catalyst. It is a strong acid dissociating extensively in solution (*hydrobromic acid*).

hydrogencarbonate (bicarbonate) A salt of *carbonic acid in which one hydrogen atom has been replaced; it thus contains the hydrogencarbonate ion HCO_3^-.

hydrogen chloride A colourless fuming gas, HCl; m.p. −114°C; b.p. −85°C. It can be prepared in the laboratory by heating sodium chloride with concentrated sulphuric acid (hence the former name *spirits of salt*). Industrially it is made directly from the elements at high temperature and used in the manufacture of PVC and other chloro compounds. It is a strong acid and dissociates fully in solution (*hydrochloric acid*).

hydrogen cyanide (hydrocyanic acid; prussic acid) A colourless liquid or gas, HCN, with a characteristic odour of almonds; r.d. 0.699 (liquid at 22°C); m.p. −14°C; b.p. 26°C. It is an extremely poisonous substance formed by the action of acids on metal cyanides. Industrially, it is made by catalytic oxidation of ammonia and methane with air and is used in producing acrylate plastics. Hydrogen cyanide is a weak acid (K_a = 2.1 × 10^{-9} mol dm^{-3}). With organic carbonyl compounds it forms *cyanohydrins.

hydrogen electrode *See* hydrogen half cell.

hydrogen fluoride A colourless liquid, HF; r.d. 0.99; m.p. −83°C; b.p. 19.5°C. It can be made by the action of sulphuric acid on calcium fluoride. The compound is an extremely corrosive fluorinating agent, which attacks glass. It is unlike the other hydrogen halides in being a liquid (a result of *hydrogen-bond formation). It is also a weaker acid than the others because the small size of the fluorine atom means that the H–F bond is shorter and stronger. Solutions of hydrogen fluoride in water are known as *hydrofluoric acid.*

hydrogen half cell (hydrogen electrode) A type of *half cell in which a metal foil is immersed in a solution of hydrogen ions and hydrogen gas is bubbled over the foil. The standard hydrogen electrode, used in measuring standard *electrode potentials, uses a platinum foil with a 1.0 M solution of hydrogen ions, the gas at 1 atmosphere pressure, and a temperature of 25°C. It is written Pt(s)|H_2(g), H^+(aq), the effective reaction being $H_2 \rightarrow 2H^+ + 2e$.

hydrogen iodide A colourless gas, HI; m.p. −51°C; b.p. −36°C. It can be made by direct combination of the elements using a platinum catalyst. It is a strong acid dissociating extensively in solution (*hydroiodic acid*). It is also a reducing agent.

hydrogen ion *See* acids; pH.

hydrogen peroxide A colourless or pale blue viscous unstable liquid, H_2O_2; r.d. 1.44; m.p. −0.89°C; b.p. 151.4°C. As with water, there is considerable hydrogen bonding in the liquid, which has a high dielectric constant. It can be made in the laboratory by adding dilute acid to barium peroxide at 0°C. Large quantities are made commercially by electrolysis of $KHSO_4.H_2SO_4$ solutions. Another industrial process involves catalytic oxidation (using nickel, palladium, or platinum with an anthraquinone) of hydrogen and water in the presence of oxygen. Hydrogen peroxide readily decomposes in light or in the presence of metal ions to give water and oxygen. It is usually supplied in solutions designated by volume strength. For example, 20-volume hydrogen peroxide would yield 20 volumes of oxygen per volume of solution. Although the *peroxides are formally salts of H_2O_2, the compound is essentially neutral. Thus, the acidity constant of the ionization

$$H_2O_2 + H_2O \rightleftharpoons H_3O^+ + HO_2^-$$

is 1.5×10^{-12} mol dm^{-3}. It is a strong oxidizing agent, hence its use as a mild antiseptic and as a bleaching agent for cloth, hair, etc. It has also been used as an oxidant in rocket fuels.

hydrogen spectrum The atomic spectrum of hydrogen is characterized by lines corresponding to radiation quanta of sharply defined energy. A graph of the frequencies at which these lines occur against the ordinal number that characterizes their position in the series of lines, produces a smooth curve indicating that they obey a formal law. In 1885 J. J. Balmer (1825–98) discovered the law having the form:

$$1/\lambda = R(1/n_1^2 + 1/n_2^2)$$

This law gives the so-called *Balmer series* of lines in the visible spectrum in which $n_1 = 2$ and $n_2 = 3,4,5\ldots$, λ is the wavelength associated with the lines, and R is the *Rydberg constant.

In the *Lyman series*, discovered by Theodore Lyman (1874–1954), $n_1 = 1$ and the lines fall in the ultraviolet. The Lyman series is the strongest feature of the solar spectrum as observed by rockets and satellites above the earth's atmosphere. In the *Paschen series*, discovered by F. Paschen (1865–1947), $n_1 = 3$ and the lines occur in the far infrared. The *Brackett series* also occurs in the far infrared, with $n_1 = 4$.

hydrogensulphate (bisulphate) A salt containing the ion HSO_4^- or an ester of the type $RHSO_4$, where R is an organic group. It was formerly called *hydrosulphate.*

hydrogen sulphide (sulphuretted hydrogen) A gas, H_2S, with an odour of rotten eggs; r.d. 1.54 (liquid); m.p. −85.5°C; b.p. −60.7°C. It is soluble in water and ethanol and may be prepared by the action of mineral acids on metal sulphides, typically hydrochloric acid on iron(II) sulphide (*see* Kipp's apparatus). Solutions in water (known as *hydrosulphuric acid*) contain the anions HS^- and minute traces of S^{2-} and are weakly acidic. Acid salts (those containing the HS^- ion) are known as *hydrogensulphides* (formerly *hydrosulphides*). In acid solution hydrogen sulphide is a mild reducing agent. Hydrogen sulphide has an important role in traditional qualitative chemical analysis, where it precipitates metals with insoluble sulphides (in acid solution: Cu, Pb, Hg, Cd, Bi, As, Sb, Sn). The formation of a black precipitate with alkaline solutions of lead salts may be used as a test for hydrogen sulphide but the characteristic smell is usually sufficient. Hydrogen sulphide is exceedingly poisonous (more toxic than hydrogen cyanide).

The compound burns in air with a blue flame to form sulphur(IV) oxide (SO_2); solutions of hydrogen sulphide exposed to the air undergo oxidation but in this case only to elemental sulphur. North Sea gas contains some hydrogen sulphide (from S-proteins in plants) as do volcanic emissions.

hydrogensulphite (bisulphite) A salt containing the ion $^-HSO_3$ or an ester of the type $RHSO_3$, where R is an organic group.

hydroiodic acid *See* hydrogen iodide.

hydrolysis A chemical reaction of a compound with water. For instance, salts of weak acids or bases hydrolyse in aqueous solution, as in

$$Na^+ \, ^-OOCCH_3 + H_2O \rightleftharpoons Na^+ + OH^- + CH_3COOH$$

The reverse reaction of *esterification is another example. *See also* solvolysis.

hydromagnesite A mineral form of basic *magnesium carbonate, $3MgCO_3.Mg(OH)_2.3H_2O$.

hydrophilic Having an affinity for water. *See* lyophilic.

hydrophobic Lacking affinity for water. *See* lyophobic.

hydroquinone *See* benzene-1,4-diol.

hydrosol A sol in which the continuous phase is water. *See* colloid.

hydrosulphate *See* hydrogensulphate.

hydrosulphide *See* hydrogen sulphide.

hydrosulphuric acid *See* hydrogen sulphide.

hydroxide A metallic compound containing the ion OH^- (*hydroxide ion*) or containing the group –OH (hydroxyl group) bound to a metal atom. Hydroxides of typical metals are basic; those of *metalloids are amphoteric.

hydroxycerussite *See* lead(II) carbonate hydroxide.

hydroxyl group The group –OH in a chemical compound.

2-hydroxypropanoic acid *See* lactic acid.

hygroscopic Describing a substance that can take up water from the atmosphere. *See also* deliquescence.

hyperfine structure *See* fine structure.

hypertonic solution A solution that has a higher osmotic pressure than some other solution. *Compare* hypotonic solution.

hypochlorite *See* chlorates.

hypochlorous acid *See* chloric(I) acid.

hypophosphorus acid *See* phosphinic acid.

hyposulphite *See* sulphinate.

hyposulphurous acid *See* sulphinic acid.

hypotonic solution A solution that has a lower osmotic pressure than some other solution. *Compare* hypertonic solution.

I

ice *See* water.

ice point The temperature at which there is equilibrium between ice and water at standard atmospheric pressure (i.e. the freezing or melting point under standard conditions). It was used as a fixed point (0°) on the Celsius scale, but the kelvin and the International Practical Temperature Scale are based on the *triple point of water.

ideal crystal A single crystal with a perfectly regular lattice that contains no impurities, imperfections, or other defects.

ideal gas (perfect gas) A hypothetical gas that obeys the *gas laws exactly. An ideal gas would consist of molecules that occupy negligible space and have negligible forces between them. All collisions made between molecules and the walls of the container or between molecules and other molecules would be perfectly elastic, because the molecules would have no means of storing energy except as translational kinetic energy.

ideal solution *See* Raoult's law.

ignition temperature The temperature to which a substance must be heated before it will burn in air.

imides Organic compounds containing the group –CO.NH.CO.– (the *imido group*).

imido group *See* imides.

imines Compounds containing the group –NH– (the *imino group*) joined to two other groups; i.e. secondary *amines.

imino group *See* imines.

Imperial units The British system of units based on the pound and the yard. The former f.p.s. system was used in engineering and was loosely based on Imperial units; for all scientific purposes *SI units are now used. Imperial units are also being replaced for general purposes by metric units.

implosion An inward collapse of a vessel, especially as a result of evacuation.

incandescence The emission of light by a substance as a result of raising it to a high temperature.

indene A colourless flammable hydrocarbon, C_9H_8; r.d. 1.01; m.p. –35°C; b.p. 182°C. Indene is an aromatic hydrocarbon with a five-membered ring fused to a benzene ring. It is present in coal tar and is used as a solvent and raw material for making other organic compounds.

indeterminacy *See* uncertainty principle.

indicator A substance used to show the presence of a chemical substance or ion by its colour. *Acid–base indicators* are compounds, such as phenolphthalein and methyl orange, that change colour on going from acidic to basic solutions. They are usually weak acids in which the un-ionized form HA has a different colour from the negative ion A^-. In solution the indicator dissociates slightly

$$HA \rightleftharpoons H^+ + A^-$$

In acid solution the concentration of H^+ is high, and the indicator is largely undissociated HA; in alkaline solutions the equilibrium is displaced to the right and A^- is formed. Useful acid–base indicators show a sharp colour change over a range of about 2 pH units. In titration, the point at which the reaction is complete is the *equivalence point* (i.e. the point at which equivalent quantities of acid and base are added). The *end point* is the point at which the indicator just changes colour. For accuracy, the two must be the same. During a titration the pH changes sharply close to the equivalence point, and the indicator used must change colour over the same range.

Other types of indicator can be used for other reactions. Starch, for example, is used in iodine titrations because of the deep blue complex it forms. *Oxidation–reduction indicators* are substances that show a reversible colour change between oxidized and reduced forms. *See also* absorption indicator.

indigo A blue vat dye, $C_{16}H_{10}N_2O_2$. It occurs as the glucoside *indican* in the leaves of plants of the genus *Indigofera*, from which it was formerly extracted. It is now made synthetically.

indium Symbol In. A soft silvery element belonging to group IIIA of the periodic table; a.n. 49; r.a.m. 114.82; r.d. 7.31 (20°C); m.p. 156.6°C; b.p. 2080±2°C. It occurs in zinc blende and some iron ores and is obtained from zinc flue dust in total quantities of about 40 tonnes per annum. Naturally occurring indium consists of 4.23% indium–113 (stable) and 95.77% indium–115 (half-life 6 × 10^{14} years). There are a further five short-lived radioisotopes. The uses of the metal are small – some special-purpose electroplates and some special fusible alloys. Several semiconductor compounds are used, such as InAs, InP, and InSb. With only three electrons in its valency shell, indium is an electron acceptor; it forms stable indium(I), indium(II), and indium(III) compounds. The element was discovered in 1863 by Reich and Richter.

inductive effect The effect of a group or atom of a compound in pulling electrons towards itself or in pushing them away. Inductive effects can be used to explain some aspects of organic reactions. For instance, electron-withdrawing groups, such as $-NO_2$, $-CN$, $-CHO$, $-COOH$, and the halogens substituted on a benzene ring, reduce the electron density on the ring and decrease its susceptibility to further (electrophilic) substitution. Electron-releasing groups, such as $-OH$, $-NH_2$, $-OCH_3$, and $-CH_3$, have the opposite effect.

inert gases *See* noble gases.

inert-pair effect An effect seen especially in groups III and IV of the periodic table, in which the heavier elements in the group tend to form compounds with a valency two lower than the expected group valency. It is used to account for the existence of thallium(I) compounds in group III and lead(II) in group IV. In forming compounds, elements in these groups promote an electron from a filled *s*-level state to an empty *p*-level. The energy required for this is more than compensated for by the extra energy gain in forming two more bonds. For the heavier elements, the bond strengths or lattice energies in the compounds are lower than those of the lighter elements. Consequently the energy compensation is less important and the lower valence states become favoured.

inhibition A reduction in the rate of a catalysed reaction by substances called *inhibitors*. In biochemical reactions, in which the catalysts are *enzymes, if the inhibitor molecules resemble the substrate molecules they may bind to the active site of the enzyme, so preventing normal enzymatic activity. Alternatively they may form a complex with the substrate-enzyme intermediate or irreversibly destroy the enzyme configuration and active-site properties. The toxic effects of many substances are produced in this way. Inhibition by reaction products (*feedback inhibition*) is important in the control of enzyme activity.

inner Describing a chemical compound formed by reaction of one part of a molecule with another part of the same molecule. Thus, a lactam is an inner amide; a lactone is an inner ester.

inner transition series *See* transition elements.

inorganic chemistry The branch of chemistry concerned with compounds of elements other than carbon. Certain simple carbon compounds, such as CO, CO_2, CS_2, and carbonates and cyanides, are usually treated in inorganic chemistry.

insulin A hormone, secreted by the islets of Langerhans in the pancreas, that promotes the uptake of glucose by body cells and thereby controls its concentration in the blood. Underproduction of insulin results in the accumulation of large amounts of glucose in the blood and its subsequent excretion in the urine. This condition, known as *diabetes mellitus*, can be treated successfully by insulin injections. Insulin is a protein, the whole structure of which is now known.

intermediate bond *See* chemical bond.

intermetallic compound A compound consisting of two or more metallic elements present in definite proportions in an alloy.

intermolecular forces Weak forces occurring between molecules. *See* van der Waals' forces; hydrogen bond.

internal conversion A process in which an excited atomic nucleus decays to the *ground state and the energy released is transferred by electromagnetic coupling to one of the bound electrons of that atom rather than being released as a photon. The coupling is usually with an electron in the K-, L-, or M-shell of the atom, and this *conversion electron* is ejected from the atom with a kinetic energy equal to the difference between the nuclear transition energy and the binding energy of the electron. The resulting ion is itself in an excited state and usually subsequently emits an Auger electron or an X-ray photon.

internal energy Symbol *U*. The total of the kinetic energies of the atoms and molecules of which a system consists and the potential energies associated with their mutual interactions. It does not include the kinetic and potential energies of the system as a whole nor their nuclear energies or other intra-atomic energies. The value of the absolute internal energy of a system in any particular state cannot be measured; the significant quantity is the change in internal energy, ΔU. For a closed system (i.e. one that is not being replenished from outside its boundaries) the change in internal energy is equal to the heat absorbed by the system (Q) from its surroundings, less the work done (W) by the system on its surroundings, i.e. $\Delta U = Q - W$. *See also* energy; heat; thermodynamics.

interstitial *See* defect.

interstitial compound A compound in which ions or atoms of a nonmetal occupy interstitial positions in a metal lattice. Such compounds often have metallic properties. Examples are found in the *carbides, *borides, and *silicides.

Invar A tradename for an alloy of iron (63.8%), nickel (36%), and carbon (0.2%) that has a very low expansivity over a a restricted temperature range. It is used in watches and other instruments to reduce their sensitivity to changes in temperature.

inversion A chemical reaction involving a change from one optically active configuration to the opposite configuration. The Walden inversion is an example. *See* nucleophilic substitution.

iodic acid Any of various oxoacids of iodine, such as iodic(V) acid and iodic(VII) acid. When used without an oxidation state specified, the term usually refers to iodic(V) acid (HIO_3).

iodic(V) acid A colourless or very pale yellow solid, HIO_3; r.d. 4.63; decomposes at 110°C. It is soluble in water but insoluble in pure ethanol and other organic solvents. The compound is obtained by oxidizing iodine with concentrated nitric acid, hydrogen peroxide, or ozone. It is a strong acid and a powerful oxidizing agent.

iodic(VII) acid (periodic acid) A hygroscopic white solid, H_5IO_6, which decomposes at 138°C and is very soluble in water, ethanol, and ethoxyethane. Iodic(VII) acid may be prepared by electrolytic oxidation of concentrated solutions of iodic(V) acid at low temperatures. It is a weak acid but a strong oxidizing agent.

iodide *See* halide.

iodine Symbol I. A dark violet nonmetallic element belonging to group VII of the periodic table (*see* halogens); a.n. 53; r.a.m. 126.9045; r.d. 4.94; m.p. 113.5°C; b.p. 183.45°C. The element is insoluble in water but soluble in ethanol and other organic solvents. When heated it gives a violet vapour that sublimes. Iodine is required as a trace element (*see* essential element) by living organisms; in animals it is concentrated in the thyroid gland as a constituent of thyroid hormones. The element is present in sea water and was formerly extracted from seaweed. It is now obtained from oil-well brines (displacement by chlorine). There is one stable isotope, iodine-127, and fourteen radioactive isotopes. It is used in medicine as a mild antiseptic (dissolved in ethanol as *tincture of iodine*), and in the manufacture of iodine compounds. Chemically, it is less reactive than the other halogens and the most electropositive (metallic) halogen. It was discovered in 1812 by Courtois.

iodine(V) oxide (iodine pentoxide) A white solid, I_2O_5; r.d. 4.79; decomposes at 310°C. It dissolves in water to give iodic(V) acid and also acts as an oxidizing agent.

iodine value A measure of the amount of unsaturation in a fat or vegetable oil (i.e. the number of double bonds). It is obtained by finding the percentage of iodine by weight absorbed by the sample in a given time under standard conditions.

iodoethane (ethyl iodide) A colourless liquid *haloalkane, C_2H_5I; r.d. 1.9; m.p. −108°C; b.p. 72°C. It is made by reacting ethanol with a mixture of iodine and red phosphorus.

iodoform *See* tri-iodomethane.

iodoform test *See* haloform reaction.

iodomethane (methyl iodide) A colourless liquid haloalkane, CH_3I; r.d. 2.28; m.p. −66.45°C; b.p. 42.4°C. It can be made by reacting methanol with a mixture of iodine and red phosphorus.

ion An atom or group of atoms that has either lost one or more electrons, making it positively charged (an anion), or gained one or more electrons, making it negatively charged (a cation). *See also* ionization.

ion exchange The exchange of ions of the same charge between a solution (usually aqueous) and a solid in contact with it. The process occurs widely in nature, especially in the absorption and retention of water-soluble fertilizers by soils. For example, if a potassium salt is dissolved in water and applied to soil, potassium ions are absorbed by the soil and sodium and calcium ions are released from it.

The soil, in this case, is acting as an ion exchanger. Synthetic *ion-exchange resins* consist of various copolymers having a cross-linked three-dimensional structure to which ionic groups have been attached. An *anionic resin* has negative ions built into its structure and therefore exchanges positive ions. A *cationic resin* has positive ions built in and exchanges negative ions. Ion-exchange resins, which are used in sugar refining to remove salts, are synthetic organic polymers containing side groups that can be ionized. In anion exchange, the side groups are ionized basic groups, such as $-NH_3^+$ to which anions X^- are attached. The exchange reaction is one in which different anions in the solution displace the X^- from the solid. Similarly, cation exchange occurs with resins that have ionized acidic side groups such as $-COO^-$ or $-SO_2O^-$, with positive ions M^+ attached.

Ion exchange also occurs with inorganic polymers such as *zeolites, in which positive ions are held at sites in the silicate lattice. These are used for water-softening, in which Ca^{2+} ions in solution displace Na^+ions in the zeolite. The zeolite can be regenerated with sodium chloride solution. *Ion-exchange membranes* are used as separators in electrolytic cells to remove salts from sea water (*see also* desalination) and in producing deionized water.

ionic bond *See* chemical bond.

ionic crystal *See* crystal.

ionic product The product of the concentrations of ions present in a given solution taking the stoichiometry into account. For a sodium chloride solution the ionic product is $[Na^+][Cl^-]$; for a calcium chloride solution it is $[Ca^{2+}][Cl^-]^2$. In pure water, there is an equilibrium with a small amount of self-ionization:

$$H_2O \rightleftharpoons H^+ + OH^-$$

The equilibrium constant of this dissociation is given by

$$K_W = [H^+][OH^-]$$

since the concentration $[H_2O]$ can be taken as constant. K_W is referred to as the ionic product of water. It has the value 10^{-14} $mol^2\,dm^{-6}$ at 25°C. In pure water (i.e. no added acid or added alkali) $[H^+] = [OH^-] = 10^{-7}$ $mol\,dm^{-3}$. *See also* solubility product; pH scale.

ionic radius A value assigned to the radius of an ion in a crystalline solid, based on the assumption that the ions are spherical with a definite size. X-ray diffraction can be used to measure the internuclear distance in crystalline solids. For example, in NaF the Na – F distance is 0.231 nm, and this is assumed to be the sum of the Na^+ and F^- radii. By making certain assumptions about the shielding effect that the inner electrons have on the outer electrons, it is possible to assign individual values to the ionic radii – Na^+ 0.096 nm; F^- 0.135 nm. In general, negative ions have larger ionic radii than positive ions. The larger the negative charge, the larger the ion; the larger the positive charge, the smaller the ion.

ionic strength Symbol *I*. A function expressing the effect of the charge of the ions in a solution, equal to the sum of the molality of each type of ion present multiplied by the square of its charge. $I = \Sigma m_i z_i^2$.

ionization The process of producing *ions. Certain molecules (*see* electrolytes) ionize in solution; for example, *acids ionize when dissolved in water (*see also* solvation):

$$HCl \rightarrow H^+ + Cl^-$$

Electron transfer also causes ionization in certain reactions; for example, sodium and chlorine react by the transfer of a valence electron from the sodium atom to the chlorine atom to form the ions that constitute a sodium chloride crystal:

$$Na + Cl \rightarrow Na^+Cl^-$$

Ions may also be formed when an atom or molecule loses one or more electrons as a result of energy gained in a collision with another particle or a quantum of radiation (*see* photoionization). This may occur as a result of the impact of *ionizing radiation or of *thermal ionization and the reaction takes the form

$$A \rightarrow A^+ + e$$

Alternatively, ions can be formed by electron capture, i.e.

$$A + e \rightarrow A^-$$

ionization gauge A vacuum gauge consisting of a three-electrode system inserted into the container in which the pressure is to be measured. Electrons from the cathode are attracted to the grid, which is positively biased. Some pass through the grid but do not reach the anode, as it is maintained at a negative potential. Some of these electrons do, however, collide with gas molecules, ionizing them and converting them to positive ions. These ions are attracted to the anode; the resulting anode current can be used as a measure of the number of gas molecules present. Pressure as low as 10^{-6} pascal can be measured in this way.

ionization potential (IP) Symbol *I*. The minimum energy required to remove an electron from a specified atom or molecule to such a distance that there is no electrostatic interaction between ion and electron. Originally defined as the minimum potential through which an electron would have to fall to ionize an atom, the ionization potential was measured in volts. It is now, however, defined as the energy to effect an ionization and is conveniently measured in electronvolts (although this is not an SI unit).

The energy to remove the least strongly bound electron is the *first ionization potential.* Second, third, and higher ionization potentials can also be measured, although there is some ambiguity in terminology. Thus, in chemistry the second ionization potential is often taken to be the minimum energy required to remove an electron from the singly charged ion; the second IP of lithium would be the energy for the process

$$Li^+ \rightarrow Li^{2+} + e$$

In physics, the second ionization potential is the energy required to remove an electron from the next to highest energy level in the neutral atom or molecule; e.g.

$$Li \rightarrow Li^{*+} + e,$$

where Li^{*+} is an excited singly charged ion produced by removing an electron from the K-shell.

ionizing radiation Radiation of sufficiently high energy to cause *ionization in the medium through which it passes. It may consist of a stream of high-energy particles (e.g. electrons, protons, alpha-particles) or short-wavelength electromagnetic radiation (ultraviolet, X-rays, gamma-rays). This type of radiation can cause extensive damage to the molecular structure of a substance either as a result of the direct transfer of energy to its atoms or molecules or as a result of the secondary electrons released by ionization. In biological tissue the effect of ionizing radiation can be very serious, usually as a consequence of the ejection of an electron from a water molecule and the oxidizing or reducing effects of the resulting highly reactive species:

$$H_2O \rightarrow e^- + H_2O^* + H_2O^+ \rightarrow$$
$$\cdot OH + H_3O^+ + \cdot H,$$

where the dot before a radical indicates an unpaired electron and an * denotes an excited species.

ion-microprobe analysis A technique for analysing the surface composition of solids. The sample is bombarded with a narrow beam (as small as 2 μm diameter) of high-energy ions. Ions ejected from the surface by sputtering are detected by mass spectrometry. The technique allows quantitative analysis of both chemical and isotopic composition for concentrations as low as a few parts per million.

ion pair A pair of oppositely charged ions produced as a result of a single ionization; e.g.

$$HCl \rightarrow H^+ + Cl^-.$$

Sometimes a positive ion and an electron are referred to as an ion pair, as in

$$A \rightarrow A^+ + e^-.$$

ion pump A type of *vacuum pump that can reduce the pressure in a container to about 1 nanopascal by passing a beam of electrons through the residual gas. The gas is ionized and the positive ions formed are attracted to a cathode within the container where they remain trapped. The pump is only useful at very low pressures, i.e. below about 1 micropascal. The pump has a limited capacity because the absorbed ions eventually saturate the surface of the cathode. A more effective pump can be made by simultaneously producing a film of metal by ion impact (sputtering), so that fresh surface is continuously produced. The device is then known as a *sputter-ion pump.*

IP *See* ionization potential.

iridium Symbol Ir. A silvery metallic *transition element (*see also* platinum metals); a.n. 77; r.a.m. 192.20; r.d. 22.42; m.p. 2410°C; b.p. 4130°C. It occurs with platinum and is mainly used in alloys with platinum and osmium. The element forms a range of iridium(III) and iridium(IV) complexes. It was discovered in 1804 by Tennant.

iron Symbol Fe. A silvery malleable and ductile metallic *transition element; a.n. 26; r.a.m. 55.847; r.d. 7.87; m.p. 1535°C; b.p. 2750°C. The main sources are the ores *haematite (Fe_2O_3), *magnetite (Fe_3O_4), limonite ($FeO(OH)_n H_2O$), ilmenite ($FeTiO_3$), siderite ($FeCO_3$), and pyrite (FeS_2). The metal is smelted in a *blast furnace to give impure *pig iron, which is further processed to give *cast iron, *wrought iron, and various types of *steel. The pure element has three crystal forms: *alpha-iron*, stable below 906°C with a body-centred-cubic structure; *gamma-iron*, stable between 906°C and 1403°C with a nonmagnetic face-centred-cubic structure; and *delta-iron*, which is the body-centred-cubic form above 1403°C. Alpha-iron is ferromagnetic up to its Curie point (768°C). The element has nine isotopes (mass numbers 52–60), and is the fourth most abundant in the earth's crust. It is required as a trace element (*see* essential element) by living organisms. Iron is quite reactive, being oxidized by moist air, displacing hydrogen from dilute acids, and combining with nonmetallic elements. It forms ionic salts and numerous complexes with the metal in the +2 or +3 oxidation states. Iron(VI) also exists in the ferrate ion FeO_4^{2-}, and the element also forms complexes in which its oxidation number is zero (e.g. $Fe(CO)_5$).

iron(II) chloride A green-yellow deliquescent compound, $FeCl_2$; hexagonal; r.d. 3.16; m.p. 670°C. It also exists in hydrated forms: $FeCl_2.2H_2O$ (green monoclinic; r.d. 2.36) and $FeCl_2.4H_2O$ (blue-green monoclinic deliquescent; r.d. 1.93). Anhydrous iron(II) chloride can be made by passing a stream of dry hydrogen chloride over the heated metal; the hydrated forms can be made using dilute hydrochloric acid or by recrystallizing with water. It is converted into iron(III) chloride by the action of chlorine.

iron(III) chloride A black-brown solid, $FeCl_3$; hexagonal; r.d. 2.9; m.p. 306°C; decomposes at 315°C. It also exists as the hexahydrate $FeCl_3.6H_2O$, a brown-yellow deliquescent crystalline substance (m.p. 37°C; b.p. 280–285°C). Iron(III) chloride is prepared by passing dry chlorine over iron wire or steel wool. The reaction proceeds with incandescence when started and iron (III) chloride sublimes as almost black iridescent scales. The compound is rapidly hydrolysed in moist air. In solution it is partly hydrolysed; hydrolysis can be suppressed by the addition of hydrochloric acid. The compound dissolves in many organic solvents, forming solutions of low electrical conductivity: in ethanol, ethoxyethane, and pyridine the molecular weight corresponds to $FeCl_3$ but is higher in other solvents corresponding to Fe_2Cl_6. The vapour is also dimerized. In many ways the compound resembles aluminium chloride, which it may replace in Friedel–Crafts reactions.

iron(II) oxide A black solid, FeO; cubic; r.d. 5.7; m.p. 369°C. It can be obtained by heating iron(II) oxalate; the carbon monoxide formed produces a reducing atmosphere thus preventing oxidation to iron(III) oxide. The compound has the sodium chloride structure, indicating its ionic nature, but the crystal lattice is deficient in iron(II) ions and it is nonstoichiometric. Iron(II) oxide dissolves readily in dilute acids.

iron(III) oxide A red-brown to black insoluble solid, Fe_2O_3; trigonal; r.d. 5.24; m.p. 1565°C. There is also a hydrated form, $Fe_2O_3xH_2O$, which is a red-brown powder; r.d. 2.44–3.60. (*See* rusting.)

Iron(III) oxide occurs naturally as *haematite and can be prepared by heating iron(III) hydroxide or iron(II) sulphate. It is readily reduced on heating with carbon or in a stream of carbon monoxide, hydrogen, or coal gas:

$$Fe_2O_3 + 3C \rightarrow 2Fe + 3CO$$

iron pyrites *See* pyrite.

iron(II) sulphate An off-white solid, $FeSO_4.H_2O$; monoclinic; r.d. 2.970. There is also a heptahydrate, $FeSO_4.7H_2O$; blue-green monoclinic; r.d. 1.898; m.p. 64°C. The heptahydrate is the best known iron(II) salt and is sometimes called *green vitriol* or *copperas*. It is obtained by the action of dilute sulphuric acid on iron in a reducing atmosphere. The anhydrous compound is very hygroscopic. It decomposes at red heat to give iron(III) oxide, sulphur trioxide, and sulphur dioxide. A solution of iron(II) sulphate is gradually oxidized on exposure to air, a basic iron(III) sulphate being deposited.

iron(III) sulphate A yellow hygroscopic compound, $Fe_2(SO_4)_3$; rhombic; r.d. 3.097; decomposes above 480°C. It is obtained by heating an aqueous acidified solution of iron(II) sulphate with hydrogen peroxide:

$$2FeSO_4 + H_2SO_4 + H_2O_2 \rightarrow Fe_2(SO_4)_3 + 2H_2O$$

On crystallizing, the hydrate $Fe_2(SO_4)_3.9H_2O$ is formed. The acid sulphate $Fe_2(SO_4)_3.H_2SO_4.8H_2O$ is deposited from solutions containing a sufficient excess of sulphuric acid.

irreversible process *See* reversible process.

irreversible reaction *See* chemical reaction.

isentropic process Any process that takes place without a change of *entropy. The quantity of heat transferred, δQ, in a reversible process is proportional to the change in entropy, δS, i.e. $\delta Q = T\delta S$, where T is the thermodynamic temperature. Therefore, a reversible *adiabatic process is isentropic, i.e. when $\delta Q = 0$, δS also equals 0.

iso- Prefix denoting that a compound is an *isomer, e.g. isopentane ($CH_3CH(CH_3)C_2H_5$, 2-methylbutane) is an isomer of pentane.

isobar A curve on a graph indicating readings taken at constant pressure.

isocyanate *See* cyanic acid.

isocyanic acid *See* cyanic acid.

isocyanide *See* isonitrile.

isocyanide test A test for primary amines by reaction with an alcoholic solution of potassium hydroxide and trichloromethane.

$$RNH_2 + 3KOH + CHCl_3 \rightarrow RNC + 3KCl + 3H_2O$$

The isocyanide RNC is recognized by its unpleasant smell. This reaction of primary amines is called the *carbylamine reaction*.

isoelectronic Describing compounds that have the same numbers of valence electrons. For example, nitrogen (N_2) and carbon monoxide (CO) are isoelectronic molecules.

isoleucine *See* amino acid.

isomerism The existence of chemical compounds (*isomers*) that have the same molecular formulae but different molecular structures or different arrangements of atoms in space. In *structural isomerism* the molecules have different molecular structures: i.e. they may be different types of compound or they may simply differ in the position of the functional group in the molecule. Structural isomers generally have different physical and chemical properties. In *stereoisomerism*, the isomers have the same formula and functional groups, but differ in the arrangement of groups in space. Optical isomerism is one form of this (*see* optical activity). Another type is *cis–trans isomerism* (formerly *geometrical isomerism*), in which the isomers have different positions of groups with respect to a double bond or central atom (see illustration).

ISOMERISM

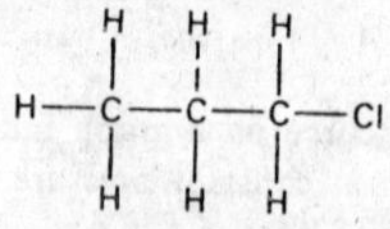

1-chloropropane

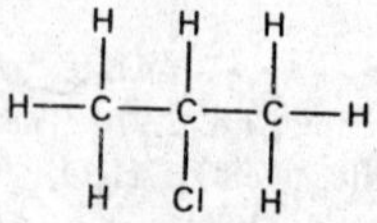

2-chloropropane

structural isomers in which the functional group has different positions

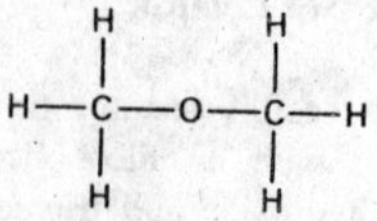

methoxymethane

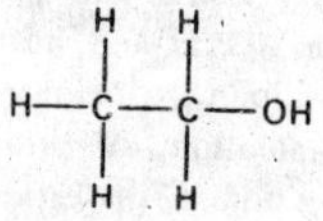

ethanol

structural isomers in which the functional groups are different

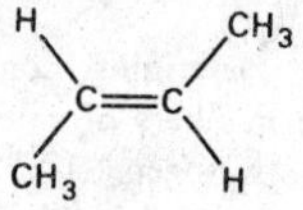

trans-but-2-ene

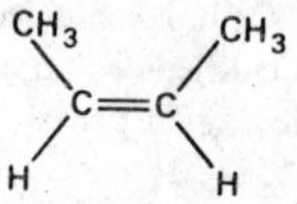

cis-but-2-ene

cis–trans isomers in which the groups are distributed on a double bond

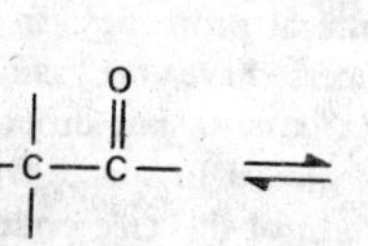

cis–trans isomers in a square-planar complex

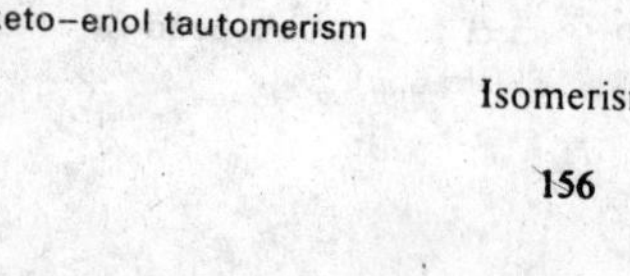

keto form

enol form

keto–enol tautomerism

Isomerism

isomers *See* isomerism.

isometric 1. (in crystallography) Denoting a system in which the axes are perpendicular to each other, as in cubic crystals. **2.** Denoting a line on a graph illustrating the way in which temperature and pressure are interrelated at constant volume.

isomorphism The existence of two or more substances (*isomorphs*) that have the same crystal structure, so that they are able to form *solid solutions.

isonitrile (isocyanide; carbylamine) An organic compound containing the group –NC, in which the bonding is to the nitrogen atom.

iso-octane *See* octane; octane number.

isoprene A colourless liquid diene, CH_2:C(CH_3)CH:CH_2. The systematic name is *2-methylbuta-1,3-diene*. It is the structural unit in *terpenes and natural *rubber, and is used in making synthetic rubbers.

isotactic polymer *See* polymer.

isothermal process Any process that takes place at constant temperature. In such a process heat is, if necessary, supplied or removed from the system at just the right rate to maintain constant temperature. *Compare* adiabatic process.

isotonic Describing solutions that have the same osmotic pressure.

isotope One of two or more atoms of the same element that have the same number of protons in their nucleus but different numbers of neutrons. Hydrogen (1 proton, no neutrons), deuterium (1 proton, 1 neutron), and tritium (1 proton, 2 neutrons) are isotopes of hydrogen. Most elements in nature consist of a mixture of isotopes. *See* isotope separation.

isotope separation The separation of the *isotopes of an element from each other on the basis of slight differences in their physical properties. For laboratory quantities the most suitable device is often the mass spectrometer. On a larger scale the methods used include gaseous diffusion (widely used for separating isotopes of uranium in the form of the gas uranium hexafluoride), distillation (formerly used to produce heavy water), electrolysis (requiring cheap electrical power), thermal diffusion (formerly used to separate uranium isotopes, but now considered uneconomic), centrifuging (a method in which there is renewed interest), and laser methods (involving the excitation of one isotope and its subsequent separation by electromagnetic means).

isotopic number (neutron excess) The difference between the number of neutrons in an isotope and the number of protons.

isotropic Denoting a medium whose physical properties are independent of direction. *Compare* anisotropic.

J

jade A hard semiprecious stone consisting either of jadeite or nephrite. *Jadeite*, the most valued of the two, is a sodium aluminium pyroxene, $NaAlSi_2O_6$. It is prized for its intense translucent green colour but white, green and white, brown, and orange varieties also occur. The only important source of jadeite is in the Mogaung region of upper Burma. *Nephrite* is one of the amphibole group of rock-forming minerals. It occurs in a variety of colours, including green, yellow, white, and black. Important sources include the Soviet Union, New Zealand, Alaska, China, and W USA.

jadeite *See* jade.

Jahn–Teller effect If a likely structure of a nonlinear molecule or ion would have degenerate orbitals (i.e. two molecular orbitals with the same energy levels) the actual structure of the molecule or ion is distorted so as to split the energy levels ('raise' the degeneracy). The effect is observed in inorganic complexes. For example, the ion $[Cu(H_2O)_6]^{2+}$ is octahedral and the six ligands might be expected to occupy equidistant positions at the corners of a regular octahedron. In fact, the octahedron is distorted, with four ligands in a square and two opposite ligands further away. If the 'original' structure has a centre of symmetry, the distorted structure must also have a centre of symmetry. The effect was predicted theoretically by H. A. Jahn and Edward Teller in 1937.

jasper An impure variety of *chalcedony. It is associated with iron ores and as a result contains iron oxide impurities that give the mineral its characteristic red or reddish-brown colour. Jasper is used as a gemstone.

jet A variety of *coal that can be cut and polished and is used for jewellery, ornaments, etc.

jeweller's rouge Red powdered haematite, iron(III) oxide, Fe_2O_3. It is a mild abrasive used in metal cleaners and polishes.

joule Symbol J. The *SI unit of work and energy equal to the work done when the point of application of a force of one newton moves, in the direction of the force, a distance of one metre. 1 joule = 10^7 ergs = 0.2388 calorie. It is named after James Prescott Joule (1818–89).

Joule's law The *internal energy of a given mass of gas is independent of its volume and pressure, being a function of temperature alone. This law applies only to *ideal gases (for which it provides a definition of thermodynamic temperature) as in a real gas intermolecular forces would cause changes in the internal energy should a change of volume occur. *See also* Joule–Thomson effect.

Joule–Thomson effect (Joule–Kelvin effect) The change in temperature that occurs when a gas expands through a porous plug into a region of lower pressure. For most real gases the temperature falls under these circumstances as the gas has to do internal work in overcoming the intermolecular forces to enable the expansion to take place. This is a deviation from *Joule's law. There is usually also a deviation from *Boyle's law, which can cause either a rise or a fall in temperature since any increase in the product of pressure and volume is a measure of external work done. At a given pressure, there is a particular temperature, called the *inversion temperature* of the gas, at which the rise in temperature from the Boyle's law deviation is balanced by the fall from the Joule's law deviation. There is then no temperature change. Above the inversion temperature the gas is heated by expansion, below it, it is cooled. The effect was discovered by James Joule working in collaboration with William Thomson (later Lord Kelvin; 1824–1907).

K

kainite A naturally occurring double salt of magnesium sulphate and potassium chloride, $MgSO_4.KCl.3H_2O$.

kalinite A mineral form of *aluminium potassium sulphate ($Al_2(SO_4)_3.K_2SO_4.24H_2O$).

kaolin (china clay) A soft white clay that is composed chiefly of the mineral kaolinite (*see* clay minerals). It is formed during the weathering and hydrothermal alteration of other clays or feldspar. Kaolin is mined in the UK, France, Czechoslovakia, and USA. Besides its vital importance in the ceramics industry it is also used extensively as a filler in the manufacture of rubber, paper, paint, and textiles and as a constituent of medicines.

katharometer An instrument for comparing the thermal conductivities of two gases by comparing the rate of loss of heat from two heating coils surrounded by the gases. The instrument can be used to detect the presence of a small amount of an impurity in air and is also used as a detector in gas chromatography.

Kekulé structure A proposed structure of *benzene in which the molecule has a hexagonal ring of carbon atoms linked by alternating double and single bonds. It was suggested in 1865 by Friedrich August Kekulé (1829–69).

kelvin Symbol K. The *SI unit of thermodynamic *temperature equal to the fraction 1/273.16 of the thermodynamic temperature of the *triple point of water. The magnitude of the kelvin is equal to that of the degree celsius (centigrade), but a temperature expressed in degrees celsius is numerically equal to the temperature in kelvins less 273.15 (i.e. °C = K − 273.15). The *absolute zero of temperature has a temperature of 0 K (−273.15°C). The former name *degree kelvin* (symbol °K) became obsolete by international agreement in 1967. The unit is named after Lord Kelvin (1824–1907).

Kelvin effect *See* Thomson effect.

keratin Any of a group of fibrous *proteins occurring in hair, feathers, hooves, and horns. Keratins have coiled polypeptide chains that combine to form supercoils of several polypeptides linked by disulphide bonds between adjacent cysteine amino acids.

kerosine *See* petroleum.

ketals Organic compounds, similar to *acetals, formed by addition of an alcohol to a ketone. If one molecule of ketone (RR′CO) reacts with one molecule of alcohol R″OH, then a *hemiketal* is formed. The rings of ketose sugars are hemiketals. Further reaction produces a full ketal ($RR'C(OR'')_2$).

keto–enol tautomerism A form of tautomerism in which a compound containing a $-CH_2-CO-$ group (the *keto form* of the molecule) is in equilibrium with one containing the $-CH{=}C(OH)-$ group (the *enol*). It occurs by migration of a hydrogen atom between a carbon atom and the oxygen on an adjacent carbon. *See* isomerism.

keto form *See* keto–enol tautomerism.

ketohexose *See* monosaccharide.

ketone body Any of three compounds, acetoacetic acid (3-oxobutanoic acid, CH_3COCH_2COOH), *β*-hydroxybutyric acid (3-hydroxybutanoic acid, $CH_3CH(OH)CH_2COOH$), and acetone or (propanone, CH_3COCH_3), produced by the liver as a result of the metabolism of body fat deposits. Ketone bodies are normally used as energy sources by peripheral tissues.

ketones Organic compounds that contain the group $-CO-$ linked to two hydrocarbon groups. The *ketone group* is a carbonyl group with two single bonds to other carbon atoms. In systematic chemical nomenclature, ketone names end with the suffix *-one*. Examples are propanone (acetone), CH_3COCH_3, and butanone (methyl ethyl ketone), $CH_3COC_2H_5$. Ketones can be made by oxidizing secondary alcohols to convert the C–OH group to C=O. Certain ketones form addition compounds with sodium hydrogensulphate(IV) (sodium hydrogensulphite). They also form addition compounds with hydrogen cyanide to give *cyanohydrins and with alcohols to give *ketals. They undergo condensation reactions to yield *oximes, *hydrazones, phenylhydrazones, and *semicarbazones. These are reactions that they share with aldehydes. Unlike aldehydes, they do not affect Fehling's solution or Tollen's reagent and do not easily oxidize. Strong oxidizing agents produce a mixture of carboxylic acids; butanone, for example, gives ethanoic and propanoic acids.

ketopentose *See* monosaccharide.

ketose *See* monosaccharide.

kieselguhr A soft fine-grained deposit consisting of the siliceous skeletal remains of diatoms, formed in lakes and ponds. Kieselguhr is used as an absorbent, filtering material, filler, and insulator.

kieserite A mineral form of *magnesium sulphate monohydrate, $MgSO_4.H_2O$.

kilo- Symbol k. A prefix used in the metric system to denote 1000 times. For example, 1000 volts = 1 kilovolt (kV).

kilogram Symbol kg. The *SI unit of mass defined as a mass equal to that of the international platinum–iridium prototype kept by the International Bureau of Weights and Measures at Sèvres, near Paris.

kimberlite A rare igneous rock that often contains diamonds. It occurs as narrow pipe intrusions but is often altered and fragmented. It consists of olivine and phlogopite mica, usually with calcite, serpentine, and other minerals. The chief occurrences of kimberlite are in South Africa, especially at Kimberley (after which the rock is named), and in the Yakutia area of Siberia.

kinematic viscosity Symbol ν. The ratio of the *viscosity of a liquid to its density. The SI unit is $m^2\ s^{-1}$.

kinetic effect A chemical effect that depends on reaction rate rather than on thermodynamics. For example, diamond is thermodynamically less stable than graphite; its apparent stability depends on the vanishingly slow rate at which it is converted. *Overvoltage in electrolytic cells is another example of a kinetic effect. *Kinetic isotope effects* are changes in reaction rates produced by isotope substitution. For example, if the slow step in a chemical reaction is the breaking of a C–H bond, the rate for the deuterated compound would be slightly lower because of the lower vibrational frequency of the C–D bond. Such effects are used in investigating the mechanisms of chemical reactions.

kinetic energy *See* energy.

kinetic theory A theory, largely the work of Count Rumford (1753–1814), James Joule (1818–89), and James Clerk Maxwell (1831–79), that explains the physical properties of matter in terms of the motions of its constituent particles. In a gas, for example, the pressure is due to the incessant impacts of the gas molecules on the walls of the container. If it is assumed that the molecules occupy negligible space, exert negligible forces on each other except during collisions, are perfectly elastic, and make only brief collisions with each other, it can be shown that the pressure p exerted by one mole of gas containing n molecules each of mass m in a container of volume V, will be given by:

$$p = nm\bar{c}^2/3V,$$

where $\bar{c}^2$ is the mean square speed of the molecules. As according to the *gas laws for one mole of gas: $pV = RT$, where T is the thermodynamic temperature, and R is the molar *gas constant, it follows that:

$$RT = nm\bar{c}^2/3$$

Thus, the thermodynamic temperature of a gas is proportional to the mean square speed of its molecules. As the average kinetic *energy of translation of the molecules is $m\bar{c}^2/2$, the temperature is given by:

$$T = (m\bar{c}^2/2)(2n/3R)$$

The number of molecules in one mole of any gas is the *Avogadro constant, N_A; therefore in this equation $n = N_A$. The ratio R/N_A is a constant called the *Boltzmann constant (k). The average kinetic energy of translation of the molecules of one mole of any gas is therefore $3kT/2$. For monatomic gases this is proportional to the *internal energy (U) of the gas, i.e.

$$U = N_A 3kT/2$$

and as $k = R/N_A$

$$U = 3RT/2$$

For diatomic and polyatomic gases the rotational and vibrational energies also have to be taken into account (*see* degrees of freedom).

In liquids, according to the kinetic theory, the atoms and molecules still move around at random, the temperature being proportional to their average kinetic energy. However, they are sufficiently close to each other for the attractive forces between molecules to be important. A molecule that approaches the surface will experience a resultant force tending to keep it within the liquid. It is, therefore, only some of the fastest moving molecules that escape; as a result the average kinetic energy of those that fail to escape is reduced. In this way evaporation from the surface of a liquid causes its temperature to fall.

In a crystalline solid the atoms, ions, and molecules are able only to vibrate about the fixed positions of a *crystal lattice; the attractive forces are so strong at this range that no free movement is possible.

Kipp's apparatus A laboratory apparatus for making a gas by the reaction of a solid with a liquid (e.g. the reaction of hydrochloric acid with iron sulphide to give hydrogen sulphide). It consists of three interconnected glass globes arranged vertically, with the solid in the middle globe. The upper and lower globes are connected by a tube and contain the liquid. The middle globe has a tube with a tap for drawing off gas. When the tap is closed, pressure of gas forces the liquid down in the bottom reservoir and up into the top, and reaction does not occur. When the tap is opened, the release in pressure allows the liquid to rise into the middle globe, where it reacts with the solid. It is named after Petrus Kipp (1808–64).

Kjeldahl's method A method for measuring the percentage of nitrogen in an organic compound. The compound is boiled with concentrated sulphuric acid and copper(II) sulphate catalyst to convert any nitrogen to ammonium sulphate. Alkali is added and the mixture heated to distil off ammonia. This is passed into a standard acid solution, and the amount of ammonia can then be found by estimating the amount of unreacted acid by titration. The amount of nitrogen in the original specimen can then be calculated. The method was developed by the Danish chemist Johan Kjeldahl (1849–1900).

Kohlrausch's law If a salt is dissolved in water, the conductivity of the (dilute) solution is the sum of two values – one depending on the positive ions and the other on the negative ions. The law, which depends on the independent migration of ions, was deduced experimentally by the German chemist Friedrich Kohlrausch (1840–1910).

Kolbe's method A method of making alkanes by electrolysing a solution of a carboxylic acid salt. For a salt Na^+RCOO^-, the carboxylate ions lose electrons at the cathode to give radicals:

$$RCOO^- - e \rightarrow RCOO\cdot$$

These decompose to give alkyl radicals

$$RCOO\cdot \rightarrow R\cdot + CO_2$$

Two alkyl radicals couple to give an alkane

$$R\cdot + R\cdot \rightarrow RR$$

The method can only be used for hydrocarbons with an even number of carbon atoms, although mixtures of two salts can be electrolysed to give a mixture of three products. The method was discovered by the German chemist Herman Kolbe (1818–84), who electrolysed pentanoic acid (C_4H_9COOH) in 1849 and obtained a hydrocarbon, which he assumed was the substance 'butyl' C_4H_9 (actually octane, C_8H_{18}).

Kovar A tradename for an alloy of iron, cobalt, and nickel with an *expansivity similar to that of glass. It is therefore used in making glass-to-metal seals, especially in circumstances in which a temperature variation can be expected.

Krebs cycle (citric acid cycle; tricarboxylic acid cycle; TCA cycle) A cyclical series of biochemical reactions that is fundamental to the metabolism of aerobic organisms, i.e. animals, plants, and many microorganisms. The enzymes of the Krebs cycle are in close association with the components of the *electron transport chain. The two-carbon acetyl coenzyme A (acetyl CoA) reacts with the four-carbon oxaloacetate to form the six-carbon citric acid. In a series of seven reactions, this is reconverted to oxaloacetate and produces two molecules of carbon dioxide. Most importantly, the cycle generates one molecule of guanosine triphosphate (GTP – equivalent to 1 ATP) and reduces three molecules of the coenzyme NAD to NADH and one molecule of the coenzyme FAD to $FADH_2$. NADH and $FADH_2$ are then oxidized by the electron transport chain to generate three and two molecules of ATP respectively. This gives a net yield of 12 molecules of ATP per molecule of acetyl CoA.

Acetyl CoA can be derived from carbohydrates (via *glycolysis), fats, or certain amino acids. (Other amino acids may enter the cycle at different stages.) Thus the Krebs cycle is the central 'crossroads' in the complex system of metabolic pathways and is involved not only in degradation and energy production but also in the synthesis of biomolecules. It is named after its principal discoverer, Sir Hans Adolf Krebs (1900–81).

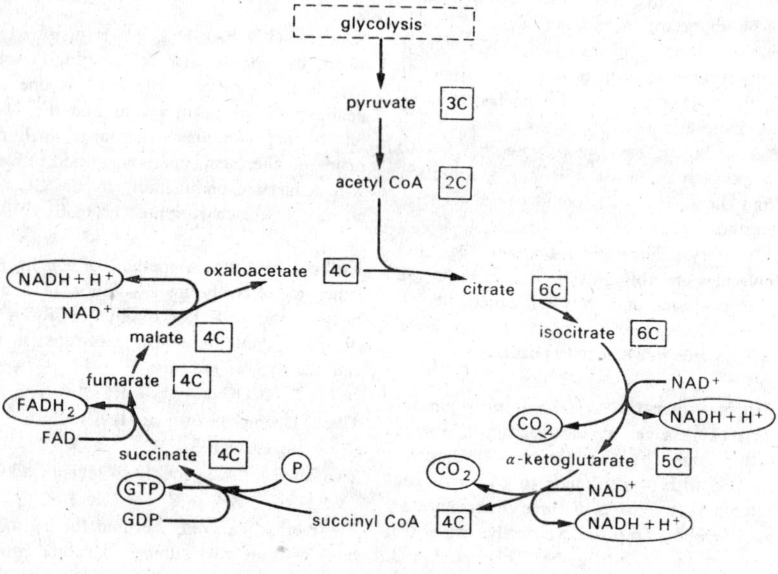

Krebs cycle

Kroll process A process for producing certain metals by reducing the chloride with magnesium metal, e.g.

$$TiCl_4 + 2Mg \rightarrow Ti + 2MgCl_2$$

krypton Symbol Kr. A colourless gaseous element belonging to group 0 (the *noble gases) of the periodic table; a.n. 36; r.a.m. 83.80; d. 3.73 g m^{-3}; m.p. −156.6°C; b.p. −152.3°C. Krypton occurs in air (0.0001% by volume) from which it can be extracted by fractional distillation of liquid air. Usually, the element is not isolated but is used with other inert gases in fluorescent lamps, etc. The element has five natural isotopes (mass numbers 78, 80, 82, 83, 84) and there are five radioactive isotopes (76, 77, 79, 81, 85). Krypton−85 (half-life 10.76 years) is produced in fission reactors and it has been suggested that an equilibrium amount will eventually occur in the atmosphere. The element is inert and forms no stable compounds (KrF_2 has been reported).

Kupfer nickel A naturally occurring form of nickel arsenide, NiAs; an important ore of nickel.

L

labelling The process of replacing a stable atom in a compound with a radioisotope of the same element to enable its path through a biological or mechanical system to be traced by the radiation it emits. In some cases a different stable isotope is used and the path is detected by means of a mass spectrometer. A compound containing either a radioactive or stable isotope is called a *labelled compound.* If a hydrogen atom in each molecule of the compound has been replaced by a tritium atom, the compound is called a *tritiated compound.* A radioactive labelled compound will behave chemically and physically in the same way as an otherwise identical stable compound, and its presence can easily be detected using a Geiger counter. This process of *radioactive tracing* is widely used in chemistry, biology, medicine, and engineering. For example, it can be used to follow the course of the reaction of a carboxylic acid with an alcohol to give an ester, e.g.

$$CH_3COOH + C_2H_5OH \rightarrow$$
$$C_2H_5COOCH_3 + H_2O$$

To determine whether the noncarbonyl oxygen in the ester comes from the acid or the alcohol, the reaction is performed with the labelled compound $CH_3CO^{18}OH$, in which the oxygen in the hydroxyl group of the acid has been 'labelled' by using the ^{18}O isotope. It is then found that the water product is $H_2{}^{18}O$; i.e. the oxygen in the ester comes from the alcohol, not the acid.

labile Describing a chemical compound in which certain atoms or groups can easily be replaced by other atoms or groups. The term is applied to coordination complexes in which ligands can easily be replaced by other ligands in an equilibrium reaction.

lactams Organic compounds containing a ring of atoms in which the group −NH.CO.− forms part of the ring. Lactams can be formed by reaction of an $-NH_2$ group in one part of a molecule with a −COOH group in the other to give a cyclic amide. They can exist in an alternative tautomeric form, the *lactim* form, in which the hydrogen atom on the nitrogen has migrated to the oxygen of the carbonyl to give −N=C(OH)−. The pyrimidine base uracil is an example of a lactam.

lactate A salt or ester of lactic acid (i.e. a 2-hydroxypropanoate).

lactic acid (2-hydroxypropanoic acid) A clear odourless hygroscopic syrupy liquid, $CH_3CH(OH)COOH$, with a sour taste; r.d. 1.206; m.p. 18°C; b.p. 122°C. It is prepared by the hydrolysis of ethanal cyanohydrin or

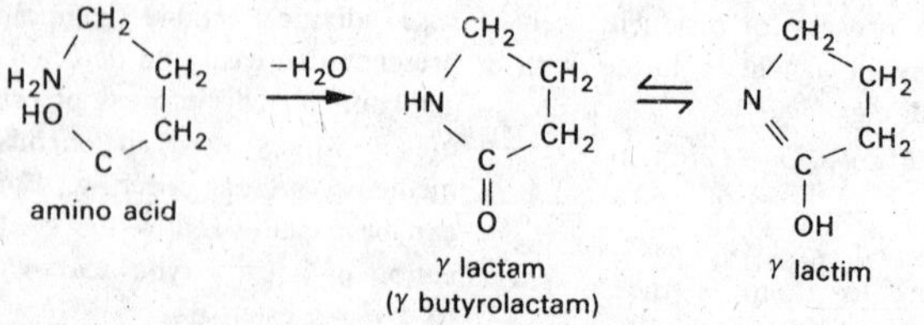

Lactam formation

the oxidation of propan-1,2-diol using dilute nitric acid. Lactic acid is manufactured by the fermentation of lactose (from milk) and used in the dyeing and tanning industries. It is an alpha hydroxy *carboxylic acid. *See also* optical activity.

Lactic acid is produced from pyruvic acid in active muscle tissue when oxygen is limited and subsequently removed for conversion to glucose by the liver. During strenuous exercise it may build up in the muscles, causing cramplike pains. It is also produced by fermentation in certain bacteria and is characteristic of sour milk.

lactims *See* lactams.

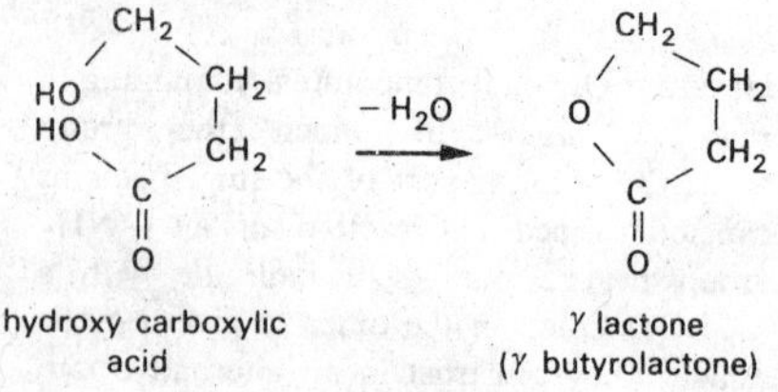

Lactone formation

lactones Organic compounds containing a ring of atoms in which the group –CO.O– forms part of the ring. Lactones can be formed (or regarded as formed) by reaction of an –OH group in one part of a molecule with a –COOH group in the other to give a cyclic ester. This type of reaction occurs with γ-hydroxy carboxylic acids such as the compound $CH_2(OH)CH_2CH_2COOH$ (the hydroxyl group is on the third carbon from the carboxyl group). The resulting γ-lactone has a five-membered ring. Similarly, δ-lactones have six-membered rings. β-lactones, with a four-membered ring, are not produced directly from β-hydroxy acids, but can be synthesized by other means.

lactose (milk sugar) A sugar comprising one glucose molecule linked to a galactose molecule. Lactose is manufactured by the mammary gland and occurs only in milk. For example, cows' milk contains about 4.7% lactose. It is less sweet than sucrose (cane sugar).

Ladenburg benzene An (erroneous) structure for *benzene proposed by Albert Ladenburg (1842–1911), in which the six carbon atoms were arranged at the corners of a triangular prism and linked by single bonds to each other and to the six hydrogen atoms.

laevorotatory Designating a chemical compound that rotates the plane of plane-polarized light to the left (anticlockwise for someone facing the oncoming radiation). *See* optical activity.

laevulose *See* fructose.

LAH Lithium aluminium hydride; *see* lithium tetrahydroaluminate (III).

lake A pigment made by combining an organic dyestuff with an inorganic compound (usually an oxide, hydroxide, or salt). Absorption of the organic compound on the inorganic substrate yields a coloured complex, as in the combination of a dyestuff with a *mordant. Lakes are used in paints and printing inks.

Lamb shift A small energy difference between two levels ($^2S_{1/2}$ and $^2P_{1/2}$) in the *hydrogen spectrum. The shift results from the quantum interaction between the atomic electron and the electromagnetic radiation. It was first explained by Willis Eugene Lamb (1913–).

lamellar solids Solid substances in which the crystal structure has distinct layers (i.e. has a layer lattice). The *micas are an example of this type of compound. *Intercalation compounds* are lamellar compounds formed by interposition of atoms, ions, etc., between the layers of an existing element or compound. For example, graphite is a lamellar solid. With strong oxidizing agents (e.g. a mixture of concentrated sulphuric and nitric acids) it forms a nonstoichiometric 'graphitic oxide', which is an intercalation compound having oxygen atoms between the layers of carbon atoms.

lamp black A finely divided (microcrystalline) form of carbon made by burning organic compounds in insufficient oxygen. It is used as a black pigment and filler.

lanolin An emulsion of purified wool fat in water, containing cholesterol and certain terpene alcohols and esters. It is used in cosmetics.

lansfordite A mineral form of *magnesium carbonate pentahydrate, $MgCO_3.5H_2O$.

lanthanides *See* lanthanoids.

lanthanoid contraction *See* lanthanoids.

lanthanoids (lanthanides; lanthanons; rare-earth elements) A series of elements in the *periodic table, generally considered to range in proton number from cerium (58) to lutetium (71) inclusive. The lanthanoids all have two outer *s*-electrons (a $6s^2$ configuration), follow lanthanum, and are classified together because an increasing proton number corresponds to increase in number of 4*f* electrons. In fact, the 4*f* and 5*d* levels are close in energy and the filling is not smooth. The outer electron configurations are as follows:

57 lanthanum (La) $5d^16s^2$
58 cerium (Ce) $4f5d^16s^2$ (or $4f^26s^2$)
59 praseodymium (Pr) $4f^36s^2$
60 neodymium (Nd) $4f^46s^2$
61 promethium (Pm) $4f^56s^2$
62 samarium (Sm) $4f^66s^2$
63 europium (Eu) $4f^76s^2$
64 gadolinium (Gd) $4f^75d^16s^2$
65 terbium (Tb) $4f^96s^2$
66 dysprosium (Dy) $4f^{10}6s^2$
67 holmium (Ho) $4f^{11}6s^2$
68 erbium (Er) $4f^{12}6s^2$
69 thulium (Tm) $4f^{13}6s^2$
70 ytterbium (Yb) $4f^{14}6s^2$
71 lutetium (Lu) $4f^{14}5d^16s^2$

Note that lanthanum itself does not have a 4*f* electron but it is generally classified with the lanthanoids because of its chemical similarities, as are yttrium (Yt) and scandium (Sc). Scandium, yttrium, and lanthanum are *d*-block elements; the lanthanoids and *actinoids make up the *f*-block.

The lanthanoids are sometimes simply called the *rare earths*, although strictly the 'earths' are their oxides. Nor are they particularly rare: they occur widely, usually together. All are silvery very reactive metals. The *f*-electrons do not penetrate to the outer part of the atom and there is no *f*-orbital participation in bonding (unlike the *d*-orbitals of the main *transition elements) and the elements form few coordination compounds. The main compounds contain M^{3+} ions. Cerium also has the highly oxidizing Ce^{4+} state and europium and ytterbium have a M^{2+} state.

The 4*f* orbitals in the atoms are not very effective in shielding the outer electrons from the nuclear charge. In going across the series the increasing nuclear charge causes a contraction in the radius of the M^{3+} ion – from 0.1061 nm in lanthanum to 0.0848 nm in lutetium. This effect, the *lanthanoid con-*

traction, accounts for the similarity between the transition elements zirconium and hafnium.

lanthanons *See* lanthanoids.

lanthanum Symbol La. A silvery metallic element belonging to group IIIB of the periodic table and often considered to be one of the *lanthanoids; a.n. 57; r.a.m. 138.91; r.d. 6.146 (20°C); m.p. 918°C; b.p. 3464°C. Its principal ore is bastnasite, from which it is separated by an ion-exchange process. There are two natural isotopes, lanthanum-139 (stable) and lanthanum-138 (half-life $10^{10}-10^{15}$ years). The metal, being pyrophoric, is used in alloys for lighter flints and the oxide is used in some optical glasses. The largest use of lanthanum, however, is as a catalyst in cracking crude oil. Its chemistry resembles that of the lanthanoids. The element was discovered by C. G. Mosander in 1839.

lapis lazuli A blue rock that is widely used as a semiprecious stone and for ornamental purposes. It is composed chiefly of the deep blue mineral *lazurite* embedded in a matrix of white calcite and usually also contains small specks of pyrite. It occurs in only a few places in crystalline limestones as a contact metamorphic mineral. The chief source is Afghanistan; lapis lazuli also occurs near Lake Baikal in Siberia and in Chile. It was formerly used to make the artists' pigment ultramarine.

lattice The regular arrangement of atoms, ions, or molecules in a crystalline solid. *See* crystal lattice.

lattice energy A measure of the stability of a *crystal lattice, given by the energy that would be released per mole if atoms, ions, or molecules of the crystal were brought together from infinite distances apart to form the lattice. *See* Born-Haber cycle.

lattice vibrations The periodic vibrations of the atoms, ions, or molecules in a *crystal lattice about their mean positions. On heating, the amplitude of the vibrations increases until they are so energetic that the lattice breaks down. The temperature at which this happens is the melting point of the solid and the substance becomes a liquid. On cooling, the amplitude of the vibrations diminishes. At *absolute zero a residual vibration persists, associated with the *zero-point energy of the substance. The increase in the electrical resistance of a conductor is due to increased scattering of the free conduction electrons by the vibrating lattice particles.

laughing gas *See* dinitrogen oxide.

lauric acid *See* dodecanoic acid.

law of chemical equilibrium *See* equilibrium constant.

law of constant composition *See* chemical combination.

law of definite proportions *See* chemical combination.

law of mass action *See* mass action.

law of multiple proportions *See* chemical combination.

law of octaves (Newlands' law) An attempt at classifying elements made by J. R. Newlands (1837-98) in 1863. He arranged 56 elements in order of increasing atomic mass in groups of eight, pointing out that each element resembled the element eight places from it in the list. He drew an analogy with the notes of a musical scale. *Newlands' octaves* were groups of similar elements distinguished in this way: e.g. oxygen and sulphur; nitrogen and phosphorus; and fluorine, chlorine, bromine, and iodine. In some cases it was necessary to put two elements in the same position. The proposal was rejected at the time. *See* periodic table.

law of reciprocal proportions *See* chemical combination.

lawrencium Symbol Lr. A radioactive metallic transuranic element belonging to the *actinoids; a.n. 103; mass number of only known isotope 257 (half-life 8 seconds). The element was identified by A. Ghiorso and associates in 1961. The alternative name *unniltrium* has been proposed.

laws of chemical combination *See* chemical combination.

layer lattice A crystal structure in which the atoms are chemically bonded in plane layers, with relatively weak forces between atoms in adjacent layers. Graphite and micas are examples of substances having layer lattices (i.e. they are *lamellar solids).

lazurite *See* lapis lazuli.

L-dopa *See* dopa.

L–D process *See* basic-oxygen process.

leaching Extraction of soluble components of a solid mixture by percolating a solvent through it.

lead Symbol Pb. A heavy dull grey soft ductile metallic element belonging to *group IV of the periodic table; a.n. 82; r.a.m. 207.19; r.d. 11.35; m.p. 327.5°C; b.p. 1740°C. The main ore is the sulphide galena (PbS); other minor sources include anglesite ($PbSO_4$), cerussite ($PbCO_3$), and litharge (PbO). The metal is extracted by roasting the ore to give the oxide, followed by reduction with carbon. Silver is also recovered from the ores. Lead has a variety of uses including building construction, lead-plate accumulators, bullets, and shot, and is a constituent of such alloys as solder, pewter, bearing metals, type metals, and fusible alloys. Chemically, it forms compounds with the +2 and +4 oxidation states, the lead (II) state being the more stable.

lead(II) acetate *See* lead(II) ethanoate.

lead–acid accumulator An accumulator in which the electrodes are made of lead and the electrolyte consists of dilute sulphuric acid. The electrodes are usually cast from a lead alloy containing 7–12% of antimony (to give increased hardness and corrosion resistance) and a small amount of tin (for better casting properties). The electrodes are coated with a paste of lead(II) oxide (PbO) and finely divided lead; after insertion into the electrolyte a 'forming' current is passed through the cell to convert the PbO on the negative plate into a sponge of finely divided lead. On the positive plate the PbO is converted to lead(IV) oxide (PbO_2). The equation for the overall reaction during discharge is:

$$PbO_2 + 2H_2SO_4 + Pb \rightarrow 2PbSO_4 + 2H_2O$$

The reaction is reversed during charging. Each cell gives an e.m.f. of about 2 volts and in motor vehicles a 12-volt battery of six cells is usually used. The lead–acid battery produces 80–120 kJ per kilogram. *Compare* nickel–iron accumulator.

lead(II) carbonate A white solid, $PbCO_3$, insoluble in water; rhombic; r.d. 6.6. It occurs as the mineral *cerussite, which is isomorphous with aragonite and may be prepared in the laboratory by the addition of cold ammonium carbonate solution to a cold solution of a lead(II) salt (acetate or nitrate). It decomposes at 315°C to lead(II) oxide and carbon dioxide.

lead(II) carbonate hydroxide (white lead; basic lead carbonate) A powder, $2PbCO_3.Pb(OH)_2$, insoluble in water, slightly soluble in aqueous carbonate solutions; r.d. 6.14; decomposes at 400°C. Lead(II) carbonate hydroxide occurs as the mineral *hydroxycerussite* (of variable composition). It was previously manufactured from lead in processes using spent tanning bark or horse manure, which released carbon dioxide. It is currently made by electrolysis of mixed solutions (e.g. ammonium nitrate, nitric acid, sulphuric acid, and acetic acid) using lead anodes. For the highest grade product the lead must be exceptionally pure (known in the trade as 'corroding lead') as small amounts of metallic impurity impart grey or pink discolorations. The material was used widely in paints, both for art work and for commerce, but it has the disadvantage of reacting with hydrogen sulphide in industrial atmospheres and producing black lead sulphide. The poisonous nature of lead compounds has also contributed to the declining importance of this material.

lead-chamber process An obsolete method of making sulphuric acid by the catalytic oxidation of sulphur dioxide with air using a potassium nitrate catalyst in water. The process was carried out in lead containers (which was expensive) and only produced dilute acid. It was replaced in 1876 by the *contact process.

lead dioxide *See* lead(IV) oxide.

lead(II) ethanoate (lead(II) acetate) A white crystalline solid, $Pb(CH_3COO)_2$, soluble in water and slightly soluble in ethanol. It exists as the anhydrous compound (r.d. 3.25; m.p. 280°C), as a trihydrate, $Pb(CH_3COO)_2.3H_2O$ (monoclinic; r.d. 2.55; loses water at 75°C), and as a decahydrate, $Pb(CH_3COO)_2.10H_2O$ (rhombic; r.d. 1.69). The common form is the trihydrate. Its chief interest stems from the fact that it is soluble in water and it also forms a variety of complexes in solution. It was once known as *sugar of lead* because of its sweet taste.

lead(IV) ethanoate (lead tetra-acetate) A colourless solid, $Pb(CH_3COO)_4$, which decomposes in water and is soluble in pure ethanoic acid; monoclinic; r.d. 2.228; m.p. 175°C. It may be prepared by dissolving dilead(II) lead(IV) oxide in warm ethanoic acid. In solution it behaves essentially as a covalent compound (no measurable conductivity) in contrast to the lead(II) salt, which is a weak electrolyte.

lead(IV) hydride *See* plumbane.

lead monoxide *See* lead(II) oxide.

lead(II) oxide (lead monoxide) A solid yellow compound, PbO, which is insoluble in water; m.p. 886°C. It exists in two crystalline forms: *litharge* (tetrahedral; r.d. 9.53) and *massicot* (rhombic; r.d. 8.0). It can be prepared by heating the nitrate, and is manufactured by heating molten lead in air. If the temperature used is lower than the melting point of the oxide, the product is massicot; above this, litharge is formed. Variations in the temperature and in the rate of cooling give rise to crystal vacancies and red, orange, and brown forms of litharge can be produced. The oxide is amphoteric, dissolving in acids to give lead(II) salts and in alkalis to give *plumbates.

lead(IV) oxide (lead dioxide) A dark brown or black solid with a rutile lattice, PbO_2, which is insoluble in water and slightly soluble in concentrated sulphuric and nitric acids; r.d. 9.375; decomposes at 290°C. Lead(IV) oxide may be prepared by the oxidation of lead(II) oxide by heating with alkaline chlorates or nitrates, or by anodic oxidation of lead(II) solutions. It is an oxidizing agent and readily reverts to the lead(II) oxidation state, as illustrated by its conversion to Pb_3O_4 and PbO on heating. It reacts with hydrochloric acid to evolve chlorine. Lead(IV) oxide has been used in the manufacture of safety matches and was widely used until the mid-1970s as an adsorbent for sulphur dioxide in pollution monitoring.

lead(II) sulphate A white crystalline solid, $PbSO_4$, which is virtually insoluble in water and soluble in solutions of ammonium salts; r.d. 6.2; m.p. 1170°C. It occurs as the mineral *anglesite*; it may be prepared in the laboratory by adding any solution containing sulphate ions to solutions of lead(II) ethanoate. The material known as *basic lead (II) sulphate* may be made by shaking together lead(II) sulphate and lead(II) hydroxide in water. This material has been used in white paint in preference to lead(II) carbonate hydroxide, as it is not so susceptible to discoloration through reaction with hydrogen sulphide. The toxicity of lead compounds has led to a decline in the use of these compounds.

lead(II) sulphide A black crystalline solid, PbS, which is insoluble in water; r.d. 7.5; m.p. 1114°C. It occurs naturally as the metallic-looking mineral *galena (the principal ore of lead). It may be prepared in the laboratory by the reaction of hydrogen sulphide with soluble lead(II) salts. Lead(II) sulphide has been used as an electrical rectifier.

lead tetra-acetate *See* lead(IV) ethanoate.

lead tetraethyl(IV) (tetraethyl lead) A colourless liquid, $Pb(C_2H_5)_4$, insoluble in water, soluble in benzene, ethanol, ether, and petroleum; r.d. 1.659; m.p. −137°C; b.p. 200°C. It may be prepared by the reaction of hydrogen and ethene with lead but a more convenient laboratory and industrial method is the reaction of a sodium–lead alloy with chloroethane. A more recent industrial process is the electrolysis of ethylmagnesium chloride (the Grignard reagent) using a lead anode and slowly running additional chloroethane onto the cathode. Lead tetraethyl is used in fuel for internal-combustion engines (along with 1,2-dibromoethane) to increase the *octane number and reduce knocking. Mounting pressure from groups concerned about environmental pollution has led to a reduction of permitted levels of lead tetraethyl in many countries.

Leblanc process An obsolete process for manufacturing sodium carbonate. The raw materials were sodium chloride, sulphuric acid, coke, and limestone (calcium carbonate), and the process involved two stages. First the sodium chloride was heated with sulphuric acid to give sodium sulphate:

$$2NaCl(s) + H_2SO_4(l) \rightarrow Na_2SO_4(s) + 2HCl(g)$$

The sodium sulphate was then heated with coke and limestone:

$$Na_2SO_4 + 2C + CaCO_3 \rightarrow Na_2CO_3 + CaS + 2CO_2$$

Calcium sulphide was a by-product, the sodium carbonate being extracted by crystallization. The process, invented in 1783 by the French chemist Nicolas Leblanc (1742–1806), was the first for producing sodium carbonate synthetically (earlier methods were from wood ash and other vegetable sources). By the end of the 19th century it had been largely replaced by the *Solvay process.

lechatelierite A mineral form of *silicon (IV) oxide, SiO_2.

Le Chatelier's principle If a system is in equilibrium, any change imposed on the system tends to shift the equilibrium to nullify the effect of the applied change. The principle, which is a consequence of the law of conservation of energy, was first stated in 1888 by Henri Le Chatelier (1850–1936). It is applied to chemical equilibria. For example, in the gas reaction

$$2SO_2 + O_2 \rightleftharpoons 2SO_3$$

an increase in pressure on the reaction mixture displaces the equilibrium to the right, since this reduces the total number of molecules present and thus decreases the pressure. The standard enthalpy change for the forward reaction is negative (i.e. the reaction is exothermic). Thus, an increase in temperature displaces the equilibrium to the left since this tends to reduce the temperature. The *equilibrium constant thus falls with increasing temperature.

Leclanché cell A primary *voltaic cell consisting of a carbon rod (the anode) and a zinc rod (the cathode) dipping into an electrolyte of a 10–20% solution of ammonium chloride. *Polarization is prevented by using a mixture of manganese dioxide mixed with crushed carbon, held in contact with the anode by means of a porous bag or pot; this reacts with the hydrogen produced. This wet form of the cell, devised in 1867 by Georges Leclanché (1839–82), has an e.m.f. of about 1.5 volts. The *dry cell based on it is widely used in torches, radios, and calculators.

leucine *See* amino acid.

leuco form *See* dyes.

Lewis acid and base *See* acid.

***l*-form** *See* optical activity.

Liebig condenser A laboratory condenser having a straight glass tube surrounded by a coaxial glass jacket through which cooling water is passed. It is named after the German organic chemist Justus von Liebig (1803–73).

ligand An ion or molecule that donates a pair of electrons to a metal atom or ion in forming a coordination *complex. Molecules that function as ligands are acting as Lewis bases (*see* acid). For example, in the complex hexaquocopper(II) ion $[Cu(H_2O)_6]^{2+}$ six water molecules coordinate to a central Cu^{2+} ion. In the tetrachloroplatinate(II) ion $[PtCl_4]^{2-}$, four Cl^- ions are coordinated to a central Pt^{2+} ion. A feature of such ligands is that they have lone pairs of electrons, which they donate to empty metal orbitals. A certain class of ligands also have empty *p*- or *d*-orbitals in addition to their lone pair of electrons and can produce complexes in which the metal has low oxidation state. A double bond is formed between the metal and the ligand: a sigma bond by donation of the lone pair from ligand to metal, and a pi bond by *back donation* of electrons on the metal to empty *d*-orbitals on the ligand. Carbon monoxide is the most important such ligand, forming metal carbonyls (e.g. $Ni(CO)_4$).

The examples given above are examples of *monodentate* ligands (literally: 'having one tooth'), in which there is only one point on each ligand at which coordination can occur. Some ligands are *polydentate*; i.e. they have two or more possible coordination points. For instance, 1,2-diaminoethane, $H_2NC_2H_4NH_2$, is a *bidentate* ligand, having two coordination points. Certain polydentate ligands can form *chelates.

ligand-field theory A modification of *crystal-field theory in which the overlap of orbitals is taken into account. *See also* complex.

ligase Any of a class of enzymes that catalyse the formation of covalent bonds using the energy released by the cleavage of ATP. Ligases are important in the synthesis and repair of many biological molecules, including DNA.

lignin A complex organic polymer that is deposited within the cellulose of plant cell walls during secondary thickening. Lignification makes the walls woody and therefore rigid.

lignite *See* coal.

lime *See* calcium oxide.

limestone A sedimentary rock that is composed largely of carbonate minerals, especially carbonates of calcium and magnesium. *Calcite and *aragonite are the chief minerals; *dolomite is also present in the dolomitic limestones. There are many varieties of limestones but most are deposited in shallow water. *Organic limestones* (e.g. *chalk) are formed from the calcareous skeletons of organisms; *precipitated limestones* include oolite, which is composed of ooliths – spherical bodies formed by the precipitation of carbonate around a nucleus; and *clastic limestones* are derived from fragments of pre-existing calcareous rocks.

limewater A saturated solution of *calcium hydroxide in water. When carbon dioxide gas is bubbled through limewater, a 'milky' precipitate of calcium carbonate is formed:

$$Ca(OH)_2(aq) + CO_2(g) \rightarrow CaCO_3(s) + H_2O(l)$$

If the carbon dioxide continues to be bubbled through, the calcium carbonate eventually redissolves to form a clear solution of calcium hydrogencarbonate:

$$CaCO_3(s) + CO_2(g) + H_2O(g) \rightarrow Ca(HCO_3)_2(aq)$$

If cold limewater is used the original calcium carbonate precipitated has a calcite structure; hot limewater yields an aragonite structure.

limonite A generic term for a group of hydrous iron oxides, mostly amorphous. *Goethite and *haematite are important constituents, together with colloidal silica, clays, and manganese oxides. Limonite is formed by direct precipitation from marine or fresh water in shallow seas, lagoons, and bogs (thus it is often called *bog iron ore*) and by oxidation of iron-rich minerals. It is used as an ore of iron and as a pigment.

linear molecule A molecule in which the atoms are in a straight line, as in carbon dioxide, O=C=O.

line spectrum *See* spectrum.

Linnz–Donnewitz process *See* basic-oxygen process.

linoleic acid A liquid polyunsaturated *fatty acid with two double bonds, $CH_3(CH_2)_4CH{:}CHCH_2CH{:}CH(CH_2)_7COOH$. Linoleic acid is abundant in many plant fats and oils, e.g. linseed oil, groundnut oil, and soya-bean oil. It is an *essential fatty acid.

linolenic acid A liquid polyunsaturated *fatty acid with three double bonds in its structure:
$CH_3CH_2CH{:}CHCH_2CH{:}CHCH_2CH{:}CH(CH_2)_7COOH$. Linolenic acid occurs in certain plant oils, e.g. linseed and soya-bean oil, and in algae. It is one of the *essential fatty acids.

linseed oil A pale yellow oil pressed from flax seed. It contains a mixture of glycerides of fatty acids, including linoleic acid and linolenic acid. It is a *drying oil, used in oil paints, varnishes, linoleum, etc.

lipase An enzyme secreted by the pancreas and the glands of the small intestine of vertebrates that catalyses the breakdown of fats into fatty acids and glycerol.

lipid Any of a diverse group of organic compounds, occurring in living organisms, that are insoluble in water but soluble in organic solvents, such as chloroform, benzene, etc. Lipids are broadly classified into two categories: *complex lipids*, which are esters of long-chain fatty acids and include the *glycerides (which constitute the *fats and *oils of animals and plants), glycolipids, *phospholipids, and *waxes; and *simple lipids*, which do not contain fatty acids and include the *steroids and *terpenes.

Lipids have a variety of functions in living organisms. Fats and oils are a convenient and concentrated means of storing food energy in plants and animals. Phospholipids and *sterols, such as cholesterol, are major components of cell membranes. Waxes provide vital waterproofing for body surfaces. Terpenes include vitamins A, E, and K, and phytol (a component of chlorophyll) and occur in essential oils, such as menthol and camphor. Steroids include the adrenal hormones, sex hormones, and bile acids.

Lipids can combine with proteins to form *lipoproteins*, e.g. in cell membranes. In bacterial cell walls, lipids may associate with polysaccharides to form *lipopolysaccharides*.

lipoic acid A vitamin of the *vitamin B complex. It is one of the *coenzymes involved in the decarboxylation of pyruvate by the enzyme pyruvate dehydrogenase. Good sources of lipoic acid include liver and yeast.

lipolysis The breakdown of storage lipids in living organisms. Most long-term energy reserves are in the form of triglycerides in fats and oils. When these are needed, e.g. during starvation, lipase enzymes convert the triglycerides into glycerol and the component fatty acids. These are then transported to tissues and oxidized to provide energy.

lipoprotein *See* lipid.

liquation The separation of mixtures of solids by heating to a temperature at which lower-melting components liquefy.

liquefaction of gases The conversion of a gaseous substance into a liquid. This is usually achieved by one of four methods or by a combination of two of them:

(1) by vapour compression, provided that the substance is below its *critical temperature;

(2) by refrigeration at constant pressure, typically by cooling it with a colder fluid in a countercurrent heat exchanger;

(3) by making it perform work adiabatically against the atmosphere in a reversible cycle;

(4) by the *Joule–Thomson effect.

Large quantities of liquefied gases are now used commercially, especially *liquefied petroleum gas and liquefied natural gas.

liquefied petroleum gas (LPG) Various petroleum gases, principally propane and butane, stored as a liquid under pressure. It is used as an engine fuel and has the advantage of causing very little cylinder-head deposits.

Liquefied natural gas (LNG) is a similar product and consists mainly of methane. However, it cannot be liquefied simply by pressure as it has a low critical temperature of 190 K and must therefore be cooled to below this temperature before it will liquefy. Once liquefied it has to be stored in well-insulated containers. It provides a convenient form in which to ship natural gas in bulk from oil wells to users. It is also used as an engine fuel.

liquid A phase of matter between that of a crystalline solid and a *gas. In a liquid, the large-scale three-dimensional atomic (or ionic or molecular) regularity of the solid is absent but, on the other hand, so is the total disorganization of the gas. Although liquids have been studied for many years there is still no comprehensive theory of the liquid state. It is clear, however, from diffraction studies that there is a short-range structural regularity extending over several molecular diameters. These bundles of ordered atoms, molecules, or ions move about in relation to each other, enabling liquids to have almost fixed volumes, which adopt the shape of their containers.

liquid crystal A substance that flows like a liquid but has some order in its arrangement of molecules. *Nematic crystals* have long molecules all aligned in the same direction, but otherwise randomly arranged. *Cholesteric* and *smectic* liquid crystals also have aligned molecules, which are arranged in distinct layers. In cholesteric crystals, the axes of the molecules are parallel to the plane of the layers; in smectic crystals they are perpendicular.

litharge *See* lead(II) oxide.

lithia *See* lithium oxide.

lithium Symbol Li. A soft silvery metal, the first member of *group I of the periodic table; a.n. 3; r.a.m. 6.939; r.d. 0.534; m.p. 180.54°C; b.p. 1340°C. It is a rare element found in spodumene ($LiAlSi_2O_6$), petalite ($LiAlSi_4O_{10}$), the mica lepidolite, and certain brines. It is usually extracted by treatment with sulphuric acid to give the sulphate, which is converted to the chloride. This is mixed with a small amount of potassium chloride, melted, and electrolysed. The stable isotopes are lithium-6 and lithium-7. Lithium-5 and lithium-8 are short-lived radioisotopes. The metal is used to remove oxygen in metallurgy and as a constituent of some Al and Mg alloys. It is also used in batteries and is a potential tritium source for fusion research. Lithium salts are used in psychomedicine. The element reacts with oxygen and water; on heating it also reacts with nitrogen and hydrogen. Its chemistry differs somewhat from that of the other group I elements because of the small size of the Li^+ ion.

lithium aluminium hydride *See* lithium tetrahydroaluminate(III).

lithium carbonate A white solid, Li_2CO_3; r.d. 2.11; m.p. 735°C; decomposes above 1200°C. It is produced commercially by treating the ore with sulphuric acid at 250°C and leaching the product to give a solution of lithium sulphate. The carbonate is then obtained by precipitation with sodium carbonate solution. Lithium carbonate is used in the prevention and treatment of manic-depressive disorders. It is also used industrially in ceramic glazes.

lithium deuteride *See* lithium hydride.

lithium hydride A white solid, LiH; cubic; r.d. 0.82; m.p. 686°C; decomposes at about 850°C. It is produced by direct combination of the elements at temperatures above 500°C. The bonding in lithium hydride is believed to be largely ionic; i.e. Li^+H^- as supported by the fact that hydrogen is released from the anode on electrolysis of the molten salt. The compound reacts violently and exothermically with water to yield hydrogen and lithium hydroxide. It is used as a reducing agent to prepare other hydrides and the ^2H isotopic compound, *lithium deuteride*, is particularly valuable for deuterating a range of organic compounds. Lithium hydride has also been used as a shielding material for thermal neutrons.

lithium hydrogencarbonate A compound, $LiHCO_3$, formed by the reaction of carbon dioxide with aqueous lithium carbonate and known only in solution. It has found medicinal uses similar to those of lithium carbonate and is sometimes included in proprietary mineral waters.

lithium hydroxide A white crystalline solid, LiOH, soluble in water, slightly soluble in ethanol and insoluble in ether. It is known as the monohydrate (monoclinic; r.d. 1.51) and in the anhydrous form (tetragonal, r.d. 1.46, m.p. 450°C; decomposes at 924°C). The compound is made by reacting lime with lithium salts or lithium ores. Lithium hydroxide is basic but has a closer resemblance to group II hydroxides than to the other group I hydroxides (an example of the first member of a periodic group having atypical properties).

lithium oxide (lithia) A white crystalline compound, Li_2O; cubic; r.d. 2.01; m.p. 1700°C. It can be obtained from a number of lithium ores; the main uses are in lubricating greases, ceramics, glass and refractories, alkaline storage batteries, and as a flux in brazing and welding.

lithium sulphate A white or colourless crystalline material, Li_2SO_4, soluble in water and insoluble in ethanol. It forms a monohydrate (monoclinic; r.d. 1.88) and an anhydrous form, which exists in α- (monoclinic), β- (hexagonal) and γ- (cubic) forms; r.d. 2.23. The compound is prepared by the reaction of the hydroxide or carbonate with sulphuric acid. It is not isomorphous with other group I sulphates and does not form alums.

lithium tetrahydroaluminate(III) (lithium aluminium hydride; LAH) A white or light grey powder, $LiAlH_4$; r.d. 0.917; decomposes at 125°C. It is prepared by the reaction of excess lithium hydride with aluminium chloride. The compound is soluble in ethoxyethane, reacts violently with water to release hydrogen, and is widely used as a powerful reducing agent in organic chemistry. It should always be treated as a serious fire risk in storage.

litmus A water-soluble dye extracted from certain lichens. It turns red under acid conditions and blue under alkaline conditions, the colour change occurring over the pH range 4.5–8.3 (at 25°C). It is not suitable for titrations because of the wide range over which the colour changes, but is used as a rough *indicator of acidity or alkalinity, both in solution and as litmus paper (absorbent paper soaked in litmus solution).

litre Symbol l. A unit of volume in the metric system regarded as a special name for the cubic decimetre. It was formerly defined as the volume of 1 kilogram of pure water at 4°C at standard pressure, which is equivalent to 1.000 028 dm^3.

lixivation The separation of mixtures by dissolving soluble constituents in water.

localized bond A *chemical bond in which the electrons forming the bond remain between (or close to) the linked atoms. *Compare* delocalization.

lodestone *See* magnetite.

logarithmic scale 1. A scale of measurement in which an increase or decrease of one unit represents a tenfold increase or decrease in the quantity measured. Decibels and pH measurements are common examples of logarithmic scales of measurement. **2.** A scale on the axis of a graph in which an increase of one unit represents a tenfold increase in the variable quantity. If a curve $y = x^n$ is plotted on graph paper with logarithmic scales on both axes, the result is a straight line of slope n, i.e. $\log y = n \log x$, which enables n to be determined.

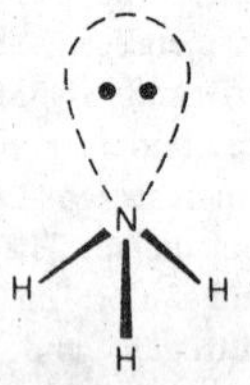

Lone pair of electrons in ammonia

lone pair A pair of electrons having opposite spin in an orbital of an atom. For instance, in ammonia the nitrogen atom has five electrons, three of which are used in forming single bonds with hydrogen atoms. The other two occupy a filled atomic orbital and constitute a lone pair. The orbital containing these electrons is equivalent to a single bond (sigma orbital) in spatial orientation, accounting for the pyramidal shape of the molecule. In the water molecule, there are two lone pairs on the oxygen atom. In considering the shapes of molecules, repulsions between bonds and lone pairs can be taken into account:

lone pair–lone pair → lone pair–bond → bond–bond.

long period *See* periodic table.

Loschmidt's constant (Loschmidt number) The number of particles per unit volume of an *ideal gas at STP. It has the value 2.687 19 × 10^{25} m^{-3} and was first worked out by Joseph Loschmidt (1821–95).

lowering of vapour pressure A reduction in the saturated vapour pressure of a pure liquid when a solute is introduced. If the solute is a solid of low vapour pressure, the decrease in vapour pressure of the liquid is proportional to the concentration of particles of solute; i.e. to the number of dissolved molecules or ions per unit volume. To a first approximation, it does not depend on the nature of the particles. *See* colligative property; Raoult's law.

L-series *See* absolute configuration.

lumen Symbol lm. The SI unit of *luminous flux equal to the flux emitted by a uniform point source of 1 candela in a solid angle of 1 steradian.

luminescence The emission of light by a substance for any reason other than a rise in its temperature. In general, atoms of substances emit *photons of electromagnetic energy when they return to the *ground state after having been in an excited state (*see* excitation). The causes of the excitation are various. If the exciting cause is a photon, the process is called *photoluminescence*; if it is an electron it is called *electroluminescence*. *Chemiluminescence* is luminescence resulting from a chemical reaction (such as the slow oxidation of phosphorus); *bioluminescence* is the luminescence produced by a living organism (such as a firefly). If the luminescence persists significantly after the exciting cause is removed it is called *phosphorescence*; if it does not it is called *fluorescence*. This distinction is arbitrary since there must always be some delay; in some definitions a persistence of more than 10 nanoseconds (10^{-8} s) is treated as phosphorescence.

lutetium Symbol Lu. A silvery metallic element belonging to the *lanthanoids; a.n. 71; r.a.m. 174.97; r.d. 9.842 (20°C); m.p. 1663°C; b.p. 3402°C. Lutetium is the least abundant of the elements and the little quantities that are available have been obtained by processing other metals. There are two natural isotopes, lutetium-175 (stable) and lutetium-176 (half-life 2.2 × 10^{10} years). There are no uses for the element, which was first identified by G. Urban in 1907.

lux Symbol lx. The SI unit of illuminance equal to the illumination produced by a luminous flux of 1 lumen distributed uniformly over an area of 1 square metre.

lye *See* potassium hydroxide.

Lyman series *See* hydrogen spectrum.

lyophilic Having an affinity for a solvent ('solvent-loving'; if the solvent is water the term *hydrophilic* is used). *See* colloid.

lyophobic Lacking any affinity for a solvent ('solvent-hating'; if the solvent is water the term *hydrophobic* is used). *See* colloid.

lysine *See* amino acid.

M

macromolecular crystal A crystalline solid in which the atoms are all linked together by covalent bonds. Carbon (in diamond), boron nitride, and silicon carbide are examples of substances that have macromolecular crystals. In effect, the crystal is a large molecule (hence the alternative description *giant-molecular*), which accounts for the hardness and high melting point of such materials.

macromolecule A very large molecule. Natural and synthetic polymers have macromolecules, as do such substances as haemoglobin. *See also* colloids.

Magnadur Tradename for a ceramic material used to make permanent magnets. It consists of sintered iron oxide and barium oxide.

Magnalium Tradename for an aluminium-based alloy of high reflectivity for light and ultraviolet radiation that contains 1–2% of copper and between 5% and 30% of magnesium. Strong and light, these alloys also sometimes contain other elements, such as tin, lead, and nickel.

magnesia *See* magnesium oxide.

magnesite A white, colourless, or grey mineral form of *magnesium carbonate, $MgCO_3$, crystallizing in the trigonal system. It is formed as a replacement mineral of magnesium-rich rocks when carbon dioxide is available. Magnesite is mined both as an ore for magnesium and as a source of magnesium carbonate. It occurs in Austria, USA, Greece, Norway, India, Australia, and South Africa.

magnesium Symbol Mg. A silvery metallic element belonging to group II of the periodic table (*see* alkaline-earth metals); a.n. 12; r.a.m. 24.321; r.d. 1.74; m.p. 651°C; b.p. 1107°C. The element is found in a number of minerals, including magnesite ($MgCO_3$), dolomite ($MgCO_3.CaCO_3$), and carnallite ($MgCl_2.KCl.6H_2O$). It is also present in sea water, and it is an *essential element for living organisms. Extraction is by electrolysis of the fused chloride. The element is used in a number of light alloys (e.g. for aircraft). Chemically, it is very reactive. In air it forms a protective oxide coating but when ignited it burns with an intense white flame. It also reacts with the halogens, sulphur, and nitrogen. Magnesium was first isolated by Bussy in 1828.

magnesium bicarbonate *See* magnesium hydrogencarbonate.

magnesium carbonate A white compound, $MgCO_3$, existing in anhydrous and hydrated forms. The anhydrous material (trigonal; r.d. 2.96) is found in the mineral *magnesite. There is also a trihydrate, $MgCO_3.3H_2O$ (rhombic; r.d. 1.85), which occurs naturally as *nesquehonite*, and a pentahydrate, $MgCO_3.5H_2O$ (monoclinic; r.d. 1.73), which occurs as *lansfordite*. Magnesium carbonate also occurs in the mixed salt *dolomite ($CaCO_3.MgCO_3$) and as *basic magnesium carbonate* in the two minerals *artinite* ($MgCO_3.Mg(OH)_2.3H_2O$) and *hydromagnesite* ($3MgCO_3.Mg(OH)_2.3H_2O$). The anhydrous salt can be formed by heating magnesium oxide in a stream of carbon dioxide:

$$MgO(s) + CO_2(g) \rightarrow MgCO_3(s)$$

Above 350°C, the reverse reaction predominates and the carbonate decomposes. Magnesium carbonate is used in making magnesium oxide and is a drying agent (e.g. in table salt). It is also used as a medical antacid and laxative (the basic carbonate is used) and is a component of certain inks and glasses.

magnesium chloride A white solid compound, $MgCl_2$. The anhydrous salt (hexagonal; r.d. 2.32; m.p. 714°C; b.p. 1412°C) can be prepared by the direct combination of dry chlorine with magnesium:

$$Mg(s) + Cl_2(g) \rightarrow MgCl_2(s)$$

The compound also occurs naturally as a constituent of carnallite ($KCl.MgCl_2$). It is a deliquescent compound that commonly forms the hexahydrate, $MgCl_2.6H_2O$ (monoclinic; r.d. 1.57). When heated, this hydrolyses to give magnesium oxide and hydrogen chloride gas. The fused chloride is electrolysed to produce magnesium and it is also used for fireproofing wood, in magnesia cements and artificial leather, and as a laxative.

magnesium hydrogencarbonate (magnesium bicarbonate) A compound, $Mg(HCO_3)_2$, that is stable only in solution. It is formed by the action of carbon dioxide on a suspension of magnesium carbonate in water:

$$MgCO_3(s) + CO_2(g) + H_2O(l) \rightarrow Mg(HCO_3)_2(aq)$$

On heating, this process is reversed. Magnesium hydrogencarbonate is one of the compounds responsible for temporary *hardness in water.

magnesium hydroxide A white solid compound, $Mg(OH)_2$; trigonal; r.d. 2.36; decomposes at 350°C. Magnesium hydroxide occurs naturally as the mineral *brucite* and can be prepared by reacting magnesium sulphate or chloride with sodium hydroxide solution. It is used in the refining of sugar and in the processing of uranium. Medicinally it is important as an antacid (*milk of magnesia*) and as a laxative.

magnesium oxide (magnesia) A white compound, MgO; cubic; r.d. 3.58; m.p. 2800°C. It occurs naturally as the mineral *periclase* and is prepared commercially by thermally decomposing the mineral *magnesite:

$$MgCO_3(s) \rightarrow MgO(s) + CO_2(g)$$

It has a wide range of uses, including reflective coatings on optical instruments and aircraft windscreens and in semiconductors. Its high melting point makes it useful as a refractory lining in metal and glass furnaces.

magnesium peroxide A white solid, MgO_2. It decomposes at 100°C to release oxygen and also releases oxygen on reaction with water:

$$2MgO_2(s) + 2H_2O \rightarrow 2Mg(OH)_2 + O_2$$

The compound is prepared by reacting sodium peroxide with magnesium sulphate solution and is used as a bleach for cotton and silk.

magnesium sulphate A white soluble compound, $MgSO_4$, existing as the anhydrous compound (rhombic; r.d. 2.66; decomposes at 1124°C) and in hydrated crystalline forms. The monohydrate $MgSO_4.H_2O$ (monoclinic; r.d. 2.45) occurs naturally as the mineral *kieserite*. The commonest hydrate is the heptahydrate, $MgSO_4.7H_2O$ (rhombic; r.d. 1.68), which is called *Epsom salt(s)*, and occurs naturally as the mineral *epsomite*. This is a white powder with a bitter saline taste, which loses $6H_2O$ at 150°C and $7H_2O$ at 200°C. It is used in sizing and fireproofing cotton and silk, in tanning leather, and in the manufacture of fertilizers, explosives, and matches. In medicine, it is used as a laxative. It is also used in veterinary medicine for treatment of local inflammations and infected wounds.

magnetic moment The ratio between the maximum torque (T_{max}) exerted on a magnet, current-carrying coil, or moving charge situated in a magnetic field and the strength of that field. It is thus a measure of the strength of a magnet or current-carrying coil. In the Sommerfeld approach this quantity (also called *electromagnetic moment* or *magnetic area moment*) is the ratio T_{max}/B. In the Kennelly approach the quantity (also called *magnetic dipole moment*) is T_{max}/H.

In the case of a magnet placed in a magnetic field of field strength H, the maximum torque T_{max} occurs when the axis of the magnet is perpendicular to the field. In the case of a coil of N turns and area A carrying a current I, the magnetic moment can be shown to be $m = T/B = NIA$ or $m = T/H = \mu NIA$. Magnetic moments are measured in A m^2.

An orbital electron has an orbital magnetic moment IA, where I is the equivalent current as the electron moves round its orbit. It is given by $I = q\omega/2\pi$, where q is the electronic charge and ω is its angular velocity. The orbital magnetic moment is therefore $IA = q\omega A/2\pi$, where A is the orbital area. If the electron is spinning there is also a spin magnetic moment (*see* spin); atomic nuclei also have magnetic moments (*see* nuclear moment).

magnetic quantum number *See* atom.

magnetism A group of phenomena associated with magnetic fields. Whenever an electric current flows a magnetic field is produced; as the orbital motion and the *spin of atomic electrons are equivalent to tiny current loops, individual atoms create magnetic fields around them, when their orbital electrons have a net *magnetic moment as a result of their angular momentum. The magnetic moment of an atom is the vector sum of the magnetic moments of the orbital motions and the spins of all the electrons in the atom. The macroscopic magnetic properties of a substance arise from the magnetic moments of its component atoms and molecules. Different materials have different characteristics in an applied magnetic field; there are four main types of magnetic behaviour:

(a) In *diamagnetism* the magnetization is in the opposite direction to that of the applied field, i.e. the susceptibility is negative. Although all substances are diamagnetic, it is a weak form of magnetism and may be masked by other, stronger, forms. It results from changes induced in the orbits of electrons in the atoms of a substance by the applied field, the direction of the change opposing the applied flux. There is thus a weak negative susceptibility (of the order of -10^{-8} m^3 mol^{-1}) and a relative permeability of slightly less than one.

(b) In *paramagnetism* the atoms or molecules of the substance have net orbital or spin magnetic moments that are capable of being aligned in the direction of the applied field. They therefore have a positive (but small) susceptibility and a relative permeability slightly in excess of one. Paramagnetism occurs in all atoms and molecules with unpaired electrons; e.g. free atoms, free radicals, and compounds of transition metals containing ions with unfilled electron shells. It also occurs in metals as a result of the magnetic moments associated with the spins of the conducting electrons.

(c) In *ferromagnetic* substances, within a certain temperature range, there are net atomic magnetic moments, which line up in such a way that magnetization persists after the removal of the applied field. Below a certain temperature, called the *Curie point* (or Curie temperature) an increasing magnetic field applied to a ferromagnetic substance will cause increasing magnetization to a high value, called the *saturation magnetization*. This is because a ferromagnetic substance consists of small (1–0.1 mm across) magnetized regions called *domains*. The total magnetic moment of a sample of the substance is the vector sum of the magnetic moments of the component domains. Within each domain the individual atomic magnetic moments are spontaneously aligned by *exchange forces*, related to whether or not the atomic electron spins are parallel or antiparallel. However, in an unmagnetized piece of ferromagnetic material the magnetic moments of the domains themselves are not aligned; when an external field is applied those domains that are aligned with the field increase in size at the expense of the others. In a very strong field all the domains are lined up in the direction of the field and provide the high observed magnetization. Iron, nickel, cobalt, and their alloys are ferromagnetic. Above the Curie point, ferromagnetic materials become paramagnetic.

(d) Some metals, alloys, and transition-element salts exhibit another form of magnetism called *antiferromagnetism*. This occurs below a certain temperature, called the *Néel temperature*, when an ordered array of atomic magnetic moments spontaneously forms in which alternate moments have opposite directions. There is therefore no net resultant magnetic moment in the absence of an applied field. In manganese fluoride, for example, this antiparallel arrangement occurs below a Néel temperature of 72 K. Below this temperature the spontaneous ordering opposes the normal tendency of the magnetic moments to align with the applied field. Above the Néel temperature the substance is paramagnetic.

A special form of antiferromagnetism is *ferrimagnetism*, a type of magnetism exhibited by the *ferrites. In these materials the magnetic moments of adjacent ions are antiparallel and of unequal strength, or the number of magnetic moments in one direction is greater than those in the opposite direction. By suitable choice of rare-earth ions in the ferrite lattices it is possible to design ferrimagnetic substances with specific magnetizations for use in electronic components.

magnetite A black mineral form of iron oxide crystallizing in the cubic system. It is a mixed iron(II)-iron(III) oxide, Fe_3O_4, and is one of the major ores of iron. It is strongly magnetic and some varieties, known as *lodestone*, are natural magnets; these were used as compasses in the ancient world. Magnetite is widely distributed and occurs as an accessory mineral in almost all igneous and metamorphic rocks. The largest deposits of the mineral occur in N Sweden.

magnetochemistry The branch of physical chemistry concerned with measuring and investigating the magnetic properties of compounds. It is used particularly for studying transition-metal complexes, many of which are paramagnetic because they have unpaired electrons. Measurement of the magnetic susceptibility allows the magnetic moment of the metal atom to be calculated, and this gives information about the bonding in the complex.

magneton A unit for measuring magnetic moments of nuclear, atomic, or molecular magnets. The *Bohr magneton* μ_B has the value of the classical magnetic moment of an electron, given by

$$\mu_B = eh/4\pi m_e = 9.274 \times 10^{-24}\ \mathrm{A\,m^2},$$

where e and m_e are the charge and mass of the electron and h is the Planck constant. The *nuclear magneton*, μ_N is obtained by replacing the mass of the electron by the mass of the proton and is therefore given by

$$\mu_N = \mu_B.m_e/m_p = 5.05 \times 10^{-27}\ \mathrm{A\,m^2}.$$

malachite A secondary mineral form of copper carbonate–hydroxide, $CuCO_3.Cu(OH)_2$. It is bright green and crystallizes in the monoclinic system but usually occurs as aggregates of fibres or in massive form. It is generally found with *azurite in association with the more important copper ores and is itself mined as an ore of copper (e.g. in Zaîre). It is also used as an ornamental stone and as a gemstone.

maleic acid *See* butenedioic acid.

malic acid (2-hydroxybutanedioic acid) A crystalline solid, $HOOCCH(OH)CH_2COOH$. L-malic acid occurs in living organisms as an intermediate metabolite in the *Krebs cycle and also (in certain plants) in photosynthesis. It is found especially in the juice of unripe fruits, e.g. green apples.

maltose (malt sugar) A sugar consisting of two linked glucose molecules that results from the action of the enzyme amylase on starch. Maltose occurs in barley seeds following germination and drying, which is the basis of the malting process used in the manufacture of beer and malt whisky.

malt sugar *See* maltose.

manganate(VI) A salt containing the ion $MnO_4{}^{2-}$. Manganate(VI) ions are darl. green; they are produced by manganate(VII) ions in basic solution.

manganate(VII) (permanganate) A salt containing the ion $MnO_4{}^{-}$. Manganate(VII) ions are dark purple and strong oxidizing agents.

manganese Symbol Mn. A grey brittle metallic *transition element, a.n. 25; r.a.m. 54.94; r.d. 7.4; m.p. 1244°C; b.p. 2040°C. The main sources are pyrolusite (MnO_2) and rhodochrosite ($MnCO_3$). The metal can be extracted by reduction of the oxide using magnesium (*Kroll process) or aluminium (*Goldschmidt process). Often the ore is mixed with iron ore and reduced in an electric furnace to produce ferromanganese for use in alloy steels. The element is quite electropositive, reacting with water and dilute acids to give hydrogen. It combines with oxygen, nitrogen, and other metals when heated. Salts of manganese contain the element in the +2 and +3 oxidation states. Manganese(II) salts are the more stable. It also forms compounds in higher oxidation states, such as manganese(IV) oxide and manganate(VI) and manganate(VII) salts. The element was discovered in 1774 by Scheele.

manganese(IV) oxide (manganese dioxide) A black oxide made by heating manganese(II) nitrate. The compound also occurs naturally as pyrolusite. It is a strong oxidizing agent, used as a depolarizing agent in voltaic cells.

manganic compounds Compounds of manganese in its +3 oxidation state; e.g. manganic oxide is manganese(III) oxide, Mn_2O_3.

manganin A copper alloy containing 13–18% of manganese and 1–4% of nickel. It has a high electrical resistance, which is relatively insensitive to temperature changes. It is therefore suitable for use in resistance wire.

manganous compounds Compounds of manganese in its +2 oxidation state; e.g. manganous oxide is manganese(II) oxide, MnO.

mannitol A polyhydric alcohol, $CH_2OH(CHOH)_4CH_2OH$, found in some plants, used as a sweetener in certain foodstuffs.

mannose A *monosaccharide, $C_6H_{12}O_6$, stereoisomeric with glucose, that occurs naturally only in polymerized forms called *mannans*. These are found in plants, fungi, and bacteria, serving as food energy stores.

manometer A device for measuring pressure differences, usually by the difference in height of two liquid columns. The simplest type is the U-tube manometer, which consists of a glass tube bent into the shape of a U. If a pressure to be measured is fed to one side of the U-tube and the other is open to the atmosphere, the difference in level of the liquid in the two limbs gives a measure of the unknown pressure.

marble A metamorphic rock composed of recrystallized *calcite or *dolomite. Pure marbles are white but such impurities as silica or clay minerals result in variations of colour. Marble is extensively used for building purposes and ornamental use; the pure white marble from Carrara in Italy is especially prized by sculptors. The term is applied commercially to any limestone or dolomite that can be cut and polished.

Markovnikoff's rule When an acid HA adds to an alkene, a mixture of products can be formed if the alkene is not symmetrical. For instance, the reaction between $C_2H_5CH{:}CH_2$ and HCl can give $C_2H_5CH_2CH_2Cl$ or $C_2H_5CHClCH_3$. In general, a mixture of products occurs in which one predominates over the other. In

1870, W. Markovnikoff proposed the rule that the main product would be the one in which the hydrogen atom adds to the carbon having the larger number of hydrogen atoms (the latter product above). This occurs when the mechanism is *electrophilic addition, in which the first step is addition of H^+. The electron-releasing effect of the alkyl group (C_2H_5) distorts the electron-distribution in the double bond, making the carbon atom furthest from the alkyl group negative. This is the atom attacked by H^+ giving the carbonium ion $C_2H_5C^+HCH_3$, which further reacts with the negative ion Cl^-.

In some circumstances *anti-Markovnikoff* behaviour occurs, in which the opposite effect is found. This happens when the mechanism involves free radicals and is common in addition of hydrogen bromide when peroxides are present.

marsh gas Methane formed by rotting vegetation in marshes.

Marsh's test A chemical test for arsenic in which hydrochloric acid and zinc are added to the sample, arsine being produced by the nascent hydrogen generated. Gas from the sample is led through a heated glass tube and, if arsine is present, it decomposes to give a brown deposit of arsenic metal. The arsenic is distinguished from antimony (which gives a similar result) by the fact that antimony does not dissolve in sodium chlorate(I) (hypochlorite). The test was devised in 1836 by the British chemist James Marsh.

martensite A solid solution of carbon in alpha-iron (*see* iron) formed when *steel is cooled too rapidly for pearlite to form from austenite. It is responsible for the hardness of quenched steel.

mascagnite A mineral form of *ammonium sulphate, $(NH_4)_2SO_4$.

mass A measure of a body's *inertia, i.e. its resistance to acceleration. According to Newton's laws of motion, if two unequal masses, m_1 and m_2, are allowed to collide, in the absence of any other forces both will experience the same force of collision. If the two bodies acquire accelerations a_1 and a_2 as a result of the collision, then $m_1a_1 = m_2a_2$. This equation enables two masses to be compared. If one of the masses is regarded as a standard of mass, the mass of all other masses can be measured in terms of this standard. The body used for this purpose is a 1-kg cylinder of platinum–iridium alloy, called the international standard of mass.

mass action The law of mass action states that the rate at which a chemical reaction takes place at a given temperature is proportional to the product of the *active masses* of the reactants. The active mass of a reactant is taken to be its molar concentration. For example, for a reaction

$$A + B \rightarrow C$$

the rate is given by

$$R = k[A][B]$$

where k is the *rate constant. The principle was introduced by C. M. Guldberg and P. Waage in 1863. It is strictly correct only for ideal gases. In real cases *activities can be used.

mass concentration *See* concentration

massicot *See* lead(II) oxide.

mass number *See* nucleon number.

mass spectrum *See* spectrum.

masurium A former name for *technetium.

Maxwell–Boltzmann distribution A law describing the distribution of speeds among the molecules of a gas. In a system consisting of N molecules that are independent of each other except that they exchange energy on collision, it is clearly impossible to say what velocity any particular molecule will have. However, statistical statements regarding certain functions of the molecules were worked out by James Clerk Maxwell (1831–79) and Ludwig Boltzmann (1844–1906). One form of their law states that $n = N\exp(-E/RT)$, where n is the number of molecules with energy in excess of E, T is the thermodynamic temperature, and R is the *gas constant.

Mcleod gauge A vacuum pressure gauge in which a relatively large volume of a low-pressure gas is compressed to a small volume in a glass apparatus. The volume is reduced to an extent that causes the pressure to rise sufficiently to support a column of fluid high enough to read. This simple device, which relies on *Boyle's law, is suitable for measuring pressures in the range 10^3 to 10^{-3} pascal.

mean free path The average distance travelled between collisions by the molecules in a gas, the electrons in a metallic crystal, the neutrons in a moderator, etc. According to the *kinetic theory the mean free path between elastic collisions of gas molecules of diameter d (assuming they are rigid spheres) is $1/\sqrt{2}n\pi d^2$, where n is the number of molecules per unit volume in the gas. As n is proportional to the pressure of the gas, the mean free path is inversely proportional to the pressure.

mean free time The average time that elapses between the collisions of the molecules in a gas, the electrons in a crystal, the neutrons in a moderator, etc. *See* mean free path.

mega- Symbol M. A prefix used in the metric system to denote one million times. For example, 10^6 volts = 1 megavolt (MV).

melamine A white crystalline compound, $C_3N_6H_6$. Melamine is a cyclic compound having a six-membered ring of alternating C and N atoms, with three NH_2 groups. It can be copolymerized with methanal to give thermosetting *melaminc resins*, which are used particularly for laminated coatings.

melting point (m.p.) The temperature at which a solid changes into a liquid. A pure substance under standard conditions of pressure (usually 1 atmosphere) has a single reproducible melting point. If heat is gradually and uniformly supplied to a solid the consequent rise in temperature stops at the melting point until the fusion process is complete.

Mendeleev's law *See* periodic law.

mendelevium Symbol Md. A radioactive metallic transuranic element belonging to the *actinoids; a.n. 101; mass number of the only known isotope 256 (half-life 1.3 hours). It was first identified by A. Ghiorso, G. T. Seaborg, and associates in 1955. The alternative name *unnilunium* has been proposed.

Mendius reaction A reaction in which an organic nitrile is reduced by nascent hydrogen (e.g. from sodium in ethanol) to a primary amine:

$$RCN + 2H_2 \rightarrow RCH_2NH_2$$

menthol A white crystalline terpene alcohol, $C_{10}H_{19}OH$; r.d. 0.89; m.p. 42°C; b.p. 212°C. It has a minty taste and is found in certain essential oils (e.g. peppermint) and used as a flavouring.

mercaptans *See* thiols.

mercapto group *See* thiols.

mercuric compounds Compounds of mercury in its +2 oxidation state; e.g. mercuric chloride is mercury(II) chloride, $HgCl_2$.

mercurous compounds Compounds of mercury in its +1 oxidation state; e.g. mercury(I) chloride is mercurous chloride, HgCl.

mercury Symbol Hg. A heavy silvery liquid metallic element belonging to the *zinc group; a.n. 80; r.a.m. 200.59; r.d. 13.55; m.p. −38.87°C; b.p. 356.58°C. The main ore is the sulphide cinnabar (HgS), which can be decomposed to the elements. Mercury is used in thermometers, barometers, and other scientific apparatus, and in dental amalgams. The element is less reactive than zinc and cadmium and will not displace hydrogen from acids. It is also unusual in forming mercury(I) compounds containing the Hg_2^{2+} ion, as well as mercury(II) compounds containing Hg^{2+} ions. It also forms a number of complexes and organomercury compounds (e.g. the *Grignard reagents).

mercury cell A primary *voltaic cell consisting of a zinc anode and a cathode of mercury(II) oxide (HgO) mixed with graphite. The electrolyte is potassium hydroxide (KOH) saturated with zinc oxide, the overall reaction being:

$$Zn + HgO \rightarrow ZnO + Hg$$

The e.m.f. is 1.35 volts and the cell will deliver about 0.3 ampere-hour per cm^3.

mercury(I) chloride A white salt, Hg_2Cl_2; r.d. 7.0; m.p. 302°C; b.p. 384°C. It is made by heating mercury(II) chloride with mercury and is used in calomel cells (so called because the salt was formerly called *calomel*) and as a fungicide.

mercury(II) chloride A white salt, $HgCl_2$; r.d. 5.4; m.p. 276°C; b.p. 303°C. It is made by reacting mercury with chlorine and used in making other mercury compounds.

mercury(II) oxide A yellow or red oxide of mercury, HgO. The red form is made by heating mercury in oxygen at 350°C; the yellow form, which differs from the red in particle size, is precipitated when sodium hydroxide solution is added to a solution of mercury(II) nitrate. Both forms decompose to the elements at high temperature. The black precipitate formed when sodium hydroxide is added to mercury(I) nitrate solution is sometimes referred to as mercury(I) oxide (Hg_2O) but is probably a mixture of HgO and free mercury.

mercury(II) sulphide A red or black compound, HgS, occurring naturally as the minerals cinnabar (red) and metacinnabar (black). It can be obtained as a black precipitate by bubbling hydrogen sulphide through a solution of mercury(II) nitrate. The red form is obtained by sublimation. The compound is also called *vermilion* (used as a pigment).

meso form *See* optical activity.

mesomerism A former name for *resonance in molecules.

meta- 1. Prefix designating a benzene compound in which two substituents are in the 1,3 positions on the benzene ring. The abbreviation *m*- is used; for example, *m*-xylene is 1,3-dimethylbenzene. *Compare* ortho-; para-. **2.** Prefix designating a lower oxo acid, e.g. metaphosphoric acid. *Compare* ortho-.

metabolism The sum of the chemical reactions that occur within living organisms. The various compounds that take part in or are formed by these reactions are called *metabolites*. In animals many metabolites are obtained by the digestion of food, whereas in plants only the basic starting materials (carbon dioxide, water, and minerals) are externally derived. The synthesis (*anabolism) and breakdown (*catabolism) of most compounds occurs by a number of reaction steps, the reaction sequence being termed a *metabolic pathway*. Some pathways (e.g.

*glycolysis) are linear; others (e.g. the *Krebs cycle) are cyclic.

metaboric acid *See* boric acid.

metal Any of a class of chemical elements that are typically lustrous solids that are good conductors of heat and electricity. Not all metals have all these properties (e.g. mercury is a liquid). In chemistry, metals fall into two distinct types. Those of the *s*- and *p*-blocks (e.g. sodium and aluminium) are generally soft silvery reactive elements. They tend to form positive ions and so are described as electropositive. This is contrasted with typical nonmetallic behaviour of forming negative ions. The *transition elements (e.g. iron and copper) are harder substances and generally less reactive. They form coordination complexes. All metals have oxides that are basic.

metaldehyde A solid compound, $C_4O_4H_4(CH_3)_4$, formed by polymerization of ethanal (acetaldehyde) in dilute acid solutions below 0°C. The compound, a tetramer of ethanal, is used in slug pellets and as a fuel for portable stoves.

metal fatigue A cumulative effect causing a metal to fail after repeated applications of stress, none of which exceeds the ultimate tensile strength. The *fatigue strength* (or *fatigue limit*) is the stress that will cause failure after a specified number (usually 10^7) of cycles. The number of cycles required to produce failure decreases as the level of stress or strain increases. Other factors, such as corrosion, also reduce the fatigue life.

metallic bond A chemical bond of the type holding together the atoms in a solid metal or alloy. In such solids, the atoms are considered to be ionized, with the positive ions occupying lattice positions. The valence electrons are able to move freely (or almost freely) through the lattice, forming an 'electron gas'. The bonding force is electrostatic attraction between the positive metal ions and the electrons. The existence of free electrons accounts for the good electrical and thermal conductivities of metals. *See also* energy bands.

metallic crystal A crystalline solid in which the atoms are held together by *metallic bonds. Metallic crystals are found in some *interstitial compounds as well as in metals and alloys.

metallized dye *See* dyes.

metallocene A type of organometallic complex in which one or more aromatic rings (e.g. $C_5H_5^-$ or C_6H_6) coordinate to a metal ion or atom by the pi electrons of the ring. *Ferrocene was the first such compound to be discovered.

metallography The microscopic study of the structure of metals and their alloys. Both optical microscopes and electron microscopes are used in this work.

metalloid (semimetal) Any of a class of chemical elements intermediate in properties between metals and nonmetals. The classification is not clear cut, but typical metalloids are boron, silicon, germanium, arsenic, and tellurium. They are electrical semiconductors and their oxides are amphoteric.

metallurgy The branch of applied science concerned with the production of metals from their ores, the purification of metals, the manufacture of alloys, and the use and performance of metals in engineering practice. *Process metallurgy* is concerned with the extraction and production of metals, while *physical metallurgy* concerns the mechanical behaviour of metals.

metamict state The amorphous state of a substance that has lost its crystalline structure as a result of the radioactivity of uranium or thorium. *Metamict minerals* are minerals whose structure has been disrupted by this process. The metamictization is caused by alpha-particles and the recoil nuclei from radioactive disintegration.

metaphosphoric acid *See* phosphoric(VI) acid.

metaplumbate *See* plumbate.

metastable state A condition of a system in which it has a precarious stability that can easily be disturbed. It is unlike a state of stable equilibrium in that a minor disturbance will cause a system in a metastable state to fall to a lower energy level. A book lying on a table is in a state of stable equilibrium; a thin book standing on edge is in metastable equilibrium. Supercooled water is also in a metastable state. It is liquid below 0°C; a grain of dust or ice introduced into it will cause it to freeze. An excited state of an atom or nucleus that has an appreciable lifetime is also metastable.

metastannate *See* stannate.

metathesis *See* double decomposition.

methacrylate A salt or ester of methacrylic acid (2-methylpropenoic acid).

methacrylate resins *Acrylic resins obtained by polymerizing 2-methylpropenoic acid or its esters.

methacrylic acid *See* 2-methylpropenoic acid.

methanal (formaldehyde) A colourless gas, HCHO; r.d. 0.815 (at −20°C); m.p. −92°C; b.p. −19°C. It is the simplest *aldehyde, made by the catalytic oxidation of methanol (500°C; silver catalyst) by air. It forms two polymers: *methanal trimer and polymethanal. *See also* formalin.

methanal trimer A cyclic trimer of methanal, $C_3O_3H_6$, obtained by distillation of an acidic solution of methanal. It has a six-membered ring of alternating $-O-$ and $-CH_2-$ groups.

methane A colourless odourless gas, CH_4; m.p. −182.5°C; b.p. −161°C. Methane is the simplest hydrocarbon, being the first member of the *alkane series. It is the main constituent of natural gas (~99%) and as such is an important raw material for producing other organic compounds. It can be converted into methanol by catalytic oxidation.

methanide *See* carbide.

methanoate (formate) A salt or ester of methanoic acid.

methanoic acid (formic acid) A colourless pungent liquid, HCOOH; r.d. 1.2; m.p. 8°C; b.p. 101°C. It can be made by the action of concentrated sulphuric acid on the sodium salt (sodium methanoate), and occurs naturally in ants and stinging nettles. Methanoic acid is the simplest of the *carboxylic acids.

methanol (methyl alcohol) A colourless liquid, CH_3OH; r.d. 0.79; m.p. −98°C; b.p. 64°C. It is made by catalytic oxidation of methane (from natural gas) using air. Methanol is used as a solvent (*see* methylated spirits) and as a raw material for making methanal (mainly for urea–formaldehyde resins). It was formerly made by the dry distillation of wood (hence the name *wood alcohol*).

methionine *See* amino acid.

methoxy group The organic group CH_3O-.

methyl acetate *See* methyl ethanoate.

methyl alcohol *See* methanol.

methylamine A colourless flammable gas, CH_3NH_2; m.p. −92°C; b.p. −7°C. It can be made by a catalytic reaction between methanol and ammonia and is used in the manufacture of other organic chemicals.

methylated spirits A mixture consisting mainly of ethanol with added methanal (~9.5%), pyridine (~0.5%), and blue dye. The additives are included to make the ethanol undrinkable so that it can be sold without excise duty for use as a solvent and a fuel (for small spirit stoves).

methylation A chemical reaction in which a methyl group (CH_3-) is introduced in a molecule. A particular example is the replacement of a hydrogen atom by a methyl group, as in a *Friedel–Crafts reaction.

methylbenzene (toluene) A colourless liquid, $CH_3C_6H_5$; r.d. 0.9; m.p. −94°C; b.p. 111°C. Methylbenzene is derived from benzene by replacement of a hydrogen atom by a methyl group. It can be obtained from coal tar or made from methylcyclohexane (extracted from crude oil) by catalytic dehydrogenation. Its main uses are as a solvent and as a raw material for producing TNT.

methyl bromide *See* bromomethane.

2-methylbuta-1,3-diene *See* isoprene.

methyl chloride *See* chloromethane.

methylene The highly reactive *carbene, $:CH_2$. The divalent CH_2 group in a compound is the *methylene group*.

methyl ethanoate (methyl acetate) A colourless volatile fragrant liquid, CH_3COOCH_3; r.d. 0.92; m.p. −98°C; b.p. 54°C. A typical *ester, it can be made from methanol and methanoic acid and is used mainly as a solvent.

methyl ethyl ketone *See* butanone.

methyl group *or* **radical** The organic group CH_3-

methyl methacrylate An ester of methacrylic acid (2-methylpropenoic acid), $CH_2{:}C(CH_3)COOCH_3$, used in making *methacrylate resins.

methyl orange An organic dye used as an acid–base *indicator. It changes from red below pH 3.1 to yellow above pH 4.4 (at 25°C) and is used for titrations involving weak bases.

methylphenols (cresols) Organic compounds having a methyl group and a hydroxyl group bound directly to a benzene ring. There are three isomeric methylphenols with the formula $CH_3C_6H_4OH$, differing in the relative positions of the methyl and hydroxyl groups. A mixture of the three can be obtained by distilling coal tar and is used as a germicide and antiseptic.

2-methylpropenoic acid (methacrylic acid) A white crystalline unsaturated carboxylic acid, $CH_2{:}C(CH_3)COOH$, used in making *methacrylate resins.

methyl red An organic dye similar in structure and use to methyl orange. It changes from red below pH 4.4 to yellow above pH 6.0 (at 25°C).

metre Symbol m. The SI unit of length, being the length of the path travelled by light in vacuum during a time interval of $1/(2.99\,792\,458 \times 10^8)$ second. This definition, adopted by the General Conference on Weights and Measures in October, 1983, replaced the 1967 definition based on the krypton lamp, i.e. 1 650 763.73 wavelengths in a vacuum of the radiation corresponding to the transition between the levels $2p^{10}$ and $5d^5$ of the nuclide krypton–86. This definition (in 1958) replaced the older definition of a metre based on a platinum–iridium bar of standard length. When the *metric system was introduced in 1791 in France, the metre was intended to be one ten-millionth of the earth's meridian quadrant passing through Paris. However, the original geodetic surveys proved the impractibility of such a standard and the original platinum metre bar, the *mètre des archives*, was constructed in 1793.

metric system A decimal system of units originally devised by a committee of the French Academy, which included J. L. Lagrange and P. S. Laplace, in 1791. It was based on the *metre, the gram defined in terms of the mass of a cubic centimetre of water, and the second. This centimetre-gram-second system (*see* c.g.s. units) later gave way for scientific work to the metre-kilogram-second system (*see* m.k.s. units) on which *SI units are based.

mica Any of a group of silicate minerals with a layered structure. Micas are composed of linked SiO_4 tetrahedra with cations and hydroxyl groupings between the layers. The general formula is $X_2Y_{4-6}Z_8O_{20}(OH,F)_4$, where X = K,Na,Ca; Y = Al,Mg,Fe,Li; and Z = Si,Al. The three main mica minerals are

*muscovite, $K_2Al_4(Si_6Al_2O_{20})(OH,F)_4$

*biotite, $K_2(Mg,Fe^{2+}$

lepidolite, $K_2(Li,Al)_{5-6}(Si_{6-7}Al_{2-1}O_{20})(OH,F)_4$.

Micas have perfect basal cleavage and the thin cleavage flakes are flexible and elastic. Flakes of mica are used as electrical insulators and as the dielectric in capacitors.

micelle An aggregate of molecules in a *colloid. For example, when soap or other *detergents dissolve in water they do so as micelles – small clusters of molecules in which the nonpolar hydrocarbon groups are in the centre and the hydrophilic polar groups are on the outside solvated by the water molecules.

micro- Symbol μ. A prefix used in the metric system to denote one millionth. For example, 10^{-6} metre = 1 micrometre (μm).

microbalance A sensitive *balance capable of weighing masses of the order 10^{-6} to 10^{-9} kg.

microscope A device for forming a magnified image of a small object. The *simple microscope* consists of a biconvex magnifying glass or an equivalent system of lenses, either hand-held or in a simple frame. The *compound microscope* uses two lenses or systems of lenses, the second magnifying the real image formed by the first. The lenses are usually mounted at the opposite ends of a tube that has mechanical controls to move it in relation to the object. An optical condenser and mirror, often with a separate light source, provide illumination of the object. The widely used *binocular microscope* consists of two separate instruments fastened together so that one eye looks through one while the other eye looks through the other. This gives stereoscopic vision. *See also* electron microscope.

migration 1. The movement of a group, atom, or double bond from one part of a molecule to another. **2.** The movement of ions under the influence of an electric field.

milk of magnesia *See* magnesium hydroxide.

milk sugar *See* lactose.

milli- Symbol m. A prefix used in the metric system to denote one thousandth. For example, 0.001 volt = 1 millivolt (mV).

mineral A naturally occurring substance that has a characteristic chemical composition and, in general, a crystalline structure. The term is also often applied generally to organic substances that are obtained by mining (e.g. coal, petroleum, and natural gas) but strictly speaking these are not minerals, being complex mixtures without definite chemical formulas. Rocks are composed of mixtures of minerals. Minerals may be identified by the properties of their crystal system, hardness (measured on the Mohs' scale), relative density, lustre, colour, cleavage, and fracture. Many names of minerals end in *-ite*.

mineral acid A common inorganic acid, such as hydrochloric acid, sulphuric acid, or nitric acid.

mirabilite A mineral form of *sodium sulphate, $Na_2SO_4.10H_2O$.

misch metal An alloy of cerium (50%), lanthanum (25%), neodymium (18%), praseodymium (5%), and other rare earths. It is used alloyed with iron (up to 30%) in lighter flints, and in small quantities to improve the malleability of iron. It is also added to copper alloys to make them harder, to aluminium alloys to make them stronger, to magnesium alloys to reduce creep, and to nickel alloys to reduce oxidation.

Mitscherlich's law (law of isomorphism) Substances that have the same crystal structure have similar chemical formulae. The law can be used to determine the formula of an unknown compound if it is isomorphous with a compound of known formula.

mixture A system of two or more distinct chemical substances. *Homogeneous mixtures* are those in which the atoms or molecules are interspersed, as in a mixture of gases or in a solution. *Heterogeneous mixtures* have distinguishable phases, e.g. a mixture of iron filings and sulphur. In a mixture there is no redistribution of valence electrons, and the components retain their individual chemical properties. Unlike compounds, mixtures can be separated by physical means (distillation, crystallization, etc.).

m.k.s. units A *metric system of units devised by A. Giorgi (and sometimes known as *Giorgi units*) in 1901. It is based on the metre, kilogram, and second and grew from the earlier *c.g.s. units. The electrical unit chosen to augment these three basic units was the ampere and the permeability of space (magnetic constant) was taken as 10^{-7} Hm^{-1}. To simplify electromagnetic calculations the magnetic constant was later changed to $4\pi \times 10^{-7}$ Hm^{-1} to give the *rationalized MKSA system*. This system, with some modifications, formed the basis of *SI units, now used in all scientific work.

mmHg A unit of pressure equal to that exerted under standard gravity by a height of one millimetre of mercury, or 133.322 pascals.

molal concentration *See* concentration.

molality *See* concentration.

molar Denoting that an extensive physical property is being expressed per *amount of substance, usually per mole. For example, the molar heat capacity of a compound is the heat capacity of that compound per unit amount of substance; in SI units it would be expressed in $J\ K^{-1}\ mol^{-1}$.

molar conductivity Symbol Λ. The conductivity of that volume of an electrolyte that contains one mole of solution between electrodes placed one metre apart.

molar heat capacity *See* heat capacity.

molarity *See* concentration.

molar volume (molecular volume) The volume occupied by a substance per unit amount of substance.

mole Symbol mol. The SI unit of *amount of substance. It is equal to the amount of substance that contains as many elementary units as there are atoms in 0.012 kg of carbon−12. The elementary units may be atoms, molecules, ions, radicals, electrons, etc., and must be specified. 1 mole of a compound has a mass equal to its *relative molecular mass expressed in grams.

molecular beam A beam of atoms, ions, or molecules at low pressure, in which all the particles are travelling in the same direction and there are few collisions between them. They are formed by allowing a gas or vapour to pass through an aperture into an enclosure, which acts as a collimator by containing several additional apertures and vacuum pumps to remove any particles that do not pass through the apertures. Molecular beams are used in studies of surfaces and chemical reactions and in spectroscopy.

molecular distillation Distillation in high vacuum (about 0.1 pascal) with the condensing surface so close to the surface of the evaporating liquid that the molecules of the liquid travel to the condensing surface without collisions. This technique enables very much lower temperatures to be used than are used with distillation at atmospheric pressure and therefore heat-sensitive substances can be distilled. Oxidation of the distillate is also eliminated as there is no oxygen present.

molecular formula *See* formula.

molecularity The number of molecules involved in forming the activated complex in a step of a chemical reaction. Reactions are said to be *unimolecular*, *bimolecular*, or *trimolecular* according to whether 1, 2, or 3 molecules are involved.

molecular orbital *See* orbital.

molecular sieve Porous crystalline substances, especially aluminosilicates (*see* zeolite), that can be dehydrated with little change in crystal structure. As they form regularly spaced cavities, they provide a high surface area for the adsorption of smaller molecules. The general formula of these substances is $M_nO.Al_2O_3.xSiO_2.yH_2O$, where *M* is a metal ion and *n* is twice the reciprocal of its valency. Molecular sieves are used as drying agents and in the separation and purification of fluids. They can also be loaded with chemical substances, which remain separated from any reaction that is taking place around them, until they are released by heating or by displacement with a more strongly adsorbed substance. They can thus be used as cation exchange mediums and as catalysts and catalyst supports.

molecular volume *See* molar volume.

molecular weight *See* relative molecular mass.

molecule One of the fundamental units forming a chemical compound; the smallest part of a chemical compound that can take part in a chemical reaction. In most covalent compounds, molecules consist of groups of atoms held together by covalent or coordinate bonds. Covalent substances that form *macromolecular crystals have no discrete molecules (in a sense, the whole crystal is a molecule). Similarly, ionic compounds do not have single molecules, being collections of oppositely charged ions.

mole fraction Symbol *X*. A measure of the amount of a component in a mixture. The mole fraction of component A is given by $X_A = n_A/N$, where n_A is the amount of substance of A (for a given entity) and *N* is the total amount of substance of the mixture (for the same entity).

Molisch's test *See* alpha-naphthol test.

molybdenum Symbol Mo. A silvery hard metallic *transition element; a.n. 42; r.a.m. 95.94; r.d. 10.22; m.p. 2610°C; b.p. 5560°C. It is found in molybdenite (MoS_2), the metal being extracted by roasting to give the oxide, followed by reduction with hydrogen. The element is used in alloy steels. Molybdenum(IV) sulphide (MoS_2) is used as a lubricant. Chemically, it is unreactive, being unaffected by most acids. It oxidizes at high temperatures and can be dissolved in molten alkali to give a range of molybdates and polymolybdates. Molybdenum was discovered in 1778 by Scheele.

Mond process A method of obtaining pure nickel by heating the impure metal in a stream of carbon monoxide at 50–60°C. Volatile nickel carbonyl ($Ni(CO)_4$) is formed, and this can be decomposed at higher temperatures (180°C) to give pure nickel. The method was invented by the German–British chemist Ludwig Mond (1839–1909).

Monel metal An alloy of nickel (60–70%), copper (25–35%), and small quantities of iron, manganese, silicon, and carbon. It is used to make acid-resisting equipment in the chemical industry.

monoclinic *See* crystal system.

monohydrate A crystalline compound having one molecule of water per molecule of compound.

monomer A molecule (or compound) that joins with others in forming a dimer, trimer, or polymer.

monosaccharide (simple sugar) A carbohydrate that cannot be split into smaller units by the action of dilute acids. Monosaccharides are classified according to the number of carbon atoms they possess: *trioses* have three carbon atoms; *tetroses*, four; *pentoses*, five; *hexoses*, six; etc. Each of these is further divided into *aldoses* and *ketoses*, depending on whether the molecule contains an aldehyde group (–CHO) or a ketone group (–CO–). For example glucose, having six carbon atoms and an aldehyde group, is an *aldohexose* whereas fructose is a *ketohexose*. These aldehyde and ketone groups confer reducing properties on monosaccharides: they can be oxidized to yield sugar acids. They also react with phosphoric acid to produce phosphate esters (e.g. in *ATP), which are important in cell metabolism. Monosaccharides can exist as either straight-chain or ring-shaped molecules. They also exhibit *optical activity, giving rise to both dextrorotatory and laevorotatory forms.

monotropy *See* allotropy.

monovalent (univalent) Having a valency of one.

mordant A substance used in certain dyeing processes. Mordants are often inorganic oxides or salts, which are absorbed on the fabric. The dyestuff then forms a coloured complex with the mordant, the colour depending on the mordant used as well as the dyestuff. *See also* lake.

morphine An alkaloid present in opium. It is an analgesic and narcotic, used medically for the relief of severe pain.

mosaic gold *See* tin(IV) sulphide.

Moseley's law The frequencies of the lines in the *X-ray spectra of the elements are related to the atomic numbers of the elements. If the square roots of the frequencies of corresponding lines of a set of elements are plotted against the atomic numbers a straight line is obtained. The law was discovered by H. G. Moseley (1887–1915).

moss agate *See* agate.

multiple proportions *See* chemical combination.

multiplet 1. A spectral line formed by more than two (*see* doublet) closely spaced lines. **2.** A group of elementary particles that are identical in all respects except that of electric charge.

Mumetal The original trade name for a ferromagnetic alloy, containing 78% nickel, 17% iron, and 5% copper, that had a high permeability and a low coercive force. More modern versions also contain chromium and molybdenum. These alloys are used in some transformer cores and for shielding various devices from external magnetic fields.

Muntz metal A form of *brass containing 60% copper, 39% zinc, and small amounts of lead and iron. Stronger than alpha-brass, it is used for hot forgings, brazing rods, and large nuts and bolts. It is named after G. F. Muntz (1794–1857).

muscovite (white mica; potash mica) A mineral form of potassium aluminosilicate, $K_2Al_4(Si_6Al_2)O_{20}(OH,F)_4$; one of the most important members of the *mica group of minerals. It is chemically complex and has a sheetlike crystal structure. It is usually silvery-grey in colour, sometimes tinted with green, brown, or pink. Muscovite is a common constituent of certain granites and pegmatites. It is also common in metamorphic and sedimentary rocks. It is widely used in industry, for example in the manufacture of electrical equipment and as a filler in roofing materials, wallpapers, and paint.

mustard gas A highly poisonous gas, $(ClCH_2CH_2)_2S$; dichlorodiethyl sulphide. It is made from ethene and disulphur dichloride (S_2Cl_2), and used as a war gas.

mutarotation Change of optical activity with time as a result of spontaneous chemical reaction.

myoglobin A globular protein occurring widely in muscle tissue as an oxygen carrier. It comprises a single polypeptide chain and a *haem group, which reversibly binds a molecule of oxygen. This is only relinquished at relatively low external oxygen concentrations, e.g. during strenuous exercise when muscle oxygen demand outpaces supply from the blood. Myoglobin thus acts as an emergency oxygen store.

N

NAD (nicotinamide adenine dinucleotide) A *coenzyme, derived from the B vitamin *nicotinic acid, that participates in many biological dehydrogenation reactions. NAD is characteristically loosely bound to the enzymes concerned. It normally carries a positive charge and can accept one hydrogen atom and two electrons to become the reduced form, *NADH*. NADH is generated during the oxidation of food; it then gives up its two electrons (and single proton) to the electron transport chain, thereby reverting to NAD^+ and generating three molecules of ATP per molecule of NADH.

NADP (*nicotinamide adenine dinucleotide phosphate*) differs from NAD only in possessing an additional phosphate group. It functions in the same way as NAD although anabolic reactions (*see* anabolism) generally use NADPH (reduced NADP) as a hydrogen donor rather than NADH. Enzymes tend to be specific for either NAD or NADP as coenzyme.

nano- Symbol n. A prefix used in the metric system to denote 10^{-9}. For example, 10^{-9} second = 1 nanosecond (ns).

naphthalene A white volatile solid, $C_{10}H_8$; r.d. 1.14; m.p. 802°C; b.p. 218°C. Naphthalene is an aromatic hydrocarbon with an odour of mothballs and is obtained from crude oil. It is a raw material for making certain synthetic resins.

NAPHTHOLS

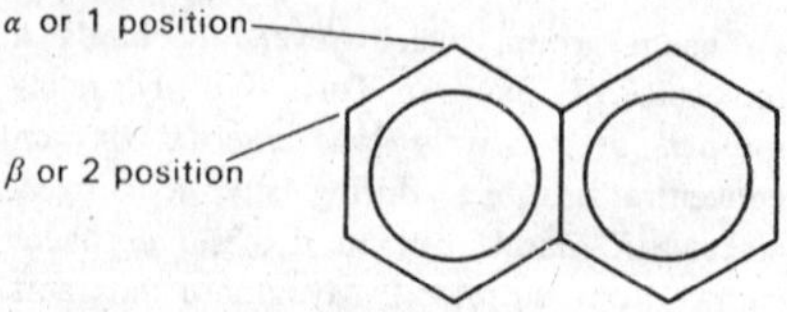

Naphthalene

naphthols Two phenols derived from naphthalene with the formula $C_{10}H_7OH$, differing in the position of the $-OH$ group. The most important is naphthalen-2-ol (β-naphthol), with the $-OH$ in the 2-position. It is a white solid (r.d. 1.2; m.p. 122°C; b.p. 285°C) used in rubber as an antioxidant. Naphthalen-2-ol will couple with diazonium salts at the 1-position to form red *azo compounds, a reaction used in testing for primary amines (by making the diazonium salt and adding naphthalen-2-ol).

naphthyl group The group $C_{10}H_7-$ obtained by removing a hydrogen atom from naphthalene. There are two forms depending on whether the hydrogen is removed from the 1- or 2-position.

nascent hydrogen A reactive form of hydrogen generated *in situ* in the reaction mixture (e.g. by the action of acid on zinc). Nascent hydrogen can reduce elements and compounds that do not readily react with 'normal' hydrogen. It was once thought that the hydrogen was present as atoms, but this is not the case. Probably hydrogen molecules are formed in an excited state and react before they revert to the ground state.

natron A mineral form of hydrated sodium carbonate, $Na_2CO_3.H_2O$.

Natta process *See* Ziegler process.

natural gas A naturally occurring mixture of gaseous hydrocarbons that is found in porous sedimentary rocks in the earth's crust, usually in association with *petroleum deposits. It consists chiefly of methane (about 85%), ethane (up to about 10%), propane (about 3%), and butane. Carbon dioxide, nitrogen, oxygen, hydrogen sulphide, and sometimes helium may also be present. Natural gas, like petroleum, originates in the decomposition of organic matter. It is widely used as a fuel and also to produce carbon black and some organic chemicals. Natural gas occurs on every continent, the major reserves occurring in the USSR, USA, Algeria, Canada, and the Middle East.

nematic crystal *See* liquid crystal.

neodymium Symbol Nd. A soft silvery metallic element belonging to the *lanthanoids; a.n. 60; r.a.m. 144.24; r.d. 7.004 (20°); m.p. 1016°C; b.p. 3068°C. It occurs in bastnasite and monazite, from which it is recovered by an ion-exchange process. There are seven naturally occurring isotopes, all of which are stable, except neodymium-144, which is slightly radioactive (half-life 10^{10}–10^{15} years). Seven artificial radioisotopes have been produced. The metal is used to colour glass violet-purple and to make it dichroic. It is also used in mischmetal (18% neodymium). It was discovered by C. A. von Welsbach in 1885.

neon Symbol Ne. A colourless gaseous element belonging to group I of the periodic table (the *noble gases); a.n. 10; r.a.m. 20.79; d. 0.9 g dm^{-3}; m.p. −248.67°C; b.p. −246.05°C. Neon occurs in air (0.0018% by volume) and is obtained by fractional distillation of liquid air. It is used in discharge tubes and neon lamps, in which it has a characteristic red glow. It forms hardly any compounds (neon fluorides have been reported). The element was discovered in 1898 by Sir William Ramsey and M. W. Travers.

neoprene A synthetic rubber made by polymerizing the compound 2-chlorobuta-1,2-diene. Neoprene is often used in place of natural rubber in applications requiring resistance to chemical attack.

nephrite *See* jade.

neptunium Symbol Np. A radioactive metallic transuranic element belonging to the *actinoids; a.n. 93; r.a.m. 237.0482. The most stable isotope, neptunium–237, has a half-life of 2.2×10^6 years and is produced in small quantities as a by-product by nuclear reactors. Other isotopes have mass numbers 229–236 and 238–241. The only other relatively long-lived isotope is neptunium–236 (half-life 5×10^3 years). The element was first produced by McMillan and Abelson in 1940.

neptunium series *See* radioactive series.

Nernst heat theorem A statement of the third law of *thermodynamics in a restricted form: if a chemical change takes place between pure crystalline solids at *absolute zero there is no change of entropy.

nesquehonite A mineral form of *magnesium carbonate trihydrate, $MgCO_3.3H_2O$.

Nessler's reagent A solution of mercury (II) iodide (HgI_2) in potassium iodide and potassium hydroxide. It is used in testing for ammonia, with which it forms a brown coloration or precipitate.

neutral Describing a compound or solution that is neither acidic nor basic. A neutral solution is one that contains equal numbers of both protonated and deprotonated forms of the solvent.

neutralization The process in which an acid reacts with a base to form a salt and water.

neutron A neutral hadron that is stable in the atomic nucleus but decays into a proton, an electron, and an antineutrino with a mean life of 12 minutes outside the nucleus. Its rest mass is slightly greater than that of the proton, being $1.674\,92 \times 10^{-27}$ kg. Neutrons occur in all atomic nuclei except normal hydrogen. The neutron was first reported in 1932 by James Chadwick (1891–1974).

neutron number Symbol N. The number of neutrons in an atomic nucleus of a particular nuclide. It is equal to the difference between the *nucleon number and the *atomic number.

Newlands' law *See* law of octaves.

newton Symbol N. The *SI unit of force, being the force required to give a mass of one kilogram an acceleration of 1 m s^{-2}. It is named after Sir Isaac Newton (1642–1727).

niacin *See* nicotinic acid.

Nichrome Tradename for a group of nickel–chromium alloys used for wire in heating elements as they possess good resistance to oxidation and have a high resistivity. Typical is Nichrome V containing 80% nickel and 19.5% chromium, the balance consisting of manganese, silicon, and carbon.

nickel Symbol Ni. A malleable ductile silvery metallic *transition element; a.n. 28; r.a.m. 58.70; r.d. 8.9; m.p. 1450°C; b.p. 2840°C. It is found in the minerals pentlandite (NiS), pyrrhoite ((Fe,Ni)S), and garnierite ($(Ni,Mg)_6(OH)_6Si_4O_{11}.H_2O$). Nickel is also present in certain iron meteorites (up to 20%). The metal is extracted by roasting the ore to give the oxide, followed by reduction with carbon monoxide and purification by the *Mond process. Alternatively electolysis is used. Nickel metal is used in special steels, in Invar, and, being ferromagnetic, in magnetic alloys, such as *Mumetal. It is also an effective catalyst, particularly for hydrogenation reactions (*see also* Raney nickel). The main compounds are formed with nickel in the +2 oxidation state; the +3 state also exists (e.g. the black oxide, Ni_2O_3). Nickel was discovered by A. F. Cronstedt in 1751.

nickel carbonyl A colourless volatile liquid, $Ni(CO)_4$; m.p. −25°C; b.p. 43°C. It is formed by direct combination of nickel metal with carbon monoxide at 50–60°C. The reaction is reversed at higher temperatures, and the reactions are the basis of the *Mond process for purifying nickel. The nickel in the compound has an oxidation state of zero, and the compound is a typical example of a complex with pi-bonding *ligands, in which filled *d*-orbitals on the nickel overlap with empty *p*-orbitals on the carbon.

nickel–iron accumulator (Edison cell; NIFE cell) A *secondary cell devised by Thomas Edison (1847–1931) having a positive plate of nickel oxide and a negative plate of iron both immersed in an electrolyte of potassium hydroxide. The reaction on discharge is

$$2NiOOH.H_2O + Fe \rightarrow 2Ni(OH)_2 + Fe(OH)_2,$$

the reverse occurring during charging. Each cell gives an e.m.f. of about 1.2 volts and produces about 100 kJ per kilogram during each discharge. *Compare* lead–acid accumulator.

nickel(II) oxide A green powder, NiO; r.d. 6.6. It can be made by heating nickel (II) nitrate or carbonate with air excluded.

nickel(III) oxide (nickel peroxide; nickel sesquioxide) A black or grey powder, Ni_2O_3; r.d. 4.8. It is made by heating nickel(II) oxide in air and used in *nickel–iron accumulators.

nickel silver *See* German silver.

nicotinamide adenine dinucleotide *See* NAD.

nicotine A colourless poisonous *alkaloid present in tobacco. It is used as an insecticide.

nicotinic acid (niacin) A vitamin of the *vitamin B complex. It can be manufactured by plants and animals from the amino acid tryptophan. The amide derivative, nicotinamide, is a component of the coenzymes *NAD and NADP. These take part in many metabolic reactions as hydrogen acceptors. Deficiency of nicotinic acid causes the disease pellagra in humans. Apart from tryptophan-rich protein, good sources are liver and groundnut and sunflower meals.

NIFE cell *See* nickel–iron accumulator.

niobium Symbol Nb. A soft ductile grey-blue metallic transition element; a.n. 41; r.a.m. 92.91; r.d. 8.57; m.p. 2468°C; b.p. 4742°C. It occurs in several minerals, including niobite ($Fe(NbO_3)_2$), and is extracted by several methods including reduction of the complex fluoride K_2NbF_7 using sodium. It is used in special steels and in welded joints (to increase strength). Niobium–zirconium alloys are used in superconductors. Chemically, the element combines with the halogens and oxidizes in air at 200°C. It forms a number of compounds and complexes with the metal in oxidation states 2, 3, or 5. The element was discovered by Charles Hatchett in 1801 and first isolated by Blomstrand in 1864. Formerly, it was called *columbium*.

nitrate A salt or ester of nitric acid.

nitration A type of chemical reaction in which a nitro group ($-NO_2$) is added to or substituted in a molecule. Nitration can be carried out by a mixture of concentrated nitric and sulphuric acids. An example is electrophilic substitution of benzene (and benzene compounds), where the electrophile is the nitryl ion NO_2^+.

nitre (saltpetre) Commercial *potassium nitrate; the name was formerly applied to natural crustlike efflorescences, occurring in some arid regions.

nitre cake *See* sodium hydrogensulphate.

nitric acid A colourless corrosive poisonous liquid, HNO_3; r.d. 1.50; m.p. −42°C; b.p. 83°C. Nitric acid may be prepared in the laboratory by the distillation of a mixture of an alkali-metal nitrate and concentrated sulphuric acid. The industrial production is by the oxidation of ammonia to nitrogen monoxide, the oxidation of this to nitrogen dioxide, and the reaction of nitrogen dioxide with water to form nitric acid and nitrogen monoxide (which is recycled). The first reaction (NH_3 to NO) is catalysed by platinum or platinum/rhodium in the form of fine wire gauze. The oxidation of NO and the absorption of NO_2 to form the product are noncatalytic and proceed with high yields but both reactions are second-order and slow. Increases in pressure reduce the selectivity of the reaction and therefore rather large gas absorption towers are required. In practice the absorbing acid is refrigerated to around 2°C and a commercial 'concentrated nitric acid' at about 67% is produced.

Nitric acid is a strong acid (highly dissociated in aqueous solution) and dilute solutions behave much like other mineral acids. Concentrated nitric acid is a strong oxidizing agent. Most metals dissolve to form nitrates but with the evolution of nitrogen oxides. Concentrated nitric acid also reacts with several nonmetals to give the oxo acid or oxide. Nitric acid is generally stored in dark brown bottles because of the photolytic decomposition to dinitrogen tetroxide. *See also* nitration.

nitric oxide *See* nitrogen monoxide.

nitrides Compounds of nitrogen with a more electropositive element. Boron nitride is a covalent compound having macromolecular crystals. Certain electropositive elements, such as lithium, magnesium, and calcium, react directly with nitrogen to form ionic nitrides containing the N^{3-} ion. Transition elements form a range of interstitial nitrides (e.g. Mn_4N, W_2N), which can be produced by heating the metal in ammonia.

nitrification A chemical process in which nitrogen (mostly in the form of ammonia) in plant and animal wastes and dead remains is oxidized at first to nitrites and then to nitrates. These reactions are effected mainly by the bacteria *Nitrosomonas* and *Nitrobacter* respectively. Unlike ammonia, nitrates are readily taken up by plant roots; nitrification is therefore a crucial part of the *nitrogen cycle. Nitrogen-containing compounds are often applied to soils deficient in this element, as fertilizer. *Compare* denitrification.

nitriles (cyanides) Organic compounds containing the group −CN bound to an organic group. Nitriles are made by reaction between potassium cyanide and haloalkanes in alcoholic solution, e.g.

$$KCN + CH_3Cl \rightarrow CH_3CN + KCl$$

An alternative method is dehydration of amides

$$CH_3CONH_2 - H_2O \rightarrow CH_3CN$$

They can be hydrolysed to amides and carboxylic acids and can be reduced to amines.

nitrite A salt or ester of nitrous acid; the nitrite ion, NO_2^-, has a bond angle of 115°.

nitrobenzene A yellow oily liquid, $C_6H_5NO_2$; r.d. 1.2; m.p. 6°C; b.p. 211°C. It is made by the *nitration of benzene using a mixture of nitric and sulphuric acids.

nitrocellulose *See* cellulose nitrate.

nitro compounds Organic compounds containing the group $-NO_2$ (the *nitro group*) bound to a carbon atom in a benzene ring. Nitro compounds are made by *nitration reactions. They can be reduced to aromatic amines (e.g. nitrobenzene can be reduced to phenyiamine).

nitrogen Symbol N. A colourless gaseous element belonging to *group V of the periodic table; a.n. 7; r.a.m. 14.0067; d. 1.2506 g dm^{-3}; m.p. −209.86°C; b.p. −195.8°C. It occurs in air (about 78% by volume) and is an essential constituent of proteins and nucleic acids in living organisms (*see* nitrogen cycle). Nitrogen is obtained for industrial purposes by fractional distillation of liquid air. Pure nitrogen can be obtained in the laboratory by heating a metal azide. There are two natural isotopes: nitrogen-14 and nitrogen-15 (about 3%). The element is used in the *Haber process for making ammonia and is also used to provide an inert atmosphere in welding and metallurgy. The gas is diatomic and relatively inert – it reacts with hydrogen at high temperatures and with oxygen in electric discharges. It also forms *nitrides with certain metals. Nitrogen was discovered in 1772 by D. Rutherford.

nitrogen cycle One of the major cycles of chemical elements in the environment. Nitrates in the soil are taken up by plant roots and may then pass along food chains into animals. Decomposing bacteria convert nitrogen-containing compounds (especially ammonia) in plant and animal wastes and dead remains back into nitrates, which are released into the soil and can again be taken up by plants (*see* nitrification). Though nitrogen is essential to all forms of life, the huge amount present in the atmosphere is not directly available to most organisms (*compare* carbon cycle). It can, however, be assimilated by some specialized bacteria and algae (*see* nitrogen fixation) and is thus made available to other organisms indirectly. Lightning flashes also make some nitrogen available to plants by causing the combination of atmospheric nitrogen and oxygen to form oxides of nitrogen, which enter the soil and form nitrates. Some nitrogen is returned from the soil to the atmosphere by denitrifying bacteria (*see* denitrification).

nitrogen dioxide *See* dinitrogen tetroxide.

nitrogen fixation A chemical process in which atmospheric nitrogen is assimilated into organic compounds in living organisms and hence into the *nitrogen cycle. The ability to fix nitrogen is limited to certain bacteria (e.g. *Azotobacter*) and blue-green algae (e.g. *Anabaena*). *Rhizobium* bacteria are able to fix nitrogen in association with cells in the roots of leguminous plants such as peas and beans, in which they form characteristic root nodules; cultivation of legumes is therefore one way of increasing soil nitrogen. Various chemical processes are used to fix atmospheric nitrogen in the manufacture of fertilizers. These include the *Birkeland–Eyde process, the cyanamide process (*see* calcium dicarbide), and the *Haber process.

nitrogen monoxide (nitric oxide) A colourless gas, NO; m.p. −90.8°C; b.p. −88.5°C. It is soluble in water, ethanol, and ether. In the liquid state nitrogen monoxide is blue in colour (r.d. 1.26). It is formed in many reactions involving the reduction of nitric acid, but more convenient reactions for the preparation of reasonably pure NO are reactions of sodium nitrite, sulphuric acid, and either sodium iodide or iron(II) sulphate. Nitrogen monoxide reacts readily with oxygen to give nitrogen dioxide and with the halogens to give the nitrosyl halides XNO (X = F,Cl,Br). It is oxidized to nitric acid by strong oxidizing agents and reduced to dinitrogen oxide by reducing agents. The molecule has one unpaired electron, which accounts for its paramagnetism

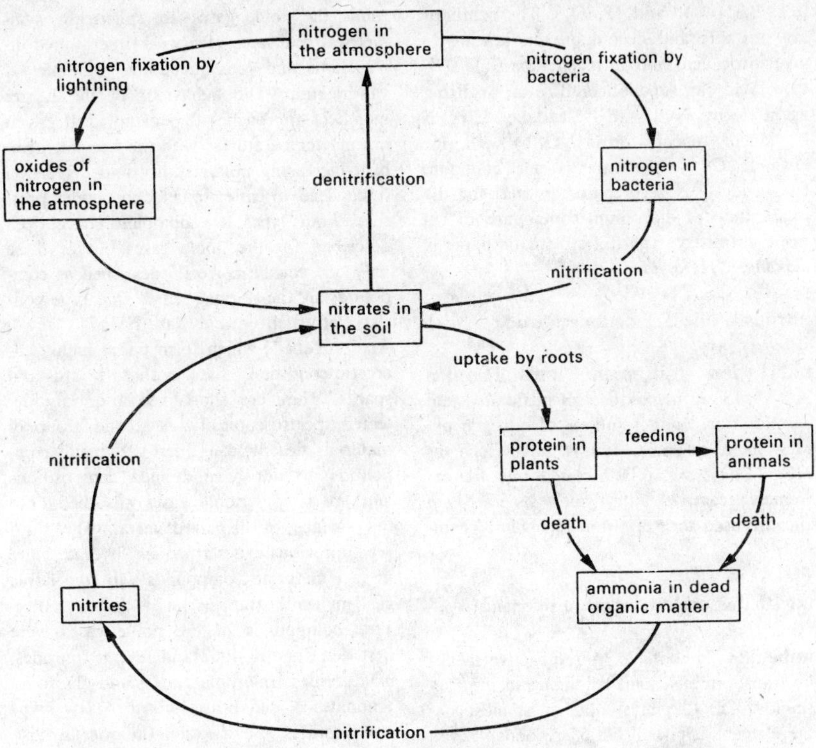

The nitrogen cycle

and for the blue colour in the liquid state. This electron is relatively easily removed to give the *nitrosyl ion* NO^+, which is the ion present in such compounds as $NOClO_4$, $NOBF_4$, $NOFeCl_4$, $(NO)_2PtCl_6$ and a ligand in complexes such as $Co(CO)_3NO$.

nitrogenous base A basic compound containing nitrogen. The term is used especially of organic ring compounds, such as adenine, guanine, cytosine, and thymine, which are constituents of nucleic acids. *See* amine salts.

nitroglycerine An explosive made by reacting 1,2,3-trihydroxypropane (glycerol) with a mixture of concentrated sulphuric and nitric acids. Despite its name and method of preparation, it is not a nitro compound, but an ester of nitric acid, $CH_2(NO_3)CH(NO_3)CH_2(NO_3)$. It is used in dynamites.

nitro group *See* nitro compounds.

nitronium ion *See* nitryl ion.

nitrosyl ion The ion NO^+. *See* nitrogen monoxide.

nitrous acid A weak acid, HNO_2, known only in solution and in the gas phase. It is prepared by the action of acids upon nitrites, preferably using a combination that removes the salt as an insoluble precipitate (e.g. $Ba(NO_2)_2$ and H_2SO_4). The solutions are unstable and decompose on heating to give nitric acid and nitrogen monoxide. Nitrous acid can function both as an oxidizing agent (forms NO) with I^- and Fe^{2+}, or as a reducing agent (forms NO_3^-) with, for example, Cu^{2+}; the latter is most common. It is widely used (prepared *in situ*) for the preparation of diazonium compounds in organic chemistry. The full systematic name is *dioxonitric(III) acid.*

nitrous oxide *See* dinitrogen oxide.

nitryl ion (nitronium ion) The ion NO_2^+, found in mixtures of nitric acid and sulphuric acid and solutions of nitrogen oxides in nitric acid. Nitryl salts, such as $NO_2^+ClO_4^-$, can be isolated but are extremely reactive. Nitryl ions generated *in situ* are used for *nitration in organic chemistry.

NMR *See* nuclear magnetic resonance.

nobelium Symbol No. A radioactive metallic transuranic element belonging to the *actinoids; a.n. 102; mass number of most stable element 254 (half-life 55 seconds). Seven isotopes are known. The element was first identified with certainty by A. Ghiorso and G. T. Seaborg in 1966. The alternative name ***unnilbium*** has been proposed.

noble gases (inert gases; rare gases; group 0 elements) A group of monatomic gaseous elements forming group 0 (sometimes called group VIII) of the *periodic table: helium (He), neon (Ne), argon (Ar), krypton (Kr), xenon (Xe), and radon (Rn). The electron configuration of helium is $1s^2$. The configurations of the others terminate in ns^2np^6 and all inner shells are fully occupied. The elements thus represent the termination of a period and have closed-shell configuration and associated high ionization energies (He 2370 to Rn 1040 kJ mol^{-1}) and lack of chemical reactivity. Being monatomic the noble gases are spherically symmetrical and have very weak interatomic interactions and consequent low enthalpies of vaporization. The behaviour of the lighter members approaches that of an ideal gas at normal temperatures; with the heavier members increasing polarizability and dispersion forces lead to easier liquefaction under pressure. Four types of 'compound' have been described for the noble gases but of these only one can be correctly described as compounds in the normal sense. One type consists of such species as HHe^+, He_2^+, Ar_2^+, $HeLi^+$, which form under highly energetic conditions, such as those in arcs and sparks. They are short-lived and only detected spectroscopically. A second group of materials described as inert-gas–metal compounds do not have defined compositions and are simply noble gases adsorbed onto the surface of dispersed metal. The third type, previously described as 'hydrates' are in fact clathrate compounds with the noble gas molecule trapped in a water lattice. True compounds of the noble gases were first described in 1962 and several fluorides, oxyfluorides, fluoroplatinates, and fluoroantimonates of xenon are known. A few krypton fluorides and a radon fluoride are also known although the short half-life of radon and its intense alpha activity restrict the availability of information. Apart from argon, the noble gases are present in the atmosphere at only trace levels. Helium may be found along with natural gas (up to 7%), arising from the radioactive decay of heavier elements (via alpha particles).

nonbenzenoid aromatics Aromatic compounds that have rings other than benzene rings. Examples are the cyclopentadienyl anion, $C_5H_5^-$, and the tropyllium cation, $C_7H_7^+$.

nonmetal Any of a class of chemical elements that are typically poor conductors of heat and electricity and that do not form positive ions. Nonmetals are electronegative elements, such as carbon, nitrogen, oxygen, phosphorus, sulphur, and the halogens. They form compounds that contain negative ions or covalent bonds. Their oxides are either neutral or acidic.

nonpolar compound A compound that has covalent molecules with no permanent dipole moment. Examples of nonpolar compounds are methane and benzene.

nonpolar solvent *See* solvent.

nonrelativistic quantum theory *See* quantum theory.

nonstoichiometric compound (Berthollide compound) A chemical compound in which the elements do not combine in simple ratios. For example, rutile (titanium(IV) oxide) is often deficient in oxygen, having such a formula as $TiO_{1.8}$.

noradrenaline (norepinephrine) A hormone produced by the adrenal glands and also secreted from nerve endings in the sympathetic nervous system as a chemical transmitter of nerve impulses. Many of its general actions are similar to those of *adrenaline, but it is more concerned with maintaining normal body activity than with preparing the body for emergencies.

Nordhausen sulphuric acid *See* disulphuric(VI) acid.

norepinephrine *See* noradrenaline.

normal Having a concentration of one gram equivalent per dm^3.

N.T.P. *See* s.t.p.

nuclear magnetic resonance (NMR) The absorption of electromagnetic radiation at a suitable precise frequency by a nucleus with a nonzero magnetic moment in an external magnetic field. The phenomenon occurs if the nucleus has nonzero *spin, in which case it behaves as a small magnet. In an external magnetic field, the nucleus's magnetic moment vector precesses about the field direction but only certain orientations are allowed by quantum rules. Thus, for hydrogen (spin of ½) there are two possible states in the presence of a field, each with a slightly different energy. Nuclear magnetic resonance is the absorption of radiation at a photon energy equal to the difference between these levels, causing a transition from a lower to a higher energy state. For practical purposes, the difference in energy levels is small and the radiation is in the radiofrequency region of the electromagnetic spectrum. It depends on the field strength.

NMR can be used for the accurate determination of nuclear moments. It can also be used in a sensitive form of magnetometer to measure magnetic fields. In medicine, NMR tomography is being developed, in which images of tissue are produced by magnetic-resonance techniques.

The main application of NMR is as a technique for chemical analysis and structure determination, known as *NMR spectroscopy*. It depends on the fact that the electrons in a molecule shield the nucleus to some extent from the field, causing different atoms to absorb at slightly different frequencies (or at slightly different fields for a fixed frequency). Such effects are known as *chemical shifts*. In an NMR spectrometer, the sample is subjected to a strong field, which can be varied in a controlled way over a small region. It is irradiated with radiation at a fixed frequency, and a detector monitors the field at the sample. As the field changes, absorption corresponding to transitions occurs at certain values, and this causes oscillations in the field, which induce a signal in the detector. The most common nucleus studied is ^1H. For instance, an NMR spectrum of ethanol (CH_3CH_2OH) has three peaks in the ratio 3:2:1, corresponding to the three different hydrogen-atom environments. The peaks also have a fine structure caused by interaction between spins in the molecule. Other nuclei can also be used for NMR spectroscopy (e.g. ^{13}C, ^{14}N, ^{19}F) although these generally have lower magnetic moment and natural abundance than hydrogen. *See also* electron spin resonance.

nucleon A *proton or a *neutron.

nucleon number (mass number) Symbol A. The number of *nucleons in an atomic nucleus of a particular nuclide.

nucleophile An ion or molecule that can donate electrons. Nucleophiles are often oxidizing agents and Lewis bases. They are either negative ions (e.g. Cl^-) or molecules that have electron pairs (e.g. NH_3). In organic reactions they tend to attack positively charged parts of a molecule. *Compare* electrophile.

nucleophilic addition A type of addition reaction in which the first step is attachment of a *nucleophile to a positive (electron-deficient) part of the molecule. *Aldehydes and *ketones undergo reactions of this type because of polarization of the carbonyl group (carbon positive).

nucleophilic substitution A type of substitution reaction in which a *nucleophile displaces another group or atom from a compound. For example, in

$$CR_3Cl + OH^- \rightarrow CR_3OH + Cl^-$$

the nucleophile is the OH^- ion. There are two possible mechanisms of nucleophilic substitution. In *S_N1 reactions,* a positive carbonium ion is first formed:

$$CR_3Cl \rightarrow CR_3^+ + Cl^-$$

This then reacts with the nucleophile

$$CR_3^+ + OH^- \rightarrow CR_3OH$$

The CR_3^+ ion is planar and the OH^- ion can attack from either side. Consequently, if the original molecule is optically active (the three R groups are different) then a racemic mixture of products results.

The alternative mechanism, the *S_N2 reaction,* is a concerted reaction in which the nucleophile approaches from the side of the R groups as the other group (Cl in the example) leaves. In this case the configuration of the molecule is inverted. If the original molecule is optically active, the product has the opposite activity, an effect known as *Walden inversion.*

nucleoside An organic compound consisting of a nitrogen-containing *purine or *pyrimidine base linked to a sugar (ribose or deoxyribose). An example is *adenosine. *Compare* nucleotide.

nucleotide An organic compound consisting of a nitrogen-containing *purine or *pyrimidine base linked to a sugar (ribose or deoxyribose) and a phosphate group. *DNA and *RNA are made up of long chains of nucleotides (i.e. *polynucleotides*). *Compare* nucleoside.

nucleus The central core of an atom that contains most of its mass. It is positively charged and consists of one or more nucleons (protons or neutrons). The positive charge of the nucleus is determined by the number of protons it contains (*see* atomic number) and in the neutral atom this is balanced by an equal number of electrons, which move around the nucleus. The simplest nucleus is the hydrogen nucleus, consisting of one proton only. All other nuclei also contain one or more neutrons. The neutrons contribute to the atomic mass (*see* nucleon number) but not to the nuclear charge. The most massive nucleus that occurs in nature is uranium–238, containing 92 protons and 146 neutrons. The symbol used for this *nuclide is $^{238}_{92}U$, the upper figure being the nucleon number and the lower figure the atomic number. In all nuclei the nucleon number (A) is equal to the sum of the atomic number (Z) and the neutron number (N), i.e. $A = Z + N$.

nuclide **1.** An atomic nucleus as characterized by its *atomic number and its *neutron number. An *isotope refers to a series of different atoms that have the same atomic number but different neutron numbers (e.g. uranium–238 and uranium–235 are isotopes of uranium), whereas a nuclide refers only to a particular nuclear species (e.g. the nuclides uranium–235 and plutonium–239 are fissile). **2.** The atom to which a specified nucleus belongs.

nylon Any of various synthetic polyamide fibres having a protein-like structure formed by the condensation between an amino group of one molecule and a carboxylic acid group of another. There are three main nylon fibres, nylon 6, nylon 6,6, and nylon 6,10. Nylon 6, for example Enkalon and Celon, is formed by the self-condensation of 6-aminohexanoic acid. Nylon 6,6, for example Bri nylon, is made by polycondensation of hexanedioic acid (adipic acid) and 1,6-diaminohexane (hexamethylenediamine) having an average formula weight between 12 000 and 15 000. Nylon 6,10 is prepared by polymerizing decanedioic acid and 1,6-diaminohexane.

O

occlusion **1.** The trapping of small pockets of liquid in a crystal during crystallization. **2.** The absorption of a gas by a solid such that atoms or molecules of the gas occupy interstitial positions in the solid lattice. Palladium, for example, can occlude hydrogen.

ochre A yellow or red mineral form of iron (III) oxide, Fe_2O_3, used as a pigment.

octadecanoate *See* stearate.

octadecanoic acid *See* stearic acid.

octadecenoic acid A straight-chain unsaturated fatty acid with the formula $C_{17}H_{33}COOH$. *Cis-octadec-9-enoic acid* (*see* oleic acid) has the formula $CH_3(CH_2)_7CH{:}CH(CH_2)_7COOH$. The glycerides of this acid are found in many natural fats and oils.

octahydrate A crystalline hydrate having eight molecules of water per molecule of compound.

octane A straight-chain liquid *alkane, C_8H_{18}; r.d. 0.7; m.p. 216°C; b.p. 399°C. It is present in petroleum. The compound is isomeric with 2,2,4-trimethylpentane, $(CH_3)_3CCH_2CH(CH_3)_2$, *iso-octane*). *See* octane number.

octane number A number that provides a measure of the ability of a fuel to resist knocking when it is burnt in a spark-ignition engine. It is the percentage by volume of iso-octane (C_8H_{18}; 2,2,4-trimethylpentane) in a blend with normal heptane (C_7H_{16}) that matches the knocking behaviour of the fuel being tested in a single cylinder four-stroke engine of standard design. *Compare* cetane number.

octanoic acid (caprylic acid) A colourless liquid straight-chain saturated *carboxylic acid, $CH_3(CH_2)_6COOH$; b.p. 237°C.

octavalent Having a valency of eight.

octave *See* law of octaves.

octet A stable group of eight electrons in the outer shell of an atom (as in an atom of an inert gas).

ohm Symbol Ω. The derived *SI unit of electrical resistance, being the resistance between two points on a conductor when a constant potential difference of one volt, applied between these points, produces a current of one ampere in the conductor. The former *international ohm* (sometimes called the 'mercury ohm') was defined in terms of the resistance of a column of mercury. The unit is named after Georg Ohm (1787–1854).

oil Any of various viscous liquids that are generally immiscible with water. Natural plant and animal oils are either volatile mixtures of terpenes and simple esters (e.g. *essential oils) or are *glycerides of fatty acids. Mineral oils are mixtures of hydrocarbons (e.g. *petroleum).

oil of vitriol *See* sulphuric acid.

oil sand (tar sand; bituminous sand) A sandstone or porous carbonate rock that is impregnated with hydrocarbons. The largest deposit of oil sand occurs in Alberta, Canada (the Athabasca tar sands); there are also deposits in the Orinoco Basin of Venezuela, the USSR, USA, Madagascar, Albania, Trinidad, and Romania.

oil shale A fine-grained carbonaceous sedimentary rock from which oil can be extracted. The rock contains organic matter – *kerogen* – which decomposes to yield oil when heated. Deposits of oil shale occur on every continent, the largest known reserves occurring in Colorado, Utah, and Wyoming in the USA. Commercial production of oil from oil shale is generally considered to be uneconomic unless the price of petroleum rises above the recovery costs for oil from oil shale. However, threats of declining conventional oil resources have resulted in considerable interest and developments in recovery techniques.

oleate A salt or ester of *oleic acid.

olefines *See* alkenes.

oleic acid An unsaturated *fatty acid with one double bond, $CH_3(CH_2)_7CH{:}CH(CH_2)_7COOH$; r.d. 0.9; m.p. 13°C. Oleic acid is one of the most abundant constituent fatty acids of animal and plant fats, occurring in butterfat, lard, tallow, groundnut oil, soyabean oil, etc. Its systematic chemical name is *cis-octadec-9-enoic acid.*

oleum *See* disulphuric(VI) acid.

oligopeptide *See* peptide.

olivine An important group of rock-forming silicate minerals crystallizing in the orthorhombic system. Olivine conforms to the general formula $(Mg,Fe)_2SiO_4$ and comprises a complete series from pure magnesium silicate (forsterite, Mg_2SiO_4) to pure iron silicate (fayalite, Fe_2SiO_4). It is green, brown-green, or yellow-green in colour.

onium ion An ion formed by adding a proton to a neutral molecule, e.g. the hydroxonium ion (H_3O^+) or the ammonium ion (NH_4^+).

opal A hydrous amorphous form of silica. Many varieties of opal occur, some being prized as gemstones. Common opal is usually milk white but the presence of impurities may colour it yellow, green, or red. Precious opals, which are used as gemstones, display the property of *opalescence* – a characteristic internal play of colours resulting from the interference of light rays within the stone. Black opal has a black background against which the colours are displayed. The chief sources of precious opals are Australia and Mexico. Geyserite is a variety deposited by geysers or hot springs. Another variety, diatomite, is made up of the skeletons of diatoms.

open chain *See* chain.

open-hearth process A traditional method for manufacturing steel by heating together scrap, pig iron, hot metal, etc., in a refractory-lined shallow open furnace heated by burning producer gas in air.

optical activity The ability of certain substances to rotate the plane of plane-polarized light as it passes through a crystal, liquid, or solution. It occurs when the molecules of the substance are asymmetric, so that they can exist in two different structural forms each being a mirror image of the other. The two forms are *optical isomers* or *enantiomers*. The existence of such forms is also known as *enantiomorphism* (the mirror images being *enantiomorphs*). One form will rotate the light in one direction and the other will rotate it by an equal amount in the other. The two possible forms are described as *dextrorotatory or *laevorotatory according to the direction of rotation, and prefixes are used to designate the isomer, as in *d*-tartaric and *l*-tartaric acids. An equimolar mixture of the two forms is not optically active. It is called a *racemic mixture* (or *racemate*) and designated by *dl*-. In addition, certain molecules can have a *meso form* in which one part of the molecule is a mirror image of the other. Such molecules are not optically active.

Molecules that show optical activity have no plane of symmetry. The commonest case of this is in organic compounds in which a carbon atom is linked to four different groups. An atom of this type is said to be a *chiral centre*. Asymmetric molecules showing optical activity can also occur in inorganic compounds. For example, an octahedral complex in which the central ion coordinates to eight different ligands would be optically active. Many naturally occurring compounds show optical isomerism and usually only one isomer occurs naturally. For instance, glucose is found in the dextrorotatory form. The other isomer, *l*-glucose, can be synthesized in the laboratory, but cannot be synthesized by living organisms. *See also* absolute configuration.

optical glass Glass used in the manufacture of lenses, prisms, and other optical parts. It must be homogeneous and free from bubbles and strain. Optical *crown glass* may contain potassium or barium in place of the sodium of ordinary crown glass and has a refractive index in the range 1.51 to 1.54. *Flint glass* contains lead oxide and has a refractive index between 1.58 and 1.72. Higher refractive indexes are obtained by adding lanthanoid oxides to glasses; these are now known as lanthanum crowns and flints.

optical isomers *See* optical activity.

optical rotary dispersion (ORD) The effect in which the amount of rotation of plane-polarized light by an optically active compound depends on the wavelength. A graph of rotation against wavelength has a characteristic shape showing peaks or troughs.

optical rotation Rotation of plane-polarized light. *See* optical activity.

orbit The path of an electron as it travels round the nucleus of an atom. *See* orbital.

orbital A region in which an electron may be found in an atom or molecule. In the original *Bohr theory of the atom the electrons were assumed to move around the nucleus in circular orbits, but further advances in quantum mechanics led to the view that it is not possible to give a definite path for an electron. According to *wave mechanics, the electron has a certain probability of being in a given element of space. Thus for a hydrogen atom the electron can be anywhere from close to the nucleus to out in space but the maximum probability occurs in a spherical shell around the nucleus with a radius equal to the Bohr radius of the atom. The probabilities of finding an electron in different regions can be obtained by solving the Schrödinger wave equation to give the wave function ψ, and the probability is then proportional to $|\psi|^2$. Thus the idea of electrons in fixed orbits has been replaced by that of a probability distribution around

ORBITAL

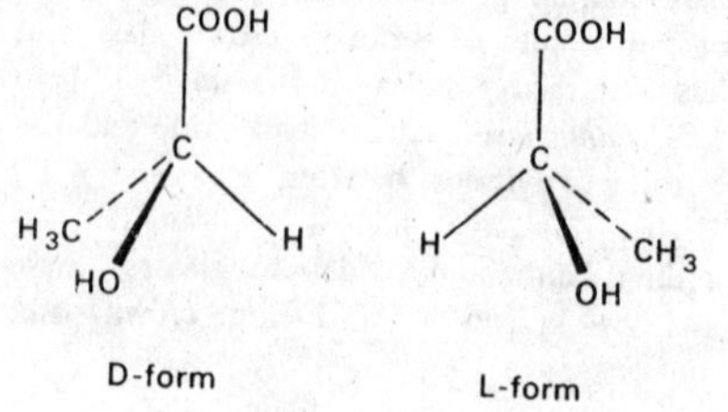

Isomers of lactic acid

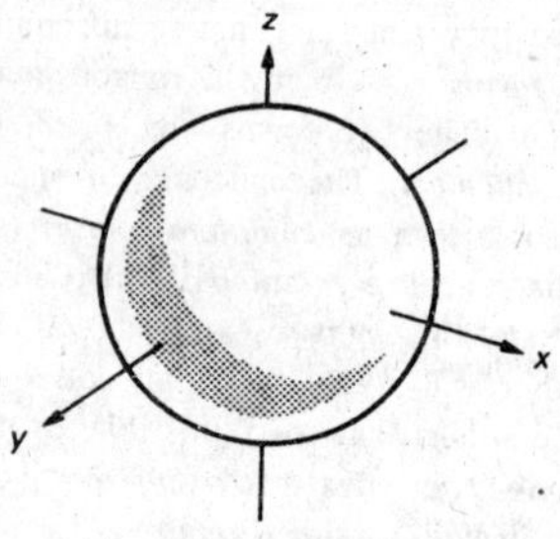

symmetrical
s–orbital

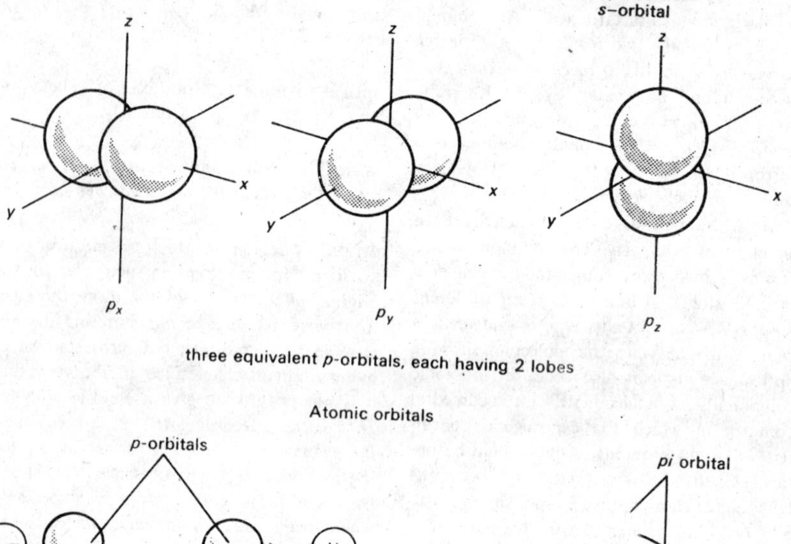

three equivalent *p*-orbitals, each having 2 lobes

Atomic orbitals

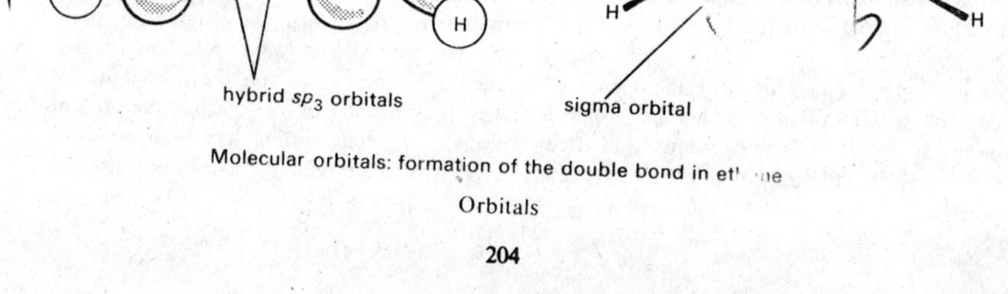

Molecular orbitals: formation of the double bond in et' ıne

Orbitals

the nucleus – an *atomic orbital*. Alternatively, the orbital can be thought of as an electric charge distribution (averaged over time). In representing orbitals it is convenient to take a surface enclosing the space in which the electron is likely to be found with a high probability.

The possible atomic orbitals correspond to subshells of the atom. Thus there is one *s*-orbital for each shell (orbital quantum number $l = 0$). This is spherical. There are three *p*-orbitals (corresponding to the three values of l) and five *d*-orbitals. The shapes of orbitals depend on the value of l. For instance, *p*-orbitals each have two lobes; most *d*-orbitals have four lobes.

In molecules, the valence electrons move under the influence of two nuclei (in a bond involving two atoms) and there are corresponding *molecular orbitals* for electrons. It is convenient in considering these to regard them as formed by overlap of atomic orbitals. In a hydrogen molecule the *s*-orbitals on the two atoms overlap and form a molecular orbital between the two nuclei. This is an example of a *sigma orbital*. In a double bond, as in ethene, one bond is produced by overlap along the line of axes to form a sigma orbital. The other is produced by sideways overlap of the lobes of the *p*-orbitals (see illustration). The resulting molecular orbital has two parts, one on each side of the sigma orbital – this is a *pi orbital*. In fact, the combination of two atomic orbitals produces two molecular orbitals with different energies. The one of lower energy is the *bonding orbital*, holding the atoms together; the other is the *antibonding orbital*, which would tend to push the atoms apart. In the case of valence electrons, only the lower (bonding) orbital is filled.

In considering the formation of molecular orbitals it is often useful to think in terms of *hybrid* atomic orbitals. For instance, carbon has in its outer shell one *s*-orbital and three *p*-orbitals. In forming methane (or other tetrahedral molecules) these can be regarded as combining to give four equivalent sp^3 hybrid orbitals, each with a lobe directed to a corner of a tetrahedron. It is these that overlap with the *s*-orbitals on the hydrogen atoms. In ethene, two *p*-orbitals combine with the *s*-orbital to give three sp^2 hybrids with lobes in a plane pointing to the corners of an equilateral triangle. These form the sigma orbitals in the C–H and C–C bonds. The remaining *p*-orbitals (one on each carbon) form the pi orbital. In ethyne, sp^2 hybridization occurs to give two hybrid orbitals on each atom with lobes pointing along the axis. The two remaining *p*-orbitals on each carbon form two pi orbitals. Hybrid atomic orbitals can also involve *d*-orbitals. For instance, square-planar complexes use sp^2d hybrids; octahedral complexes use sp^3d^2.

orbital quantum number *See* atom.

order In the expression for the rate of a chemical reaction, the sum of the powers of the concentrations is the overall order of the reaction. For instance, in a reaction

$$A + B \rightarrow C$$

the rate equation may have the form

$$R = k[A][B]^2$$

This reaction would be described as *first order* in A and *second order* in B. The overall order is three. The order of a reaction depends on the mechanism and it is possible for the rate to be independent of concentration (*zero order*) or for the order to be a fraction. *See also* molecularity; pseudo order.

ore A naturally occurring mineral from which a metal can be extracted, usually on a commercial basis. The metal may be present in the ore as the native metal, but more commonly it occurs in a combined form as an oxide, sulphide, sulphate, silicate, etc.

ore dressing *See* beneficiation.

organic chemistry The branch of chemistry concerned with compounds of carbon.

organo- Prefix used before the name of an element to indicate compounds of the elements containing organic groups (with the element bound to carbon atoms). For example, lead(IV) tetraethyl is an organolead compound.

organometallic compound A compound in which a metal atom or ion is bound to an organic group. Organometallic compounds may have single metal–carbon bonds, as in the aluminium alkyls (e.g. $Al(CH_3)_3$). In some cases, the bonding is to the pi electrons of a double bond, as in complexes formed between platinum and ethene, or to the pi electrons of a ring, as in ferrocene.

ornithine (orn) An *amino acid, $H_2N(CH_2)_3CH(NH_2)COOH$, that is not a constituent of proteins but is important in living organisms as an intermediate in the reactions of the *urea cycle and in arginine synthesis.

ornithine cycle *See* urea cycle.

orpiment A natural yellow mineral form of arsenic(III) sulphide, As_2S_3. The name is also used for the synthetic compound, which is used as a pigment.

ortho- 1. Prefix indicating that a benzene compound has two substituted groups in the 1,2 positions (i.e. on adjacent carbon atoms). For instance, orthodichlorobenzene is 1,2-dichlorobenzene. **2.** Prefix formerly used to indicate the most hydrated form of an acid. For example, phosphoric(V) acid, H_3PO_4, was called orthophosphoric acid to distinguish it from the lower metaphosphoric acid, HPO_3 (which is actually $(HPO_3)_n$).

orthoboric acid *See* boric acid.

orthoclase *See* feldspars.

orthohydrogen *See* hydrogen.

orthophosphoric acid *See* phosphoric(V) acid. .

orthoplumbate *See* plumbate.

orthorhombic *See* crystal system.

orthosilicate *See* silicate.

orthostannate *See* stannate.

osmiridium A hard white naturally occurring alloy consisting principally of osmium (17–48%) and iridium (49%). It also contains small quantities of platinum, rhodium, and ruthenium. It is used for making small items subject to wear, e.g. electrical contacts or the tips of pen nibs.

osmium Symbol Os. A hard blue-white metallic *transition element; a.n. 76; r.a.m. 190.2; r.d. 22.57; m.p. 3045°C; b.p. 5027°C. It is found associated with platinum and is used in certain alloys with platinum and iridium (*see* osmiridium). Osmium forms a number of complexes in a range of oxidation states.

osmium(IV) oxide (osmium tetroxide) A yellow solid, OsO_4, made by heating osmium in air. It is used as an oxidizing agent in organic chemistry, as a catalyst, and as a fixative in electron microscopy.

osmometer *See* osmosis.

osmosis The passage of a solvent through a *semipermeable membrane* separating two solutions of different concentrations. A semipermeable membrane is one through which the molecules of a solvent can pass but the molecules of most solutes cannot. There is a thermodynamic tendency for solutions separated by such a membrane to become equal in concentration, the water (or other solvent) flowing from the weaker to the stronger solution. Osmosis will stop when the two solutions reach equal concentration, and can also be stopped by applying a pressure to the liquid on the stronger-solution side of the membrane. The pressure required to stop the flow from a pure solvent into a solution is a characteristic of the solution, and is called the *osmotic pressure* (symbol Π). Osmotic pressure depends only on the concentration of particles in the solution, not on their nature (i.e. it is a *colligative property). For a solution of n moles in volume V at thermodynamic temperature T, the osmotic pressure is given by $\Pi V = RT$, where R is the gas constant. Osmotic-pressure measurements are used in finding the relative molecular masses of compounds, particularly macromolecules. A device used to measure osmotic pressure is called an *osmometer*.

The distribution of water in living organisms is dependent to a large extent on osmosis, water entering the cells through their membranes. A cell membrane is not truly semipermeable as it allows the passage of certain solute molecules; it is described as *differentially permeable*.

osmotic pressure *See* osmosis.

Ostwald's dilution law An expression for the degree of dissociation of a weak electrolyte. For example, if a weak acid dissociates in water

$$HA \rightleftharpoons H^+ + A^-$$

the dissociation constant K_a is given by

$$K_a = \alpha^2 n/(1 - \alpha)V$$

where α is the degree of dissociation, n the initial amount of substance (before dissociation), and V the volume. If α is small compared with 1, then $\alpha^2 = KV/n$; i.e. the degree of dissociation is proportional to the square root of the dilution. The law was first put forward by W. Ostwald (1853–1932) to account for electrical conductivities of electrolyte solutions.

overpotential A potential that must be applied in an electrolytic cell in addition to the theoretical potential required to liberate a given substance at an electrode. The value depends on the electrode material and on the current density. It is a kinetic effect occurring because of the significant activation energy for electron transfer at the electrodes, and is particularly important for the liberation of such gases as hydrogen and oxygen. For example, in the electrolysis of a solution of zinc ions, hydrogen (E = 0.00 V) would be expected to be liberated at the cathode in preference to zinc (E = −0.76 V). In fact, the high overpotential of hydrogen on zinc (about 1 V under suitable conditions) means that zinc can be deposited instead.

oxalate A salt or ester of *oxalic acid.

oxalic acid (ethanedioic acid) A crystalline solid, $(COOH)_2$, that is slightly soluble in water. Oxalic acid is strongly acidic and very poisonous. It occurs in certain plants, e.g. sorrel and the leaf blades of rhubarb.

oxidant *See* oxidizing agent.

oxidation *See* oxidation–reduction.

oxidation number (oxidation state) *See* oxidation–reduction.

oxidation–reduction (redox) Originally, *oxidation* was simply regarded as a chemical reaction with oxygen. The reverse process – loss of oxygen – was called *reduction*. Reaction with hydrogen also came to be regarded as reduction. Later, a more general idea of oxidation and reduction was developed in which oxidation was loss of electrons and reduction was gain of electrons. This wider definition covered the original one. For example, in the reaction

$$4Na(s) + O_2(g) \rightarrow 2Na_2O(s)$$

the sodium atoms lose electrons to give Na^+ ions and are oxidized. At the same time, the oxygen atoms gain electrons and are reduced. These definitions of oxidation and reduction also apply to reactions that do not involve oxygen. For instance in

$$2Na(s) + Cl_2(g) \rightarrow 2NaCl(s)$$

the sodium is oxidized and the chlorine reduced. Oxidation and reduction also occurs at the electrodes in *cells.

This definition of oxidation and reduction applies only to reactions in which electron transfer occurs – i.e. to reactions involving ions. It can be extended to reactions between covalent compounds by using the concept of *oxidation number* (or *state*). This is a measure of the electron control that an atom has in a compound compared to the atom in the pure element. An oxidation number consists of two parts:

(1) Its sign, which indicates whether the control has increased (negative) or decreased (positive).

(2) Its value, which gives the number of electrons over which control has changed.

The change of electron control may be complete (in ionic compounds) or partial (in covalent compounds). For example, in SO_2 the sulphur has an oxidation number +4, having gained partial control over 4 electrons compared to sulphur atoms in pure sulphur. The oxygen has an oxidation number –2, each oxygen having lost partial control over 2 electrons compared to oxygen atoms in gaseous oxygen. Oxidation is a reaction involving an increase in oxidation number and reduction involves a decrease. Thus in

$$2H_2 + O_2 \rightarrow 2H_2O$$

the hydrogen in water is +1 and the oxygen –2. The hydrogen is oxidized and the oxygen is reduced.

The oxidation number is used in naming inorganic compounds. Thus in H_2SO_4, sulphuric(VI) acid, the sulphur has an oxidation number of +6. Compounds that tend to undergo reduction readily are *oxidizing agents; those that undergo oxidation are *reducing agents.

oxides Binary compounds formed between elements and oxygen. Oxides of nonmetals are covalent compounds having simple molecules (e.g. CO, CO_2, SO_2) or giant molecular lattices (e.g. SiO_2). They are typically acidic or neutral. Oxides of metals are ionic, containing the O^{2-} ion. They are generally basic or *amphoteric. Various other types of ionic oxide exist (*see* ozonides; peroxides; superoxides).

oxidizing acid An acid that can act as a strong oxidizing agent as well as an acid. Nitric acid is a common example. It is able to attack metals, such as copper, that are below hydrogen in the electromotive series, by oxidizing the metal:

$$2HNO_3 + Cu \rightarrow CuO + H_2O + 2NO_2$$

This is followed by reaction between the acid and the oxide:

$$2HNO_3 + CuO \rightarrow Cu(NO_3)_2 + H_2O$$

oxidizing agent (oxidant) A substance that brings about oxidation in other substances. It achieves this by being itself reduced. Oxidizing agents contain atoms with high oxidation numbers; that is the atoms have suffered electron loss. In oxidizing other substances these atoms gain electrons.

oximes Compounds containing the group C:NOH, formed by reaction of an aldehyde or ketone with hydroxylamine (H_2NOH). Ethanal (CH_3CHO), for example, forms the oxime CH_3CH:NOH.

oxo- Prefix indicating the presence of oxygen in a chemical compound.

oxo acid An *acid in which the acidic hydrogen atom(s) are bound to oxygen atoms. Sulphuric acid is an example: the two acidic hydrogens are on the –OH groups bound to the sulphur. *Compare* binary acid.

oxonium ion An ion of the type R_3O^+, in which R indicates hydrogen or an organic

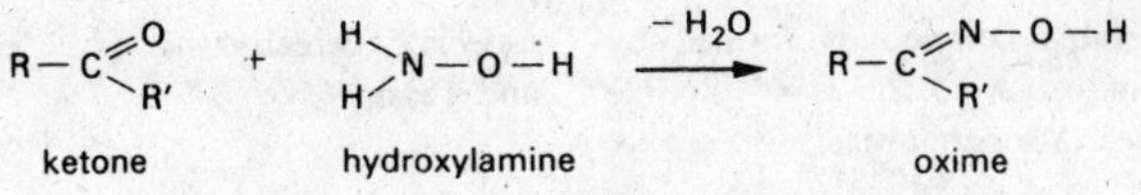

Formation of an oxime from a ketone
The same reaction occurs with an aldehyde ($R' = H$)

group. The hydroxonium ion, H_3O^+, is formed when *acids dissociate in water.

oxo process An industrial process for making aldehydes by reaction between alkanes, carbon monoxide, and hydrogen (cobalt catalyst using high pressure and temperature).

oxyacetylene burner A welding or cutting torch that burns a mixture of oxygen and acetylene (ethyne) in a specially designed jet. The flame temperature of about 3300°C enables all ferrous metals to be welded. For cutting, the point at which the steel is to be cut is preheated with the oxyacetylene flame and a powerful jet of oxygen is then directed onto the steel. The oxygen reacts with the hot steel to form iron oxide and the heat of this reaction melts more iron, which is blown away by the force of the jet.

oxygen Symbol O. A colourless odourless gaseous element belonging to *group VI of the periodic table; a.n. 8; r.a.m. 15.9994; d. 1.429 g dm^{-3}; m.p. −214.4°C; b.p. −183°C. It is the most abundant element in the earth's crust (49.2% by weight) and is present in the atmosphere (28% by volume). Atmospheric oxygen is of vital importance for all organisms that carry out aerobic respiration. For industrial purposes it is obtained by fractional distillation of liquid air. It is used in metallurgical processes, in high-temperature flames (e.g. for welding), and in breathing apparatus. The common form is diatomic (*dioxygen*, O_2); there is also a reactive allotrope *ozone (O_3). Chemically, oxygen reacts with most other elements forming *oxides. The element was discovered by Priestley in 1774.

oxyhaemoglobin *See* haemoglobin.

ozone (trioxygen) A colourless gas, O_3, soluble in cold water and in alkalis; m.p. −192.7°C; b.p. −111.9°C. Liquid ozone is dark blue in colour and is diamagnetic (dioxygen, O_2, is paramagnetic). The gas is made by passing oxygen through a silent electric discharge and is usually used in mixtures with oxygen. It is produced in the stratosphere by the action of high-energy ultraviolet radiation on oxygen and its presence there acts as a screen for ultraviolet radiation (*see* ozone layer). It is a powerful oxidizing agent and is used to form ozonides by reaction with alkenes and subsequently by hydrolysis to carbonyl compounds.

ozone layer (ozonosphere) A layer of the *earth's atmosphere in which most of the atmosphere's ozone is concentrated. It occurs 15–50 km above the earth's surface and is virtually synonymous with the stratosphere. In this layer most of the sun's ultraviolet radiation is absorbed by the ozone molecules, causing a rise in the temperature of the stratosphere and preventing vertical mixing so that the stratosphere forms a stable layer. By absorbing most of the solar ultraviolet radiation the ozone layer protects living organisms on earth. The fact that the ozone layer is thinnest at the equator is believed to account for the high equatorial incidence of skin cancer as a result of exposure to unabsorbed solar ultraviolet radiation.

ozonides **1.** A group of compounds formed by reaction of ozone with alkali metal hydroxides and formally containing the ion

O_3^-. **2.** Unstable compounds formed by the addition of ozone to the C=C double bond in alkenes. *See* ozonolysis.

ozonolysis A reaction of alkenes with ozone to form an ozonide. It was once used to investigate the structure of alkenes by hydrolysing the ozonide to give aldehydes or ketones. For instance

$$R_2C{:}CHR' \rightarrow R_2CO + R'CHO$$

These could be identified, and the structure of the original alkene determined.

P

palladium Symbol Pd. A soft white ductile *transition element (*see also* platinum metals); a.n. 46; r.a.m. 106.4; r.d. 12.26; m.p. 1551±1°C; b.p. 3140±1°C. It occurs in some copper and nickel ores and is used in jewellery and as a catalyst for hydrogenation reactions. Chemically, it does not react with oxygen at normal temperatures. It dissolves slowly in hydrochloric acid. Palladium is capable of occluding 900 times its own volume of hydrogen. It forms few simple salts, most compounds being complexes of palladium(II) with some palladium(IV). It was discovered by Woolaston in 1803.

palmitate (hexadecanoate) A salt or ester of palmitic acid.

palmitic acid (hexadecanoic acid) A saturated fatty acid, $CH_3(CH_2)_{14}COOH$; r.d. 0.85; m.p. 63°C; b.p. 351°C. Glycerides of palmitic acid occur widely in plant and animal oils and fats.

pantothenic acid A vitamin of the *vitamin B complex. It is a constituent of coenzyme A, which performs a crucial role in the oxidation of fats, carbohydrates, and certain amino acids. Deficiency rarely occurs because the vitamin occurs in many foods, especially cereal grains, peas, egg yolk, liver, and yeast.

papain A protein-digesting enzyme occurring in the fruit of the West Indian papaya tree (*Carica papaya*). It is used as a digestant and in the manufacture of meat tenderizers.

paper chromatography A technique for analysing mixtures by *chromatography, in which the stationary phase is absorbent paper. A spot of the mixture to be investigated is placed near one edge of the paper and the sheet is suspended vertically in a solvent, which rises through the paper by capillary action carrying the components with it. The components move at different rates, partly because they absorb to different extents on the cellulose and partly because of partition between the solvent and the moisture in the paper. The paper is removed and dried, and the different components form a line of spots along the paper. Colourless substances are detected by using ultraviolet radiation or by spraying with a substance that reacts to give a coloured spot (e.g. ninhydrin gives a blue coloration with amino acids). The components can be identified by the distance they move in a given time.

para- 1. Prefix designating a benzene compound in which two substituents are in the 1,4 positions, i.e. directly opposite each other, on the benzene ring. The abbreviation *p-* is used; for example, *p*-xylene is 1,4-dimethylbenzene. *Compare* ortho-; meta-. **2.** Prefix denoting the form of diatomic molecules in which the nuclei have opposite spins, e.g. parahydrogen. *Compare* ortho-.

paraffin *See* petroleum.

paraffins *See* alkanes.

paraffin wax *See* petroleum.

paraformaldehyde *See* methanal.

parahydrogen *See* hydrogen.

paraldehyde *See* ethanal.

partial pressure *See* Dalton's law.

partition If a substance is in contact with two different phases then, in general, it will have a different affinity for each phase. Part of the substance will be absorbed or dissolved by one and part by the other, the relative amounts depending on the relative affinities. The substance is said to be *partitioned* between the two phases. For example, if two immiscible liquids are taken and a third compound is shaken up with them, then an equilibrium is reached in which the concentration in one solvent differs from that in the other. The ratio of the concentrations is the *partition coefficient* of the system. The *partition law* states that this ratio is a constant for given liquids.

partition coefficient *See* partition.

pascal The *SI unit of pressure equal to one newton per square metre.

Paschen series *See* hydrogen spectrum.

passive Describing a solid that has reacted with another substance to form a protective layer, so that further reaction stops. The solid is said to have been 'rendered passive'. For example, aluminium reacts spontaneously with oxygen in air to form a thin layer of *aluminium oxide, which prevents further oxidation. Similarly, pure iron forms a protective oxide layer with concentrated nitric acid and is not dissolved further.

***p*-block elements** The block of elements in the periodic table consisting of the main groups III (B to Tl), IV (C to Pb), V (N to Bi), VI (O to Po), VII (F to At) and 0 (He to Rn). The outer electronic configurations of these elements all have the form ns^2np^x where $x = 1$ to 6. Members at the top and on the right of the *p*-block are nonmetals (C, N, P, O, F, S, Cl, Br, I, At). Those on the left and at the bottom are metals (Al, Ga, In, Tl, Sn, Pb, Sb, Bi, Po). Between the two, from the top left to bottom right, lie an ill-defined group of metalloid elements (B, Si, Ge, As, Te).

peacock ore *See* bornite.

pearl ash *See* potassium carbonate.

pearlite *See* steel.

penicillin An antibiotic derived from the mould *Penicillium notatum*; specifically it is known as *penicillin G* and belongs to a class of similar substances called penicillins. They produce their effects by disrupting synthesis of the bacterial cell wall, and are used to treat a variety of infections caused by bacteria.

pentahydrate A crystalline hydrate containing five molecules of water per molecule of compound.

pentane A straight-chain alkane hydrocarbon, C_5H_{12}; r.d. 0.63; m.p. −129.7°C; b.p. 36.1°C. It is obtained by distillation of petroleum.

pentanoic acid (valeric acid) A colourless liquid *carboxylic acid, $CH_3(CH_2)_3COOH$; r.d. 0.9; m.p. −34°C; b.p. 185°C. It is used in the perfume industry.

pentavalent (quinquevalent) Having a valency of five.

pentlandite A mineral consisting of a mixed iron–nickel sulphide, $(Fe,Ni)_9S_8$, crystallizing in the cubic system; the chief ore of nickel. It is yellowish-bronze in colour with a metallic lustre. The chief occurrence of the mineral is at Sudbury in Ontario, Canada.

pentose A sugar that has five carbon atoms per molecule. *See* monosaccharide.

pentyl group *or* **radical** The organic group $CH_3CH_2CH_2CH_2CH_2^-$, derived from pentane.

pepsin An enzyme, secreted by cells lining the interior of the vertebrate stomach, that catalyses the breakdown of proteins.

peptide Any of a group of organic compounds comprising two or more amino acids linked by *peptide bonds*. These bonds are formed by the reaction between adjacent carboxyl (–COOH) and amino ($-NH_2$) groups with the elimination of water (see illustration). *Dipeptides* contain two amino acids, *tripeptides* three, and so on. *Polypeptides contain more than ten and usually 100–300. Naturally occurring *oligopeptides* (of less than ten amino acids) include the tripeptide glutathione and the pituitary hormones vasopressin and oxytocin, which are octapeptides. Peptides also result from protein breakdown, e.g. during digestion.

per- Prefix indicating that a chemical compound contains an excess of an element, e.g. a peroxide.

perchlorate *See* chlorates.

perchloric acid *See* chloric(VII) acid.

perdisulphuric acid *See* peroxosulphuric (VI) acid.

perfect solution *See* Raoult's law.

period *See* periodic table.

periodic acid *See* iodic(VII) acid.

periodic law The principle that the physical and chemical properties of elements are a periodic function of their proton number. The concept was first proposed in 1869 by the Russian chemist Dimitri Mendeleev (1834–1907), using relative atomic mass rather than proton number, as a culmination of efforts to rationalize chemical properties by J. W. Döbereiner (1817), J. A. R. Newlands (1863), and Lothar Meyer (1864). One of the major successes of the periodic law was its ability to predict chemical and physical properties of undiscovered elements and unknown compounds that were later confirmed experimentally. *See* periodic table.

periodic table A table of elements arranged in order of increasing proton number to show the similarities of chemical elements with related electronic configurations. (The original form was proposed by Dimitri Mendeleev in 1869 using relative atomic masses.) In the modern *short form* (see Appendix) the *lanthanoids and *actinoids are not shown. The elements fall into vertical columns, known as *groups*. Going down a group, the atoms of the elements all have the same outer shell structure, but an increasing number of inner shells. Traditionally, the alkali metals are shown on the left of the table and the groups are numbered IA to VIIA, IB to VIIB, and 0 (for the noble gases). It is now more common to classify all the elements in the middle of the table as *transition elements and to regard the nontransition elements as *main-group* elements, numbered from I to VII, with the noble gases in group 0. Horizontal rows in

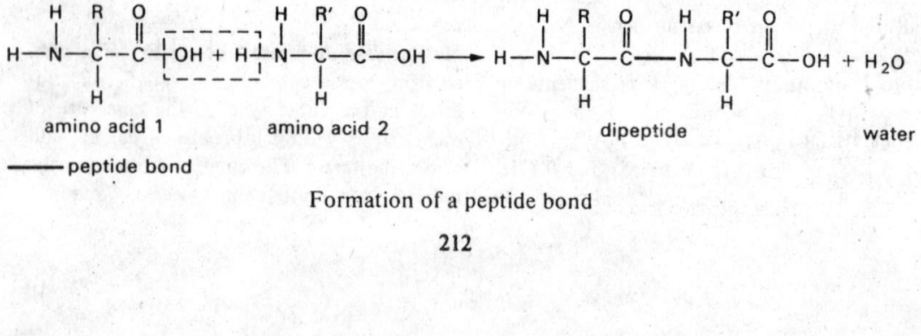

Formation of a peptide bond

the table are *periods*. The first three are called *short periods*; the next four (which include transition elements) are *long periods*. Within a period, the atoms of all the elements have the same number of shells, but with a steadily increasing number of electrons in the outer shell. The periodic table can also be divided into four *blocks* depending on the type of shell being filled: the **s*-block, the **p*-block, the **d*-block, and the **f*-block.

There are certain general features of chemical behaviour shown in the periodic table. In moving down a group, there is an increase in metallic character because of the increased size of the atom. In going across a period, there is a change from metallic (electropositive) behaviour to nonmetallic (electronegative) because of the increasing number of electrons in the outer shell. Consequently, metallic elements tend to be those on the left and towards the bottom of the table; nonmetallic elements are towards the top and the right.

There is also a significant difference between the elements of the second short period (lithium to fluorine) and the other elements in their respective groups. This is because the atoms in the second period are smaller and their valence electrons are shielded by a small $1s^2$ inner shell. Atoms in the other periods have inner *s*- and *p*-electrons shielding the outer electrons from the nucleus. Moreover, those in the second period only have *s*- and *p*-orbitals available for bonding. Heavier atoms can also promote electrons to vacant *d*-orbitals in their outer shell and use these for bonding. *See also* diagonal relationship; inert-pair effect.

Permalloys A group of alloys of high magnetic permeability consisting of iron and nickel (usually 40–80%) often with small amounts of other elements (e.g. 3–5% molybdenum, copper, chromium, or tungsten). They are used in thin foils in electronic transformers, for magnetic shielding, and in computer memories.

permanent gas A gas, such as oxygen or nitrogen, that was formerly thought to be impossible to liquefy. A permanent gas is now regarded as one that cannot be liquefied by pressure alone at normal temperatures (i.e. a gas that has a critical temperature below room temperature).

permanent hardness *See* hardness of water.

permanganate *See* manganate(VII).

permonosulphuric(VI) acid *See* peroxosulphuric(VI) acid.

Permutit Tradename for a *zeolite used for water softening.

peroxides 1. A group of inorganic compounds that contain the $O_2{}^{2-}$ ion. They are notionally derived from hydrogen peroxide, H_2O_2, but these ions do not exist in aqueous solution due to extremely rapid hydrolysis to OH^-

peroxodisulphuric acid *See* peroxosulphuric(VI) acid.

peroxomonosulphuric(VI) acid *See* peroxosulphuric(VI) acid.

peroxosulphuric(VI) acid The term commonly refers to *peroxomonosulphuric(VI) acid*, H_2SO_5, which is also called *permonosulphuric(VI) acid* and *Caro's acid*. It is a crystalline compound made by the action of hydrogen peroxide on concentrated sulphuric acid. It decomposes in water and the crystals decompose, with melting, above 45°C. The compound *peroxodisulphuric acid*, $H_2S_2O_8$, also exists (formerly called *perdisulphuric acid*). It is made by the high-current electrolysis of sulphate solutions. It decomposes at 65°C (with melting) and is hydrolysed in water to give the mono acid and sulphuric acid. Both peroxo acids are very powerful oxidizing agents. *See also* sulphuric acid (for structural formulas).

Perspex Tradename for a form of *polymethylmethacrylate.

peta- Symbol P. A prefix used in the metric system to denote one thousand million million times. For example, 10^{15} metres = 1 petametre (Pm).

petrochemicals Organic chemicals obtained from petroleum or natural gas.

petroleum A naturally occurring oil that consists chiefly of hydrocarbons with some other elements, such as sulphur, oxygen, and nitrogen. In its unrefined form petroleum is known as *crude oil* (sometimes *rock oil*). Petroleum is believed to have been formed from the remains of living organisms that were deposited, together with rock particles and biochemical and chemical precipitates, in shallow depressions, chiefly in marine conditions. Under burial and compaction the organic matter went through a series of processes before being transformed into petroleum, which migrated from the source rock to become trapped in large underground reservoirs beneath a layer of impermeable rock. The petroleum often floats above a layer of water and is held under pressure beneath a layer of *natural gas.

Petroleum reservoirs are discovered through geological exploration: commercially important oil reserves are detected by exploratory narrow-bore drilling. The major known reserves of petroleum are in Saudi Arabia, USSR, China, Kuwait, Iran, Iraq, Mexico, USA, United Arab Emirates, Libya, and Venezuela. The oil is actually obtained by the sinking of an oil well. Before it can be used it is separated by fractional distillation in oil refineries. The main fractions obtained are:

(1) *Refinery gas* A mixture of methane, ethane, butane, and propane used as a fuel and for making other organic chemicals.

(2) *Gasoline* A mixture of hydrocarbons containing 5 to 8 carbon atoms, boiling in the range 40–180°C. It is used for motor fuels and for making other chemicals.

(3) *Kerosine* (or *paraffin oil*) A mixture of hydrocarbons having 11 or 12 carbon atoms, boiling in the range 160–250°C. Kerosine is a fuel for jet aircraft and for oil-fired domestic heating. It is also cracked to produce smaller hydrocarbons for use in motor fuels.

(4) *Diesel oil* (or *gas oil*) A mixture of hydrocarbons having 13 to 25 carbon atoms, boiling in the range 220–350°C. It is a fuel for diesel engines.

The residue is a mixture of higher hydrocarbons. The liquid components are obtained by vacuum distillation and used in lubricating oils. The solid components (*paraffin wax*) are obtained by solvent extraction. The final residue is a black tar containing free carbon (*asphalt* or *bitumen*).

petroleum ether A colourless volatile flammable mixture of hydrocarbons (not an ether), mainly pentane and hexane. It boils in the range 30–70°C and is used as a solvent.

pewter An alloy of lead and tin. It usually contains 63% tin; pewter tankards and food containers should have less than 35% of lead so that the lead remains in solid solution with the tin in the presence of weak acids in the food and drink. Copper is sometimes added to increase ductility and antimony is added if a hard alloy is required.

pH *See* pH scale.

phase A homogeneous part of a heterogeneous system that is separated from other parts by a distinguishable boundary. A mixture of ice and water is a two-phase system. A solution of salt in water is a single-phase system.

phase diagram A graph showing the relationship between solid, liquid, and gaseous *phases over a range of conditions (e.g. temperature and pressure). *See* steel (illustration).

phase rule For any system at equilibrium, the relationship $P + F = C + 2$ holds, where P is the number of distinct phases, C the number of components, and F the number of degrees of freedom of the system. The relationship derived by Josiah Willard Gibbs in 1876, is often called the *Gibbs phase rule*.

phase space *See* statistical mechanics.

phenol (carbolic acid) A white crystalline solid, C_6H_5OH; r.d. 1.1; m.p. 42°C; b.p. 182°C. It is made by the *cumene process or by the *Raschig process and is used to make a variety of other organic chemicals. *See also* phenols.

phenolphthalein A dye used as an acid-base *indicator. It is colourless below pH 8 and red above pH 9.6. It is used in titrations involving weak acids and strong bases. It is also used as a laxative.

phenols Organic compounds that contain a hydroxyl group (–OH) bound directly to a carbon atom in a benzene ring. Unlike normal alcohols, phenols are acidic because of the influence of the aromatic ring. Thus, phenol itself (C_6H_5OH) ionizes in water:

$$C_6H_5OH \rightarrow C_6H_5O^- + H^+$$

Phenols are made by fusing a sulphonic acid salt with sodium hydroxide to form the sodium salt of the phenol. The free phenol is liberated by adding sulphuric acid.

phenylalanine *See* amino acid.

phenylamine (aniline; aminobenzene) A colourless oily liquid aromatic *amine, $C_6H_5NH_2$, with an 'earthy' smell; r.d. 1.027; m.p. –6.2°C; b.p. 185°C. The compound turns brown on exposure to sunlight. It is basic, forming the *phenylammonium* (or *anilinium*) *ion*, $C_6H_5NH_3^+$, with strong acids. It is manufactured by the reduction of nitrobenzene or by the addition of ammonia to chlorobenzene using a copper(II) salt catalyst at 200°C and 55 atm. The compound is used extensively in the rubber industry and in the manufacture of drugs and dyes.

phenylammonium ion The ion $C_6H_5NH_3^+$, derived from *phenylamine.

phenylethene (styrene) A liquid hydrocarbon, $C_6H_5CH{:}CH_2$; r.d. 0.9; m.p. –31°C; b.p. 145°C. It can be made by dehydrogenating ethylbenzene and is used in making polystyrene.

phenyl group The organic group C_6H_5-, present in benzene.

phenylhydrazones *See* hydrazones.

phenylmethanol (benzyl alcohol) A liquid aromatic alcohol, $C_6H_5CH_2OH$; r.d. 1.04; m.p. –15.3°C; b.p. 205.4°C. It is used mainly as a solvent.

3-phenylpropenoic acid *See* cinnamic acid.

Phillips process A process for making high-density polyethene by polymerizing ethene at high pressure (30 atmospheres) and 150°C. The catalyst is chromium(III) oxide supported on silica and alumina.

phlogiston theory A former theory of combustion in which all flammable objects were supposed to contain a substance called *phlogiston*, which was released when the object burned. The existence of this hypothetical substance was proposed in 1669 by Johann Becher, who called it 'combustible earth' (*terra pinguis*: literally 'fat earth'). For example, according to Becher, the conversion of wood to ashes by burning was explained on the assumption that the original wood consisted of ash and *terra pinguis*, which was released on burning. In the early 18th century Georg Stahl renamed the substance *phlogiston* (from the Greek for 'burned') and extended the theory to include the calcination (and corrosion) of metals. Thus, metals were thought to be composed of *calx* (a powdery residue) and phlogiston; when a metal was heated, phlogiston was set free and the calx remained. The process could be reversed by heating the metal over charcoal (a substance believed to be rich in phlogiston, because combustion almost totally consumed it). The calx would absorb the phlogiston released by the burning charcoal and become metallic again.

The theory was finally demolished by Antoine Lavoisier, who showed by careful experiments with reactions in closed containers that there was no *absolute* gain in mass – the gain in mass of the substance was matched by a corresponding loss in mass of the air used in combustion. After experiments with Priestley's dephlogisticated air, Lavoisier realized that this gas, which he named oxygen, was taken up to form a calx (now called an oxide). The role of oxygen in the new theory was almost exactly the opposite of phlogiston's role in the old. In combustion and corrosion phlogiston was released; in the modern theory, oxygen is taken up to form an oxide.

phosgene *See* carbonyl chloride.

phosphagen A compound found in animal tissues that provides a reserve of chemical energy in the form of high-energy phosphate bonds. The most common phosphagens are creatine phosphate, occurring in vertebrate muscle and nerves, and arginine phosphate, found in most invertebrates. During tissue activity (e.g. muscle contraction) phosphagens give up their phosphate groups, thereby generating *ATP from ADP. The phosphagens are then reformed when ATP is available.

phosphates Salts based formally on phosphorus(V) oxoacids and in particular salts of *phosphoric(V) acid, H_3PO_4. A large number of polymeric phosphates also exist, containing P–O–P bridges. These are formed by heating the free acid and its salts under a variety of conditions; as well as linear polyphosphates, cyclic polyphosphates and or cross-linked polyphosphates ultraphosphates are known.

phosphatide *See* phospholipid.

phosphide A binary compound of phosphorus with a more electropositive element. Phosphides show a wide range of properties. Alkali and alkaline earth metals form ionic phosphides, such as Na_3P and Ca_3P_2, which are readily hydrolysed by water. The other transition-metal phosphides are inert metallic-looking solids with high melting points and electrical conductivities.

phosphine A colourless highly toxic gas, PH_3; m.p. –133°C; b.p. –87.7°C; slightly soluble in water. Phosphine may be prepared by reacting water or dilute acids with calcium phosphide or by reaction between yellow phosphorus and concentrated alkali. Solutions of phosphine are neutral but phosphine does react with some acids to give phosphonium salts containing PH_4^+ ions, analogous to the ammonium ions. Phosphine prepared in the laboratory is usually contaminated with diphosphine and is spontaneously flammable but the pure compound is not so. Phosphine can function as a ligand in binding to transition-metal ions. Dilute gas mixtures of very pure phosphine and the rare gases are used for doping semiconductors.

phosphinic acid (hypophosphorus acid) A white crystallline solid, H_3PO_2; r.d. 1.493; m.p. 26.5°C; decomposes above

130°C. It is soluble in water, ethanol, and ethoxyethane. Salts of phosphinic acid may be prepared by boiling white phosphorus with the hydroxides of group I or group II metals. The free acid is made by the oxidation of phosphine with iodine. It is a weak monobasic acid in which it is the –O–H group that is ionized to give the ion $H_2PO_2^-$. The acid and its salts are readily oxidized to the orthophosphate and consequently are good reducing agents.

phosphite *See* phosphonic acid.

phospholipid (phosphatide) One of a group of lipids having both a phosphate group and one or more fatty acids. *Glycerophospholipids* are based on *glycerol; the three hydroxyl groups are esterified with two fatty acids and a phosphate group, which may itself be bound to one of a variety of simple organic groups. *Sphingophospholipids* are based on the alcohol sphingosine and contain only one fatty acid linked to an amino group. With their hydrophilic polar phosphate groups and long hydrophobic hydrocarbon 'tails', phospholipids readily form membrane-like structures in water (*see* micelle). They are a major component of cell membranes.

phosphonate *See* phosphonic acid.

phosphonic acid (phosphorous acid; orthophosphorous acid) A colourless to pale-yellow deliquescent crystalline solid, H_3PO_3; r.d. 1.65; m.p. 73.6°C; decomposes at 200°C; very soluble in water and soluble in alcohol. Phosphonic acid may be crystallized from the solution obtained by adding ice-cold water to phosphorus(III) oxide or phosphorus trichloride. The structure of this material is unusual in that it contains one direct P–H bond and is more correctly written $(HO)_2HPO$. The acid is dibasic, giving rise to the ions $H_2PO_3^-$ and HPO_3^{2-} (*phosphonates*; formerly *phosphites*), and has moderate reducing properties. On heating it gives phosphine and phosphoric(V) acid.

phosphonium ion The ion PH_4^+, or the corresponding organic derivatives of the type R_3PH^+, RPH_3^+. The phosphonium ion PH_4^+ is formally analogous to the ammonium ion NH_4^+ but PH_3 has a much lower proton affinity than NH_3 and reaction of PH_3 with acids is necessary for the production of phosphonium salts.

phosphor A substance that is capable of *luminescence (including phosphorescence). Phosphors that release their energy after a short delay of between 10^{-10} and 10^{-4} second are sometimes called *scintillators*.

phosphor bronze An alloy of copper containing 4% to 10% of tin and 0.05% to 1% of phosphorus as a deoxidizing agent. It is used particularly for marine purposes and where it is exposed to heavy wear, as in gear wheels. *See also* bronze.

phosphorescence *See* luminescence.

phosphoric(V) acid (orthophosphoric acid) A white rhombic solid, H_3PO_4; r.d. 1.834; m.p. 42.35°C; loses water at 213°C; very soluble in water and soluble in ethanol. Phosphoric(V) acid is very deliquescent and is generally supplied as a concentrated aqueous solution. It is the most commercially important derivative of phosphorus, accounting for over 90% of the phosphate rock mined. It is manufactured by two methods; the *wet process*, in which the product contains some of the impurities originally present in the rock and applications are largely in the fertilizer industry, and the *thermal process*, which produces a much purer product suitable for the foodstuffs and detergent industries. In the wet process the phosphate rock, $Ca_3(PO_4)_2$, is treated with sulphuric acid and the calcium sulphate removed either as gypsum or the hemihydrate. In the thermal process, molten phosphorus is sprayed and burned in a mixture of air and steam. Phosphoric(V) acid is a weak tribasic acid, which is best visualized as $(HO)_3PO$. Its full systematic name is *tetraoxo-phosphoric(V) acid.* It gives rise to three series of salts containing *phosphate(V)* ions based on the anions $[(HO)_2PO_2]^-$, $[(HO)PO_3]^{2-}$, and $PO_4{}^{3-}$. These salts are acidic, neutral, and alkaline in character respectively and phosphate ions often feature in buffer systems. There is also a wide range of higher acids and acid anions in which there is some P–O–P chain formation. The simplest of these is *pyrophosphoric acid* (technically *heptaoxodiphosphoric(V) acid*), $H_4P_2O_7$, produced by heating phosphoric (V) acid (solid) and phosphorus(III) chloride oxide. *Metaphosphoric acid* is a glassy polymeric solid $(HPO_2)_x$.

phosphorous acid *See* phosphonic acid.

phosphorus Symbol P. A nonmetallic element belonging to *group V of the periodic table; a.n. 15; r.a.m. 30.9738; r.d. 1.82 (α-white), 2.20 (red); m.p. 44.1°C (α-white); b.p. 280°C (α-white). It occurs in various phosphate rocks, from which it is extracted by heating with carbon (coke) and silicon (IV) oxide in an electric furnace (1500°C). Calcium silicate and carbon monoxide are also produced. Phosphorus has a number of allotropic forms. The α-white form consists of P_4 tetrahedra (there is also a β-white form stable below −77°C). If α-white phosphorus is dissolved in lead and heated at 500°C a violet form is obtained. Red phosphorus, which is a combination of violet and white phosphorus, is obtained by heating α-white phosphorus at 250°C with air excluded. There is also a black allotrope, which has a graphite-like structure, made by heating white phosphorus at 300°C with a mercury catalyst. The element is highly reactive. If forms metal *phosphides and covalently bonded phosphorus(III) and phosphorus(V) compounds. Phosphorus is an *essential element for living organisms. It was discovered by Brandt in 1669.

phosphorus(III) bromide (phosphorus tribromide) A colourless fuming liquid, PBr_3; r.d. 2.85; m.p. −40°C; b.p. 173°C. It is prepared by passing bromine vapour over phosphorus but avoiding an excess, which would lead to the phosphorus(V) bromide. Like the other phosphorus(III) halides, PBr_3 is pyramidal in the gas phase. In the liquid phase the P–Br bonds are labile; for example, PBr_3 will react with PCl_3 to give a mixture of products in which the halogen atoms have been redistributed. Phosphorus (III) bromide is rapidly hydrolysed by water to give phosphonic acid and hydrogen bromide. It reacts readily with many organic hydroxyl groups and is used as a reagent for introducing bromine atoms into organic molecules.

phosphorus(V) bromide (phosphorus pentabromide) A yellow readily sublimable solid, PBr_5, which decomposes below 100°C and is soluble in benzene and carbon tetrachloride (tetrachloromethane). It may be prepared by the reaction of phosphorus(III) bromide with bromine or the direct reaction of phosphorus with excess bromine. It is very readily hydrolysed to give hydrogen bromide and phosphoric(V) acid. An interesting feature of this material is that in the solid state it has the structure $[PBr_4]^+Br^-$. It is used in organic chemistry as a brominating agent.

phosphorus(III) chloride (phosphorus trichloride) A colourless fuming liquid, PCl_3; r.d. 1.57; m.p. −112°C; b.p. 75.5°C. It is soluble in ether and in carbon tetrachloride but reacts with water and with ethanol. It may be prepared by passing chlorine over excess phosphorus (excess chlorine contaminates the product with phosphorus (V) chloride). The molecule is pyramidal in the gas phase and possesses weak electron-pair donor properties. It is hydrolysed violently by water to phosphonic acid and hydrogen chloride. Phosphorus(III) chloride is an important starting point for the synthesis of a variety of inorganic and organic derivatives of phosphorus.

phosphorus(V) chloride (phosphorus pentachloride) A yellow-white rhombic solid, PCl_5, which fumes in air; r.d. 3.6; m.p. 148°C (under pressure); sublimes at 160–162°C. It is decomposed by water to give hydrogen chloride and phosphoric(V) acid. It is soluble in organic solvents. The compound may be prepared by the reaction of chlorine with phosphorus(III) chloride. Phosphorus(V) chloride is structurally interesting in that in the gas phase it has the expected trigonal bipyramidal form but in the solid phase it consists of the ions $[PCl_4]^+[PCl_6]^-$. The same ions are detected when phosphorus(V) chloride is dissolved in polar solvents. It is used in organic chemisty as a chlorinating agent.

phosphorus(III) chloride oxide (phosphorus oxychloride; phosphoryl chloride) A colourless fuming liquid, $POCl_3$; r.d. 1.67; m.p. 2°C; b.p. 105.3°C. It may be prepared by the reaction of phosphorus(III) chloride with oxygen or by the reaction of phosphorus(V) oxide with phosphorus(V) chloride. Its reactions are very similar to those of phosphorus(III) chloride. Hydrolysis with water gives phosphoric(V) acid. Phosphorus(III) chloride oxide has a distorted tetrahedral shape and can act as a donor towards metal ions, thus giving rise to a series of complexes.

phosphorus(III) oxide (phosphorus trioxide) A white or colourless waxy solid, P_4O_6; r.d. 2.13; m.p. 23.8°C; b.p. 173.8°C. It is soluble in ether, chloroform, and benzene but reacts with cold water to give phosphonic acid, H_3PO_3, and with hot water to give phosphine and phosphoric(V) acid. The compound is formed when phosphorus is burned in an oxygen-deficient atmosphere (about 50% yield). As it is difficult to separate from white phosphorus by distillation, the mixture is irradiated with ultraviolet radiation to convert excess white phosphorus into the red form, after which the oxide can be separated by dissolution in organic solvents. Although called a trioxide for historical reasons, phosphorus(III) oxide consists of P_4O_6 molecules of tetrahedral symmetry in which each phosphorus atom is linked to the three others by an oxygen bridge. The chemistry is very complex. Above 210°C it decomposes into red phosphorus and polymeric oxides. It reacts with chlorine and bromine to give oxo-halides and with alkalis to give phosphonates (*see* phosphonic acid).

phosphorus(V) oxide (phosphorus pentoxide; phosphoric anhydride) A white powdery and extremely deliquescent solid, P_4O_{10}; r.d. 2.39; m.p. 580°C under pressure; sublimes at 360°C. It reacts violently with water to give phosphoric(V) acid. It is prepared by burning elemental phosphorus in a plentiful supply of oxygen, then purified by sublimation. The hexagonal crystalline form consists of P_4O_{10} molecular units; these have the phosphorus atoms arranged tetrahedrally, each P atom linked to three others by oxygen bridges and having in addition one terminal oxygen atom. The compound is used as a drying agent and as a dehydrating agent; for example, amides are converted into nitrites and sulphuric acid is converted to sulphur trioxide.

phosphorus oxychloride *See* phosphorus (III) chloride oxide.

phosphorus pentabromide *See* phosphorus (V) bromide.

phosphorus pentachloride *See* phosphorus (V) chloride.

phosphorus tribromide *See* phosphorus (III) bromide.

phosphorus trichloride *See* phosphorus(III) chloride.

phosphorus trioxide *See* phosphorus(III) oxide.

phosphoryl chloride *See* phosphorus(III) chloride oxide.

photochemical reaction A chemical reaction caused by light or ultraviolet radiation. The incident photons are absorbed by reactant molecules to give excited molecules or free radicals, which undergo further reaction.

photochemistry The branch of chemistry concerned with *photochemical reactions.

photochromism A change of colour occurring in certain substances when exposed to light. Photochromic materials are used in sunglasses that darken in bright sunlight.

photoconductive effect *See* photoelectric effect.

photoelectric effect The liberation of electrons from a metal surface exposed to electromagnetic radiation. The number of electrons emitted depends on the intensity of the radiation. The kinetic energy of the electrons emitted depends on the frequency of the radiation. The effect is a quantum process in which the radiation is regarded as a stream of *photons, each having an energy hf, where h is the Planck constant and f is the frequency of the radiation. A photon can only eject an electron if the photon energy exceeds the *work function, ϕ, of the solid, i.e. if $hf_0 = \phi$ an electron will be ejected; f_0 is the minimum frequency (or *threshold frequency*) at which ejection will occur. For many metals the photoelectric effect occurs at ultraviolet frequencies or above, but for some materials (having low work functions) it occurs with light. The maximum kinetic energy, E_m, of the photoelectron is given by *Einstein's equation: $E_m = hf - \phi$.

Apart from the liberation of electrons from metals other phenomena are also referred to as photoelectric effects. These are the *photoconductive effect* and the *photovoltaic effect*. In the photoconductive effect, an increase in the electrical conductivity of a semiconductor is caused by radiation as a result of the excitation of additional free charge carriers by the incident photons. *Photoconductive cells*, using such photosensitive materials as cadmium sulphide, are widely used as radiation detectors and light switches (e.g. to switch on street lighting).

In the photovoltaic effect, an e.m.f. is produced between two layers of different materials as a result of irradiation. The effect is made use of in *photovoltaic cells*, most of which consist of *p–n* semiconductor junctions. When photons are absorbed near a *p–n* junction new free charge carriers are produced (as in photoconductivity); however, in the photovoltaic effect the electric field in the junction region causes the new charge carriers to move, creating a flow of current in an external circuit without the need for a battery.

photoelectron spectroscopy A technique for determining the *ionization potentials of molecules. The sample is a gas or vapour irradiated with a narrow beam of ultraviolet radiation (usually from a helium source at 58.4 nm, 21.21 eV photon energy). The photoelectrons produced in accordance with *Einstein's equation are passed through a slit into a vacuum region, where they are deflected by magnetic or electrostatic fields to give an energy spectrum. The photoelectron spectrum obtained has peaks corresponding to the ionization potentials of the molecule (and hence the orbital energies). The technique also gives information on the vibrational energy levels of the ions formed. *ESCA* (electron spectroscopy for chemical analysis) is a similar analytical technique in which a beam of X-rays is used. In this case, the electrons ejected are from the inner shells of the atoms. Peaks in the electron spectrum for a particular element show characteristic chemical shifts, which depend on the presence of other atoms in the molecule.

photoionization The *ionization of an atom or molecule as a result of irradiation by electromagnetic radiation. For a photoionization to occur the incident photon of the radiation must have an energy in excess of the *ionization potential of the species being irradiated. The ejected photoelectron will have an energy, E, given by $E = hf - I$, where h is the Planck constant, f is the frequency of the incident radiation, and I is the ionization potential of the irradiated species.

photoluminescence *See* luminescence.

photolysis A chemical reaction produced by exposure to light or ultraviolet radiation. Photolytic reactions often involve free radicals, the first step being homolytic fission of a chemical bond. *See* flash photolysis.

photon A particle with zero rest mass consisting of a *quantum of electromagnetic radiation. The photon may also be regarded as a unit of energy equal to hf, where h is the *Planck constant and f is the frequency of the radiation in hertz. Photons travel at the speed of light. They are required to explain the photoelectric effect and other phenomena that require light to have particle character,

photosensitive substance **1.** Any substance that when exposed to electromagnetic radiation produces a photoconductive, photoelectric, or photovoltaic effect. **2.** Any substance, such as the emulsion of a photographic film, in which electromagnetic radiation produces a chemical change.

photosynthesis The chemical process by which green plants synthesize organic compounds from carbon dioxide and water in the presence of sunlight. It occurs in the chloroplasts (most of which are in the leaves) and there are two principal series of reactions. In the *light reactions*, which require the presence of light, energy from sunlight is absorbed by *photosynthetic pigments (chiefly the green pigment *chlorophyll) and converted into chemical energy. In the ensuing *dark reactions*, which can take place either in light or darkness, this chemical energy is used in the production of simple organic compounds from carbon dioxide and water. Further chemical reactions convert these compounds into chemicals useful to the plant. Photosynthesis can be summarized by the equation:

$$CO_2 + 2H_2O \rightarrow [CH_2O] + H_2O + O_2$$

Since virtually all other forms of life are directly or indirectly dependent on plants for food, photosynthesis is the basis for all life on earth. Furthermore virtually all the atmospheric oxygen has originated from oxygen released during photosynthesis.

photosynthetic pigments The plant pigments responsible for the capture of light energy during the light reactions of *photosynthesis. The green pigment *chlorophyll is the principal light receptor, absorbing blue and red light. However the *carotenoids and various other pigments also absorb light energy and pass this on to the chlorophyll molecules.

pH scale A logarithmic scale for expressing the acidity or alkalinity of a solution. To a first approximation, the pH of a solution can be defined as $-\log_{10}c$, where c is the concentration of hydrogen ions in moles per cubic decimetre. A neutral solution at 25°C has a hydrogen-ion concentration of 10^{-7} mol dm^{-3}, so the pH is 7. A pH below 7 indicates an acid solution; one above 7 indicates an alkaline solution. More accurately, the pH depends not on the concentration of hydrogen ions but on their *activity, which cannot be measured experimentally. For practical purposes, the pH scale is defined by using a hydrogen electrode in the solution of interest as one half of a cell, with a reference electrode (e.g. a calomel electrode) as the other half cell. The pH is then given by $(E - E_R)F/2.303RT$, where E is the e.m.f. of the cell and E_R the standard electrode potential of the reference electrode. In practice, a glass electrode is more convenient than a hydrogen electrode.

pH stands for 'potential of hydrogen'. The scale was introduced by S. P. Sørensen in 1909.

phthalic acid A colourless crystalline dicarboxylic acid, $C_6H_4(COOH)_2$; r.d. 1.6; m.p. 207°C. The two –COOH groups are substituted on adjacent carbon atoms of the ring, the technical name being *benzene-1,2-dicarboxylic acid.* The acid is made from *phthalic anhydride* (benzene-1,2-dicarboxylic anhydride, $C_8H_4O_3$), which is made by the catalytic oxidation of naphthalene. The anhydride is used in making plasticizers and polyester resins.

phthalic anhydride *See* phthalic acid.

physical chemistry The branch of chemistry concerned with the effect of chemical structure on physical properties. It includes chemical thermodynamics and electrochemistry.

physics The study of the laws that determine the structure of the universe with reference to the matter and energy of which it consists. It is concerned not with chemical changes that occur but with the forces that exist between objects and the interrelationship between matter and energy. Traditionally, the study was divided into separate fields: heat, light, sound, electricity and magnetism, and mechanics. Since the turn of the century, however, quantum mechanics and relativistic physics have become increasingly important; the growth of modern physics has been accompanied by the studies of atomic physics, nuclear physics, and particle physics. The physics of astronomical bodies and their interactions is known as *astrophysics*, the physics of the earth is known as *geophysics*, and the study of the physical aspects of biology is called *biophysics*.

physisorption *See* adsorption.

pi bond *See* orbital.

pico- Symbol p. A prefix used in the metric system to denote 10^{-12}. For example, 10^{-12} farad = 1 picofarad (pF).

picrate A salt or ester of picric acid.

picric acid (2,4,6-trinitrophenol) A yellow highly explosive nitro compound, $C_6H_2(NO_2)_3$; r.d. 1.8; m.p. 122°C.

pi electron An electron in a pi orbital. *See* orbital.

pig iron The impure form of iron produced by a blast furnace, which is cast into pigs (blocks) for converting at a later date into cast iron, steel, etc. The composition depends on the ores used, the smelting procedure, and the use to which the pigs will later be put.

pi orbital *See* orbital.

pipette A graduated tube used for transferring measured volumes of liquid.

pirsonnite A mineral consisting of a hydrated mixed carbonate of sodium and calcium, $Na_2CO_3.CaCO_3.2H_2O$.

pitch A black or dark-brown residue resulting from the distillation of coal tar, wood tar, or petroleum (bitumen). The term is also sometimes used for the naturally occurring petroleum residue (asphalt). Pitch is used as a binding agent (e.g. in road tars), for waterproofing (e.g. in roofing felts), and as a fuel.

pitchblende *See* uraninite.

pK value A measure of the strength of an acid on a logarithmic scale. The pK value is given by $\log_{10}(1/K_a)$, where K_a is the acid dissociation constant. pK values are often used to compare the strengths of different acids.

Planck constant Symbol *h*. The fundamental constant equal to the ratio of the energy of a quantum of energy to its frequency. It has the value $6.626\,196 \times 10^{-34}$ J s. It is named after Max Planck (1858–1947).

plane-polarized light *See* polarization of light.

plaster of Paris The hemihydrate of *calcium sulphate, $2CaSO_4.H_2O$, prepared by heating the mineral gypsum. When ground to a fine powder and mixed with water, plaster of Paris sets hard, forming interlocking crystals of gypsum. The setting results in an increase in volume and so the plaster fits tightly into a mould. It is used in pottery making, as a cast for setting broken bones, and as a constituent of the plaster used in the building industry.

plasticizer A substance added to a synthetic resin to make it flexible. *See* plastics.

plastics Materials that can be shaped by applying heat or pressure. Most plastics are made from polymeric synthetic *resins, although a few are based on natural substances (e.g. cellulose derivatives or shellac). They fall into two main classes. *Thermoplastic materials* can be repeatedly softened by heating and hardened again on cooling. *Thermosetting materials* are initially soft, but change irreversibly to a hard rigid form on heating. Plastics contain the synthetic resin mixed with such additives as pigments, plasticizers (to improve flexibility), antioxidants and other stabilizers, and fillers.

platinum Symbol Pt. A silvery white metallic *transition element (*see also* platinum metals); a.n. 78; r.a.m. 195.09; r.d. 21.37; m.p. 1772°C; b.p. ~3800°C. It occurs in some nickel and copper ores and is also found native in some deposits. The main source is the anode sludge obtained in copper–nickel refining. The element is used in jewellery, laboratory apparatus (e.g. thermocouples, electrodes, etc.), electrical contacts, and in certain alloys (e.g. with iridium or rhodium). It is also a hydrogenation catalyst. The element does not oxidize nor dissolve in hydrochloric acid. Most of its compounds are platinium(II) or platinium(IV) complexes.

platinum black Black finely divided platinum metal produced by vacuum evaporation and used as an absorbent and a catalyst.

platinum metals The three members of the second and third transition series immediately proceeding silver and gold: ruthenium (Ru), rhodium (Rh), and palladium (Pd); and osmium (Os), iridium (Ir), and platinum (Pt). These elements, together with iron, cobalt, and nickel, were formerly classed as group VIII of the periodic table. The platinum-group metals are relatively hard and resistant to corrosion and are used in jewellery and in some industrial applications (e.g. electrical contacts). They have certain chemical similarities that justify classifying them together. All are resistant to chemical attack. In solution they form a vast range of complex ions. They also form coordination compounds with carbon monoxide and other pi-bonding ligands. A number of complexes can be made in which a hydrogen atom is linked directly to the metal. The metals and their organic compounds have considerable catalytic activity. *See also* transition elements.

pleochroic Denoting a crystal that appears to be of different colours, depending on the direction from which it is viewed. It is caused by polarization of light as it passes through an anisotropic medium.

plumbago *See* carbon.

plumbane (lead(IV) hydride) An extremely unstable gas, PbH_4, said to be formed by the action of acids on magnesium–lead alloys. It was first reported in 1924, although doubts have since been expressed about the existence of the compound. It demonstrates the declining stability of the hydrides in group IV. More stable organic derivatives are known; e.g. trimethyl plumbane, $(CH_3)_3PbH$.

plumbate A compound formed by reaction of lead oxides (or hydroxides) with alkali. The oxides of lead are amphoteric (weakly acidic) and react to give plumbate ions. With the lead(IV) oxide, reaction with molten alkali gives the plumbate(IV) ion

$$PbO_2 + 2OH^- \rightarrow PbO_3^{2-} + H_2O$$

In fact, various ions are present in which the lead is bound to hydroxide groups, the principal one being the hexahydroxoplumbate(IV) ion $Pb(OH)_6^{2-}$. This is the negative ion present in crystalline 'trihydrates' of the type $K_2PbO_3.3H_2O$. Lead(II) oxide gives the trihydroxoplumbate(II) ion in alkaline solutions

$$PbO(s) + OH^-(aq) + H_2O(l) \rightarrow Pb(OH)_3^{2-}(aq)$$

Plumbate(IV) compounds were formerly referred to as *orthoplumbates* (PbO_4^{4-}) or *metaplumbates* (PbO_3^{2-}). Plumbate(II) compounds were called *plumbites.*

plumbic compounds Compounds of lead in its higher (+4) oxidation state; e.g. plumbic oxide is lead(IV) oxide, PbO_2.

plumbite *See* plumbate.

plumbous compounds Compounds of lead in its lower (+2) oxidation state; e.g. plumbous oxide is lead(II) oxide, PbO.

plutonium Symbol Pu. A dense silvery radioactive metallic transuranic element belonging to the *actinoids; a.n. 94; mass number of most stable isotope 244 (half-life 7.6×10^7 years); r.d. 19.84; m.p. 641°C; b.p. 3232°C. Thirteen isotopes are known, by far the most important being plutonium–239 (half-life 2.44×10^4 years), which undergoes nuclear fission with slow neutrons and is therefore a vital power source for nuclear weapons and some nuclear reactors. About 20 tonnes of plutonium are produced annually by the world's nuclear reactors. The element was first produced by Seaborg McMillan, Kennedy, and Wahl in 1940.

poise A *c.g.s. unit of viscosity equal to the tangential force in dynes per square centimetre required to maintain a difference in velocity of one centimetre per second between two parallel planes of a fluid separated by one centimetre. 1 poise is equal to 10^{-1} N s m^{-2}

poison 1. Any substance that is injurious to the health of a living organism. **2.** A substance that prevents the activity of a catalyst. **3.** A substance that absorbs neutrons in a nuclear reactor and therefore slows down the reaction. It may be added intentionally for this purpose or may be formed as a fission product and need to be periodically removed.

polar compound A compound that is either ionic (e.g. sodium chloride) or that has molecules with a large permanent dipole moment (e.g. water).

polariscope (polarimeter) A device used to study optically active substances (*see* optical activity). The simplest type of instrument consists of a light source, collimator, polarizer, and analyser. The specimen is placed between polarizer and analyser, so that any rotation of the plane of polarization of the light can be assessed by turning the analyser.

polarization **1.** The process of confining the vibrations of the vector constituting a transverse wave to one direction. In unpolarized radiation the vector oscillates in all directions perpendicular to the direction of propagation. *See* polarization of light. **2.** The formation of products of the chemical reaction in a *voltaic cell in the vicinity of the electrodes resulting in increased resistance to current flow and, frequently, to a reduction in the e.m.f. of the cell. *See also* depolarization. **3.** The partial separation of electric charges in an insulator subjected to an electric field. **4.** The separation of charge in a polar *chemical bond.

polarization of light The process of confining the vibrations of the electric vector of light waves to one direction. In unpolarized light the electric field vibrates in all directions perpendicular to the direction of propagation. After reflection or transmission through certain substances (*see* Polaroid) the electric field is confined to one direction and the radiation is said to be *pl*
larized light. The plane of plane-polarized light can be rotated when it passes through certain substances (*see* optical activity).

In *circularly polarized light*, the tip of the electric vector describes a circular helix about the direction of propagation with a frequency equal to the frequency of the light. The magnitude of the vector remains constant. In *elliptically polarized light*, the vector also rotates about the direction of propagation but the amplitude changes; a projection of the vector on a plane at right angles to the direction of propagation describes an ellipse. Circularly and elliptically polarized light are produced using a retardation plate.

polar molecule A molecule that has a dipole moment; i.e. one in which there is some separation of charge in the *chemical bonds, so that one part of the molecule has a positive charge and the other a negative charge.

Polaroid A doubly refracting material that plane-polarizes unpolarized light passed through it. It consists of a plastic sheet strained in a manner that makes it birefringent by aligning its molecules. Sunglasses incorporating a Polaroid material absorb light that is vibrating horizontally – produced by reflection from horizontal surfaces – and thus reduce glare.

polar solvent *See* solvent.

pollution An undesirable change in the physical, chemical, or biological characteristics of the natural environment, brought about by man's activities. It may be harmful to human or nonhuman life. Pollution may affect the soil, rivers, seas, or the atmosphere. There are two main classes of pollutants: those that are *biodegradable* (e.g. sewage), i.e. can be rendered harmless by natural processes and need therefore cause no permanent harm if adequately dispersed or treated; and those that are *nonbiodegradable* (e.g. heavy metals (such as lead) and *DDT), which eventually accumulate in the environment and may be concentrated in food chains. Other forms of pollution in the environment include noise (e.g. from jet aircraft, traffic, and industrial processes) and thermal pollution (e.g. the release of excessive waste heat into lakes or rivers causing harm to wildlife). Recent pollution problems include the disposal of radioactive waste; *acid rain* resulting from industrial emissions of sulphates; increasing levels of human waste; and high levels of carbon dioxide in the atmosphere. Attempts to contain or prevent pollution include strict regulations concerning factory emissions, the use of smokeless fuels, and the banning of certain pesticides.

polonium Symbol Po. A rare radioactive metallic element of group VIA of the periodic table; a.n. 84; r.a.m. 210; r.d. 9.32; m.p. 254°C; b.p. 962°C. The element occurs in uranium ores to an extent of about 100 micrograms per 1000 kilograms. It has 27 isotopes, more than any other element. The longest-lived isotope is polonium–209 (half-life 103 years). Polonium has attracted attention as a possible heat source for spacecraft as the energy released as it decays is 1.4×10^5 J kg^{-1} s^{-1}. It was discovered by Marie Curie in 1898 in a sample of pitchblende.

poly- Prefix indicating a polymer, e.g. polyethene. Sometimes brackets are used in polymer names to indicate the repeated unit, e.g. poly(ethene).

polyamide A type of condensation polymer produced by the interaction of an amino group of one molecule and a carboxylic acid group of another molecule to give a protein-like structure. The polyamide chains are linked together by hydrogen bonding.

polychloroethene (PVC; polyvinyl chloride) A tough white solid material, which softens with the application of a plasticizer, manufactured from chloroethene by heating in an inert solvent using benzoyl peroxide as an initiator, or by the free-radical mechanism initiated by heating chloroethene under water with potassium persulphate or hydrogen peroxide. The polymer is used in a variety of ways, being easy to colour and resistant to fire, chemicals, and weather.

polycyclic Denoting a compound that has two or more rings in its molecules. Polycyclic compounds may contain single rings (as in phenylbenzene, $C_6H_5.C_6H_5$) or fused rings (as in naphthalene, $C_{10}H_8$).

polydioxoboric(III) acid *See* boric acid.

polyester A condensation polymer formed by the interaction of polyhydric alcohols and polybasic acids. Linear polyesters are saturated thermoplastics and linked by dipole–dipole attraction as the carbonyl groups are polarized. They are extensively used as fibres (e.g. *Terylene*). Unsaturated polyesters readily copolymerize to give thermosetting products. They are used in the manufacture of glass-fibre products.

polyethene (polyethylene; polythene) A flexible waxy translucent polyalkene thermoplastic made in a variety of ways producing a polymer of varying characteristics. In the ICI process, ethene containing a trace of oxygen is subjected to a pressure in excess of 1500 atmospheres and a temperature of 200°C. Low-density polyethene (r.d. 0.92) has a formula weight between 50 000 and 300 000, softening at a temperature around 110°C, while the high-density polythene (r.d. 0.945–0.96) has a formula weight up to 3 000 000, softening around 130°C. The low-density polymer is less crystalline, being more atactic. Polyethene is used as an insulator; it is acid resistant and is easily moulded and blown. *See* Phillips process; Ziegler process.

polyethylene *See* polyethene.

polyhydric alcohol An *alcohol that has several hydroxyl groups per molecule.

polymer A substance having large molecules consisting of repeated units (the monomers). There are a number of natural polymers, such as polysaccharides. Synthetic polymers are extensively used in *plastics. Polymers do not have a definite formula since they consist of chains of different lengths. The various types of polymer are shown in the illustration.

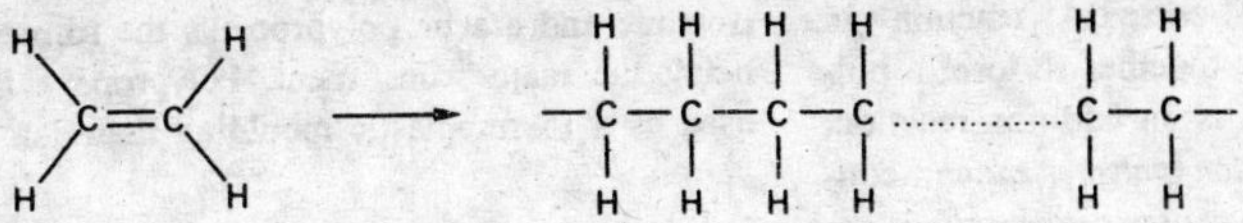

Addition polymerization of ethene to form polyethene a homopolymer

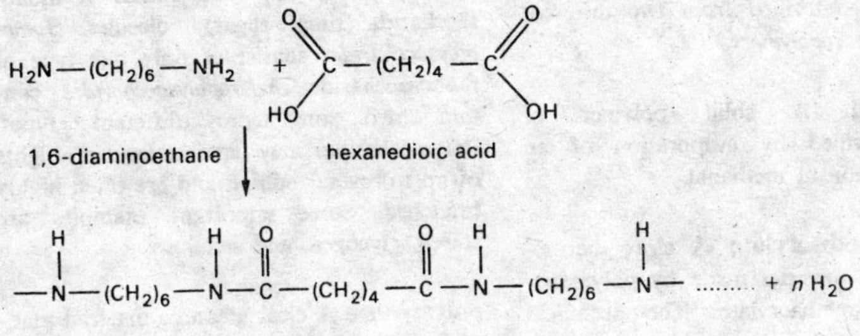

Condensation polymerization to form nylon: a heteropolymer

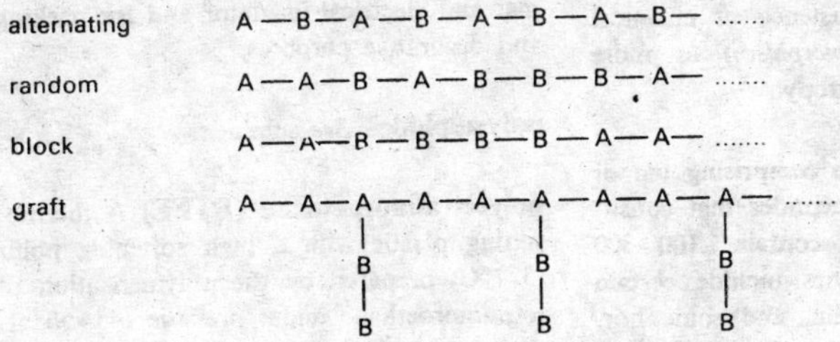

Types of copolymer depending on the arrangement of the monomers A and B

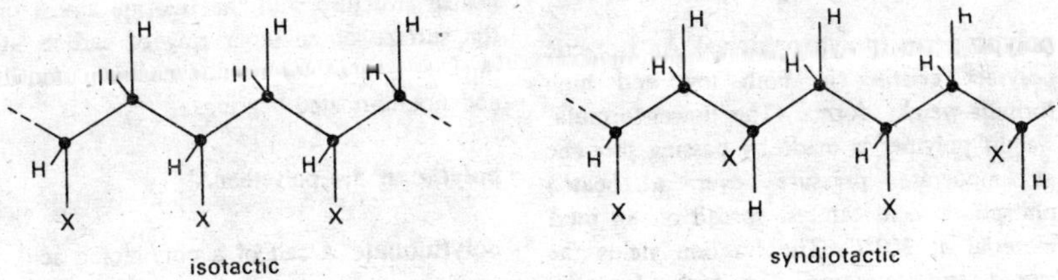

Types of stereospecific polymer

polymerization A chemical reaction in which molecules join together to form a polymer. If the reaction is an addition reaction, the process is *addition polymerization*; condensation reactions cause *condensation polymerization*, in which a small molecule is eliminated during the reaction. Polymers consisting of a single monomer are *homopolymers*; those formed from two different monomers are *copolymers*.

polymethanal A solid polymer of methanal, formed by evaporation of an aqueous solution of methanal.

polymethylmethacrylate A clear thermoplastic acrylic material made by polymerizing methyl methacrylate. The technical name is *poly(methyl 2-methylpropenoate)*. It is used in such materials as *Perspex*.

polymorphism The existence of chemical substances in two (*dimorphism*) or more physical forms. *See* allotropy.

polypeptide A *peptide comprising ten or more amino acids. Polypeptides that constitute proteins usually contain 100–300 amino acids. Shorter ones include certain antibiotics, e.g. gramicidin, and some hormones, e.g. ACTH, which has 39 amino acids. The properties of a polypeptide are determined by the type and sequence of its constituent amino acids.

polypropene (polypropylene) An isotactic polymer existing in both low and high formula-weight forms. The lower-formula-weight polymer is made by passing propene at moderate pressure over a heated phosphoric acid catalyst spread on an inert material at 200°C. The reaction yields the trimer and tetramer. The higher-formula-weight polymer is produced by passing propene into an inert solvent, heptane, which contains a trialkyl aluminium and a titanium compound. The product is a mixture of isotactic and atactic polypropene, the former being the major constituent. Polypropene is used as a thermoplastic moulding material.

polypropylene *See* polypropene.

polysaccharide Any of a group of carbohydrates comprising long chains of monosaccharide (simple-sugar) molecules. *Homopolysaccharides* consist of only one type of monosaccharide; *heteropolysaccharides* contain two or more different types. Polysaccharides may have molecular weights of up to several million and are often highly branched. Some important examples are starch, glycogen, and cellulose.

polystyrene A clear glasslike material manufactured by free-radical polymerization of phenylethene (styrene) using benzoyl peroxide as an initiator. It is used as both a thermal and electrical insulator and for packing and decorative purposes.

polysulphides *See* sulphides.

polytetrafluoroethane (PTFE) A thermosetting plastic with a high softening point (327°C) prepared by the polymerization of tetrafluoroethane under pressure (45–50 atmospheres). The reaction requires an initiator, ammonium peroxosulphate. The polymer has a low coefficient of friction and its 'anti-stick' properties are probably due to its helical structure with the fluorine atoms on the surface of an inner ring of carbon atoms. It is used for coating cooking utensils and nonlubricated bearings.

polythene *See* polyethene.

polythionate A salt of a polythionic acid.

polythionic acids Oxo acids of sulphur in which the general formula is $HO.SO_2.S_n.SO_2.OH$, where $n = 0–4$. *See also* sulphuric acid.

polyurethane A polymer containing the urethane group –NH.CO.O–, prepared by reacting di-isocyanates with appropriate diols or triols. A wide range of polyurethanes can be made, and they are used in adhesives, durable paints and varnishes, plastics, and rubbers. Addition of water to the polyurethane plastics turns them into foams.

polyvinyl chloride *See* polychloroethene.

porphyrin Any of a group of related organic compounds characterized by the possession of a cyclic group of four linked nitrogen-containing rings (a *pyrrole* nucleus). Porphyrins differ in the nature of their side-chain groups. They include the chlorophylls and the haem groups of haemoglobin, myoglobin, and the cytochromes.

potash Any of a number of potassium compounds, such as the carbonate or the hydroxide.

potash alum *See* aluminium potassium sulphate; alums.

potash mica *See* muscovite.

potassium Symbol K. A soft silvery metallic element belonging to group I of the periodic table (*see* alkali metals); a.n. 19; r.a.m. 39.098; r.d. 0.87; m.p. 63.7°C; b.p. 774°C. The element occurs in seawater and in a number of minerals, such as sylvite (KCl), carnallite ($KCl.MgCl_2.6H_2O$), and kainite ($MgSO_4.KCl.3H_2O$). It is obtained by electrolysis. The metal has few uses but potassium salts are used for a wide range of applications. Potassium is an essential element for living organisms. Chemically, it is highly reactive, resembling sodium in its behaviour and compounds. It also forms an orange-coloured superoxide, KO_2, which contains the O_2^- ion. Potassium was discovered by Sir Humphry Davy in 1807.

potassium–argon dating A *dating technique for certain rocks that depends on the decay of the radioisotope potassium–40 to argon–40, a process with a half-life of about 1.27×10^{10} years. It assumes that all the argon–40 formed in the potassium-bearing mineral accumulates within it and that all the argon present is formed by the decay of potassium–40. The mass of argon–40 and potassium–40 in the sample is estimated and the sample is then dated from the equation:

$$^{40}Ar = 0.1102\ ^{40}K(e^{\lambda t} - 1),$$

where λ is the decay constant and t is the time in years since the mineral cooled to about 300°C, when the ^{40}Ar became trapped in the crystal lattice. The method is effective for micas, feldspar, and some other minerals.

potassium bicarbonate *See* potassium hydrogencarbonate.

potassium bichromate *See* potassium dichromate.

potassium bromide A white or colourless crystalline solid, KBr, slightly hygroscopic and soluble in water and very slightly soluble in ethanol; cubic; r.d. 2.73; m.p. 734°C; b.p. 1435°C. Potassium bromide may be prepared by the action of bromine on hot potassium hydroxide solution or by the action of iron(III) bromide or hydrogen bromide on potassium carbonate solution. It is used widely in the photographic industry and is also used as a sedative. Because of its range of transparency to infrared radiation, KBr is used both as a matrix for solid samples and as a prism material in infrared spectroscopy.

potassium carbonate (pearl ash; potash) A translucent (granular) or white (powder) deliquescent solid known in the anhydrous and hydrated forms. K_2CO_3 (monoclinic; r.d. 2.4; m.p. 891°C) decomposes without boiling. $2K_2CO_3.3H_2O$ (monoclinic; r.d.

2.04) dehydrates to $K_2CO_3.H_2O$ above 100°C and to K_2CO_3 above 130°C. It is prepared by the Engel–Precht process in which potassium chloride and magnesium oxide react with carbon dioxide to give the compound *Engel's salt*, $MgCO_3.KHCO_3.4H_2O$. This is decomposed in solution to give the hydrogencarbonate, which can then be calcined to K_2CO_3. Potassium carbonate is soluble in water (insoluble in alcohol) with significant hydrolysis to produce basic solutions. Industrial uses include glasses and glazes, the manufacture of soft soaps, and in dyeing and wool finishing. It is used in the laboratory as a drying agent.

potassium chlorate A colourless crystalline compound, $KClO_3$, which is soluble in water and moderately soluble in ethanol; monoclinic; r.d. 2.33; m.p. 360°C; decomposes above 400°C giving off oxygen. The industrial route to potassium chlorate involves the fractional crystallization of a solution of potassium chloride and sodium chlorate but it may also be prepared by electrolysis of hot concentrated solutions of potassium chloride. It is a powerful oxidizing agent finding applications in weedkillers and disinfectants and, because of its ability to produce oxygen, it is used in explosives, pyrotechnics, and matches.

potassium chloride A white crystalline solid, KCl, which is soluble in water and very slightly soluble in ethanol; cubic; r.d. 1.98; m.p. 772°C; sublimes at 1500°C. Potassium chloride occurs naturally as the mineral *sylvite* (KCl) and *carnallite* ($KCl.MgCl_2.6H_2O$); it is produced industrially by fractional crystallization of these deposits or of solutions from lake brines. It has the interesting property of being more soluble than sodium chloride in hot water but less soluble in cold. It is used as a fertilizer, in photography, and as a source of other potassium salts, such as the chlorate and the hydroxide. It has low toxicity.

potassium chromate A bright yellow crystalline solid, K_2CrO_4, soluble in water and insoluble in alcohol; rhombic; r.d. 2.73; m.p. 971°C; decomposes without boiling. It is produced industrially by roasting powdered chromite ore with potash and limestone and leaching the resulting cinder with hot potassium sulphate solution. Potassium chromate is used in leather finishing, as a textile mordant, and in enamels and pigments. In the laboratory it is used as an analytical reagent and as an indicator. Like other chromium(III) compounds it is toxic when ingested or inhaled.

potassium chromium sulphate (chrome alum) A violet or ruby-red crystalline solid, $K_2SO_4.Cr_2(SO_4)_3.24H_2O$, soluble in water and insoluble in ethanol; cubic or octahedral; r.d. 1.826; m.p. 89°C; loses $10H_2O$ at 100°C, $12H_2O$ at 400°C. Six water molecules surround each of the chromium(III) ions and the remaining ones are hydrogen bonded to the sulphate ions. Like all alums, the compound may be prepared by mixing equimolar quantities of the constituent sulphates. *See* alums.

potassium cyanide (cyanide) A white crystalline or granular deliquescent solid, KCN, soluble in water and in ethanol and having a faint characteristic odour of almonds (due to hydrolysis forming hydrogen cyanide at the surface); cubic; r.d. 1.52; m.p. 634°C. It is prepared industrially by the absorption of hydrogen cyanide in potassium hydroxide. The compound is used in the extraction of silver and gold, in some metal-finishing processes and electroplating, as an insecticide and fumigant (source of HCN), and in the preparation of cyanogen derivatives. In the laboratory it is used in analysis, as a reducing agent, and as a stabilizing *ligand for low oxidation states. The salt itself is highly toxic and aqueous solutions of potassium cyanide are strongly hydrolysed to give rise to the slow release of equally toxic hydrogen cyanide gas.

potassium dichromate (potassium bichromate) An orange-red crystalline solid, $K_2Cr_2O_7$, soluble in water and insoluble in alcohol; monoclinic or triclinic; r.d. 2.67; monoclinic changes to triclinic at 241.6°C; m.p. 396°C; decomposes above 500°C. It is prepared by acidification of crude potassium chromate solution (the addition of a base to solutions of potassium dichromate reverses this process). The compound is used industrially as an oxidizing agent in the chemical industry and in dyestuffs manufacture, in electroplating, pyrotechnics, glass manufacture, glues, tanning, photography and lithography, and in ceramic products. Laboratory uses include application as an analytical reagent and as an oxidizng agent. Potassium dichromate is toxic and considered a fire risk on account of its oxidizing properties.

potassium dioxide *See* potassium superoxide.

potassium hydride A white or greyish white crystalline solid, KH; r.d. 1.43–1.47. It is prepared by passing hydrogen over heated potassium and marketed as a light grey powder dispersed in oil. The solid decomposes on heating and in contact with moisture and is an excellent reducing agent. Potassium hydride is a fire hazard because it produces hydrogen on reaction with water.

potassium hydrogencarbonate (potassium bicarbonate) A white crystalline solid, $KHCO_3$, soluble in water and insoluble in ethanol; r.d. 2.17; decomposes about 120°C. It occurs naturally as *calcinite* and is prepared by passing carbon dioxide into saturated potassium carbonate solution. It is used in baking, soft-drinks manufacture, and in CO_2 fire extinguishers. Because of its buffering capacity, it is added to some detergents and also used as a laboratory reagent.

potassium hydrogentartrate (cream of tartar) A white crystalline acid salt, HOOC $(CHOH)_2COOK$. It is obtained from deposits on wine vats (argol) and used in baking powders.

potassium hydroxide (caustic potash; lye) A white deliquescent solid, KOH, often sold as pellets, flakes, or sticks, soluble in water and in ethanol and very slightly soluble in ether; rhombic; r.d. 2.02; m.p. 405°C; b.p. 1320°C. It is prepared industrially by the electrolysis of concentrated potassium chloride solution but it can also be made by heating potassium carbonate or sulphate with slaked lime, $Ca(OH)_2$. It closely resembles sodium hydroxide but is more soluble and is therefore preferred as an absorber for carbon dioxide and sulphur dioxide. It is also used in the manufacture of soft soap, other potassium salts, and in Ni–Fe and alkaline storage cells. Potassium hydroxide is extremely corrosive to body tissues and especially damaging to the eyes.

potassium iodate A white crystalline solid, KIO_3, soluble in water and insoluble in ethanol; monoclinic; r.d. 3.9; m.p. 561°C. It may be prepared by the reaction of iodine with hot concentrated potassium hydroxide or by careful electrolysis of potassium iodide solution. It is an oxidizing agent and is used as an analytical reagent. Some potassium iodate is used as a food additive.

potassium iodide A white crystalline solid, KI, with a strong bitter taste, soluble in water, ethanol, and acetone; cubic; r.d. 3.12; m.p. 686°C; b.p. 1330°C. It may be prepared by the reaction of iodine with hot potassium hydroxide solution followed by separation from the iodate (which is also formed) by fractional crystallization. In solution it has the interesting property of dissolving iodine to form the triiodide ion I_3^-, which is brown. Potassium iodide is widely used as an analytical reagent, in photography, and also as an additive to table salt to prevent goitre and other disorders due to iodine deficiency.

potassium manganate(VII) (potassium permanganate) A compound, $KMnO_4$, forming purple crystals with a metallic sheen, soluble in water (intense purple solution), acetone, and methanol, but decomposed by ethanol; r.d. 2.70; decomposition begins slightly above 100°C and is complete at 240°C. The compound is prepared by fusing manganese(IV) oxide with potassium hydroxide to form the manganate and electrolysing the manganate solution using iron electrodes at about 60°C. An alternative route employs production of sodium manganate by a similar fusion process, oxidation with chlorine and sulphuric acid, then treatment with potassium chloride to crystallize the required product.

Potassium manganate(VII) is widely used as an oxidizing agent and as a disinfectant in a variety of applications, and as an analytical reagent.

potassium monoxide A grey crystalline solid, K_2O; cubic; r.d. 2.32; decomposition occurs at 350°C. It may be prepared by the oxidation of potassium metal with potassium nitrate. It reacts with ethanol to form potassium ethoxide (KOC_2H_5), and with liquid ammonia to form potassium hydroxide and potassamide (KNH_2).

potassium nitrate (saltpetre) A colourless rhombohedral or trigonal solid, KNO_3, soluble in water, insoluble in alcohol; r.d. 2.109; transition to trigonal form at 129°C; m.p. 334°C; decomposes at 400°C. It occurs naturally as *nitre* and may be prepared by the reaction of sodium nitrate with potassium chloride followed by fractional crystallization. It is a powerful oxidizing agent (releases oxygen on heating) and is used in gunpowder and fertilizers.

potassium nitrite A white or slightly yellow deliquescent solid, KNO_2, soluble in water and insoluble in ethanol; r.d. 1.91; m.p. 300°C; may explode at 600°C. Potassium nitrite reacts with cold dilute mineral acids to give nitrous acid and is also able to behave as a reducing agent (if oxidized to the nitrate) or as an oxidizing agent (if reduced to nitrogen). It is used in organic synthesis because of its part in diazotization, and in detecting the presence of the amino groups in organic compounds.

potassium permanganate *See* potassium manganate(VII).

potassium sulphate A white crystalline powder, K_2SO_4, soluble in water and insoluble in ethanol; rhombic or hexagonal; r.d. 2.66; m.p. 1072°C. It occurs naturally as *schönite* (Strassfurt deposits) and in lake brines, from which it is separated by fractional crystallization. It has also been produced by the Hargreaves process, which involves the oxidation of potassium chloride with sulphuric acid. In the laboratory it may be obtained by the reaction of either potassium hydroxide or potassium carbonate with sulphuric acid. Potassium sulphate is used in cements, in glass manufacture, as a food additive, and as a fertilizer (source of K^+) for chloride-sensitive plants, such as tobacco and citrus.

potassium sulphide A yellow-red or brown-red deliquescent solid, K_2S, which is soluble in water and in ethanol but insoluble in diethyl ether; cubic; r.d. 1.80; m.p. 840°C. It is made industrially by reducing potassium sulphate with carbon at high temperatures in the absence of air. In the laboratory it may be prepared by the reaction of hydrogen sulphide with potassium hydroxide. The pentahydrate is obtained on crystallization. Solutions are strongly alkaline due to hydrolysis. It is used as an analytical reagent and as a depilatory. Potassium sulphide is generally regarded as a hazardous chemical with a fire risk; dusts of K_2S have been known to explode.

potassium sulphite A white crystalline solid, K_2SO_3, soluble in water and very sparingly soluble in ethanol; r.d. 1.51; decomposes on heating. It is a reducing agent and is used as such in photography and in the food and brewing industries, where it prevents oxidation.

potassium superoxide (potassium dioxide) A yellow paramagnetic solid, KO_2, produced by burning potassium in an excess of oxygen; it is very soluble (by reaction) in water, soluble in ethanol, and slightly soluble in diethyl ether; m.p. 490°C. When treated with cold water or dilute mineral acids, hydrogen peroxide is obtained. The compound is a powerful oxidizing agent and on strong heating releases oxygen with the formation of the monoxide, K_2O.

potential barrier A region containing a maximum of potential that prevents a particle on one side of it from passing to the other side. According to classical theory a particle must possess energy in excess of the height of the potential barrier to pass it. However, in quantum theory there is a finite probability that a particle with less energy will pass through the barrier (*see* tunnel effect). A potential barrier surrounds the atomic nucleus and is important in nuclear physics; a similar but much lower barrier exists at the interface between semiconductors and metals and between differently doped semiconductors. These barriers are important in the design of electronic devices.

potentiometric titration A titration in which the end point is found by measuring the potential on an electrode immersed in the reaction mixture.

powder metallurgy A process in which powdered metals or alloys are pressed into a variety of shapes at high temperatures. The process started with the pressing of powdered tungsten into incandescent lamp filaments in the first decade of this century and is now widely used for making self-lubricating bearings and cemented tungsten carbide cutting tools.

The powders are produced by atomization of molten metals, chemical decomposition of a compound of the metal, or crushing and grinding of the metal or alloy. The parts are pressed into moulds at pressures ranging from 140×10^6 Pa to 830×10^6 Pa after which they are heated in a controlled atmosphere to bond the particles together (*see* sintering).

praseodymium Symbol Pr. A soft silvery metallic element belonging to the *lanthanoids; a.n. 59; r.a.m. 140.91; r.d. 6.769 (20°C); m.p. 934°C; b.p. 3512°C. It occurs in bastnasite and monazite, from which it is recovered by an ion-exchange process. The only naturally occurring isotope is praseodymium-141, which is not radioactive; however, fourteen radioisotopes have been produced. It is used in mischmetal, a rare-earth alloy containing 5% praseodymium, for use in lighter flints. Another rare-earth mixture containing 30% praseodymium is used as a catalyst in cracking crude oil. The element was discovered by C. A. von Welsbach in 1885.

precipitate A suspension of small solid particles produced in a liquid by chemical reaction.

precipitation 1. All liquid and solid forms of water that are deposited from the atmosphere; it includes rain, drizzle, snow, hail, dew, and hoar frost. **2.** The formation of a precipitate.

precursor A compound that leads to another compound in a series of chemical reactions.

pressure The force acting on unit area of a surface or the ratio of force to area. It is measured in *pascals in SI units. *Absolute* *pressure* is pressure measured on a gauge that reads zero at zero pressure rather than at atmospheric pressure. *Gauge pressure* is measured on a gauge that reads zero at atmospheric pressure.

pressure gauge Any device used to measure *pressure. Three basic types are in use: the liquid-column gauge (e.g. the mercury barometer and the manometer), the expanding-element gauge (e.g. the Bourdon gauge and the aneroid barometer), and the electrical transducer. In the last category the strain gauge is an example. Capacitor pressure gauges also come into this category. In these devices, the pressure to be measured displaces one plate of a capacitor and thus alters its capacitance.

primary alcohol *See* alcohols.

primary amine *See* amines.

primary cell A *voltaic cell in which the chemical reaction producing the e.m.f. is not satisfactorily reversible and the cell cannot therefore be recharged by the application of a charging current. *See* Daniell cell; Leclanché cell; Weston cell; mercury cell. *Compare* secondary cell.

producer gas (air gas) A mixture of carbon monoxide and nitrogen made by passing air over very hot carbon. Usually some steam is added to the air and the mixture contains hydrogen. The gas is used as a fuel in some industrial processes.

product *See* chemical reaction.

progesterone A hormone, produced primarily by the corpus luteum of the ovary but also by the placenta, that prepares the inner lining of the uterus for implantation of a fertilized egg cell. If implantation fails, the corpus luteum degenerates and progesterone production ceases accordingly. If implantation occurs, the corpus luteum continues to secrete progesterone, under the influence of luteinizing hormone and prolactin, for several months of pregnancy, by which time the placenta has taken over this function. During pregnancy, progesterone maintains the constitution of the uterus and prevents further release of eggs from the ovary. Small amounts of progesterone are produced by the testes. *See also* progestogen.

progestogen One of a group of naturally occurring or synthetic hormones that maintain the normal course of pregnancy. The best known is *progesterone. In high doses progestogens inhibit secretion of luteinizing hormone, thereby preventing ovulation, and alter the consistency of mucus in the vagina so that conception tends not to occur. They are therefore used as major constituents of oral contraceptives.

prolactin (lactogenic hormone; luteotrophic hormone; luteotrophin) A hormone produced by the anterior pituitary gland. In mammals it stimulates the mammary glands to produce milk and the corpus luteum of the ovary to secrete the hormone *progesterone.

proline *See* amino acid.

promethium Symbol Pm. A soft silvery metallic element belonging to the *lanthanoids; a.n. 61; r.a.m. 145; r.d. 7.26 (20°C); m.p. 1042°C; b.p. 3000°C. The only naturally occurring isotope, promethium-147, has a half-life of only 2.52 years. Eighteen other radioisotopes have been produced, but they have very short half-lives. The only known source of the element is nuclear-waste material. Promethium-147 is of interest as a beta-decay power source but the promethium-146 and -148, which emit penetrating gamma radiation, must first be removed. It was discovered by J. A. Marinsky, L. E. Glendenin, and C. D. Coryell in 1947.

promoter A substance added to a catalyst to increase its activity.

proof A measure of the amount of alcohol (ethanol) in drinks. *Proof spirit* contains 42.28% ethanol by weight (about 57% by volume). Degrees of proof express the percentage of proof spirit present, so 70° proof spirit contains 0.7 × 57% alcohol.

propanal (propionaldehyde) A colourless liquid *aldehyde, C_2H_5CHO; m.p. −185.2°C; b.p. 48.8°C.

propane A colourless gaseous hydrocarbon, C_3H_8; m.p. −190°C; b.p. −42°C. It is the third member of the *alkane series and is obtained from petroleum. Its main use is as bottled gas for fuel.

propanoic acid (propionic acid) A colourless liquid *carboxylic acid, CH_3CH_2COOH; r.d. 0.99; m.p. −20.8°C; b.p. 141°C. It is used to make calcium propanate – an additive in bread.

propanol Either of two *alcohols with the formula C_3H_7OH. Propan-1-ol is $CH_3CH_2CH_2OH$ and propan-2-ol is $CH_3CH(OH)CH_3$. Both are colourless volatile liquids. Propan-2-ol is used in making propanone (acetone).

propanone (acetone) A colourless flammable volatile compound, CH_3COCH_3; r.d. 0.79; m.p. −95.4°C; b.p. 56.2°C. The simplest *ketone, propanone is miscible with water. It is made by oxidation of propan-2-ol (*see* propanol) or is obtained as a by-product in the manufacture of phenol from cumene; it is used as a solvent and as a raw material for making plastics.

propenal (acrolein) A colourless pungent liquid unsaturated aldehyde, CH_2:CHCHO; r.d. 0.84; m.p. −87°C; b.p. 53°C. It is made from propene and can be polymerized to give acrylate resins.

propene (propylene) A colourless gaseous hydrocarbon, CH_3CH:CH_2; m.p. −81°C; b.p. 48.8°C. It is an *alkene obtained from petroleum by cracking alkanes. Its main use is in the manufacture of polypropene.

propenoate (acrylate) A salt or ester of *propenoic acid.

propenoic acid (acrylic acid) An unsaturated liquid *carboxylic acid, CH_2:CHCOOH; m.p. 7°C; b.p. 141°C. It readily polymerizes and it is used in the manufacture of *acrylic resins.

propenonitrile (acrylonitrile; vinyl cyanide) A colourless liquid, H_2C:CHCN; r.d. 0.81; m.p. −83.5°C. It is an unsaturated nitrile, made from propene and used to make acrylic resins.

propionaldehyde *See* propanal.

propylene *See* propene.

propyl group The organic group $CH_3CH_2CH_2$–.

prostaglandin Any of a group of organic compounds derived from *essential fatty acids and causing a range of physiological effects in animals. Prostaglandins have been detected in most body tissues. They act at very low concentrations to cause the contraction of smooth muscle; natural and synthetic prostaglandins are used to induce abortion or labour in humans and domestic animals. Two prostaglandin derivatives have antagonistic effects on blood circulation: *thromboxane* A_2 causes blood clotting while *prostacyclin* causes blood vessels to dilate. Inflammation in allergic reactions and other diseases is also thought to involve prostaglandins.

prosthetic group A tightly bound nonpeptide inorganic or organic component of a protein. Prosthetic groups may be lipids, carbohydrates, metal ions, phosphate groups, etc. Some *coenzymes are more correctly regarded as prosthetic groups.

protactinium Symbol Pa. A radioactive metallic element belonging to the *actinoids; a.n. 91; r.a.m. 231.036; r.d. 15.37 (calculated); m.p. <1600°C (estimated). The most stable isotope, protactinium-231, has a half-life of 3.43×10^4 years; ten other radioisotopes are known. Protactinium-231 occurs in all uranium ores as it is a member of the uranium series. Protactinium has no practical applications; it was discovered by Lise Meitner and Otto Hahn in 1917.

protamine Any of a group of proteins of relatively low molecular weight found in association with the chromosomal *DNA of vertebrate male germ cells. They contain a single polypeptide chain comprising about 67% arginine. Protamines are thought to protect and support the chromosomes.

protease (peptidase; proteinase; proteolytic enzyme) Any enzyme that catalyses the splitting of proteins into smaller *peptide fractions and amino acids, a process known as *proteolysis*. Examples are *pepsin and *trypsin. Several proteases, acting sequentially, are normally required for the complete digestion of a protein to its constituent amino acids.

protein Any of a large group of organic compounds found in all living organisms. Proteins comprise carbon, hydrogen, oxygen, and nitrogen and most also contain sulphur; molecular weights range from 6000 to several million. Protein molecules consist of one or several long chains (*polypeptides) of *amino acids linked in a characteristic sequence. This sequence is called the *primary structure* of the protein. These polypeptides may undergo coiling or pleating, the nature and extent of which is described as the *secondary structure*. The three-dimensional shape of the coiled or pleated polypeptides is called the *tertiary structure*. *Quaternary structure* specifies the structural relationship of the component polypeptides.

Proteins may be broadly classified into globular proteins and fibrous proteins. Globular proteins have compact rounded molecules and are usually water-soluble. Of prime importance are the *enzymes, proteins that catalyse biochemical reactions. Other globular proteins include the antibodies, which combine with foreign substances in the body; the carrier proteins, such as haemoglobin; the storage proteins (e.g. casein in milk and albumin in egg white), and certain hormones (e.g. insulin). Fibrous proteins are generally insoluble in water and consist of long coiled strands or flat sheets, which confer strength and elasticity. In this category are keratin and collagen. Actin and myosin are the principal fibrous proteins of muscle, the interaction of which brings about muscle contraction.

When heated over 50°C or subjected to strong acids or alkalis, proteins lose their specific tertiary structure and may form insoluble coagulates (e.g. egg white). This usually inactivates their biological properties.

protein synthesis The process by which living cells manufacture proteins from their constituent amino acids, in accordance with the genetic information carried in the DNA of the chromosomes. This information is encoded in messenger *RNA, which is transcribed from DNA in the nucleus of the cell: the sequence of amino acids in a particular protein is determined by the sequence of nucleotides in messenger RNA. At the ribosomes the information carried by messenger RNA is translated into the sequence of amino acids of the protein in the process of translation.

proteolysis The enzymic splitting of proteins. *See* protease.

proteolytic enzyme *See* protease.

proton An elementary particle that is stable, bears a positive charge equal in magnitude to that of the *electron, and has a mass of $1.672\,614 \times 10^{-27}$ kg, which is 1836.12 times that of the electron. The proton is a hydrogen ion and occurs in all atomic nuclei.

protonic acid An *acid that forms positive hydrogen ions (or, strictly, oxonium ions) in aqueous solution. The term is used to distinguish 'traditional' acids from Lewis acids or from Lowry–Br o/nsted acids in non-aqueous solvents.

proton number *See* atomic number.

prussic acid *See* hydrogen cyanide.

pseudoaromatic A compound that has a ring of atoms containing alternating double and single bonds, yet does not have the characteristic properties of *aromatic compounds. Such compounds do not obey the Huckel rule. Cyclooctatetraene (C_8H_8), for instance, has a ring of eight carbon atoms with conjugated double bonds, but the ring is not planar and the compound acts like an alkene, undergoing addition reactions.

pseudohalogens A group of compounds, including cyanogen $(CN)_2$ and thiocyanogen $(SCN)_2$, that have some resemblance to the halogens. Thus, they form hydrogen acids (HCN and HSCN) and ionic salts containing such ions as CN^- and SCN^-.

pseudo order An order of a chemical reaction that appears to be less than the true order because of the experimental conditions used. Pseudo orders occur when one reactant is present in large excess. For example, a reaction of substance A undergoing hydrolysis may appear to be proportional only to [A] because the amount of water present is so large.

PTFE *See* polytetrafluoroethane.

ptyalin An enzyme that digests carbohydrates (*see* amylase). It is present in mammalian saliva and is responsible for the initial stages of starch digestion.

pumice A porous volcanic rock that is light and full of cavities due to expanding gases that were liberated from solution in the lava while it solidified. Pumice is often light enough to float on water. It is usually acid (siliceous) in composition, and is used as an abrasive and for polishing.

pump A device that imparts energy to a fluid in order to move it from one place or level to another or to raise its pressure (*compare* vacuum pump). *Centrifugal pumps* and turbines have rotating impellers, which increase the velocity of the fluid, part of the energy so acquired by the fluid then being converted to pressure energy. Displacement pumps act directly on the fluid, forcing it to flow against a pressure. They include piston, plunger, gear, screw, and cam pumps.

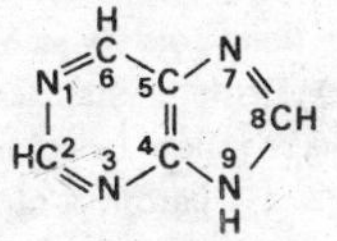

Purine

purine An organic nitrogenous base, sparingly soluble in water, that gives rise to a group of biologically important derivatives, notably *adenine and *guanine, which occur in nucleotides and nucleic acids (DNA and RNA).

PVC *See* polychloroethene.

pyridine A colourless liquid with a strong unpleasant smell, C_5H_5N; r.d. 0.9; m.p. −42°C; b.p. 115°C. Pyridine is an aromatic heterocyclic compound present in coal tar. It is used in making other organic chemicals.

pyridoxine *See* vitamin B complex.

Pyridine

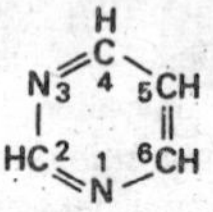

Pyrimidine

pyrimidine An organic nitrogenous base, sparingly soluble in water, that gives rise to a group of biologically important derivatives, notably *uracil, *thymine, and *cytosine, which occur in *nucleotides and nucleic acids (DNA and RNA).

pyrite (iron pyrites) A mineral form of iron(II) sulphide, FeS_2. Superficially it resembles gold in appearance, hence it is also known as *fool's gold*, but it is harder and more brittle than gold (which may be cut with a knife). Pyrite crystallizes in the cubic system, is brass yellow in colour, has a metallic lustre, and a hardness of 6–6.5 on the Mohs' scale. It is the most common and widespread of the sulphide minerals and is used as a source of sulphur for the production of sulphuric acid. Sources include the Rio Tinto mines in Spain.

pyro- Prefix denoting an oxo acid that could be obtained from a lower acid by dehydration of two molecules. For example, pyrosulphuric acid is $H_2S_2O_7$ (i.e. $2H_2SO_4$ minus H_2O).

pyroboric acid *See* boric acid.

pyroelectricity The property of certain crystals, such as tourmaline, of acquiring opposite electrical charges on opposite faces when heated. In tourmaline a rise in temperature of 1 K at room temperature produces a polarization of some 10^{-5} $C\,m^{-2}$.

pyrolysis Chemical decomposition occurring as a result of high temperature.

pyrometric cones *See* Seger cones.

pyrometry The measurement of high temperatures (beyond the range of thermometers) using a *pyrometer*. Modern *narrow-band* or *spectral* pyrometers use infrared-sensitive photoelectric cells behind filters that exclude visible light. In the *optical pyrometer* (or disappearing filament pyrometer) the image of the incandescent source is focused in the plane of a tungsten filament that is heated electrically. A variable resistor is used to adjust the current through the filament until it blends into the image of the source, when viewed through a red filter and an eyepiece. The temperature is then read from a calibrated ammeter or a calibrated dial on the variable resistor. In the *total-radiation pyrometer* radiation emitted by the source is focused by a concave mirror onto a blackened foil to which a thermopile is attached. From the e.m.f. produced by the thermopile the temperature of the source can be calculated.

pyrophoric Igniting spontaneously in air. *Pyrophoric alloys* are alloys that give sparks when struck. *See* misch metal.

pyrophosphoric acid *See* phosphoric(V) acid.

pyrosilicate *See* silicate.

pyrosulphuric acid *See* disulphuric(VI) acid.

pyroxenes A group of ferromagnesian rock-forming silicate minerals. They are common in basic igneous rocks but may also be developed by metamorphic processes in gneisses, schists, and marbles. Pyroxenes have a complex crystal chemistry; they are composed of continuous chains of silicon and oxygen atoms linked by a variety of other elements. They are related to the *amphiboles, from which they differ in cleavage angles. The general formula is $X_{1-p}Y_{1+p}Z_2O_6$, where X = Ca,Na; Y = Mg,Fe^{2+},Mn,Li,Al,Fe^{3+},Ti; and Z = Si,Al. Orthorhombic pyroxenes (*orthopyroxenes*), $(Mg,Fe)_2Si_2O_6$, vary in composition between the end-members enstatite ($Mg_2Si_2O_6$) and orthoferrosilite ($Fe_2Si_2O_6$). Monoclinic pyroxenes (*clinopyroxenes*), the larger group, include diopside, $CaMgSi_2O_6$; hedenbergite, $CaFe^{2+}Si_2O_6$; johannsenite, $CaMnSi_2O_6$; augite, $(Ca,Mg,Fe,Ti,Al)_2(Si,Al)_2O_6$; aegirine, $NaFe^{3+}Si_2O_6$; jadeite (*see* jade); and pigeonite $(Mg,Fe^{2+},Ca)(Mg,Fe^{2+})Si_2O_6$.

pyruvic acid (2-oxopropanoic acid) A colourless liquid organic acid, $CH_3COCOOH$; m.p. 13°C. It is an important intermediate compound in metabolism, being produced during glycolysis.

Q

quadrivalent Having a valency of four.

qualitative analysis *See* analysis.

quantitative analysis *See* analysis.

quantum The minimum amount by which certain properties, such as energy or angular momentum, of a system can change. Such properties do not, therefore, vary continuously, but in integral multiples of the relevant quantum. This concept forms the basis of the *quantum theory. In waves and fields the quantum can be regarded as an excitation, giving a particle-like interpretation to the wave or field. Thus, the quantum of the electromagnetic field is the *photon and the graviton is the quantum of the gravitational field. *See* quantum mechanics.

quantum mechanics A system of mechanics that was developed from *quantum theory and is used to explain the properties of atoms and molecules. Using the energy *quantum as a starting point it incorporates Heisenberg's *uncertainty principle and the de Broglie wavelength to establish the wave–particle duality on which *Schrödinger's equation is based. This form of quantum mechanics is called *wave mechanics*. An alternative but equivalent formalism, *matrix mechanics*, is based on mathematical operators.

quantum number *See* atom; spin.

quantum state The state of a quantized system as described by its quantum numbers. For instance, the state of a hydrogen *atom is described by the four quantum numbers n, l, m, m_s. In the ground state they have values 1, 0, 1, and ½ respectively.

quantum statistics A statistical description of a system of particles that obeys the rules of *quantum mechanics rather than classical mechanics. In quantum statistics, energy states are considered to be quantized; if the particles are treated as indistinguishable, *Bose–Einstein statistics* apply and the particles are called *bosons*. All known bosons have an angular momentum nh, where n is zero or an integer and h is the Planck constant. For identical bosons the *wave function is always symmetric. For the particular case in which not more than one particle may appear in any of the cells into which the particles are distributed, *Fermi–Dirac statistics* apply and the particles are called *fermions*. All known fermions have a total angular momentum $(n + ½)h$ and any wave function that involves identical fermions is always antisymmetric.

quantum theory The theory devised by Max Planck (1858–1947) in 1900 to account for the emission of the black-body radiation from hot bodies. According to this theory energy is emitted in quanta (*see* quantum), each of which has an energy equal to $h\nu$, where h is the *Planck constant and ν is the frequency of the radiation. This theory led to the modern theory of the interaction between matter and radiation known as *quantum mechanics, which generalizes and replaces classical mechanics and Maxwell's electromagnetic theory. In *nonrelativistic quantum theory* particles are assumed to be neither created nor destroyed, to move slowly relative to the speed of light, and to have a mass that does not change with velocity. These assumptions apply to atomic and molecular phenomena and to some aspects of nuclear physics. *Relativistic quantum theory* applies to particles that have zero rest mass or travel at or near the speed of light.

quartz The most abundant and common mineral, consisting of crystalline silica (silicon dioxide, SiO_2), crystallizing in the trigonal system. It has a hardness of 7 on the Mohs' scale. Well-formed crystals of quartz are six-sided prisms terminating in six-sided pyramids. Quartz is ordinarily colourless and transparent, in which form it is known as *rock crystal*. Coloured varieties, a number of which are used as gemstones, include *amethyst, citrine quartz (yellow), rose quartz (pink), milk quartz (white), smoky quartz (grey-brown), *chalcedony, *agate, and *jasper. Quartz occurs in many rocks, especially igneous rocks such as granite and quartzite (of which it is the chief constituent), metamorphic rocks such as gneisses and schists, and sedimentary rocks such as sandstone and limestone. The mineral has the property of being piezoelectric and hence is used to make oscillators for clocks, radios, and radar instruments. It is also used in optical instruments and in glass, glaze, and abrasives.

quaternary ammonium compounds *See* amine salts.

quenching 1. (in metallurgy) The rapid cooling of a metal by immersing it in a bath of liquid in order to improve its properties. Steels are quenched to make them harder but some nonferrous metals are quenched for other reasons (copper, for example, is made softer by quenching). **2.** (in physics) The process of inhibiting a continuous discharge in a *Geiger counter so that the incidence of further ionizing radiation can cause a new discharge. This is achieved by introducing a quenching vapour, such as ether or a halogen gas, into the tube.

quicklime *See* calcium oxide.

quinhydrone electrode A *half-cell consisting of a platinum electrode in an equimolar solution of quinone (cyclohexadiene-1,4-dione) and hydroquinone (benzene-1,4-diol). It depends on the oxidation–reduction reaction

$$C_6H_4(OH)_2 \rightleftharpoons C_6H_4O_2 + 2H^+ + 2e^-$$

quinol *See* benzene-1,4-diol.

quinone 1. *See* cyclohexadiene-1,4-dione. **2.** Any similar compound containing C=O groups in an unsaturated ring.

R

racemate *See* racemic mixture.

racemic mixture (racemate) A mixture of equal quantities of the *d*- and *l*-forms of an optically active compound. Racemic mixtures are denoted by the prefix *dl* (e.g. *dl*-lactic acid). A racemic mixture shows no *optical activity.

racemization A chemical reaction in which an optically active compound is converted into a *racemic mixture.

rad *See* radiation units.

radiation **1.** Energy travelling in the form of electromagnetic waves or photons. **2.** A stream of particles, especially alpha- or beta-particles from a radioactive source or neutrons from a nuclear reactor.

radiation units Units of measurement used to express the activity of a radionuclide and the dose of ionizing radiation. The units *curie*, *roentgen*, *rad*, and *rem* are not coherent with SI units but their temporary use with SI units has been approved while the derived SI units *becquerel*, *gray*, and *sievert* become familiar.

The becquerel (Bq), the SI unit of activity, is the activity of a radionuclide decaying at a rate, on average, of one spontaneous nuclear transition per second. Thus 1 Bq = 1 s^{-1}. The former unit, the curie (Ci), is equal to 3.7 × 10^{10} Bq. The curie was originally chosen to approximate the activity of 1 gram of radium-226.

The gray (Gy), the SI unit of absorbed dose, is the absorbed dose when the energy per unit mass imparted to matter by ionizing radiation is 1 joule per kilogram. The former unit, the rad (rd), is equal to 10^{-2} Gy.

The sievert (Sv), the SI unit of dose equivalent, is the dose equivalent when the absorbed dose of ionizing radiation multiplied by the stipulated dimensionless factors is 1 J kg^{-1}. As different types of radiation cause different effects in biological tissue a weighted absorbed dose, called the *dose equivalent*, is used in which the absorbed dose is modified by multiplying it by dimensionless factors stipulated by the International Commission on Radiological Protection. The former unit of dose equivalent, the rem (originally an acronym for *r*oentgen *e*quivalent *m*an), is equal to 10^{-} Sv.

In SI units, exposure to ionizing radiation is expressed in coulombs per kilogram, the quantity of X- or gamma-radiation that produces ion pairs carrying 1 coulomb of charge of either sign in 1 kilogram of pure dry air. The former unit, the roentgen (R), is equal to 2.58 × 10^{-4} C kg^{-1}

radical A group of atoms, either in a compound or existing alone. *See* free radical; functional group.

radioactive age The age of an archaeological or geological specimen as determined by a process that depends on a radioactive decay. *See* carbon dating; fission-track dating; potassium–argon dating; rubidium–strontium dating; uranium–lead dating.

radioactive series A series of radioactive nuclides in which each member of the series is formed by the decay of the nuclide before it. The series ends with a stable nuclide. Three radioactive series occur naturally, those headed by thorium–232 (*thorium series*), uranium–235 (*actinium series*), and uranium–238 (*uranium series*). All three series end with an isotope of lead. The *neptunium series* starts with the artificial isotope plutonium–241, which decays to neptunium–237, and ends with thallium–81

radioactive tracing *See* labelling.

radioactivity The spontaneous disintegration of certain atomic nuclei accompanied by the emission of alpha particles (helium nuclei), beta particles (electrons), or gamma radiation (short-wave electromagnetic waves).

Natural radioactivity is the result of the spontaneous disintegration of naturally occurring radioisotopes; these radioisotopes can be arranged in three *radioactive series. The rate of disintegration is uninfluenced by chemical changes or any normal changes in their environment. However, radioactivity can be induced in many nuclides by bombarding them with neutrons or other particles. *See also* ionizing radiation; radiation units.

radiocarbon dating *See* carbon dating.

radiochemistry The branch of chemistry concerned with radioactive compounds and with ionization. It includes the study of compounds of radioactive elements and the preparation and use of compounds containing radioactive atoms. *See* labelling; radiolysis.

radioisotope (radioactive isotope) An isotope of an element that is radioactive. *See* labelling.

radiolysis The use of ionizing radiation to produce chemical reactions. The radiation used includes alpha particles, electrons, neutrons, X-rays, and gamma rays from radioactive materials or from accelerators. Energy transfer produces ions and excited species, which undergo further reaction. A particular feature of radiolysis is the formation of short-lived solvated electrons in water and other polar solvents.

radiometric dating (radioactive dating) *See* dating techniques; radioactive age.

radionuclide (radioactive nuclide) A *nuclide that is radioactive.

radium Symbol Ra. A radioactive metallic element belonging to *group II of the periodic table; a.n. 88; r.a.m. 226.0254; r.d. ~5; m.p. 700°C; b.p. 1140°C. It occurs in uranium ores (e.g. pitchblende). The most stable isotope is radium–226 (half-life 1602 years), which decays to radon. It is used as a radioactive source in research and, to some extent, in radiotherapy. The element was isolated from pitchblende in 1898 by Marie and Pierre Curie.

radon Symbol Rn. A colourless radioactive gaseous element belonging to group 0 of the periodic table (the *noble gases); a.n. 86; r.a.m. 222; d. 9.73 g dm^{-3}; m.p. −71°C; b.p. −61.8°C. At least 20 isotopes are known, the most stable being radon–222 (half-life 3.8 days). It is formed by decay of radium–226 and undergoes alpha decay. It is used in radiotherapy. As a noble gas, radon is practically inert, although radon fluoride can be made. It was first isolated by Ramsey and Gray in 1908.

raffinate A liquid purified by solvent extraction.

r.a.m. *See* relative atomic mass.

Raney nickel A spongy form of nickel made by the action of sodium hydroxide on a nickel–aluminium alloy. The sodium hydroxide dissolves the aluminium leaving a highly active form of nickel with a large surface area. The material is a black pyrophoric powder saturated with hydrogen. It is an extremely efficient catalyst, especially for hydrogenation reactions at room temperature. It was discovered in 1927 by the American chemist M. Raney.

ranksite A mineral consisting of a mixed sodium carbonate, sodium sulphate, and potassium chloride, $2Na_2CO_3.9Na_2SO_4.KCl$.

Raoult's law The partial vapour pressure of a solvent is proportional to its mole fraction. If p is the vapour pressure of the solvent (with a substance dissolved in it) and X the mole fraction of solvent (number of moles of solvent divided by total number of moles) then $p = p_0X$, where p_0 is the vapour pressure of the pure solvent. A solution that obeys Raoult's law is said to be an *ideal solution*. In general the law holds only for dilute solutions, although some mixtures of liquids obey it over a whole range of concentrations. Such solutions are *perfect solutions* and occur when the intermolecular forces between molecules of the pure substances are similar to the forces between molecules of one and molecules of the other. Deviations in Raoult's law for mixtures of liquids cause the formation of *azeotropes. The law was discovered by the French chemist François Raoult (1830–1901).

rare-earth elements *See* lanthanoids.

rarefaction A reduction in the pressure of a fluid and therefore of its density.

rare gases *See* noble gases.

Raschig process An industrial process for making chlorobenzene (and phenol) by a gas-phase reaction between benzene vapour, hydrogen chloride, and oxygen (air) at 230°C

$$2C_6H_6 + 2HCl + O_2 \rightarrow 2H_2O + 2C_6H_5Cl$$

The catalyst is copper(II) chloride. The chlorobenzene is mainly used for making phenol by the reaction

$$C_6H_5Cl + H_2O \rightarrow HCl + C_6H_5OH$$

This reaction proceeds at 430°C with a silicon catalyst.

Raschig synthesis *See* hydrazine.

rate constant (velocity constant) Symbol *k*. The constant in an expression for the rate of a chemical reaction in terms of concentrations (or activities). For instance, in a simple unimolecular reaction

$$A \rightarrow B$$

the rate is proportional to the concentration of A, i.e.

$$\text{rate} = k[A]$$

where *k* is the rate constant, which depends on the temperature. The equation is the *rate equation* of the reaction, and its form depends on the reaction mechanism.

rate-determining step The slowest step in a chemical reaction that involves a number of steps. In such reactions, there is often a single step that is appreciably slower than the other steps, and the rate of this determines the overall rate of the reaction.

rationalized units A system of units in which the defining equations have been made to conform to the geometry of the system in a logical way. Thus equations that involve circular symmetry contain the factor 2π, while those involving spherical symmetry contain the factor 4π. *SI units are rationalized; c.g.s. units are unrationalized.

rayon A textile made from cellulose. There are two types, both made from wood pulp. In the viscose process, the pulp is dissolved in carbon disulphide and sodium hydroxide to give a thick brown liquid containing cellulose xanthate. The liquid is then forced through fine nozzles into acid, where the xanthate is decomposed and a cellulose filament is produced. The product is *viscose rayon*. In the acetate process cellulose acetate is made and dissolved in a solvent. The solution is forced through nozzles into air, where the solvent quickly evaporates leaving a filament of *acetate rayon*.

reactant *See* chemical reaction.

reaction *See* chemical reaction.

reactive dye *See* dyes.

reagent A substance reacting with another substance. Laboratory reagents are compounds, such as sulphuric acid, hydrochloric acid, sodium hydroxide, etc., used in chemical analysis or experiments.

realgar A red mineral form of arsenic(II) sulphide, As_2S_2.

real gas A gas that does not have the properties assigned to an *ideal gas. Its molecules have a finite size and there are forces between them (*see* equation of state).

rearrangement A type of chemical reaction in which the atoms in a molecule rearrange to form a new molecule.

reciprocal proportions *See* chemical combination.

recombination process The process in which a neutral atom or molecule is formed by the combination of a positive ion and a negative ion or electron; i.e. a process of the type:

$$A^+ + B^- \rightarrow AB.$$

or

$$A^+ + e^- \rightarrow A$$

In recombination, the neutral species formed is usually in an excited state, from which it can decay with emission of light or other electromagnetic radiation.

rectification The process of purifying a liquid by *distillation. *See* fractional distillation.

rectified spirit A constant-boiling mixture of *ethanol (95.6°) and water; it is obtained by distillation.

red lead *See* dilead(II) lead(IV) oxide.

redox *See* oxidation–reduction.

reducing agent (reductant) A substance that brings about reduction in other substances. It achieves this by being itself oxidized. Reducing agents contain atoms with low oxidation numbers; that is the atoms have gained electrons. In reducing other substances, these atoms lose electrons.

reductant *See* reducing agent.

reduction *See* oxidation–reduction.

refinery gas *See* petroleum.

refining The process of purifying substances or extracting substances from mixtures.

refluxing A laboratory technique in which a liquid is boiled in a container attached to a condenser (*reflux condenser*), so that the liquid continuously flows back into the container. It is used for carrying out reactions over long periods in organic synthesis.

reforming The conversion of straight-chain alkanes into branched-chain alkanes by *cracking or by catalytic reaction. It is used in petroleum refining to produce hydrocarbons suitable for use in gasoline. Benzene is also manufactured from alkane hydrocarbons by catalytic reforming. *Steam reforming* is a process used to convert methane (from natural gas) into a mixture of carbon monoxide and hydrogen, which is used to synthesize organic chemicals. The reaction

$$CH_4 + H_2O \rightarrow CO + 3H_2$$

occurs at about 900°C using a nickel catalyst.

Regnault's method A technique for measuring gas density by evacuating and weighing a glass bulb of known volume, admitting gas at known pressure, and reweighing. The determination must be carried out at constant known temperature and the result corrected to standard temperature and pressure. The method is named after the French chemist Henri Victor Regnault (1810–78).

relative atomic mass (atomic weight; r.a.m.) Symbol A_r. The ratio of the average mass per atom of the naturally occurring form of an element to 1/12 of the mass of a carbon–12 atom.

relative density (r.d.) The ratio of the *density of a substance to the density of some reference substance. For liquids or solids it is the ratio of the density (usually at 20°C) to the density of water (at its maximum density). This quantity was formerly called *specific gravity*. Sometimes relative densities of gases are used; for example, relative to dry air, both gases being at s.t.p.

relative molecular mass (molecular weight) Symbol M_r. The ratio of the average mass per molecule of the naturally occurring form of an element or compound to 1/12 of the mass of a carbon–12 atom. It is equal to the sum of the relative atomic masses of all the atoms that comprise a molecule.

rem *See* radiation units.

rennin An enzyme secreted by cells lining the stomach in mammals that is responsible for clotting milk. It acts on a soluble milk protein (*caseinogen*), which it converts to the insoluble form casein. This ensures that milk remains in the stomach long enough to be acted on by protein-digesting enzymes.

resin A synthetic or naturally occurring *polymer. Synthetic resins are used in making *plastics. Natural resins are acidic chemicals secreted by many trees (especially conifers) into ducts or canals. They are found either as brittle glassy substances or dissolved in essential oils. Their functions are probably similar to those of gums and mucilages.

resolution The process of separating a racemic mixture into its optically active constituents. In some cases the crystals of the two forms have a different appearance, and the separation can be done by hand. In general, however, physical methods (distillation, crystallization, etc.) cannot be used because the optical isomers have identical physical properties. The most common technique is to react the mixture with a compound that is itself optically active, and then separate the two. For instance, a racemic mixture of *l*-A and *d*-A reacted with *l*-B, gives two compounds AB that are not optical isomers (they are diastereoisomers) and can be separated and reconverted into the pure *l*-A and *d*-A. Biological techniques using bacteria that convert one form but not the other can also be used.

resonance The representation of the structure of a molecule by two or more conventional formulae. For example, the formula of methanal can be represented by a covalent structure $H_2C{=}O$, in which there is a double bond in the carbonyl group. It is known that in such compounds the oxygen has some negative charge and the carbon some positive charge. The true bonding in the molecule is somewhere between $H_2C{=}O$ and the ionic compound $H_2C^+O^-$. It is said to be a *resonance hybrid* of the two, indicated by

$$H_2C{=}O \leftrightarrow H_2C^+O^-$$

The two possible structures are called *canonical forms*, and they need not contribute equally to the actual form. Note that the double-headed arrow does not imply that the two forms are in equilibrium.

retinol *See* vitamin A.

retort **1.** A laboratory apparatus consisting of a glass bulb with a long neck. **2.** A vessel used for reaction or distillation in industrial chemical processes.

reverberatory furnace A metallurgical furnace in which the charge to be heated is kept separate from the fuel. It consists of a shallow hearth on which the charge is heated by flames that pass over it and by radiation reflected onto it from a low roof.

reverse osmosis A method of obtaining pure water from water containing a salt, as in *desalination. Pure water and the salt water are separated by a semipermeable membrane and the pressure of the salt water is raised above the osmotic pressure, causing water from the brine to pass through the membrane into the pure water.

This process requires a pressure of some 25 atmospheres, which makes it difficult to apply on a large scale.

reversible process Any process in which the variables that define the state of the system can be made to change in such a way that they pass through the same values in the reverse order when the process is reversed. It is also a condition of a reversible process that any exchanges of energy, work, or matter with the surroundings should be reversed in direction and order when the process is reversed. Any process that does not comply with these conditions when it is reversed is said to be an *irreversible process.* All natural processes are irreversible, although some processes can be made to approach closely to a reversible process.

R_F value (in chromatography) The distance travelled by the solvent front divided by the distance travelled by a given component. For a given system at a known temperature, it is a characteristic of the component and can be used to identify components.

rhe A unit of fluidity equal to the reciprocal of the *poise.

rhenium Symbol Re. A silvery-white metallic *transition element; a.n. 75; r.a.m. 186.2; r.d. 21.0; m.p. 3180°C; b.p. 5620°C. The element is obtained as a by-product in refining molybdenum, and is used in certain alloys (e.g. rhenium–molybdenum alloys are superconducting). The element forms a number of complexes with oxidation states in the range 1–7.

rheology The study of the deformation and flow of matter.

rheopexy The process by which certain thixotropic substances set more rapidly when they are stirred, shaken, or tapped. Gypsum in water is such a *rheopectic substance.*

rhodium Symbol Rh. A silvery-white metallic *transition element; a.n. 45; r.a.m. 102.9; r.d. 12.4; m.p. 1966°C; b.p. 3727°C. It occurs with platinum and is used in certain platinum alloys (e.g. for thermocouples) and in plating jewellery and optical reflectors. Chemically, it is not attacked by acids (dissolves only slowly in aqua regia) and reacts with nonmetals (e.g. oxygen and chlorine) at red heat. Its main oxidation state is +3 although it also forms complexes in the +4 state. The element was discovered in 1803 by W. H. Wollaston.

riboflavin *See* vitamin B complex.

ribonucleic acid *See* RNA.

ribose A *monosaccharide, $C_5H_{10}O_5$, rarely occurring free in nature but important as a component of *RNA (ribonucleic acid). Its derivative *deoxyribose*, $C_5H_{10}O_4$, is equally important as a constituent of *DNA (deoxyribonucleic acid), which carries the genetic code in chromosomes.

ring A closed chain of atoms in a molecule. In compounds, such as naphthalene, in which two rings share a common side, the rings are *fused rings. Ring closures* are chemical reactions in which one part of a chain reacts with another to form a ring, as in the formation of *lactams and *lactones.

RNA (ribonucleic acid) A complex organic compound (a nucleic acid) in living cells that is concerned with *protein synthesis. In some viruses, RNA is also the hereditary material. Most RNA is synthesized in the nucleus and then distributed to various parts of the cytoplasm. An RNA molecule consists of a long chain of *nucleotides in which the sugar is *ribose and the bases are adenine, cytosine, guanine, and uracil (*compare* DNA).

Rochelle salt Potassium sodium tartrate tetrahydrate, $KNaC_4H_4O_6.4H_2O$. A colour-

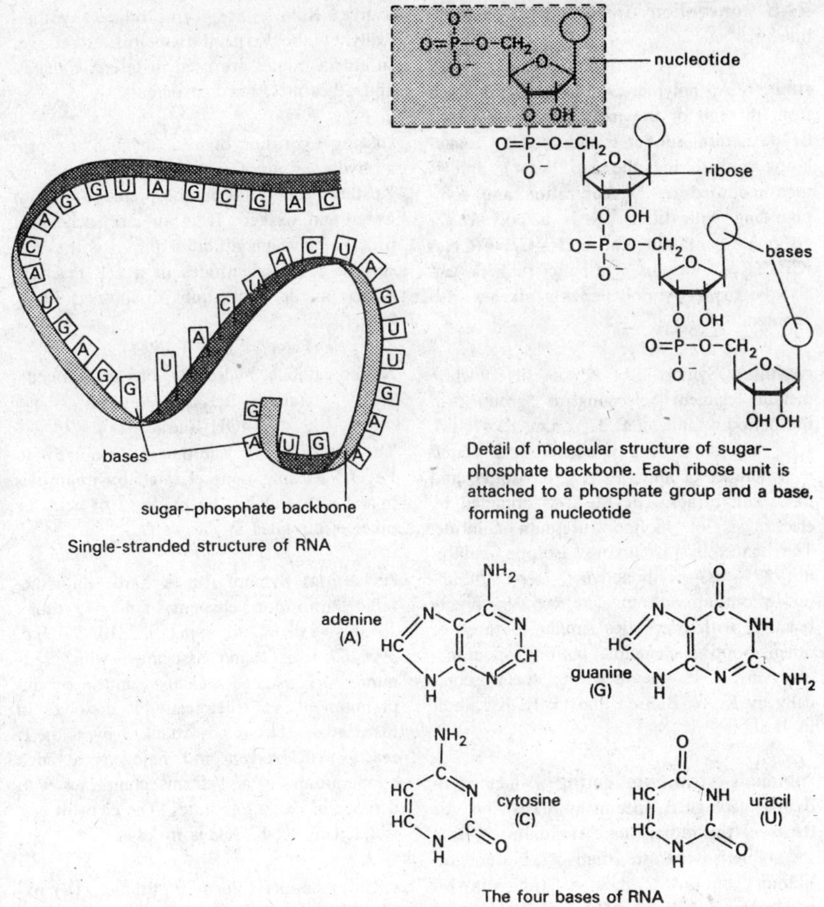

Single-stranded structure of RNA

Detail of molecular structure of sugar–phosphate backbone. Each ribose unit is attached to a phosphate group and a base, forming a nucleotide

The four bases of RNA

Molecular structure of RNA

less crystalline salt used for its piezoelectric properties.

rock An aggregate of mineral particles that makes up part of the earth's crust. It may be consolidated or unconsolidated (e.g. sand, gravel, mud, shells, coral, and clay).

rock crystal *See* quartz.

rock salt *See* halite.

roentgen The former unit of dose equivalent (*see* radiation units). It is named after the discoverer of X-rays, W. K. Roentgen (1845–1923).

Rose's metal An alloy of low melting point (about 100°C) consisting of 50% bismuth, 25–28% lead, and 22–25% tin.

R–S convention *See* absolute configuration.

rubber A polymeric substance obtained from the sap of the tree *Hevea brasiliensis*. Crude natural rubber is obtained by coagulating and drying the sap (latex), and is then modified by *vulcanization and compounding with fillers. It is a polymer of *isoprene containing the unit $-CH_2C(CH_3)$ $:CHCH_2-$. Various synthetic rubbers can also be made by polymerizing alkenes. *See* neoprene.

rubidium Symbol Rb. A soft silvery-white metallic element belonging to *group I of the periodic table; a.n. 37; r.a.m. 85.47; r.d. 1.53; m.p. 38.4°C; b.p. 688°C. It is found in a number of minerals (e.g. lepidolite) and in certain brines. The metal is obtained by electrolysis of molten rubidium chloride. The naturally occurring isotope rubidium-87 is radioactive (*see* rubidium-strontium dating). The metal is highly reactive, with properties similar to those of other group I elements, igniting spontaneously in air. It was discovered spectroscopically by R. W. Bunsen and G. R. Kirchhoff in 1861.

rubidium–strontium dating A method of dating geological specimens based on the decay of the radioisotope rubidium-87 into the stable isotope strontium-87. Natural rubidium contains 27.85% of rubidium-87, which has a half-life of 4.7×10^{11} years. The ratio $^{87}Rb/^{87}Sr$ in a specimen gives an estimate of its age (up to several thousand million years).

ruby The transparent red variety of the mineral *corundum, the colour being due to the presence of traces of chromium. It is a valuable gemstone, more precious than diamonds. The finest rubies are obtained from Mogok in Burma, where they occur in metamorphic limestones; Sri Lanka and Thailand are the only other important sources. Rubies have been produced synthetically by the Verneuil flame-fusion process. Industrial rubies are used in lasers, watches, and other precision instruments.

rusting Corrosion of iron (or steel) to form a hydrated iron(III) oxide $Fe_2O_3.xH_2O$. Rusting occurs only in the presence of both water and oxygen. It is an electrochemical process in which different parts of the iron surface act as electrodes in a cell reaction. At the anode, iron atoms dissolve as Fe^{2+} ions:

$$Fe(s) \rightarrow Fe^{2+}(aq) + 2e$$

At the cathode, hydroxide ions are formed:

$$O_2(aq) + 2H_2O(l) + 4e \rightarrow 4OH^-(aq)$$

The $Fe(OH)_2$ in solution is oxidized to Fe_2O_3. Rusting is accelerated by impurities in the iron and by the presence of acids or other electrolytes in the water.

ruthenium Symbol Ru. A hard white metallic *transition element; a.n. 44; r.a.m. 101.07; r.d. 12.41; m.p. 2310°C; b.p. 3900°C. It is found associated with platinum and is used as a catalyst and in certain platinum alloys. Chemically, it dissolves in fused alkalis but is not attacked by acids. It reacts with oxygen and halogens at high temperatures. It also forms complexes with a range of oxidation states. The element was isolated by K. K. Klaus in 1844.

rutile A mineral form of titanium(IV) oxide, TiO_2.

Rydberg spectrum An absorption spectrum of a gas in the ultraviolet region, consisting of a series of lines that become closer together towards shorter wavelengths, merging into a continuous absorption region. The absorption lines correspond to electronic transitions to successively higher energy levels. The onset of the continuum corresponds to photoionization of the atom or molecule, and can thus be used to determine the ionization potential.

S

saccharide *See* sugar.

saccharose *See* sucrose.

Sachse reaction A reaction of methane at high temperature to produce ethyne:

$$2CH_4 \rightarrow C_2H_2 + 3H_2$$

The reaction occurs at about 1500°C, the high temperature being obtained by burning part of the methane in air.

sacrificial protection (cathodic protection) The protection of iron or steel against corrosion (*see* rusting) by using a more reactive metal. A common form is galvanizing (*see* galvanized iron), in which the iron surface is coated with a layer of zinc. Even if the zinc layer is scratched, the iron does not rust because zinc ions are formed in solution in preference to iron ions. Pieces of magnesium alloy are similarly used in protecting pipelines, etc.

sal ammoniac *See* ammonium chloride.

salicylic acid (1-hydroxybenzoic acid) A naturally occurring carboxylic acid found in certain plants, HOC_6H_4COOH; r.d. 1.4; m.p. 157°C. It is used in making aspirin and in the foodstuffs and dyestuffs industries.

saline Describing a chemical compound that is a salt, or a solution containing a salt. *See also* physiological saline.

salinometer An instrument for measuring the salinity of a solution. There are two main types: one is a type of *hydrometer to measure density; the other is an apparatus for measuring the electrical conductivity of the solution.

sal soda Anhydrous *sodium carbonate, Na_2CO_3.

salt A compound formed by reaction of an acid with a base, in which the hydrogen of the acid has been replaced by metal or other positive ions. Typically, salts are crystalline ionic compounds such as Na^+Cl^- and $NH_4{}^+NO_3{}^-$. Covalent metal compounds, such as $TiCl_4$, are also often regarded as salts.

salt bridge An electrical connection made between two half cells. It usually consists of a glass U-tube filled with agar jelly containing a salt, such as potassium chloride. A strip of filter paper soaked in the salt solution can also be used.

salt cake Industrial *sodium sulphate.

saltpetre *See* nitre.

samarium Symbol Sm. A soft silvery metallic element belonging to the *lanthanoids; a.n. 62; r.a.m. 150.35; r.d. 7.52 (20°C); m.p. 1073°C; b.p. 1791°C. It occurs in monazite and bastnatite. There are seven naturally occurring isotopes, all of which are stable except samarium-147, which is weakly radioactive (half-life 2.5×10^{11} years). The metal is used in special alloys for making nuclear-reactor parts as it is a neutron absorber. Samarium oxide (Sm_2O_3) is used in small quantities in special optical glasses. The largest use of the element is in the ferromagnetic alloy $SmCo_5$, which produces permanent magnets five times stronger than any other material. The element was discovered by François Lecoq de Boisbaudran in 1879.

sand Particles of rock with diameters in the range 0.06–2.00 mm. Most sands are composed chiefly of particles of quartz, which are derived from the weathering of quartz-bearing rocks.

Sandmeyer reaction A reaction of diazonium salts used to prepare chloro- or bromo-substituted aromatic compounds. The method is to diazotize an aromatic amide at low temperature and add an equimolar solution of the halogen acid and copper(I) halide. A complex of the diazonium salt and copper halide forms, which decomposes when the temperature is raised. The copper halide acts as a catalyst in the reaction of the halide ions from the acid, for example

$$C_6H_5N_2{}^+(aq) + Cl^-(aq) + CuCl(aq) \rightarrow C_6H_5Cl(l) + N_2(g) + CuCl(aq)$$

The reaction was discovered in 1884 by the German chemist Traugott Sandmeyer (1854–1922). *See also* Gattermann reaction.

sandwich compound A transition-metal complex in which a metal atom or ion is 'sandwiched' between two rings of atoms. *Ferrocene was the first such compound to be prepared. *See also* metallocene.

saponification The reaction of esters with alkalis to give alcohols and salts of carboxylic acids:

$$RCOOR' + OH^- \rightarrow RCOO^- + R'OH$$

See esterification; soap.

sapphire Any of the gem varieties of *corundum except ruby, especially the blue variety, but other colours of sapphire include yellow, brown, green, pink, orange, and purple. Sapphires are obtained from igneous and metamorphic rocks and from alluvial deposits. The chief sources are Sri Lanka, Kashmir, Burma, Thailand, East Africa, the USA, and Australia. Sapphires are used as gemstones and record-player styluses. They are synthesized by the Verneuil flame-fusion process.

saturated 1. (of a compound) Consisting of molecules that have only single bonds (i.e. no double or triple bonds). Saturated compounds can undergo substitution reactions but not addition reactions. *Compare* unsaturated. **2.** (of a solution) Containing the maximum equilibrium amount of solute at a given temperature. In a saturated solution the dissolved substance is in equilibrium with undissolved substance; i.e. the rate at which solute particles leave the solution is exactly balanced by the rate at which they dissolve. A solution containing less than the equilibrium amount is said to be *unsaturated*. One containing more than the equilibrium amount is *supersaturated*. Supersaturated solutions can be made by slowly cooling a saturated solution. Such solutions are metastable; if a small crystal seed is added the excess solute crystallizes out of solution. **3.** (of a vapour) *See* vapour pressure.

saturation *See* supersaturation.

***s*-block elements** The elements of the first two main groups of the *periodic table; i.e. groups IA (Li, Na, K, Rb, Cs, Fr) and IIA (Be, Mg, Ca, Sr, Ba, Ra). The outer electronic configurations of these elements all have inert-gas structures plus outer ns^1 (IA) or ns^2 (IIA) electrons. The term thus excludes elements with incomplete inner *d*-levels (transition metals) or with incomplete inner *f*-levels (lanthanoids and actinoids) even though these often have outer ns^2 or occasionally ns^1 configurations. Typically, the *s*-block elements are reactive metals forming stable ionic compounds containing M^+ or M^{2+} ions. *See* alkali metals; alkaline-earth metals.

scandium Symbol Sc. A rare soft silvery metallic element belonging to group IIIB of the periodic table; a.n. 21; r.a.m. 44.956; r.d. 2.985 (alpha form), 3.19 (beta form); m.p. 1540°C; b.p. 2850°C. Scandium often occurs in *lanthanoid ores, from which it can be separated on account of the greater solubility of its thiocyanate in ether. The only natural isotope, which is not radioactive, is scandium-45, and there are nine radioactive isotopes, all with relatively short half-lives. Because of the metal's high reactivity and high cost no substantial uses have been found for either the metal or its compounds. Predicted in 1869 by Mendeleev, and then called *ekaboron*, the oxide (called *scandia*) was isolated by Nilson in 1879.

scanning electron microscope *See* electron microscope.

scheelite A mineral form of calcium tungstate, $CaWO_4$, used as an ore of tungsten. It occurs in contact metamorphosed deposits and vein deposits as colourless or white tetragonal crystals.

Schiff's base A compound formed by a condensation reaction between an aromatic amine and an aldehyde or ketone, for example

$$RNH_2 + R'CHO \rightarrow RN{:}CHR' + H_2O$$

The compounds are often crystalline and are used in organic chemistry for characterizing aromatic amines (by preparing the Schiff's base and measuring the melting point). They are named after the German chemist Hugo Schiff (1834–1915).

Schiff's reagent A reagent used for testing for aldehydes and ketones; it consists of a solution of fuchsin dye that has been decolorized by sulphur dioxide. Aliphatic aldehydes restore the pink immediately, whereas aromatic ketones have no effect on the reagent. Aromatic aldehydes and aliphatic ketones restore the colour slowly.

schönite A mineral form of potassium sulphate, K_2SO_4.

Schrödinger equation An equation used in wave mechanics (*see* quantum mechanics) for the wave function of a particle. The time-independent Schrödinger equation is

$$\Delta^2\psi + 8\pi^2 m(E - U)\psi/h^2 = 0$$

where ψ is the wave function; Δ^2 the Laplace operator, h the Planck constant, m the particle's mass, E its total energy, and U its potential energy.

secondary alcohol *See* alcohols.

secondary amine *See* amines.

secondary cell A *voltaic cell in which the chemical reaction producing the e.m.f. is reversible and the cell can therefore be charged by passing a current through it. *See* accumulator. *Compare* primary cell.

second-order reaction *See* order.

sedimentation The settling of the solid particles through a liquid either to produce a concentrated slurry from a dilute suspension or to clarify a liquid containing solid particles. Usually this relies on the force of gravity, but if the particles are too small or the difference in density between the solid and liquid phases is too small, a *centrifuge may be used. In the simplest case the rate of sedimentation is determined by Stokes's law, but in practice the predicted rate is rarely reached. Measurement of the rate of sedimentation in an *ultracentrifuge can be used to estimate the size of macromolecules.

seed A crystal used to induce other crystals to form from a gas, liquid, or solution.

Seger cones (pyrometric cones) A series of cones used to indicate the temperature inside a furnace or kiln. The cones are made from different mixtures of clay, limestone, feldspars, etc., and each one softens at a different temperature. The drooping of the vertex is an indication that the known softening temperature has been reached and thus the furnace temperature can be estimated.

selenides Binary compounds of selenium with other more electropositive elements. Selenides of nonmetals are covalent (e.g. H_2Se). Most metal selenides can be prepared by direct combination of the elements. Some are well-defined ionic compounds (containing Se^{2-}), while others are nonstoichiometric interstitial compounds (e.g. Pd_4Se, $PdSe_2$).

selenium Symbol Se. A metalloid element belonging to group VI of the periodic table; a.n. 34; r.a.m. 78.96; r.d. 4.79 (grey); m.p. 217°C (grey); b.p. 684.9°C. There are a number of allotropic forms, including grey, red, and black selenium. It occurs in sulphide ores of other metals and is obtained as a by-product (e.g. from the anode sludge in electrolytic refining). The element is a semiconductor; the grey allotrope is light-sensitive and is used in photocells, xerography, and similar applications. Chemically, it resembles sulphur, and forms compounds with selenium in the +2, +4, and +6 oxidation states. Selenium was discovered in 1817 by J. J. Berzelius.

selenium cell Either of two types of *photoelectric cell; one type relies on the photoconductive effect, the other on the photovoltaic effect (*see* photoelectric effect). In the photoconductive selenium cell an external e.m.f. must be applied; as the selenium changes its resistance on exposure to light, the current produced is a measure of the light energy falling on the selenium. In the photovoltaic selenium cell, the e.m.f. is generated within the cell. In this type of cell, a thin film of vitreous or metallic selenium is applied to a metal surface, a transparent film of another metal, usually gold or platinum, being placed over the selenium. Both types of cell are used as light meters in photography.

Seliwanoff's test A biochemical test to identify the presence of ketonic sugars, such as fructose, in solution. It was devised by the Russian chemist F. F. Seliwanoff. A few drops of the reagent, consisting of resorcinol crystals dissolved in equal amounts of water and hydrochloric acid, are heated with the test solution and the formation of a red precipitate indicates a positive result.

semicarbazones Organic compounds containing the unsaturated group $=C{:}N.NH.CO.NH_2$. They are formed when aldehydes or ketones react with semicarbazide ($H_2N.NH.CO.NH_2$). Semicarbazones are crystalline compounds with relatively high melting points. They are used to identify aldehydes and ketones in quantitative analysis: the semicarbazone derivative is made and identified by its melting point. Semicarbazones are also used in separating ketones from reaction mixtures: the derivative is crystallized out and hydrolysed to give the ketone.

semimetal *See* metalloid.

semipermeable membrane A membrane that is permeable to molecules of the solvent but not the solute in *osmosis. Semipermeable membranes can be made by supporting a film of material (e.g. cellulose) on a wire gauze or porous pot.

semipolar bond *See* chemical bond.

septivalent (heptavalent) Having a valency of seven.

sequestration The process of forming coordination complexes of an ion in solution. Sequestration often involves the formation of chelate complexes, and is used to prevent the chemical effect of an ion without removing it from the solution (e.g. the sequestration of Ca^{2+} ions in water softening). It is also used as a way of supplying ions in a protected form, e.g. the use of sequestered iron solutions for plants in regions having alkaline soil.

serine *See* amino acid.

serpentine Any of a group of hydrous magnesium silicate minerals with the general composition $Mg_3Si_2O_5(OH)_4$. Serpentine is monoclinic and occurs in two main forms: *chrysotile*, which is fibrous and the chief source of *asbestos; and *antigorite*, which occurs as platy masses. It is generally green or white with a mottled appearance, sometimes resembling a snakeskin – hence the name. It is formed through the metamorphic alteration of ultrabasic rocks rich in olivine, pyroxene, and amphibole. *Serpentinite* is a rock consisting mainly of serpentine; it is used as an ornamental stone.

sesqui- Prefix indicating a ratio of 2:3 in a chemical compound. For example, a sesquioxide has the formula M_2O_3.

sexivalent (hexavalent) Having a valency of six.

sherardizing The process of coating iron or steel with a zinc corrosion-resistant layer by heating the iron or steel in contact with zinc dust to a temperature slightly below the melting point of zinc. At a temperature of about 371°C the two metals amalgamate to form internal layers of zinc–iron alloys and an external layer of pure zinc. The process was invented by Sherard Cowper-Coles (d. 1935).

short period *See* periodic table.

sial The rocks that form the earth's continental crust. These are granite rock types rich in *si*lica (SiO_2) and *al*uminium (Al), hence the name. *Compare* sima.

side chain *See* chain.

side reaction A chemical reaction that occurs at the same time as a main reaction but to a lesser extent, thus leading to other products mixed with the main products.

siderite A brown or grey-green mineral form of iron(II) carbonate, $FeCO_3$, often with magnesium and manganese substituting for the iron. It occurs in sedimentary deposits or in hydrothermal veins and is an important iron ore. It is found in England, Greenland, Spain, N Africa, and the USA.

siemens Symbol S. The SI unit of electrical conductance equal to the conductance of a circuit or element that has a resistance of 1 ohm. $1\ S = 10^{-1}\ \Omega$. The unit was formerly called the mho or reciprocal ohm. It is named after Sir William Siemens (1823–83).

sievert The SI unit of dose equivalent (*see* radiation units).

sigma electron An electron in a sigma orbital. *See* orbital.

silane (silicane) 1. A colourless gas, SiH_4, which is insoluble in water; d. 1.44 g dm^{-3}; r.d. 0.68 (liquid); m.p. −185°C; b.p. −112°C. Silane is produced by reduction of silicon tetrachloride using lithium tetrahydridoaluminate(III). It is also formed by the reaction of magnesium silicide (Mg_2Si) with acids, although other silicon hydrides are also produced at the same time. Silane itself is stable in the absence of air but is spontaneously flammable, even at low temperatures. It is used for controlled silicon doping of semiconductors in the electronics industry. It is also a reducing agent and has been used for the removal of corrosion in inaccessible plants (e.g. pipes in nuclear reactors). **2.** (*or* **silicon hydride)** Any of a class of compounds of silicon and hydrogen. They have the general formula Si_nH_{2n+2}. The first three in the series are silane itself (SiH_4), *disilane* (Si_2H_6), and *trisilane* (Si_3H_8). The compounds are analogous to the alkanes but are much less stable and only the lower members of the series can be prepared in any quantity (up to Si_6H_{14}). No silicon hydrides containing double or triple bonds exist (i.e. there are no analogues of the alkenes and alkynes).

silica *See* silicon(IV) oxide.

silica gel A rigid gel made by coagulating a sol of sodium silicate and heating to drive off water. It is used as a support for catalysts and also as a drying agent because it readily absorbs moisture from the air. The gel itself is colourless but, when used in desiccators, etc., a blue cobalt salt is added. As moisture is taken up, the salt turns pink, indicating that the gel needs to be regenerated (by heating).

silicane *See* silane.

silicate Any of a group of substances containing negative ions composed of silicon and oxygen. The silicates are a very extensive group and natural silicates form the major component of most rocks (*see* silicate minerals). The basic structural unit is the tetrahedral SiO_4 group. This may occur as a simple discrete $SiO_4{}^{4-}$ anion as in the *orthosilicates*, e.g. *phenacite* (Be_2SiO_4) and *willemite* (Zn_2SiO_4). Many larger silicate species are also found. These are composed of SiO_4 tetrahedra linked by sharing oxygen atoms as in the *pyrosilicates*, $Si_2O_7{}^{6-}$, e.g. $Sc_2Si_2O_7$. The linking can extend to such forms as benitoite, $BaTiSi_3O_9$, or alternatively infinite chain anions, which are single strand (*pyroxenes) or double strand (*amphiboles). Spodumene, $LiAl(SiO_3)_2$, is a pyroxene and the asbestos minerals are amphiboles. Infinite two-dimensional sheets are also possible, as in the various *micas and the linking can extend to full three-dimensional framework structures, often with substituted trivalent atoms in the lattice. The *zeolites are examples of this.

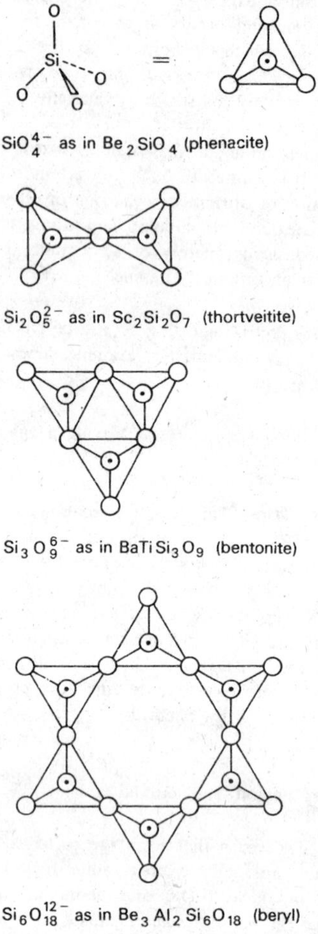

Structure of some discrete silicon ions

silicate minerals A group of rock-forming minerals that make up the bulk of the earth's outer crust (about 90%) and constitute one-third of all minerals. All silicate minerals are based on a fundamental structural unit – the SiO_4 tetrahedron (*see* silicate). They consist of a metal (e.g. calcium, magnesium, aluminium) combined with silicon and oxygen. The silicate minerals are classified on a structural basis according to how the tetrahedra are linked together. The six groups are: nesosilicates (e.g. olivine and *garnet); sorosilicates (e.g. hemimorphite); cyclosilicates (e.g. axinite, *beryl, and *tourmaline); inosilicates (e.g. *amphiboles and *pyroxenes); phyllosilicates (e.g. *micas, *clay minerals, and *talc); and tektosilicates (e.g. *feldspars and *feldspathoids). Many

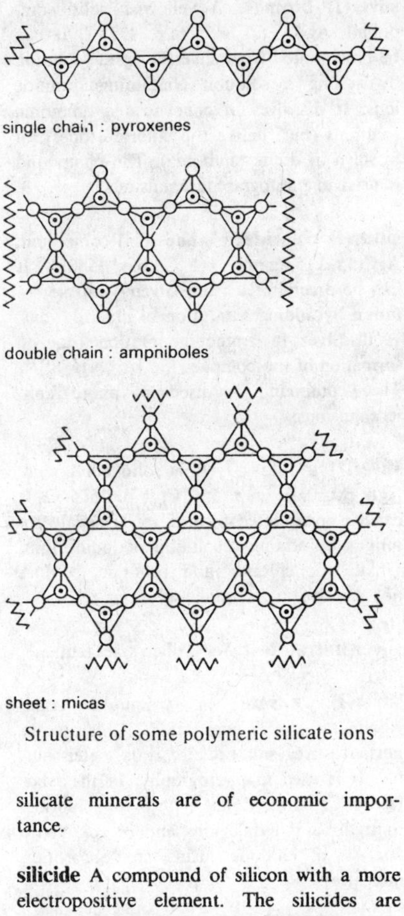

Structure of some polymeric silicate ions

silicate minerals are of economic importance.

silicide A compound of silicon with a more electropositive element. The silicides are structurally similar to the interstitial carbides but the range encountered is more diverse. They react with mineral acids to form a range of *silanes.

silicon Symbol Si. A metalloid element belonging to *group IV of the periodic table; a.n. 14; r.a.m. 28.086; r.d. 2.33; m.p. 1410°C; b.p. 2355°C. Silicon is the second most abundant element in the earth's crust (25.7% by weight) occurring in various forms of silicon(IV) oxide (e.g. *quartz) and in *silicate minerals. The element is extracted by reducing the oxide with carbon in an electric furnace and is used extensively for its semiconductor properties. It has a diamond-like crystal structure; an amorphous form also exists. Chemically, silicon is less reactive than carbon. The element combines with oxygen at red heat and is also dissolved by molten alkali. There is a large number of organosilicon compounds (e.g. *siloxanes) although silicon does not form the range of silicon–hydrogen compounds and derivatives that carbon does (*see* silanes). The element was identified by Lavoisier in 1787 and first isolated in 1823 by Berzelius.

silicon carbide (carborundum) A black solid compound, SiC, insoluble in water and soluble in molten alkali; r.d. 3.217; m.p. *c.* 2700°C. Silicon carbide is made by heating silicon(IV) oxide with carbon in an electric furnace (depending on the grade required sand and coke may be used). It is extremely hard and is widely used as an abrasive. The solid exists in both zinc blende and wurtzite structures.

silicon dioxide *See* silicon(IV) oxide.

silicones Polymeric compounds containing chains of silicon atoms alternating with oxygen atoms, with the silicon atoms linked to organic groups. A variety of silicone materials exist, including oils, waxes, and rubbers. They tend to be more resistant to temperature and chemical attack than their carbon analogues.

silicon hydride *See* silane.

silicon(IV) oxide (silicon dioxide; silica) A colourless or white vitreous solid, SiO_2, insoluble in water and soluble (by reaction) in hydrofluoric acid and in strong alkali; m.p. 1610°C; b.p. 2230°C. The following forms occur naturally: *cristobalite* (cubic or tetragonal crystals; r.d. 2.32); *tridymite* (rhombic; r.d. 2.26); *quartz (hexagonal; r.d.

2.63–2.66); *lechatelierite* (r.d. 2.19). Quartz has two modifications: α-quartz below 575°C and β-quartz above 575°C; above 870°C β-quartz is slowly transformed to tridymite and above 1470°C this is slowly converted to cristobalite. Various forms of silicon(IV) oxide occur widely in the earth's crust; yellow sand for example is quartz with iron(III) oxide impurities and flint is essentially amorphous silica. The gemstones amethyst, opal, and rock crystal are also forms of quartz.

Silica is an important commercial material in the form of *silica brick*, a highly refractive furnace lining, which is also resistant to abrasion and to corrosion. Silicon(IV) oxide is also the basis of both clear and opaque silica glass, which is used on account of its transparency to ultraviolet radiation and its resistance to both thermal and mechanical shock. A certain proportion of silicon(IV) oxide is also used in ordinary glass and in some glazes and enamels. It also finds many applications as a drying agent in the form of *silica gel.

siloxanes A group of compounds containing silicon atoms bound to oxygen atoms, with organic groups linked to the silicon atoms, e.g. $R_3SiOSiR_3$, where R is an organic group. *Silicones are polymers of siloxanes.

silver Symbol Ag. A white lustrous soft metallic *transition element; a.n. 47; r.a.m. 107.87; r.d. 10.5; m.p. 961.93°C; b.p. 2212°C. It occurs as the element and as the minerals argentite (Ag_2S) and horn silver (AgCl). It is also present in ores of lead and copper, and is extracted as a by-product of smelting and refining these metals. The element is used in jewellery, tableware, etc., and silver compounds are used in photography. Chemically, silver is less reactive than copper. A dark silver sulphide forms when silver tarnishes in air because of the presence of sulphur compounds. Silver(I) ionic salts exist (e.g. $AgNO_3$, AgCl) and there are a number of silver(II) complexes.

silver(I) bromide A yellowish solid compound, AgBr; r.d. 6.5; m.p. 432°C. It can be precipitated from silver(I) nitrate solution by adding a solution containing bromide ions. It dissolves in concentrated ammonia solutions (but, unlike the chloride, does not dissolve in dilute ammonia). The compound is used in photographic emulsions.

silver(I) chloride A white solid compound, AgCl; r.d. 5.6; m.p. 445°C; b.p. 1550°C. It can be precipitated from silver(I) nitrate solution by adding a solution of chloride ions. It dissolves in ammonia solution (due to formation of the complex ion $[Ag(NH_3)_2]^+$). The compound is used in photographic emulsions.

silver(I) iodide A yellow solid compound, AgI; r.d. 6.01; m.p. 556°C; b.p. 1506°C. It can be precipitated from silver(I) nitrate solutions by adding a solution of iodide ions. Unlike the chloride and bromide, it does not dissolve in ammonia solutions.

silver-mirror test *See* Tollen's reagent.

silver(I) nitrate A colourless solid, $AgNO_3$; r.d. 4.3; m.p. 212°C. It is an important silver salt because it is water-soluble. It is used in photography. In the laboratory, it is used as a test for chloride, bromide, and iodide ions and in volumetric analysis of chlorides using an *absorption indicator.

silver(I) oxide A brown slightly water-soluble amorphous powder, Ag_2O; r.d. 7.14. It can be made by adding sodium hydroxide solution to silver(I) nitrate solution. Silver(I) oxide is strongly basic and is also an oxidizing agent. It is used in certain reactions in preparative organic chemistry; for example, moist silver(I) oxide converts haloalkanes into alcohols; dry silver oxide converts haloalkanes into ethers. The compound decomposes to the elements at 160°C and can be reduced by hydrogen to silver. With ozone it gives the oxide AgO (which is diamagnetic and probably $Ag^{I}Ag^{III}O_2$).

sima The rocks that form the earth's oceanic crust and underlie the upper crust. These are basaltic rock types rich in *si*lica (SiO_2) and *ma*gnesium (Mg), hence the name. The sima is denser and more plastic than the *sial that forms the continental crust.

single bond *See* chemical bond.

sintered glass Porous glass made by sintering powdered glass, used for filtration of precipitates in gravimetric analysis.

sintering The process of heating and compacting a powdered material at a temperature below its melting point in order to weld the particles together into a single rigid shape. Materials commonly sintered include metals and alloys, glass, and ceramic oxides. Sintered magnetic materials, cooled in a magnetic field, make especially retentive permanent magnets.

SI units Système International d'Unités: the international system of units now recommended for all scientific purposes. A coherent and rationalized system of units derived from the *m.k.s. units, SI units have now replaced *c.g.s. units and *Imperial units. The system has seven *base units* and two *supplementary units* (see Appendix), all other units being derived from these nine units. There are 18 derived units with special names. Each unit has an agreed symbol (a capital letter or an initial capital letter if it is named after a scientist, otherwise the symbol consists of one or two lower-case letters). Decimal multiples of the units are indicated by a set of prefixes; whenever possible a prefix representing 10 raised to a power that is a multiple of three should be used.

slag Material produced during the *smelting or refining of metals by reaction of the flux with impurities (e.g. calcium silicate formed by reaction of calcium oxide flux with silicon dioxide impurities). The liquid slag can be separated from the liquid metal because it floats on the surface. *See also* basic slag.

slaked lime *See* calcium hydroxide.

slurry A paste consisting of a suspension of a solid in a liquid.

smectic *See* liquid crystal.

smelting The process of separating a metal from its ore by heating the ore to a high temperature in a suitable furnace in the presence of a reducing agent, such as carbon, and a fluxing agent, such as limestone. Iron ore is smelted in this way so that the metal melts and, being denser than the molten *slag, sinks below the slag, enabling it to be removed from the furnace separately.

smoke A fine suspension of solid particles in a gas.

S_N1 reaction *See* nucleophilic substitution.

S_N2 reaction *See* nucleophilic substitution.

SNG Substitute (or synthetic) natural gas; a mixture of gaseous hydrocarbons produced from coal, petroleum, etc., and suitable for use as a fuel. Before the discovery of natural gas *coal gas was widely used as a domestic and industrial fuel. This gave way to natural gas in the early part of this century in the US and other countries where natural gas was plentiful. The replacement of coal gas occurred somewhat later in the UK and other parts of Europe. More recently, interest has developed in ways of manufacturing hydrocarbon gas fuels. The main sources are coal and the naphtha fraction of petroleum. In the case of coal three methods have been used: (1) pyrolysis – i.e. more efficient forms of destructive distillation, often with further hydrogenation of the hydrocarbon products; (2) heating the coal with hydrogen and catalysts to give hydrocarbons – a process known as *hydroliquefaction* (*see also* Bergius process); (3) producing carbon monoxide and hydrogen and obtaining hydrocarbons by the *Fischer–Tropsch process. SNG from naptha is made by steam *reforming.

soap A substance made by boiling animal fats with sodium hydroxide. The reaction involves the hydrolysis of *glyceride esters of fatty acids to glycerol and sodium salts of the acids present (mainly the stearate, oleate, and palmitate), giving a soft semisolid with *detergent action. Potassium hydroxide gives a more liquid product (*soft soap*). By extension, other metal salts of long-chain fatty acids are also called soaps. *See also* saponification.

soda Any of a number of sodium compounds, such as caustic soda (NaOH) or, especially, washing soda ($Na_2CO_3.10H_2O$).

soda ash Anhydrous *sodium carbonate, Na_2CO_3.

soda lime A mixed hydroxide of sodium and calcium made by slaking lime with caustic soda solution (to give NaOH + Ca $(OH)_2$) and recovering greyish white granules by evaporation. The material is produced largely for industrial adsorption of carbon dioxide and water, but also finds some applications in pollution and effluent control. It is also used as a laboratory drying agent.

sodamide *See* sodium amide.

sodium Symbol Na. A soft silvery reactive element belonging to group I of the periodic table (*see* alkali metals); a.n. 11; r.a.m. 22.9898; r.d. 0.97; m.p. 97.5°C; b.p. 892°C. Sodium occurs as the chloride in sea water and in the mineral halite. It is extracted by electrolysis in a *Downs cell. The metal is used as a reducing agent in certain reactions and liquid sodium is also a coolant in nuclear reactors. Chemically, it is highly reactive, oxidizing in air and reacting violently with water (it is kept under oil). It dissolves in liquid ammonia to form blue solutions containing solvated electrons. Sodium is a major element required by living organisms. The element was first isolated by Humphry Davy in 1807.

sodium acetate *See* sodium ethanoate.

sodium aluminate A white solid, $NaAlO_2$ or $Na_2Al_2O_4$, which is insoluble in ethanol and soluble in water giving strongly alkaline solutions; m.p. 1800°C. It is manufactured by heating bauxite with sodium carbonate and extracting the residue with water, or it may be prepared in the laboratory by adding excess aluminium to hot concentrated sodium hydroxide. In solution the ion $Al(OH)_4^-$ predominates. Sodium aluminate is used as a mordant, in the production of zeolites, in effluent treatment, in glass manufacture, and in cleansing compounds.

sodium amide (sodamide) A white crystalline powder, $NaNH_2$, which decomposes in water and in warm ethanol, and has an odour of ammonia; m.p. 210°C; b.p. 400°C. It is produced by passing dry ammonia over metallic sodium at 350°C. It reacts with red-hot carbon to give sodium cyanide and with nitrogen(I) oxide to give sodium azide.

sodium azide A white or colourless crystalline solid, NaN_3, soluble in water and slightly soluble in alcohol; hexagonal; r.d. 1.846; decomposes on heating. It is made by the action of nitrogen(I) oxide on hot sodamide ($NaNH_2$) and is used as an organic reagent and in the manufacture of detonators.

sodium benzenecarboxylate (sodium benzoate) A colourless crystalline or white amorphous powder, C_6H_5COONa, soluble in water and slightly soluble in ethanol. It is made by the reaction of sodium hydroxide with benzoic acid and is used in the dyestuffs industry and as a food preservative. It was formerly used as an antiseptic.

sodium benzoate *See* sodium benzenecarboxylate.

sodium bicarbonate *See* sodium hydrogencarbonate.

sodium bisulphate *See* sodium hydrogensulphate.

sodium bisulphite *See* sodium hydrogensulphite.

sodium bromide A white crystalline solid, NaBr, known chiefly as the dihydrate (monoclinic; r.d. 2.17), and as the anhydrous salt (cubic; r.d. 3.20; m.p. 747°C; b.p. 1390°C). The dihydrate loses water at about 52°C and is very slightly soluble in alcohol. Sodium bromide is prepared by the reaction of bromine on hot sodium hydroxide solution or of hydrogen bromide on sodium carbonate solution. It is a sedative and is also used in photographic processing and in analytical chemistry.

sodium carbonate Anhydrous sodium carbonate (*soda ash, sal soda*) is a white powder, which cakes and aggregates on exposure to air due to the formation of hydrates. The monohydrate, $Na_2CO_3.H_2O$, is a white crystalline material, which is soluble in water and insoluble in alcohol; r.d. 1.55; loses water at 109°C; m.p. 851°C. The decahydrate, $Na_2CO_3.10H_2O$, (*washing soda*) is a translucent efflorescent crystalline solid; r.d. 1.44; loses water at 32–34°C to give the monohydrate; m.p. 851°C. Sodium carbonate may be manufactured by the *Solvay process or by suitable crystallization procedures from any one of a number of natural deposits, such as:

trona $5(Na_2CO_3.NaHCO_3.2H_2O)$,
natron $(Na_2CO_3.10H_2O)$,
ranksite $(2Na_2CO_3.9Na_2SO_4.KCl)$,
pirsonnite $(Na_2CO_3.CaCO_3.2H_2O)$, and
gaylussite $(Na_2CO_3.CaCO_3.5H_2O)$.

The method of extraction is very sensitive to the relative energy costs and transport costs in the region involved. Sodium carbonate is used in photography, in cleaning, in pH control of water, in textile treatment, glasses and glazes, and as a food additive and volumetric reagent. *See also* sodium sesquicarbonate.

sodium chlorate(V) A white crystalline solid, $NaClO_3$; cubic; r.d. 2.49; m.p. 250°C. It decomposes above its melting point to give oxygen and sodium chloride. The compound is soluble in water and in ethanol and is prepared by the reaction of chlorine on hot concentrated sodium hydroxide. Sodium chlorate is a powerful oxidizing agent and is used in the manufacture of matches and soft explosives, in calico printing, and as a garden weedkiller.

sodium chloride (common salt) A colourless crystalline solid, NaCl, soluble in water and very slightly soluble in ethanol; cubic; r.d. 2.17; m.p. 801°C; b.p. 1413°C. It occurs as the mineral *halite (rock salt) and in natural brines and sea water. It has the interesting property of a solubility in water that changes very little with temperature. It is used industrially as the starting point for a range of sodium-based products (e.g. Solvay process for Na_2CO_3, Castner–Kellner process for NaOH), and is known universally as a preservative and seasoner of foods. Sodium chloride has a key role in biological systems in maintaining electrolyte balances.

sodium cyanide A white or colourless crystalline solid, NaCN, deliquescent, soluble in water and in liquid ammonia, and slightly soluble in ethanol; cubic; m.p. 564°C; b.p. 1496°C. Sodium cyanide is now made by absorbing hydrogen cyanide in sodium hydroxide or sodium carbonate solution. The compound is extremely poisonous because it reacts with the iron in haemoglobin in the blood, so preventing oxygen reaching the tissues of the body. It is used in the extraction of precious metals and in electroplating industries. Aqueous solutions are alkaline due to salt hydrolysis.

sodium dichromate A red crystalline solid, $Na_2Cr_2O_7.2H_2O$, soluble in water and insoluble in ethanol. It is usually known as the dihydrate (r.d. 2.52), which starts to lose water above 100°C; the compound decomposes above 400°C. It is made by melting chrome iron ore with lime and soda ash and acidification of the chromate thus formed. Sodium dichromate is cheaper than the corresponding potassium compound but has the disadvantage of being hygroscopic. It is used as a mordant in dyeing, as an oxidizing agent in organic chemistry, and in analytical chemistry.

sodium dihydrogenorthophosphate *See* sodium dihydrogenphosphate(V).

sodium dihydrogenphosphate(V) (sodium dihydrogenorthophosphate) A colourless crystalline solid, NaH_2PO_4, soluble in water and insoluble in alcohol, known as the monohydrate (r.d. 2.04) and the dihydrate (r.d. 1.91). The dihydrate loses one water molecule at 60°C and the second molecule of water at 100°C, followed by decomposition at 204°C. The compound may be prepared by treating sodium carbonate with an equimolar quantity of phosphoric acid or by neutralizing phosphoric acid with sodium hydroxide. It is used in the preparation of sodium phosphate (Na_3PO_4), in baking powders, as a food additive, and as a constituent of buffering systems. Both sodium dihydrogenphosphate and trisodium phosphate enriched in ^{32}P have been used to study phosphate participation in metabolic processes.

sodium dioxide *See* sodium superoxide.

sodium ethanoate (sodium acetate) A colourless crystalline compound, CH_3COONa, which is known as the anhydrous salt (r.d. 1.52; m.p. 324°C) or the trihydrate (r.d. 1.45; loses water at 58°C). Both forms are soluble in water and in ethoxyethane, and slightly soluble in ethanol. The compound may be prepared by the reaction of ethanoic acid (acetic acid) with sodium carbonate or with sodium hydroxide. Because it is a salt of a strong base and a weak acid, sodium ethanoate is used in buffers for pH control in many laboratory applications, in foodstuffs, and in electroplating. It is also used in dyeing, soaps, pharmaceuticals, and in photography.

sodium fluoride A crystalline compound, NaF, soluble in water and very slightly soluble in ethanol; cubic; r.d. 2.56; m.p. 993°C; b.p. 1695°C. It occurs naturally as villiaumite and may be prepared by the reaction of sodium hydroxide or of sodium carbonate with hydrogen fluoride. The reaction of sodium fluoride with concentrated sulphuric acid may be used as a source of hydrogen fluoride. The compound is used in ceramic enamels and as a preservative agent for fermentation. It is highly toxic but in very dilute solution (less than 1 part per million) it is used in the fluoridation of water for the prevention of tooth decay on account of its ability to replace OH groups with F groups in the material of dental enamel.

sodium formate *See* sodium methanoate.

sodium hexafluoraluminate A colourless monoclinic solid, Na_3AlF_6, very slightly soluble in water; r.d. 2.9; m.p. 1000°C. It changes to a cubic form at 580°C. The compound occurs naturally as the mineral *cryolite but a considerable amount is manufactured by the reaction of aluminium fluoride wth alumina and sodium hydroxide or directly with sodium aluminate. Its most important use is in the manufacture of aluminium in the *Hall–Heroult cell. It is also used in the manufacture of enamels, opaque glasses, and ceramic glazes.

sodium hydride A white crystalline solid, NaH; cubic; r.d. 0.92; decomposes above 300°C (slow); completely decomposed at 800°C. Sodium hydride is prepared by the reaction of pure dry hydrogen with sodium at 350°C. Electrolysis of sodium hydride in molten LiCl/KCl leads to the evolution of hydrogen; this is taken as evidence for the ionic nature of NaH and the presence of the hydride ion (H^-). It reacts violently with water to give sodium hydroxide and hydrogen, with halogens to give the halide and appropriate hydrogen halide, and ignites spontaneously with oxygen at 230°C. It is a powerful reducing agent with several laboratory applications.

sodium hydrogencarbonate (bicarbonate of soda; sodium bicarbonate) A white crystalline solid, $NaHCO_3$, soluble in water and slightly soluble in ethanol; monoclinic; r.d. 2.159; loses carbon dioxide above 270°C. It is manufactured in the *Solvay process and may be prepared in the laboratory by passing carbon dioxide through sodium carbonate or sodium hydroxide solution. Sodium hydrogencarbonate reacts with acids to give carbon dioxide and, as it does not have strongly corrosive or strongly basic properties itself, it is employed in bulk for the treatment of acid spillage and in medicinal applications as an antacid. Sodium hydrogencarbonate is also used in baking powders (and is known as *baking soda*), dry-powder fire extinguishers, and in the textiles, tanning, paper, and ceramics industries. The hydrogencarbonate ion has an important biological role as an intermediate between atmospheric CO_2/H_2CO_3 and the carbonate ion $CO_3{}^{2-}$. For water-living organisms this is the most important and in some cases the only source of carbon.

sodium hydrogensulphate (sodium bisulphate) A colourless solid, $NaHSO_4$, known in anhydrous and monohydrate forms. The anhydrous solid is triclinic (r.d. 2.435; m.p. >315°C). The monohydrate is monoclinic and deliquescent (r.d. 2.103; m.p. 59°C). Both forms are soluble in water and slightly soluble in alcohol. Sodium hydrogensulphate was originally made by the reaction between sodium nitrate and sulphuric acid, hence its old name of *nitre cake*. It may be manufactured by the reaction of sodium hydroxide with sulphuric acid, or by heating equimolar proportions of sodium chloride and concentrated sulphuric acid. Solutions of sodium hydrogensulphate are acidic. On heating the compound decomposes (via $Na_2S_2O_7$) to give sulphur trioxide. It is used in paper making, glass making, and textile finishing.

sodium hydrogensulphite (sodium bisulphite) A white solid, $NaHSO_3$, which is very soluble in water (yellow in solution) and slightly soluble in ethanol; monoclinic; r.d. 1.48. It decomposes on heating to give sodium sulphate, sulphur dioxide, and sulphur. It is formed by saturating a solution of sodium carbonate with sulphur dioxide. The compound is used in the brewing industry and in the sterilization of wine casks. It is a general antiseptic and bleaching agent. *See also* aldehydes.

sodium hydroxide (caustic soda) A white transluscent deliquescent solid, NaOH, soluble in water and ethanol but insoluble in ether; r.d. 2.13; m.p. 318°C; b.p. 1390°C. Hydrates containing 7, 5, 4, 3.5, 3, 2, and 1 molecule of water are known.

Sodium hydroxide was formerly made by the treatment of sodium carbonate with lime but its main source today is from the electrolysis of brine using mercury cells or any of a variety of diaphragm cells. The principal product demanded from these cells is chlorine (for use in plastics) and sodium hydroxide is almost reduced to the status of a by-product. It is strongly alkaline and finds many applications in the chemical industry, particularly in the production of soaps and paper. It is also used to adsorb acidic gases, such as carbon dioxide and sulphur dioxide, and is used in the treatment of effluent for the removal of heavy metals (as hydroxides) and of acidity. Sodium hydroxide solutions are extremely corrosive to body tissue and are particularly hazardous to the eyes.

sodium iodide A white crystalline solid, NaI, very soluble in water and soluble in both ethanol and ethanoic acid. It is known in both the anhydrous form (cubic; r.d. 3.67; m.p. 661°C; b.p. 1304°C) and as the dihydrate (monoclinic; r.d. 2.45). It is prepared by the reaction of hydrogen iodide with sodium carbonate or sodium hydroxide in solution. Like potassium iodide, sodium iodide in aqueous solution dissolves iodine to form a brown solution containing the I_3^- ion. It finds applications in photography and is also used in medicine as an expectorant and in the administration of radioactive iodine for studies of thyroid function and for treatment of diseases of the thyroid.

sodium methanoate (sodium formate) A colourless deliquescent solid, HCOONa, soluble in water and slightly soluble in ethanol; monoclinic; r.d. 1.92; m.p. 253°C; decomposes on further heating. The monohydrate is also known. The compound may be produced by the reaction of carbon monoxide with solid sodium hydroxide at 200°C and 10 atmospheres pressure; in the laboratory it can be conveniently prepared by the reaction of methanoic acid and sodium hydroxide. Its uses are in the production of oxalic acid (ethanedioic acid) and methanoic acid and in the laboratory it is a convenient source of carbon monoxide.

sodium monoxide A whitish-grey deliquescent solid, Na_2O; r.d. 2.27; sublimes at 1275°C. It is manufactured by oxidation of the metal in a limited supply of oxygen and purified by sublimation. Reaction with water produces sodium hydroxide. Its commercial applications are similar to those of sodium hydroxide.

sodium nitrate (Chile saltpetre) A white solid, $NaNO_3$, soluble in water and in ethanol; trigonal; r.d. 2.261; m.p. 306°C; decomposes at 380°C. A rhombohedral form is also known. It is obtained from deposits of caliche or may be prepared by the reaction of nitric acid with sodium hydroxide or sodium carbonate. It was previously used for the manufacture of nitric acid by heating with concentrated sulphuric acid. Its main use is in nitrate fertilizers.

sodium nitrite A yellow hygroscopic crystalline compound, $NaNO_2$, soluble in water, slightly soluble in ether and in ethanol; rhombohedral; r.d. 2.17; m.p. 271°C; decomposes above 320°C. It is formed by the thermal decomposition of sodium nitrate and is used in the preparation of nitrous acid (reaction with cold dilute hydrochloric acid). Sodium nitrite is used in organic *diazotization and as a corrosion inhibitor.

sodium orthophosphate *See* trisodium phosphate(V).

sodium peroxide A whitish solid (yellow when hot), Na_2O_2, soluble in ice-water and decomposed in warm water or alcohol; r.d. 2.80; decomposes at 460°C. A crystalline octahydrate (hexagonal) is obtained by crystallization from ice-water. The compound is formed by the combustion of sodium metal in excess oxygen. At normal temperatures it reacts with water to give sodium hydroxide and hydrogen peroxide. It is a powerful oxidizing agent reacting with iodine vapour to give the iodate and periodate, with carbon at 300°C to give the carbonate, and with nitrogen(II) oxide to give the nitrate. It is used as a bleaching agent in wool and yarn processing, in the refining of oils and fats, and in the production of wood pulp.

sodium sesquicarbonate A white crystalline hydrated double salt, $Na_2CO_3.NaHCO_3.2H_2O$, soluble in water but less alkaline than sodium carbonate; r.d. 2.12; decomposes on heating. It may be prepared by crystallizing equimolar quantities of the constituent materials; it also occurs naturally as *trona* and in Searles Lake brines. It is widely used as a detergent and soap builder and, because of its mild alkaline properties, as a water-softening agent and bath-salt base. *See also* sodium carbonate.

sodium sulphate A white crystalline compound, Na_2SO_4, usually known as the anhydrous compound (orthorhombic; r.d. 2.67; m.p. 888°C) or the decahydrate (monoclinic; r.d. 1.46; loses water at 100°C). The decahydrate is known as *Glauber's salt*. A metastable heptahydrate ($Na_2SO_4.7H_2O$) also exists. All forms are soluble in water, dissolving to give a neutral solution. The compound occurs naturally as

mirabilite ($Na_2SO_4.10H_2O$),
threnardite (Na_2SO_4), and
glauberite ($Na_2SO_4.CaSO_4$).

Sodium sulphate may be produced industrially by the reaction of magnesium sulphate with sodium chloride in solution followed by crystallization, or by the reaction of concentrated sulphuric acid with solid sodium chloride. The latter method was used in the *Leblanc process for the production of alkali and has given the name *salt cake* to impure industrial sodium sulphate. Sodium sulphate is used in the manufacture of glass and soft glazes and in dyeing to promote an even finish. It also finds medicinal application as a purgative and in commercial aperient salts.

sodium sulphide A yellow-red solid, Na_2S, formed by the reduction of sodium sulphate with carbon (coke) at elevated temperatures. It is a corrosive and readily oxidized material of variable composition and usually contains polysulphides of the type Na_2S_2, Na_2S_3, and Na_2S_4, which cause the variety of colours. It is known in an anhydrous form (r.d. 1.85; m.p. 1180°C) and as a nonahydrate, $Na_2S.9H_2O$ (r.d. 1.43; decomposes at 920°C). Other hydrates of sodium sulphide have been reported. The compound is deliquescent, soluble in water with extensive hydrolysis, and slightly soluble in alcohol. It is used in wood pulping, dyestuffs manufacture, and metallurgy on account of its reducing properties. It has also been used for the production of sodium thiosulphate (for the photographic industry) and as a depilatory agent in leather preparation. It is a strong skin irritant.

sodium sulphite A white solid, Na_2SO_3, existing in an anhydrous form (r.d. 2.63) and as a heptahydrate (r.d. 1.59). Sodium sulphite is soluble in water and because it is readily oxidized it is widely used as a convenient reducing agent. It is prepared by reacting sulphur dioxide with either sodium carbonate or sodium hydroxide. Dilute mineral acids reverse this process and release sulphur dioxide. Sodium sulphite is used as a bleaching agent in textiles and in paper manufacture. Its use as an antioxidant in some canned foodstuffs gives rise to a slightly sulphurous smell immediately on opening, but its use is prohibited in meats or foods that contain vitamin B_1. Sodium sulphite solutions are occasionally used as biological preservatives.

sodium superoxide (sodium dioxide) A whitish-yellow solid, NaO_2, formed by the reaction of sodium peroxide with excess oxygen at elevated temperatures and pressures. It reacts with water to form hydrogen peroxide and oxygen.

sodium thiosulphate (hypo) A colourless efflorescent solid, $Na_2S_2O_3$, soluble in water but insoluble in ethanol, commonly encountered as the pentahydrate (monoclinic; r.d. 1.73; m.p. 42°C), which loses water at 100°C to give the anhydrous form (r.d. 1.66). It is prepared by the reaction of sulphur dioxide with a suspension of sulphur in boiling sodium hydroxide solution. Aqueous solutions of sodium thiosulphate are readily oxidized in the presence of air to sodium tetrathionate and sodium sulphate. The reaction with dilute acids gives sulphur and sulphur dioxide. It is used in the photographic industry and in analytical chemistry.

soft soap *See* soap.

soft water *See* hardness of water.

sol A *colloid in which small solid particles are dispersed in a liquid continuous phase.

solder An alloy used to join metal surfaces. A *soft solder* melts at a temperature in the range 200–300°C and consists of a tin–lead alloy. The tin content varies between 80% for the lower end of the melting range and 31% for the higher end. *Hard solders* contain substantial quantities of silver in the alloy. *Brazing solders* are usually alloys of copper and zinc, which melt at over 800°C.

solid A state of matter in which there is a three-dimensional regularity of structure, resulting from the proximity of the component atoms, ions, or molecules and the strength of the forces between them. True solids are crystalline (*see also* amorphous). If a crystalline solid is heated, the kinetic energy of the components increases. At a specific temperature, called the *melting point*, the forces between the components become unable to contain them within the crystal structure. At this temperature, the lattice breaks down and the solid becomes a liquid.

solid solution A crystalline material that is a mixture of two or more components, with ions, atoms, or molecules of one component replacing some of the ions, atoms, or molecules of the other component in its normal crystal lattice. Solid solutions are found in certain alloys. For example, gold and copper form solid solutions in which some of the copper atoms in the lattice are replaced by gold atoms. In general, the gold atoms are distributed at random, and a range of gold–copper compositions is possible. At a certain composition, the gold and copper atoms can each form regular individual lattices (referred to as *superlattices*). Mixed crystals of double salts (such as alums) are also examples of solid solutions. Compounds can form solid solutions if they are isomorphous (*see* isomorphism).

solubility The quantity of solute that dissolves in a given quantity of solvent to form a saturated solution. Solubility is measured in kilograms per metre cubed, moles per kilogram of solvent, etc. The solubility of a substance in a given solvent depends on the temperature. Generally, for a solid in a liquid, solubility increases with temperature; for a gas, solubility decreases. *See also* concentration.

solubility product Symbol K_s. The product of the concentrations of ions in a saturated solution. For instance, if a compound A_xB_y is in equilibrium with its solution

$$A_xB_y(s) \rightleftharpoons xA^+(aq) + yB^-(aq)$$

the equilibrium constant is

$$K_c = [A^+]^x[B^-]^y/[A_xB_y]$$

Since the concentration of the undissolved solid can be put equal to 1, the solubility product is given by

$$K_s = [A^+]^x[B^-]^y$$

The expression is only true for sparingly soluble salts. If the product of ionic concentrations in a solution exceeds the solubility product, then precipitation occurs.

solute The substance dissolved in a solvent in forming a *solution.

solution A homogeneous mixture of a liquid (the *solvent) with a gas or solid (the *solute*). In a solution, the molecules of the solute are discrete and mixed with the molecules of solvent. There is usually some interaction between the solvent and solute molecules (*see* solvation). Two liquids that can mix on the molecular level are said to be *miscible*. In this case, the solvent is the major component and the solute the minor component. *See also* solid solution.

solvation The interaction of ions of a solute with the molecules of solvent. For instance, when sodium chloride is dissolved in water the sodium ions attract polar water molecules, with the negative oxygen atoms pointing towards the positive Na^+ ion. Solvation of transition-metal ions can also occur by formation of coordinate bonds, as in the hexaquocopper(II) ion $[Cu(H_2O)_6]^{2+}$. Solvation is the process that causes ionic solids to dissolve, because the energy released compensates for the energy necessary to break down the crystal lattice. It occurs only with polar solvents. Solvation in which the solvent is water is called *hydration*.

Solvay process (ammonia–soda process) An industrial method of making sodium carbonate from calcium carbonate and sodium chloride. The calcium carbonate is first heated to give calcium oxide and carbon dioxide, which is bubbled into a solution of sodium chloride in ammonia. Sodium hydrogencarbonate is precipitated:

$$H_2O + CO_2(g) + NaCl(aq) + NH_3(aq) \rightarrow NaHCO_3(s) + NH_4Cl(aq)$$

The sodium hydrogencarbonate is heated to give sodium carbonate and carbon dioxide. The ammonium chloride is heated with calcium oxide (from the first stage) to regenerate the ammonia. The process was patented in 1861 by the Belgian chemist Ernest Solvay (1838–1922).

solvent A liquid that dissolves another substance or substances to form a *solution. *Polar solvents* are compounds such as water and liquid ammonia, which have dipole moments and consequently high dielectric constants. These solvents are capable of dissolving ionic compounds or covalent compounds that ionize (*see* solvation). *Nonpolar solvents* are compounds such as ethoxyethane and benzene, which do not have permanent dipole moments. These do not dissolve ionic compounds but will dissolve nonpolar covalent compounds.

solvent extraction The process of separating one constituent from a mixture by dissolving it in a solvent in which it is soluble but in which the other constituents of the mixture are not. The process is usually carried out in the liquid phase, in which case it is also known as *liquid–liquid extraction*. In liquid–liquid extraction, the solution containing the desired constituent must be immiscible with the rest of the mixture. The process is widely used in extracting oil from oil-bearing materials.

solvolysis A reaction between a compound and its solvent. *See* hydrolysis.

sorption *Absorption of a gas by a solid.

sorption pump A type of vacuum pump in which gas is removed from a system by absorption on a solid (e.g. activated charcoal or a zeolite) at low temperature.

species A chemical entity, such as a particular atom, ion, or molecule.

specific 1. Denoting that an extensive physical quantity so described is expressed per unit mass. For example, the *specific latent heat* of a body is its latent heat per unit mass. When the extensive physical quantity is denoted by a capital letter (e.g. *L* for latent heat), the specific quantity is denoted by the corresponding lower-case letter (e.g. *l* for specific latent heat). **2.** In some older physical quantities the adjective 'specific' was added for other reasons (e.g. specific gravity, specific resistance). These names are now no longer used.

specific activity *See* activity.

specific gravity *See* relative density; specific.

specific heat capacity *See* heat capacity.

spectrograph *See* spectroscope.

spectrometer Any of various instruments for producing a spectrum and measuring the wavelengths, energies, etc., involved. A simple type, for visible radiation, is a spectroscope equipped with a calibrated scale allowing wavelengths to be read off or calculated. In the X-ray to infrared region of the electromagnetic spectrum, the spectrum is produced by dispersing the radiation with a prism or diffraction grating (or crystal, in the case of hard X-rays). Some form of photoelectric detector is used, and the spectrum can be obtained as a graphical plot, which shows how the intensity of the radiation varies with wavelength. Such instruments are also called *spectrophotometers*. Spectrometers also exist for investigating the gamma-ray region and the microwave and radio-wave regions of the spectrum (*see* electron spin resonance; nuclear magnetic resonance). Instruments for obtaining spectra of particle beams are also called spectrometers (*see* spectrum; photoelectron spectroscopy).

spectrophotometer *See* spectrometer.

spectroscope An optical instrument that produces a *spectrum for visual observation. The first such instrument was made by R. W. Bunsen; in its simplest form it consists of a hollow tube with a slit at one end by which the light enters and a collimating lens at the other end to produce a parallel beam, a prism to disperse the light, and a telescope for viewing the spectrum (see illustration). In the *spectrograph*, the spectroscope is provided with a camera to record the spectrum. For a broad range of spectroscopic work, from the ultraviolet to the infrared, a diffraction grating is used instead of a prism. *See also* spectrometer.

spectroscopy The study of methods of producing and analysing *spectra using *spectroscopes, *spectrometers, spectrographs, and spectrophotometers. The interpretations of the spectra so produced can be used for chemical analysis, examining atomic and molecular energy levels and molecular structures, and for determining the composition and motions of celestial bodies.

spectrum **1.** A distribution of entities or properties arrayed in order of increasing or decreasing magnitude. For example, a beam of ions passed through a mass spectrograph, in which they are deflected according to their charge-to-mass ratios, will have a range of masses called a *mass spectrum*. A *sound spectrum* is the distribution of energy over a range of frequencies of a particular source. **2.** A range of electromagnetic energies arrayed in order of increasing or decreasing wavelength or frequency (*see* electromagnetic spectrum). The *emission spectrum* of a body or substance is the characteristic range of radiations it emits when it is heated, bombarded by electron or ions, or absorbs photons. The *absorption spectrum* of a substance is produced by examining, through the substance and through a spectroscope, a continuous spectrum of radiation. The energies removed from the continuous spectrum by the absorbing medium show up as black lines or bands; with a substance capable of emitting a spectrum these are in exactly the same positions in the spectrum as the emission lines and bands would occur in the emission spectrum.

Emission and absorption spectra may show a *continuous spectrum*, a *line spectrum*, or a *band spectrum*. A continuous spectrum contains an unbroken sequence of frequencies over a relatively wide range; it is produced by incandescent solids, liquids, and compressed gases. Line spectra are discontinuous lines produced by excited atoms and ions as they fall back to a lower energy level. Band spectra (closely grouped bands of lines) are characteristic of molecular gases or chemical compounds. *See also* spectroscopy.

speculum An alloy of copper and tin formerly used in reflecting telescopes to make the main mirror as it could be cast, ground, and polished to make a highly reflective surface. It has now been largely replaced by silvered glass for this purpose.

sphalerite (zinc blende) A mineral form of zinc sulphide, ZnS, crystallizing in the cubic system; the principal ore of zinc. It is usually yellow-brown to brownish-black in colour and occurs, often with galena, in metasomatic deposits and also in hydrothermal veins and replacement deposits. Sphalerite is mined on every continent, the chief sources including the USA, Canada, Mexico, the USSR, Australia, Peru, and Poland.

spiegel (spiegeleisen) A form of *pig iron containing 15–30% of manganese and 4–5% of carbon. It is added to steel in a Bessemer converter as a deoxidizing agent and to raise the manganese content of steel.

spin (intrinsic angular momentum) Symbol *s*. The part of the total angular momentum of a particle, atom, nucleus, etc., that can continue to exist even when the particle is apparently at rest, i.e. when its translational motion is zero and therefore its orbital angular momentum is zero. A molecule, atom, or nucleus in a specified energy level, or a particular elementary particle, has a particular spin, just as it has a particular charge or mass. According to *quantum theory, this is quantized and is restricted to multiples of $h/2\pi$, where h is the *Planck constant. Spin is characterized by a quantum number s. For example, for an electron $s = \pm\frac{1}{2}$, implying a spin of $+h/4\pi$ when it is spinning in one direction and $-h/4\pi$ when it is spinning in the other. Because of their spin, charged particles also have their own intrinsic magnetic moments and in a magnetic field the spin of the particles lines up at an angle to the direction of the field, precessing around this direction.

spinel A group of oxide minerals with the general formula $F^{2+}R_2{}^{3+}O_4$, where F^{2+} = Mg, Fe, Zn, Mn, or Ni and R^{3+} = Al, Fe, or Cr, crystallizing in the cubic system. The spinels are divided into three series: spinel ($MgAl_2O_4$), *magnetite, and *chromite. They occur in high-temperature igneous or metamorphic rocks.

spirits of salt Hydrogen chloride, so-called because it can be made by adding sulphuric acid to common salt (sodium chloride).

spontaneous combustion Combustion in which a substance produces sufficient heat within itself, usually by a slow oxidation process, for ignition to take place without the need for an external high-temperature energy source.

sputtering The process by which some of the atoms of an electrode (usually a cathode) are ejected as a result of bombardment by heavy positive ions. Although the process is generally unwanted, it can be used to produce a clean surface or to deposit a uniform film of a metal on an object in an evacuated enclosure.

square-planar Describing a *coordination compound in which four ligands positioned at the corners of a square coordinate to a metal ion at the centre of the square.

stabilization energy The amount by which the energy of a delocalized chemical structure is less than the theoretical energy of a structure with localized bonds. It is obtained by subtracting the experimental heat of formation of the compound (in kJ mol^{-1}) from that calculated on the basis of a classical structure with localized bonds.

stable equilibrium *See* equilibrium.

staggered conformation *See* conformation.

stainless steel A form of *steel containing at least 11–12% of chromium, a low percentage of carbon, and often some other elements, notably nickel and molybdenum. Stainless steel does not rust or stain and therefore has a wide variety of uses in industrial, chemical, and domestic environments. A particularly successful alloy is the steel known as 18–8, which contains 18% Cr, 8% Ni, and 0.08% C.

stalactites and stalagmites Accretions of calcium carbonate in limestone caves. Stalactites are tapering cones or pendants that hang down from the roofs of caves; stalagmites are upward projections from the cave floor and tend to be broader at their bases than stalactites. Both are formed from drips of water containing calcium carbonate in solution and may take thousands of years to grow.

standard cell A *voltaic cell, such as a *Clarke cell, or *Weston cell, used as a standard of e.m.f.

standard electrode An electrode (a half cell) used in measuring electrode potential. *See* hydrogen half cell.

standard electrode potential *See* electrode potential.

standard solution A solution of known concentration for use in volumetric analysis.

standard state A state of a system used as a reference value in thermodynamic measurements. Standard states involve a reference value of pressure (usually 1 atmosphere, 101.325 kPa) or concentration (usually 1 M). Thermodynamic functions are designated as 'standard' when they refer to changes in which reactants and products are all in their standard and their normal physical state. For example, the standard molar enthalpy of formation of water at 298 K is the enthalpy change for the reaction

$$H_2(g) + \tfrac{1}{2}O_2(g) \rightarrow H_2O(l)$$

$\Delta H_{298} = -285.83$ kJ mol^{-1}. Note the superscript is used to denote standard state and the temperature should be indicated.

standard temperature and pressure *See* s.t.p.

stannane *See* tin(IV) hydride.

stannate A compound formed by reaction of tin oxides (or hydroxides) with alkali. Tin oxides are amphoteric (weakly acidic) and react to give stannate ions. Tin(IV) oxide with molten alkali gives the stannate(IV) ion

$$SnO_2 + 2OH^- \rightarrow SnO_3^{2-} + H_2O$$

In fact, there are various ions present in which the tin is bound to hydroxide groups, the main one being the hexahydroxostannate (IV) ion, $Sn(OH)_6^{2-}$. This is the negative ion present in crystalline 'trihydrates' of the type $K_2Sn_2O_3.3H_2O$.

Tin(II) oxide gives the trihydroxostannate (II) ion in alkaline solutions

$$SnO(s) + OH^-(aq) + H_2O(l) \rightarrow Sn(OH)_3^-(aq)$$

Stannate(IV) compounds were formerly referred to as *orthostannates* (SnO_4^{4-}) or *metastannates* (SnO_3^{2-}). Stannate(II) compounds were called *stannites*.

stannic compounds Compounds of tin in its higher (+4) oxidation state; e.g. stannic chloride is tin(IV) chloride.

stannite *See* stannate.

stannous compounds Compounds of tin in its lower (+2) oxidation state; e.g. stannous chloride is tin(II) chloride.

starch A *polysaccharide consisting of various proportions of two glucose polymers, *amylose and *amylopectin. It occurs widely in plants, especially in roots, tubers, seeds, and fruits, as a carbohydrate energy store. Starch is therefore a major energy source for animals. When digested it ultimately yields glucose. Starch granules are insoluble in cold water but disrupt if heated to form a gelatinous solution. This gives an intense blue colour with iodine solutions and starch is used as an *indicator in certain titrations.

state of matter One of the three physical states in which matter can exist, i.e. *solid, *liquid, or *gas. Plasma is sometimes regarded as the fourth state of matter.

stationary phase *See* chromatography.

stationary state A state of a system when it has an energy level permitted by *quantum mechanics. A transition from one stationary state to another can only occur by the emission or absorption of an appropriate quanta of energy in the form of photons.

statistical mechanics The branch of physics in which statistical methods are applied to the microscopic constituents of a system in order to predict its macroscopic properties. The earliest application of this method was Boltzmann's attempt to explain the thermodynamic properties of gases on the basis of the statistical properties of large assemblies of molecules.

In classical statistical mechanics, each particle is regarded as occupying a point in *phase space*, i.e. to have an exact position and momentum at any particular instant. The probability that this point will occupy any small volume of the phase space is taken to be proportional to the volume. The Maxwell–Boltzmann law gives the most probable distribution of the particles in phase space.

With the advent of quantum theory, the exactness of these premises was disturbed (by the Heisenberg uncertainty principle). In the *quantum statistics that evolved as a result, the phase space is divided into cells, each having a volume h^f, where h is the Planck constant and f is the number of degrees of freedom of the particles. This new concept led to Bose–Einstein statistics, and for particles obeying the Pauli exclusion principle, to Fermi–Dirac statistics.

steam distillation A method of distilling liquids that are immiscible with water by bubbling steam through them. It depends on the fact that the vapour pressure (and hence the boiling point) of a mixture of two immiscible liquids is lower than the vapour pressure of either pure liquid.

steam point The temperature at which the maximum vapour pressure of water is equal to the standard atmospheric pressure (101 325 Pa). On the Celsius scale it has the value 100°C.

stearate (octadecanoate) A salt or ester of stearic acid.

stearic acid (octadecanoic acid) A solid saturated *fatty acid, $CH_3(CH_2)_{16}COOH$; r.d. 0.94; m.p. 69.6°C; b.p. 376°C (with decomposition). It occurs widely (as *glycerides) in animal and vegetable fats.

steel Any of a number of alloys consisting predominantly of iron with varying proportions of carbon (up to 1.7%) and, in some cases, small quantities of other elements (*alloy steels*), such as manganese, silicon, chromium, molybdenum, and nickel. Steels con-

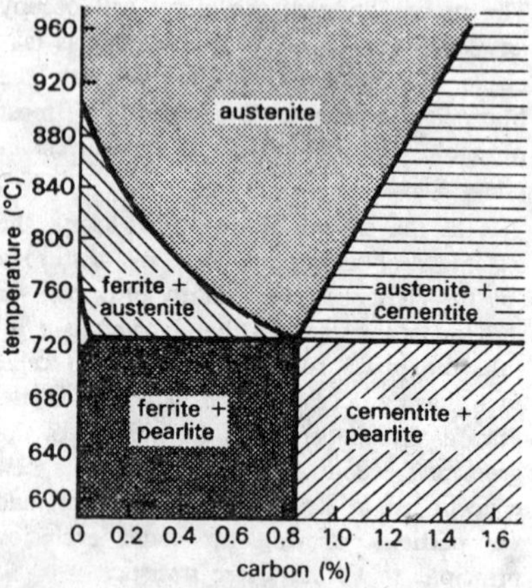

Phase diagram for steel

taining over 11–12% of chromium are known as *stainless steels.

Carbon steels exist in three stable crystalline phases: *ferrite* has a body-centred cubic crystal, *austenite* has a face-centred cubic crystal, and *cementite* has an orthorhombic crystal. *Pearlite* is a mixture of ferrite and cementite arranged in parallel plates. The phase diagram shows how the phases form at different temperatures and compositions.

Steels are manufactured by the *basic-oxygen process (L–D process), which has largely replaced the *Bessemer process and the *open-hearth process, or in electrical furnaces.

step A single stage in a chemical reaction. For example, the addition of hydrogen chloride to ethene involves three steps:

$$HCl \rightarrow H^+ + Cl^-$$

$$H^+ + C_2H_4 \rightarrow CH_3CH_2{}^+$$

$$CH_3CH_2{}^+ + Cl^- \rightarrow CH_3CH_2Cl$$

steradian Symbol sr. The supplementary *SI unit of solid angle equal to the solid angle that encloses a surface on a sphere equal to the square of the radius of the sphere.

stere A unit of volume equal to 1 m^3. It is not now used for scientific purposes.

stereochemistry The branch of chemistry concerned with the structure of molecules and the way the arrangement of atoms and groups affects the chemical properties.

stereoisomerism *See* isomerism.

stereoregular Describing a *polymer that has a regular pattern of side groups along its chain.

stereospecific Describing chemical reactions that give products with a particular arrangement of atoms in space. An example of a stereospecific reaction is the *Ziegler process for making polyethene.

steric effect An effect in which the rate or path of a chemical reaction depends on the size or arrangement of groups in a molecule.

steric hindrance An effect in which a chemical reaction is slowed down or prevented because large groups on a reactant molecule hinder the approach of another reactant molecule.

steroid Any of a group of lipids derived from a saturated compound called cyclopentanoperhydrophenanthrene, which has a nucleus of four rings. Some of the most important steroid derivatives are the steroid alcohols, or sterols. Other steroids include the bile acids, which aid digestion of fats in the intestine; the sex hormones (androgens and oestrogens); and the corticosteroid hormones, produced by the adrenal cortex. *Vitamin D is also based on the steroid structure.

sterol Any of a group of *steroid-based alcohols having a hydrocarbon side-chain of 8–10 carbon atoms. Sterols exist either as free sterols or as esters of fatty acids. Animal sterols (*zoosterols*) include cholesterol and lanosterol. The major plant sterol (*phytosterol*) is beta-sitosterol, while fungal sterols (*mycosterols*) include ergosterol.

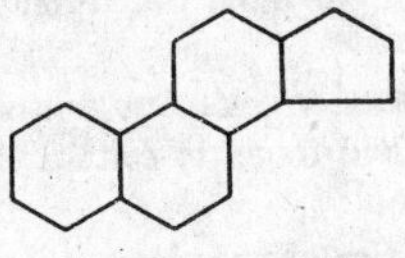

steroid nucleus

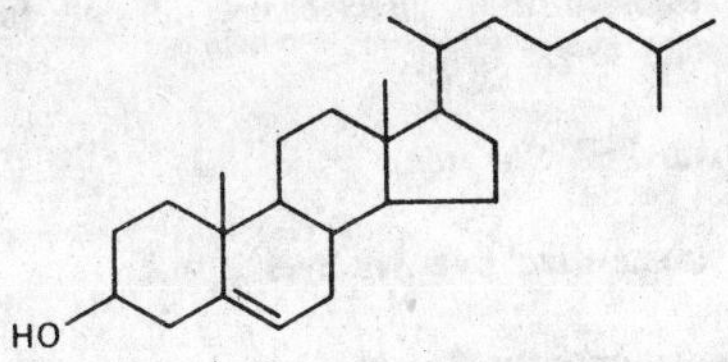

cholesterol (a sterol)

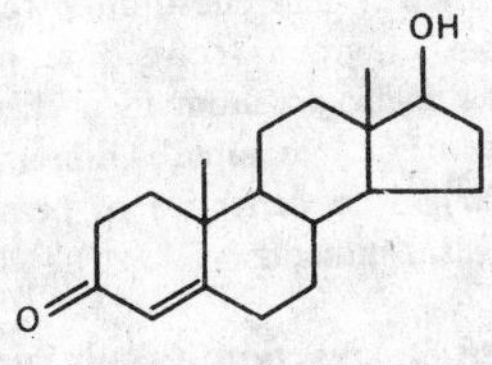

testosterone (an androgen)

Steroid structure

stoichiometric Describing chemical reactions in which the reactants combine in simple whole-number ratios.

stoichiometric coefficient *See* chemical equation.

stoichiometric compound A compound in which atoms are combined in exact whole-number ratios. *Compare* nonstoichiometric compound.

stoichiometric mixture A mixture of substances that can react to give products with no excess reactant.

stoichiometric sum *See* chemical equation.

stoichiometry The relative proportions in which elements form compounds or in which substances react.

s.t.p. Standard temperature and pressure, formerly known as *N.T.P.* (normal temperature and pressure). The standard conditions used as a basis for calculations involving quantities that vary with temperature and pressure. These conditions are used when comparing the properties of gases. They are 273.15 K (or 0°C) and 101 325 Pa (or 760.0 mmHg).

straight chain *See* chain.

strong acid An *acid that is completely dissociated in aqueous solution.

strontia *See* strontium oxide.

strontianite A mineral form of *strontium carbonate, $SrCO_3$.

strontium Symbol Sr. A soft yellowish metallic element belonging to group II of the periodic table (*see* alkaline-earth elements); a.n. 38; r.a.m. 87.62; r.d. 2.54; m.p. 800°C; b.p. 1300°C. The element is found in the minerals strontianite ($SrCO_3$) and celestine ($SrSO_4$). It can be obtained by roasting the ore to give the oxide, followed by reduction with aluminium (i.e. the *Goldschmidt process). The element, which is highly reactive, is used in certain alloys and as a vacuum getter. The isotope strontium-90 is present in radioactive fallout (half-life 28 years), and can be metabolized with calcium so that it collects in bone. Strontium was discovered by Klaproth and Hope in 1798 and isolated by Humphry Davy in 1808.

strontium bicarbonate *See* strontium hydrogencarbonate.

strontium carbonate A white solid, $SrCO_3$; orthorhombic; r.d. 3.7; decomposes at 1770°C. It occurs naturally as the mineral *strontianite* and is prepared industrially by boiling celestine (strontium sulphate) with ammonium carbonate. It can also be prepared by passing carbon dioxide over strontium oxide or hydroxide or by passing the gas through a solution of strontium salt. It is a phosphor, used to coat the glass of cathode-ray screens, and is also used in the refining of sugar, as a slagging agent in certain metal furnaces, and to provide a red flame in fireworks.

strontium chloride A white compound, $SrCl_2$. The anhydrous salt (cubic; r.d. 3.05; m.p. 872°C; b.p. 1250°C) can be prepared by passing chlorine over heated strontium. It is deliquescent and readily forms the hexahydrate, $SrCl_2.6H_2O$ (r.d. 2.67). This can be made by neutralizing hydrochloric acid with strontium carbonate, oxide, or hydroxide. Strontium chloride is used for military flares.

strontium hydrogencarbonate (strontium bicarbonate) A compound, $Sr(HCO_3)_2$, which is stable only in solution. It is formed by the action of carbon dioxide on a suspension of strontium carbonate in water. On heating, this process is reversed.

strontium oxide (strontia) A white compound, SrO; r.d. 4.7; m.p. 2430°C, b.p. 3000°C. It can be prepared by the decomposition of heated strontium carbonate, hydroxide, or nitrate, and is used in the manufacture of other strontium salts, in pigments, soaps and greases, and as a drying agent.

strontium sulphate A white solid, $SrSO_4$; r.d. 3.96; m.p. 1605°C. It can be made by dissolving strontium oxide, hydroxide, or carbonate in sulphuric acid. It is used as a pigment in paints and ceramic glazes and to provide a red colour in fireworks.

structural formula *See* formula.

strychnine A colourless poisonous crystalline alkaloid found in certain plants.

styrene *See* phenylethene.

sublimate A solid formed by sublimation.

sublimation A direct change of state from solid to gas.

subshell *See* atom.

substantive dye *See* dyes.

substantivity The affinity of a dye for its substrate.

substituent 1. An atom or group that replaces another in a substitution reaction. **2.** An atom or group regarded as having replaced a hydrogen atom in a chemical derivative. For example, dibromobenzene ($C_6H_4Br_2$) is a derivative of benzene with bromine substituents.

substitution reaction (displacement reaction) A reaction in which one atom or molecule is replaced by another atom or molecule. *See* electrophilic substitution: nucleophilic substitution.

substrate The substance upon which an *enzyme acts in biochemical reactions.

succinic acid (butanedioic acid) A crystalline solid, $HOOC(CH_2)_2COOH$, that is soluble in water. It occurs in living organisms as an intermediate in metabolism.

sucrose (cane sugar; beet sugar; saccharose) A sugar comprising one molecule of glucose linked to a fructose molecule. It oc curs widely in plants and is particularly abundant in sugar cane and sugar beet (15–20%), from which it is extracted and refined for table sugar. If heated to 200°C, sucrose becomes caramel.

sugar (saccharide) Any of a group of water-soluble *carbohydrates of relatively low molecular weight and typically having a sweet taste. The simple sugars are called *monosaccharides. More complex sugars comprise between two and ten monosaccharides linked together: *disaccharides contain two, trisaccharides three, and so on. The name is often used to refer specifically to *sucrose (table sugar).

sugar of lead *See* lead(II) ethanoate.

sulpha drugs *See* sulphonamides.

sulphanes Compounds of hydrogen and sulphur containing chains of sulphur atoms. They have the general formula H_2S_n. The simplest is hydrogen sulphide, H_2S; other members of the series are H_2S_2, H_2S_3, H_2S_4, etc. *See* sulphides.

sulphate A salt or ester of sulphuric(VI) acid. Organic sulphates have the formula R_2SO_4, where R is an organic group. Sulphate salts contain the ion SO_4^{2-}.

sulphides **1.** Inorganic compounds of sulphur with more electropositive elements. Compounds of sulphur with nonmetals are covalent compounds, e.g. hydrogen sulphide (H_2S). Metals form ionic sulphides containing the S^{2-} ion; these are salts of hydrogen sulphide. *Polysulphides* can also be produced containing the polymeric ion S_x^{2-}. **2.** (*or* **thio ethers**) Organic compounds that contain the group –S– linked to two hydrocarbon groups. Organic sulphides are named from the linking groups, e.g. dimethyl sulphide (CH_3SCH_3), ethyl methyl sulphide ($C_2H_5SCH_3$). They are analogues of ethers in which the oxygen is replaced by sulphur (hence the alternative name) but are generally more reactive than ethers. Thus they react with halogen compounds to form *sulphonium compounds and can be oxidized to *sulphoxides.

sulphinate (dithionite; hyposulphite) A salt containing the negative ion $S_2O_4^{2-}$, usually formed by the reduction of sulphites with excess SO_2. Solutions are not very stable and decompose to give thiosulphate and hydrogensulphite ions. The structure is $^-O_2S\text{-}SO_2$

sulphininic acid (dithionous acid; hyposulphurous acid) An unstable acid, $H_2S_2O_4$, known in the form of its salts (sulphinates). *See also* sulphuric acid.

sulphite A salt or ester derived from sulphurous acid. The salts contain the trioxosulphate(IV) ion SO_3^{2-}. Sulphites generally have reducing properties.

sulphonamides Organic compounds containing the group $-SO_2.NH_2$. The sulphonamides are amides of sulphonic acids. Many have antibacterial action and are also known as *sulpha drugs*, including

sulphadiazine, $NH_2C_6H_4SO_2NHC_4H_3N_2$,
sulphathiazole, $NH_2C_6H_4SO_2NHC_5H_2NS$,

and several others. They act by preventing bacteria from reproducing and are used to treat a variety of bacterial infections, especially of the gut and urinary system.

sulphonate A salt or ester of a sulphonic acid.

sulphonation A type of chemical reaction in which a $-SO_3H$ group is substituted on a benzene ring to form a *sulphonic acid. The reaction is carried out by refluxing with concentrated sulphuric(VI) acid for a long period. It can also occur with cold disulphuric(VI) acid ($H_2S_2O_7$). Sulphonation is an example of electrophilic substitution in which the electrophile is a sulphur trioxide molecule, SO_3.

sulphonic acids Organic compounds containing the $-SO_2.OH$ group. Sulphonic acids are formed by reaction of aromatic hydrocarbons with concentrated sulphuric acid. They are strong acids, ionizing completely in solution to form the sulphonate ion, $-SO_2.O^-$.

sulphonium compounds Compounds containing the ion R_3S^+ (sulphonium ion), where R is any organic group. Sulphonium compounds can be formed by reaction of organic sulphides with halogen compounds. For example, diethyl sulphide, $C_2H_5SC_2H_5$, reacts with chloromethane, CH_3Cl, to give diethylmethylsulphonium chloride, $(C_2H_5)_2.CH_3.S^+Cl^-$.

sulphoxides Organic compounds containing the group $=S=O$ (*sulphoxide group*) linked to two other groups, e.g. dimethyl sulphoxide, $(CH_3)_2SO$.

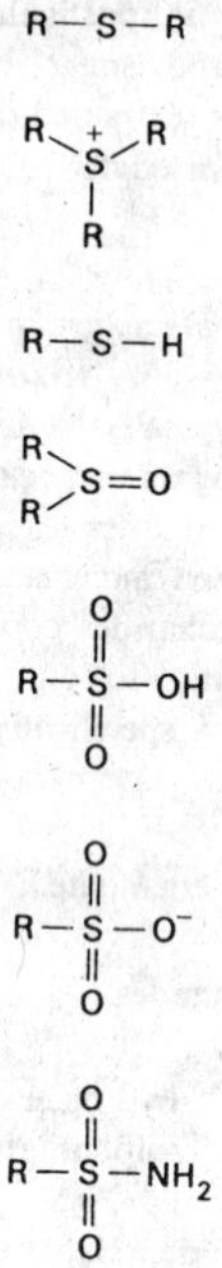

sulphide (thio ether)
sulphonium ion
thiol (mercaptan)
sulphoxide
sulphonic acid
sulphonate ion
sulphonamide

Examples of organic sulphur compounds

sulphur Symbol S. A yellow nonmetallic element belonging to *group VI of the periodic table; a.n. 16; r.a.m. 32.06; r.d. 2.07 (rhombic); m.p. 112.8°C; b.p. 444.674°C. The element occurs in many sulphide and sulphate minerals and native sulphur is also found in Sicily and the USA (obtained by the *Frasch process). It is an essential element for living organisms.

Sulphur has various allotropic forms. Below 95.6°C the stable crystal form is rhombic; above this temperature the element transforms into a triclinic form. These crystalline forms both contain cyclic S_8 molecules. At temperatures just above its melting point, molten sulphur is a yellow liquid containing S_8 rings (as in the solid form). At about 160°C, the sulphur atoms form chains and the liquid becomes more viscous and dark brown. If the molten sulphur is cooled quickly from this temperature (e.g. by pouring into cold water) a reddish-brown solid known as *plastic sulphur* is obtained. Above 200°C the viscosity decreases. Sulphur vapour contains a mixture of S_2, S_4, S_6, and S_8 molecules. *Flowers of sulphur* is a yellow powder obtained by subliming the vapour. It is used as a plant fungicide. The element is also used to produce sulphuric acid and other sulphur compounds.

sulphur dichloride *See* disulphur dichloride.

sulphur dichloride dioxide (sulphuryl chloride) A colourless liquid, SO_2Cl_2; r.d. 1.67; m.p. −54.1°C; b.p. 69°C. It decomposes in water but is soluble in benzene. The compound is formed by the action of chlorine on sulphur dioxide in the presence of an iron(III) chloride catalyst or sunlight. It is used as a chlorinating agent and a source of the related fluoride, SO_2F_2.

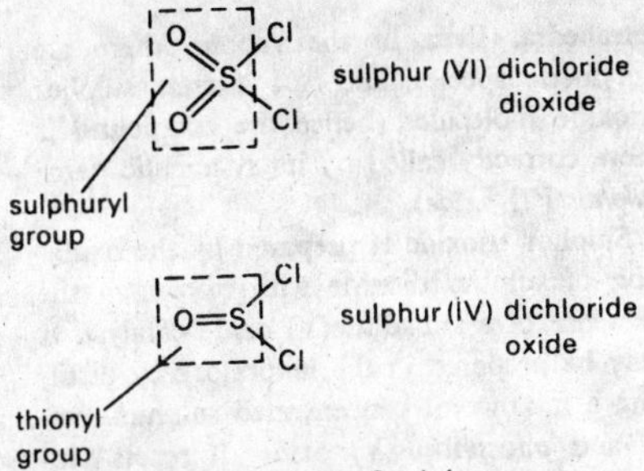

Oxychlorides of sulphur

sulphur dichloride oxide (thionyl chloride) A colourless fuming liquid, $SOCl_2$; m.p. −99.5°C; b.p. 75.7°C. It hydrolyses rapidly in water but is soluble in benzene. It may be prepared by the direct action of sulphur on chlorine monoxide or, more commonly, by the reaction of phosphorus (V) chloride with sulphur dioxide. It is used as a chlorinating agent in synthetic organic chemistry (replacing −OH groups with Cl).

sulphur dioxide (sulphur(IV) oxide) A colourless liquid or pungent gas, SO_2, formed by sulphur burning in air; r.d. 1.43 (liquid); m.p. −72.7°C; b.p. −10°C. It can be made by heating iron sulphide (pyrites) in air. The compound is a reducing agent and is used in bleaching and as a fumigant and food preservative. Large quantities are also used in the *contact process for manufacturing sulphuric acid. It dissolves in water to give a mixture of sulphuric and sulphurous acids.

sulphuretted hydrogen *See* hydrogen sulphide.

sulphuric acid (oil of vitriol) A colourless oily liquid, H_2SO_4; r.d. 1.84; m.p. 10.36°C; b.p. 338°C. The pure acid is rarely used; it is commonly available as a 96−98% solution (m.p. 3.0°C). The compound also forms a range of hydrates: $H_2SO_4.H_2O$ (m.p. 8.62°C); $H_2SO_4.2H_2O$ (m.p. −38/39°C); $H_2SO_4.6H_2O$ (m.p. −54°C); $H_2SO_4.8H_2O$ (m.p. −62°C). Its full systematic name is *tetraoxosulphuric(VI) acid.*

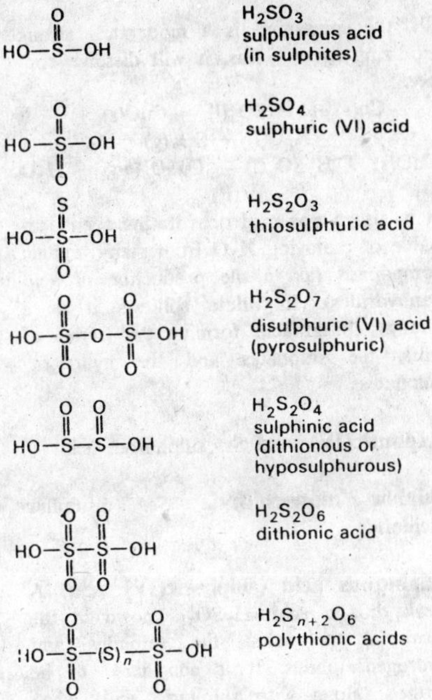

Structures of some oxo acids of sulphur

Until the 1930s, sulphuric acid was manufactured by the *lead-chamber process, but this has now been replaced by the *contact process (catalytic oxidation of sulphur dioxide). More sulphuric acid is made in the UK than any other chemical product; production levels (UK) are commonly 12 000 to 13 000 tonnes per day. It is extensively used in industry, the main applications being fertilizers (32%), chemicals (16%), paints and pigments (15%), detergents (11%), and fibres (9%).

In concentrated sulphuric acid there is extensive hydrogen bonding and several competing equilibria, to give species such as H_3O^+, HSO_4^-, $H_3SO_4^+$, and $H_2S_2O_7$. Apart from being a powerful protonating agent (it protonates chlorides and nitrates producing hydrogen chloride and nitric acid), the compound is a moderately strong oxidizing agent. Thus, it will dissolve copper:

$$Cu(s) + H_2SO_4(l) \rightarrow CuO(s) + H_2O(l) + SO_2(g)$$

$$CuO(s) + H_2SO_4(l) \rightarrow CuSO_4(aq) + H_2O(l)$$

It is also a powerful dehydrating agent, capable of removing H_2O from many organic compounds (as in the production of acid *anhydrides). In dilute solution it is a strong dibasic acid forming two series of salts, the sulphates and the hydrogensulphates.

sulphuric(IV) acid *See* sulphurous acid.

sulphur monochloride *See* disulphur dichloride.

sulphurous acid (sulphuric(IV) acid) A weak dibasic acid, H_2SO_3, known in the form of its salts: the sulphites and hydrogensulphites. It is considered to be formed (along with sulphuric acid) when sulphur dioxide is dissolved in water. It is probable, however, that the molecule H_2SO_3 is not present and that the solution contains hydrated SO_2. It is a reducing agent. The systematic name is *trioxosulphuric(IV) acid. See also* sulphuric acid.

sulphur(IV) oxide *See* sulphur dioxide.

sulphur(VI) oxide *See* sulphur trioxide.

sulphur trioxide (sulphur(VI) oxide) A colourless fuming solid, SO_3, which has three crystalline modifications. In decreasing order of stability these are: α, r.d. 1.97; m.p. 16.83°C; b.p. 44.8°C; β, m.p. 16.24°C; sublimes at 50°C; r.d. 2.29; γ, m.p. 16.8°C; b.p. 44.8°C. All are polymeric, with linked SO_4 tetrahedra: the γ-form has an icelike structure and is obtained by rapid quenching of the vapour; the β-form has infinite helical chains; and the α-form has infinite chains with some cross-linking of the SO_4 tetrahedra. Even in the vapour, there are polymeric species, and not discrete sulphur trioxide molecules (hence the compound is more correctly called by its systematic name *sulphur(VI) oxide*).

Sulphur trioxide is prepared by the oxidation of sulphur dioxide with oxygen in the presence of a vanadium(V) oxide catalyst. It may be prepared in the laboratory by distilling a mixture of concentrated sulphuric acid and phosphorus(V) oxide. It reacts violently with water to give sulphuric(VI) acid and is an important intermediate in the preparation of sulphuric acid and oleum.

sulphuryl chloride *See* sulphur dichloride dioxide.

sulphuryl group The group $=SO_2$, as in *sulphur dichloride oxide.

sulphydryl group *See* thiols.

superlattice *See* solid solution.

supernatant liquid The clear liquid remaining when a precipitate has settled.

superoxides A group of inorganic compounds that contain the O_2^- ion. They are formed in significant quantities only for sodium, potassium, rubidium, and caesium. They are very powerful oxidizing agents and react vigorously with water to give oxygen gas and OH^- ions. The superoxide ion has an unpaired electron and is paramagnetic and coloured (orange).

superphosphate A commercial phosphate mixture consisting mainly of monocalcium phosphate. Single-superphosphate is made by treating phosphate rock with sulphuric acid; the product contains 16–20% 'available' P_2O_5:

$$Ca_{10}(PO_4)_6F_2 + 7H_2SO_4 = 3Ca(H_2PO_4)_2 + 7CaSO_4 + 2HF.$$

Triple-superphosphate is made by using phosphoric(V) acid in place of sulphuric acid; the product contains 45–50% 'available' P_2O_5:

$$Ca_{10}(PO_4)_6F_2 + 14H_3PO_4 = 10Ca(H_2PO_4)_2 + 2HF$$

superplasticity The ability of some metals and alloys to stretch uniformly by several thousand percent at high temperatures, unlike normal alloys, which fail after being stretched 100% or less. Since 1962, when this property was discovered in an alloy of zinc and aluminium (22%), many alloys and ceramics have been shown to possess this property. For superplasticity to occur, the metal grain must be small and rounded and the alloy must have a slow rate of deformation.

supersaturated solution *See* saturated.

supersaturation 1. The state of the atmosphere in which the relative humidity is over 100%. This occurs in pure air where no condensation nuclei are available. Supersaturation is usually prevented in the atmosphere by the abundance of condensation nuclei (e.g. dust, sea salt, and smoke particles). **2.** The state of any vapour whose pressure exceeds that at which condensation usually occurs (at the prevailing temperature).

supplementary units *See* SI units.

surface tension Symbol γ. The property of a liquid that makes it behave as if its surface is enclosed in an elastic skin. The property results from intermolecular forces: a molecule in the interior of a liquid experiences a force of attraction from other molecules equally from all sides, whereas a molecule at the surface is only attracted by molecules below it in the liquid. The surface tension is defined as the force acting over the surface per unit length of surface perpendicular to the force. It is measured in newtons per metre. It can equally be defined as the energy required to increase the surface area by one square metre, i.e. it can be measured in joules per metre squared (which is equivalent to $N\,m^{-1}$).

The property of surface tension is responsible for the formation of liquid drops, soap bubbles, and meniscuses, as well as the rise of liquids in a capillary tube (*capillarity*), the absorption of liquids by porous substances, and the ability of liquids to wet a surface.

surfactant (surface active agent) A substance, such as a *detergent, added to a liquid to increase its spreading or wetting properties by reducing its *surface tension.

suspension A mixture in which small solid or liquid particles are suspended in a liquid or gas.

sylvite (sylvine) A mineral form of *potassium chloride, KCl.

syndiotactic *See* polymer.

synthesis The formation of chemical compounds from more simple compounds.

synthesis gas *See* Haber process.

synthetic Describing a substance that has been made artificially; i.e. one that does not come from a natural source.

Système International d'Unités *See* SI units.

T

tactic polymer *See* polymer.

talc A white or pale-green mineral form of magnesium silicate, $Mg_3Si_4O_{10}(OH)_2$, crystallizing in the triclinic system. It forms as a secondary mineral by alteration of magnesium-rich olivines, pyroxenes, and amphiboles of ultrabasic rocks. It is soaplike to touch and very soft, having a hardness of 1 on the Mohs' scale. Massive fine-grained talc is known as *soapstone* or *steatite*. Talc in powdered form is used as a lubricant, as a filler in paper, paints, and rubber, and in cosmetics, ceramics, and French chalk. It occurs chiefly in the USA, USSR, France, and Japan.

tannic acid A yellowish complex organic compound present in certain plants. It is used in dyeing as a mordant.

tannin One of a group of complex organic chemicals commonly found in leaves, unripe fruits, and the bark of trees. Their function is uncertain though the unpleasant taste may discourage grazing animals. Some tannins have commercial uses, notably in the production of leather and ink.

tantalum Symbol Ta. A heavy blue-grey metallic *transition element; a.n. 73; r.a.m. 180.948; r.d. 16.63; m.p. 2996°C; b.p. 5427°C. It is found with niobium in the ore columbite–tantalite $(Fe,Mn)(Ta,Nb)_2O_6$. It is extracted by dissolving in hydrofluoric acid, separating the tantalum and niobium fluorides to give K_2TaF_7, and reduction of this with sodium. The element contains the stable isotope tantalum–181 and the long-lived radioactive isotope tantalum–180 (0.012%; half-life $>10^7$ years). There are several other short-lived isotopes. The element is used in certain alloys and in electronic components. Tantalum parts are also used in surgery because of the unreactive nature of the metal (e.g. in pins to join bones). Chemically, the metal forms a passive oxide layer in air. It forms complexes in the +2, +3, +4, and +5 oxidation states. Tantalum was identified in 1802 by Ekeberg and first isolated in 1820 by Berzelius.

tar Any of various black semisolid mixtures of hydrocarbons and free carbon, produced by destructive distillation of *coal or by *petroleum refining.

tar sand *See* oil sand.

tartaric acid A crystalline naturally occurring carboxylic acid, $(CHOH)_2(COOH)_2$; r.d. 1.8; m.p. 170°C. It can be obtained from tartar (potassium hydrogen tartrate) deposits from wine vats, and is used in baking powders and as a foodstuffs additive. The compound is optically active (*see* optical activity). The systematic name is *2,3-dihydroxybutanedioic acid*.

tartrate A salt or ester of *tartaric acid.

tautomerism A type of *isomerism in which the two isomers (*tautomers*) are in equilibrium. *See* keto–enol tautomerism.

TCA cycle *See* Krebs cycle.

technetium Symbol Tc. A radioactive metallic *transition element; a.n. 43; m.p. 2171°C; b.p. 4876°C. The element can be detected in certain stars and is present in the fission products of uranium. It was first made by Perrier and Segrè by bombarding molybdenum with deuterons to give technetium–97. The most stable isotope is technetium–99 (half-life 2.12×10^5 years); this is used to some extent in labelling for medical diagnosis. There are sixteen known isotopes. Chemically, the metal has properties intermediate between manganese and rhenium.

Teflon Tradename for a form of *polytetrafluoroethene.

tellurides Binary compounds of tellurium with other more electropositive elements. Compounds of tellurium with nonmetals are covalent (e.g. H_2Te). Metal tellurides can be made by direct combination of the elements and are ionic (containing Te^{2-}) or non-stoichiometric interstitial compounds (e.g. Pd_4Te, $PdTe_2$).

tellurium Symbol Te. A silvery metalloid element belonging to *group VI of the periodic table; a.n. 52; r.a.m. 127.60; r.d. 6.24 (crystalline); m.p. 451°C; b.p. 1390±3°C. It occurs mainly as *tellurides in ores of gold, silver, copper, and nickel and it is obtained as a by-product in copper refining. There are eight natural isotopes and nine radioactive isotopes. The element is used in semiconductors and small amounts are added to certain steels. Tellurium is also added in small quantities to lead. Its chemistry is similar to that of sulphur. It was discovered by Franz Müller in 1782.

temperature The property of a body or region of space that determines whether or not there will be a net flow of heat into it or out of it from a neighbouring body or region and in which direction (if any) the heat will flow. If there is no heat flow the bodies or regions are said to be in *thermodynamic equilibrium* and at the same temperature. If there is a flow of heat, the direction of the flow is from the body or region of higher temperature. Broadly, there are two methods of quantifying this property. The empirical method is to take two or more reproducible temperature-dependent events and assign *fixed points* on a scale of values to these events. For example, the Celsius temperature scale uses the freezing point and boiling point of water as the two fixed points, assigns the values 0 and 100 to them, respectively, and divides the scale between them into 100 degrees. This method is serviceable for many practical purposes (*see* temperature scales), but lacking a theoretical basis it is awkward to use in many scientific contexts. In the 19th century, Lord Kelvin proposed a thermodynamic method to specify temperature, based on the measurement of the quantity of heat flowing between bodies at different temperatures. This concept relies on an absolute scale of temperature with an *absolute zero of temperature, at which no body can give up heat. He also used Sadi Carnot's concept of an ideal frictionless perfectly efficient heat engine (*see* Carnot cycle). This Carnot engine takes in a quantity of heat q_1 at a temperature T, and exhausts heat q_2 at T_2, so that $T_1/T_2 = q_1/q_2$. If T_2 has a value fixed by definition, a Carnot engine can be run between this fixed temperature and any unknown temperature T_1, enabling T_1 to be calculated by measuring the values of q_1 and q_2. This concept remains the basis for defining *thermodynamic temperature*, quite independently of the nature of the working substance. The unit in which thermodynamic temperature is expressed is the *kelvin. In practice thermodynamic temperatures cannot be measured directly; they are usually inferred from measurements with a gas thermometer containing a nearly ideal gas. This is possible because another aspect of thermodynamic temperature is its relationship to the *internal energy of a given amount of substance. This can be shown most simply in the case of an ideal monatomic gas, in which the internal energy per mole (U) is equal to the total kinetic energy of translation of the atoms in one mole of the gas (a monatomic gas has no rotational or vibrational energy). According to *kinetic theory, the thermodynamic temperature of such a gas is given by $T = 2U/3R$, where R is the universal *gas constant.

temperature scales A number of empirical scales of *temperature have been in use: the *Celsius scale is widely used for many purposes and in certain countries the *Fahrenheit scale is still used. These scales both rely on the use of *fixed points*, such as the freezing point and the boiling point of water, and the division of the *fundamental interval* between these two points into units of temperature (100 degrees in the case of the Celsius scale and 180 degrees in the Fahrenheit scale).

However, for scientific purposes the scale in use is the *International Practical Temperature Scale (1968)*, which is designed to conform as closely as possible to thermodynam-

	T/K	t/°C
triple point of equilibrium hydrogen	13.81	−259.34
temperature of equilibrium hydrogen when its vapour pressure is 25/76 standard atmosphere	17.042	−256.108
b.p. of equilibrium hydrogen	20.28	−252.87
b.p. of neon	27.102	−246.048
triple point of oxygen	54.361	−218.789
b.p. of oxygen	90.188	−182.962
triple point of water	273.16	0.01
b.p. of water	373.15	100
f.p. of zinc	692.73	419.58
f.p. of silver	1235.08	961.93
f.p. of gold	1337.58	1064.43

Temperature scales

ic temperature and is expressed in the unit of thermodynamic temperature, the *kelvin. The eleven fixed points of the scale are given in the table, with the instruments specified for interpolating between them. Above the freezing point of gold, a radiation pyrometer is used, based on Planck's law of radiation. The scale is expected to be refined in the late 1980s.

tempering The process of increasing the toughness of an alloy, such as steel, by heating it to a predetermined temperature, maintaining it at this temperature for a predetermined time, and cooling it to room temperature at a predetermined rate. In steel, the purpose of the process is to heat the alloy to a temperature that will enable the excess carbide to precipitate out of the supersaturated solid solution of *martensite and then to cool the saturated solution fast enough to prevent further precipitation or grain growth. For this reason steel is quenched rapidly by dipping into cold water.

temporary hardness *See* hardness of water.

tera- Symbol T. A prefix used in the metric system to denote one million million times. For example, 10^{12} volts = 1 teravolt (TV).

terbium Symbol Tb. A silvery metallic element belonging to the *lanthanoids; a.n. 65; r.a.m. 158.92; r.d. 8.23 (20°C); m.p. 1365°C; b.p. 3230°C. It occurs in apatite and xenotime, from which it is obtained by an ion-exchange process. There is only one natural isotope, terbium−159, which is stable. Seventeen artificial isotopes have been identified. There are virtually no uses for this element although its potentialities are still being explored. It was discovered by C. G. Mosander in 1843.

ternary compound A chemical compound containing three different elements.

terpenes A group of unsaturated hydrocarbons present in plants (*see* essential oil). Terpenes consist of isoprene units, $CH_2{:}C(CH_3)CH{:}CH_2$. Monoterpenes have two units, $C_{10}H_{16}$, sesquiterpenes three units, $C_{15}H_{24}$, diterpenes four units, $C_{20}H_{32}$, etc.

tertiary alcohol *See* alcohols.

tertiary amine *See* amines.

tervalent (trivalent) Having a valency of three.

Terylene Tradename for a type of *polyester used in synthetic fibres.

tesla Symbol T. The SI unit of magnetic flux density equal to one weber of magnetic flux per square metre, i.e. 1 T = 1 Wb m^{-2}. It is named after Nikola Tesla (1870–1943), Croatian-born US electrical engineer.

tetrachloroethene A colourless nonflammable volatile liquid, $CCl_2{:}CCl_2$; r.d. 1.6; m.p. −22°C; b.p. 121°C. It is used as a solvent.

tetrachloromethane (carbon tetrachloride) A colourless volatile liquid with a characteristic odour, virtually insoluble in water but miscible with many organic liquids, such as ethanol and benzene; r.d. 1.586; m.p. −23°C; b.p. 76.8°C. It is made by the chlorination of methane (previously by chlorination of carbon disulphide). The compound is a good solvent for waxes, lacquers, and rubbers and the main industrial use is as a solvent, but safer substances (e.g. 1,1,1-trichloroethane) are increasingly being used. Moist carbon tetrachloride is partly decomposed to phosgene and hydrogen chloride and this provides a further restriction on its use.

tetraethyl lead *See* lead tetraethyl(IV).

tetragonal *See* crystal system.

tetrahedral angle The angle between the bonds in a *tetrahedral compound (approximately 109° for a regular tetrahedron).

tetrahedral compound A compound in which four atoms or groups situated at the corners of a tetrahedron are linked (by covalent or coordinate bonds) to an atom at the centre of the tetrahedron. *See also* complex.

tetrahydrate A crystalline hydrate containing four molecules of water per molecule of compound.

tetrahydroxomonoxodiboric(III) acid *See* boric acid.

tetraoxophosphoric(V) acid *See* phosphoric(V) acid.

tetraoxosulphuric(IV) acid *See* sulphuric acid.

tetravalent (quadrivalent) Having a valency of four.

thallium Symbol Tl. A greyish metallic element belonging to *group IIIA of the periodic table; a.n. 81; r.a.m. 204.39; r.d. 11.85 (20°C); m.p. 303.3°C; b.p. 1460°C. It occurs in zinc blende and some iron ores and is recovered in small quantities from lead and zinc concentrates. The naturally occurring isotopes are thallium-203 and thallium-205; eleven radioisotopes have been identified. It has few uses – experimental alloys for special purposes and some minor uses in electronics. The sulphate has been used as a rodenticide. Thallium(I) compounds resemble those of the alkali metals. Thallium(III) compounds are easily reduced to the thallium(I) state and are therefore strong oxidizing agents. The element was discovered by Sir William Crookes in 1861.

thermal capacity *See* heat capacity.

thermal equilibrium *See* equilibrium.

thermite A stoichiometric powdered mixture of iron(III) oxide and aluminium for the reaction:

$$2Al + Fe_2O_3 \rightarrow Al_2O_3 + 2Fe$$

The reaction is highly exothermic and the increase in temperature is sufficient to melt the iron produced. It has been used for localized welding of steel objects (e.g. railway lines) in the *Thermit process*. Thermite is also used in incendiary bombs.

thermochemistry The branch of physical chemistry concerned with heats of chemical reaction, heats of formation of chemical compounds, etc.

thermodynamics The study of the laws that govern the conversion of energy from one form to another, the direction in which heat will flow, and the availability of energy to do work. It is based on the concept that in an isolated system anywhere in the universe there is a measurable quantity of energy called the *internal energy (U) of the system. This is the total kinetic and potential energy of the atoms and molecules of the system of all kinds that can be transferred directly as heat; it therefore excludes chemical and nuclear energy. The value of U can only be changed if the system ceases to be isolated. In these circumstances U can change by the transfer of mass to or from the system, the transfer of heat (Q) to or from the system, or by the work (W) being done on or by the system. For an adiabatic ($Q = 0$) system of constant mass, $\Delta U = W$. By convention, W is taken to be positive if work is done on the system and negative if work is done by the system. For nonadiabatic systems of constant mass, $\Delta U = Q + W$. This statement, which is equivalent to the law of conservation of energy, is known as the *first law of thermodynamics*.

All natural processes conform to this law, but not all processes conforming to it can occur in nature. Most natural processes are irreversible, i.e. they will only proceed in one direction (*see* reversible process). The direction that a natural process can take is the subject of the *second law of thermodynamics*, which can be stated in a variety of ways. R. Clausius (1822–88) stated the law in two ways: "heat cannot be transferred from one body to a second body at a higher temperature without producing some other effect" and "the entropy of a closed system increases with time". These statements introduce the thermodynamic concepts of *temperature (T) and *entropy (S), both of which are parameters determining the direction in which an irreversible process can go. The temperature of a body or system determines whether heat will flow into it or out of it; its entropy is a measure of the unavailability of its energy to do work. Thus T and S determine the relationship between Q and W in the statement of the first law. This is usually presented by stating the second law in the form $\Delta U = T\Delta S - W$.

The second law is concerned with changes in entropy (ΔS). The *third law of thermodynamics* provides an absolute scale of values for entropy by stating that for changes involving only perfect crystalline solids at *absolute zero, the change of the total entropy is zero. This law enables absolute values to be stated for entropies.

One other law is used in thermodynamics. Because it is fundamental to, and assumed by, the other laws of thermodynamics it is usually known as the *zeroth law of thermodynamics*. This states that if two bodies are each in thermal equilibrium with a third body, then all three bodies are in thermal equilibrium with each other. *See also* enthalpy; free energy.

thermoluminescence *Luminescence produced in a solid when its temperature is raised. It arises when free electrons and holes, trapped in a solid as a result of exposure to ionizing radiation, unite and emit photons of light. The process is made use of in *thermoluminescent dating*, which assumes that the number of electrons and holes trapped in a sample of pottery is related to the length of time that has elapsed since the pottery was fired. By comparing the luminescence produced by heating a piece of pottery of unknown age with the luminescence produced by heating similar materials of known age, a fairly accurate estimate of the age of an object can be made.

thermoluminescent dating *See* thermoluminescence.

thermometer An instrument used for measuring the *temperature of a substance. A number of techniques and forms are used in thermometers depending on such factors as the degree of accuracy required and the range of temperatures to be measured, but they all measure temperature by making use of some property of a substance that varies with temperature. For example, *liquid-in-glass thermometers* depend on the expansion of a liquid, usually mercury or alcohol coloured with dye. These consist of a liquid-filled glass bulb attached to a partially filled capillary tube. In the *bimetallic thermometer* the unequal expansion of two dissimilar metals that have been bonded together into a narrow strip and coiled is used to move a pointer round a dial. The *gas thermometer*, which is more accurate than the liquid-in-glass thermometer, measures the variation in the pressure of a gas kept at constant volume. The *resistance thermometer* is based on the change in resistance of conductors or semiconductors with temperature change. Platinum, nickel, and copper are the metals most commonly used in resistance thermometers.

thermoplastic *See* plastics.

thermosetting *See* plastics.

thermostat A device that controls the heating or cooling of a substance in order to maintain it at a constant temperature. It consists of a temperature-sensing instrument connected to a switching device. When the temperature reaches a predetermined level the sensor switches the heating or cooling source on or off according to a predetermined program. The sensing thermometer is often a bimetallic strip that triggers a simple electrical switch. Thermostats are used for space-heating controls, in water heaters and refrigerators, and to maintain the environment of a scientific experiment at a constant temperature.

thiamin(e) *See* vitamin B complex.

thin-layer chromatography A technique for the analysis of liquid mixtures using *chromatography. The stationary phase is a thin layer of an absorbing solid (e.g. alumina) prepared by spreading a slurry of the solid on a plate (usually glass) and drying it in an oven. A spot of the mixture to be analysed is placed near one edge and the plate is stood upright in a solvent. The solvent rises through the layer by capillary action carrying the components up the plate at different rates (depending on the extent to which they are absorbed by the solid). After a given time, the plate is dried and the location of spots noted. It is possible to identify constituents of the mixture by the distance moved in a given time. The technique needs careful control of the thickness of the layer and of the temperature.

thiocyanate A salt or ester of cyanic acid.

thiocyanic acid An unstable gas, HSCN.

thio ethers *See* sulphides.

thiol group *See* thiols.

thiols (mercaptans; thio alcohols) Organic compounds that contain the group –SH (called the *thiol group*, *mercapto group*, or *sulphydryl group*). Thiols are analogues of alcohols in which the oxygen atom is replaced by a sulphur atom. They are named according to the parent hydrocarbon; e.g. ethane thiol (C_2H_5SH). A characteristic property is their strong disagreeable odour. For example the odour of garlic is produced by ethane thiol. Unlike alcohols they are acidic, reacting with alkalis and certain metals to form saltlike compounds. The older name, mercaptan, comes from their ability to react with ('seize') mercury.

thionyl chloride *See* sulphur dichloride oxide.

thionyl group The group =SO, as in *sulphur dichloride oxide.

thiosulphate A salt containing the ion $S_2O_3^{2-}$ formally derived from thiosulphuric acid. Thiosulphates readily decompose in acid solution to give elemental sulphur and hydrogensulphite (HSO_3^-) ions.

thiosulphuric acid An unstable acid, $H_2S_2O_3$, formed by the reaction of sulphur trioxide with hydrogen sulphide. *See also* sulphuric acid.

thiourea A white crystalline solid, $(NH_2)_2CS$; r.d. 1.4; m.p. 180°C. It is used as a fixer in photography.

thoria *See* thorium.

thorium Symbol Th. A grey radioactive metallic element belonging to the *actinoids; a.n. 90; r.a.m. 232.038; r.d. 11.5–11.9 (17°C); m.p. 1740–1760°C; b.p. 4780–4800°C. It occurs in monazite sand in Brazil, India, and USA. The isotopes of thorium have mass numbers from 223 to 234 inclusive; the most stable isotope, thorium–232, has a half-life of 1.39×10^{10} years. It has an oxidation state of (+4) and its chemistry resembles that of the other actinoids. It can be used as a nuclear fuel for breeder reactors as thorium–232 captures slow neutrons to breed uranium–233. Thorium dioxide (*thoria*, ThO_2) is used on gas mantles and in special refractories. The element was discovered by J. J. Berzelius in 1829.

thorium series *See* radioactive series.

threnardite A mineral form of *sodium sulphate, Na_2SO_4.

threonine *See* amino acid.

thulium Symbol Tm. A soft grey metallic element belonging to the *lanthanoids; a.n. 69; r.a.m. 168.934; r.d. 9.321 (20°C); m.p. 1545°C; b.p. 1950°C. It occurs in apatite and xenotime. There is one natural isotope, thulium–169, and seventeen artificial isotopes have been produced. There are no uses for the element, which was discovered by P. T. Cleve in 1879.

thymine A *pyrimidine derivative and one of the major component bases of *nucleotides and the nucleic acid *DNA.

tin Symbol Sn. A silvery malleable metallic element belonging to *group IV of the periodic table; a.n. 50; r.a.m. 118.69; r.d. 7.29; m.p. 231.97°C; b.p. 2270°C. It is found as tin(IV) oxide in ores, such as cassiterite, and is extracted by reduction with carbon. The metal (called *white tin*) has a powdery nonmetallic allotrope *grey tin*, into which it changes below 18°C. The formation of this allotrope is called *tin plague*; it can be reversed by heating to 100°C. The natural element has 21 isotopes (the largest number of any element); five radioactive isotopes are also known. The metal is used as a thin protective coating for steel plate and is a constituent of a number of alloys (e.g. phosphor bronze, gun metal, solder, Babbitt metal, and pewter). Chemically it is reactive. It combines directly with chlorine and oxygen and displaces hydrogen from dilute acids. It also dissolves in alkalis to form *stannates. There are two series of compounds with tin in the +2 and +4 oxidation states.

tin(II) chloride A white solid, $SnCl_2$, soluble in water and ethanol. It exists in the anhydrous form (rhombic; r.d. 3.95; m.p. 246°C; b.p. 652°C) and as a dihydrate,

$SnCl_2.2H_2O$ (monoclinic; r.d. 2.71; m.p. 37.7°C). The compound is made by dissolving metallic tin in hydrochloric acid and is partially hydrolysed in solution.

$$Sn^{2+} + H_2O \rightleftharpoons SnOH^+ + H^+$$

Excess acid must be present to prevent the precipitation of basic salts. In the presence of additional chloride ions the pyramidal ion $[SnCl_3]^-$ is formed; in the gas phase the $SnCl_2$ molecule is bent. It is a reducing agent in acid solutions and oxidizes slowly in air:

$$Sn^{2+} \rightarrow Sn^{4+} + 2e$$

tin(IV) chloride A colourless fuming liquid, $SnCl_4$, hydrolysed in cold water, decomposed by hot water, and soluble in ethers; r.d. 2.226; m.p. −33°C; b.p. 114°C. Tin(IV) chloride is a covalent compound, which may be prepared directly from the elements. It dissolves sulphur, phosphorus, bromine, and iodine, and there is evidence for the presence of species such as $SnCl_2I_2$. In hydrochloric acid and in chloride solutions the coordination is extended from four to six by the formation of the $SnCl_6{}^{2-}$ ion.

tincture A solution with alcohol as the solvent (e.g. tincture of iodine).

tin(IV) hydride (stannane) A highly reactive and volatile gas (b.p. −53°), SnH_4, which decomposes on moderate heating (150°C). It is prepared by the reduction of tin chlorides using lithium tetrahydridoaluminate(III) and is used in the synthesis of some organo-tin compounds. The compound has reducing properties.

tin(IV) oxide (tin dioxide) A white solid, SnO_2, insoluble in water; tetrahedral; r.d. 6.95; m.p. 1630°C; sublimes at about 1850°C. Tin(IV) oxide is trimorphic: the common form, which occurs naturally as the ore *cassiterite, has a rutile lattice but hexagonal and rhombic forms are also known. There are also two so-called dihydrates, $SnO_2.2H_2O$, known as α- and β-stannic acid. These are essentially tin hydroxides. Tin (IV) oxide is amphoteric, dissolving in molten alkalis to form *stannates; in the presence of sulphur, thiostannates are produced.

tin plague *See* tin.

tin(II) sulphide A grey-black cubic or monoclinic solid, SnS, virtually insoluble in water; r.d. 5.22; m.p. 882°C; b.p. 1230°C. It has a layer structure similar to that of black phosphorus. Its heat of formation is low and it can be made by heating the elements together. Above 265°C it slowly decomposes (disproportionates) to tin(IV) sulphide and tin metal. The compound reacts with hydrochloric acid to give tin(II) chloride and hydrogen sulphide.

tin(IV) sulphide (mosaic gold) A bronze or golden yellow crystalline compound, SnS_2, insoluble in water and in ethanol; hexagonal; r.d. 4.5; decomposes at 600°C. It is prepared by the reaction of hydrogen sulphide with a soluble tin(IV) salt or by the action of heat on thiostannic acid, H_2SnS_3. The golden-yellow form used for producing a gilded effect on wood is prepared by heating tin, sulphur, and ammonium chloride.

titania *See* titanium(IV) oxide.

titanium Symbol Ti. A white metallic *transition element; a.n. 22; r.a.m. 47.9; r.d. 4.507; m.p. 1660±10°C; b.p. 3280°C. The main sources are rutile (TiO_2) and, to a lesser extent, ilmenite ($FeTiO_3$). The element also occurs in numerous other minerals. It is obtained by heating the oxide with carbon and chlorine to give $TiCl_4$, which is reduced by the *Kroll process. The main use is in a large number of strong light corrosion-resistant alloys for aircraft, ships, chemical plant, etc. The element forms a passive oxide coating in air. At higher temperatures it reacts with oxygen, nitrogen, chlorine, and other nonmetals. It dissolves in dilute acids. The main compounds are titanium(IV) salts and complexes; titanium(II) and titanium(III) compounds are also known. The element was first discovered by Gregor in 1789.

titanium dioxide *See* titanium(IV) oxide.

titanium(IV) oxide (titania; titanium dioxide) A white oxide, TiO_2, occurring naturally in various forms, particularly the mineral rutile. It is used as a white pigment and as a filler for plastics, rubber, etc.

titration A method of volumetric analysis in which a volume of one reagent is added to a known volume of another reagent slowly from a burette until an end point is reached (*see* indicator). The volume added before the end point is reached is noted. If one of the solutions has a known concentration, that of the other can be calculated.

TNT *See* trinitrotoluene.

tocopherol *See* vitamin E.

Tollen's reagent A reagent used in testing for aldehydes. It is made by adding sodium hydroxide to silver nitrate to give silver(I) oxide, which is dissolved in aqueous ammonia (giving the complex ion $[Ag(NH_3)_2]^+$). The sample is warmed with the reagent in a test tube. Aldehydes reduce the complex Ag^+ ion to metallic silver, forming a bright silver mirror on the inside of the tube (hence the name *silver-mirror test*). Ketones give a negative result.

toluene *See* methylbenzene.

topaz A variably coloured aluminium silicate mineral, $Al_2(SiO_4)(OH,F)_2$, that forms orthorhombic crystals. It occurs chiefly in acid igneous rocks, such as granites and pegmatites. Topaz is valued as a gemstone because of its transparency, variety of colours (the wine-yellow variety being most highly prized), and great hardness (8 on the Mohs' scale). When heated, yellow or brownish topaz often becomes a rose-pink colour. The main sources of topaz are Brazil, the USSR, and the USA.

torr A unit of pressure, used in high-vacuum technology, defined as 1 mmHg. 1 torr is equal to 133.322 pascals. The unit is named after Evangelista Torricelli (1609–47).

total-radiation pyrometer *See* pyrometry.

tourmaline A group of minerals composed of complex cyclosilicates containing boron with the general formula $NaR_3^{2+}Al_6B_3Si_6O_{27}(H,F)_4$, where R = Fe^{2+}, Mg, or (Al + Li). The crystals are trigonal, elongated, and variably coloured, the two ends of the crystals often having different colours. Tourmaline is used as a gemstone and because of its double refraction and piezoelectric properties is also used in polarizers and some pressure gauges.

trace element *See* essential element.

tracing (radioactive tracing) *See* labelling.

transamination A biochemical reaction in amino acid metabolism in which an amine group is transferred from an amino acid to a keto acid to form a new amino acid and keto acid. The coenzyme required for this reaction is pyridoxal phosphate.

trans effect An effect in the substitution of inorganic square-planar complexes, in which certain ligands in the original complex are able to direct the incoming ligand into the trans position. The order of ligands in decreasing trans-directing power is:
$CN^- > NO_2 > I^- > Br^- > Cl^- > NH_3 > H_2O$.

transition elements A set of elements in the *periodic table in which filling of electrons in an inner *d*- or *f*-level occurs. With increasing proton number, electrons fill atomic levels up to argon, which has the electron configuration $1s^2 2s^2 2p^6 3s^2 3p^6$. In this shell, there are 5 *d*-orbitals, which can each contain 2 electrons. However, at this point the subshell of lowest energy is not the 3*d* but the 4*s*. The next two elements, potassium and calcium, have the configurations $[Ar]4s^1$ and $[Ar]4s^2$ respectively. For the next element, scandium, the 3*d* level is of lower energy than the 4*p* level, and scandium has the configuration $[Ar]3d^1 4s^2$. This filling of the inner *d*-level continues up to zinc $[Ar]3d^{10} 4s^2$, giving the first transition series. There is a further series of this type in the next period of the table: between yttrium ($[Kr]4d5s^2$) and cadmium ($[Kr]4d^{10} 5s^2$). This is the second transition series. In the next period of the table the situation is rather more complicated. Lanthanum has the configuration $[Xe]5d^1 6s^2$. The level of lowest energy then becomes the 4*f* level and the next element, cerium, has the configuration $[Xe]4f^1 5d^1 6s^2$. There are 7 of these *f*-orbitals, each of which can contain 2 electrons, and filling of the *f*-levels continues up to lutetium ($[Xe]4f^{14} 5d^1 6s^2$). Then the filling of the 5*d* levels continues from hafnium to mercury. The series of 14 elements from cerium to lutetium is a 'series within a series', sometimes called an *inner transition series*. This one is the *lanthanoid series. In the next period there is a similar inner transition series, the *actinoid series, from thorium to lawrencium. Then filling of the *d*-level continues from element 104 onwards.

In fact, the classification of chemical elements is valuable only in so far as it illustrates chemical behaviour, and it is conventional to use the term 'transition elements' in a more restricted sense. The elements in the inner transition series from cerium (58) to lutetium (71) are called the lanthanoids; those in the series from thorium (90) to lawrencium (103) are the actinoids. These two series together make up the *f*-block in the periodic table. It is also common to include scandium, yttrium, and lanthanum with the lanthanoids (because of chemical similarity) and to include actinium with the actinoids. Of the remaining transition elements, it is usual to speak of three *main transition series*: from titanium to copper; from zirconium to silver; and from hafnium to gold. All these elements have similar chemical properties that result from the presence of unfilled *d*-orbitals in the element or (in the case of copper, silver, and gold) in the ions. The elements from 104 to 109 and the undiscovered elements 110 and 111 make up a fourth transition series. The elements zinc, cadmium, and mercury have filled *d*-orbitals both in the elements and in compounds, and are usually regarded as nontransition elements (*see* group II elements).

The elements of the three main transition series are all typical metals (in the nonchemical sense), i.e. most are strong hard materials that are good conductors of heat and electricity and have high melting and boiling points. Chemically, their behaviour depends on the existence of unfilled *d*-orbitals. They exhibit variable valency, have coloured compounds, and form *coordination compounds. Many of their compounds are paramagnetic as a result of the presence of unpaired electrons. Many of them are good catalysts. They are less reactive than the *s* and *p* block metals.

transition point (transition temperature) **1.** The temperature at which one crystalline form of a substance changes to another form. **2.** The temperature at which a substance changes phase. **3.** The temperature at which a substance becomes superconducting. **4.** The temperature at which some other change, such as a change of magnetic properties, takes place.

transition state (activated complex) The association of atoms of highest energy formed during a chemical reaction. The transition state can be regarded as a short-lived intermediate that breaks down to give the products. For example, in a S_N2 substitution reaction, one atom or group approaches the molecule as the other leaves. The transition state is an intermediate state in which both attacking and leaving groups are partly bound to the molecule, e.g.

$$B + RA \rightarrow B\text{---}R\text{---}A \rightarrow BR + A$$

In the theory of reaction rates, the reactants are assumed to be in equilibrium with this activated complex, which decomposes to the products.

transmission electron microscope *See* electron microscope.

transport number Symbol *t*. The fraction of the total charge carried by a particular type of ion in the conduction of electricity through electrolytes.

transuranic elements Elements with an atomic number greater than 92, i.e. elements above uranium in the *periodic table.

triacylglycerol *See* triglyceride.

triazine *See* azine.

triboluminescence *Luminescence caused by friction; for example, some crystalline substances emit light when they are crushed as a result of static electric charges generated by the friction.

tribromomethane (bromoform) A colourless liquid *haloform, $CHBr_3$; r.d. 2.9; m.p. 8°C; b.p. 150°C.

tricarbon dioxide (carbon suboxide) A colourless gas, C_3O_2, with an unpleasant odour; r.d. 1.114 (liquid at 0°C); m.p. −111.3°C; b.p. 7°C. It is the acid anhydride of malonic acid, from which it can be prepared by dehydration using phosphorus (V) oxide. The molecule is linear (O:C:C:C:O).

tricarboxylic acid cycle *See* Krebs cycle.

trichloroethanal (chloral) A liquid aldehyde, CCl_3CHO; r.d. 1.51; m.p. −57.5°C; b.p. 97.8°C. It is made by chlorinating ethanal and used in making DDT. *See also* 2,2,2-trichloroethanediol.

2,2,2-trichloroethanediol (chloral hydrate) A colourless crystalline solid, $CCl_3CH(OH)_2$; r.d. 1.91; m.p. 57°C; b.p. 96.3°C. It is made by the hydrolysis of trichloroethanal and is unusual in having two −OH groups on the same carbon atom. Gem diols of this type are usually unstable; in this case the compound is stabilized by the presence of the three Cl atoms. It is used as a sedative.

trichloromethane (chloroform) A colourless volatile sweet-smelling liquid *haloform, $CHCl_3$; r.d. 1.48; m.p. −63.5°C; b.p. 61°C. It can be made by chlorination of methane (followed by separation of the mixture of products) or by the haloform reaction. It is an effective anaesthetic but can cause liver damage and it has now been replaced by other halogenated hydrocarbons. Chloroform is used as a solvent and raw material for making other compounds.

triclinic *See* crystal system.

tridymite A mineral form of *silicon(IV) oxide, SiO_2.

triglyceride (triacylglycerol) An ester of glycerol (propane-1,2,3-triol) in which all three hydroxyl groups are esterified with a fatty acid. Triglycerides are the major constituent of fats and oils and provide a concentrated food energy store in living organisms as well as cooking fats and oils, margarines, soaps, etc. Their physical and chemical properties depend on the nature of their constituent fatty acids. In *simple triglycerides* all three fatty acids are identical; in *mixed triglycerides* two or three different fatty acids are present.

trihydric alcohol *See* triol.

tri-iodomethane (iodoform) A yellow volatile solid sweet-smelling *haloform, CHI_3; r.d. 4.1; m.p. 115°C. It is made by the haloform reaction.

tri-iron tetroxide (ferrosoferric oxide) A black magnetic oxide, Fe_3O_4; r.d. 5.2. It is formed when iron is heated in steam and also occurs naturally as the mineral *magnetite. The oxide dissolves in acids to give a mixture of iron(II) and iron(III) salts.

trimethylaluminium (aluminium trimethyl) A colourless liquid, $Al(CH_3)_3$, which ignites in air and reacts with water to give aluminium hydroxide and methane, usually with extreme vigour; r.d. 0.752; m.p. 0°C; b.p. 130°C. Like other aluminium alkyls it may be prepared by reacting a Grignard reagent with aluminium trichloride. Aluminium alkyls are used in the *Ziegler process for the manufacture of high-density polyethene (polythene).

2,4,6-trinitrophenol *See* picric acid.

trinitrotoluene (TNT) A yellow highly explosive crystalline solid, $CH_3C_6H_2(NO_2)_3$; r.d. 1.6; m.p. 81°C. It is made by nitrating toluene (methylbenzene), the systematic name being 1-methyl-2,4,6-trinitrobenzene.

triol (trihydric alcohol) An *alcohol containing three hydroxyl groups per molecule.

trioxoboric(III) acid *See* boric acid.

trioxosulphuric(IV) acid *See* sulphurous acid.

trioxygen *See* ozone.

triple bond *See* chemical bond.

triple point The temperature and pressure at which the vapour, liquid, and solid phases of a substance are in equilibrium. For water the triple point occurs at 273.16 K and 611.2 Pa. This value forms the basis of the definition of the *kelvin and the thermodynamic *temperature scale.

trisilane *See* silane.

trisodium phosphate(V) (sodium orthophosphate) A colourless crystalline compound, Na_3PO_4, soluble in water and insoluble in ethanol. It is known both as the decahydrate (octagonal; r.d. 2.54) and the dodecahydrate (trigonal; r.d. 1.62) The dodecahydrate loses water at about 76°C and the decahydrate melts at 100°C. Trisodium phosphate may be prepared by boiling sodium carbonate with the stoichiometric amount of phosphoric acid and subsequently adding sodium hydroxide to the disodium salt thus formed. It is useful as an additive for high-pressure boiler feed water (for removal of calcium and magnesium as phosphates), in emulsifiers, as a water-softening agent, and as a component in detergents and cleaning agents. Sodium phosphate labelled with the radioactive isotope ^{32}P is used in the study of the role of phosphate in biological processes and is also used (intravenously) in the treatment of polycythaemia.

tritiated compound *See* labelling.

tritium Symbol T. An isotope of hydrogen with mass number 3; i.e. the nucleus contains 2 neutrons and 1 proton. It is radioactive (half-life 12.3 years), undergoing beta decay to helium-3. Tritium is used in *labelling.

trivalent (tervalent) Having a valency of three.

trona A mineral form of sodium sesquicarbonate, consisting of a mixed hydrated sodium carbonate and sodium hydrogencarbonate, $Na_2CO_3.NaHCO_3.2H_2O$.

tropyllium ion The positive ion $C_7H_7^+$, having a ring of seven carbon atoms. The ion is symmetrical and has characteristic properties of *aromatic compounds.

trypsin An enzyme that digests proteins (*see* protease). It is secreted in an inactive form (*trypsinogen*) by the pancreas into the duodenum. There, trypsinogen is acted on by an enzyme (*enterokinase*) produced in the duodenum to yield trypsin. The active enzyme plays an important role in the digestion of proteins in the anterior portion of the small intestine.

trypsinogen *See* trypsin.

tryptophan *See* amino acid.

tungsten Symbol W. A white or grey metallic *transition element (formerly called *wolfram*); a.n. 74; r.a.m. 183.85; r.d. 19.3; m.p. 3410°C; b.p. 5660°C. It is found in a number of ores, including the oxides wolframite, $(Fe,Mn)WO_4$, and scheelite, $CaWO_4$. The ore is heated with concentrated sodium hydroxide solution to form a soluble *tungstate*. The oxide WO_3 is precipitated from this by adding acid, and is reduced to the metal using hydrogen. It is used in various alloys, especially high-speed steels (for cutting tools) and in lamp filaments. Tungsten forms a protective oxide in air and can be oxidized at high temperature. It does not dissolve in dilute acids. It forms compounds in which the oxidation state ranges from +2 to +6. The metal was first isolated by J. J. and F. d'Elhuyer in 1783.

tungsten carbide A black powder, WC, made by heating powdered tungsten metal with lamp black at 1600°C. It is extremely hard (9.5 on Mohs' scale) and is used in dies and cutting tools. A ditungsten carbide, W_2C, also exists.

tunnel effect An effect in which electrons are able to tunnel through a narrow potential barrier that would constitute a forbidden region if the electrons were treated as classical particles. That there is a finite probability of an electron tunnelling from one classically allowed region to another arises as a consequence of *quantum mechanics. The effect is made use of in the tunnel diode.

turpentine An oily liquid extracted from pine resin. It contains pinene, $C_{10}H_{16}$, and other terpenes and is mainly used as a solvent.

turquoise A mineral consisting of a hydrated phosphate of aluminium and copper, $CuAl_6(PO_4)_4(OH)_8.4H_2O$), that is prized as a semiprecious stone. It crystallizes in the triclinic system and is generally blue in colour, the 'robin's egg' blue variety being the most sought after. It usually occurs in veinlets and as masses and is formed by the action of surface waters on aluminium-rich rocks. The finest specimens are obtained from Iran.

tyrosine *See* amino acid.

U

ultracentrifuge A high-speed centrifuge used to measure the rate of sedimentation of colloidal particles or to separate macromolecules, such as proteins or nucleic acids, from solutions. Ultracentrifuges are electrically driven and are capable of speeds up to 60 000 rpm.

ultramicroscope A form of microscope that uses the Tyndall effect to reveal the presence of particles that cannot be seen with a normal optical microscope. Colloidal particles, smoke particles, etc., are suspended in a liquid or gas in a cell with a black background and illuminated by an intense cone of light that enters the cell from the side and has its apex in the field of view. The particles then produce diffraction-ring systems, appearing as bright specks on the dark background.

ultraviolet radiation (UV) Electromagnetic radiation having wavelengths between that of violet light and long X-rays, i.e. between 400 nanometres and 4 nm. In the range 400–300 nm the radiation is known as the *near ultraviolet*. In the range 300–200 nm it is known as the *far ultraviolet*. Below 200 nm it is known as the *extreme ultraviolet* or the *vacuum ultraviolet*, as absorption by the oxygen in the air makes the use of evacuated apparatus essential. The sun is a strong emitter of UV radiation but only the near UV reaches the surface of the earth as the ozone in the atmosphere absorbs all wavelengths below 290 nm.

Most UV radiation for practical use is produced by various types of mercury-vapour lamps. Ordinary glass absorbs UV radiation and therefore lenses and prisms for use in the UV are made from quartz.

uncertainty principle (Heisenberg uncertainty principle; principle of indeterminism) The principle that it is not possible to know with unlimited accuracy both the position and momentum of a particle. This principle, discovered in 1927 by Werner Heisenberg (1901–76), is usually stated in the form: $\Delta x \Delta p_x > h/2\pi$, where Δx is the uncertainty in the x-coordinate of the particle, Δp_x is the uncertainty in the x-component of the particle's momentum, and h is the *Planck constant. An explanation of the uncertainty is that in order to locate a particle exactly, an observer must be able to bounce off it a photon of radiation; this act of location itself alters the position of the particle in an unpredictable way. To locate the position accurately, photons of short wavelength would have to be used. These would have associated large momenta and cause a large effect on the position. On the other hand, using long-wavelength photons would have less effect on the particle's position, but would be less accurate because of the longer wavelength. The principle has had a profound effect on scientific thought as it appears to upset the classical relationship between cause and effect at the atomic level.

uniaxial crystal A double-refracting crystal (*see* double refraction) having only one *optic axis.

unimolecular reaction A chemical reaction or step involving only one molecule. An example is the decomposition of dinitrogen tetroxide:

$$N_2O_4 \rightarrow 2NO_2$$

Molecules colliding with other molecules acquire sufficient activation energy to react, and the activated complex only involves the atoms of a single molecule.

unit A specified measure of a physical quantity, such as length, mass, time, etc., specified multiples of which are used to express magnitudes of that physical quantity. For scientific purposes previous systems of units have now been replaced by *SI units.

unit cell The group of particles (atoms, ions, or molecules) in a crystal that is repeated in three dimensions in the *crystal lattice. *See also* crystal system.

univalent (monovalent) Having a valency of one.

universal constants *See* fundamental constants.

universal indicator A mixture of acid–base *indicators that changes colour (e.g. red-yellow-orange-green-blue) over a range of pH.

unsaturated 1. (of a compound) Having double or triple bonds in its molecules. Unsaturated compounds can undergo addition reactions as well as substitution. *Compare* saturated. **2.** (of a solution) *See* saturated.

unstable equilibrium *See* equilibrium.

uracil A *pyrimidine derivative and one of the major component bases of *nucleotides and the nucleic acid *RNA.

uraninite A mineral form of uranium(IV) oxide, containing minute amounts of radium, thorium, polonium, lead, and helium. When uraninite occurs in a massive form with a pitchy lustre it is known as *pitchblende*, the chief ore of uranium. Uraninite occurs in Saxony (East Germany), Romania, Norway, the UK (Cornwall), E Africa (Zaîre), USA, and Canada (Great Bear Lake).

uranium Symbol U. A white radioactive metallic element belonging to the *actinoids; a.n. 92; r.a.m. 238.03; r.d. 19.05 (20°C); m.p. 1132±1°C; b.p. 3818°C. It occurs as *uraninite, from which the metal is extracted by an ion-exchange process. Three isotopes are found in nature: uranium–238 (99.28%), uranium–235 (0.71%), and uranium–234 (0.006%). As uranium–235 undergoes nuclear fission with slow neutrons it is the fuel used in nuclear reactors and nuclear weapons; uranium has therefore assumed enormous technical and political importance since their invention. It was discovered by M. H. Klaproth in 1789.

uranium(VI) fluoride (uranium hexafluoride) A volatile white solid, UF_6; r.d. 5.1; m.p. 64.5°C. It is used in the separation of uranium isotopes by gas diffusion.

uranium hexafluoride *See* uranium(VI) fluoride.

uranium–lead dating A group of methods of *dating certain rocks that depends on the decay of the radioisotopes uranium–238 to lead–206 (half-life 4.5×10^9 years) or the decay of uranium–235 to lead–207 (half-life 7.1×10^8 years). One form of uranium–lead dating depends on measuring the ratio of the amount of helium trapped in the rock to the amount of uranium present (since the decay $^{238}U \rightarrow {}^{206}Pb$ releases eight alpha-particles). Another method of calculating the age of the rocks is to measure the ratio of radiogenic lead (^{206}Pb, ^{207}Pb, and ^{208}Pb) present to nonradiogenic lead (^{204}Pb). These methods give reliable results for ages of the order 10^7–10^9 years.

uranium(IV) oxide A black solid, UO_2; r.d. 10.9; m.p. 3000°C. It occurs naturally as *uraninite and is used in nuclear reactors.

uranium series *See* radioactive series.

urea (carbamide) A white crystalline solid, $CO(NH_2)_2$; r.d. 1.3; m.p. 133°C. It is soluble in water but insoluble in certain organic solvents. Urea is the major end product of nitrogen excretion in mammals, being synthesized by the *urea cycle. Urea is synthesized industrially from ammonia and carbon dioxide for use in *urea–formaldehyde resins and pharmaceuticals, as a source of nonprotein nitrogen for ruminant livestock, and as a nitrogen fertilizer.

urea cycle (ornithine cycle) The series of biochemical reactions that converts ammonia to *urea during the excretion of metabolic nitrogen. Urea formation occurs in mammals and, to a lesser extent, in some other animals. The liver converts ammonia to the much less toxic urea, which is excreted in solution in urine.

urea–formaldehyde resins Synthetic resins made by copolymerizing urea with formaldehyde (methanal). They are used as adhesives or thermosetting plastics.

urethane resins (polyurethanes) Synthetic resins containing the repeating group –NH–CO–O–. There are numerous types made by copolymerizing isocyanate esters with polyhydric alcohols. They have a variety of uses in plastics, paints, and solid foams.

uric acid The end product of purine breakdown in most primates, birds, terrestrial reptiles, and insects and also (except in primates) the major form in which metabolic nitrogen is excreted. Being fairly insoluble, uric acid can be expelled in solid form, which conserves valuable water in arid environments. The accumulation of uric acid in the synovial fluid of joints causes gout.

UV *See* ultraviolet radiation.

V

vacancy *See* defect.

vacuum A space in which there is a low pressure of gas, i.e. relatively few atoms or molecules. A *perfect vacuum* would contain no atoms or molecules, but this is unobtainable as all the materials that surround such a space have a finite *vapour pressure. In a *soft* (or *low*) *vacuum* the pressure is reduced to about 10^{-2} pascal, whereas a *hard* (or *high*) vacuum has a pressure of 10^{-2}–10^{-7} pascal. Below 10^{-7} pascal is known as an *ultrahigh vacuum*. *See also* vacuum pump.

vacuum distillation Distillation under reduced pressure. The depression in the boiling point of the substance distilled means that the temperature is lower, which may prevent the substance from decomposing.

vacuum pump A pump used to reduce the gas pressure in a container. The normal laboratory rotary oil-seal pump can maintain a pressure of 10^{-1} Pa. For pressures down to 10^{-7} Pa a *diffusion pump is required. *Ion pumps can achieve a pressure of 10^{-9} Pa and a *cryogenic pump combined with a diffusion pump can reach 10^{-13} Pa.

valence *See* valency.

valence band *See* energy bands.

valence electron An electron in one of the outer shells of an atom that takes part in forming chemical bonds.

valency (valence) The combining power of an atom or radical, equal to the number of hydrogen atoms that the atom could combine with or displace in a chemical compound (hydrogen has a valency of 1). It is equal to the ionic charge in ionic compounds; for example, in Na_2S, sodium has a valency of 1 (Na^+) and sulphur a valency of 2 (S^{2-}). In covalent compounds it is equal to the number of bonds formed; in CO_2 both carbon and oxygen have a valency of 2.

valine *See* amino acid.

vanadium Symbol V. A silvery-white metallic *transition element; a.n. 23; r.a.m. 50.94; r.d. 6.1; m.p. 1890°C; b.p. 3380°C. It occurs in a number of complex ores, including vanadinite ($Pb_5Cl(VO_4)_3$) and carnotite ($K_2(ClO_2)_2(VO_4)_2$). The pure metal can be obtained by reducing the oxide with calcium. The element is used in a large number of alloy steels. Chemically, it reacts with nonmetals at high temperatures but is not affected by hydrochloric acid or alkalis. It forms a range of complexes with oxidation states from +2 to +5. Vanadium was discovered in 1801 by del Rio, who allowed himself to be persuaded that what he had discovered was an impure form of chromium. The element was rediscovered and named by Sefström in 1880.

vanadium(V) oxide (vanadium pentoxide) A crystalline compound, V_2O_5, used extensively as a catalyst in industrial gas-phase oxidation processes.

vanadium pentoxide *See* vanadium(V) oxide.

van der Waals' equation *See* equation of state.

van der Waals' force An attractive force between atoms or molecules, named after J. D. van der Waals (1837–1923). The force accounts for the term a/V^2 in the van der Waals equation (*see* equation of state). These forces are much weaker than those arising from valence bonds and are inversely proportional to the seventh power of the distance between the atoms or molecules. They are the forces responsible for nonideal behaviour of gases and for the lattice energy of molecular crystals. There are three factors causing such forces: (1) dipole–dipole interaction, i.e. electrostatic attractions between two molecules with permanent dipole moments; (2) dipole-induced dipole interactions, in which the dipole of one molecule polarizes a neighbouring molecule; (3) dispersion forces arising because of small instantaneous dipoles in atoms.

van't Hoff factor Symbol *i*. A factor appearing in equations for *colligative properties, equal to the ratio of the number of actual particles present to the number of undissociated particles. It was first suggested by Jacobus van't Hoff (1852–1911).

van't Hoff's isochore An equation for the variation of equilibrium constant with temperature

$$(\mathrm{d}\log_e K)/\mathrm{d}T = \Delta H/RT^2$$

where T is the thermodynamic temperature and ΔH the enthalpy of the reaction.

vapour density The density of a gas or vapour relative to hydrogen, oxygen, or air. Taking hydrogen as the reference substance, the vapour density is the ratio of the mass of a particular volume of a gas to the mass of an equal volume of hydrogen under identical conditions of pressure and temperature. Taking the density of hydrogen as 1, this ratio is equal to half the relative molecular mass of the gas.

vapour pressure The pressure exerted by a vapour. All solids and liquids give off vapours, consisting of atoms or molecules of the substances that have evaporated from the condensed forms. These atoms or molecules exert a vapour pressure. If the substance is in an enclosed space, the vapour pressure will reach a maximum value that depends only on the nature of the substance and the temperature. This maximum value occurs when there is a dynamic equilibrium between the atoms or molecules escaping from the liquid or solid and those that strike the surface of the liquid or solid and return to it. The vapour is then said to be a *saturated vapour* and the pressure it exerts is the *saturated vapour pressure*.

verdigris A green patina of basic copper salts formed on copper. The composition of verdigris varies depending on the atmospheric conditions, but includes the basic carbonate $CuCO_3.Cu(OH)_2$, the basic sulphate $CuSO_4.Cu(OH)_2.H_2O$, and sometimes the basic chloride $CuCl_2.Cu(OH)_2$.

vermiculite *See* clay minerals.

vicinal (vic) Designating a molecule in which two atoms or groups are linked to adjacent atoms. For example, 1,2-dichloroethane (CH_2ClCH_2Cl) is a vic dihalide.

Victor Meyer's method A method of measuring vapour density, devised by Victor Meyer (1848–97). A weighed sample in a small tube is dropped into a heated bulb with a long neck. The sample vaporizes and displaces air, which is collected over water and the volume measured. The vapour density can then be calculated.

villiaumite A mineral form of sodium fluoride, NaF.

vinyl acetate *See* ethenyl ethanoate.

vinyl chloride *See* chloroethene.

vinyl group The organic group $CH_2{:}CH-$.

virial equation A gas law that attempts to account for the behaviour of real gases, as opposed to an ideal gas. It takes the form

$$pV = RT + Bp + Cp^2 + Dp^3 + \ldots,$$

where *B*, *C*, and *D* are known as *virial coefficients*.

viscosity A measure of the resistance to flow that a fluid offers when it is subjected to shear stress. For a Newtonian fluid, the force, *F*, needed to maintain a velocity gradient, dv/dx, between adjacent planes of a fluid of area *A* is given by: $F = \eta A(dv/dx)$, where η is a constant, called the coefficient of viscosity. In SI units it has the unit pascal second (in the c.g.s. system it was measured in *poise). Non-Newtonian fluids, such as clays, do not conform to this simple model. *See also* kinematic viscosity.

vitamin One of a number of organic compounds required by living organisms in relatively small amounts to maintain normal health. There are some 14 generally recognized major vitamins: the water-soluble *vitamin B complex (containing 9) and *vitamin C and the fat-soluble *vitamin A, *vitamin D, *vitamin E, and *vitamin K. Most B vitamins and vitamin C occur in plants, animals, and microorganisms; they function typically as *coenzymes. Vitamins A, D, E, and K occur only in animals, especially vertebrates, and perform a variety of metabolic roles. Animals are unable to manufacture many vitamins themselves and must have adequate amounts in the diet. Foods may contain vitamin precursors (called *provitamins*) that are chemically changed to the actual vitamin on entering the body. Many vitamins are destroyed by light and heat, e.g. during cooking.

vitamin A (retinol) A fat-soluble vitamin that cannot be synthesized by mammals and other vertebrates and must be provided in the diet. Green plants contain precursors of the vitamin, notably carotenes, that are converted to vitamin A in the intestinal wall and liver. The aldehyde derivative of vitamin A, *retinal*, is a constituent of the visual pigment rhodopsin. Deficiency affects the eyes, causing night blindness, xerophthalmia, and eventually total blindness. The role of vitamin A in other aspects of metabolism is less clear.

vitamin B complex A group of water-soluble vitamins that characteristically serve as components of *coenzymes. Plants and many microorganisms can manufacture B vitamins but dietary sources are essential for most animals. Heat and light tend to destroy B vitamins.

Vitamin B_1 (*thiamin(e)*) is a precursor of the coenzyme thiamine pyrophosphate, which functions in carbohydrate metabolism. Deficiency leads to beriberi in humans and to polyneuritis in birds. Good sources include brewer's yeast, wheatgerm, beans, peas, and green vegetables.

Vitamin B_2 (*riboflavin*) occurs in green vegetables, yeast, liver, and milk. It is a constituent of the coenzymes *FAD and

FMN, which have an important role in the metabolism of all major nutrients as well as in the oxidative phosphorylation reactions of the electron transport chain. Deficiency of B_2 causes inflammation of the tongue and lips and mouth sores.

Vitamin B_6 (pyridoxine) is widely distributed in cereal grains, yeast, liver, milk, etc. It is a constituent of a coenzyme (pyridoxal phosphate) involved in amino acid metabolism. Deficiency causes retarded growth, dermatitis, convulsions, and other symptoms.

Vitamin B_{12} (cyanocobalamin) is manufactured only by microorganisms and natural sources are entirely of animal origin. Liver is especially rich in it. One form of B_{12} functions as a coenzyme in a number of reactions, including the oxidation of fatty acids and the synthesis of DNA. It also works in conjunction with *folic acid (another B vitamin) in the synthesis of the amino acid methionine and it is required for normal production of red blood cells. Vitamin B_{12} can only be absorbed from the gut in the presence of a glycoprotein called intrinsic factor; lack of this factor or deficiency of B_{12} results in pernicious anaemia.

Other vitamins in the B complex include *nicotinic acid, *pantothenic acid, *folic acid, *biotin, and *lipoic acid. *See also* choline.

vitamin C (ascorbic acid) A colourless crystalline water-soluble vitamin found especially in citrus fruits and green vegetables. Most organisms synthesize it from glucose but man and other primates and various other species must obtain it from their diet. It is required for the maintenance of healthy connective tissue; deficiency leads to scurvy. Vitamin C is readily destroyed by heat and light.

vitamin D A fat-soluble vitamin occurring in the form of two steroid derivatives: *vitamin D_2 (ergocalciferol*, or *calciferol*), found in yeast; and *vitamin D_3 (cholecalciferol*), which occurs in animals. Vitamin D_2 is formed from a steroid by the action of ultraviolet light and D_3 is produced by the action of sunlight on a cholesterol derivative in the skin. Fish-liver oils are the major dietary source. The active form of vitamin D is manufactured in response to the secretion of parathyroid hormone, which occurs when blood calcium levels are low. It causes increased uptake of calcium from the gut, which increases the supply of calcium for bone synthesis. Vitamin D deficiency causes rickets in growing animals and osteomalacia in mature animals. Both conditions are characterized by weak deformed bones.

vitamin E (tocopherol) A fat-soluble vitamin consisting of several closely related compounds, deficiency of which leads to a range of disorders in different species, including muscular dystrophy, liver damage, and infertility. Good sources are cereal grains and green vegetables. Vitamin E prevents the oxidation of unsaturated fatty acids in cell membranes, so maintaining their structure.

vitamin K A fat-soluble vitamin consisting of several related compounds that act as coenzymes in the synthesis of several proteins necessary for blood clotting. Deficiency of vitamin K, which leads to extensive bleeding, is rare because a form of the vitamin is manufactured by intestinal bacteria. Green vegetables and egg yolk are good sources.

volt Symbol V. The SI unit of electric potential, potential difference, or e.m.f. defined as the difference of potential between two points on a conductor carrying a constant current of one ampere when the power dissipated between the points is one watt. It is named after Alessandro Volta (1745–1827).

voltaic cell (galvanic cell) A device that produces an e.m.f. as a result of chemical reactions that take place within it. These reactions occur at the surfaces of two electrodes, each of which dips into an electrolyte. The first voltaic cell, devised by Alessandro Volta (1745–1827), had electrodes of two different metals dipping into brine. *See* primary cell; secondary cell.

voltameter (coulometer) 1. An electrolytic cell formerly used to measure quantity of electric charge. The increase in mass (m) of the cathode of the cell as a result of the deposition on it of a metal from a solution of its salt enables the charge (Q) to be determined from the relationship $Q = m/z$, where z is the electrochemical equivalent of the metal. **2.** Any other type of electrolytic cell used for measurement.

volume Symbol V. The space occupied by a body or mass of fluid.

volumetric analysis A method of quantitative analysis using measurement of volumes. For gases, the main technique is in reacting or absorbing gases in graduated containers over mercury, and measuring the volume changes. For liquids, it involves *titrations.

vulcanite (ebonite) A hard black insulating material made by the vulcanization of rubber with a high proportion of sulphur (up to 30%).

vulcanization A process for hardening rubber by heating it with sulphur or sulphur compounds.

W

Wacker process A process for the manufacture of ethanal by the air oxidation of ethene. A mixture of air and ethene is bubbled through a solution containing palladium(II) chloride and copper(II) chloride. The Pd^{2+} ions form a complex with the ethene in which the ion is bound to the pi electrons in the C=C bond. This decreases the electron density in the bond, making it susceptible to nucleophilic attack by water molecules. The complex formed breaks down to ethanal and palladium metal. The Cu^{2+} ions oxidize the palladium back to Pd^{2+}, being reduced to Cu^{+} ions in the process. The air present oxidizes Cu^{+} back to Cu^{2+}. Thus the copper(II) and palladium(II) ions effectively act as catalysts in the process, which is now the main source of ethanal and, by further oxidation, ethanoic acid. It can also be applied to other alkenes.

warfarin 3-(alpha-acetonylbenzyl)-4-hydroxycoumarin: a synthetic anticoagulant used both therapeutically in clinical medicine and, in lethal doses, as a rodenticide.

washing soda *Sodium carbonate decahydrate, $Na_2CO_3.10H_2O$.

water A colourless liquid, H_2O; r.d. 1.000 (4°C); m.p. 0.000°C; b.p. 100.000°C. In the gas phase water consists of single H_2O molecules in which the H-O-H angle is 105°. The structure of liquid water is still controversial; hydrogen bonding of the type H_2O ... H-O-H imposes a high degree of structure and current models supported by X-ray scattering studies have short-range ordered regions, which are constantly disintegrating and re-forming. This ordering of the liquid state is sufficient to make the density of water at about 0°C higher than that of the relatively open-structured ice; the maximum density occurs at 3.98°C. This accounts for the well-known phenomenon of ice floating on water and the contraction of water below ice, a fact of enormous biological significance for all aquatic organisms.

Ice has nine distinct structural modifications of which ordinary ice, or ice I, has an open structure built of puckered six-membered rings in which each H_2O unit is tetrahedrally surrounded by four other H_2O units.

Because of its angular shape the water molecule has a permanent dipole moment and in addition it is strongly hydrogen bonded and has a high dielectric constant. These properties combine to make water a powerful solvent for both polar and ionic compounds. Species in solution are frequently strongly hydrated and in fact ions frequently written as, for example, Cu^{2+} are essentially $[Cu(H_2O)_6]^{2+}$. Crystalline *hydrates are also common for inorganic substances; polar organic compounds, particularly those with O-H and N-H bonds, also form hydrates.

Pure liquid water is very weakly dissociated into H_3O^+ and OH^- ions by self ionization:

$$H_2O \rightleftharpoons H^+ + OH^-$$

(*see* ionic product) and consequently any species that increases the concentration of the positive species, H_3O^+, is acidic and species increasing the concentration of the negative species, OH^-, are basic (*see* acid). The phenomena of ion transport in water and the division of materials into *hydrophilic* (water loving) and *hydrophobic* (water hating) substances are central features of almost all biological chemistry. A further property of water that is of fundamental importance to the whole planet is its strong absorption in the infrared range of the spectrum and its transparency to visible and near ultraviolet radiation. This allows solar radiation to reach the earth during hours of daylight but restricts rapid heat loss at night. Thus atmospheric water prevents violent diurnal oscillations in the earth's ambient temperature.

water gas A mixture of carbon monoxide and hydrogen produced by passing steam over hot carbon (coke):

$$H_2O(g) + C(s) \rightarrow CO(g) + H_2(g)$$

The reaction is strongly endothermic but the reaction can be used in conjunction with that for *producer gas for making fuel gas. The main use of water gas before World War II was in producing hydrogen for the *Haber process. Here the above reaction was combined with the *water-gas shift reaction* to increase the amount of hydrogen:

$$CO + H_2O \rightleftharpoons CO_2 + H_2$$

Most hydrogen for the Haber process is now made from natural gas by steam *reforming.

water glass A viscous colloidal solution of sodium silicates in water used to make silica gel and as a size and preservative.

water of crystallization Water present in crystalline compounds in definite proportions. Many crystalline salts form hydrates containing 1, 2, 3, or more molecules of water per molecule of compound, and the water may be held in the crystal in various ways. Thus, the water molecules may simply occupy lattice positions in the crystal, or they may form bonds with the anions or the cations present. In copper sulphate pentahydrate ($CuSO_4.5H_2O$), for instance, each copper ion is coordinated to four water molecules through the lone pairs on the oxygen to form the *complex $[Cu(H_2O)_4]^{2+}$. Each sulphate ion has one water molecule held by hydrogen bonding. The difference between the two types of bonding is demonstrated by the fact that the pentahydrate converts to the monohydrate at 100°C and only becomes anhydrous above 250°C. *Water of constitution* is an obsolete term for water combined in a compound (as in a metal hydroxide $M(OH)_2$ regarded as a hydrated oxide $MO.H_2O$).

water softening *See* hardness of water.

watt Symbol W. The SI unit of power, defined as a power of one joule per second. In electrical contexts it is equal to the rate of energy transformation by an electric current of one ampere flowing through a conductor the ends of which are maintained at a potential difference of one volt. The unit is named after James Watt (1736–1819).

wave function A function $\psi(x,y,z)$ appearing in *Schrödinger's equation in wave mechanics. The wave function is a mathematical expression involving the coordinates of a particle in space. If the Schrödinger equation can be solved for a particle in a given system (e.g. an electron in an atom) then, depending on the boundary conditions, the solution is a set of allowed wave functions (*eigenfunctions*) of the particle, each corresponding to an allowed energy level (*eigenvalue*). The physical significance of the wave function is that the square of its absolute value, $|\psi|^2$, at a point is proportional to the probability of finding the particle in a small element of volume, d*x*d*y*d*z*, at that point. For an electron in an atom, this gives rise to the idea of atomic and molecular *orbitals.

wave mechanics *See* quantum mechanics.

wax Any of various solid or semisolid substances. There are two main types. Mineral waxes are mixtures of hydrocarbons with high molecular weights. Paraffin wax, obtained from *petroleum, is an example. Waxes secreted by plants or animals are mainly esters of fatty acids and usually have a protective function.

weak acid An *acid that is only partially dissociated in aqueous solution.

weber Symbol Wb. The SI unit of magnetic flux equal to the flux that, linking a circuit of one turn, produces in it an e.m.f. of one volt as it is reduced to zero at a uniform rate in one second. It is named after Wilhelm Weber (1804–91).

Weston cell (cadmium cell) A type of primary *voltaic cell, which is used as a standard; it produces a constant e.m.f. of 1.0186 volts at 20°C. The cell is usually made in an H-shaped glass vessel with a mercury anode covered with a paste of cadmium sulphate and mercury(I) sulphate in one leg and a cadmium amalgam cathode covered with cadmium sulphate in the other leg. The electrolyte, which connects the two electrodes by means of the bar of the H, is a saturated solution of cadmium sulphate. In some cells sulphuric acid is added to prevent the hydrolysis of mercury sulphate.

white arsenic *See* arsenic(III) oxide.

white mica *See* muscovite.

white spirit A liquid mixture of hydrocarbons obtained from petroleum, used as a solvent for paint ('turpentine substitute').

Williamson's synthesis Either of two methods of producing ethers, both named after the British chemist Alexander Williamson (1824–1904).

1. The dehydration of alcohols using concentrated sulphuric acid. The overall reaction can be written

$$2ROH \rightarrow H_2O + ROR$$

The method is used for making ethoxyethane ($C_2H_5OC_2H_5$) from ethanol by heating at 140°C with excess of alcohol (excess acid at 170°C gives ethene). Although the steps in the reaction are all reversible, the ether is distilled off so the reaction can proceed to completion. This is *Williamson's continuous process*. In general, there are two possible mechanisms for this synthesis. In the first (favoured by primary alcohols), an alkylhydrogen sulphate is formed

$$ROH + H_2SO_4 \rightleftharpoons ROSO_3H + H_2O$$

This reacts with another alcohol molecule to give an oxonium ion

$$ROH + ROSO_3H \rightarrow ROHR^+$$

This loses a proton to give ROR.

The second mechanism (favoured by tertiary alcohols) is formation of a carbonium ion

$$ROH + H^+ \rightarrow H_2O + R^+$$

This is attacked by the lone pair on the other alcohol molecule

$$R^+ + ROH \rightarrow ROHR^+$$

and the oxonium ion formed again gives the product by loss of a proton.

The method can be used for making symmetric ethers (i.e. having both R groups the same). It can successfully be used for mixed ethers only when one alcohol is primary and the other tertiary (otherwise a mixture of the three possible products results).

2. A method of preparing ethers by reacting a haloalkane with an alkoxide. The reaction, discovered in 1850, is a nucleophilic substitution in which the negative alkoxide ion displaces a halide ion; for example:

$$RI + {}^{-}OR' \rightarrow ROR' + I^{-}$$

A mixture of the reagents is refluxed in ethanol. The method is particularly useful for preparing mixed ethers, although a possible side reaction under some conditions is an elimination to give an alcohol and an alkene.

witherite A mineral form of *barium carbonate, $BaCO_3$.

Wöhler's synthesis A synthesis of urea performed by the German chemist Friedrich Wöhler (1800–82) in 1828. He discovered that urea ($CO(NH_2)_2$) was formed when a solution of ammonium isocyanate (NH_4NCO) was evaporated. At the time it was believed that organic substances such as urea could be made only by living organisms, and its production from an inorganic compound was a notable discovery. It is sometimes (erroneously) cited as ending the belief in vitalism.

wolfram *See* tungsten.

wolframite (iron manganese tungsten) A mineral consisting of a mixed iron–manganese tungstate, $(FeMn)WO_4$, crystallizing in the monoclinic system; the principal ore of tungsten. It commonly occurs as blackish or brownish tabular crystal groups. It is found chiefly in quartz veins associated with granitic rocks. China is the major producer of wolframite.

wood alcohol *See* methanol.

Wood's metal A low-melting (71°C) alloy of bismuth (50%), lead (25%), tin (12.5%), and cadmium (12.5%). It is used for fusible links in automatic sprinkler systems. The melting point can be changed by varying the composition.

Woodward–Hoffmann rules Rules governing the formation of products during certain types of organic concerted reactions. The theory of such reactions was put forward in 1969 by the American chemists Robert Burns Woodward (1917–79) and Roald Hoffmann (1937–), and is concerned with the way that orbitals of the reactants change continuously into orbitals of the products during reaction and with conservation of orbital symmetry during this process. It is sometimes known as *frontier-orbital theory*.

work function A quantity that determines the extent to which thermionic or photoelectric emission will occur according to the Richardson equation or Einstein's photoelectric equation. It is sometimes expressed as a potential difference (symbol ϕ) in volts and sometimes as the work to be done by the exciting electron (symbol W) in electronvolts or joules. The former has been called the *work function potential* and the latter the *work function energy*.

work hardening An increase in the hardness of metals as a result of working them cold. It causes a permanent distortion of the crystal structure and is particularly apparent with iron, copper, aluminium, etc., whereas with lead and zinc it does not occur as these metals are capable of recrystallizing at room temperature.

wrought iron A highly refined form of iron containing 1–3% of slag (mostly iron silicate), which is evenly distributed throughout the material in threads and fibres so that the product has a fibrous structure quite dissimilar to that of crystalline cast iron. Wrought iron rusts less readily than other forms of metallic iron and it welds and works more easily. It is used for chains, hooks, tubes, etc.

Wurtz reaction A reaction to prepare alkanes by reacting a haloalkane with sodium:

$$2RX + 2Na \rightarrow 2NaX + RR$$

The haloalkane is refluxed with sodium in dry ether. The method is named after the French chemist Charles-Adolphe Wurtz (1817–84). The analogous reaction using a haloalkane and a haloarene, for example:

$$C_6H_5Cl + CH_3Cl + 2Na \rightarrow 2NaCl + C_6H_5CH_3$$

is called the *Fittig reaction* after the German chemist Rudolph Fittig (1835–1910).

X

xanthates Salts or esters containing the group $-SCS(OR)$, where R is an organic group. Cellulose xanthate is an intermediate in the manufacture of *rayon by the viscose process.

xenon Symbol Xe. A colourless odourless gas belonging to group 0 of the periodic table (*see* noble gases); a.n. 54; r.a.m. 131.30; d 5.887 g dm^{-3}; m.p. −111.9°C; b.p. −107.1°C. It is present in the atmosphere (0.00087%) from which it is extracted by distillation of liquid air. There are nine natural isotopes with mass numbers 124, 126, 128–132, 134, and 136. Seven radioactive isotopes are also known. The element is used in fluorescent lamps and bubble chambers. Several compounds of xenon are now known, including $XePtF_6$, XeF_2, XeF_4, $XeSiF_6$, XeO_2F_2, and XeO_3. The element was discovered in 1898 by Ramsey and Travers.

X-ray crystallography The use of *X-ray diffraction to determine the structure of crystals or molecules. The technique involves directing a beam of X-rays at a crystalline sample and recording the diffracted X-rays on a photographic plate. The diffraction pattern consists of a pattern of spots on the plate, and the crystal structure can be worked out from the positions and intensities of the diffraction spots. X-rays are diffracted by the electrons in the molecules and if molecular crystals of a compound are used, the electron density distribution in the molecule can be determined.

X-ray diffraction The diffraction of X-rays by a crystal. The wavelengths of X-rays are comparable in size to the distances between atoms in most crystals, and the repeated pattern of the crystal lattice acts like a diffraction grating for X-rays. Thus, a crystal of suitable type can be used to disperse X-rays in a spectrometer. X-ray diffraction is also the basis of X-ray crystallography.

X-ray fluorescence The emission of *X-rays from excited atoms produced by the impact of high-energy electrons, other particles, or a primary beam of other X-rays. The wavelengths of the fluorescent X-rays can be measured by an X-ray spectrometer as a means of chemical analysis. X-ray fluorescence is used in such techniques as *electron-probe microanalysis.

X-rays Electromagnetic radiation of shorter wavelength than ultraviolet radiation and longer wavelength than gamma radiation. The range of wavelengths is 10^{-11} m to 10^{-9} m. Atoms of all the elements emit a characteristic *X-ray spectrum* when they are bombarded by electrons. The X-ray photons are emitted when the incident electrons knock an inner orbital electron out of an atom. When this happens an outer electron falls into the inner shell to replace it, losing potential energy (ΔE) in doing so. The wavelength λ of the emitted photon will then be given by $\lambda = ch/\Delta E$, where c is the speed of light and h is the Planck constant.

X-rays can pass through many forms of matter and they are therefore used medically and industrially to examine internal structures. X-rays are produced for these purposes by an X-ray tube.

X-ray spectrum *See* X-rays.

xylenes *See* dimethylbenzenes.

Y

yeasts A group of unicellular fungi many of which belong to the Ascomycetes. Certain species of the genus *Saccharomyces* are used in the baking and brewing industries.

ytterbium Symbol Yb. A silvery metallic element belonging to the *lanthanoids; a.n. 70; r.a.m. 173.04; r.d. 6.966 (20°C); m.p. 819°C; b.p. 1196°C. It occurs in gadolinite, monazite, and xenotime. There are seven natural isotopes and ten artificial isotopes are known. There are no uses for the element, which was discovered by J. D. G. Marignac in 1878.

yttrium Symbol Y. A silvery-grey metallic element belonging to group IIIB of the periodic table; a.n. 39; r.a.m. 88.905; r.d. 4.469 (20°C); m.p. 1522°C; b.p. 3338°C. It occurs in uranium ores and in *lanthanoid ores, from which it can be extracted by an ion exchange process. The natural isotope is yttrium–89, and there are 14 known artificial isotopes. The metal is used in superconducting alloys and in alloys for strong permanent magnets (in both cases, with cobalt). The oxide (Y_2O_3) is used in colour-television phosphors, neodymium-doped lasers, and microwave components. Chemically it resembles the lanthanoids, forming ionic compounds containing Y^{3+} ions. The metal is stable in air below 400°C. It was discovered in 1828 by Friedrich Wöhler.

Z

Zeeman effect The splitting of the lines in a spectrum when the source of the spectrum is exposed to a magnetic field. It was discovered in 1896 by P. Zeeman (1865–1943). In the *normal Zeeman effect* a single line is split into three if the field is perpendicular to the light path or two lines if the field is parallel to the light path. This effect can be explained by classical electromagnetic principles in terms of the speeding up and slowing down of orbital electrons in the source as a result of the applied field. The *anomolous Zeeman effect* is a complicated splitting of the lines into several closely spaced lines, so called because it does not agree with classical predictions. This effect is explained by quantum mechanics in terms of electron spin.

zeolite A natural or synthetic hydrated aluminosilicate with an open three-dimensional crystal structure, in which water molecules are held in cavities in the lattice. The water can be driven off by heating and the zeolite can then absorb other molecules of suitable size. Zeolites are used for separating mixtures by selective absorption – for this reason they are often called *molecular sieves*. They are also used in sorption pumps for vacuum systems and certain types (e.g. *Permutit*) are used in ion-exchange (e.g. water-softening).

zero order *See* order.

zeroth law of thermodynamics *See* thermodynamics.

Ziegler process An industrial process for the manufacture of high-density polyethene using catalysts of titanium(IV) chloride ($TiCl_4$) and aluminium alkyls (e.g. triethylaluminium, $Al(C_2H_5)_3$). The process was introduced in 1953 by the German chemist Karl Ziegler (1898–1973). It allowed the manufacture of polythene at lower temperatures (about 60°C) and pressures (about 1 atm.) than used in the original process. Moreover, the polyethene produced had more straight-chain molecules, giving the product more rigidity and a higher melting point than the earlier low-density polyethene. The reaction involves the formation of a titanium alkyl in which the titanium can coordinate directly to the pi bond in ethene.

In 1954 the process was developed further by the Italian chemist Giulio Natta (1903–79), who extended the use of Ziegler's catalysts (and similar catalysts) to other alkenes. In particular he showed how to produce stereospecific polymers of propene.

Ziesel reaction A method of determining the number of methoxy ($-OCH_3$) groups in an organic compound. The compound is heated wih excess hydriodic acid, forming an alcohol and iodomethane

$$R-O-CH_3 + HI \rightarrow ROH + CH_3I$$

The iodomethane is distilled off and led into an alcoholic solution of silver nitrate, where it precipitates silver iodide. This is filtered and weighed, and the number of iodine atoms and hence methoxy groups can be calculated. The method was developed by S. Ziesel in 1886.

zinc Symbol Zn. A blue-white metallic element; a.n. 30; r.a.m. 65.38; r.d. 7.1; m.p. 419.57°C; b.p. 907°C. It occurs in sphalerite (or zinc blende, ZnS), which is found associated with the lead sulphide, and in smithsonite ($ZnCO_3$). Ores are roasted to give the oxide and this is reduced with carbon (coke) at high temperature, the zinc vapour being condensed. Alternatively, the oxide is dissolved in sulphuric acid and the zinc obtained by electrolysis. There are five stable isotopes (mass numbers 64, 66, 67, 68, and 70) and six radioactive isotopes are known. The metal is used in galvanizing and in a number of alloys (brass, bronze, etc.). Chemically it is a reactive metal, combining with oxygen and other nonmetals and reacting with dilute acids to release hydrogen. It also dissolves in alkalis to give *zincates. Most of its compounds contain the Zn^{2+} ion.

zincate A salt formed in solution by dissolving zinc or zinc oxide in alkali. The formula is often written $ZnO_2^{\ 2-}$ although in aqueous solution the ions present are probably complex ions in which the Zn^{2-} is coordinated to OH^- ions. $ZnO_2^{\ 2-}$ ions may exist in molten sodium zincate, but most solid 'zincates' are mixed oxides.

zinc blende A mineral form of *zinc sulphide, ZnS, the principal ore of zinc (*see* sphalerite). The *zinc-blende structure* is the crystal structure of this compound (and of other compounds). It has zinc atoms surrounded by four sulphur atoms at the corners of a tetrahedron. Each sulphur is similarly surrounded by four zinc atoms. The crystals belong to the cubic system.

zinc chloride A white crystalline compound, $ZnCl_2$. The anhydrous salt, which is deliquescent, can be made by the action of hydrogen chloride gas on hot zinc; r.d. 2.9; m.p. 290°C; b.p. 732°C. It has a relatively low melting point and sublimes easily, indicating that it is a molecular compound rather than ionic. Various hydrates also exist. Zinc chloride is used as a catalyst, dehydrating agent, and flux for hard solder. It was once known as *butter of zinc*.

zinc group The group of elements in the periodic table consisting of zinc (Zn), cadmium (Cd), and mercury (Hg). *See* group II elements.

zincite A mineral form of *zinc oxide, ZnO.

zinc oxide A powder, white when cold and yellow when hot, ZnO; r.d. 5.5; m.p. 1975°C. It occurs naturally as a reddish orange ore *zincite*, and can also be made by oxidizing hot zinc in air. It is amphoteric, forming *zincates with bases. It is used as a pigment (*Chinese white*) and a mild antiseptic in zinc ointments. An archaic name is *philosopher's wool.*

zinc sulphate A white crystalline water-soluble compound made by heating zinc sulphide ore in air and dissolving out and recrystallizing the sulphate. The common form is the heptahydrate, $ZnSO_4.7H_2O$; r.d. 1.9. This loses water above 30°C to give the hexahydrate and more water is lost above 100°C to form the monohydrate. The anhydrous salt forms at 450°C and this decomposes above 500°C. The compound, which was formerly called *white vitriol*, is used as a mordant and as a styptic (to check bleeding).

zinc sulphide A yellow-white water-soluble solid, ZnS. It occurs naturally as *sphalerite (*see also* zinc blende) and wurtzite. The compound sublimes at 1180°C. It is used as a pigment and phosphor.

zirconia *See* zirconium.

zirconium Symbol Zr. A grey-white metallic *transition element; a.n. 40; r.a.m. 91.22; r.d. 6.44; m.p. 1853°C; b.p. 4376°C. It is found in zircon ($ZrSiO_4$; the main source) and in baddeleyite (ZnO_2). Extraction is by chlorination to give $ZrCl_4$ which is purified by solvent extraction and reduced with magnesium (Kroll process). There are five natural isotopes (mass numbers 90, 91, 92, 94, and 96) and six radioactive isotopes are known. The element is used in nuclear reactors (it is an effective neutron absorber) and in certain alloys. The metal forms a passive layer of oxide in air and burns at 500°C. Most of its compounds are complexes of zirconium(IV). *Zirconium(IV) oxide* (*zirconia*) is used as an electrolyte in fuel cells. The element was identified in 1789 by Klaproth and was first isolated by Berzelius in 1824.

zirconium(IV) oxide *See* zirconium.

zone refining A technique used to reduce the level of impurities in certain metals, alloys, semiconductors, and other materials. It is based on the observation that the solubility of an impurity may be different in the liquid and solid phases of a material. To take advantage of this observation, a narrow molten zone is moved along the length of a specimen of the material, with the result that the impurities are segregated at one end of the bar and the pure material at the other. In general, if the impurities lower the melting point of the material they are moved in the same direction as the molten zone moves, and vice versa.

zwitterion (ampholyte ion) An ion that has a positive and negative charge on the same group of atoms. Zwitterions can be formed from compounds that contain both acid groups and basic groups in their molecules. For example, aminoethanoic acid (the amino acid glycine) has the formula $H_2N.CH_2.COOH$. However, under neutral conditions, it exists in the different form of the zwitterion $^+H_3N.CH_2.COO^-$, which can be regarded as having been produced by an internal neutralization reaction (transfer of a proton from the carboxyl group to the amino group). Aminoethanoic acid, as a consequence, has some properties characteristic of ionic compounds; e.g. a high melting point and solubility in water. In acid solutions, the positive ion $^+H_3NCH_2COOH$ is formed. In basic solutions, the negative ion $H_2NCH_2COO^-$ predominates. The name comes from the German *zwei*, two.

Appendix 1 SI units

Table 1.1 Base and supplementary SI units

Physical quantity	*Name*	*Symbol*
length	metre	m
mass	kilogram	kg
time	second	s
electric current	ampere	A
thermodynamic temperature	kelvin	K
luminous intensity	candela	cd
amount of substance	mole	mol
*plane angle	radian	rad
*solid angle	steradian	sr

*supplementary units

Table 1.2 Derived SI units with special names

Physical quantity	*Name of SI unit*	*Symbol of SI unit*
frequency	hertz	Hz
energy	joule	J
force	newton	N
power	watt	W
pressure	pascal	Pa
electric charge	coulomb	C
electric potential difference	volt	V
electric resistance	ohm	Ω
electric conductance	siemens	S
electric capacitance	farad	F
magnetic flux	weber	Wb
inductance	henry	H
magnetic flux density (magnetic induction)	tesla	T
luminous flux	lumen	lm
illuminance	lux	lx
absorbed dose	gray	Gy
activity	becquerel	Bq
dose equivalent	sievert	Sv

Table 1.3 Decimal multiples and submultiples to be used with SI units

Submultiple	*Prefix*	*Symbol*	*Multiple*	*Prefix*	*Symbol*
10^{-1}	deci	d	10	deca	da
10^{-2}	centi	c	10^2	hecto	h
10^{-3}	milli	m	10^3	kilo	k
10^{-6}	micro	μ	10^6	mega	M
10^{-9}	nano	n	10^9	giga	G
10^{-12}	pico	p	10^{12}	tera	T
10^{-15}	femto	f	10^{15}	peta	P
10^{-18}	atto	a	10^{18}	exa	E

Table 1.4 Conversion of units to SI units

From	*To*	*Multiply by*
in	m	2.54×10^{-2}
ft	m	0.3048
sq. in	m^2	6.4516×10^{-4}
sq. ft	m^2	9.2903×10^{-2}
cu. in	m^3	1.63871×10^{-5}
cu. ft	m^3	2.83168×10^{-2}
l(itre)	m^3	10^{-3}
gal(lon)	m^3	$4.546\ 09 \times 10^{-3}$
gal(lon)	l(itre)	4.546 09
miles/hr	m s^{-1}	0.477 04
km/hr	m s^{-1}	0.277 78
lb	kg	0.453 592
g cm^{-3}	kg m^{-3}	10^3
lb/in^3	kg m^{-3}	$2.767\ 99 \times 10^4$
dyne	N	10^{-5}
kgf	N	9.806 65
poundal	N	0.138 255
lbf	N	4.448 22
mmHg	Pa	133.322
atmosphere	Pa	$1.013\ 25 \times 10^5$
hp	W	745.7
erg	J	10^{-7}
eV	J	$1.602\ 10 \times 10^{-19}$
kW h	J	3.6×10^6
cal	J	4.1868